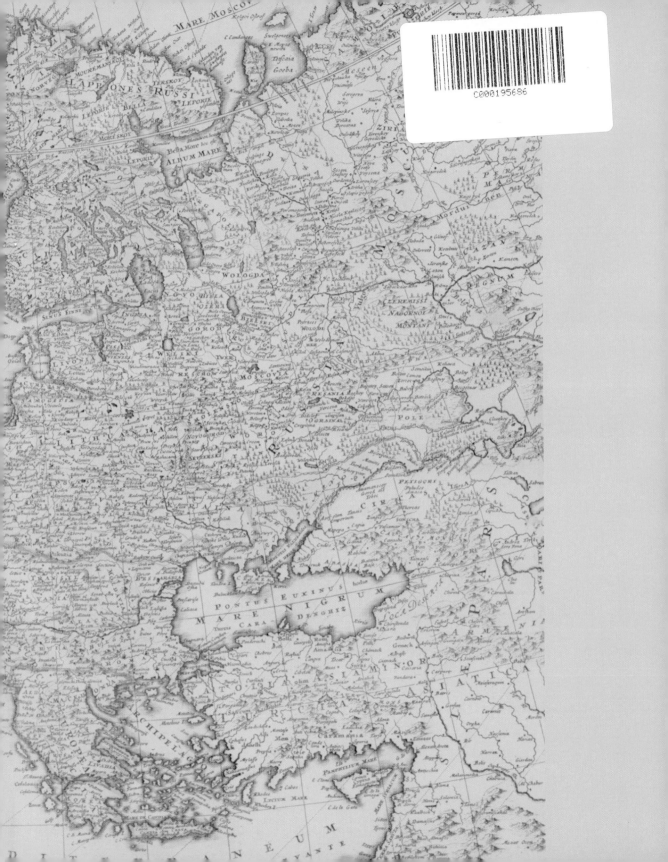

Swedenborg's Secret

The Meaning and Significance of the Word of God,
the Life of the Angels, and Service to God

A Biography

Lars Bergquist

The Swedenborg Society
Swedenborg House
20-21 Bloomsbury Way
London WC1A 2TH

—

2005

Previously published in Swedish, in 1999, by Bokförlaget Natur och Kultur
under the title *Swedenborgs Hemlighet*

Bible quotations are printed from The New King James Version
by permission of the publisher Thomas Nelson Inc.

Endpapers: Map of Europe by J B Homann, 1706,
by permission of the British Library. Shelfmark: Maps.k.Top.4.74

Published by:
The Swedenborg Society
Swedenborg House
20-21 Bloomsbury Way
London WC1A 2TH

Book design: Stephen McNeilly
Typeset at Swedenborg House
Printed and bound in Great Britain at the University Press,
Cambridge

ISBN 0 85448 143 5
British Library Cataloguing-in-Publication Data
A catalogue record for this book is available
from the British Library

Acknowledgements

The English edition of my biography *Swedenborg's Secret*, originally published in Swedish in 1999 as *Swedenborgs Hemlighet*, is the result of the patient and expert work of the Revd Norman Ryder. Developing the text from a preliminary English translation, made by the Revd Kurt P Nemitz, Mr Ryder has, with my modest contribution, tried to adapt the book to an international public, correcting mistakes and inconsistencies in the original text.

Lars Bergquist

Contents

Contents

List of black and white illustrations

| List of colour plates |

Introduction

'They call this Swedenborgianism, for my part I call it true Christianity [...] '
Letter from Emanuel Swedenborg to Gabriel Beyer, 12 April 1770. [1]

From natural science to theosophy

During the first part of his life Emanuel Swedenborg was an active inventor, mining expert, scientist, public official, and member of the Swedish Parliament.* At the same time he wrote books treating of the philosophy of nature, of nature's essence and the relationship between spirit and matter, and of the origin of the universe. His key concepts throughout his life were will, duty, use, and knowledge based on solid experience. Simultaneously with these dispassionate sober words, we find in the middle-aged scientist a religious conviction and an emphasis on intuition and dreams as a means to knowledge. His studies became increasingly directed towards the soul, its place and role in our body, and its relation to our knowledge and love. He was in good company: the philosophers Descartes, Malebranche, Leibniz, and Wolff were occupied with similar problems.

His final work on the philosophy of nature dealt precisely with locating the soul and giving an anatomical demonstration of God's way of working in man. In the years 1744-5

* Until his ennoblement in 1719, Emanuel was known by his family's surname 'Swedberg'. We have used the name 'Swedenborg' in the earlier chapters to avoid confusion between Emanuel and his father Jesper Swedberg.

---

he went through a crisis that changed his life. My attempt to describe Swedenborg's eighty-four years on earth focuses primarily on this crisis and the ensuing theosophical period.

Catastrophe and epiphany

Catastrophe, a breakdown, often exposes what would otherwise be hidden. In the case of Swedenborg's life the crisis is documented in his diary published in 1859 as 'Swedenborg's Dreams', here referred to as the *Dream Diary*.[2] We do not know much of his private life, but here we come close to him. His journal contains records of his dreams and visions, and his reflections on them. At the same time, we gain information on his daily life and circle of acquaintances. His notes culminate in a call: he was to write a 'divine book', and the material for this work was not to be 'others' notions', not 'trash' that he had collected from books. Everything was to be taken from 'his own'.

Here is the beginning of the second period of his life. It is characterized by his theosophy: I use the word in its etymological sense, 'knowledge of God'. His doctrine can be seen as a protest against a petrified Christianity and against a world more and more materialistically fixated, bound and tied to the senses and their experience, but also against a philosophical idealism that seeks to derive a conception of the 'essential' nature of being from an idea.

Against this he placed the intuitive insight of dreams and visions. Already before the crisis he was certain as to the soul's divine origin and its nature; the question was where the soul had its bodily seat, and how it functioned. The soul received and 'embodied' God's inflow into man.

The notion of the soul as a vessel for divine influence was in fact decisive for escaping the dead end that a mechanically based world order involves. We must be able to prove our belief that there are other truths than those verities offered by the microscope and the measuring rule. This kind of truth we must find within ourselves, in our own *anima*, a classic Christian thought. In a different context Marcel Proust describes this turning inward:

> I [...] examine my own mind. It alone can discover the truth. But how? What an abyss of uncertainty, whenever the mind feels overtaken by itself; when it, the seeker, is at the same time the dark region through which it must go seeking and where all its equipment will

avail it nothing. Seek? More than that: create. It is face to face with something which does not yet exist, which it alone can make actual, which it alone can bring into the light of day.[3]

We leave Proust: divine grace gave Swedenborg the gift of penetrating and beholding the invisible. Heaven was opened. He felt he saw how the finite led to the infinite and vice versa. He thought he could distinguish the links in what, in an older time, had been called a 'golden chain' connecting the Divine with the human. The high and the low, the sublime and the ordinary, mirrored each other, a recurrent theme in Swedenborg's theosophy.

Worldly and divine knowledge

Human reason on one side, divine inspiration on the other. Both were needed as tools for the structure he sought to erect, the true Christian religion. It was a matter of explaining what was dark, and of answering the many questions that the Bible and Christian dogmas left open. What did the Creation story mean? How should the evil in the world be explained? What happens to man after death? Shall we be lying in the grave until the day of the Last Judgement? And through what process does sober knowledge pass over into faith that reason cannot fathom?

He composed his great explanation over a span of twenty-seven years. All the questions were answered in the Bible, but the true meaning of the texts was hidden. The Christian church had built its doctrines on man's own natural understanding, but true comprehension required both rational mind and divine guidance. And God had given him, Emanuel Swedenborg, an ability to interpret the Word correctly: his soul stood in contact with otherwise hidden sources of knowledge.

Day after day, year after year, he worked on his grand interpretation of divine providence's unfathomable ways. Towards the end of his life, he had a vision. He saw a temple with the inscription '*Nunc licet*' ('Now it is permitted') over its entrance. He interpreted this as meaning, 'Now it is permitted to enter with the understanding into the mysteries of faith'.[4] His life's work was finished.

At its core, Swedenborg's doctrine is very simple. God's love is present in all human beings. Man is a field of battle, ever receptive of inflowing forces. We are free to take them in or to reject them: our will is always free. It is a matter of 'looking to the Lord and turning and fleeing from sin, because it is evil'.

To understand Swedenborg's colossal panorama of heaven and hell, one must first perceive this fundamental theme as having an underlying pattern. All the details, sublime, ridiculous, intelligent, and absurd, need to be seen as elements and extensions of this basic idea. The constant shift between egotistical and unselfish love stands in the centre of his work. Swedenborg's psychology is essentially a description of human states, determined by our nearness to or distance from God. Without this view, Swedenborg's revelations become uninteresting. I quote from Erik Sandström, a follower of Swedenborg:

> As dead information the revelation about the reality of the spiritual world becomes [. . .] completely worthless [. . .] But seen as a painting of one or another reality we carry within ourselves, the revelation takes life and becomes priceless in the death march of our doubting, de-Christianized world. [5]

The joy of teaching

Religious texts can often be read as poetry. Swedenborg's prose is characterized by demonstrations and proofs. There is seldom a 'lyrical silence' between his lines; instead he turns himself directly to the understanding and will. He writes ceaselessly, as if he were driven. The consolation and confidence he presents to his readers take the form of explanations.

In the midst of his constant work with questions of the divine and celestial he led a busy earthly life. He was often politically active as a member of the Diet,* always defending the power of the Parliament against royal infringements. The 'world' he rejected only when it totally dominated man: when the selfish will was put in the place of God as the aim of all endeavours. Love for God and the neighbour was the constant goal: we must fight and overcome our temptations. In his published writings he seldom describes his own experience of such attacks. However, they are present in his journal written between 1745 and 1765, and then in such strong trials that he must let them be embodied in the forms of deceased acquaintances to be able to dispel them.

* The term 'Diet' refers to the system of goverment in Sweden during Swedenborg's day.

In his message there is little room for common human feelings of sadness: melancholy, worry, despair occur in most cases as evil spirits, tribulations to be chased away.

Suffering seems scarcely more than suggested in his work and then usually as a feeling associated with temptation. 'O bloody, wounded head', Christ's suffering and self-sacrifice is overshadowed by the view of divine victory. The spiritual joy that man can experience seems to make the academically-inclined writer disinterested in or immune to physical pain: it was scarcely in harmony with his positive view of the world, and when writing about death, he is always composed, calm, and filled with confidence.

Two spheres of life

Martin Lamm, at the beginning of the twentieth century, wrote an excellent biography of Swedenborg [6] emphasizing his scientific work and his work on the philosophy of nature. Although he devoted relatively little interest to Swedenborg's almost thirty-year long theosophical period, one of the chief thoughts in his book is the organic connection between Swedenborg's science, philosophy, and theosophy. These three subjects formed a continuous fabric.

This thesis had already been advanced by Swedenborg himself. In one of his countless conversations with heavenly beings, an angel points out that spiritual and natural truths are interconnected. Emanuel Swedenborg, Assessor in the Royal Board of Mines, had been chosen by the Lord to do research in both the natural and spiritual realms. The one reflected the other.

Nevertheless, the continuity must not be exaggerated. Swedenborg the scientist by no means went straight towards an interpretation of the Bible that he felt was inspired by God, nor to the galleries of the spirit world. He changed his mechanistic view of the world to an organic one; his view of heavenly relationships changed, as did his opinions of people he met in paradise and hell. In no way did he glide from one sphere of life to the other. However, for anyone who focuses attention upon his religious thinking, it is natural to point to those sides of his earlier life that can throw light on its later stage.

The text and the Book of Revelation

My source has been Swedenborg's own texts. His scientific, philosophical, and religious concepts anticipate or refer to each other, illuminating his intellectual and religious universe. One thought clarifies another. The eye wanders over the pages of his almost endless production. The reader gradually gains the feeling that he has found his way into a temple of echoes where the same heavenly whispers and calls are either amplified or weakened, depending on where the speaker is standing. The starting point was the call, the vocation. Its concrete form was determined, I believe, by his fascination with the dark, haunting scenery of the Book of Revelation. As for so many others, the apocalyptic text acted like a challenge. Here he had found the right questions to ask and an indication of the direction to take in seeking the answers.

Most of his theosophical writing is present already in his first great work, *Arcana Coelestia (Arcana Caelestia),* which can be translated as Heavenly Secrets, published anonymously in Latin in eight volumes from 1749 to 1756; twelve volumes were required for the English version. The work constitutes a commentary on Genesis and Exodus together with accounts of the 'marvellous things heard and seen in the world of spirits and the heaven of angels'.

Figures in the background

The first part of his life I attempt to describe chronologically. The theosophical period is treated more thematically.

The texts can scarcely be understood without a view of the Swedenborgian stage. In the foreground we see his father, the pious, dominating, vital, and childlike Jesper Swedberg, first a pastor, then a professor at the University of Uppsala, and finally bishop of the Skara diocese in the south of Sweden. There is an oft-noted, remarkable similarity between the messages of father and son.

We meet other actors. Without any claims at completeness, I draw forward from the wings a line of persons who form the supporting cast, explaining Swedenborg's own appearance. We catch glimpses of ancient church fathers and philosophers, as well as thinkers and theologians more or less contemporary with Swedenborg, among them well-known, significant personalities within the pietistic sphere.

This is a biography, not an academic work. I seldom or never attempt to give a thorough, broad account of the different topics of relevance for Swedenborg's life and thinking.

Such an in-depth account would easily fill as many volumes as his own *Arcana Caelestia*. I give an account only of the explanatory factors that in my opinion are near at hand for understanding his work, why he writes as he does.

It is seldom a matter of explanations in terms of cause and effect. I attempt to limit myself to reminders about the context of the times and recurring underlying themes. Perhaps my book can stimulate a deeper research into some of the seldom or never discussed problems on which I touch, above all, the relation to radical Pietism in Germany and England. I devote a great deal of attention to the significance of the Book of Revelation for understanding Swedenborg's thinking, a virgin subject awaiting special research. A third area is Swedenborg's special mode of hermeneutics.

In Swedenborg's world we also meet individuals active in practical affairs, remote from his own philosophical and spiritual problems. Swedenborg was not only a scientist and theosopher. He was the principal representative of his newly ennobled family and as such participated in meetings of the Swedish Parliament. At times he owned interests in mines, significant for the Swedish economy. He lived in the midst of Sweden's 'Period of Freedom', when practically all political power was in the hands of the Diet. Swedenborg was related to, a friend of, or acquainted with several of the most important actors on the political stage. His engagement in questions regarding Sweden's foreign policy and fiscal and constitutional problems also belongs to a description of his life. His negative experiences with corrupt Swedish politicians probably contributed to his reports of the settlings of accounts with hypocritical spirits made in the spiritual realm, recorded in his great journal.

Healthy or sick?

Swedenborg's perspective is that of the Baroque Age. His scenery continues on from the earthly theatre directly into a waiting heaven. The visible was a model for the invisible. His vision of life and death involve a withdrawal from the concrete and tangible. Truth was clothed in a disguise: it was not enough to mirror reality, behind or above it lay higher relationships that only the spiritually-oriented individual could sense or distinguish. We must never give up on what is dark or difficult to grasp. Each and every one must seek his or her own picture of the world, his or her own explanation.

Like so many others in the history of Christianity, Swedenborg saw the world as inhabited by angels, spirits and demons. They played a great role in his doctrine. Above all, he communicated with them and regarded himself as able to visit their world 'in spirit'. Wise or insane? Healthy or sick? Religious truth or poetic fantasy?

'As, God be thanked, I have both a sound faith and sound reason, it may well be inferred what my judgment is about this man', reported Carl Gustaf Tessin, a well-known member of the Swedish government, after a visit to Swedenborg at his home on Hornsgatan in Stockholm. He continued: 'I do not know if I should call a weak-minded man happy or unhappy, a man who finds delight in what he imagines'.[7] The Swedish physician Emil Kleen wrote a large biography containing a wealth of information whose main theme was that Swedenborg was clearly insane:

> During the whole of the religious part of his active life he suffered from a now clinically well-known incurable mental illness [...] After going through the different phases of this sickness's characteristic development he clearly exhibited a paranoia with hallucinations, but without dementia, or, in other words, the special form of paranoia that now since Kraepelin is called parafrenia.[8]

The Swedish author and poet Olof Lagercrantz sees Swedenborg's religious works as a 'poem about a strange land with unusual laws and customs [...] one of the mightiest structures of thought that Western literature possesses', and followers of Swedenborg consider him a 'spiritual Columbus', a divinely-inspired discoverer of new and spiritual continents. Now that I have attempted to immerse myself in his works the question of his mental health has fallen to the side and lost interest for me. Instead, like many others I have been filled with wonder at his power, and the unheard of panorama of life and death he painted. If one takes Swedenborg's world of thought as insanity, there is a method there that is still worth studying.

The animate world

Death for Swedenborg became a drama in life, and life a play in death. He was raised in a time and in a home where angels were present. His father Jesper Swedberg always felt that he lived in an animate world. This was true also for Christian Scriver, author of the famous *Siäle-Skatt* (*Treasure for the Soul*), for Swedberg an indispensable devotional book, after the Bible the most important of all books ever written. The intensity in this belief in a spiritual presence seems hard for most today to understand. A passage from Scriver can be taken as an example:

> You are sealed with the seal of the living God, you are the Highest's sanctuary and dwelling, the one he has chosen for his resting place. His holy angels, the clear and shining flames of fire, hover around and above you with their burning love, they lead you in all your ways, they serve you when you eat, and wait on you when you are seated at the table, they watch around your bed when you sleep, they sorrow with you when you are grieved, and strengthen you when you are in need and anxious, they rejoice over your joy [. . .] they hear and see you with gladness when you serve your and their God [. . .] [9]

Thus from his earliest childhood Swedenborg was a man with a Christian anchorage, equipped with an unusually strong will to put all he knew into one grand picture. He was an intensive reader, totally engaged in the Biblical texts with which he worked. He read the Pentateuch, the Prophets, the Psalms, the Gospels, the Apostle Paul, and the Book of Revelation with care and reflection for twenty-seven years from his call to his death. He found himself associated with great protagonists of the Bible: we read him debating with Paul over the period of a whole year. Heavenly figures, deceased acquaintances and famous reformers, like Luther and Calvin, frequented his lonely earthly house.

Points of departure in radical Pietism

I began to read Swedenborg in my youth but in spite of diligent efforts could not understand him. I saw him as a solitary, eighteenth century dreamer who worked out a personal philosophy in which individual elements were recognizable but the whole hung in the air, and therefore became just a curiosity piece. For my part it was not primarily a matter of his journeys into the supernatural that was of interest, but his interpretation of the Bible, the doctrine itself. Certainly one could see a reaction to that day's religious orthodoxy or to natural theology's tendency to let revelation fade away into a reverence for Creation's ingenuity; but such references explain details, not the whole. Gradually I found the sought-after connection in radical Pietism's desire for renewal and return to what I thought was an original Christianity, distant from dogmatic subtlety, with the Gospel as a measuring rule, and with Christ's impending advent as a promise and a warning. Swedenborg continued and in his special way developed the lines of thought present in part in his father's teaching, anchored in Johann Arndt and Christian Scriver, and further developed by Gottfried Arnold and Johann Conrad Dippel.

The horizon gives perspective. But a biography can only give a fragment from a life, and this applies to my treatment of Swedenborg's religion and its place in the Europe of the 1700s.

The enchanted forest

My many years' work with Swedenborg has been interleaved with epiphanies. The reading of his almost endless production carries the mind into new regions and studies that in their turn carry one further to new questions and new fields. The French author Paul Valéry had a similar experience. He wrote a preface to the French translation of Martin Lamm's biography of Swedenborg. Before he read Lamm's book he had only a superficial knowledge of the Swedish theosopher and his work:

> I approached without knowing that I was pushing on into an enchanted forest where every step stirred ideas that flew up like unexpected birds, where shimmering hypotheses, echoes, and psychological chases ran together at every crossroad, and where the eye glimpses mysteriously renewed vistas, in the midst of which the hunter seeking rational answers gets encouraged, lost, and then finds the track again, only to lose it from sight [. . .] [10]

But the time spent in this enchanted forest is not lost, Valéry continues: 'I love the hunt for its own sake, and there are few hunts so captivating and changing as the hunt for the Mystery of Swedenborg' (*J'aime la chasse pour la chasse, et il y a peu de chasses plus prenantes et plus diverses que la chasse au Mystére de Swedenborg*).

Swedenborg's Secret

The church, the bishop, and the son

Chapter One

The serious world

Emanuel's father, Jesper Swedberg, was one of the truly great prelates in the short era when Sweden held a dominant political and military position in Northern Europe. He was born in 1653 in the region of Dalecarlia, a few miles east of the town of Falun, on a farm named 'Sveden' from which he took his surname. He was the son of the *bergsman,* Daniel Isaksson, a mine-owner who in time became relatively affluent. His mother, named Anna Petersdotter Bullenaesia, came from a family of clergymen; her father was a pastor, Petrus Bullenaesius, their family name being a latinized form of the name of their hometown, Bollnäs.

They were pious, simple, forceful people. In his old age Swedberg often spoke of his longing for a vanished sense of earnest, guiding principles. He felt that he was living in a fallen era, with dangerous French ideals that threatened the simplicity of the old Swedish style of living. 'But my dear God! Where do you now find again the earnest, serious world of old?', he asked. 'In that ancient seriousness I was educated and confirmed', he wrote in his autobiography, *Jesper Swedbergs Lefwernes Beskrifning* (*Description of my Life*), an account composed for his children in the 1720s, each of them receiving a handwritten copy. [1]

1

Swedberg was ordained a priest in 1683, after sixteen years of study at Uppsala and Lund. He was soon appointed regimental preacher to the Stockholm Royal Cavalry Regiment, and in the same year he married Sara Behm, daughter of a deceased mine-owner and Assessor in the Royal Board of Mines, Albrecht de Behm. They had nine children before she died in 1696 after twelve years of marriage. Their oldest son, Albrecht, died ten days later. The other Swedberg children were Daniel, who died in infancy; Anna, who married the

Fig. 1. Jesper Swedberg. Oil painting, Upsala.

librarian, bishop, and archbishop Eric Benzelius; Emanuel; Eliezer, who died at the age of twenty-seven; Hedvig, who married Lars Benzelstierna; Katharina, who married the priest Jonas Unge; Jesper, who became an army officer; and Margaretha, who married a landed gentleman Anders Lundstedt. Jesper junior, who married Christina Silfverswärd, became the ancestor of the present Swedenborg family line.

Sara Behm was wealthy, and through her and Swedberg's own paternal heritage the estate became opulent. His marriage with Sara Behm was a gift of God:

From God's mild hand I was given a wife, wealthy in property and money, and besides this rich in virtue, the fear of God, having a serious character, piety, modesty. *Serious*, I say: she never plumed herself on her riches, but was humble in thought, speech, behaviour, and attire; her ways were not the ways of the world.[2]

God's anointed

Jesper Swedberg seems usually to have had exceptionally good relations with King Charles XI. His attitude towards the Swedish king and queen was biblically coloured: the ruler had received his power from God, and reigned by divine grace. The king supported him throughout life, in spite of Jesper's severe priestly reproaches for occasional royal deviations from the Ten Commandments.

In 1703 Swedberg was named bishop of the diocese of Skara, six years after the death of Charles XI. When it came to the new monarch, Charles XII, the relationship was different. The king's defeat at Poltava in 1709 and his long exile in Turkey were in themselves already a disaster. If the king were to succeed in his plans for a Swedish-Turkish alliance against the Russians it would be an unnatural union between Christians and pagans, contrary to divine will. This was one of the chief thoughts in a book published in 1711 by the bishop. The title is eloquent: *Gudelige Döds Tankar, them en christen altid, helst i thessa dödeliga krigs-och pestilens tider bör hafwa skrifne och utgifne* (*Godly thoughts at death which a Christian should have always in mind in these times of deadly wars and pestilence*).

The bishop wrote a special prayer against this unholy union:

Help us, God, our Saviour [...] save and forgive us all our sins, for your name's sake! Why do you let the pagans and Turks say, "Where now is their God?" Who knows if the Tartars, Turks, and pagans [...] who up to this time never heard and saw such great things as you, our gracious God, have done through our dear King, your anointed [...] are not saying to each other, "Let us see if his God is able to help him now!" If he is not supported they would say, "His God was not strong enough to help him!"[3]

In printed poems and prayers he repeated his condemnation of the 'unholy alliance' with the Turks. Sweden's misfortunes were God's punishment. He prayed urgently for the king's speedy return to Sweden, where he ought to marry and bring children into the world.

The exiled monarch cannot have looked with favour on his bishop's intrusion into the political scene. Swedberg's standing with Charles XII was presumably further worsened by the fact that in a parliamentary commission in 1713 the bishop had recommended immediate peace negotiations with the enemies of the kingdom.[4] This Diet had been assembled in a manner contrary to the constitution and to the will of the king, then practically a prisoner in Turkey. By royal order the Parliament was forbidden to meet, and dissolved.

The monarch was known for his good memory. When Charles XII returned to Sweden in 1715, the royal sun no longer shone over the prelate in the episcopal seat at Brunsbo. This became clearly evident during a visit that Swedberg made to Lund in 1717.[5] Without authorization he had preached before the king, and, in his own words, without sparing his criticism. Charles XII reacted: the Bishop should keep to his own diocese. Furthermore, 'He does not preach as well as he did for the dear deceased king, because he himself is now old'.

The rejected hymn book

As regimental chaplain, professor, dean of Uppsala Cathedral, during a period as Rector of the University of Uppsala and not least as bishop of the diocese of Skara, Swedberg manifested an incredible energy as clergyman, teacher, Bible translator, author of hymns, linguist, administrator, economist, and diligent travelling examiner and inspector in his diocese for more than thirty years. His solid economy permitted extensive publications. 'I would be able to fill a wheel-barrow with the books I have written', he noted.

Foremost among them was a new Swedish hymn book, whose contents he himself had written to a great extent. He undertook this work in secret, but with the king's permission. Little by little he widened his circle of co-workers and reviewers. The book was printed in 1694, but was not accepted by all Swedish bishops. A series of hymns contained lines of thought that, according to his critics, conflicted with the accepted confessions of faith. Twenty-thousand copies were confiscated, most of them left to moulder in the vaults of the Royal Archives in Stockholm. In 1695 a new hymn book was published by order of the king, edited by the bishops, and for the most part consisting of material from the rejected Swedberg book. He had financed the printing of the book himself, and even if the king did pay half the costs the withdrawal was a heavy financial blow. In his autobiography he regards ill will from personal opponents as the cause of the whole affair: it was an expression of 'disfavour, injustice, anger, and envy' by the high dignitaries of the church. The words about disfavour and anger perhaps referred to his colleagues' unwillingness to accept the pious devotion, coloured by conservative pietism, reflected in several of Swedberg's hymns.

His priestly critics did not, however, seem to have protested against a small portion of the edition being exported to the Swedish congregations in Delaware, by royal order standing under the control of Jesper Swedberg. Perhaps the need for doctrinal purity was less pressing in the overseas colonies.

But Swedberg recovered from the blow. He was still supported by his king. Undeterred, he continued his authorship: he wrote meditations, books on Christian doctrine, a Latin-Swedish dictionary, a Swedish grammar, an extensive collection of sermons, and a modernized translation of the Bible. According to Henry William Tottie's biography, his published works number almost fifty. Most were printed at the press in Skara that he had set up after his arrival.

The Excuses of the Unrepentant

Of all Jesper Swedberg's works his autobiography, *Description of my Life,* gives the clearest picture of his religious profile. From our perspective his faith is of interest because it bears similarities with that of his famous son. However, it must at once be emphasized that they are in no way identical. In summary, we may maintain that the bishop's fundamental thoughts on matters of faith became starting points or stimulating mementoes in his son's theosophical universe. His memories of Bishop Swedberg's world, of the space in which his father spiritually lived, and his continual association with God and angels became important elements in Emanuel Swedenborg's life.

For him it was a matter of moving towards a life in agreement with the demands of the Gospels constantly, every waking hour of the day.[6] With both father and son we find the same pietistically-coloured emphasis on the significance of good works, in opposition to the seventeenth century's objective, formally structured preaching. Time and again, in every conceivable context, the bishop emphasized the necessary connection between doctrine and life: 'God wants a faith of the heart and a faith of deeds', he called out from the pulpits in his diocese. What he called 'great-faith' or 'brain-faith' will never be enough.

All are invited to the well-known marriage spoken of in the Gospels, he wrote in an essay that could be read for a hundred years in the Swedish hymn book under the title *Betrachtelser om the Obotferdigas Förhinder* (*Reflections on the Excuses of the Unrepentant*). The majority refused, finding different pretexts to refrain from Christian life.

Vicarious suffering

Justification and its relation to faith and works was a primary question both for the bishop and for his son. It was theologically coupled with the question of vicarious suffering for mankind.

Jesper Swedberg's constant emphasis on the significance of good works for a Christian's salvation did not, naturally, negate the sacrificial work of Christ's suffering and death. However, in the Swedish church of the seventeenth century this central notion often came to be interpreted as a vicarious suffering which resulted in forgiveness granted in advance. Christ had allowed himself to die for the sake of our sins; man's personal way of life thus became of secondary importance.

But this was not at all the intended meaning of the biblical text. Both father and son constantly emphasized the danger of this false interpretation of the Easter suffering. The opposite was the case, wrote the bishop in 1709 in his book *Ungdoms Regel och Ålderdoms Spegel* (*The Rule for Youth and the Mirror for Old Age*):

> […] we should not think, nor could we think, that Christ Jesus, God's son, has redeemed with such terrible pain and death for us to live self-indulgently, luxuriantly, and in contempt of him, dishonouring him. In no way: rather, he shall have honour, joy, service, and praise from us.[7]

Emanuel Swedenborg agreed with his father.

The praise of wisdom

In the same book, *The Rule for Youth and the Mirror for Old Age*, Jesper Swedberg described at length the divinely inspired wisdom. It is, together with his memoirs, the document in which the bishop comes closest to us: its pages breathe his dynamism, power, and childlike piety. We can assume that Emanuel carefully studied the 578 pages in small octavo. He translated into Latin his father's poetical version of the famous last chapter in Ecclesiastes; it became a little booklet, printed separately that same year, 1709.[8] The last chapter of Solomon's book is perhaps the most famous text on the vanity and transitory nature of existence. It teaches that mankind, already in its youth, must be aware of the brevity of life and of the mental and physical decline that comes with old age. Such early insight turns Swedenborg's attention to the divine:

> Remember now your Creator in the days of your youth,
> Before the difficult days come,
> And the years draw near when you say,
> "I have no pleasure in them".

'Remember your Creator in the days of your youth': this is the prelude. King Solomon continues:

> Before the silver cord is loosed,
> Or the golden bowl is broken,
> Or the pitcher is shattered at the fountain,
> Or the wheel broken at the well.[9]

It was this sombre insight about the way of all flesh that the bishop hoped would be a 'rule for youth', making old age easier to endure.

Wisdom as a complement and counterpart to love would be one of Swedenborg's great themes. Wisdom and love partner each other; we do not need to seek for wisdom—it is present, by definition, in the believing and loving person. Wisdom is not stored like a concept in the memory; rather it is expressed as an attitude towards life and, even more, as a way of life.

Swedberg's guardian angels

We also find that Jesper Swedberg had a faith in angels coloured by the Psalms and the Book of Revelation.[10] He felt himself protected and led, throughout his life, by heavenly messengers. In his childhood he claimed to have been saved from drowning by their intervention and while at Uppsala an angel seemed to guide his studies. In his autobiography he recounts this supernatural experience. While sitting and studying in his room an angel suddenly stood at his side and asked what he was reading. Swedberg answered with a few names, among them Johann Arndt and Christian Scriver, whose books he valued highly. "Do you understand what you are reading in the Bible?" the visitor asked. Swedberg replied, "How can I understand without having someone explaining it to me?" The angel then told him what to read. The conversation concluded with biblical injunctions. The first words were the overture to the Book of Revelation, 'Blessed is he who reads and those who hear the words of this prophecy, and keep those things which are written in it', and then the words of John's Gospel on the significance of Christian deeds, 'If you know these things, happy are you if you do them'. The angel blessed him, and disappeared. Swedberg, we read, followed the advice he had been given, as well as the concluding exhortations.

This and other events of a similar nature caused the bishop never to undertake anything of importance throughout his life without first singing a few lines to his angel guardian:

Your holy, gentle angel,
May he never turn from me,
Driving away the devil's cunning,
Who daily tries
To bring me to a fall.
Help that he may do no danger
Nor seduce my soul
In this vale of tears. [11]

The angels' task of protecting and preserving man is analysed in detail in Swedberg's essay *Festum Magnum, Stora syndares store högtid* (*The Holy Day of all Sinners*), printed in Skara in 1724. [12] Angels are ministering spirits, 'sent to serve those who would inherit blessedness'. He often cites the ninety-first Psalm, with God's command to the heavenly beings, 'to keep you in all your ways. They shall bear you up in *their* hands, lest you dash your foot against a stone. You shall tread upon the lion and the cobra, the young lion and the serpent you shall trample under foot'.

On several occasions Swedberg refers to Christian Scriver's *Treasure for the Soul*, the collection of essays and sermons that played an influential role in Pietism, and whose first edition appeared in 1675-92 in five volumes. Swedberg loved this book: 'After the Holy Bible there is in my judgement no more valuable or useful book in my library'. Scriver's life was inspired:

> The holy angels, the pure spirits, shall bear us poor, sinful, fragile human beings in their hands. But why am I amazed at the angels' service, since for our sake the Son has taken upon himself the form of a servant, and served us with His blood and life? As it says here of man that many angels have been commanded to have watch over him, the prophet elsewhere says: 'The angel of the Lord encamps around those who fear him, and delivers them'. Without doubt [he says this] as a sign that the angels together protect men and women [...] against the power of the devil and of hell [...] [13]

Scriver also refers to the apostle Peter's words about the angels' 'desire' to 'look into' the Evangel. In Scriver's interpretation: 'the holy angels look with delight into the Gospel's secret and the riches of God's grace, which are promised through the prophets and presented and offered to the world through the apostles'.

The faithful soul's communion with Christ

One of the bishop's most characteristic thoughts concerned the *unio mystica*, the spiritual and secret union and communion that exists between Christ and a faithful soul.[14] Here was 'the Christian's greatest secret and highest happiness, greater and more splendid than any man or angel can express', he stressed to the congregations in his diocese. This union can never be explained, we read, only experienced. It was comparable to the 'union between bridegroom and bride'.

We find this secret, mysterious union in the Old Testament, where it can be seen as an example of the communion that Christ offers to mankind. The exodus from Egypt, the promise of the land of Canaan, and the wandering through the desert should be seen as an expression of the Christian church's mystical union with Christ. It also involved other events during Israel's later history.

But the significance of the mystical union manifested itself above all in the New Testament. Christ's life on earth, from his baptism in the river Jordan to his death on the cross, attained its real meaning when man entered into his words and works. The Gospels were not merely accounts of Christ dying for mankind. The Christian should himself die with him who was crucified. Only in that way was sin's power in the flesh conquered.

As we shall see, this preaching of the bishop is virtually identical with Emanuel Swedenborg's way of viewing and interpreting the Bible and the Christian message. The death of the 'old man', then revival and rebirth to a new life also became Emanuel's central message. Christ, dying on the cross, was a victor. Man, overcoming temptations, could also attain victory, with God's help.

Life after death

After death we should wait for judgement in a 'sweet sleep', wrote the bishop. At the same time one's soul would be carried to 'Abraham's bosom', according to Luke. 'Man's soul lives in God's pleasure, the body sleeps until judgement day. Then shall God glorify him: his joy shall be eternal'. These are the words in one of the songs that could appropriately be sung at Swedish funerals.

Sleeping or awake? The bishop's thoughts on this difficult question were quite clear. In his book, *The Rule for Youth and the Mirror for Old Age,* we are given this information:

> The body is consigned to the earth and becomes earth. But the soul, which cannot perish or decay like flesh, comes without waiting straight to God. Therefore, as soon as the soul is separated from the body, it comes before the face of God to give account of itself. If its account is good, the soul enters into eternal joy. If the account is bad, the soul comes into the terrifying place of eternal suffering. But the body goes into the earth, where it decays, and lies there till Judgement Day, to be united then to the soul again. Such is the difference between body and soul [...] [15]

The soul is spiritual and immortal, 'and consequently must return to God again, as it has come forth'. The bishop quotes Christ's answer to the repentant robber on the cross: 'Today you will be with Me in Paradise'.

The deceased and the blessed pray for the living, he wrote in his autobiography. His oldest son, Albrecht, who died ten days after his mother in June 1696, had promised on his death bed to pray for his father, brothers, and sisters when he had left this earthly realm. 'And I know for certain', the bishop wrote, 'that he [Albrecht] had never heard talk of such things in all his living days'.[16] The promise should remind Albrecht's siblings about life in the communion of saints:

> Yes, I believe that the saints have maintained their memories and Christian love, but now free from all incompleteness and weakness, and purer and stronger. Thus they remember what happened on earth while they lived here and what conditions were reigning here when they left us. Thus they remember and bring to mind their nearest relatives, whom they have left behind in this vale of tears. And this without any negative feelings or anxiety: but with complete joy and the delight of sincere love. [17]

The thought of a continual communication between the living and the dead would become a leading theme in Swedenborg's theosophy.

The meaning of the biblical Word

Father and son also shared the conviction that the Sacred Scripture is holy, and that it is man's duty to seek 'the real meaning of God's spirit'.[18] Swedberg's own Bible studies had driven him to write a commentary on the Pentateuch, based on the original Hebrew texts. It was destroyed together with other manuscripts in a fire at the bishop's residence in 1712. Swedberg, as always full of vitality, wrote a new commentary, finished four years later. He had the manuscript bound and sent to the university library at Uppsala. Here it would be well protected: 'because if it comes into private hands, the women will probably put it under their pies and muffins'.[19]

Swedberg's 'exegesis' was presumably of a philological character. He seems to have adopted the Lutheran view that the Bible should be its own interpreter. Having entered his duties as professor at Uppsala, he preached a sermon criticizing interpretations of the

Bible that went beyond the literal meaning. Perhaps this polemic was prompted by Cartesianism. According to the French philosopher, biblical texts were composed in such a simple way so that they could be understood by everyone, but there was also a hidden, higher meaning. A dangerous line of reasoning, said the bishop from his pulpit:

> All, especially teachers and servants of God's Word, should revere and follow the truth of God's words, and not their own clever discoveries and human interpretations. Many harassed and anxious souls could come to the thought: when God's Word speaks of the universal grace and will of God the Father, and that all will be blessed [by Him] [...] still this would not be the real truth, but words spoken *ad captum vulgi* [accommodated to the simple-minded masses]. Begone, begone with such highly dangerous and damned learning! [20]

And what about the words we do not understand? When we consider the matter deeply it would, according to the bishop, gradually become clear. He did not live to read his son's interpretation of the Scripture. It is possible he would have accepted most, if not all, of Emanuel's message.

Dream and truth

Faith in miracles and omens characterized Jesper Swedberg's life. Rumours and reports of miracles and mysterious healings of the sick inspired him to sermons that would recur later in his many books. He was often criticized and derided for his leaning to the supernatural. An example of his naïve faith in miracles, and of his self-esteem, is this account of the divine music once heard in a village in the province of Skåne:

> I cannot be silent about what took place in 1673 when I ascended the pulpit to preach for the first time [in my life]. Coming before the Hoby congregation [...] I preached as well as I could by the grace of God. In that country very young men go up to the holy place [of the altar]: I had not yet completed my 20th year. It was the third Sunday after Holy Trinity, when the gladdening message about the lost sheep is taken up. At sundown that day a great sound of music playing was heard in the church, and clear voices singing godly hymns, which all there in the village [...] unanimously reported and attested to. But there were no

organs, no instruments, and no one playing, nor was there any human being in the church. It was a strong reminder for me to represent that holy angelic office with the greatest reverence and care [...] [21]

Jesper Swedberg's world was animated with living spirits: 'Chests and cupboards creak' when wicked things are going on in the room; 'they are anxious and sigh when ungodliness has taken the upper hand, angered God, and distressed the angels'. [22] And dreams, he wrote, are an important source of information.

Father and son

There were plenty of tragic deaths and catastrophes in the bishop's life. But he never broke; he went on in the conviction that, nevertheless, he was protected from above. In his memoirs he seems very pleased with himself, a characteristic that was also noted by his contemporaries. The pious hymn writer and archbishop Haquin Spegel wrote a few lines about this side of the bishop of Skara:

And if anything to his credit here has been omitted
He knows himself how highly he is gifted. [23]

With his strong personality, he must have left his mark on his many children, without exception. Long after the bishop's death, Swedenborg saw his father in a dream that he noted in his *Experientiae Spirituales* (*The Spiritual Diary*). Speaking to the bishop's spirit he had explained the relationship between father and son:

In a dream appeared to me my father in the life of the body, and in the dream I spoke (to the effect) that a son need not recognize his father for father after he has become his own master (*sui juris*). While being educated by him therefore in his house, then (his father) should be recognized as father because he is then in place of the Lord: nor does the son then know what to do save from the information and guidance (*manuductione*) (given him by) the father. But when he goes forth from his (father's) house and becomes his own master so as to be able to guide himself from his own mind and know what to do, then the Lord is his father. These things I spoke in a dream, and I awoke: and then there seemed to me a long roll (that was) round, which stretched (*perrexit*) lengthwise (*longitudine*) from heaven. (It was) formed of long sticks (arrranged) about each other in the circum-ference, lengthwise (*secundum longitudinem*), and bound together by most beautiful textures of various colours: the colours were bright blue [. . .] [24]

The angels in the innermost heaven give just such gifts to colleagues lower in rank, he continues. The many-coloured ribbons all have a special meaning. Those who receive them perceive things that can never be expressed in words. The scroll leads the thoughts to a central scene in the Book of Revelation's fifth chapter:

And I saw in the right hand of Him who sat on the throne a scroll written inside and on the back, sealed with seven seals. Then I saw a strong angel proclaiming with a loud voice, 'Who is worthy to open the scroll, and to loose its seals?' And no one in heaven or on the earth or under the earth was able to open the scroll, or to look at it. So I wept much, because no one was found worthy to open and to read the scroll, or to look at it.

Was it his father who handed Emanuel the scrolled book with the beautiful colours? Perhaps not even the dreamer himself was clear about this.

Growth and studies

Chapter Two

Birth, godparents, and baptism

Emanuel Swedenborg was born in Stockholm in St James's parish on 29 January 1688, the date being reckoned according to the old Julian calendar. The Gregorian system was first introduced into Sweden in 1753 and time was moved forward eleven days; so according to our calendar his birthday falls on 9 February.[1] His father owned a house on what is now Regeringsgatan in the centre of the city, where the family lived. The property, which was later incorporated into a larger house, stood there as number 18 until the great urban demolition of the 1960s.

As we have seen, Emanuel was the third in what was to be a large troop of children and before their mother Sara Behm died, aged 30, she had brought nine children into the world. Their father was chaplain of the Stockholm Royal Cavalry Regiment. He was not only the regiment's chaplain and preacher, but he also taught the soldiers how to read. He stood in favour with Charles XI and was soon appointed preacher to the Court.

Infant mortality was high and baptism, therefore, was an urgent matter. Godparents played an important role, both socially and religiously. Jesper Swedberg and his wife Sara were rich, on their way into the tightly bound net that formed the Swedish upper-class. Good economy and family connections were the surest means to ease the climb in society.

Emanuel's godparents were Professor Anders Nordenhielm, tutor, for the past two years, of the future King Charles XII; Maria Sylvia Wagner, wife of the officiating clergyman; Auditor-General Fahlström, a childhood friend of Jesper; Ingrid Behm, widowed sister of Sara; Johan Reenstierna, Sara's cousin; and Margareta Troila, a friend of the child's parents.[2]

The ceremony took place in St James's Church. The old Catholic baptismal formula was still in use. The godparents answered the priest's questions in the child's place, affirming a renunciation of the devil and his works and accepted the articles in the official confession of faith.

And so to the name: the bishop wanted his children to have one baptismal name. The contemporary custom of naming the newborn after grandfathers or grandmothers had no biblical foundation. A child should be given a name anchored in the Bible.[3] The boy was to be named Emanuel. It means 'God with us', wrote Swedberg in his memoirs many years later. With this name the child would always remember God's presence, he continued, and with this also would come 'the exacting, holy, and secret union with our generous and gracious God that we stand in through faith'. The father was to be proud of his son: 'God, blessed be his name, has also up to this moment certainly been with him'.[4]

A religious childhood

The young Emanuel must have been unusually studious. In a letter to Dr Gabriel Beyer in 1769 he describes his childhood, and how from the age of four to ten his thoughts had constantly centred upon God, salvation, and man's spiritual affections and battles. He writes:

[…] several times [I] made observations at which my father and mother wondered, saying that angels must be speaking through me. From my 6th to my 12th year my delight was to discourse with priests concerning faith: that its life is love, and that the love that gives life is love to the neighbour; and also that God gives faith to every one, but that only those receive it who practice that love […] The learned faith, namely that God the Father imputes the justice of His Son to whomsoever He wills and whenever He pleases, even to those who have done no penance and repentance——of this I then knew nothing, and had I known it, it would then, as now, have been far above my comprehension.[5]

During childhood he also seems to have experimented with his way of breathing. In his great journal from 1745-65 he describes the morning and evening prayers in his parental home, and how he had come to reduce his inhaling in order to enhance his concentration.[6] As we shall see, this practice became as important for the Swedish spirit-seer as for so many other mystics, regardless of their religion.

Even allowing for exaggeration the child was religiously gifted and his childhood impressions played a great role. In *Arcana Caelestia*, written when he was 60 years old, he dwells in detail on the importance of early Christian education, apparently referring to his own upbringing:

> The truths that a person learns and believes in his earliest years when he is a young child but which later on he either endorses, has doubts about, or refuses to accept, are in particular these: There is a God, and He is one; He created everything; He rewards those who do what is good and punishes those who do things that are bad; there is life after death, when the bad go to hell and the good go to heaven [...]; also, people ought to pray every day and to do so in a humble way [...][7]

Such basic knowledge should be given to everyone at an early age; it was a matter of simple fundamental statements, such as the practical father-bishop can be assumed to have taught his children.

In summary: as a child Emanuel must have been impressed by the Christian message and its application, in a manner out of the ordinary. Another factor of importance for understanding the man, already mentioned in the previous chapter, was the continual presence of the supernatural in Swedberg's home. *Numen adest*, God is here, Carl Linnaeus wrote over his door in the Hammarby estate close to Uppsala. The bishop could have painted the same quotation from Horace on his wall.

The move to Uppsala and Sara Behm's death

In September 1692, when Emanuel was four years old, Jesper Swedberg was appointed professor of theology at Uppsala; a few months later he also became rector of the university. He was the king's man. The royal letter notifying him of the professorship was laudatory:

Your person has come to our gracious attention [...] inasmuch as we have followed with
pleasure the special industry in all the offices [...] that you hereto have been entrusted with;
and your extraordinary zeal for God's honour [...] your learning and ability [...] [8]

Four years later, in 1696, Emanuel's mother Sara Behm died, followed days later by his
oldest brother Albrecht, aged twelve years. We do not know what these deaths meant for the
many children. Emanuel, eight years old at the time, never mentions his mother by name
in either his letters or his other writings. The professor had an epitaph for her printed in the
children's name, now disappeared. In his autobiography he quotes a few lines from this
document:

We miss our dear mother, who knelt and prayed for us. Still, as our brother said on his last
day, that he would pray for father and mother, so now will our dear mother pray for us, with
greater perfection and strength and even more earnestly than before. [9]

Would the grown-up Emanuel perhaps preserve the memory of the pious Sara Behm
and Albrecht, their prayers, and the professor's consoling words at their graves? Is there
here perhaps one of the many factors that contributed to the future assessor's teaching
about angels, and to his many visits into the society of the saints, where memory and love
were of 'greater perfection and strength' than on earth?

Studies for a well-paid tutor

Jesper Swedberg had a remarkable talent for teaching. That Emanuel began his studies
of Latin and Greek very early, perhaps at the age of seven or eight, says very much. His
first tutor was a cousin, the orphaned Johan Moraeus, later a physician and father of the
girl who became Linnaeus's wife, Sara Moraea.

Moraeus was an excellent teacher, Jesper Swedberg told his students in his farewell
speech when, in 1703, he had been appointed Bishop of Skara. They were told that 'a
learned and God-fearing preceptor is like having a Joseph in the house, with whom boun-
teous blessing follows':

Listen now to a secret stratagem. I have a young son, who at the age of five had learned as much as my neighbour's son has learned in ten [years]. The boys have the same wits, sit at their books for the same amount of time. What makes the difference? My neighbour is parsimonious [...] He gives the preceptor no more than food and 50 dalers in copper coin a year, uses him for the most part for chores around the house. As a result, he gets the preceptor we would expect, one that is not particularly learned [...] a bad teacher [...] I promise my preceptor 240 copper dalers a year, four times more. And I show him great respect: as a result I get a preceptor for my son who in actual fact has four times as much learning, manners, and ability. He knows four times as much and is four times better when instructing my son to read and write [...] When my son sees that I honour his preceptor, along with me he honours him too, and likes him very well. And then not a little has been gained. [10]

Swedberg was a rich man: whether his neighbour could pay as much as the generous professor is a question he leaves unanswered. The essential point for us is Swedberg's words about this unusually receptive son.

Emanuel's younger brother Jesper would never join in the words of praise for the teachers his father had arranged for them. On the contrary, he had been 'frightened away from the books' by a tutor who was too strict. Jesper was 'a little wild' by nature, his father wrote in his memoirs and he was sent to Delaware in America to strengthen his character. After his return in 1724, he joined the Swedish army until his marriage three years later. [11]

Jesper Swedberg's new marriage; happy days of security

After a year of mourning for Sara Behm bishop Swedberg re-married. His new wife was Sara Bergia, a priest's daughter from Dalecarlia and the childless wealthy widow of a local judge. The professor was forty years old, his wife's age is unknown. She became a good stepmother for the seven siblings: Anna, the oldest in the group, Emanuel, Hedvig, Eliezer, Katharina, Jesper, and Margaretha. According to their father she loved Emanuel especially, and wanted to favour him in her will; but on her death bed, the father persuaded her to make a more equitable division.

The new marriage was a happy one. Emanuel and his brothers and sisters grew up in a harmonious, economically secure environment. Sweden enjoyed peace; later, during the wars and catastrophes of the eighteenth century, these years must have seemed like a faraway time of balance and safety. These were the final years of the ever-victorious Charles XI. Sweden was one of Europe's great powers, controlling Finland, the Baltic Provinces, and a large part of Pomerania, and thus ensuring Swedish dominance over the Baltic Sea. The king died in 1697 and was succeeded by Charles XII his fifteen-year old son, who was declared to be of age by the four Estates of the Diet. At his coronation in Stockholm Cathedral in December he himself put the crown on his head, without the customary symbolic assistance of the Archbishop. His reign would be known for autocracy and permanent war, without the Diet ever being summoned or heard.

The wealthy rector and professor had a house built for himself and his family on Central Square in Uppsala. Another well-known professor was a neighbour, Olof Rudbeck Senior, a botanist, anatomist, and historian. Encouraged by Charles XI, Rudbeck had sought to show that the North, particularly Sweden, was the sunken Atlantis from which the whole world's spiritual and physical formation had gone forth. The Latin title of the work, in four folio volumes, was simply *Atlantica*, sub-titled 'Atland or Mannheim from which Japheth's descendants [...] and all the families of the whole world [...] issued [...]'. It has been called an 'archaeological novel': an attempt to give ancestry and roots to Sweden, the new great power in Europe, that would outshine the claims of the old, continental powers to ranking places in Europe's history. In the writings of Swedenborg's mature years we sometimes see shadows of Rudbeckian ideas. Above all we find a striving for syntheses, whose daring sometimes reminds us of his far-reaching notions.

Jesper Swedberg as teacher, and an eleven-year-old student

The academic learning of that day writes Sten Lindroth, a well-known expert on the history of Swedish science, rested on three foundations: Lutheran doctrine, classical humanism, and scholastic philosophy.[12] Classical humanism was essentially knowledge of and familiarity with the latter period of classical antiquity, with emphasis on the Stoics and Epicureans, Plato and Aristotle. Here Latin was the first language, and Greek the second. Latin was also the *lingua franca* of learned studies, an 'Esperanto' for oral and written communications with continental European scientists and with those who held worldly power.

Overseen by his father and with the help of Johan Moraeus, Emanuel was initiated into the languages he needed for his university studies. Jesper Swedberg had his own prescription for learning Latin, documented in his textbook from 1709, entitled *Dextra sors docensi et dicendi seu Ludus Literarius* (*Lucky Draw, or Literary Game*): Latin should not be pounded in, but be absorbed as in a 'play school':

> Then I can certainly vouch for what I have already tried with my boys. And I have the experience that in one year's time, thanks to God's blessing, these boys, with pleasure and enjoyment, have learned more in an easy-going, enjoyable, unforced, and gentle way than I could have taught them in five years using a stern, driving, and unyielding method. It comforts me also to write that using this method I bolster many a young, discouraged heart, giving courage to study.[13]

The professor's 'literary game' consisted of short, simple Latin phrases that the student was to learn by heart. They included verses from the Bible, classical sentences, and adages which become gradually more difficult, supplied with Swedish translations. They were presented in groups of one hundred short sentences, arranged in alphabetical order. An example: in the second set of phrases, beginning with the letter 'P', one learned the following:

> *Parisios stolidum si quis transmittat asellum*
> *Si fuit hic asinus, non ibi sit equus.*

Swedberg's translation:

> If you want to send a dumb ass to Paris,
> the ass can still in no way become a horse.

Emanuel was enrolled in Uppsala University in 1699. He was then eleven years old. His brothers Eliezer and Jesper were registered in 1703 at the ages of twelve and nine respectively. All three belonged to the association of students from the provinces of Västmanland and Dalecarlia, of which their father was the inspector.

21

In five years, according to Professor Swedberg, Emanuel had learned as much as his neighbour's son in ten. As regards the course of his studies, we can assume that he followed his father's recommendations, at least during the first years. As mentioned he had found, as a child, great delight in discussions about God and the divine love. His father had gathered a comprehensive theological library and encouraged appropriate reading in the subject. It should be noted that a good fundamental knowledge in theology was required of all students, whether they were going to be priests or not.

Jesper Swedberg's students should also know Greek, the language of the New Testament. At the age of twelve, on 14 September 1700, Emanuel was given a copy of the 1623 Greek-Latin lexicon which the professor had acquired in 1674. His studies in Greek came into use in an academic essay on the sayings of Publius Syrus Mimus and Seneca, which Emanuel defended in a disputation in June 1709.

Of definite significance for his son's later years in life was Professor Swedberg's concern for the Hebrew language. Hebrew did not take a long time to learn, 'well within a quarter of a year, if one devotes as much energy to it as one devotes to other foreign languages'. Swedberg explained the use of Hebrew studies as follows:

I have the thought, and I believe I am not unreasonable when [...] maintaining, that all Christians who apply themselves to book learning, or to learn a foreign language, ought to know some Hebrew, the language God Himself and His holy angels have spoken to the holy patriarchs and fathers, and in which God has left us His holy will regarding our temporal and eternal happiness; now this, I think, is something worth learning and knowing [...] [14]

With these fatherly thoughts in his mind we can assume that Emanuel acquired at least some knowledge of the language of the Old Testament. Later in life this knowledge, presumably sunk in the depths of his memory, was recalled to become the basis for his further studies. At the end of his life, the Hebrew text of the Bible became his chief reading.

The teaching at Uppsala University

Emanuel probably attended most of the courses held by the professors, with the exception, perhaps, of jurisprudence. [15] His own father's lectures on theological subjects presumably were on his schedule. Jesper Swedberg had pietistic sympathies, emphasizing man's personal devotion and love to God, manifested in his daily life, as the essence of Christianity. As the Swedish historian of science Tore Frängsmyr has pointed out there were at least three other professors of theology who shared his opinion.[16] Like Jesper Swedberg they preached a kind of revivalism without attacking the church, in contrast to the movement's comparatively radical branch that was regarded as upsetting to society. These mildly pietistic teachings at Uppsala University are worth keeping in mind with regard to Emanuel's future development. It may also be worth noting that his fellow students, encouraged by their professor, presented papers on topics ranging from natural theology to the existence and characteristics of angels. These papers, always in Latin, assert that the existence of angels could be proved.

Most of the subjects were associated with the classics. Diplomacy was read using Pliny's laws for public life as a fundamental text, history was taught with the help of ancient handbooks. The professor of poetry explained Virgil's *Aeneid*. 'But not only Virgil', he wrote in the course description. Using the *Aeneid*, he would 'first take his listeners by hand and […] lead them to a knowledge of the nature and structure of epic poetry. Privately, taking Ovid, Horace, and others as a point of departure he will demonstrate the art of writing poetry'.

There were also lectures on philosophy, with emphasis on Plato, Aristotle, and Plotinus: in the following pages we shall see the traces of this early learning. But the students were also given some orientation in contemporary thinking. The young Emanuel above all must have come into contact with René Descartes' philosophy, an acquaintance with importance for his own way of thinking in the future.

The study of Lutheranism and the philosophical heritage must have made him familiar with the scholastic method. Scholasticism attempted to adjust Greek philosophy to Christian faith. For Aristotle, the concept agreed with the thing: truth was what one could deduce, or rule out, from the concept. During the Middle Ages people had begun to apply these rules of thought to fundamental Christian ideas: the results could be apparently faultless, but logical statements derived from the simple message of the Gospels easily went astray. The question of how many angels could find room on the head of a pin is often used as an example by polemicists on the subject.

Emanuel presumably became aware of the dangers of the method at an early stage.

Knowledge should be grounded in mathematics, geometry, and personal observation, and never simply be a result of a conceptual exercise. In books and unpublished notes he often warns about the risks of scholasticism: human reason interprets derived concepts as confirmations while in actual fact these deal with something quite different.

Jesper Swedberg, Bishop of Skara

In 1702 Jesper Swedberg was named Bishop of Skara, west of Lake Vättern in the south of Sweden; Charles XII signed the appointment in Praga, a village on the outskirts of Warsaw. The episcopal seat, Brunsbo, was located about a mile from the town. It was the year before the great fire at Uppsala when many dwellings were ravaged by the flames, among them the house owned by the Swedberg family. The following year, 1703, the newly appointed bishop was to leave Uppsala together with Sara Bergia and presumably also with his daughters Hedvig, Katharina, and Margaretha. Left in the town was the oldest daughter, sixteen-year-old Anna, who some months later was to marry the university librarian Eric Benzelius junior, son of the Archbishop of Sweden with the same name. The three sons, Emanuel, Eliezer, and Jesper, also remained in Uppsala.

The house on Central Square was repaired or rebuilt. Anna and Eric Benzelius were to live there, as did Emanuel and presumably also his brothers and their tutor. We know that Benzelius's two younger brothers Gustaf and Henrik also lived under the same roof: at least for part of the time.

Life with Anna and Eric Benzelius: science and mathematics

For seven years, from the time he was fourteen till he was twenty-one, Emanuel would be in the company of his sister and her learned husband. Bishop Swedberg, through his vital and practical religious engagement, had laid the foundation for the mature Swedenborg's outlook on life. Now Eric Benzelius became his model, influencing him intellectually. Benzelius was a polymath, a humanist with strong scientific interests, and later a noted politician with ties to the Hat Party. With royal support he had visited France, Germany, and England, and met Leibniz, Malebranche, Thomasius, and several other of the day's great lights of learning. He was a strong personality, with wider perspectives than most of his colleagues at the University.

Throughout his life, Benzelius corresponded with his acquaintances on the continent and in England.[17] He was a distinguished bibliophile, enriching the University's library with almost 3,000 volumes, and a linguist, with Greek and Latin as two of his many specialities. As we shall see further on, in the 1730s Swedenborg, now a middle-aged man, gave a tribute to his brother-in-law that can only be compared with the words of praise he dedicated to his father. But later he radically changed his opinion of his famous brother-in-law.

Fig. 2. Jesper Swedberg pictured in a copper etching. Under the portrait there is a verse in Swedish and German: Here stands Herr Swedberg's picture in copper etching shown/Whose learning and understanding, and zeal for Christ's flock,/Is widely found renowned in Svea's kingdom/And in cedar wood with eternal memory praised.

Benzelius seems to have contributed to awakening the interest in mathematics, physics, and science in general that distinguished the young Emanuel Swedenborg. In a letter from Brunsbo written by Emanuel to his brother-in-law in July 1709 we read that his choice of

Fig. 3. The 'Gustavianum' was given its present shape by Olof Rudbeck snr, who added the cupola to the roof. Beneath he built an eight-cornered 'anatomical theatre': a hall for dissections. This building contained also the university's library and two auditoriums for lectures and other academic events. In the larger of these two halls Emanuel Swedenborg defended his paper on Publius Syrus Mimus on 1 June 1709. According to a letter to Eric Benzelius it had been his intention to present certain of his scientific findings to receive a master's degree. However this never happened.

science was made 'on your advice and with your approval'. Here was perhaps a path for him: he could become a *mechanicus* like the famous Christopher Polhammar. His tutor Johan Moraeus studied medicine: perhaps he also contributed to the novice's interest in subjects that seem to have been far from the bishop's sphere of interest.

It would have been natural for the bishop's pious son to have taken the path to the priesthood. But throughout his life he stammered, a 'mild stuttering' as it was usually described, especially when he became excited or emotional. It was scarcely suitable for a priest of a church, where the 'service of the Divine Word' was celebrated, and in which the sermons, not the sacraments, were the central elements. As we shall see, this speech difficulty also made him dubious about the academic path, where oral instruction was far more important than it is today.

Descartes' appeal

Only a few decades after Descartes death in Stockholm, the French philosopher's doctrines had become a matter of dispute at Uppsala. His mechanistic view of the world was anathema to the powerful theological faculty; Charles XI was petitioned to forbid the teaching of his ideas at the university. Nonetheless the king decreed, in 1689, that the new Cartesian as well as the old classical philosophy should be allowed, but with one condition: philosophical criticism of the Bible was forbidden.

Descartes' philosophy was a union of rationalism and metaphysical idealism. The first and fundamental question had regard to the nature of knowledge: how could we know that our theoretical thought-structures were an objective reality and not simply subjective ideas? We can escape the abyss of subjectivity only if we can find a fixed point; this basis was in thought itself. *Cogito ergo sum*, I think, therefore I am. With the help of correct thinking and correct observation we can build up an accurate picture of the world. When we contemplate and study nature we find that it follows mechanical laws; mechanics forms a system, comprehensible to everyone. Here are principles and fundamental concepts freed from potentially misleading sense impressions. Our seeing, hearing, feeling go back to invisible motions and vibrations. We should be able to formulate a theory about a world of particles where everything functions like a machine. Here we find only extension, quality, and movement.

These thoughts are the basis of Descartes' philosophy of nature. We find mechanical structures far beyond the world we can observe with the naked eye. Everything is in motion in accordance with clearly distinguishable laws. But in what direction, and with what purpose? If we want to give a clear and unambiguous interpretation of our world, we must consider everything as a necessary consequence of a series of earlier states of being: therefore as elements in a development governed by laws. With the help of mathematics, mechanics, and geometry everything can be derived. The question about the earlier states leads on to the problem of the origin of the universe. As a consequence we find a Cartesian cosmogony.

The conclusions and observations of the thinking doubter were, however, insufficient. We need a comprehensive reality that includes the cogitating man. For Descartes this was the Divine, the Absolute Truth. God's existence is evident from our idea of the Divine, he said, making a connection with a classic thought. We imagine God as perfect, he must therefore exist, since this perspective includes existence. God must be truthful: consequently he guarantees the truths at which we arrive as carefully testing, doubting human beings. We see clearly and unmistakably that the outer causes of what we experience with our senses are 'extension' and 'movement'. We also understand that these characteristics must be seen and formulated as simply and clearly as possible. Once again, everything material can be understood and explained by mathematics, the laws of mechanics, and geometry. Nature functions like a clock.

To the theologians schooled in Aristotle, the Cartesian conception seemed to oppose the idea of God's presence in, through, and over everything in nature. The human soul was now placed outside the laws of nature and her kingdom; but as in older times, philosophy ought to be seen as a 'helping hand of religion'. Descartes' mechanical thinking was not a help, but a threat.

We return to cosmogony, the theory of the world's origin. For Descartes, God is truth, power, and movement. He is the infinite and the finite. The universe had arisen from his infinity. In the world of God and mechanics, the vortex and the spiral were the fundamental divine forms. At the centre of the vortex there was a compression: here was the bridge between the infinite and the finite, the origin of matter. It is to be noted that matter, formed in this manner, consisted of mechanically-active elements that affected each other by their movements.

And the soul? It was a substance in man standing under God, with a connecting link in the brain's pineal gland. Body and soul were two essentially different quantities. The one had nothing to do with the other, even if they co-existed in a human being. The soul, being enlightened by divine intelligence, helps us to correct our groping reasoning. God had once and for all 'programmed' our soul with his truth.

Descartes' philosophy must have acted like a challenge to young students and researchers. It stimulated studies in mathematics, geometry, physics, and the laws of mechanics. With sufficient knowledge, mental power, and good instruments, tremendous tasks were awaiting, with unparalleled stores of information and discoveries; world-wide fame was within reach for the right man.

Finale in Uppsala: the Stoic man

On 1 June 1709 in the great hall of the Gustavianum Emanuel Swedenborg defended the Latin dissertation that would mark the crown and conclusion of his ten years of study at the university. The essay, comprising sixty-two pages, was entitled *Selectae Sententiae* (*Selected Sentences*). His teacher had been Johan Eenberg, Professor of Practical Philosophy, who had died a short time prior to this event, and the presiding official for the disputation became instead Fabian Törner who held the chair in Theoretical Philosophy. The opponents were acquaintances: Anders Rhyzelius, at least periodically resident in the house on Central Square, and Jonas Unge, who would in due time marry Emanuel's younger sister Katharina. Bishop Swedberg had travelled up from Skara in honour of the day.

The essay was lyrically dedicated to his father. It was his son's delight, we read, to resemble his parent in writing and thoughts. The bishop, now fifty-six years old, was moving quickly into old age: Emanuel praised God that Jesper Swedberg's life had been lengthened to the 'snow white locks and wrinkled forehead' of this respectable age. Now the son could only hope that through the family's prayers the bishop's days might be yet more numerous.

The sweetened words of praise were in the style of the times, but Emanuel certainly had reason to praise the professor and bishop, not only as a father and teacher, but also as instrumental for his thesis. This becomes evident when we compare the essay's structure of moral-psychological statements with the methods of instruction in the Swedberg home.

The sixty-two pages were taken up with 176 *loci communes*, useful statements worthy of thought, attributed to Publius Syrus Mimus. He was a freed slave born in Syria, living during the century before our era. He moved to Rome and became known for his popular comedies, which explains the name Mimus; but for posterity Syrus is known for his sentences regarding moral-psychological matters: about 700 fragments of them were collected and copied over the centuries, finally to be printed in several editions. They were based on deep insight into human psychology, usually with a strong element of Stoic thinking. Existence was governed by a universal intelligence; consequently man should attempt to develop a strong will, self-control, and virtue.

It was customary that the presiding official, the head teacher of the candidate, would himself supervise and either wholly or partially write the document being presented. We do not know how much of the sixty-two pages should be ascribed to the deceased Professor Eenberg, but according to the preface Emanuel had himself carefully worked on his essay, requiring 'a great deal of midnight-oil in his lamp'.

The sentences of the Stoics are often laconically worded and difficult to interpret. Emanuel quotes an authority on this subject: their style of writing was like pricks with a needle. To explain the meaning of Syrus's short sentences Swedenborg now compared his utterances with those of classical authors and with the notes of the great humanist Erasmus. For further elucidation of the texts he also presented the well-known linguist Scaliger's Greek translation of the sentences.

Emanuel was certainly unusually well-prepared for this type of interpretation. At an early age his scholarly father had exercised his son in the art of identifying, interpreting, and commenting on Latin sentences. Once again we learn from his father's words:

> Finally, listen [. . .] to how I used to play this game with my boys. They each learned their particular lesson every day, its words and what they meant. In the evening, after dinner, they drew lots out of the little box in which they lay hidden, each with its own number on it. The lot showed the number of the sentence, along with its reward or fine. Then, if they knew it, they received the stipulated reward, or were freed from the penalty that an earlier incorrect answer had incurred. If they didn't know, then they got nothing: in fact, the penalty laid on them would be carried on their account to the end period. I kept a small journal of debits and credits, winnings and losses. Towards market day I would make a proper accounting with them. They then also received their payment, with a reminder to use their money well [. . .] [18]

Publius Syrus emphasized the significance of the will, man's ability to govern his own life, the importance of restraint and moderation, the necessity of facing death in the right way. As a typical example we can take the forty-seventh sentence: 'whatever man's mind commands to itself, it obtains'. This is a convinced Stoic's conception, Emanuel comments: the Stoics regard the mind as the governor of the body, its conqueror. By 'mind' we should understand man's nature or reason, his virtue, his power of judgement. These are the ideas that lead our actions, and to which all things are subordinated:

> consequently, if anyone in sound senses wants war, honour, learned studies, or anything else, neither dangers, fortune, nor death can make him refrain from what he intensely desires [. . .] [19]

You gain what you want, you see what you want to see: this is in the spirit of Seneca; but we can also hear echoes from Descartes: the soul steers the ways of the body. The Stoic-Cartesian view of man, emphasizing free will, good works, and reason's decisive significance, would forever characterize the author of the essay on Publius Syrus Mimus. It was one of the great thoughts in the neo-Stoicism and Classicism of the seventeenth century. We shall have occasion to return to these ideas.

Farewell to Uppsala: Poltava and waiting at Brunsbo

After the disputation Emanuel and his father, together with Eric and Anna Benzelius's four-year-old son Eric, and perhaps Eliezer and Jesper, travelled down by coach to Västergötland and Brunsbo where Sara Bergia was waiting. Emanuel's former tutor Johan Moraeus was also in the house; in 1705 he had concluded his studies of medicine in France and now worked as a physician in Skara, living with the bishop and his wife.

In May Jesper Swedberg had requested permission and a passport for Emanuel to make a foreign tour for his studies. Such an undertaking belonged to the education of the time: if the student had money, he made a 'grand tour' to the continent and England; if not he might go as a tutor with someone of better means. Jesper Swedberg had made such a tour at his own expense, and Eric Benzelius had travelled with the help of a royal scholarship. Usually this tour came at the end of academic studies: students from far-away Sweden gained some international experience, and could make useful contacts.

At Brunsbo Emanuel began a long correspondence with Eric Benzelius; the preserved letters are our foremost source of knowledge about his activities and thoughts during the years after his time at Uppsala. In a letter to his brother-in-law dated 13 July 1709 we read that he planned to travel to England in fourteen days. Could he obtain recommendations to some of Benzelius's acquaintances in the Royal Society? In England he would devote himself to science and generally make observations of use for the future. He was now studying the history of natural science of the previous century.[20]

But Emanuel's departure was delayed. On 28 June 1709 the Swedish army had been defeated by the Russians at Poltava in the Ukraine. News of this had not reached Brunsbo when the letter to his brother-in-law was written. Approximately 14,000 Swedes were taken prisoner, and the king was compelled to flee to Turkey together with a small force. In

Copenhagen the Swedish defeat was looked upon as a sign that the time was ripe to invade Skåne, the southern region of Sweden, which had been lost by the Danes in 1658. To meet the threatened Danish invasion, General Magnus Stenbock gathered a new army in the autumn. The presence of Danish warships around the Swedish coast made Emanuel's passage to England impossible.

In the midst of the chaos of war life went on at Brunsbo. Jesper Swedberg had his book *The Rule for Youth and the Mirror for Old Age* printed. Emanuel taught himself to bind books, which he reported in the same letter written on 13 July.[21] Earlier the industrious student had taught himself to play the organ; now, he wrote to his brother-in-law in March 1710, he improved his skills so that he could at times replace the organist; but he was wasting his time in the episcopal residence, where no one was interested in his science. Benzelius had met Polhammar: could he, Emanuel, while waiting for better times possibly assist the great mechanic in his work at the Stjernsund factory in Dalecarlia?

In February 1710 Magnus Stenbock and his army defeated the Danes in a battle at Helsingborg. The immediate threat to Sweden seemed to diminish, even if the Danes rallied to new efforts to regain the lost province. Several months after the battle, in April, the impatient student at Brunsbo was informed that a merchant ship, in spite of the risks, was going to sail from Gothenburg to England. Emanuel left Brunsbo and Sweden at the beginning of May.

The 'Grand Tour': England, Holland, France

Chapter Three

Difficulties of a passage: privateers, bad weather, quarantine violation and a tourist in London

The voyage from Gothenburg to London became adventurous, difficult, and dangerous, full of hardships. Later in life Swedenborg became a favoured passenger for the captains plying the same route because his presence aboard seemed to guarantee an easy passage. I quote from his own travel journal:

In 1710 I travelled to Gothenburg, from there by ship to London. On the way to London my life was in danger four times:

1) On an English sand bank in a dark fog, when I thought all was lost because the sand bank was only some inches from the ship.

2) Privateers came aboard, and although one suspected they were Danish, they made themselves out to be French.

3) From an English patrol ship the evening afterwards, that had gathered from signals in the dusk that we were the same privateer ship, for we were fired on the whole day, but without any particular damage.

4) Outside London some Swedes boarded the ship from a yacht, persuading me to travel with them into the city, when nonetheless all who were on the ship had been

commanded to stay there for six weeks, because they had already heard that the plague
had begun in Sweden. But as I did not obey the order of quarantine, they were searching
for me. I escaped the rope, but with the admonition that no one afterwards, daring to do
something similar, would escape. [1]

Among the Swedes enticing him to leave the ship ahead of time was a young Swedish
theological student from Uppsala, Sven Bredberg. He kept a detailed journal, with
information about Emanuel Swedenborg's first days in England. [2] Once ashore, they
rode for two hours on horseback the sixteen miles to Gravesend and then continued by
boat to London.

Together with Bredberg and a few other students from Uppsala, among them Eric
Alstrin, Emanuel quickly visited the capital's scenic sites. On 13 October he could report
to Benzelius that he had seen all that was worth seeing.

Isaac Casaubon

When visiting Westminster Abbey Swedenborg stopped before the tomb of the humanist
Isaac Casaubon. He became so touched by the sight of it that he wrote a poem in Latin
to the memory of the deceased:

Death has dissolved you into dust,
but you are still whole in our hearts. [3]

For Swedenborg and his contemporaries, Casaubon, more or less forgotten in our time,
was the very symbol of humanistic learning, having made classical Greek and Latin
literature more accessible than ever before. He was also known as a spokesman for
Christian ecumenicism; like the Bible translator and theologian Sebastian Castellio [4]
and the philosopher and diplomat Hugo Grotius he worked for Christian unity, based on
the fundamental thoughts in the primitive church, far from dogmatic theology. The
dream of Christian unity was part of the times, and Emanuel Swedenborg would later
urge the churches to unite in charity and love rather than emphasize the differences in
their official creeds. [5]

In Polhammar's tracks

The report of the visit to Westminster Abbey and the poem to Casaubon are given in the third of Emanuel's many letters to Eric Benzelius. These letters are the most important source of knowledge about his activities during his four-year tour abroad. The letters to his father have disappeared. Gone also is the original manuscript of the journal that he kept during this period.

These letters clearly show that his primary interest concerned science, above all, its practical applications. His role models seem to have been the inventive engineer Christopher Polhammar, ennobled with the name Polhem, and his brother-in-law Eric Benzelius. Polhem became famous through his ingenious clocks, canals, locks, and hoisting equipment; all his inventions were founded on the laws of mechanics, formulated by the inventor in a well-known 'mechanical alphabet'. Mechanics rested on mathematics, or could be most clearly described with the aid of that science. The world's secrets and possibilities for development could be, if not fully understood, at least described by the use of numbers and algebra. Man could deduce laws for how things functioned, confirmed by observation thanks to continually improving instruments, such as the microscope, the telescope, the quadrant, and the sextant.

In a letter Benzelius had encouraged his brother-in-law to concentrate on *mathesis*, mathematics and science. No such encouragement was needed, Emanuel answered. He had an 'immoderate desire' to broaden his knowledge in this area, especially in astronomy and mechanics.[6] He had read Isaac Newton's *Philosophiae Naturalis Principia Mathematica* (*Mathematical Principles of Natural Philosophy*), and he very much wanted to visit the great man.[7] We do not know if any encounter ever took place, but he did meet other scientists. The language of conversation was Latin. He tried to learn English and it is likely that he could understand and make himself understood in that language. However, it appears that he never really became proficient in speaking English.

The Royal Society and applied science

As a practically minded man Swedenborg had come to the right land and city. London was the home of the Royal Society which received its constitution in 1662. Its purpose was concrete and directed toward usefulness. The society's motto was taken from Horace:

Nullius in verba — 'no one should feel bound by previous authorities'. English scientists should go forward by experiments and mathematical thinking that could be of use to England as the great power she had now become through shipping, trade, and her rich colonial resources. Lectures were arranged and competitions announced, involving the great English scientists, where Newton himself occasionally functioned as chairman.

In his letters the restlessly active youth reports meetings and discussions with the astronomers Edmund Halley and John Flamsteed, the physician and botanist Hans Sloane, the geologist John Woodward, and not least William Whiston, mathematician and astronomer, theologian and opponent of the Trinitarian doctrine. Whiston wrote a book, famous in his time, on the simple and exemplary Christianity that existed before the Council of Nicea, 325 A.D. It was published during Emanuel's visit to England. Later in life Swedenborg considered the Nicean doctrine of God's 'three essences' as one of the roots of the Christian world's decline and confusion. But Whiston's mathematics and work with the problem of finding the key to longitude at sea stood at the centre of the young man's interests.

This focus on applied science was met with vivid interest at Uppsala. The plague had spread in Sweden and tuition at the university was temporarily suspended. Several of the teachers under the leadership of Benzelius and Polhem formed, as we shall see, an academic association called *Collegium Curiosorum,* The Guild of the Curious, whose task was to increase scientific knowledge and publish experiments undertaken in that field. Swedenborg became the guild's correspondent, recommending and buying books, as well as instruments requested by the professors.

Swedenborg lived with craftsmen whose specialities interested him and he 'stole' (in his own words) his landlords' professional knowledge.[8] Having learned sufficient English he attended lectures, concentrating on his own special interests. He busied himself with mathematics and the design of various practical inventions. His brother-in-law should know that he has been very industrious: 'Since my investigations have prevented me from being as sociable and useful as usual, and tired me out somewhat, for a brief while I took up the study of poetry', we read in a letter dated 15 August 1712.[9]

In short, Swedenborg went his own way and worked alone. Had he wanted university education, he could have gone to Oxford or Cambridge.

Religion on hold

The early eighteenth century in England was not only a time of natural science. An intensive religious and philosophical debate was also going on, at the centre of which was the problem of how a rationally thinking man should relate his insights to the Christian revelation. For Ralph Cudworth and the Cambridge Platonists, as well as for John Locke, John Toland, and Isaac Newton, this problem became the equation that would later engage the natural philosopher and theosopher Swedenborg. The doctrine of the Trinity was also being intensely discussed, with Locke among those who emphasized God's unity; but such questions were not touched upon in Emanuel's letters.

Thus, philosophical and religious problems lie at the focal point of the young Swedenborg's attention. Between the lines in his letters to Benzelius, there are glimpses that indicate that he more or less consciously steered away from the intense religious atmosphere in which he had grown up. Another point is that the receptive youth had probably rightly understood the combatants on the religious battlefield. Soon after his arrival he informed his brother-in-law of the day's great subject of conversation in the capital.

A mutual animosity prevailed between the Church of England and the Dissenters. Everybody in London was talking of an open conflict, where one of the primary figures was the clergyman Henry Sacheverell. Swedenborg told Benzelius that 'his name is on everyone's lips, everywhere people are talking about him, and his book is being read in every coffee house'; but he gave no details of the subject.[10]

The strife concerning Sacheverell should have interested the newly arrived Swedenborg. In two sermons the priest had attacked Whig Government Ministers for neglecting the interests of the Church of England. He charged them with indulgence towards the deistic ideas promoted by Locke, Toland, and Newton. The strife was actually, as Swedenborg must have recognized, about the implications of religious tolerance and its limits. Scarcely thirty years later these problems would become one of his own preoccupations.

Swedenborg and the problem of longitude

Six years before Swedenborg's arrival in London, the British Parliament had set up a competition with three large prizes of £20,000, £15,000, and £10,000 to be awarded to those who could solve one of the most important problems of a seafaring nation: how to calculate longitude at sea. The problem would occupy Swedenborg for most of his life, but without success.

In order to determine a ship's location at sea the intersection between latitude and longitude must be found. Latitude was relatively easy to determine but longitude posed a special problem: one must know the difference between the time on board ship and the time at a particular point on land. In principle one ought to be able to know the time from a clock but because of the ship's motion the clocks were seldom correct. There was, however, another method. With the help of a predecessor to the sextant one could measure the angles between different celestial bodies, and then compare the measured angle with the angle tabulated for observations made in London, at different times of the day. In this way the time difference could be determined; but the system had great disadvantages, not least that the measuring and calculating was a lengthy task.

Fig. 4. This portrait is thought to portray Swedenborg when young, but this cannot be determined with any certainty. We can regard the picture as portraying a young man in a good social position at the beginning of the 1700s.

For young Swedenborg the secret of determining longitude clearly had an irresistible appeal, as also had the prospect of the fame that would come with the prize. In no way was he alone in this: the problem became like the *perpetuum mobile*, a mania that could drive a person insane. In one of Hogarth's genre pictures from London about twenty years later, one sees such an inventor in his own corner in the Bedlam asylum.

Swedenborg's method was a simplification of the astronomical method. He had found, he wrote to his brother-in-law in August 1711, a method for measuring with the help of the moon.[11] Several others were on the same track, and the only problem was that reliable tables of the moon's orbit did not yet exist. However, he had visited the astronomer John Flamsteed, who explained that after many years of observations he could now put together tables for the moon's movements that could give complete and infallible clarity. 'If this is true, I have won the whole prize', Emanuel explained. But still it was not entirely clear that he could win the prize he deserved, he told his brother-in-law. Englishmen were proud and would rather not see a foreigner take home the victory. They had dismissed his project as impossible and therefore he had decided to refrain from further discussion with them. Perhaps he could send his theory to the astronomer Abbé Bignon in Paris for comment, after his calculations had been reviewed by specialists at Uppsala.

He would never lose faith in his method. His procedures started from observation of the moon's position in relation to chosen fixed stars, but according to contemporary expertise this method was practically impossible. He published his findings first in 1716 in his own magazine *Daedalus Hyperboreus (The Northern Inventor),* and then in Uppsala in 1718 and in Amsterdam in 1721, 1727, 1754, and 1766. In the last year, 1766, he also made a presentation to the Royal Society, but without success. At home in Stockholm he wrote to the Royal Academy of Sciences requesting that his paper be published in the Academy's proceedings.[12] The secretary attempted to convince Swedenborg of the method's impossibility. The paper was sent for review to the Uppsala professor of astronomy Fredrik Mallet; the opinion of the Academy was negative.

It should be mentioned that the astronomical method of finding the longitude had lost any likelihood of winning the prize by the end of the 1750s. An Englishman, John Harrison, had then constructed the first of a series of marine chronometers, accurate clocks which were insensitive to the motion of the sea. In 1773 the Board of Longitude of the Admiralty awarded him the main prize in the competition.

The longitude project is of interest primarily by virtue of the fact that it seems to throw light on an aspect of Swedenborg's personality. His faith in his own ability was equally as large as his determination. He had glimpsed the solution to a problem, developed it, and then pursued his idea with great persistence throughout the whole of his adult life. Here, and in far more significant contexts as well, we find this faith in himself, his task, and his call. Then, with this faith he adapted his thinking to what it required. A discursive pursuit, with questions and answers, was foreign to him. A few months later he wrote some illuminating lines in a letter from Paris to his brother-in-law: 'In this place I avoid company with Swedes and with all who can in the least way discourage me in my studies'. A spoken exchange of ideas with its mutual correction, praise, and criticism never seems to have been cherished by Swedenborg, as either a scientist or a theosopher. Perhaps this reticence was a part of his personality, possibly strengthened by his speech defect.

The fire in Brunsbo

We do not know much about how the bishop regarded his son's scientific studies. Emanuel complained in a letter to Benzelius about his father's lack of understanding of his economic needs. The money he had brought with him was not enough: should he live like 'the maid in Skåne?' he wondered. The servant girl in question had asserted that by the grace of God she could live without food; Bishop Swedberg had visited her, piously attesting the miracle.[13]

The scarcity of his allowance might have been connected with the fire that struck Brunsbo, the episcopal residence, on 11 February 1712. The house burned down and with it, according to the bishop, 'Almost all my temporal goods'. It was God's punishment for his sins, he said in his autobiography.[14] Everything was foreseen in the divine plan. He refers to the Gospel of Matthew: 'The very hairs of your head are all numbered, and not a sparrow falls to the ground without the will of my heavenly Father'.

Emanuel was informed of the catastrophe. Almost everything had burned up, but not a copper plate on which was engraved Jesper Swedberg's portrait.

It was a miracle. Why had not the fire melted or damaged the plate? To comfort his father Emanuel wrote three short verses, all included in the collection of Latin poems entitled *Ludus Heliconius* (*Heliconian Sport*). Here is a translation of the most eloquent of them:

Hear a miracle! This engraved image was covered in flames,
When the house burnt down, but the image was not injured.

Look, spectator, and see the piety of the lips,

The loftiness and dignity of this man!

See the learning and strength reflected in this picture!

The love in his face, warming us all!

It would have been a crime if the plate been destroyed

and if the flames had not turned from his visage.

Women at Oxford: poetry and relaxation

We read of the ambitious, disciplined, and constantly working student. Did he have traits of character other than will and ambition? He did write poems to comfort his father robbed by the fire, but he also wrote other poems, seldom or never read. His early poetic products, all in Latin, have been thoroughly analysed by the Swedish Latinist Hans Helander. [15] Most of them are pieces of skilful handiwork in the style of the time.

It is typical of the young Swedenborg that his poems are written as the result of determination, a conscious decision to compose poetry, not from any inner compulsion. At this time his studies and especially his cogitations on the longitude problem had tired him: he decided to rest by writing Latin poetry. A few more lines from the just mentioned letter to Benzelius may be quoted. Writing poetry would be refreshing, and perhaps also contribute to his fame: 'by it […] I might gain something of a reputation […] And by this poetry I hope to improve my skill, as much might be expected of me: of which time and others may be the judges'.

His hopes for further renown through writing poetry were never fulfilled. Most of his poems show a thorough knowledge of Latin, not least as Catullus, Horace, and Ovid used the language. For us the poems are of interest because they increase our knowledge of the young author, of his human side that we can only glimpse occasionally elsewhere in his works. An example is his 'Ludus Extemporalis' ('Improvised Play'), included in the previously mentioned small collection of poems that he called *Ludus Heliconius*, first published in Greifswald in 1714, and again in Skara in 1716.

The poem is dedicated to 'A', by which is presumably understood Erik Alstrin, a student of theology among those who met Emanuel when he arrived in London in the autumn of 1710. Alstrin had studied at Oxford and would soon return to Uppsala. Swedenborg visited him, and the two of them took a stroll that included a visit to the quarter where girls waited in the window for gentlemen to visit. Actually, there were three in the group, we read in the poem: Swedenborg himself, 'A', — and Phoebus Apollo, god of poets and youth. The two young men were filled with a quantity of wine, and one of them was compelled to unburden himself hastily of what he had consumed. The event takes the form of a dream, clouded in the mist of wine. One of them, the composer, gives his attention to a willing girl. The scenes become increasingly advanced in the long poem: ninty-eight lines of verse, written in elegiac couplets. Hans Helander has read the poem as an account of a kind of dance, with erotic overtones.[16] We may perhaps go further than this: the choice of words, the place, and the mood lead the thoughts on to intercourse with two women, a girl and her mother.

I remember how she looked back and reservedly consented,

and readied herself with bent knees,

lowering her thighs as girls do

and her body willingly too, thinking to please

as if it would be charming and enticing

to bend this part of her body in that way.

For if only this part of a girl is pliant and movable,

she then thinks that she will please many men.

It was as if she were girded with grass

as if she were dressed in the flowers of May.

(Lo! The reed-pen, the page and my Muse, as I sing,

are girded by honey-dropping flowers and masses of herbs.

And now as I sang my verses about this girl, by chance

a bee approached and stole from the scented flowers,

and thus he took the sweetness of the Nymph's fame,

drawing nectar as was his wont.

I do not know whether he drank a little juice from the Nymph,

but he disturbed the rhythm of my verses all the time.

But then he fled, lo! And I saw that both his thighs were yellow

---

as he flew home to his hive.)

Soon the girl withdrew within her walls,

then I glimpsed instead a woman's face, an old one.

The evening removed her white hairs and many wrinkles

and made her cheeks youthful and maidenly.

Then, I remember, that one of us wanted his knee

to be movable and pliant,

since the aged mother was obliging to him with all her body

twice with her feet and twice with her hair.

Her hair fell uncombed over her forehead,

her age lent her head dignity and gravity.

But I became silent, you know this, and sat without talking,

with something of doubtful gravity in my face.

The Muse was still there in my mind

and turned my thoughts towards herself,

and whatever I found in my mind, the Muse forbade

it from my mouth, that it may not be converted into sounds and voices.

Since the Muse in this way mocked the poet and laughed at him,

I said, "Watch out, you will be punished for being adverse!"

Without entering upon the question of the poem's lyrical quality we may stress that it testifies to the composer's knowledge of classical Latin, and to his interest in women. This interest is also manifest in some other poems, and is evident in *The Spiritual Diary*, a journal covering the period 1745-65. The document that lets us gain most clearly an idea of the role of sexuality in his private life is the so-called *Swedenborgs Drömmar* (*Dream Diary*), first published in 1859, containing notes concerning his religious crisis in 1744-5. His interest in the power of sexual attraction comes to light later on in his theosophy, especially in *Delitiae Sapientiae de Amore Conjugiali* (*Conjugial Love*), published in 1768, and we also hear echoes of experiences of the kind sensed in the poem in other areas of his authorship:

The man who is ruled by bodily desire or craving scarcely consults his reason and is only darkly conscious of himself [...] for the body is in the world and therefore far from heaven, where true reason dwells [...][17]

Academic disputes and their great victors: departure from England

In the *Dream Diary* the middle-aged and penitent writer identified and analysed the motives for his ceaseless scientific activity. The balance sheet was negative: he had worked to be spoken of, honoured as the one who knew best, attracted by 'voluptuousness, riches and vanity'.

Even if ambition and lust for fame naturally existed in small Uppsala, it could not produce anything similar to the mighty professorial battles that Swedenborg could witness in England. The resounding crash of these encounters was amplified by the entrance of the royal power supporting one side or the other, and by the fact that national interests were at stake. Who actually had devised differential calculus, Newton or Leibniz? Who was the first with the clearest lunar tables, the best although incomplete method of reckoning longitude, Flamsteed, Halley, or Frenchmen like Abbé Bignon and Jacques Cassini? Ernst Benz has given a detailed account of these quarrels in his biography of Swedenborg.[18]

The one in England who received the victor's crown after all the battles was rewarded in a princely fashion by Swedish standards. In his *Letters on England* in 1733-4 Voltaire described Newton's burial as an affair of state, unthinkable in his own homeland and, one can add, presumably not in most other regions either. Swedenborg's ambition must have been spurred by the possibilities of the European fame he thought himself able to gain. In his letter to Benzelius in August 1712, already mentioned, he explained his own temporary lack of success with his method of determining longitude. He had not received enough 'encouragement', and therefore was going to put the matter aside. But just wait!

I intend, however, to take up *mathesis* again, after some time, though I am also continuing right now. And if I should be encouraged in this subject I intend to make more *inventiones* than anyone in our *aetate* [age]. But without encouragement it's torturing oneself *et non profecturis litora bubus arare* [and it's no use ploughing sand with oxen].[19]

Holland: the envoy-mathematician

Swedenborg left England after a two-and-half year stay. He had originally thought to continue directly to France from England, but he now took his route through Holland, where he sojourned for about five months. His primary purpose was presumably to become acquainted with the land: a cultured European must have visited The Hague, Amsterdam, and Leiden. The University of Leiden was famous throughout Europe. The pious and pietistically inclined entomologist Jan Swammerdam had worked there, as well as the physician Herman Boerhaave. Swammerdam's manuscripts of his work on the classification of insects had just been published by Boerhaave with the title *Biblia Naturae* (*The Books of Nature*), a copy of which would later be found in Swedenborg's personal library. Emanuel's great interest was mathematics and science. The Swedish minister in The Hague, Baron Johan Palmquist, was reputed to have been a most capable mathematician.

At the same time as Swedenborg was making his stay in Holland, the peace congress that brought to a conclusion the War of the Spanish Succession was being held in Utrecht. Sweden's role in the European game of power, with her army defeated and her king a prisoner in Turkey, was less significant than before. Palmquist certainly had time for discussions of the longitude problem and other subjects with Swedenborg, who later told Benzelius about his time in Holland:

> When I was in Holland, and most of the time in Utrecht at the peace conference, I was in great favour with Ambassador Palmquist, who had me at his house every day; with whom I sat, discussing algebra. He is a great mathematician and a great algebraist. He insisted that I proceed on my journey, since I intend, next spring, to return to Leiden, where there is a fine observatory and the most beautiful brass quadrant that I have ever seen. It cost 2,000 guilders, when new; and yet there is no *observator* there. I will ask leave of the university to make observations there for two or three months, I can easily obtain this, which Palmquist also said. In Leiden I learned glass-grinding and I now have all the equipment and basins for this.[20]

His enthusiasm for the Swedish diplomat took poetic expression in the form of a complimentary poem dedicated to him: 'To a Famous Man upon the Arrival of His Wife and Newborn Child in Utrecht in 1713'. The poem is typical of the young scholar and poet, and his baroque-style predilection for analogies. As Hans Helander emphasizes, there is an inclination in the poetry of that day, and not least in Swedenborg's Latin poetry, to let clear statements reflect other concepts or events, beyond the poems' literal 'actual' meaning. Thus there can be innuendoes, as in the poem about the girl in Oxford, or more explicit double-meanings.

The name 'Palmquist', meaning palm-twig, lent itself in the poem to a picture of a dove with a palm branch in its beak. The ambassador's wife arrives in Utrecht with her newborn child to meet her husband and together they build a nest of inexpressible happiness, an olive tree! For Swedenborg the poet, the arrival and the meeting between husband, wife, and the new-born child become a picture of happiness. Utrecht likewise becomes a symbol: the city of peace.

As we shall see, this multi-layered mode of expression relates to the Swedenborgian theory of correspondences, the key that opened the seals to the inner, hidden meaning of the biblical texts.

France: poems and prose

Jesper Swedberg had warned about the Swedish tendency to admire, uncritically, everything French. He had been in Paris barely a month, but the 'French vanity' had not suited his taste and was not for him: 'A Dalecarlian is not accustomed to this. The more he is serious, the better does he think, speak, and act'.[21]

The future bishop had come to Paris in 1684, when making his own grand European tour; his son Emanuel arrived in May 1713. On both occasions Louis XIV was in power; the king did not die until 1715. Now Swedenborg would learn French, he informed his brother-in-law, 'this useful and fashionable language'. But mainly he would establish connections with the great French scientists and experts in the areas where he himself would be working.

However, immediately after his arrival he became sick. It is not known why. He was in bed for six weeks. We may note that, aside from his period of confusion in London in the summer of 1744, this was the only time in his eighty-four years that we hear anything of a long illness. His friend the merchant John Christian Cuno later described the eighty-year old Swedenborg as a wonder of health, with twice the vitality of a younger man.

This vitality is reflected in his programme for the ten or eleven months he was to pass in Paris after his sickness. The biographer Ernst Benz has already discussed in detail the young Swedenborg's visits to the capital city. Emanuel now had a better starting point than when he came to London; letters of introduction from Eric Benzelius opened doors. In his meetings he could now refer to his English contacts and his knowledge of British science. The continual scientific rivalry between England and France presumably made him an interesting go-between.

The great names swirl past: Abbé Jean Paul Bignon, publisher of the famous *Journal des Savants* (*Journal of Scholars*), the mathematician Paul Varignon, the astronomer Philippe de la Hire, as well as Benzelius's colleagues at the great libraries.

Emanuel presented his longitude theory, clearly with as little success as in England. And the fashionable language? What linguistic skills did he acquire? He spoke French and High German, said Cuno in his memoirs. In Paris for the first time, his learned conversations were probably in Latin, at least at the beginning.

Nothing indicates that Swedenborg left Paris with the same obvious relief as did his father. France and French politics would later come to be of great significance to him in his role as a member of the House of Nobles and the Diet, as well as for his role as author of voluminous and costly theosophical works.

A piece in prose, fables dealing with his sojourn in Paris, has been preserved. Late in the summer of 1714, when dwelling in the German city of Rostock, he wrote to his brother-in-law that he had composed some fables in Latin in the style of Ovid. He published them the following year in Greifswald, a few months before he managed to return home to Skåne and his waiting father in Skara, calling this new proof of his poetic ability *Camena Borea* (*The Northern Muse*). It consisted of twenty-two short, interwoven stories. Beneath the surface, hidden in the course of events, lies an account of a political nature, which has been analysed by Helander. [22] I shall return to this prose work in the following chapter.

The scene of the second fable in this collection is the forest at Versailles, not far from Paris. Apart from its contents, full of secrets, the piece testifies to Swedenborg's delight in the castle, the park, and the statues. He describes his surroundings with a clarity we rarely meet in his writings. There is a sculpture by Girardon representing 'Apollo's Bath': this work of art had originally been the starting point for a collection of poems, we read. But the pages were torn out of the poet's hands by a gust of wind and transformed into a bat. Swedenborg took this as a sign: he abandoned the lyrical form and rewrote his poems in prose, but in a form less open and accessible than in the first version. He had understood that the content of his poems were better in darkness than in the light of day.

His great educational journey ran toward its conclusion. He seems to have followed no more of a particular academic path in England and on the continent than he had in Sweden at Uppsala. Encouraged by Benzelius, he let himself be led by his interests in science and technology. He focused now on 'practical discoveries', from locks to beer barrels to megaphones and automatic weapons.

Poetry and politics

Chapter Four

> Your people, O Lord, have behaved themselves in such a way that you must be their enemy
> [...] We are besieged all-around, humiliated, speaking from out of the earth, muttering in
> the dust [...] Those dispersing us are as many as the grains of dust, and the tyrants numerous
> as [...] chaff [...] Many say about our soul: There is no salvation in God.
>
> Johan Runius: *Refuge in need, or the Kingdom of Sweden's humble*
> *supplication to God Almighty* [...] *etc.* (1709-10)[1]

1714: the political situation

Charles XII had been in Bender in Turkish Bessarabia since 1709. After the catastrophe at Poltava on 30 June the king had crossed over the Dnieper river, together with a small escort. In Bender he was waiting for his army and planned to continue to the Crimea where the Sultan would be his ally. Some days after the battle of Poltava he learned that his whole army had surrendered to the Russians at Perevolotjna.

The defeat resulted in Sweden's loss of the military base it needed for protecting its boundaries and territory. The king himself had lost his aura of invincibility; he was no Alexander on the way to conquering the world. He understood, naturally, that the capitulation would make his earlier successes more or less meaningless and that his allies would easily lose courage. We do not know if he foresaw the consequences his debacle would have on Swedish internal politics.

He could have returned home, rallied a new army, and perhaps been able to repair the damage that had been done, but he chose to remain in Turkish Bender. He hoped to draw the Turks into war against Russia. In this way Peter the Great's attention would be diverted from the Baltic and Finland. For four years the king tried, from his refuge in

49

Bessarabia, to follow the Byzantine intrigues in Constantinople. The Turks made three attacks against Russia during this time but without any tangible consequences for Sweden.

Gradually the Sultan tired of his royal guest and tried to compel him to leave the country; the result was a skirmish in Bender on 1 February 1713, that concluded with the king's imprisonment, mostly in Demotika, close to Adrianople (Edivne). In Constantinople, Turkey's hold on the king was considered a political advantage; but the foreign policy situation changed, and he was permitted to leave Demotika on 1 September 1714. Followed by 1,500 men from Bender, Swedes, Cossacks, and Turkish creditors, he rode through Siebenbürgen but soon left his main force behind. Accompanied by two attendants, he travelled, partly in carriages, partly on horseback, via Vienna, Frankfurt am Main, and Kassel; he returned to Swedish territory, Stralsund in Pomerania, on 22 November, accompanied by one officer. He had then travelled 2,152 kilometres in fourteen days, having been away from Sweden an equal number of years.

He knew, of course, that Finland and the Baltic provinces had been occupied by the Russians: he now received a detailed assessment of the situation. After Magnus Stenbock's surrender at Tönning in Schleswig-Holstein in 1713 there was practically no Swedish army. The greater part of the Swedish territories in Germany were in enemy hands; the remaining regions were now occupied by troops from Denmark, Prussia, and Saxony, and on 1 September 1715 their siege of Stralsund began. During the night of 13 December Charles XII succeeded in making a voyage over to Ale Stenar in the province of Skåne. The following day Stralsund surrendered. Lund, a small town known for its university, became the king's residence during the greater part of the three remaining years of his life.

Swedish opposition to the King: royal prohibition of the Diet of 1713-4

The king's long absence, the continual defeats after 1709, culminating in Stenbock's capitulation and the Russian conquest of Finland, together with the plague, bad harvests, and continual conscriptions and levies, had naturally created a widespread sense of hopelessness in the land. The people wanted peace, but every suggestion from Stockholm about a compromising peace treaty had been rejected by the distant monarch, called 'the iron-head' by the Turks.

Charles XII ruled dictatorially as sovereign by God's grace; he summoned no Diet from the time he entered into power in 1697 until his death in 1718. In October 1713 the government under the leadership of Arvid Horn, with the king's sister Ulrika Eleonora as a member, decided to assemble the Diet but the resolution was explicitly revoked by courier from Bender the following spring. Nevertheless, the representatives of the four Estates had then written to the king, declaring that a conclusion to the war was considered an unavoidable necessity.

One of the most zealous and convinced spokesmen for peace was Bishop Jesper Swedberg. In the minutes of the Parliament's Secret Committee from 1714 the great prelate pleaded for peace as soon as possible. He described the cruelty of the Russians in the Baltic provinces, Sweden's impoverishment, the despair of the population. Even if the sovereign had the right of decision, it was impossible to wait: 'So we must now, without further delay, in the Lord's name carry this issue into execution'.[2]

Emanuel Swedenborg's journey home: poems on war and autocracy

The correspondence between Eric Benzelius and Emanuel continued. It now dealt mostly with Emanuel's future. The dismemberment of the Swedish realm and political questions in general were scarcely touched on. This need not be interpreted as a lack of interest: it could be risky to discuss politics in an open correspondence.

Swedenborg had left Paris in May or June 1714. During his stay in The Hague a letter from his father reached him, urging him to return home as soon as possible. He continued to Hanover, where he intended to visit the great Leibniz, but the philosopher had travelled to Vienna. From Hanover he went north, through Hamburg to the Hanseatic town of Rostock on the Baltic Sea, arriving at the end of August to stay for a few weeks. Here, if not earlier, he must have heard of the Russian ravages in Finland and of the alarming proximity of Russian warships to the Swedish coast in the Uppland province. At the beginning of September he wrote a long letter from Rostock to his brother-in-law. It dealt for the most part with practical inventions he had made, to which we shall return later. At the same time there were a few lines about his compositions in which he had described contemporary political events clothed in fables:

Now I have time to put my poetic productions in order. They consist only of a few fables, like those of Ovid. Beneath these fables is hidden all that has happened in Europe during the past fourteen or fifteen years. In this way one is free to joke about serious things and make fun of heroes and people from our own country.[3]

This was the manuscript that he had had printed in the spring of 1715 in the small, then Swedish, university town of Greifswald: *Camena Borea*. He did not put his full name on the title page, cautiously contenting himself with his initials and the descriptive apposition 'Swedish': *Ab E. S. Sueco*.[4]

This noteworthy little work is preserved in only a few copies. The fables were practically bypassed by researchers until 1988, when Hans Helander published a thorough and careful analysis of the content within these Ovid-style stories.[5] The young Swedenborg's hidden criticism of absolute monarchy and the king's inability or unwillingness to refrain from continual new offensive actions gives a key to understanding the older Swedenborg's position on domestic politics. We also gain an early expression of his later very strong criticism of Charles XII.

Thus in cryptic form the fables present the main events in the great Nordic war: the many defeats and the king's captivity. The work takes the form of a question that should also be read as a wish: a dream of the cessation of absolute monarchy and a return to the old Swedish system, in which Sweden was governed by King and Diet united together.

'Now we are on the wrong path' was the message easily deciphered for the few who had access to the essay. The king, the fable's Leo, the Lion, had been presented with a choice. Would he devote himself to Pallas Athene, the goddess of intelligent and rational conflict and at the same time patron of peaceful work and discoveries? Or should he choose Mars, the god of war, under whose banner he could achieve continually increasing power and glory? The Lion chose conquest and battle as the path for his life. *Coronis*, the fable's code name for Sweden, wept in despair over the decision of the lion king.

In *Camena Borea* there is a key figure with the mysterious name *Dejodes*. Helander interprets the word as a symbol for peace and a code name for those who were advocating a return to the old form of government before the time of absolute monarchy. In the next to last of the total of twenty-two fables, Minerva (the Roman counterpart of Pallas Athena) gives birth to a son: this is *Dejodes* who has already appeared in the book. Helander is doubtful about the meaning of the name itself. It might be a combination of a Greek verb and a Latin substantive: *dänióou*, meaning to strike or destroy, and *odium*, denoting hatred or a hater of violence.

It is possible, but we could also guess a different, more specific signification, related to Swedenborg's later statements about the preferred form of government.[6] Key words could be *Deus*, *Ecclesia*, *Justitia*, *Ordo*, *Dominium*, *Oeconomia*, *Senatus*: the Latin terms for God, church, justice, order, rule, purposeful administration, Diet. The words form an acronym: *Dejodes* could then be interpreted symbolically, as a motto for a new Sweden with old and tested values: 'For God and the church, justice and order, a new form of government, through the control and government of the Diet'.

The whole text was dangerous. Regardless of the exact interpretation, we have before us something resembling a programme for restoration, applicable in a situation where the king seems to have lost his kingdom and perhaps disappeared forever from the Swedish scene. Emanuel Swedenborg was by no means the only one with such thoughts; similar views have been attributed to his brother-in-law Eric Benzelius, as well as to many others.

Festivus Applausus: a welcoming ovation

Had *Camena Borea* come into the hands of the monarch, royal disfavour would certainly have fallen upon the author and his career would have been 'nipped in the bud'. The fables had evidently been written entirely or in part already in Paris and were later edited for printing in Greifswald, presumably at the same time as he took to the printer the collection of poems mentioned in the previous chapter.

The king had arrived at Stralsund on 22 November. Like many other Swedes with a mastery of Latin, Swedenborg hurried to write and print a greeting in Latin prose to the returning Lion. It was entitled *Festivus Applausus* (*Festival Ode to Charles XII*). The full title translated into English reads: 'A Joyful Ovation on the arrival of Charles XII, the Phoenix of the old Gothic nation, and the Ruler of our northern region, in his own Pomerania on 22 November 1714'.

Hans Helander has also reviewed and commented on this third youthful production in Greifswald.[7] He emphasizes that the little book is an example of a special baroque and panegyric genre, often used at this time. The barely hidden criticism of the king in *Camena Borea* was one thing, an ovation of welcome to the Lord's anointed king on his return was another, almost a matter of protocol. Thus the genre would determine the content. The purpose put the old demand for *sinceritas*, for upright honesty, in the shade.

Helander also quotes a reflection that Swedenborg made much later in a travel journal, an observation made on a long trip abroad 1736-9, dealing with the causes of the great well-being of the Netherlands:

> The primary reason is said to be that it is a *republic*, in which our Lord seem to have greater pleasure than in kingdoms with a *sovereign* [...] from which it follows that they do not lose courage or rational thoughts from fear, timidity, or concern for the future, but in full freedom, with spirit unoppressed, can dedicate their souls, and elevate them to the honour of the Highest, who will have no shared worship; at the least, under *sovereignties* oppressed minds are encouraged to flatteries and falseness, speaking and acting differently from what they think, and when such a custom becomes *inrooted by habit*, it seems natural.

Perhaps for the sake of his career Swedenborg simply felt it necessary to doff his hat to the unexpected arrival, all the more since his fables published at the same time could be interpreted as saying it would be best to be rid of the absent king. Emanuel Swedenborg was, as stated, very ambitious.

Departure and return to Sweden

Emanuel had come from Greifswald to Stralsund late in the spring of 1715. The Governor, Baron Casten Feif, was one of the officials who stood nearest to the king, in Bender as well as in Stralsund. In July, scarcely a month before the allied siege began, he had received a letter from Bishop Swedberg asking for a favour for his son. The bishop recommended him as being capable in Oriental and European languages, and being particularly accomplished in 'poetry and mathematics'. He was now returning home after his long studies abroad, and intended to build an observatory at Kinnekulle near Skara, where he would continue his work on the determination of longitude at sea, a task of the greatest importance for which 'foreign powers' had promised great rewards to the one who would first solve the problem. If there were any opening for his son at any university, the bishop would be grateful if the governor would keep his son in mind.[8]

Feif certainly did not have much time to think over how a poetically accomplished mathematician could be used, but it was in the company of Feif's wife that Emanuel would return to his native land in July—'with the help of God', he noted in his travel journal.

It is worth noting that Emanuel's younger brother Jesper, an ensign in the regiment of Jönköping, was in Stralsund during the siege. He was attached to General Dücker, the commandant of the Swedish forces in the town. Swedenborg never mentions this brother in his correspondence.

Brunsbo, as we have said, burnt down in 1712. But that same year the house had already been 'extensively and magnificently rebuilt'. It became much better than before —presumably the finest episcopal residence in Sweden, Swedberg noted in his autobiography.[9] The moral of this he found in the prophet Isaiah:

When God will gladden His servant [. . .] He says: 'Through you the old wastes shall be rebuilt. And you shall lay a foundation which shall last forever. And you shall be called he who builds destroyed estates, who makes highways, so that one may dwell there [. . .]'[10]

With the king in Sweden: journal editor and inventor

Chapter Five

As proposed *Daedalus Hyperboreus* should probably be dedicated to his Majesty if conditions remain as they are. Perhaps, then, one must deal with several Potentates in the country, more than Sweden can endure. It seems to me that Sweden is being brought down and will soon fall *in agone* [into a death struggle], when her limbs will kick for the last time. Many are said to wish that the pain may be short and that we may be delivered. Yet, we probably cannot expect better, *si Spiritus Illum maneat* [if the Spirit would preserve him].

> Letter from Emanuel Swedenborg to Eric Benzelius, 1 June 1716. [1]

Homecoming, inventions

In the spring or summer of 1715 the returning son travelled from Skåne to Brunsbo and his waiting father. In August, he wrote to Eric Benzelius about his own future: did his brother-in-law see any possibilities of a post for him at the university? Further: he had sent a list of his inventions to the bishop, who had either lost them or sent them to his son-in-law. Had he received these designs? He listed what they were about:

Three sketches and methods of water pumps whereby a large quantity of water could in a short time [. . .] be pumped out. 2. A machine for hoisting loads, using water, as easily and smoothly as done when using *potentias mechanicas* [mechanical power]. 3. Several kinds of sluices that could be built where there was no fall of water, and still boats could be raised over hills, sandbanks, etc. 4. A gun machine that will shoot 10 or 11 thousand shots an hour, the details of which I have carefully described and calculated algebraically. I also intended to describe a kind of boat in which one could travel underwater wherever one wanted, as well as a machine to build a blast furnace wherever one had still water [. . .] together with several kinds of air guns, which once loaded could shoot 60 to 70 shots in succession [. . .] [2]

57

These inventions could be of use, he wrote; he hoped to have 'the opportunity to set one or two of them into operation'. His brother-in-law was also told that he was going to travel to the hills of Kinnekulle, not far from Skara, to look for a suitable place for an observatory. From this site he intended to make observations during the coming winter to confirm his theory about how best to find the longitude at sea.

The last lines of the letter are an obscure intimation to the effect that he was now inclined to take his fate in his own hands: 'What further success I may have in my plans, my dear brother will be the first to know. I ask to have that freedom [...] '.

What did he mean? We can only guess. In Sweden of that day, almost anything of significance had to proceed by way of the king. If the absolute ruler, still residing in Ystad, could be persuaded to take an interest in Emanuel, his future would be secure.

Collegium Curiosorum and Polhem's inventions

We go back in time five years. The year 1710 had been full of misfortunes for the kingdom of Sweden. The king was virtually a captive and in exile in Turkey. Both Latvia and Estonia were in Russian hands, as also were Viborg and Kexholm in eastern Finland. Denmark had allied itself with Prussia against Sweden and was preparing to invade Skåne, the territory of southern Sweden. The plague was ravaging Stockholm and Sweden's other larger cities. To add to these misfortunes came years with extremely bad harvests.

At Uppsala University, the majority of the students had left the city in fear of being smitten with the plague, but the professors seemed to have remained. It was then that Eric Benzelius, with his untiring vitality, took the initiative and founded The Guild of the Curious, in Latin *Collegium Curiosorum*. Co-fellows were professors with scientific interests, among them the physician Lars Roberg, the botanist Olof Rudbeck Jr, Harald and Johan Wallerius, father and son, both successively professors of mathematics. The Society's purpose was to further Swedish research, with the emphasis on practical science. Similar associations had been set up in other countries, above all the Royal Society in London. This English Royal Society was directed towards practical observations, that is, experiments and inventions that could be of use to society. The same purpose was to apply to the *Collegium Curiosorum*. In particular, there was a desire to spread the thoughts and inventions of Christopher Polhammar, regarded as the great universal genius, later as the 'father of Swedish mechanics'. Polhammar would soon change his name: he was ennobled in 1716, and then called himself Polhem.

Daedalus Hyperboreus: Swedenborg as journal editor

During his long visit abroad, ruminating on his own inventions, Emanuel Swedenborg had also been helpful to the learned fellows of the *Collegium Curiosorum* as a correspondent and purchaser of scientific instruments.

Even if Swedenborg had his own plans for the future, it seems that it was actually Benzelius who put him on the right track, when in a letter written towards the end of 1715 he mentioned the question of the publication of a new periodical. Its purpose would be to further practical science in the land impoverished by war. This would be done through the publishing, analysis, and above all dissemination of knowledge about Christopher Polhem's many inventions. Would this be something for Emanuel to undertake?

Swedenborg was in Stockholm when he received the letter. This happened on 1 December 1715, just at the time when news of the king's flight from Stralsund reached the city. The country's lamentable condition stands in contrast to Swedenborg's euphoria over the proposal. He wrote in a comprehensible French but with idiosyncratic sentence structure. His choice of language, he seems to be saying, corresponds with his exhilaration.[3]

Swedenborg was delighted with the letter. He had read it six or seven times and would continue reading it. The proposal pleased him in the highest degree. It would be a pleasure for him to publish the great mechanic's constructions and to provide the articles with beautiful illustrations, as ornaments in the 'golden tapestry of this joint effort'. His brother-in-law had obviously started from the assumption that Swedenborg himself would cover the costs from his own resources. Gladly, the editor-to-be replied, but this presumed Benzelius's assistance, who must write to the bishop and recommend the project: a few words from his son-in-law would carry more weight than a thousand from his son himself.

Swedenborg at once made contact with Polhem, presenting the project and a mathematical analysis of some of Polhem's essays. The inventor replied in a friendly tone:

It has been a particular joy and delight to look over the highly honoured Herr Swedberg's beautiful plan to publish, at his own effort and expense, the curiosities and useful things in mathematical physics and mechanics that the *Collegium Curiosorum* and he himself have collected, for which you earn and deserve much thanks and praise, if not right now while the day is as yet cloudy for the Kingdom, then I suspect from following generations when the just God once again lets the sun of his grace rise.[4]

The bishop seems to have opened his purse. Perhaps Emanuel received an advance payment of his father's part of the inheritance that came from his mother Sara Behm. However he acquired it, he soon received money enough. And two years later the bishop completed the payment, giving his children all their inheritance from her, including his portion as surviving spouse.

Thus Emanuel Swedenborg became both editor and financier of the journal that the *Collegium Curiosorum* would publish in the years 1716-8. Six issues were printed with the title *Daedalus Hyperboreus*.

The classically educated circle of readers understood at once the cryptic title's import. 'Daedalus' means dexterous in Greek, and *Daidalos* was the name of the mythical architect and inventor who together with his son Icarus was said to have flown out of prison to Crete with the aid of wings fastened with wax. The builder saved himself, while his son crashed into the sea; Icarus had, symbolically, flown too high, and the fastening had melted in the sun.

The *Collegium's* journal, then, was to spread knowledge of Polhem's inventions. The famous mechanic came to play a determining role in Emanuel Swedenborg's life. This applies first and foremost to the intellectual plane, for Polhem's gift for practical engineering was paired with an interest in medicine, psychology, politics, philosophy, and religion. His knowledge of mathematics and physics, his faith in reason and man's ability, as well as his rational and concrete way of approaching all problems, must have made a deep impression on Swedenborg. It applies also to the critique that Polhem made in connection with the journal's publication, which he directed towards what he found to be the editor's all too rapidly composed, sometimes superficial or inadequately supported propositions and solutions.

His dependence on Polhem seems to extend long beyond the publication of *Daedalus Hyperboreus*. The great mechanic's thoughts are close to Swedenborg's later theories in physics and natural philosophy. We shall return to the apprentice's dependence on the master in the next chapter.

Secondly, Polhem came to serve the bishop's ambitious son as a lever and fulcrum for his career. Polhem would be responsible for the new publication's projects and ideas, while Swedenborg would analyse their theoretical basis, thus becoming known and recognized: it would be a mutually beneficial project.

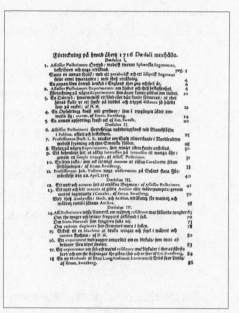

Fig. 5. *Daedalus Hyperboreus*. Title page and list of the articles published in 1716.

At this time Polhem was engaged at the iron works in Stjernsund in Dalecarlia. He supervised the manufacturing, in which his technical specialities were the production of locks and clocks. Swedenborg visited him in January or February and presumably then became acquainted with the two oldest daughters in the house, Maria, eighteen years old, and Emerentia, thirteen.

Interlude on Eliezer's death and his widow's marriages

Eliezer Swedberg, born a year after Emanuel, died in 1716 at twenty-seven years of age. Eliezer had taken the practical route, through his father's agency, becoming the manager and owner of the estate that had been part of the bishop's own inheritance from his parents, among them the property of 'Sveden', a farm close to the town of Falun. He is the least known in the crowd of children and seldom mentioned in Jesper Swedberg's writings. He was a simple, unlearned man, Swedenborg states in *The Spiritual Diary*, the journal he would keep in the years 1745-65, and he was also unstable and worldly-minded. The following has regard to his deceased brother:

> They believe that the all of heaven consists in perception, and are averse to such things as belong to intelligence. They were shown that they can be as easily led by the evil as by the good, and that they can have innumerable opinions about one thing, and not know which is true. They suppose that only is true which inflows, and which they thus perceive. It was shown them, by turning the thing over [. . .] Those in heaven who shine above the rest, are those who have studied the truths of faith, and at the same time have lived according to them; for the knowledges of truth and good enter into light there, and are in the light. But they who are in knowledges, and in a life of evil, are in hell; for knowledges, with them, have not entered the life, because they have not entered the will, and thus produced good.[5]

At the time of his death Eliezer was newly married to Elisabeth Brink, widowed since 1714 and first married to the owner of the foundry Riddarhyttan in Västmanland. In the same year that Eliezer died she purchased Jesper Swedberg's portion of his father's estate Sveden and resold it to Johan Moraeus, instructor and cousin of the young Emanuel.[6] In 1739 Moraeus's daughter Sara Elisabeth would become the wife of Carl Linnaeus: the money she inherited from the Swedberg family contributed to the originally-poor Linnaeus's well-being.

After Eliezer's death Elisabeth married for the third time, now to Anders Swab, a colleague of Swedenborg in the Board of Mines. He was the son of Anton Swab and Christina Arrhusia—the Christina who as a widow would later enter into marriage with

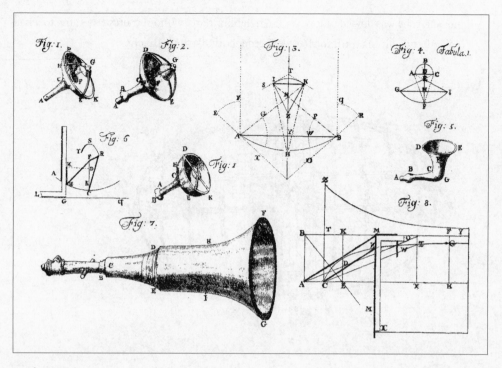

Fig. 6. *Daedalus Hyperboreus*. The illustrations above show Polhem's design for an 'ear-tube', a hearing aid.

Bishop Jesper Swedberg. Anders Swab left the earth in 1731; Elisabeth Brink was then forty-seven years old. In 1735 she married a fourth time, again to one of the officials in the Board of Mines, Johan Bergenstierna.

Sweden was sparsely populated. In the enormous Swedish and Finnish territory dwelt perhaps two million people. The educated upper class, including nobles, priests, and wealthy burghers, amounted to perhaps a few thousand families. Everyone knew everybody; their circles overlapped through marriage, politics, and business.

In passing it may be noted that neither Swab nor Bergenstierna were among Swedenborg's favourites. Swab was a hypocrite who had attempted to frustrate him in every possible way. He was an evil man, Swedenborg wrote in his great journal: his demonstrated Christianity was only a way to gain worldly power. And Bergenstierna was no better; he was devoid of love for the neighbour and without mercy. He came to a bad end; after death his spirit tormented Swedenborg like a toothache.[7]

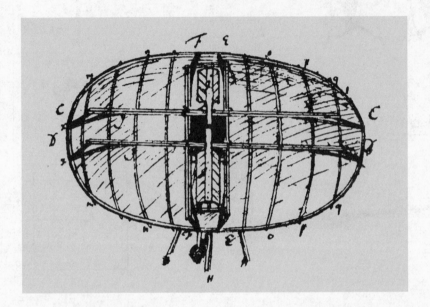

Fig. 7. In the fourth issue of *Daedalus Hyperboreus*, Swedenborg published an essay, entitled 'Sketch of a machine to fly in the air'. The text was not illustrated, but a sketch is kept in the Diocesan Library in Linköping. The project was based on an imitation of the way birds fly. The wings of Swedenborg's apparatus were to function approximately like a propeller: 'It would do no harm to tilt the wings slightly backwards like the wings on a windmill and give it power'. He was clearly conscious of the difficulty of the project. One could only proceed by trial and error, he wrote: 'As an example it should be noted that there was a man in Strängnäs who [...] fell from the tower in a strong gust, and was saved by the coat he had on, coming down to earth uninjured, which should give us more reason [...] to think further [...] When the first trials are made an arm or a leg may be at risk'.

The first four issues — a call upon the king

The journal project took shape. The text would be in the mother tongue, following the example of the Royal Society's famous *Philosophical Transactions*; Latin did not fit the needs of men focusing on the practical matters of life. The first number came out in January 1716. According to the sub-title, the magazine would contain 'experiments and observations in physics and mathematics made by the Honourable Assessor Polhammar and other ingenious persons in Sweden, and now for all time given for general use'. The reader found three articles by Polhem on hearing aids and the characteristics of sound. Besides this there were also some articles by the editor himself. They treated of experiments in acoustics that ought to be done in the country—a 'thunder horn', a megaphone—and hoisting equipment for use in mines. During the year three more issues were published. All were dominated by Polhem's and the young Swedenborg's productions. In the last we find Emanuel's theory on the correct way to find longitude at sea.

Thus, during 1716 a total of four issues were published. Together they would be a suitable gift for the technically-interested warrior-king. A set was bound in a volume, given a new title page and a dedication to Charles XII, written by the editor. Swedenborg extolled Polhem's merits, but at the same time in no way hid his own light under a bushel. The royal reader would find, it stated, numerous items that were the fruit of Swedenborg's own research:

[. . .] my own experiments, which I have sought to develop through persistent, careful consideration, both at home as well as during an expensive, five-year trip to those foreign places where *studia mathematica* are most popular and most highly valued. This is only the beginning, Most Gracious King; there is yet much more left that is hidden away and which one presumes will contribute to the well-being of Your Royal Majesty's kingdom, particularly to the improvement of manufacturing, navigation, artillery, and marksmanship. If this merits Your Majesty's royal grace, it will certainly stir many others to humbly disclose their thoughts and offer them to Your Royal Majesty's most gracious good pleasure.

I remain to the hour of my death, Your Majesty, my most gracious King's most humble and most faithful subject, Emanuel Swedberg.[8]

On the title page the king found a newly written poem by the editor:

Behold! Daedalus ascends into the heights against the wind,
and escapes the snares of King Minos set on the ground.

So, ride on the wind, Daedalus, with this art of yours:
avoid the traps laid by the low-minded crowd!

At this time, the king had moved his headquarters from Ystad to Lund. In November Polhem received a call to present himself for a conversation with His Majesty, the subject envisaged being the construction of a dam for a dry-dock for Swedish warships in Karlskrona on the south-eastern coast. Now the great mechanic asked his apprentice to accompany him on the journey to the royal residence. The proposal fitted perfectly. At the turn of the month, from November to December, Polhem and Swedenborg journey-ed on horseback to Brunsbo, where they stayed for a few days. From there they continued to Lund.

On one of the first days in December the travellers appeared before the king. The bound issues of *Daedalus Hyperboreus* with their dedication were put in the hands of the mathematically and technically interested monarch. Perhaps he was also given a few copies of Swedenborg's *Festivus Applausus*, as a further proof of faithful loyalty.

Swedenborg—Assessor, Polhem—nobleman

The inventor owed a debt of gratitude to his editor and amanuensis: the time had come for encouragement. On 6 December Polhem wrote to the king proposing that Swedenborg should now be appointed Assessor in the Board of Mines. Polhem's penmanship was poor —the document is written in what resembles Swedenborg's own, earlier handwriting.

Mechanics were important for the improvement of the fatherland, it read, and it was necessary to take care of people with the right gifts and talents:

At the present time I know of no one who seems to have a better aptitude for mechanics than Emanuel Swedberg [. . .] Therefore, with the deepest humility, I want to lay before Your Majesty my humble thought: would it not be more useful to bestow an honourable position on a person who has an aptitude for mechanics, than to let so useful a subject find other employment? And since there is a requirement in the Royal Board of Mines for nothing less than someone who understands mechanics equally as well as mining legislation [. . .] someone who is able to select and examine new candidates for positions at the mines, and also test their work and proposals, I therefore submit for Your Majesty's gracious consideration if this Swedberg, who otherwise has made himself capable of being an academic professor, might not be promoted to the position of Assessor in the said Board, and thereby render greater service to Your Majesty than at a university.[9]

Now events moved quickly. Four days later Emanuel Swedenborg was appointed as Extraordinary Assessor in the Board of Mines, although without pay until several years later. But the new Assessor found the appointment unclear as regards his right to a seat

Fig. 8. Polhem's famous hoisting machinery for the Stora Kopparberg mine. From *Daedalus Hyperboreus*, no. 2.

and vote with colleagues in the department. There were men in the King's Council who were jealous of him, he wrote to Benzelius; the question of remuneration, therefore, had been left open. Consequently, as Emanuel wrote to Benzelius at the end of December, he returned the warrant of appointment to the king with a request for a clearer statement of his rights and status. A reworded warrant was issued by the king, dated 10 December, concerning which Swedenborg commented to his brother-in-law: 'Those who had sought the worst for me were glad that they came away with their honour and reputation intact, so close had they come to burning their fingers'.[10]

Over Christopher Polhem the royal sun shone even more warmly. On the same day that Swedenborg received his appointment, Polhem was given the rank of Councillor in the Board of Commerce. Five days later he was ennobled.

The monarch's mathematics

Daedalus Hyperboreus was kept on the king's desk for three weeks, Benzelius was informed. The gift had given rise to a series of questions and discussions, where the king showed himself to be a dedicated mathematician. In a letter written in the 1730s to Göran Nordberg, a former military chaplain to Charles XII and a Russian prisoner at Poltava, Swedenborg described the following conversation he had had at Lund, in the shadow of the war. Nordberg later inserted the text in his well-known biography of the king:

On our successive visits to the Royal Office there were usually discussions, with the king present, dealing particularly with mechanics and aspects of its rules and powers, together with pertinent calculations, as well as regarding geometry and arithmetic, with numerous other matters of natural science. The great man displayed a particular delight and pleasure in questioning us about one thing and another, as if without being noticeable he wanted to learn what we knew. However, now and then, he still let himself show that he was not so ignorant in these matters as he pretended — which put us on guard against bringing up something general and trivial, or mentioning something we were un-certain about.[11]

Swedenborg gives an account of the king's exceptional ability at mental calculations — 'inconceivable to me' — and then presents a royal proposal for a new system of arithmetic based on the number eight instead of ten. Eight, the king felt, was a mathematically appealing number: in contrast to ten it was divisible without fractions. The two visitors countered that on the one hand eight was too high a number, and on the other using this number it would be too difficult to learn the basics of mathematics. Multiplication and division would be seriously complicated: the multiplication tables would then consist of not less than four thousand and ninety-six numbers, instead of the usual system which only went up to eighty or ninety.

But the king would not give in. He returned to the matter and gave Polhem and his protégé the task of writing a memorandum on his system and its application. After making many calculations Swedenborg, in spite of earlier objections, seems to have found the concept workable. In 1718 he wrote a small tract on the king's proposal, entitled *En ny Räkenkonst, som omwexlas wid 8 i stelle then wahnliga wid thalet 10* [...] (*A new arithmetic in which 8 is used instead of 10, whereby all calculations relating to money, weight, measures, and dimensions are done much more easily*): but the king died, and the tract was never printed.

The king was 'a man of deeper thought and penetration than anyone can imagine', Swedenborg wrote to Nordberg. The monarch considered anyone ignorant of mathematics 'as only half a man'. The assessor's overall judgement of the sovereign's personality and ability is very positive. What would have happened if he had been able to rule his kingdom in peace and rest? Swedenborg's answer:

He [would] presumably have brought study and science to a higher level and flower than they had ever been in Sweden before or presumably ever would be afterwards, since he personally seemed to want to put himself at the head of the troop of the learned and encourage each and every one of them to use his own insight to reach such a high professional level in these matters [...]

As we shall see, this positive view of the king came to be changed in the decade 1740-50. In *The Spiritual Diary* Swedenborg describes Charles XII as possessed by the desire for power; all his other characteristics faded away in the shadow of his passion for ruling over all and everything.

Docks, canals, and saltworks

As newly-named Assessor and Polhem's assistant, Swedenborg was drawn into three large projects promoted by the king and of economic and strategic significance to the country. It was a matter first of building a dry-dock on Lindholm Island at Karlskrona. Swedenborg scouted the site at the beginning of 1717. It was a complicated engineering project, necessitating great dams facing the Baltic. Polhem visited Karlskrona during the summer and had a provisional dam built to dry out the site. At the end of the year, the great mechanic left the work in the hands of others.

The second project concerned buildings for the production of salt at the Gullmar Fjord in the south-western province of Bohuslän. Here also a dam arrangement was necessary, and the required apparatus was designed by Polhem. To finance the project a company was formed with royal approval and Swedenborg explored places favourable for use; but for economic reasons the plans came to nothing.

The third project first became a reality in 1832 when the Göta canal was finished. This involved creating a navigable waterway between the North Sea and the Baltic, Gothenburg and Stockholm. The different water levels required locks, and here Polhem's mechanical genius came into use. On account of the poor economic times wooden parts were used, which later were to be replaced by iron.

Swedenborg's cooperation with Polhem during 1717-8 was presumably not free of friction. He told Benzelius that next year 'if everything stands then as it does now', he, Emanuel, was thinking of building his own lock, standing under 'his own command'. Working independently would be advantageous from many points of view, he added. [12]

The last year of absolute monarchy: warships on land

During 1718, the last year of the Carolinian Era, Swedenborg was feverishly active. His ambitions seem boundless: simultaneously with all his practical undertakings, he wrote a textbook on algebra and several essays of a technical character. When his brother-in-law warned him about those envious of him Swedenborg answered that 'envy makes me smile rather than worry'. The reason: 'I've always tried to be *invidiosus* (worthy of envy) and with time will probably be still more so'. He continued:

I wish I had many new ideas, yes, a new idea to put in writing every day of the year—the world would be pleased by it. In every generation there are certainly those who follow the beaten track, sticking with what is old, but in a whole century perhaps six to ten who come up with new things founded on sound reasons [...] [13]

The kingdom of Sweden was now largely in enemy hands. Rather than seeking to recover lost territories, the king chose to attempt to take Norway, then under Danish rule. In spite of the failure of a Swedish surprise attack against Norway in 1716, he seems to have looked upon the country as an easy prey, giving him a trump card in subsequent peace negotiations.

A new army was rallied among the few men left in the population capable of bearing arms. In July 1718 Polhem was asked by General Carl Gustaf Dücker's officers about transporting Swedish ships overland, to the bordering River Idefjord between Sweden and Norway, north of the town of Strömstad. The warships would be needed when the Swedes were to attack the Norwegian fort of Fredrikssten, situated on a hill near Fredrikshald (Halden). The normal route by way of the Skagerrack was closed by Danish warships.

We do not know if this solution to the problem came from Polhem or Swedenborg, only that the master sent his assistant to help with carrying out the transportation of 'two galleys, five large boats, and a sloop' over a stretch of almost fifteen miles. Swedenborg had brushwood and oak planks laid out as a roadbed for rollers. Three hundred soldiers were occupied in the seven-week task, finished on 5 September. [14] He does not mention the matter in his letters to Benzelius; perhaps he had orders to keep it secret.

Royal disgrace?

His relations with the king seem to have deteriorated. Had the monarch read his political fables? Here was good reason for royal disfavour. Perhaps Swedenborg had opposed an order to join the army? In a letter to his brother-in-law written at the beginning of December 1718, he described his last dealings with Charles XII, without yet knowing about the king's death at Fredrikshald on 30 November:

Thank God I have escaped the campaign in Norway, in which I came near to being enrolled if I had not used intrigues to get out of it. [15]

In *The Spiritual Diary* Swedenborg mentions his falling out of favour during the last days of the king's life, a disgrace ordained by God's providence:

> Many transactions between me and Charles XII were recounted; and it was then plainly shown, that the Providence of the Lord was in the minutest details, and that all things which were going to happen to him, in life, and after death, were foreseen and provided for. Further, that, unless the state had been changed from favourable into angry, with Charles XII, one (of us) would certainly have perished. This occurred with many circumstances, which it is not allowed to relate. Hence, it was evident, that, with the Lord, all things are present, and that providence is in the minutest details of all things. [16]

During the autumn Swedish troops marched into the Norwegian territory from the south and east. The war would not last long. On 30 November King Charles was fatally shot while standing in a trench in front of Fredrikssten fortress. The Swedish army left Norwegian soil in disorder.

From twelve to one

With Charles XII's death a new epoch began. In the introductory words of the royal appointment of Emanuel Swedenborg in 1716, we find a description of the Swedish realm inherited by Charles XII from his father in 1697:

> We Charles, by God's grace, King of Sweden, Gothland, and Vendland: Grand Duke of Finland, Duke of Skåne, Estonia, Livland, Carelia, Bremen, Verden, Stettin, Pomerania, Cassüben and Wend, Prince of Rügen: Lord of Ingermanland and Wismar [...]

At the king's death, however, Finland, the Baltic provinces, Carelia, Bremen, Verden, Stettin, the greater part of Pomerania, Rügen, Ingermanland, and Wismar were in enemy hands. Sweden, paralysed and waiting for peace with Russia, finally came to terms with the victorious neighbour in 1721 at the Finnish town of Nystad. The canal project was abandoned, and the publication of *Daedalus Hyperboreus* ceased after the printing of the last two issues in 1717 and 1718.

It was not only Sweden's era as a great power that was at an end. The days of absolute monarchy were past. The royal dictatorship was succeeded by a parliamentary system, where the four Estates—nobility, clergy, burghers, and farmers—took over most of the power. This new epoch, in Sweden known as the 'Period of Freedom', was to last from 1719 to 1772, the year of Swedenborg's death. For Emanuel Swedenborg, who soon would be ennobled, Parliament became a political arena where he would play a prominent role.

Everything was altered. A well-known epigram speaks of the shift of the throne from Charles XII, first to his sister Ulrika Eleonora and soon to her husband Fredrik I. A new chronology had begun: 'King Charles we have just buried. King Fredrik we now crown. So now our Swedish clock has gone from XII to I'.

The genius's apprentice:
Polhem and Emanuel Swedenborg

Chapter Six

If what one mind alone knows cannot be compared with what two minds have both observed [...] our whole philosophy of nature would consist of mere words and nothing more. Experiments give us the history of material and the changes in its movements [in everything except mathematics and mechanics]; however, things that can be measured must be made intelligible through similes and comparisons. For how could one discover that undulations in the air produce hearing or sound if one could not compare the ripples on still water with similar wave motions in the air?

Christopher Polhem [1]

Polhem's school

Soon after his return to his native land in 1715 Emanuel Swedenborg had become magazine publisher and assistant to the great Christopher Polhem, 'the Archimedes of the North'. Polhem was twenty years his senior, and possessed a brilliant engineering talent together with interests in natural philosophy. His insights were acquired through hard work: the account of his educational path gives a picture of a will and a constitution of iron. For Swedenborg work with Polhem became a more than three-year schooling. The great mechanic's practical and geometrically-structured cosmogony, and his conception of geometry, mathematics, and natural science in general, must have captivated his apprentice as much as they did Eric Benzelius, also an admirer of the ingenious engineer.

Human thought and divine motion

Polhem appears to have studied and assimilated Descartes thoroughly. The great Frenchman had, as we have seen, divided the realm of human thought in two: critical, testing thought, anchored in the observations of the senses, could build theoretical as well as practical knowledge. The world presupposes a creator: this was common sense. But when facing the

Divine, critical and testing thought could not function in the same way as when dealing with the material world. In the last analysis man was directed to 'revelation'.

Polhem characterized these two realms in his own way. Two principles explain God and the universe: *motion* and *matter*. God must be thought of as *immaterial* motion: the infinite and eternal, beyond space and time. Even if human reason protests against the thought of motion without matter, that concept must be accepted, according to a 'discourse' dated 1711:

> The existence of light and colour is inconceivable for a blind person; now, it is equally inconceivable for us that motion can exist without matter. Consequently, lacking a sixth sense in this subject, we must still believe that motion is separate from matter, although this cannot be intellectually grasped. [2]

From God, the Infinite, 'matter' went forth. This must be understood as occurring in a series from the infinitely and inconceivably small to the inconceivably and infinitely large: in the smallest of all created entities there was always motion and force.

How could there be any connection between the Infinite and a finite? Polhem answered in somewhat the same way as Descartes had, with a guess:

> [...] as far as human reason can go, and as far as knowledge of God's Word and the Sacred Scripture tell us, we find that at the very first God, through his powerful word, created mere matter, and then gave it life and movement so that it might as if of itself split apart and produce countless forms [...] [3]

But the question remained: how could 'God's powerful word' bring about this connection that human thought can never grasp? Here he acknowledged the impossibility:

> In short, as great as is the difference between man and God himself, so great is the difference between the finite and the infinite being, and as impossible as it is for a human being to enter into God's own wisdom, so impossible is it also for a human being to step over the boundary of the finite and into the Infinite, and so inconceivable is it to find an intermediary

between something and nothing, I mean between the very smallest entity that geometrical progression can run to, and zero, which is the end point of all progression, so impossible is it also to find an intermediary between the material and immaterial.[4]

For Polhem all motion, and matter in all its forms, were infinite and indestructible: nothing disappears. But human reason cannot definitely determine if nature from the beginning, 'at the first moment of creation', was so designed that from that point on the divine work could continue by itself, or whether this creation still proceeds because of God's continuing judgements. Like Descartes he refers to the omniscience of the 'divine watchmaker':

[…] as far as human reason can see, nature is of itself completely capable of carrying out the effect and action that God at the first moment of creation planned and decreed it should perform, no otherwise than as a clock produces its effect, chiming and displaying the time according to the watchmaker's intention. Nevertheless, it lies in God's power to change and correct this when it pleases him […]

Nature's catechism and the mechanical world

How do we acquire knowledge of the divine element in our existence? The answer was obvious, in Polhem's opinion. In a letter to Benzelius in November 1712, he explained, that 'the helping, firm support [needed] for all of the work of religion' is to be found 'in mathematical physics'.[5] First and foremost it is a matter of rightly understanding the process of creation. There is in fact no contradiction whatever between Moses' account and the features of nature. And once man has correctly learned to see God's hand in the creation of the world, the main elements of Christian doctrine follow of themselves.

Like Descartes, Polhem looked upon nature as geometrically and mathematically structured. Nature, created by God, can be understood and analysed in all its aspects. For Descartes and seventeenth century France, *l'honnête homme*, the educated and intelligently reasoning human being, through the process of reflection was capable of personally coming to ethical and religious insights, satisfying both to the person himself and to society. Common sense was related to mathematics and geometry.

According to Polhem, everything in the material world could be explained mechanically, as a result of pressure or impact. All changes were spatial, and consequently could be explained and described in both geometrical and mathematical terms. This also applied to the life of the human soul. Descartes had explained the movements of the human body by 'animal spirits' produced in the blood:

> which are like a very subtle wind, or rather like a very pure and lively flame which, rising continually in great abundance from the heart to the brain, goes by means of the nerves into the muscles and gives movement to all the limbs [. . .] [6]

Polhem adopted this Cartesian idea of animal spirits. They functioned as bearers and mediating agencies of power, and their energy consisted of tremulations, vibrations, that could go on beyond their bodily centre. Thought was material, and functioned mechanically, he wrote in an essay entitled, 'The Being of Spirits':

> And just as hearing can go through a wall, and sight through the hardest diamond, it can also be stated with certainty that nothing can hinder the free passage of thoughts [. . .] It is as a result of this activity that two very good friends can know about each other many thousands of miles away [. . .] Yes, what can we say about dreams other than that the fine particles which have been set in motion linger as does light after one has seen the sun and come into the darkness [. . .] Yes, what can we say of the phantoms of the deceased, ghosts, and similar things other than that between the best of friends the finest materials of thought are in motion, producing their effect [. . .] [7]

Particles, vacuum, and animal spirits

Polhem's thinking was always concrete: all abstractions should be anchored in facts and common sense. 'Without comparisons and parallels one doesn't go far in physics', Polhem told Benzelius in a memorandum in 1722, accompanied by many examples.[8]

This desire to make things concrete caused him to question Descartes' famous method, the way of logical thought and doubt. Polhem's chief objection seems to have concerned the theoretical foundation of Cartesian ideas: they were not built on experiments. Above all he criticized Descartes' concept of matter as an originally motionless mass, without a vacuum. No: matter consisted of small round bodies, and between these 'corpuscles' there was empty space. These round balls were in continuous motion, and a vacuum between them was a necessary precondition for their motion and rotation in space. It was precisely this motion that brought about the changes that, following the laws of mechanics, build up our world. Each particle rotated around its axis with an eternal, unchanging power, the motion of which was initiated from the Infinite. But the single particle was incomplete; it began to function only when united with another, and then with yet more. As a result their inborn speed diminished, and they were changed to bodies having their own existence.

The genius's apprentice

Working with Christopher Polhem must have been most promising for a young man aiming at a future in mathematics, mechanics, and physics. Emanuel Swedenborg's world of ideas would for a long time be characterized by methods and ideas that were very close to Polhem's. This applies above all to his mechanical view of the world, the thought that all can be explained by laws of motion and force, and that these explanations should apply also to the nature and role of the divine. Here Polhem's significance can only be suggested. As a concluding concrete example of the apprentice's dependence on the master we can take the concept of material 'tremulations' as the means for the transfer of thoughts from one individual to another. As we have seen, Polhem, in his essay 'The Being of Spirits', had explained a psychic phenomenon as the result of 'vibrations'. In the sixth and last issue of *Daedalus Hyperboreus*, dated 1717 but not printed until the following year, we meet these thoughts in an article by Emanuel Swedenborg, 'Bewis at wårt lefwande wesende består merendels i små Darringar, thet är Tremulationer' ('Proof that our innermost being consists for the most part of small vibrations, that is, tremulations'). Here we can read the following:

It often happens that one person comes to think about another, and that he then knows what the other is doing and thinking. This [involves the fact that] his membranes are vibrating from the motions in membranes in the other person's brain, in the same way that one string [on a musical instrument] affects another when they are both tuned to the same note.[9]

We shall return to these 'small vibrations' in the chapter on the question of Swedenborg's presumed clairvoyant faculty.

Life after the king's death: Polhem and his daughters, ennoblement, the search for a career

Chapter Seven

Polhem's shadow

Emanuel Swedenborg had become the great mechanic's official assistant since their joint meeting with the king in Lund in December 1716. After the monarch's death their work together ceased. The country was impoverished and there was no longer any money for mechanical constructions. Perhaps the assistant left his master of his own accord: Polhem had a difficult nature, often or continually involved in disputes about pay, allowances, and reimbursements of different kinds. He was hot-headed, irritable, and conscious of his superior talent in a way that must have been trying for those around him. We have already seen that the apprentice's desire to work under the brilliant engineer had weakened. They had been brought together by the magazine project that Swedenborg financed. The last issue was dated April-June 1717, but was not published until October 1718, a month before the king's death. There was discussion about producing a new issue but without result.

Polhem realized that something had happened and in April 1719 wrote a letter to Benzelius about this matter. Communication with Swedenborg, whose 'lively *ingenio*' he valued, had now ceased. They had had a series of discussions and a correspondence that they mutually enjoyed. Polhem continues:

[...] the fact that both of these have ceased for some time troubles me about his health, because three of my letters that I wrote to him in Stockholm have been returned unopened, and as I understand it the first place he would go to is Uppsala; and so I gratefully ask you to convey my greetings [to him] there, or by letter to wherever he may now be staying, and ask him to respond to my request that he delight me with one of his pleasant letters, which are all the more welcome at our house since as, he knows, he has given us reason to love him as our own dear son. [1]

What had happened? Had he simply tired of his difficult employer?

The suitor's rejection

At the end of his great journey abroad in 1715, Emanuel was twenty-seven years old. He had a natural interest in women. His sisters were already married. What would happen to him? We may assume that following the custom of the time he would be looking for a wife with a good social position and preferably also with some fortune. Adding new branches to the family tree was important: advancement and social position were to a great extent dependent on having the right family connections.

Polhem had two daughters who as far as their age was concerned could come under consideration: Maria, born in 1698, and Emerentia, five years younger. Swedenborg had met both girls on a visit to Polhem at the Stjernsund iron works in 1715 or 1716, and in Stockholm in 1717. A marriage between Maria and the gifted and well-to-do Emanuel would have been acceptable to both families.

The king was of the same opinion, according to an account given by the Danish General Christian Tuxen in a letter to August Nordenskjöld, who keenly subscribed to Swedenborg's message. Around 1770 Tuxen had asked Swedenborg if he had ever thought of marrying. Swedenborg's answer has given rise to a whole body of literature. His words are repeated here:

> This led me jocosely to ask him, whether he had ever been married, or desirous of marry-
> ing. He answered No; but that once in his youth he had been on the road to matrimony;
> King Charles XII having recommended the famous Polhem to give him his daughter.

On my asking what obstacle had prevented it, he replied: "She would not have me, as she had promised herself to another person to whom she was more attached". I then craved his pardon if I had been too inquisitive. [He answered, ask whatever question you please, I shall answer in truth. I then inquired, whether in his youth he could keep free from temptations with regard to the sex? He replied, "Not altogether; in my youth I had a mistress in Italy".] [2]

The question of marriage between Maria and Emanuel was probably discussed without her knowledge. But already in the summer of 1717 we find that she had another man in her thoughts, the District Court Judge Herman Mallmin. According to Maria he had only one fault: he had no permanent position. Polhem wrote a letter asking the king to give Mallmin a stable appointment: 'By your Majesty's doing me this kind service [...] I would be able to be of greater use, so that many thousand dalers will be recouped by my having a freer and more relaxed mind in the tasks entrusted to me'. [3] In spite of these arguments, the king did not consider Maria's marriage as an urgent matter of state, and nothing became of the hoped-for match.

Swedenborg probably knew nothing about this. Similarly, Maria's engagement in 1718 to the courtier Martin Ludvig Manderström is said to have come as a surprise. In a letter to Benzelius dated 14 September he wonders 'what people will say about it, since it is my post'. Emanuel thus indicates that he had been promised Maria by her father. Now he turns his eyes instead towards Emerentia. Emanuel continues, 'His second daughter is, in my opinion, much prettier'. [4] Maria's wedding was celebrated that same year, a few weeks before the king's death.

Emerentia Polhem, 'much prettier', was only fourteen years old in 1717. There is an unconfirmed story about a written contract between Polhem and Swedenborg in which the father promised to try to obtain his younger daughter's consent to a marriage when she became older. Swedenborg had the letter in hand but when Emerentia learned about it she was in despair. Her brother, pitying his sister, stole and destroyed the letter, and Swedenborg soon refrained from courting her.

Perhaps these disappointed hopes for marriage should be taken into consideration as a reason for the break in the cooperation between teacher and student.

These unsuccessful plans for marriage are perhaps of marginal importance from the perspective of the young Swedenborg's relationship with Polhem. More important is the deep and lasting impression Polhem's way of thinking made on the young man.

Swedenborg the nobleman

In Sweden of old, the bishops had a high social position. *Ex officio* they all had a role in government, in the Estate of the Clergy. They ranked directly after barons, and thus stood above ordinary noblemen. As a reward for their father's episcopal merits, their children were customarily ennobled. In two communications, in February and April 1716, Jesper Swedberg, ever solicitous for himself and his family, had petitioned the king for nobility for his wife and children, and in addition for his sons-in-law. These letters seem to have gone unanswered. As already stated, Charles XI's former favourite was less popular with Charles XII: at the discontinued Diet in 1713 Jesper Swedberg had been among those who had called for immediate peace negotiations, over the king's head. The monarch was known for his good memory.

But now Charles XII was dead. His sister Ulrika Eleonora had been chosen to be Sweden's ruling queen by the Diet in 1719. The queen, little interested in political matters, wanted to turn the crown over to her husband, Fredrik of Hesse, which required a decision by the Diet. From the queen's perspective this was primarily a matter of gaining the assent of the House of Nobles. Already in 1719 she could perhaps count on the support of the majority of the leaders in the House; their backing seemed to be secured when, in the spring of 1719, she ennobled more than a hundred families of commoners. This was a matter that for the most part concerned officers and government officials——among them Emanuel Swedenborg and his siblings——as well as the children of other bishops in the country. Jesper Swedberg's wish had thus been fulfilled, although not for the commoners who had married his daughters.

The decision was signed on 23 May 1719, and the head of the family, Emanuel Swedenborg, was introduced and given a seat and voice in the House of Nobles in the following year. In the list of registered, untitled families the house of Swedenborg was given the number 1598.

Figures on the coat of arms

Heraldry is a science of symbols. The Swedenborg family was given an entirely episcopal shield, a heraldic commemoration of the great Swedish prelate. A lion rampant on a visored helmet is the crest. In the context of this clerical heraldry the animal leads the thoughts to the 'Lion of Judah' from which a prince a shall go forth, according to the Book of Revelation, with power to open the scroll, breaking its seals. As a sign of this ability the lion also has a key in its paw. From the helmet its mantle drapes down in decorative folds. The shield has two horizontal fields. In the smaller, which lies above, we find the mitre, the bishop's head-dress with its ribbons.

Fig. 9. The Swedenborg coat of arms.

The second field is divided into two parts. In one of the segments are two iron bars on a red background, enclosing two silver keys. The bars are a reminder of the Swedberg family's involvement in mining. The keys, like the mitre, are an episcopal symbol: the keys of heaven. They refer to Christ's words to Peter in Matthew 16:19: 'and I will give you the keys of the kingdom of heaven, and whatever you bind on earth will be bound in heaven, and whatever you loose on earth will be loosed in heaven'. It may be pointed out that Swedenborg later forcefully denied such 'power of the keys', the symbol of which he came to bear on his shield.

The second segment provides a geographical reminder of the family's native region. A burning mountain, or perhaps foundry, symbolizes the province of Västmanland. At the base of the mountain we find the silver arrow, emblem of the Dalecarlia province, the bishop's homeland.

Thus the coat of arms recounts that it was issued to Jesper Swedberg, rewarded for long and faithful service. This is emphasized also in the royal letter to the bishop regarding his ennoblement. He had made himself 'deserving of some further sign of grace':

Because we well know [. . .] that he is a pious man, who fills his office with honour, of whom it may be said that he neither could nor would long for any change in his status. Nevertheless, for his comfort and for remembrance to following generations, desiring to improve his wife's and children's status, and so their sons' and daughters' in like degree, we herewith and by power of this letter patent and our royal power and authority and grace and favour have willingly granted and given Jesper Swedberg's legitimate living and direct heirs, both male and female, the status and worth of nobility, together with the following crest and shield.[5]

On 22 March 1720 Fredrik of Hesse was elected king of Sweden; the vote of the House of Nobles had been unanimous. Both father and son participated in the Diet.[6] They soon returned to Brunsbo, where the newly inaugurated member of the House of Nobles continued his studies.

The Board of Mines and the salary question

The question of paid employment and a role for the future was still unresolved for Emanuel Swedenborg. He was an Extraordinary Assessor in the Royal Board of Mines, but without salary. It was not unusual that someone would be given a position in a governmental department without regular recompense; a newcomer was put on a waiting list for a paid vacancy. The unpaid official had no influence on decisions of the Board, which were taken by the ordinary officials only. At the time of his appointment in 1716, Swedenborg had already experienced the Board's scant sympathy for the royal favourite. Now the king was dead and Swedenborg's popularity in the department sank even further. We shall return to this problem that would increasingly worry him during the first years of the 1720s.

It was a question of prestige and influence. Swedenborg was not dependent on a salary for his daily bread, neither then nor later. He had already inherited a part of his mother's wealth. In March 1720 his stepmother Sara Bergia also died; she had no children, and Emanuel's financial position became further strengthened.

Studies, projects in an ungrateful country

Using Brunsbo as a base during the years 1719 and 1720 Swedenborg was engaged entirely in studies and writing. His vitality and desire to make a name for himself in the learned world are obvious. The subjects varied: in 1719 alone he published several essays: 'Om Jordenes och Planeternas Gång och Stånd' ('On the motion and position of the earth and the planets'); 'Om Wattnens Högd, och förra werldens starcka ebb och flod' ('On the depth of water and strong tides in the primeval world'); 'Förslag til Wårt Mynts och Måls Indelning, så at rekningen kan lettas och alt bråk afskaffas' ('Proposal concerning our coins and measurements'); 'Underrettelse om docken, slysswercken, och saltwercket' ('Description of docks, locks, and saltworks'). He also wrote a number of essays that were not published, on mining management, on the organization of a literary society in place of the defunct Guild of the Curious, on tremulations, and on geometry and algebra.

His letters to Benzelius overflow with ideas and proposals. 'Does God have his seat in the sun?' Swedenborg wonders. He studies chemistry: Boyle, Becker, Hjärne, Lémery. He learns from the experiments of others. His method then, in 1720, was the same that he was to use later:

> [...] It seems to me, that an endless number of experiments is a good foundation to build upon, in order to make use of the labor and expenditure of other men, that is, to work with the head, over that on which others have worked with their hands [...][7]

What would become of all this? Speculations and arts are unprofitable in Sweden, he wrote to his brother-in-law in November 1719. They have no value for 'a lot of political blockheads' who look upon them as *'scholasticum* which must stand far in the background while their supposed finesse and intrigues push to the front'.[8] In a letter dated 1 December 1719 he told Benzelius that he considered leaving the country:

> If fortune so ordains that I can get together the required means, and if […] I have been able to gain some credit abroad [through inventions and articles], then my mind is toying with the idea of going abroad and seeking my fortune in my craft, which consists in all that has to do with the advancement of mining, and with mines, etc. For he may be regarded as a fool who is a free and independent fellow, and has his name in foreign lands, and yet remains here in a darkness (and freezes to boot) where the *Erynnider*, *Invidiae* [the Envies] and Pluto have set their abode, and are those who dispose of all rewards […] [9]

Speech defect and a professorship?

Why did Swedenborg not take the academic route? Teaching at a university would have been a sensible role with ample scope for a man with his wide interests. At an earlier stage he seems to have been interested in this path but now it seems to have lost all attraction.

The question became an actuality in 1724, after the death of the professor of astronomy at Uppsala Nils Celsius, father of the inventor of the hundred-degree thermometer. Eric Benzelius at once saw an opening for his relative but Swedenborg declined with this self-portrait in his letter in response:

> My *affaire* has now been *Geometrica*, *Metallica* and *Chymica*, and it is a far cry between them and *astronomica*. To abandon that with which I think to perform a good use, would be indefensible. Besides that, I have not the *donum docendi* [the gift of teaching], as my Brother knows, by reason of the *naturella difficultate* of speech. I hope, therefore, that the Academy does not put me in nomination […] Therefore, in case any one in the Consistory should give thought to me, a great friendship would be shown me if my Brother [saw to it] that the answer was an absolute No![10]

Furthermore, he said, they were considering him for a paid position in the Board.

This is the first and as far as is known the only time that Swedenborg himself referred to his speech difficulty, mentioned by several of his acquaintances. His stuttering varied from one occasion to another: he seems to have been able to avoid it by speaking slowly. We presume that it is precisely this speech difficulty that explains why we do not know of any occasion in Swedenborg's long and well-documented life when he spoke publicly. In the political arena he put his proposals in writing. And on spiritual matters? As Olof Lagercrantz has pointed out, it is only in his dreams and visions that he is able to articulate and explain his thoughts orally, and when necessary convince his opponents. During earthly conversations, when asked about his ideas and experiences he usually refrained from detailed answers, referring instead to his books.

Polhem in eternity

When he published Polhem's articles, the rays of royal grace beamed upon Emanuel Swedenborg, and it was due to Polhem's stepping in that he gained his position as Assessor in the Board of Mines. Polhem's ideas and his way of thinking had, as already mentioned, been of the greatest importance when Swedenborg was trying to form his own future; but their work together eventually broke off. At this time, 1718-20, there were scarcely any fundamental differences between them regarding their general outlook.

Immediately after Polhem's death, Swedenborg recorded that he met the teacher of his youth. The notes Swedenborg made about this meeting and Polhem's interests contain elements that may also throw light on his own development:

That mechanician, inasmuch as, in the life of the body, he constantly medi[t]ated how to construct *moving* machines, and succeeded therein above others, because he was endowed with such a genius, had, in the life of the body, confirmed himself in the belief that there was no God; that everything was from nature; that the living [soul] in man and beast is something mechanical [...] He did not wish to know what is the life after death, what the internal man, what heaven and hell, what the Divine is other than dead nature, what Providence is other than the blind fate of nature and chance. He had confirmed himself against these. But, because the imaginative power which he possessed in the body still remains, therefore he learns and teaches there, how various things can be created, such as birds, mice, cats, also human infants. He does this by a working-up and formation of some mass, and, then, by means of ideas of thoughts, there thence appear such things [. . .] He was shown that all others, by means of imagination and phantasy, can present a similar effect, and that this is child's play; but still, he continues, as if stupid, to fashion such things, and new ones, from his mass; [. . .] and he was also seen in the dark chamber sitting upon the dead bones which were in the coffin [. . .] [11]

On several occasions in his journal Swedenborg returned to the subject of the teacher of his youth. The problem with Polhem, he noted, was the same that he had found with the philosopher Christian Wolff. [12] They could only think in a material way; they could not reason without reference to space, time, and people, and they were never able to learn the spiritual language that is spoken in heaven, and which is understood only by the spiritual, inner man.

The Board of Mines: radical pietism and the beginning of a natural philosophy

Chapter Eight

The Royal Board of Mines

In 1716 Swedenborg had been appointed Assessor in the Royal Board of Mines with the status of 'Assessor Extraordinary' meaning he was paid no salary. The appointment, scarcely popular among the officials of the Board, was a royal favour to a relatively young man with no academic qualifications or practical experience. We find his name in the records of the Board for thirty-one years, and a few words about this institution are therefore appropriate.

During the seventeenth century several 'boards', that is, governmental agencies, were established with the purpose of serving as executive organizations implementing royal policy. They were corporate bodies in which decisions were made by the majority of the small circle of members of each board in plenary meeting with the President as chairman. This collegiate system implied that all decisions should profit from the knowledge of specialists in all fields of the board's activities. The oversight of the board members into all of their institution's responsibilities also guaranteed justice and objectivity in their decisions. At the Board of Mines there was a President and a Vice-President, two counsellors, and five assessors: all permanent members with the right to vote.

The task of the Board of Mines was primarily the general survey and control of the

Swedish mining industry. The smelting of iron and to a lesser degree of silver and copper was of vital importance for the Swedish economy: the production of pig iron in the 1700s corresponded to more than 70% of the nation's exports. A second task of the department was to serve as a Court of Appeal. In the mining districts there were special local courts, dealing with problems related to the industry; appeals against their decisions could be made to the Board in Stockholm.

Fig. 10. The Royal Board of Mines in an allegorical engraving from 1736. It gives a picture of governmental support and control of all areas of the mining industry, 'from the search for new ore deposits to the export of finished products'. Svante Lindqvist, *Technology on Trial*, p. 104. The etching is from the Board's collection: *Statutes for Mine Management: 1347-1735*.

The officials of the Board were often mine owners, whose personal interest was regarded as positive since it gave them a vigilant concern for the stability and improvement of the industry. The officials formed a closed circle into which many had ascended from lower positions in the mines or on the Board. It was difficult to be accepted as a member, and those admitted had to wait for a vacancy in the circle of permanent members before receiving payment.

A cuckoo in the nest

Swedenborg was met very coolly by the officials of the Board. He had been appointed as an 'extraordinary' member, without salary and right to vote; in order to become a full member he had to give proof of his abilities. His febrile publishing activity in mining science and mechanics during the years following the king's sudden death at Fredrikshald in 1718 should be seen against this background. In a letter to Benzelius written in November 1719 he described his undertakings:

> What I have been working at is, firstly, an exact description of our Swedish smelting and blast furnaces; and secondly, a theory or investigation concerning fire and hearths. To achieve these goals I first procured all that could be found out from smiths, charcoal burners, roasters, smelting masters, etc. On the basis of such facts the theories are founded, and I hope to have made a number of inventions therein, which in time will be likely to prove to be useful; as, for example, to be able to make fire in new stoves, so that the wood and charcoal which serves for a single day can give more heat for six days. Vice-President Hjärne has given his entire approval to this, and on request, it can be demonstrated by practical experiments. [1]

The second journey abroad

On 30 August 1721 peace was concluded between Sweden and Russia at Nystad in Finland. The great 'Nordic War' was over and Sweden was forced to withdraw from its Baltic provinces, Ingermanland, the islands Dagö and Ösel, and parts of the provinces of Carelia and Viborg. The new city of St Petersburg near the estuary of the Neva, formerly Swedish territory, was already under construction having been begun in 1703.

In June the same year, Swedenborg left the country for the second time, on this occasion for a year and three months. He was accompanied by his cousin, the physician Johan Hesselius. Before his departure from Helsingborg he wrote a letter, composed in humble terms, to the President of the Board of Mines; he declared that he was about to undertake a journey, the purpose of which was to give him a deeper knowledge of the mining industry on the Continent. He now asked the Board and its President for instructions; if there were any particular areas that he should investigate, he would be grateful to be told about it. The letter was submitted for consideration but no answer was given.[2]

In Swedenborg's posthumously published account of his journeys we read that he travelled from Copenhagen to Hamburg and then to Amsterdam, where he published a book, entitled *Prodromus Principiorum Rerum Naturalium sive Novorum Tentaminum Chymiam et Physicam* (*Some Specimens of a Work on the Principles of Chemistry with Other Treatises*). He does not mention that a year later, in Leipzig and Schiffbeck near Hamburg, he printed yet another book, *Miscellanea Observata* (*Miscellaneous Observations*). Further he published separately an expanded version of his theory, first printed in *Daedalus Hyperboreus*, entitled *Methodus Nova Inveniendi Longitudines Locorum Terra Marique ope Lunae* (*A New Method of Finding the Longitude of Places on Land and Sea by Lunar Observations*). All these works were published anonymously. They were in Latin, like almost everything he published during his long life.

His intense publishing activity was probably related to his wish to qualify himself for a paid post in the Board of Mines, with a right to vote; but perhaps he was also considering working abroad, if necessary. In a letter to Benzelius, written in December 1719, he reiterated that Sweden scarcely seemed to offer him a future; it would be better to seek his fortune outside the country than to 'sit freezing in the darkness'.

In his book about the basic principles of natural things we find echoes of Descartes and Polhem. Descartes had explained that the easy and simple method of reasoning used in geometry could be applied to all human knowledge: everything in science hung together in a geometrical way. Geometry dealt with relations and proportions, and the same was true of mathematics. Physics, chemistry, and geometry had been raised to new heights by scientists of the day. This was especially the case with geometry:

For what are physics and chemistry? What is their nature, if not *a peculiar mechanism*? What is there in nature, *which is not geometrical*? What is the variety of experiments, but a variety of *position*, *figure*, *weight*, and *motion* in particles? Since then we have several thousand experiments, indicating the nature of the various metals, salts, and elements, and these bodies consist entirely of groups of particles, varying in their shapes and positions in which, again, there is a certain geometrical arrangement, for these reasons we have grounds for concluding that these subjects may at last be demonstrated. To this end, I have collected experiments from the best authorities [...] [3]

Hesselius, his cousin, studying medicine in Harderwijk, joined Swedenborg in Amsterdam at the end of December. There, at Russian expense, just before Christmas as it occurs according to the Gregorian calendar, a feast had been arranged to celebrate the peace at Nystad and the victorious Czar Peter, who in his eagerness to westernize his nation had now assumed the title of 'Emperor'. There were fireworks, and food and wine were distributed in the streets. Banners painted with a triumphant poem on the Russian victory were displayed in the city. Swedenborg reported to Benzelius his viewing of this saddening celebration: he enclosed a copy of the Russian poem with suggestions of alterations making it more favourable to Sweden and the deceased monarch. [4]

Swedenborg travelled further to Aachen and Cologne, inspecting all mines in that region. In Leipzig, he edited his *Miscellaneous Observations*, which he was to publish the following year in the same city. He continued his studies in Saxony. We read the following:

> From Hamburg back to Brunswick, Goslar, and all the mines in the Hartz mountains [...]
> The father-in-law of a son of the Emperor [of Germany] and of a son of the Czar, Duke
> Ludwig Rudolph, who resided in Blankenburg, graciously defrayed all my expenses, and on
> my taking leave of him, he presented me with a gold medal and a large silver coffee-pot,
> besides bestowing on me many other marks of his favour. [5]

Diligence's reward

The books that Swedenborg printed in Germany in 1721 should have convinced the members of the Board of the Extraordinary Assessor's energy and ambitions in the areas of physics, chemistry, geology, and philosophy. Here were articles on the best way to retain heat in dwellings, a new method of constructing air pumps, a procedure for analysing alloyed metals, on stalactites, the use of geometry and mechanics, on the nature of matter, and how to build docks for ships. In addition to this there was a short essay on the impossibility of transmuting other metals into gold, the longstanding aim of the alchemists. Did he know that the newly appointed President of the Board of Mines, Gustaf Bonde, was a keen alchemist?

In the all-embracing volumes we find a view of science as practical and useful. The reader finds the same concreteness, desire for clarity, and anchorage in observation and experience that also characterized Christopher Polhem. As has often been pointed out, Swedenborg's talent was more of a practical than a theoretical nature, more technical than mathematical.

His diligence bore fruit. Almost seven years after his appointment he was granted, in April 1723, the same right to vote as the other members of the Board of Mines; not quite a year later he was nominated as an ordinary, salaried Assessor.

Apart from his scientific and technical merits, documented in his books, Swedenborg's position and work as a member of the Diet made him useful to the Board. Up to the year 1723, he had presented to the sessions of the Diet no less than four 'humble memoranda' that were of direct interest to his department; they concerned the balance of trade, the monetary system and the value of money, the correct policy as regards Swedish copper and iron mines, and the construction of Swedish rolling mills. When the Diet assembled in January 1723, Swedenborg was elected as a member of the so-called Mining Deputation, the committee that considered the subjects falling under the jurisdiction of the Board of Mines.

Swedenborg and the steam engine

In a letter from Rostock written in September 1714 Swedenborg had sent his brother-in-law a list of fourteen 'mechanical inventions' that he had made during his time abroad. Number five was a steam engine:

> A machine which uses fire to lift water. It should be built at blast furnaces where there is no falling water, but the water is still. The fire in the hearth would give power to the water wheels.[6]

Thus it was a question of heat energy producing mechanical energy, writes Svante Lindqvist in his book *Technology on Trial*, dealing with the introduction of steam power into Sweden.[7] According to Lindqvist, Swedenborg had gained the idea from an article in the Royal Society's *Philosophical Transactions* for 1699. The inventor was Thomas Savery, and the first functioning machine was constructed by the Englishman Thomas Newcomen and used for pumping water out of mines.

One of Swedenborg's first major responsibilities on the Board had regard to the steam engine. The Swedish envoy in The Hague, Joakim Fredrik Preis, had been visited by an Irishman named John O'Kelly with the proposal that Sweden engage him to build an apparatus for pumping out mines, similar to a machine he had already constructed in Liége. Preis, informing the government about the matter, sent a drawing done by the Irishman and reported what he knew about the inventor and the use of his machine.

Fig. 11. As Assessor in the Board of Mines, one of Swedenborg's initial assignments was to evaluate the first steam engine put into practical use.

The Board assigned Swedenborg to make a technical evaluation of Savery and Newcomen's machine. In his report Swedenborg weighed the advantages and disadvantages. On the negative side was the fact that the machine could not be used everywhere in Sweden, that it required special technical training, and that the traditional technique was virtually meeting the need. On the other hand, the machine was an example of interesting new technology, and it could be used in places where there was no running water, and where fuel was easily accessible. Furthermore, the machine was stronger than those driven in the traditional way.

The Board's answer to the government's proosal was composed in accordance with the report that Swedenborg had submitted. It was an interesting discovery, but not yet suitable for Swedish circumstances. The Board would, however, appreciate information regarding the costs of setting up a Newcomen machine. Some years later the Swedish merchant and engineer Mårten Triewald constructed the first 'fire and air machine' in the country.

Breckling and Dippel: radical pietism comes to Sweden

We leave steam engines and mining management for events relating to the pietistic movement. During the 1720s so-called radical pietism became active in a way that was conceived to be a menace to order and stability in the country. Here it was not, as in the older, conservative pietism, a question mainly of spiritual renewal within the framework of the Church. The leading representatives of the radical wing challenged the traditional views as to the Church, the official confessions of faith, the doctrine of the atonement, and the concept of the Trinity. Man's regeneration, and the personal relationship with God that resulted from the individual's new life, became the determining factor for his salvation.

In August 1724 Jesper Swedenborg, Emanuel's younger brother, returned from his exile in America called home by their father. The bishop had written to his prodigal son in April, telling him that he had inherited a share in the Starbo iron works from his step-mother. He should now come home and if possible marry a woman with a good dowry. In the postscript to the letter Jesper read that his father was now about to publish a book, entitled *Festum Magnum, Stora syndares store högtid* (*The Grand Celebration, the Great Feast for Sinners*). He would dedicate this book to Jesper, provided that he was willing to pay the cost of printing it. There is no indication in the book that Jesper accepted the paternal offer.

At Brunsbo the bishop asked his returned son for help in copying books in his library. Among them was a small volume in German that Jesper translated into Swedish as *Then sidste basun öfwer Tyskland til at upweckia werlden ifrå syndenenes sömn, som uti then fördömeliga säkerheten insenckt är* (*The Last Trumpet over Germany to awaken the World from the Sleep of Sin, in which it has found a false and reprehensible Security*). It was printed at his father's expense in Skara, but without the author's name. In a preface dedicated to General Carl Gustaf Dücker, Jesper described his stormy youth, his military service, and his life in America.

The author was Friedrich Breckling, a radical pietist belonging to the same group as Gottfried Arnold and his student Johann Conrad Dippel. The book was a sermon on repentance, a final appeal to a nation and its leaders, sunk in the sleep of sin and dangerous security. Bishop Swedberg's initiative in having the little book printed was certainly due to the fact that in his opinion Breckling's warning to sinful Germany also applied to Sweden.

Swedberg did not approve of the new times, the new form of government, or rule by political parties; he particularly disliked the French influence and vanity, and subsequent conceitedness appearing everywhere. Conversion, spiritual transformation, and a new moral life stood at the centre both of his own book *The Grand Celebration* and of Breckling's condemnation of German ungodliness. The bishop was not a radical pietist, but by publishing Breckling he was on dangerous ground, even though the name of the author had been omitted. The majority of the Estate of priests in the Diet looked upon 'privatization' of the Christian faith with suspicion. Salvation from sin was the common responsibility of the church, its priests, and the congregations. During the diet of 1726-7 the Estate of the priests, concerned about their power being threatened by pietism, had gained an important victory with a new bill forbidding 'conventicles', that is, meetings of private groups for worship. Repeated offences against this prohibition could lead to exile. Bishop Swedberg did not participate in this decision; he was absent from the Diet because of weakness due to his old age.

That same year, 1726, one of radical pietism's leading German spokesmen, Johann Conrad Dippel, arrived in Sweden. He soon established contacts with several officials in the Board of Mines, among them Emanuel Swedenborg. The priesthood sounded the alarm and Dippel was expelled in December 1728. Dippel's preaching had been well-known among both priests and laymen. A pious student influenced by Dippel, Sven Rosén, was exiled. Two other students were arrested, Thomas Leopold and Johannes Stendahl.[8] The latter was exiled after ten years in prison but Leopold refused to recant his radical pietistic conviction. This brought him forty-three years in prison; he died in 1771 in the Bohus fortress, seventy-seven years old. Leopold and Stendahl's judge in the first instance was the professor of theology at the University of Lund, Jacob Benzelius, Eric Benzelius's brother.

Outlines of a philosophy of nature

In the later part of the 1720s Emanuel Swedenborg's work in the Board of Mines must have taken up most of his time. Simultaneously he was developing a philosophy of nature, fully articulated in his great work, published in 1734, on the origin of the cosmos, *Principia Rerum Naturalium sive Novorum tentaminum phaenomena mundi elementaris philosophice explicandi* (*The Principia; or, The First Principles of Natural Things, being attempts toward a philosophical explanation of the elementary world*).

The primary sources for the study of his development during this period are the works published in 1721. They deal not only with technical matters but also with what today would be called theoretical physics. Here we distinguish two lines of thought which would have great significance during his whole life.

First, he conceived of *movement* as the original basis of matter: not, as the ancient Greek philosophers thought, the movement of atoms, but a *state* of movement. These states derived from the 'Supreme Divine', forming a kind of centre of power, where movement took form in accord with the laws and geometry of mechanics. Externally the material world functioned like a machine.

This *movement* had given rise to the solar system as well as to the smallest particles that fill the universe. These particles should be thought of as bubbles or balls, and between these rounded entities there was necessarily a space. An empty universe was unthinkable, he maintained in contrast to Newton; impulses and forces must be carried on and through concrete substances, they *push* themselves forward, as advocated by Descartes and Polhem.

Secondly, we meet in these early works the concept of *spirals* or whirls as the basic form in which matter comes into being. The spiral, postulated by Descartes, formed the central concept of Swedenborg's *Principia*. This geometrical figure offers a picture of how power, emanating from a centre, circles around its own axis, and finally returns to its point of departure.

In 1729 Swedenborg finished a small work, published posthumously, entitled *Sit felix faustumque—Principia Rerum Naturalium ab experimentis et Geometria Sive ex Priori Educta* (*Lesser Principia*). We might consider the manuscript as a preparation for the great *Principia* and as a continuation of his thoughts on geometry published in 1721. This manuscript is worth noting: it is yet another proof of Swedenborg's ambitious, multi-faceted intelligence, both his practical, engineering side and his desire to combine his practical experience with philosophical and physical speculation.

Inheritance and finances

During the 1720s Swedenborg must have devoted a great deal of time to private financial matters. During these years he received, like his five surviving siblings, three rather large inheritances, of a probable total value of around 50,000 riksdalers. For comparison, it can be noted that Swedenborg's annual salary for 1724, when he first became an ordinary assessor in the Board of Mines, amounted to 2,400 riksdalers. In 1730, when he received a full salary, it was raised to 3,600 riksdalers.

The first inheritance came from his stepmother Sara Bergia who died childless in 1720, leaving her property to the bishop's children. Here Swedenborg received a share in the Starbo, Marnäs, and Prästhyttan iron works in Dalecarlia: each share worth approximately 6,000 riksdalers. The second inheritance came from his mother Sara Behm, a legacy which had been held in trust by the bishop since her death in 1696. According to a preserved document he received approximately 6,500 riksdalers. The third inheritance was property that came from Swedenborg's uncle, Lieutenant Albrecht de Behm, who had died in 1700. Behm had owned the large Axmar iron works in Gästrikland, which after his death had been managed by Swedenborg's aunt Brita de Behm. Swedenborg inherited a fifth of the business. When his aunt took over the whole establishment in 1728, Swedenborg received probably close to 30,000 riksdalers.

These amounts, the approximate character of which must be underlined, were calculated in the 1920s by Frans G Lindh.[9] The considerable inheritances Swedenborg received in the 1720s are, as will be shown in the chapter 'Money from Paris and a good king', of importance for our understanding of his finances during his later years.

Why should we care about Poland's affairs?

Chapter Nine

> [. . .] then another said to me,
> Why the devil should trouble thee
> Poland's affairs? Pling, plingeli, plong.
> Don't play Polish but learn along
> To hold your tongue. Pling, plingeli, plong!

C M Bellman: *Fredman's Epistle, no. 45*

Sweden, Poland, and French interests

'Why do we care about Poland's affairs?' the Swedish poet Bellman asked in one of his epistles in the 1780s. The question had come up at a restaurant in Stockholm, in a discussion between the watchmaker Fredman and his friends. They presumably did not know much about Swedish foreign policy. They were wrong, and right. A strong, independent Poland was of concern to Sweden as a shield against ever-threatening Russia. Charles XII was interested in Poland's affairs in the highest degree, as were all of those who held power in Europe during the 1700s. With the help of Swedish arms and Arvid Horn's diplomatic skill the king pushed through a coronation in Warsaw in 1705, he himself sitting incognito among the viewers. The new monarch was named Stanislaw Leszczyñski, a man who then seemed able to guarantee that in the future his land really would be the buffer against Russia that Sweden needed; but after the defeat at Poltava, Stanislaw was forced to leave Poland. For several years his court was given refuge in Kristianstad, in the south of Sweden. In time he came to France where one of his daughters, Maria Leszczyñska, married Louis XV and became the Queen of France.

The view of Poland as a possible guarantee of European stability was one of the foundations of French foreign policy for a long time. England, 'perfidious Albion', ruled the sea, and Russia was an unpredictable ruler of the immense landmass to the east. Besides this there was the Hapsburg empire, a classical element in the French nightmare.

It was a matter of knitting alliances with lands that had approximately the same geopolitical interests as France. For the French king, it was a long game with the same pieces: Poland, Sweden, and Turkey. Other powers came into the game at times, but soon chose other allies.

France's foreign policy could never be neglected. In the 1730s and 1740s France was 'l'arbitre de l'Europe', Europe's watchman, in the opinion of King Frederick II of Prussia, the brother of the Swedish Queen Lovisa Ulrika. When the War of the Polish Succession was brought to a close in 1738, France was allied with Spain and Naples, Poland and Turkey; and besides this, reconciliation had been made with the Emperor in Vienna. Sweden received help from France in pulling the chestnuts out of the fire after the short and unfortunate war with Russia in 1741 to 1743. Up to the end of the 1750s and from 1769 on to the French Revolution, French stage-managers and French money could often be glimpsed behind Swedish internal and external politics.

France: rule of the Swedish Estates and Polish anarchy

From the French perspective, during this time the unpredictable and leaderless political systems in both Sweden and Poland were a great concern. Poland was a democracy, led by the 'schlachta', its absurdly large aristocracy. Intrigues, internal power plays, corruption, group interests, and an elected king who was usually powerless in relationship to all this seemed to lead to anarchy; in Sweden the words 'Polish diet' became synonymous with chaos and lawlessness. Sweden was regarded by France as on her way to a similar situation. Through her government by the Estates, which had grown ever stronger over the years, the land had come to a 'metaphysical administration', wrote the Duc de Choiseul to the French ambassador in Stockholm: 'A metaphysical administration that can only be defensible and possible if all Swedes are as wise and virtuous as Plato'.[1]

After Poltava, the Elector of Saxony Fredrik August was elected with Russian help to the throne of Poland. When he died in 1733 it was, naturally, the strong wish in Versailles that Stanislaw Leszczyński should once again take possession of the throne. Louis XV and his advisor and Prime Minister Cardinal de Fleury promised subsidies and military power. Fifty-six years old and dressed like an assistant to a Polish businessman,[2] the deposed monarch arrived in Warsaw, where on 11 September he was chosen again as king by the assembled Sejm, the Diet. More than 5,000 noblemen, displeased with this election, waited threateningly on the other side of Weichsel, and the Russian regiments rushed forward. The Sejm was scattered and Stanislaw withdrew to the north, towards Danzig, to wait for the promised French help. The Russian troops approached, a citizen guard was set up, and helped by Swedish officers Stanislaw drilled the few troops he had been able to raise. Danzig was surrounded by Russian troops. From a redoubt outside the city a lookout searched for the French fleet but, apart from an effort as death-defying as doomed, no French help ever came. In June 1734 the king fled through the wooded fields around Weichsel to Königsberg, disguised as a peasant. His guide over the swampy ground was the Swedish Colonel and French Lieutenant General Johan Stenflycht.

The escape was successful. The king came by stages through Germany to Kristianstad; and Stenflycht continued his improbable, simultaneous career as French and Polish politician and military man.

In 1733, in Stockholm, the dynamic French ambassador Count Charles Louis de Casteja, on orders from Versailles, had already begun a campaign for Swedish support for re-seating Stanislaw Leszczyñski on the Polish throne. De Casteja argued that this was in Sweden's interest for, with Stanislaw as king of Poland, she could regain much of her previous position of power, and this so much the more since in the case of a Russian defeat the Baltic provinces, now under Russia, could be restored to their rightful ruler, the Swedish kingdom. Therefore de Casteja requested that Swedish troops be sent to Danzig. Substantial subsidies were promised.

Stockholm was not entirely uninterested. Arvid Horn asked for more details and set out precise conditions. At the same time he made it clear to de Casteja that the matter required the approval of the Diet. De Casteja's pledges fluctuated more and more as the months passed. The Swedes became by contrast all the more precise in their demands.

The French side was in actually in the process of changing priorities. The political situation called for war against the Austrian Empire, in alliance with Russia. This was the beginning of what is commonly called the War of the Polish Succession.

It is usually said that de Casteja's request for help for Stanislaw Leszczyñski formed the starting point for the polarization in Swedish politics that took shape in the birth of two factions, termed the Hats and the Caps. Put simply, the Hats wanted revenge on the Russians, to regain the Baltic provinces, to make an alliance with Poland, and thereby to gain control over the river estuaries of the Baltic Sea. This could only be done with outside support and France the helper stood ready. The 'hat' referred to a plumed helmet, the symbol for one who was alert and ever-ready, who acted with panache and confidence. Against the Hats stood, or lay, the listless politicians, slumbering with their nightcaps over their eyes. The Caps, according to their opponents, lacked a sense of history, and were without vision. They slept, assured that all was completely secure, if only one avoided changing foreign policy. For the Caps, represented in all four Estates, war must be avoided; Russia, well-managed, could be an asset instead of a danger.

Swedenborg on foreign policy

In the Swedish Diet, questions of foreign policy were handled by the powerful 'Secret Committee', which consisted of members from the Estates of the Nobles, Clergy, and Burghers ——the Estate of the Peasants was regarded as not having the qualifications or the interest for such problems, though they had to be heard on matters of taxation.[3] In 1734, while the siege of Danzig was in progress and King Stanislaw was still in the city, Swedenborg wrote a draft of a memorandum to the Secret Committee on his view of Swedish foreign policy.[4] It had to do with the Polish question and future support for the Polish monarch who had been popular among Swedish officers and politicians since Charles XII's time. The document has not been preserved in the Diet's archives; perhaps it never came before the committee. We must make use of the outline which is at the Royal Academy of Sciences in Stockholm. Like everything he wrote, his contribution is laid out in a series of points.

The first four points were general warnings against confidence in what appear to be favourable foreign policy and military situations. Everything must be seen in a larger context, looking ahead ten to twenty years. Sweden was surrounded by hungry neighbours. With bad luck, a Swedish military engagement could activate a series of misfortunes, in which Russia took Finland, Denmark recovered the southern Swedish region of Skåne, and Prussia gained control of the remaining part of Swedish Pomerania. Sweden was no longer a strong military power, and her economy did not permit a long, drawn-out war.

'There is little to expect from France',[5] Swedenborg wrote. Promises are one thing but when it comes to war more is needed. The Secret Committee must also realize that in 1734 Russia is more powerful than before, partly due to what she had taken from Sweden. The Russian army is better trained and equipped; it has foreign officers and has learned European tactics and strategy.

Further, Sweden's fortune in war has previously depended upon the armies having been led by kings, from Gustav Vasa to Charles XII. They spurred on their troops by their example and presence; but when the king no longer stands in the lead, Swedish soldiers are no better than those from other lands. The events after Charles XII's death in Norway in 1718 were a clear example.

Swedenborg then dealt with the key question that was increasingly discussed during the 1730s among younger officers and officials: regaining the lost territory of Livland (present-day Estonia and Latvia):

> The recapture of Livland would certainly be a great gain. But I consider it a still greater gain
> that now Livland is not Swedish […] In my thinking as long as we had Livland, Sweden was
> constantly threatened by war with our neighbours […] We had to be continually on guard,
> against Russia as well as against Poland and others. Now, however, this danger no longer
> exists, since we have already stood away from what could have involved us in conflicts with
> others. A war, or equipping an army and a fleet, would take more out of Sweden's treasury
> than Livland could bring in over a period of many years.[6]

After the peace at Fredrikshamn in 1809 and the loss of Finland to Russia, Esaias Tegnér spoke of 'the recapturing of Finland within Sweden's boundaries'. Swedenborg was of the same mind, but now with regard to the Baltic territories: the losses the country had suffered could be compensated for by a well-run economy and the encouragement of the mining industry and trade. This would do far more for Sweden's financial position than a Swedish Livland:

For a country's wealth does not depend on the size of its surface area or the number of its provinces, but on flourishing trade. And now since there is really no risk of being attacked, we can increase our commerce and our shipping and cultivate our land. In this way we can make ourselves much stronger. By doing this we would be taking Holland as our model. [7]

Besides, by making an attack Sweden would be breaking treaties previously entered into, something that is not usual in Swedish politics, he continues.

And the Polish affair? People had said that it was a matter of honour for Sweden to support King Stanislaw, he writes in the next paragraph. But Sweden had made no guarantees for whom Poland elects; and again, he repeats his call to Swedish politicians to follow Holland's example.

Therefore, Swedenborg advised the 'Secret Committee', refrain from all armed intervention, even as regards to supplying armed auxiliaries for another power. Here, he is clearly refering to France. He has one reservation. A Swedish-Russian agreement could be proposed with conditions that one would not expect to be acceptable in St Petersburg. Then, at some time in the future, should the foreign policy situation be totally changed by Russia's being attacked, Sweden could return to its formerly rejected proposal. She could justify beginning an 'affair' as the offended party, though it would be important to make preparations now to ensure that she had a strong enough military power for this eventuality.

One can guess that the hypothetical case was tactically motivated—he offered a sop to the committee's paper tigers. Turning to the same quarter, Swedenborg addresses those who felt that Sweden's European reputation was bad, and therefore a little war would show that Sweden was still a factor to reckon with. His counter argument was the same as he had already stated.

Here, in the document's eleventh paragraph, Swedenborg proposes a declaration of neutrality on approximately the same principles that scarcely a hundred years later would be the guide for Karl XIV Johan:

If one weighs the great advantage that war might possibly give against that which neutrality offers, for my humble part I find that the position of neutrality offers infinitely greater advantages. But for us to see this our thoughts must rise above our immediate present time.

Our neighbours are always going to consider us with fear when they see our thrift and immense wealth, and further, when they find that we are debt-free, that our army is in good condition and our arsenals and fortifications are filled with weapons, and lastly, when they realize that the four Estates of our Diet are united. Here is the best way to make our land strong. And the results are visible to everyone [...] [8]

In the twelfth paragraph, Swedenborg makes an analysis of Sweden's situation between two mighty alliances: Russia and the Austrian Empire on one side, France and Spain on the other. As regards Poland's affairs it would seem clear that we should support France: the Russian empire should certainly be hindered from becoming mightier than it already had done by also gaining power *de facto* over Poland. If Danzig were to fall, Russia would come to control the sea trade in the Baltic. If Sweden were to engage itself successfully in the Polish crisis, in the long run the result would be that Russia and Austria would make sure that the Polish throne was again occupied by a vassal king who suited them. A weak Sweden was desirable to both of these powers, not least to the empire. From a general point of view, every advance of Swedish possessions on the Continent always risked leading to a war of revenge.

In Poland, Sweden could never win anything during King Stanislaw's lifetime. The war had to be brought to an end and the Polish economy put on its feet. And as regards the control of Danzig, the sea powers and other states will see to it that Russia's key position will not last forever, Swedenborg wrote.

The draft omits the following four points, paragraphs 13-16. If it is not a case of mis-numbering, we can assume that the author had treated of Denmark, Swedish Pomerania, Prussia, and France. A close and friendly relationship with Paris and Copenhagen would reasonably be in line with Swedenborg's pattern for Swedish policy.

In the following three paragraphs Swedenborg warned against emotional thinking in foreign policy. Every Swede very much wanted to see King Stanislaw re-established on his throne: he was an old friend to Sweden, and a sympathetic man. But in the European game it was better to wait and see which side had the greatest possibility of winning. Doing this would also make clear what the most advantageous direction would be for one's own policy. In the current situation France presented an attractive prospect for

Swedish involvement; but here also one must be realistic: no one knew if or when the promises would be kept.

In the final paragraph, the author described the play of the great powers as resembling a chess game. By having a Polish king owing allegiance to the Austrian Empire, a Russian flank was secured. In such a situation Russia and the Empire could make common cause against the Turks. Under all circumstances such an action should be reckoned with. Even if Stanislaw were to come to power in Poland, he was already old and his health was poor, and he was only a pawn in the play of the great powers. But making guesses about what the situation would be ten to twenty years ahead was like gambling in the lottery: 'A person who wins once easily thinks that his luck will continue, and that winnings lie ahead in the future'.

The balance sheet: well-run economy and cautious foreign policy

For Louis XV's France, Poland's position as a barrier siding with France against Russia was a political goal that became an actuality through the death of Fredrik August of Saxony in 1733. The thinking in Versailles was that for stability's sake the Polish elected monarchy should be made hereditary. Ten years later the French monarch, working through his own secret diplomacy, would conspire to have the Polish throne occupied by a Frenchman. The king's man would be a relative, the Prince de Conti, and when he was securely on the throne his duty would be first and foremost to free himself from Russian influence over the land. At the same time he would transform the Polish anarchy into a central monarchy modelled on France. But in 1733-4, Sweden together with Prussia and Turkey were considered capable of strengthening and rounding out the Polish bulwark. It was in fact the so-called 'French system', directed by both Russia and the Austrian Empire.

The careful Arvid Horn disassociated himself from the French proposals. No Swedish engagement on behalf of the cause of Poland and France ever came about, even though Gustaf III later played with the thought of running in the election in 1764, which would be the last Polish election of a monarch, and for security's sake had suitable apparel tailored for the role. Swedenborg was certainly not alone in his argument. It was well thought through, and his memorandum was presumably not without political significance.

Swedenborg's position at this time is of interest because the political drama shows personal characteristics that we have not seen earlier as clearly as here. He is careful, has balanced judgement, and stands off from emotional thinking in essential questions. Rather than acting with bravura he puts patient work into Swedish everyday life, working for political unity by building up a strong economy, based on trade and shipping.

And France? A good relationship with that great power was axiomatic for Swedenborg. Sweden should have the best connections possible with both East and West, but for Swedenborg, as a member of the Diet, France was an especially significant ally. The two nations had common foreign policy and cultural interests. Later, for Swedenborg the theosopher, there was also another factor, one that was at least as significant. As we shall see, his sympathies for France hung together with his sympathy for the king. Louis XV, he felt, was an instrument of Providence. France, through her monarch, had a divine call. By rejecting the Pope's claim to religious and political power, France would show the way for the Catholic world.

Beginning of the beginning: *Principia*

Chapter Ten

All are parts of one stupendous whole
Whose body nature is, and God the soul.

Alexander Pope: *An Essay on Man*

Divine passages

In ancient Rome the god Janus was pictured with two faces, one looking forwards, one backwards. This divinity, turned in two directions, became the watchman of all gates: a guard over what goes in and what goes out, over crossing and passage. The Janus face and gate could have stood as a symbol for Swedenborg's thinking at the beginning of the 1730s. He was trying to define the point which served as 'a kind of medium between what is infinite and what is finite':

It first originates from the Infinite, and then gives origin to things finite. On the one hand it acknowledges the Infinite, and on the other the finite; thus it stands between the two, and looks as it were both ways, having respect as well to the immense Infinite as to the immense finite; and in reference to its existence, may be said to participate of the nature of both. It may be compared to Janus with two faces, who looks two ways at once, or at each universe.[1]

From a divine perspective

In 1730 Swedenborg was forty-two years old. His vitality seems boundless: the years were filled with mining, engineering, travels, and politics. He went abroad for studies in 1733-4:

visiting Prussia, Saxony, Bohemia, Kassel, and Brunswick. He returned in July 1734, in time for the already described session of the Diet, significant for foreign policy. At the same time he was industriously engaged with questions of natural philosophy. They were related to the same problems that we have met already in his *Some Specimens of a Work on the Principles of Chemistry with Other Treatises*, printed in Amsterdam in 1721, and in his manuscript from 1729. Natural philosophy dealt with problems like the essence of nature, the distinction between life and dead matter. He successively elaborated his hypothesis of the Janus-like primal entity, both infinite and finite. From this entity as a starting point, everything living, everything material, could be deduced. Behind, *a tergo*, to use the words of the Book of Exodus, was the Infinite: unapproachable and inexpressible. Nevertheless, man should always regard himself and the whole of creation from the perspective of the Infinite, which for Swedenborg was equivalent to God.

Philosophy and minerals

His studies led to a work of three folio volumes in Latin, published in 1734 in Dresden and Leipzig; each volume was dedicated to a local ruler: Ludwig Rudolph, Duke of Brunswick; Wilhelm, Duke of Hesse; and King Fredrik I of Sweden, Wilhelm's brother. The overall title of the three volumes is *Philosophical and Mineralogical Works*. From Swedenborg's perspective, philosophy and mining science were complementary realms.

The first volume is entitled *Principia; or first principles of natural things, being new attempts towards a philosophical explanation of the elementary world*. It is usually referred to as the *Principia*, the principles regarding the main problems of natural philosophy. The contents of the following two volumes are quite different. Here he concentrates on iron and copper, describing European mines, processes for smelting the minerals, and technical procedures of different kinds. At the end of these two works we find reports of chemical processes and experiments made on the Continent.

Iron and copper

It was above all the works on iron and copper that made Swedenborg known in Europe. The books were reviewed and translated entirely or partially into French, German, Spanish, and Swedish. It must have seemed natural that it was a Swedish specialist who produced this great map of the science of mining. Swedish iron dominated the European market; and the copper mine at Falun had been the chief supplier of this metal to the Continent during the 1500s and 1600s.

Fig. 12. This etching is taken from the frontispiece to Swedenborg's *Principia*. The portrait, with Swedenborg as live model, was done in Dresden. According to the German-Dutch businessman J C Cuno, Swedenborg looked the same even in his eighties.

Later Swedenborg's life was to be devoted primarily to divine tasks, in strong contrast to the earthly, technical, mineralogical speciality demonstrated in these two works. Here we read of the Swedish blast furnaces, appropriate temperatures, refining of iron, magnetic analysis of ore, assaying the quality of steel, and pulverized iron. He reports his own and others' observations with the same eagerness that we meet later in his descriptions of heaven and hell.

His descriptions convey his delight in working. As an example we may take his report of a descent into the famous copper mine at Falun:

Consider what great quantities of copper this mine […] has brought forth for thousands of long years and that are yet being born from its inexhaustible womb […] In short, the whole floor of this mine, all its doors, walls, chambers, halls, and pillars, all its open surfaces gleam in all directions with this wonderful vein's glittering, golden rays. The visitor could believe that he had been carried to Venus herself, when the goddess stood as a bride in an exquisitely decorated chamber, and there happily welcomed her guests from Falun. [2]

The living mountain

Minerals and philosophy were connected with each other. Swedenborg's many sub-terranean explorations at home and in other countries convinced him that the principles governing the vegetable kingdom applied also to the realm of minerals. The rocks were alive, and an outflow of a higher power. In the subterranean realm there was a mysterious movement, resulting in slow changes. Metals are born to grow, be purified, and mature. Salts, stones, sand, and particles of clay are continually subject to transformation. Here we gain Swedenborg's picture of the earth's development and formation:

> [...] for descend as low as we may, even to the reputed regions of Tartarus and Pluto, we never find in the course of our passage any one thing absolutely similar to another. We are always meeting something new, something different; and every new and different substance is only an indication of some different change. Look at the vegetable kingdom; how varied! how pleasing! how delightful! because of this variety! And why so varied, but in consequence of the variety prevailing in the mineral kingdom, which contains its origin, root, and essence?[3]

And the vegetable kingdom in its turn gives nourishment to the animal kingdom, *regnum animale*, a Latin term that can also mean the 'soul's kingdom'.

Beginning of the beginning

We return to the *Principia* and the boundary between spirit and matter. If we search for the cause of all causes, as Swedenborg did, we come into the same situation as when calculating the number represented by *pi*. If we do not stop at 3.14, we can go on calculating to eternity. Seeking, consequently, must be limited; Swedenborg set a boundary at what he called the Infinite. From this assumed infinity the first point had arisen, an entity at once immaterial and material.

Above everything material, he thus assumes, there must exist a being inaccessible to direct knowledge and without boundaries. It is a classical thought, occurring in Plotinus and much later in the writings of Descartes, Leibniz, and Wolff.

Certain characteristics could, according to Swedenborg, be ascribed to the infinite being. The first material particle, the origin of the world of the senses, must have been brought into being by motion from the Infinite. In this limitless being there must be a will, an action, and an intelligence that desires to bring about an effect in one certain way, and not in another; and this will is related to the first stage of matter:

> If then it be admitted that the first simple [substance] was produced by motion from the Infinite, we are at the same time bound to suppose that in the producing cause there was something of a will that it should be produced; something of an active quality, which produced it; and something of an intelligent nature, determining that it should be produced in such a manner [...]; in a word, something infinitely intelligent, infinitely provident, infinitely active, and infinitely productive. Hence, this first point could not exist by chance, nor by itself, but by something that exists by itself [...][4]

There must be a foreseen plan according to which the effects produced are successively changed in a given series, he continues. All the elements in a series must of necessity exist in the first motion's substance: 'for in the Infinite's simple and original movement future and later occurrences cannot be considered other than as actually present and already existing'.

Cosmogony and the first points

The beginning of the universe was an innumerable number of points, developing in the same way.

The point is power, always in motion, obeying the laws of mechanics. It is roused to action in the most perfect of all forms of motion, the spiral. As for Descartes, the spiral was a key concept in Swedenborg's thinking. The points wind themselves upwards and then to their beginning, forming globe-like figures. For Swedenborg these spiral-structures became the first or simple finites, moving in spirals as 'continual, eternal circles from the centre to the periphery, without limit, end, or angle'. The spiral motions give rise to passive and active particles. A tension arises between them that at a certain stage leads to their unification. This tension was a condition for the continuation of the process. The thought of the passive element's unity with the active as a requirement for all completion would follow Swedenborg through his whole life.

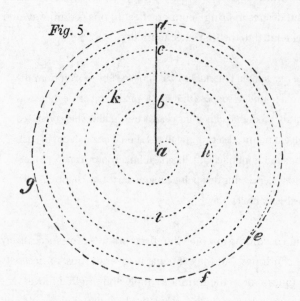

Fig. 13. An innumerable number of 'natural points' breaks forth from the Divine infinity. These points have a force, an effort towards motion. The resulting motion, which is thus thought to come from God, cannot be other than perfect. The perfect motion is a circle. The effort to perfection creates an eternal motion from the centre to the periphery, and then back to the starting point. It is consequently a matter of spirals, not on a plane, as when one throws a stone into water, but in space. They form figures in a kind of heavenly geometry, figures which in turn give rise to earthly geometry, and thereby to the spiral. (Cf. David Dunér: *Swedenborgs Spiral*)

God in creation

The theory of the Infinite's path to the finite and the building up of what is finite thus became Swedenborg's general model for the origin and development of matter. At one moment in time our solar system and the planet where we live had been created by the Infinite, and the laws valid in this process should be applicable to all areas of the universe.

The particles in the cloud of matter, forming the nebulas, move in whirls around the sun. The movement throws out particles that cover the sun and form a rind that gradually breaks apart. The fragments lie around the sun, gathering into planets. They move apart from the sun in spirals and travel around the sun in circles, first quickly, then ever more slowly.

Swedenborg's cosmological model has much in common with the theories of Wolff. It has also been pointed out that its general structure resembles the cosmogony later

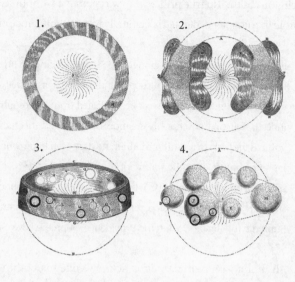

Fig. 14. The origin of the solar system according to the *Principia*. In a burning sun coarser particles rise up to the surface, which finally was covered by such entities (1). In time the sun's shell bursts (2) and forms clusters around the sun's equator (3). The movement of the circle brings about an explosion, and the planets are born, circling around the sun (4).

formulated by Kant and Laplace. Essential for Swedenborg was presumably the fact that through his cosmogony he saw himself to be on the trail of a greater truth.

God and cosmos

The connection between the Infinite and the finite became Swedenborg's predominating question during the 1730s. In the *Principia* he had described the development of matter from the Infinite through a process from the simple to increasingly composite entities. Regarded from an earthly perspective this chain of development had a continuation on a higher plane, but beyond the human faculty of perception. As we have seen, a will was attributed to the Infinite, as well as an intelligent activity with the ability to foresee all things. It is clear in the *Principia* that by these attributes he attempted to give a suggestion of God's being—an enterprise often essayed during the century of the Enlightenment.

Swedenborg's point of departure and philosophical perspective was determined by his religious faith. No true philosophy was possible without assuming a Supreme Being, he wrote in a chapter dedicated specifically to the significance of religion for correct thinking:

> For without the utmost devotion to the Supreme Being no one can be a complete and truly learned philosopher. True philosophy and contempt of the Deity are two opposites. Veneration for the Infinite Being can never be separated from philosophy [. . .] The philosopher sees, indeed, that God governs his creation by rules and mechanical laws, and that the soul governs the body in a similar manner; he may even know what those rules and mechanical laws are; but to know the nature of that Infinite Being [. . .] is an attainment beyond the sphere of his limited capacity. When, therefore, the philosopher has arrived at the end of his studies [. . .] he must there stop; for he can never know the nature of the Infinite Being, of his Supreme Intelligence, Supreme Providence, Supreme Love, Supreme Justice [. . .][5]

All that a wise man can do is acknowledge his nothingness. His total dedication to supernatural reason fills his whole soul. The mere thought sends a tremulation through his inner membranes and senses, writes Swedenborg. He experiences an inner motion, 'frightening but nevertheless full of delight'.

Creation is divine, like the forms of geometry and the transfer of power by mechanical means. This is a deistic thought typical of Swedenborg's time: God is far from the world, and never intervenes in its affairs.

We can only try to be rational, with the divine nature as the model. But as we shall see, Swedenborg's view of the world was not quite so simple.

Principles for a theosophy

In the year 1734, the *Principia* and the two volumes on iron and copper were printed. The same year, in parallel with the three folio volumes, he published yet another work: *Prodromus Philosophiae Ratiocinantis de Infinito et Causa Finali Creationis* (*The Infinite, or the Forerunner of a Reasoning Philosophy concerning the Infinite and final cause of Creation*). It was accompanied by a small postscript that he called *De Mechanismo Operationis Animae et Corporis* (*Mechanism of the Interaction of the Soul and the Body*).

The new book, usually called *The Infinite*, was intended to be a reminder that the *Principia* should be read as a description of the origin of the universe, and as such as a hypothesis with a value of its own that also has implications on a higher level. It could be seen as a model for the kingdom of God in heaven and on earth. Here was a key that gave human reason the possibility of understanding the Infinite, the essence of God's being. The earthly mirrors what is above the earth, and vice versa. The thought is a perennial one, repeated through the centuries. 'That which is below is that which is above; and that which is above is that which is below', we read in the alchemists' famous *The Emerald Table*.[6]

In the nature of God lies the key to the meaning of creation and consequently to the purpose of man's life. Swedenborg attempted to describe the Infinite as power and rational purpose. How does this involve Swedenborg the man? He would develop the thought in *The Infinite*, but still only as a prologue to the drama he would compose later in life.

The dedication to Eric Benzelius

The Infinite opens with a dedication to his brother-in-law Eric Benzelius, bishop of the diocese of Linköping since 1731. It is written in unusually warm words, atypical of the habitually reserved author, always careful to keep his distance from his subject:

> I revere in you a wisdom that corresponds to your high rank, and which is worthy of your high esteem [...] You have been a source both useful and beneficial to me personally. It was due to your advice and your wish that my attention [...] was directed to the present subject, and therewith to similar areas [...] And it was at your instruction that I took up these studies. I hope therefore that you will recognize the truth in this fruit of my, perhaps imperfect, mental power——a result which in some part belongs to you.

This testifies to Benzelius's importance as a mentor, having led the young Swedenborg to his thoughts on the Infinite as the cause and the provider for the universe. But these general ideas are one thing, different are the far-reaching conclusions that Swedenborg was to draw from them later in life.

God's Son: man's conjunction with infinity

The concept of an Infinite giving rise to the finite requires a connection between them: and to escape reasoning in a circle we are compelled to give this link the same character as its unknown origin.

But this seems impossible, since the Infinite is unearthly, radically different from our world. Reason says that we must believe in a final cause, a 'sufficient cause', in the words of Leibniz and Wolff. Pursuing the chain of causes we must stop somewhere; the belief in the existence of a Creator gives a natural frame to our research and reasoning.

In his *Principia* Swedenborg, concentrating on the interplay of powers and the life of geometric forms, described the world as a mechanically-functioning machine. In *The Infinite* he concentrated instead on man, God's most complicated and most elevated creation. The question of the connection between God and man cannot be answered as long as we are unable to describe the Infinite. This insight led Swedenborg to theology and the Gospels. He felt that he found the connection in Christ, God's only begotten Son. The Son was of the same nature as the Father — he *was* the Father: 'he who has seen me has seen the Father'. But he was also a human being. In other words: at the same time Infinite and finite, God and man.

Thus Swedenborg resorted to revelation for help; through Christ's coming to earth the picture of God became concrete. At last mankind was given an insight into the victorious God. Christ's death on the cross completed the picture of divine love.

This attempt to define the unknown is perhaps the most significant approach to the supernatural world that the scientist Swedenborg made, writes Inge Jonsson. From this little work on the Infinite, Swedenborg's interest gradually turns from nature and her mechanical functioning to man and his purpose and meaning.

After 1745 Swedenborg would again and again turn against the classical, easily misleading definition of the Trinity as three persons in one. The Father, the Son, and the Holy Spirit were the three essentials of one and the same Infinite being, and the Father could be comprehended only in the figure of the risen Christ. Perhaps the origin of Swedenborg's later unipersonal thinking lies just here, in the emphasis on God-Christ as a link between spirit and matter. Here was the 'Divine Human', the Janus figure that opened the passage between the two worlds, the Word that became flesh, God descending into the world he had created and creates.

Interaction between the soul and body

The latter part of *The Infinite*, as the full title explains, deals with the interaction between the body and soul. If the soul was regarded as something not-physical, the question seemed rationally impossible. Here the philosopher met the same difficulty as between the Infinite and the finite.

In his philosophical explanation of the origin of matter Swedenborg had assumed that the mathematical point constituted the bridge between the Infinite and the finite. From this point power went out in the form of a spiral. It is to be noted that the spiral always returned to its point of origin. The circle was closed.

Like the point, man's soul was at the same time both spiritual and natural. It was the organ in man that was turned to receive the Divine. In the God-fearing man the finest parts of the soul were activated so that he could receive the inflow that corresponded to the state of his mind. In Swedenborg's view this receiving function existed in the cortex of the brain; here were the body's finest membranes, which alone via the blood could receive and transfer the divine inflow. 'A membrane thin as a soap-bubble separates the world of imagination from the reality of truth', wrote the Swedish author Lars Gyllensten in one of his novels, *Palatset i Parken* (*The Palace in the Park*).[7] Through this membrane man's reason was strengthened; his soul became, for Swedenborg, the bearer of the power going out from God.

Thus the infinite power flowing into the soul terminates in the same way as does all movement from the Highest Source, returning to the threshold to the Infinite. Through his soul man is immortal, a 'machine with a soul'. We shall meet this thought in all the works he would write later.

Future research: his father's death

Swedenborg now found himself on the tracks he had to follow. The connecting relation between the Infinite and the finite fell under the same law as the relation between soul and body; the physical relationship corresponded to the act of God's becoming man through the Son. In the *Principia* as well as in *The Infinite* he promised a continuation with more penetrating analyses. In the last part of the latter work he sketched out a research programme that would embrace the entire human anatomy with emphasis on the sense organs' mode of functioning: 'Through this we shall finally be in a position to draw definite conclusions about the actual geometry and mechanism that characterizes this perfect entity'.[8]

In 1734, then, he had published four volumes, travelled from Germany to Sweden, and taken an active part in the Diet. The following year he was in Stockholm. During the spring of 1735 saddening reports must have reached him from Brunsbo. In 1730 the bishop's residence had been ravaged by fire a second time, and yet again he had lost his library and his manuscripts waiting to be printed. The seventy-six year old man's already weakened health deteriorated after this new catastrophe. In the summer of 1735 Jesper Swedberg died at Brunsbo, that had been rebuilt again. The funeral took place at the beginning of the year 1736.

Bishop Swedberg: his death and funeral

Chapter Eleven

Your soul dwells in a house of clay, an earthen hut that must soon tumble down, of which you are reminded daily by your own eyes, which are becoming dim; by your ears, which are becoming deaf; by your face, which is becoming wrinkled; by your teeth, which are becoming decayed; by your tendons, which are becoming loose; by your hands, which are becoming shaky. Yes, your weak feet let you know that they soon need to rest in the grave; your grey hairs show that they will soon leave a bare head; your short sleep which you take in the long nights forebodes the long sleep which lies before you beneath the earth.

Jesper Swedberg: Reflections on the Excuses of the Unrepentant

Jesper Swedberg's death

Bishop Jesper Swedberg died on 26 July 1735, nearly eighty-two years old. He had been in good physical health his whole life, though in his seventies his memory deteriorated. In 1730 Brunsbo, the episcopal seat, had burned down for the second time. He took this new loss calmly, it was said in the account of his life that he wrote to be read at his funeral, but afterwards his hands trembled, making writing difficult.[1] In July 1735 he had felt that his life was moving towards its close, and he took to his bed. We do not know if Swedenborg was present during his last days. The members of the Board of Mines customarily took vacation at the height of summer, and his departure from Stockholm is not mentioned in the minutes. Before his death the bishop 'was given the Lord's holy supper, said a loving goodbye to his dear wife, commended her, his children, and all who survived him to God [...] and lastly besought his God and Saviour for grace and a gentle death, which he then in stillness, with reverent sighs, patiently and gladly awaited'.

Burial usually took place as soon as possible after the time of death; but for some reason unknown to us the bishop's family was to wait a long six months for his funeral. The ceremony was held on 29 January in the following year. We read in the minutes of the Board of Mines that Assessor Swedenborg, with his Majesty's permission, was absent from 19 January to 1 March.[2] The same consent was given to his fellow Assessor and relative Lars Benzelstierna, the brother of Eric Benzelius, at one time married to Swedenborg's sister Hedvig, who had died in 1728. They travelled down to Brunsbo and the church at Varnhem where, close to the outer walls, the bishop had buried his second wife and prepared his own resting place. The church dates from the 1200s and was once part of a Cistercian monastery with royal graves from the medieval Erik dynasty.

Fig. 15. Jesper Swedberg at the age of 78, in an oil painting in Hovsjö chapel, close to the bishop's birthplace.

In his autobiography Jesper Swedberg had given careful and strict instructions for the ceremony at his burial. [3] His choice of hymns and the text for what was then called the 'funeral address' can be seen as a symbolic summary of his view of life and of death as a passage to another and better existence.

There should be no instrumental music in the church, wrote the bishop, only 'solemn and divine hymns shall be sung', without an organ. The service should begin with 'O Lord God of heaven, Our refuge Thou art', a paraphrase of Psalm 90 written by a German priest. In the Psalter it is called 'a prayer of Moses, the man of God', and its theme is the eternity of God, and man's frailty. Jesper Swedberg, as an experienced liturgist, had wanted to open his final service with a reminder of the eternal contrast between God's majesty and man's lowliness:

For now, our age is short,

quickly slips our lifetime by:

it has called down your wrath.

In this vale of tears we end

our time, so soon like an empty tale.

We could no longer live:

our days are seventy years,

though rarely may be eighty;

Still all is sadness, anguish,

soon hastily departing.

The transitory nature of all earthly things is one of the great religious and artistic *leitmotifs* of the first centuries after the Reformation. In Sweden we find the literary development of this theme in the official Book of Hymns as well as in secular poetry. One of the best-known Swedish poems from the early part of the 1700s is 'The World's Vanities', written by Johan Runius:

What is the world?

Only frivolity,

Pleasure, honour, riches.

What is desire?

What is force?

Only a blast of wind,

An empty shell and maggots' nest.

This is the Baroque Age's ethic and aesthetic. Finite man is only an actor, soon melted into air, but the finite passes over into the infinite, the earthly scene continues up into heaven by an invisible transition.

Jacob Benzelius's funeral sermon and Swedenborg's journal

The bishop had left instructions to the priest at Varnhem church to dwell upon this theme in his funeral sermon: 'The text shall be: I believe [in] the Community of the Saints, the forgiveness of sins, the resurrection of the flesh, and eternal life. Amen!' Read in the bishop's way, with his constant emphasis on the paradoxical element in the relationship between God and man, love opposed to sin, and transcendence set against immanence, the Community of the Saints became a picture of a community between man and the Divine, both mystical and earthly. For Swedberg the idea of the kingdom of God also involved a worldly task, a moral mission. In his constant polemic against man's moral incapacity as a dangerous resignation, he had always maintained that only faith combined with Christian deeds could lead to justification.

The sermon itself was usually followed by a short biography of the deceased. 'I think I know my own self best, so I am making the account of my life, so far as I both honestly can and should justify it to God [...] And it shall be read from the pulpit, word for word, without modifications, neither shortened nor lengthened.'

An open coffin was customary at burials, but Swedberg gave orders that the lid should be closed, so that 'no one may view my decline'.

At the distance of more than two hundred and fifty years the choice of preacher seems astonishing. The most natural candidates would have been Eric Benzelius, Bishop of Linköping, and Jonas Unge, formerly the priest at Varnhem and later vicar in Lidköping,

Fig. 16. Jacob Benzelius (1683-1742) was the brother of Eric appointed Archbishop of Sweden in 1744. He was one of the most active opponents of the growing radical pietism, who had proposed a law to the 1734 Diet prohibiting all 'Godless doctrines', that he alleged were being spread in the kingdom. The result was the religious decree of 1735 that established the right of interfering against those who confessed false interpretations of the official evangelical Christianity as well as against those who could be suspected of holding such ideas. His appointment to conduct Jesper Swedberg's funeral may be interpreted as an indication that the departed bishop was regarded even after death as a dangerous opponent to orthodoxy: the funeral sermon was a politically delicate task.

The painting is by J H Scheffel, 1738: now in the Chapter House of Uppsala Cathedral.

for both had married daughters of the deceased. Instead, the role was taken by Jacob Benzelius, Eric's younger brother and Bishop of Gothenburg, a known opponent of all forms of pietism, anchored in the official orthodoxy. In the 1720s he had been one of the driving forces behind cruel judicial sentences on well-known Swedish pietists, imprisoned for life. But Jesper Swedberg had scarcely hidden his sympathies towards the leading ideas of moderate pietism.

Benzelius's sermon can be read as an anti-pietistic document of church politics. Redemption was possible only in the church and congregation: 'Here, here, here!' he hammered out from the pulpit; the message was clearly a polemic against the private meetings held outside the churches and defended by Swedberg even though they had been officially forbidden. And salvation? Blessed is the man 'to whom God ascribes righteousness, without works': Benzelius developed Luther's thoughts about the absurdity of salvation through good deeds, but said they 'who have believed in God strive for good works'.

The autobiography that Swedberg himself had written did not appear in Benzelius's own printed account of what had taken place at the burial in spite of the instruction given by the deceased concerning its being read. There were several sentences in this text that were scarcely in line with the preacher's thoughts. Swedberg had emphasized that he always visited the congregations in the diocese annually, preached, and questioned the parishioners about their knowledge. He went on:

> And always led and attested to the *practice of godliness*. And condemned the common 'great faith'. And this in consideration of the *talents* for which we shall one day give account to God.

Benzelius thus passed over Swedberg's continual polemic against his colleagues and parishioners who contented themselves with 'faith alone'. Faith was one thing, its fruits another, and there was no automatic link between the two. A life of action in Christ was not only Swedberg's thought, it was also one of the primary theses of the pietists.

Nonetheless the bishop gave his tribute to the deceased. A pious and capable man, said Benzelius, a powerful worker, 'mighty in the Scriptures, never greedy, stubborn, bitter':

He held that hour lost when he had done nothing good. He remembered that when iron becomes dull and loses its sharpness one must then industriously whet it again [...] The sum total of his upbuilding work was the doctrine of faith and its fruit, a life pleasing to God [...].

In the church sat Emanuel Swedenborg, forty-eight years old that very day. What did he think of the speaker in the pulpit? Surely, he would not have listened with pleasure to the words of his relative by marriage. In his much later *The Spiritual Diary* few figures are treated as harshly as Jacob Benzelius. He was entirely incapable of receiving the Divine, we read: he was led by influences from hell; consequently Swedenborg found him 'deep down, among the demons'. Swedenborg also had long conversations with him about 'faith alone' and succeeded in convincing him that present-day Christianity rested upon a mistaken conviction that it was Christ's suffering on the cross that saved man from his evil, not the way he had been leading his life. But Benzelius, in spite of his theoretical insight, never properly understood the question; his evil nature and false thinking prevailed.[4] There are several descriptions of his arrogance in this journal. Here is an example from about 1759:

What phantasies are could be evident from a certain one who was in phantasies; for he seemed of himself to mount into a chariot, and the chariot to be changed into an elephant; he also seemed to himself to be seated on the elephant and the next moment to be thrown down by the elephant's trunk, and also to be trampled upon. After he rose up, they [that is, the bystanders] spoke to him, saying that those things were visions and not realities. He replied that he knew they were visions, but that, still, since he saw them with his eyes and felt the pain of the trampling and of the throwing down, it cannot be otherwise than real. The spirits reasoned with him at considerable length [...] but yet he could not be convinced that it was not real, because he actually saw and felt it. It was Jacob Benzelius.[5]

'For now we see through a glass, darkly; but then face to face'[6]

After the sermon and the biography, the renowned hymn by the pastor of the Hamburg church Philip Nicolai, 'So beautifully shines the morning star', was to be sung. It treated of the heavenly wedding, a special kind of Christian love poetry, in which God's Son is presented as 'my King and my Bride'. In later verses the heavenly marriage is described as a union between a soul afflicted with love and her bridegroom; this occurs in the presence of the heavenly hosts 'who rejoice exceedingly that the Bride has become free from Satan's tyranny. Therefore with my hands I clapped, Amen! Amen!'

'While the hymn is being sung I am to be borne to the grave', Swedberg had instructed. At the same time the priest should bring the funeral service to its conclusion with the customary words: 'From earth you have come, and earth you shall again become. Jesus Christ your Saviour shall raise you up at the last day'.

The ceremony at the grave was soon finished. The bishop had instructed that it should not last more than two hours, beginning at 12 noon if he were to die in the winter and be buried during the dark time of the year. In Varnhem, it was 2 o'clock on this January day. One more song, and the mourners were to return to the church. According to Swedberg's instructions the ceremony was to be concluded, as customary, with a well-known hymn, 'In heaven, in heaven', sung 'at the altar by a handsome priest, who sings well'. It describes life in paradise as a blessed, continued vision of God by an ever increasing cloud of witnesses:

In heaven, in heaven,
Where God himself dwells,
Shall we see him
In blessedness so great,
Face to face,
Face to face,
Near the Lord Sebaoth!

After the burial, the mourners went to a modest meal in the vicinity. In his instructions the bishop had directed, with a special 'nota bene' in the margin, that the repast should be moderate without much wine: 'More good ale, but definitely no sweets'. The money saved on this was to go to the poor in the Skärcke parish where Varnhem was situated and in nearby Åsaka. This, the instruction said, 'was more seemly, more Christian, and more pleasing to God'.

Leave of absence from the Board and a journey abroad

Swedenborg was back at his post on 1 March.[7] As usual, there was a meeting virtually every day of the week; according to the minutes for 1736 there were conferences on 23 days in March. His opinions on different questions appear often in the documents: hearings on promotions, reviews, and decisions on legal and economic issues. In May he petitioned his colleagues for a leave of absence for three to four years, to go abroad to continue the great work that he had published in 1734. It would be impossible to combine this task with service in Stockholm. He proposed that a substitute be appointed, who would be paid half of Swedenborg's salary, he himself retaining the remainder. The Board agreed with his request, which then went to the king for final decision.

His application for leave of absence was soon approved at the highest level. Swedenborg paid a parting visit to the king and queen at Karlsberg castle and said farewell to the members of the Diet. He was not just any Assessor: he was a man with highly-placed relatives and friends, and with a certain international reputation. On 10 July he left Stockholm for Amsterdam by boat.[8]

Philosophical notes

Chapter Twelve

Swedenborg's reading

Swedenborg's chief interest in his youth had been science. At the same time he seems to have always held fast to a Christian faith, even if its intensity varied. The *Principia* and *The Infinite*, both from 1734, contain natural philosophy with clear religious elements. Soon he would begin his search for man's soul using what he called a 'rational psychology', a doctrine about man's soul and its God-given faculty of understanding; but apparently it then became clear to him that the task he had taken on required insights into what philosophers and theologians had thought about the subject through the ages. At the beginning of the 1740s he made detailed notes and copied passages from his readings, excerpting long pieces from Plato, Aristotle, Plotinus, Augustine, Descartes, Locke, Malebranche, Leibniz, Wolff, and many others. In English translation these notes fill more than 500 pages. It is a philosopher's notebook, conveying a clear picture of Swedenborg's industry and interest. From this mass of material we select a few of the more important thoughts.

Malebranche and 'vision in God'

One of Descartes' best-known disciples was the French philosopher and theologian Nicolas

Malebranche, whose teaching certainly came to be of great significance for the truth-seeking assessor. Inge Jonsson has demonstrated the importance of Malebranche's teaching about the relationship between the body and soul for Swedenborg's doctrine of correspondences. After studying Descartes for many years, in 1674 Malebranche published a work in six parts: *Recherche de la Verité* (*Search for Truth*). In Descartes he had found a physiological psychology that emphasized the spiritual nature of man's soul. Descartes had given a mechanical explanation for both bodily and rational functions: activities like breathing and digestion functioned according to given laws in the same rational way as do memory, sense impressions, or the life of the senses. For Malebranche this picture of the human mechanism became a proof of God's continual presence in human memory, thoughts, and feelings. Here, according to the French philosopher, was the fatal blow to the naturalism of Aristotle and the Schoolmen, and so to the belief that in all forms there is an indwelling physical striving towards further development.

In summary, without God as a causal spiritual power the human clockwork would never function. It is only in and through the Divine that we can really understand; and in this God-given mind, called soul by Malebranche, we find the explanation of the classical problem of how spirit is related to the body.

Divine truths show themselves as models and archetypes for our thinking, provided that we turn our attention and love towards God. Our will is free. In fact, our freedom consists precisely in our ability to turn the will, which is love, to God. Thus our seeing rightly is seeing in God, *la vision en Dieu* (the vision of God).

If we turn our will to God, a higher knowledge streams into our souls and we understand the hidden, higher meaning of natural experience, opening itself to the pious man. Our sensory consciousness is always coloured by our state of mind and by our relationship with God. In the same view, our ideas of the world of the senses become facets of our picture of the Creator, just as movements of the will on the earthly plane become steps in our movement towards the Divine. God makes himself known through thoughts and movements in the soul, and his appearance as love and wisdom is naturally adapted to the individual's situation. This is the individual's will, 'the occasion', from which came the name 'occasionalism' for Malebranche's doctrine about this relationship between God and man, soul and body.

Faith and reason must always work together, writes Malebranche. Faith shows us man's unhappy condition, and his present inability to direct his will wholly towards God. God's grace through Christ makes it possible to approach this lost, blessed state; and by using our understanding we can analyse the conditions for man's freedom and God's grace.

The work of God's grace in man cannot be made clear without an analysis of man's will. For Malebranche the will is the natural motion towards what is good. This requires continual choices in situations where what is good presents itself to the intellect as idea and feeling. Sin diminishes freedom. With the first human beings, before sin's entry into the world, there was total freedom. The presence of what belongs to the body and the material world was not the threat to freedom with which we now live. But in spite of this dominance, through Christ's entrance into the world as a sequel to the Fall we can now enjoy grace. It pours down upon all, regardless of moral quality. Its reception differs from case to case depending on the occasion and the relationship of the individual to Christ and his message.

For the French philosopher reason and fate were paired in approximately the same way as in Swedenborg's later works, and here we also glimpse the concept of 'correspondence', so important for Swedenborg.[1] His notes from the French priest's *Search for Truth*, which was in his private library, are abundant.

Heavenly correspondences and God in nature

During the decades following Malebranche's contribution to philosophy an intensive debate was carried on, especially in England, about the deistic concept of 'God in nature'. For many during the Enlightenment the concept of God seemed as distant as it was indeterminable: God had withdrawn after creating the world. But was not the correct information about God present in man's reason and in the knowledge that he could gather from nature? Revelation of Christ's appearance in the world and the concept of atonement were perhaps not necessary for faith. Nature itself provided knowledge about the Creator's existence and wisdom. This view developed into the conviction that all religious truth could be confirmed by observation and reason. This was the chief thought of 'deism': a conviction of the absolute rationality of the Christian message and the belief that it is mirrored in man and nature. A 'physical theology' was developed as a support to the argument of the deists. God's infinite wisdom in nature, within botany, chemistry, physics, mathematics, stood forth in its perfection as the picture of the Divine. The divine revelation in the biblical text could also be seen from this rational perspective.

We meet the same idea about the rationality of Christianity in the fourth book of John Locke's *Essay concerning Human Understanding*, and several other writings, studiously excerpted by Swedenborg. The true, genuine Christian revelation was always sensible and judicious, and that which eventually clashes with reason is false from a Christian perspective. The Christian doctrine then becomes very simple and easily understood. It is so clear and morally self-evident that all people can be saved regardless of what faith they have held.

Locke's famous book was published in 1690. The following year Locke published his *The Reasonableness of Christianity*. Five years later another piece with a similar purpose was written by the Irish priest, John Toland, *Christianity not Mysterious*. The title can stand as an emblem for British deism. Everything in Christian doctrine and dogmatics was intelligible, according to Toland. It was only the doctrine of the Holy Supper in its Catholic and Protestant forms that must be rejected: his understanding could not accept the dogma concerning the sacramental character of Communion.

The notion of the Divine revealing itself in nature has certainly been one of mankind's constant companions. With the microscope, telescope, and ever more subtle analyses in chemistry, physics, and biology this belief naturally came into focus more than previously. Newton himself thought that he saw providence in his theories and discoveries. In a well-known letter he wrote of the purpose behind his famous *Principia*:

> When I wrote my dissertation on our system I was thinking also about such principles as could make many inclined to believe in a divine being; and nothing can make me happier than to find that my work has been of use for this purpose. But if I have thereby been of any service to mankind in general, this is due solely to my own industry and patient thinking.[2]

'Use' became a watchword during Swedenborg's century for philosophers, biologists, and botanists, and in the political economy as well. The utility, the rational purpose of all things became a key that opened the doors to the secrets of creation as well as of material well-being. This idea stands at the centre of the Englishman William Derham's well-known work *Physico-Theology, a Demonstration of the Being and Attributes of God, from His Works of Creation*, translated into Swedish in 1736. In Sweden the concept of God in nature found its best-known expression in Carl Linnaeus's contribution to the science of botany. In the later editions of his famous *Systema Naturae* we meet his lines on the divine and universal wisdom:

Gripped with reverence I saw the infinite, omniscient, and almighty God on the back when he went past, and became dizzy! I traced his footsteps over nature's field and noticed in everything, even in those things I could scarcely discern, an infinite wisdom and might, an unfathomable perfection. Yes, I saw how all animals are supported by vegetation, the ground by the whole earth; how the earth circled night and day around the life-giving sun; how the sun, planets, and stars each rolled as if on its axle, in uncountable number and endless breadth, and how they were maintained in the void by the inconceivable first motion, the being of all things, the spring and governor of all causes, the Lord and Master of this world. If you want, call him Fate, this is not wrong, for everything hangs on his finger; call him Nature if you will, call him Providence, and you will also have spoken correctly, for everything has come from him; he is utterly and entirely mind […] vision […] hearing […] soul […] a being who has established and built all this; who always glimmers before our eyes without being visible, who can be comprehended only by thought, for such a great Majesty resides on such a holy throne, which nothing can approach save the soul alone […][3]

Ultimately everything has a rational purpose, and so serves man, wrote Linnaeus in his *Cui Bono? (What Good does it serve?)* Here are the concluding lines:

And now man has been created to honour his Creator: God has also manifested himself to man through revelations and what he has created: all things have a unique and wonderful form: all things are created to be of use at length to man […] For the omniscient Creator has created nothing in vain, but for a specific purpose, or to be of service to someone […] *Everything he has created is good.*

For Swedenborg, too, the Divine would 'glimmer everywhere' before his eyes; but while Linnaeus proposed a 'classification' of all things in nature based on external characteristics, Swedenborg maintained that such systems should be guided by utility, and by the connection of natural things with heavenly realities. In several works Swedenborg would argue strongly against the ideas of his famous countryman and relative, yet without ever mentioning Linnaeus's name.

Leibniz and the world of monads

In Swedenborg's day the most significant philosophers were the Germans Gottfried Wilhelm von Leibniz and his disciple Christian von Wolff. Swedenborg's reading of both these thinkers is clearly reflected in his notes.

Leibniz was the master, a man whose mentality and wide range of interests resembled Swedenborg's own constant and many-sided activity. Leibniz, who in addition to many other specialities was also an expert mathematician, set up an equation in which God and his creation stood on opposite sides of the equals mark. Everything could then be reduced to absolute agreement. The Creator had once and for all determined that spirit and matter should be in complete accord. The divine clockmaker had set both clocks to the same time and wound them up, and together they struck the same hour.

Seen through the clock maker's magnifying glass, the whole world consists of infinitely small spiritual and indivisible entities, 'monads', each and every one *'infiniment subtil'* (infinitely subtle). The monads mirror the world with greater or lesser clarity. They are different states of mind, sleeping or more or less awake, and always without contact with each other, 'without windows'. Every monad perceives that part of the universe to which it is tied; each and every one of these 'subtle' particles is thus a tiny, concentrated universe. The monads that form a mountain see nothing else than the mountain; those that make up man's organs, and together form the human body, do not see outside the bodily parts where they have their abode. The most perspicacious monad in man is that of the soul. At the apex of this universe of windowless, spiritual atoms stands God, the perfect monad, omniscient and all embracing. Life should consist of a continually rising insight, a widened perspective, where the monad, in spite of its windowlessness, discerns in itself ever more of the Divine, the 'central monad'.

Death in the sense of disappearing was an impossibility in a world consisting of monads. As with Calderón, life was a dream, or a play. We waken when we die and put off our masks. Properly speaking, we should not speak at all of death. What happens is simply that the living leave their clothing. A new theatre begins, with an entrance onto a new stage. The dead appear in a different play, as 'equally subtle and well-directed' as the previous one.

The limited monad, the one that dimly mirrors the whole, has its own particular task in the universe. The world must contain things of all kinds, even limited, twisted perspectives. Limitation, a narrow field of vision, is according to Leibniz what we call evil. Evil, consequently, is unavoidable. But we must remember that in the great whole what is good outweighs all else; goodness is built into creation itself. Everything works together for the best. *O felix culpa!* says a hymn from the Middle Ages: O, blessed crime, how could we be saved by Christ's sacrificial death without Judas's treason?

The monad contains in itself its own development, the principle of its own existence. The adherents of the so-called pre-formation theory maintained that all of the chicken's characteristics could be known from the egg. In the same way, Leibniz's monad carried its own future within itself. On the other hand, for him the variety in life could be traced back to a single unity, like a mathematical number.

For the sake of clarity it should be pointed out that to Swedenborg this thought was untenable, as regards both simple and complicated, lower and higher entities. He conceived of all development as conditioned by a relationship of opposites, the interaction between active and passive. The process of life goes from the simple to the composite; and a simple entity in its turn always consists of dualities. In Swedenborg's metaphysics the highest entity is a union of love and wisdom. In Leibniz's thinking the divine monad is multiplicity, a composite containing everything in itself.

Thus in Leibniz there is no influence of the spiritual element on the bodily one, or the other way around. A 'pre-established harmony' prevails. The problem of the relationship of spirit to matter was solved for those who accepted the monad theory. But Swedenborg held fast to his conviction that the world consists of living spirit and material body, a dualism dictated by his cosmogony and religious conviction. The harmony was not pre-established; it was established differently, and functioned successively in a continual process. Man's will is free and he is able to influence his spiritual situation; Christianity is for Swedenborg the religion of spiritual freedom.

Wolff, philosopher in decline

The abundantly productive philosopher Christian Wolff was a faithful disciple of Leibniz. In his many works he sought to present the master's philosophy in a scholarly and systematic manner. Everything should be presented, if possible, as clearly and objectively as in a mathematical formula. God's existence could be proved, as well as the origin of the universe and the agreement of science, with a rational theology. The soul, the object of Swedenborg's continual search, would according to Wolff soon be accessible to human knowledge. If only we had a sufficiently effective microscope, we would be able to see it with our own eyes.

Theology, likewise, should be presented with the clarity that characterizes mathematics. Subjective experience and the divine purpose of existence is an individual matter. The scientist should proceed methodically. His thinking and mode of presentation should be a matter of demonstration. All concepts must be clear and distinct. Definitions should be 'geometrically' formulated, so that the basis upon which they are built stands out clearly. When this is done, we can prove the divine logic of existence through deductions. Definition and deduction became keywords, as much in metaphysics as in physics.

In Wolff's cosmology the world is seen as a chain of finite, interconnected entities. Their nature and character is evident from the first entity. Everything functions, as with Leibniz, like a giant clock. Physical entities are made up of non-spatial substances; here we meet Leibniz's monads, but now termed 'atoms of nature'. The atoms are independent but nevertheless interconnected in the whole that is the universe. They, like all else, must have a final cause, which is God.

In every atom or monad there is a soul, Wolff wrote in his *Psychologia Rationalis* (*Rational Psychology*). The soul's power is measured by its ability to imagine the world. With Wolff, as with Leibniz, there are slumbering and more or less awake atoms/monads. The soul's ability is determined by its bodily covering and by its will. All truth lies within it, as it is without contact with other souls. God, the highest soul, comprises and surveys them all. Leibniz's often sweeping and elegant hypotheses were given a professorial precision by Wolff, clearly appealing to the academics of that day. In our eyes, however, the text's effect is diminished by tiring verbosity and constant repetitions.

In the 1730s, Swedenborg was an eager reader of Wolff, whose ideas we find in *Principia* and *The Infinite*. Swedenborg himself paid his debt of gratitude in a postscript to *Principia*:

> I cannot conclude, however, without referring to the name of Christian von Wolff, who has given so much attention to the cultivation of his intellectual powers, and who has so much contributed to the advance of true philosophy by his various scientific and experimental researches. I refer particularly to his [...] *Ontology* and his *Cosmology*, which I have read and which have served in a high degree to confirm my views. But the principles I have laid down in this work [...] had been written two years before I could consult his works. In the revision of the present volume, I acknowledge myself much in debt to him. If anyone will take the trouble to compare the two, he will find that the principles I have here advanced and applied to the world and its series almost exactly coincide with the metaphysical and general axioms of this illustrious author.

Several of Wolff's books were in Swedenborg's library. In Wolff's *Rational Psychology* published in 1734, and his *Natural Theology* from 1736-7, Swedenborg found, among other things, arguments for his own doctrine about a rational and divine purpose on all levels of creation.

Swedenborg's dependence on Wolff has been thoroughly analysed by Inge Jonsson, who emphasizes especially Swedenborg's close ties to Wolff as regards the use of the concept of series and degrees. By this means the Swedenborgian doctrine of correspondences was built to a certain extent on the German philosopher's writing. Swedenborg's conviction that the human soul could be assigned to a place and function in the body was probably also stimulated by the industrious Wolff.

For the reader of Swedenborg's theosophical writings Wolff's presence is evident above all in the mode of expression. The Latin of the scientist and philosopher was living, often coloured by Ovid. *De Cultu et Amore Dei* (*The Worship and Love of God*) displays his stylistic ability. His theosophical works, in contrast, are characterized by Wolff's 'mathematical', demonstrative method. In them the writer's personality and literary skill often disappear in long Latin sentences where, in Wolff's manner, he attempts to define his starting points as clearly as possible, in order to link the conclusions in long logical chains. The recurring definitions of frequently appearing concepts often result in tiring repetitions, like lectures on spiritual mathematics. The development of thought is often geometric, with continual proportional analogies: 'A is related to B as C is to D'.

Thus Wolff should be honoured for his ontological and cosmological theories, according to Swedenborg, but later in life he would dissociate himself from the way the German philosopher made deductions from abstractly constructed concepts to describe the characteristics of the Divine.

After 1744-5, Swedenborg definitely put Christian Wolff into eternal shade. Wolff had never understood the central element 'in the truths pertaining to nature', he wrote in *The Spiritual Diary*, 'still less [the central element] in the truths of faith'.[4] Wolff, like so many other scholars, 'confirmed himself', that is, affirmed his own ideas: from the theses he proposed, he drew conclusions whose main purpose seemed to be to make himself well-known. This was an invalid approach. Higher knowledge was revelation, obtained only by the man who had made himself receptive through love to God and practical action.

In Swedenborg's later visions, Wolff met a gloomy fate after death. He had in actuality never believed in God, only in nature. A child of his time, he was a sceptic who denied providence, the immortality of the soul, and the Last Judgement. However, out of concern for his position he had falsely presented himself as a believing Christian:

> The atheists are the most learned [. . .] the more knowledge they have the greater is their trust in themselves and their stock of false proofs. Learning for them becomes a path to mental illness. [Wolff] loved money [. . .] and wanted to be acclaimed 'the light of Europe' [. . . After death] he was let into his own evil, and consequently cast into hell.[5]

Wolff became inflated with his own imagined intelligence, Swedenborg wrote elsewhere.[6] Swedenborg felt himself persecuted by him and some Swedes of the same mind, Eric Benzelius and his brothers Lars and Gustav Benzelstierna. After their deaths they tormented him with a persistent itching of the anus. They had been conceited and overbearing in their false convictions. 'We physicians have had other revelations', wrote the sceptical Kleen: 'we usually call this symptom haemorrhoidal itching'.[7]

Newton's vacuum

During his first visit to England in 1710-3, Swedenborg, according to a letter to Benzelius, intently studied Isaac Newton's famous *Mathematical Principles of Natural Philosophy*. The book, usually referred to as *Principia*, like Swedenborg's own work from 1734, had come out in 1687, the year before Swedenborg's birth; a copy was in his library in Stockholm.

Only a few quotations from Newton are in Swedenborg's great collection of excerpts. Presumably he was well acquainted with Newton's position on several of the problems related to the connection between body and soul, God and man. Here the question about the vacuum came into the picture.

Newton's view was that there is no matter between the bodies in the universe, only a vacuum. Time and space cannot exist outside the place they themselves form, he wrote in his *Principia*. He continued his thought:

In what has regard to order, everything exists in time, and the concrete situation and order of a thing must be sought in space. It is this quality of space and time that determines a thing's being. It would be absolutely absurd to think that entities as they originally existed were in motion. [8]

In the extension of this thought lies the idea that the characteristics of space and time in a given body were independent of all else in the universe. There was a vacuum between the bodies; they were not organically connected. Descartes, as we have seen, had proclaimed that there was no such thing as a vacuum. Everything was connected, in mutual interaction.

One of the difficulties in understanding Newton's theory of gravitation was connected with the question of how an attracting force could exist in a vacuum. For Swedenborg the idea of an absolutely empty space was already impossible for religious reasons. There must be some form of substance that binds man with the Divine: God could not be imagined acting in nothing. Thus matter, space, and time must constitute a unity close to the sphere of divine infinity.

At an early stage Swedenborg had spoken of 'vibrations', tremulations, as the agencies conveying energy from body to body. In a vacuum such a connection would be impossible. On the spiritual plane it took the form of a rhythm. We can think and act as elements in a universal motion. Man's breathing can be brought into harmony with heaven, which is Christ's body. This theme returns in our chapter on breathing and vision.

The dangerous philosophy

How much of modern philosophy did Swedenborg learn when he was young and how much did he remember during the years of the 1720s and 1730s when his power and vitality were at their height? Inge Jonsson has warned of the tendency in Swedenborgian literature to consider him as a giant of knowledge, a man with an encyclopedic cognizance. When he quotes philosophers and church fathers in his works his references are often based on learned summaries of his day, more than on his own studies of primary sources.

Naturally, he was an educated man, in the sense of the word at that day. His excerpts made around 1740 show industrious philosophical studies from Plato, Aristotle, the neo-Platonists, and Augustine to the great names of his own day. They were related to his own studies, he was searching for arguments to support the lines of thought he was already pursuing. He wanted to be a 'true philosopher'. He explained what this involved in his *Principia*:

> By a true philosopher we understand a man who […] is enabled to arrive at the real causes and to the knowledge of those things in the mechanical world which are invisible and remote from the senses; and who is afterwards capable of reasoning *a priori*, or from first principles or causes, concerning the world and its phenomena […] and who can thus, from a central point, take a survey of the whole mundane system, and of its mechanical and philosophical laws. [9]

There was also another and yet more important requirement that the true philosopher and lover of wisdom must fulfil. We read in the same paragraph: 'Without the utmost devotion to the Supreme Being, no one can be a complete and truly learned philosopher. True philosophy and contempt for the Deity are incompatible…'

Swedenborg always turned away from empty knowledge, cognizance isolated from an existentially meaningful context. After his religious crisis in 1744-5 philosophy was never among his favourites in the field of knowledge. Three years later, in 1748, he warned explicitly about philosophy in *The Spiritual Diary*:

> I was talking with spirits about the different sciences and how they develop human minds: among other things, philosophy. As for philosophy, every aspect of it up until now has done nothing but cast shadows over minds, and thus has closed off the way to a contemplation of deeper matters, as well as of universal principles. For it consists solely of terms, and of disputes about them——even more so does rationalistic philosophy, which constricts ideas in such a way that the mind dwells upon nothing but petty details and scholastic dust. Besides, philosophy does not simply obstruct our clear view of inner things; it blinds us, completely rejecting faith. Therefore, in the other life, a philosopher who […] had given himself to this kind of thinking is now stupid […] and by far the least knowledgeable […] [10]

It should be added that, generally speaking, after 1745 Swedenborg probably did not read worldly literature at all, in any case not after he resigned from the Board of Mines in 1747. His letter to the Prime Minister Anders Johan von Höpken from 1760 is telling. Swedenborg sent him Swammerdam's famous *Biblia Naturae* as a gift. The owner did not need the book: it was no longer of use to him since his 'thoughts had turned from *naturalia* to *spiritualia*'. [11]

The kingdom of the soul

Chapter Thirteen

Everything is testimony to something higher, if we listen with the intensity of an hallucination. In everything a power is manifested, an infectious, moving seduction, a mysterious and summoning message; but only if we look with the ardent, unbound freedom of the lover.

Lars Gyllensten: *Diarium Spirituale*, p. 64

Fainting spells in Amsterdam

Swedenborg arrived in Amsterdam in the summer of 1736, where he began work on what he called *Oeconomia Regni Animalis* (*The Economy of the Animal Kingdom*). He had the first part of it printed in 1740 and a second during the following year, both anonymously. In this new book he treated subjects that he had touched upon earlier but peripherally; now the mining engineer and philosopher appeared as a physiologist and anatomist. The book is a description of his expeditions into man's inner regions in search of the secretive *anima*, the ever-elusive soul: a pursuit also leading him into the territory of theology and to several of the principal elements of the theosophy that would later become his vocation.

He seems to have set out upon this new path in a state of great psychic tension. Later, in his *Dream Diary*, written in 1743-4, he gave a picture of his intense commitment and way of working:

In the morning when I woke up, there came again upon me such a swoon or *deliquium* [fainting fit] as I had six or seven years ago in Amsterdam, when I began the oecon. Regni anim. [*The Economy of the Animal Kingdom*]; but it was much more subtle, so that I seemed to be near death. It came upon me as I saw the light and threw me on my face. Gradually it passed off, while I fell into brief slumbers, so this *deliquium* was more inward and deeper; but soon it ceased. *This means that my head is thoroughly cleaned and rinsed from all that might obstruct these thoughts, as happened last time, when it gave me the power of penetration, especially with the pen*, which this time too was represented to me insofar as I seemed to be writing with a fine hand.[1]

He reports other, similar experiences, above all a light that suddenly showed itself when, after pondering a matter for a long time, he understood the connection or the solution to a problem.

Journeys into the interior

Swedenborg lived in the first days of the glory of the microscope that allowed ever-new discoveries through increasingly stronger lenses. New facts were brought forth, not least in the realm of anatomy. Swedenborg described his method in the preface to his book. First, if man is to investigate the operation of the functions of the human body, all relevant fields of science must be marshalled, not only anatomy and medicine, but science as a whole. Secondly, to be meaningful, all the experiences of science must be inserted into an overall picture of creation's 'unbroken chain of means and ends', or in other words, be relative to God's plan and purpose for life.

To achieve his goal Swedenborg therefore systematically recounted the observations of the great scientists of his day. He himself refrained from actual anatomical research; we read that pride in his own observations risked rendering him unable to see the light shed by discoveries of others.

Therefore on the basis of facts and relationships gathered from different areas he would now attempt to formulate syntheses and summarizing evaluations. Here intuition came into play: the power of imagination was important. This gift was especially developed in artists, he wrote, but he himself was well acquainted with its significance and effect. When man on the basis of knowledge gained from experience and after long cogitation finally understands a relationship he has the feeling of seeing everything in a new light. It is for a moment, he says, as if the seeker had recovered the faculty of understanding possessed by the first human beings in paradise and everyone who has experienced this joy knows that it is higher and greater than all bodily pleasures.

This higher form of knowledge is impeded, however, by sensual delights and by thoughts about earthly concerns, and particularly by self-love. Egotism limits the horizon and deafens reason. In his later writings he often provides illustrations of these obstacles to real insight.

The blood and the human body

In Goethe's drama *Faust* we hear Mephistopheles' famous words to Faust about the human blood: *ein ganz besonderer Saft* (a liquid of a wholly special kind). The contents and tasks of the blood in the organism was a topical issue in the seventeenth and eighteenth centuries. For Swedenborg the secret of life was hidden in this red liquid:

> That the blood is a concrete of substances of various natures, and more especially of the fluid in which the soul resides, and of which the soul is the life, is a subject which the reader will see further explained […] there is nothing which has a more intimate presence in the animal kingdom, and a greater degree of potency, than the blood; nay, that from changes of its state results are produced which affect the very sphere of the thoughts.[2]

The quality of the blood changed. The finest blood-like fluid was to be found in the 'spirituous fluid' of the brain, that functioned as the vehicle for the divine inflow that has been streaming through man and his world ever since matter came into being. From this fluid were propagated the beginnings of the blood's cruder forms: the 'pure' blood and the 'red'. Through these liquids the character and will of the soul was pumped further out into the human organism:

> […] every action of the body is the soul's action, so far as it is the action of the will […] But as the soul cannot descend without intermediates into the ultimate compositions and effects of its body […] therefore it follows, that *next to the soul, in the order of forces and substances, is the spirituous fluid; next, the purer blood; and next, the red blood; which last is thus as it were the corporeal soul of its own little world* […] And on the nature,

constitution, determination, and continuity of the blood depend the fortunes and condition of the animal [the soul's] life [...].[3]

The heart circulates the red blood that washes through all the organs. Swedenborg, with his particular angle of approach, is always interested in nourishment and cleansing. The blood receives the 'treasures of the atmosphere', as well as man's food, and vice versa there is a continual cleansing: the kidneys filter elements from the blood that would otherwise have been poisonous.

Swedenborg's anatomical studies foreshadow the models of man's spiritual development that he was later to present. Blood correctly nourished and cleansed here becomes an image of the regenerated man's right love when he has left his earth-bound life:

That 'blood' means heavenly things, and in the highest sense means the Lord's Human Essence, and so Love itself, which is His mercy towards the human race, becomes clear from the sacredness that the Jewish representative Church was required to attach to blood.[4]

In the finest blood, the *spirituous fluid*, the power of the soul was active, according to Swedenborg, pulsating in harmony with the breathing of the lungs, but without a direct connection with the heart. The heart and the brain functioned synchronously only in those instances where the brain had decided to subordinate itself to the control of the red blood, and thereby to the 'fires of the body'. Later he saw the relationship in another way: the brain and the heart determined man's love, the brain and the lungs were decisive for his knowledge and wisdom. As we shall see, the proper coordination of heart and lungs was important for Swedenborg's teaching of the significance of breathing for proper concentration on higher things.

The egg and *epigenesis*

After composing his studies of the blood Swedenborg took up yet another thought that would be echoed in his later writings. Scientists of that time debated two opinions as to the development of embryos. Those who favoured the 'preformation' theory argued that a chicken's whole path of development existed in the egg. The same applied to the human realm: the fertilized egg 'determined' and 'preformed' in all essential respects the way that the resulting human being would develop.

The theory of preformation stood in conflict with the whole idea behind Swedenborg's anatomical research, for the further extension of the theory taught that the early structures of the human body limited both the will's ability to act and the role of providence.

Preformation theory was countered by another concept, the theory of *epigenesis*: here the successive development of the organs was considered to be the result of other physical elements outside the egg, interacting with its contents. Swedenborg acknowledged the significance of these elements, but for him the creating power, the soul, was the most important factor.

He maintained that the human soul and will determine the shaping of our life; the determining factor is man's receptivity to the divine inflow. We can never explain the development of plants, animals, or man simply by what is material; and man, the most fully developed entity in creation, possesses through his free will the possibility of deviating from paths to which his mental faculties would seem to direct him:

> For the Author of Nature has reserved to himself the supremacy over it and all things, both in regard to power, presence, knowledge, and providence, which supremacy he exercises according to the law, that so far as the soul is dependent upon him, so far is it perfect in every faculty, and conducted to universal and absolute ends, and its lower powers and degrees, by its means, are the same; but so far as it ceases to be his image and likeness, so far it becomes imperfect in all its faculties, and lapses away from the nobler ends.[5]

Series and degrees

To explain the process by which the creative power from the Infinite reached the finite Swedenborg used a theory that he called the 'doctrine of series and degrees'. The 'world-soul' descended by branchings ever more complex and distant from their origin. This occurred, in his opinion, by a process that could be likened to a flight of stairs where every step implies three movements. Leading and initiating every step is an *end*, or purpose; to reach this goal a *cause* must be at hand, making the third and last level possible: this is the result, the *effect*, the *use*, the *completion* of the three-stage process.

And this goal in its turn leads to a new end and a new cause of continued development in a new stage, in continually new processes, all further distant from the original wholeness in the vicinity of the Infinite. The power from the Infinite, which according to Swedenborg's *Principia* was order and divine providence, is in action on every step of this descent. End, cause, and effect may be more or less strong on every level, with variations in intensity and clarity, like those of daylight.

And to this descent from the simple and sublime power corresponds a human ability to ascend and, with the help of empirical knowledge and syntheses, return to its source. Man's striving towards increased clarity of higher purpose and origin must have its starting point in the purpose that motivates every step, and the cause then becomes the quest he pursues. The effect is the answer, more or less clear, though he can never attain a complete knowledge of the world of the Infinite, the averted face of Janus.

The enigma of the soul and the poverty of language

In the second part of *The Economy of the Animal Kingdom* the concluding chapter describes his search for man's *anima*, or soul. Swedenborg had a notion of a connection from the cerebral cortex into the brain itself; these movements, transmitted through membranes, appeared to constitute the soul. He concentrated his attention upon the 'transporting fluid', the finest blood. But the result was unsatisfactory: in spite of all his efforts he had not been able to present the precise facts he had hoped for. The soul's location could certainly be sensed, as well as its function. For Swedenborg the soul was both material and immaterial, something '*infiniment subtil*' (infinitely subtle), to quote Leibniz. It functioned as a material receptacle for an inflow of divine love and wisdom; but how this *influxus* occurred lay beyond man's ability to understand. In an analogy with the life-giving power of the earth's sun, we read, we might envisage a spiritual sun, an active power that makes passive matter fruitful.

To grasp these vague concepts, an exact knowledge of the soul's place and form in the material world was required. Such knowledge could be achieved only if we could formulate a general concept, describing the first stage from which it originated, its earthly source of power and this in turn presupposed the finding of linguistic terms that could capture the complexity lying behind the reality.

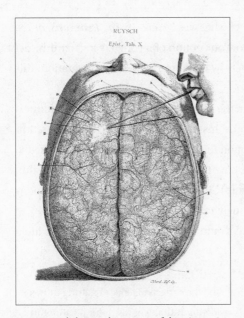

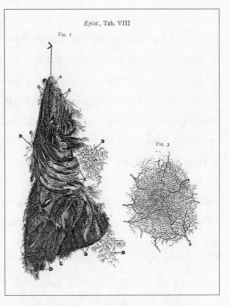

Fig. 17. Fredrik Ruysch's picture of the *pia mater*, the cerebral cortex. It covers the brain like a thin membrane. (Ruysch's *Opera Omnia Anatomico-medico-chirurgica*. Epist. Tab X; cf. Swedenborg's *The Cerebrum*, vol. II.)

Fig. 18. Swedenborg's conclusions as to the nature and location of the soul appear to be related to the Dutch anatomist Fredrik Ruysch's well-known anatomical plates. Here are Ruysch's drawings with the following explanation, given by Swedenborg: 'Part of the *pia mater* in its entrance into the brain. This does not happen in slightly curved movements [...] but takes place in a spiral form'.[6]

But human language was inadequate for such a task. Swedenborg, like other contemporary philosophers, dreamed of a kind of hieroglyphic language where every symbol contained a number of ideas; such words or tokens should be capable of being handled as mathematical entities. But his thoughts of a calculus of the soul never went further than the conceptual stage.

Correspondences: words as messengers in disguise

The doctrine of series and degrees was an important tool for a man with Swedenborg's ambitions, providing a rational explanation of the chain of concepts that bound together heaven and earth, God and man. But this connection must be made more concrete. How did man see the higher and heavenly form of what was lower? In *The Economy of the Animal Kingdom* Swedenborg described how our notion of a concrete and earthly fact or situation could be elevated to higher levels by using our power of imagination; this ability is always related to our *state of mind*.

Swedenborg's thoughts were formulated in the second part of the book. It is his famous 'doctrine of correspondences', which became his *organon*, his tool for interpreting existence.[7] The correspondence of what is upon the earth to what is above was related to the fact that all material phenomena always have their final cause in the spiritual realm. Thus he distanced himself from strictly scientific thinking, replacing exact observations and his deductions with what he saw as divinely inspired truths.

He would often describe this new knowledge and how he had acquired it. Here are a few lines written ten years later:

The representation of spiritual things by natural, and the correspondence of natural things with spiritual, may also be known from the consideration that what is natural cannot in any sense come into being without a cause prior to itself. Its cause exists in that which is spiritual. Nothing natural exists which does not have its cause there. Natural forms are effects and cannot appear as causes, let alone as the causes of causes, or first origins. Instead they take the forms they do from the use they perform in the place where they belong.[8]

Practically speaking, all things in the material world were but footprints, signs. Words, sentences, things, and relationships, from the lowest to the most sublime, bear witness to something higher, perceived by the attentive observer. In the text of the Bible, both the characters and their greed and aspirations to power and honour, bodily failings and bodily health, troubles and successes, were for the ardent and faithful, above all, components in a higher design. Behind earthly existence there is a hidden meaning.

Charles Baudelaire's poem 'Correspondances' is perhaps the best-known literary example of the Swedenborgian doctrine of correspondence and its poetic fruitfulness:

Nature is a temple where living pillars
sometimes release indistinct words;

man passes there through forests of symbols

that observe him with intimate glances.[9]

The soul after death and God's heavenly city

Swedenborg's eschatology, his teaching about the life after death, is to a certain extent present at the end of *The Economy of the Animal Kingdom*. The soul partakes of the divine power and therefore can never die. After death the soul lives on in the human form it had during its earthly existence, but is now free from all physical defects. In the light of heaven it passes its own sentence upon the way it had lived on earth:

> Now if no action or word, however insignificant, will perish; and if the soul, as order, and as intelligence, will nicely perceive in the veriest singulars, what itself contains that agrees with the truth, and what is repugnant thereto, then, in the bright light and most present glory of a wisdom, by which it is exalted to the degree of intelligence of which it is capable, it cannot fail [...] to call itself to account, and to pronounce its own sentence. In the same way as when [...] the eye is injured, the pain is exquisite in proportion to the intensity of the light [...] though all the time the light itself is blameless and excellent. [10]

In the heavens there is a community of souls, he continued, and the earthly city of God is a nursery for this community, which is the end purpose of all ends.

The book concludes with a jubilant fanfare. The essential points to be noted are Swedenborg's conviction regarding the celestial meaning of existence, the possibility of God's kingdom on earth, and eternal life in a heavenly community of saintly men and women. He considers himself as living in the eternal kingdom of the soul, with the Bible as his guide and source of all truth:

> The Holy Scripture is the code of rules [...] any sincere soul, which permits the Spirit of God to govern it, may draw them from this pure fountain, pure enough for the use and service of the members of the city of God all over the world, without violating any form of ecclesiastical government. [11]

The closing words of *The Economy of the Animal Kingdom* can be seen as an overture to his own theosophical authorship: 'It is foretold that the kingdom of God shall come; that at last the guests shall be assembled to the marriage supper; that the wolf shall lie down with the lamb, the leopard with the kid, the lion with the ox; that the young child shall play with the asp'.

In Venice's 'beautiful palace'

Swedenborg's intensive search for greater clarity on the problem of the soul went on during his long sojourn abroad from 1736 to 1740. He studied anatomical handbooks and perhaps took part in anatomical dissections that were carried out at a school for surgery near his dwelling in Paris. He began a work on the human brain. In 1738 he arrived in Venice, where he continued to write on the same subject; the manuscript, first published in 1812, grew to nearly 1,500 pages.

'In Venice, concerning the beautiful palace', he wrote five or six years later concerning a dream. [12] He did not explain what he had seen, but we gain a glimpse of his experiences in his notes of his travels from 1736 to 1739. He arrived on 19 April from Padua in company with a Count Barck. He describes the impressive ceremonies and illuminated canals in connection with the reception of an ambassador. It was Ascension Day, 15 May 1738:

> [...] saw the celebration that usually takes place at Ascension. Was also out [...] and saw how the sea was consecrated. Men and women were wearing masks for fourteen days. There were also operas. Every Saturday music was to be heard in the monastery Incurabile & Pieta. I lodged near Ponte Rialto together with Herr Firencrantz. [13]

What music did he hear? We can guess Vivaldi's, who was the organist at St. Mark's Church. Perhaps Pergolesi's?

After Swedenborg's death his relatives presented his manuscripts to the Royal Academy of Sciences in Stockholm, where they are still preserved. Before the travel journal was handed over to the Academy, someone removed the pages after the entry just cited; these sheets were probably related to his life in Venice. In the *Dream Diary* he later recorded erotically charged experiences. Perhaps there were similar notes from his time in that city?

The Animal Kingdom, the *Dream Diary*: crisis and true love

Chapter Fourteen

From about ten-thirty in the evening to around half an hour after midnight. FIRE. Abraham's God, Isaac's God, Jacob's God, not the philosophers' and scientists' God. Joy, joy, joy, tears of joy. Jesus Christ, Jesus Christ […] That I might now never be separated from him […] Utter and lovely abandonment. Eternal in joy for one day of abandonment on earth.

The *Memorial* of Blaise Pascal

Bishop Swedberg and the right choice

'I n good time a man must choose a certain *vitae genus* [way of living], and then remain steadfastly in it and advance what it involves with all his energy', the Bishop wrote in his letter of farewell to the students in the Västmanland-Dala student association in Uppsala. He had been the association's inspector but left the post on 1 May 1703 when he moved to Brunsbo as Bishop of the Skara diocese. Among those whom he was addressing was his own son Emanuel, then a fifteen year old student. Above all, the fear of God was necessary:

In what you read, what you learn, what you undertake, let this be your goal: the fear of God, virtue, and what is useful in God's congregation and society in general. When you so pursue your studies, the Holy Spirit, who gives understanding and blessing, will be with you. And soon also eternal wisdom will come, joining in the fellowship. And then a man will be so learned and wise that he shall be content in all circumstances, then he shall cheerfully overcome all difficulty. The Bible must be your handbook: you must be at home in it. [1]

The exhortation to make an early choice of a course of life, with appropriate behaviour and perseverance, was certainly in agreement with Swedenborg's thinking, both in his youth and in later days. He later changed his path radically, leaving his service in the Royal Board of Mines and his writing regarding mining science and philosophy in favour of more than twenty-five years work inspired by dreams and visions. But he believed that he had experienced a divine government and logic in the course of his life. God's spirit had been with him ever since his youth, he wrote in the journal he kept of his dreams during 1743-4. Growing old he recognized ideas from his earlier stages in life:

> Then I perceived that things were brought forth in my thoughts, which had been put into them long before, so that I thereby found the truth of the Word of God: that there is not the least word or thought that is not known to God [...] [2]

The bishop's words about the importance of reading the Bible fell into good soil. All the way from the period of the *Dream Diary* till his death twenty-eight years later Swedenborg does not seem to have read much other than the Bible and his own massive indexes of the Scriptures. During the life-crisis, that will be described, we find from his notes that he studied intently the first books of the Pentateuch, and the Gospels, the Epistles, and the Book of Revelation.

The Russian war: the political situation and Swedenborg's departure to Holland

The spring of 1743 found Sweden in a deep crisis. The Hat government had declared war against Russia two years earlier, desiring to exploit a presumed state of Russian weakness to gain revenge for territorial losses at the peace of Nystad in 1721; but the war concluded in a humiliating defeat and catastrophe. After capitulating at Helsingfors in 1742, the Swedish troops were forced to depart from Finland and peace negotiations were carried on at the town of Åbo (or Turku, as it is known in English).

Would Sweden be forced to withdraw from the whole eastern half of the kingdom? In the Swedish-Russian game there was only one Swedish card of any value. The Swedish king, Fredrik I of Hesse, tired and dissipated, devoted himself to indulgence in an apparently insatiable passion for women; he was childless and presumably would die soon. In this situation the Swedish negotiators could pay for Finland with the guarantee of a successor to the throne friendly to Russia, the Prince-Bishop of Lübeck, Adolf Fredrik of Holstein Gottorp, who was related to the Empress of Russia, and thus supported by that country. In Copenhagen, on the other hand, the Danish king wanted to see his son as the successor to the Swedish throne, a thought that had many Swedish supporters.

Because of the war's unfortunate outcome, the Diet had been gathered in an extraordinary session in Stockholm since August 1742. Swedenborg participated in the parliamentary meetings as head of his family. In the preserved lists of those who attended his name appears in connection with approximately a third of the sessions of the House of Nobles. The Hats had chosen two generals as scapegoats for the defeat, both former officers under Charles XII: Henrik Magnus von Buddenbrock and Carl Emil Lewenhaupt. They were brought before a military tribunal and executed in August 1743. We do not know Swedenborg's opinion on the matter.

His circle of acquaintances consisted for the most part of Hats. We can assume that the assessor and philosopher had been negative towards a revenge of the kind that the Hat party wanted, even if he did not express himself publicly on the matter. Calm, order, stability were key words in Swedenborg's political vocabulary. We have no reason to believe that he had given up the thoughts described in his 1734 'project'. The memories of the absolute rule of the Caroline monarchy and of the dismembering of the kingdom towards the end of the long period of war never left him.

Thus the choice of Adolf Fredrik as king was controversial. Dissatisfaction with the German candidate to succeed to the throne, and with the war and the government, led to a general rebellion in Dalecarlia. Seven thousand men from that province marched down to Stockholm to set up camp on what is now Gustav Adolf's Square, directly in front of the royal palace. They would rather see a Danish prince on the throne than a German.

But the peace negotiations went their own way on the other side of the Gulf of Bothnia, and peace was concluded on 16 June: Finland would remain Swedish, but with some territorial losses in the east. The Russian condition, which the Swedish negotiators accepted, had been that Adolf Frederik would be chosen as the successor to the throne. The insurgents from Dalecarlia marched home again. As a painful reminder of the catastrophe, 12,000 Russian troops were stationed on the Swedish coast: their task was to ward off any possible Danish attack against Sweden.

The day after the peace was concluded, Swedenborg sought a two-year leave of absence from the Board and permission to go abroad. According to the application the purpose of his journey was to print a work that he was now finishing, and to consult foreign libraries. He would have preferred to stay at home in these unsettled times, to work for the general welfare and look after his own property. The journey was scarcely pleasant, he wrote:

> I am compelled to expose myself to dangers and discomfort, particularly in these agitated times, to expose myself to headaches and indescribable work, and in addition to subject myself to criticism, far from mild. But in spite of everything I am driven by an inner urge and wish to bring something of importance to light in my lifetime [...] Something that can be of use to the world in general [...] and to the honour of my fatherland. [3]

The work he was going to publish was to be entitled *Regnum Animale* (*The Animal Kingdom*). We have already met its fundamental thesis in *The Economy of the Animal Kingdom*: that there is an 'outer' and an 'inner' man. The outer understands and acquires what is communicated to him by his five senses. The inner, on the other hand, can assimilate something better, a higher, heavenly knowing. The purpose of this new book was precisely to demonstrate this twofold division, now with the help of objective facts revealed by science, and to describe the bridge between the two that showed itself to man when he was living in faith, hope, and love. The kingdom of the soul—the new work would demonstrate—was at the same time both the realm of the earthly senses and that of the soul.

Manuscript in the baggage

While the war was raging in the eastern half of the kingdom, the industrious assessor had certainly already finished the greater part of the work that motivated his foreign journey. In addition he had, in 1742, been occupied with a treatise entitled *Psychologia Rationalis* (*Rational Psychology*, also called *The Soul*). This book, which was never published during his lifetime, was a further attempt to determine the soul's location and role. Here, there are two important points.

First, Swedenborg sees the soul as something other than mere motions in the cortex of the brain. It must have a reality of its own, separate from the brain, which like all flesh was doomed to destruction. He concentrated increasingly on the soul as will, or love. As always, he tried to apply a broad perspective of the whole, where the divine will or purpose dominated, even if the thought was not fully developed. In this religiously coloured view of the soul we meet his constant conviction concerning man's free will.

Secondly, we detect in his manuscript his continued pondering on how the soul, a finite element, could be linked to the Divine. He would describe this dilemma in *Arcana Caelestia*, ten years later, when through 'inner vision' he had found the solution to the problem.

The *Dream Diary* and its structure

Swedenborg left Stockholm on 21 July 1743. He was fifty-five years old, and had twenty-nine years of life before him.

The industrious traveller usually kept a journal while on his many European journeys. Now he had a little octavo notebook in his baggage, bound in parchment, with pockets on the inside of the binding. A number of the pages have been torn out. 138 sheets remain, on 108 of which Swedenborg recorded, mainly, his notes concerning his dreams during the years 1743 to 1744. The notebook, called the *Dream Diary*, is preserved in the Royal Library in Stockholm.

The diary was first published in Stockholm in 1859. Chiefly because of its unusually outspoken erotic elements it occasioned scandal and debate. Swedenborg was mentally ill and a sex maniac, opined his detractors. His defenders maintained that it was a question of strictly personal mental observations, 'made by a man in his night clothes'. Its thoughts and expressions were the stuff of dreams about something different and higher.

The *Dream Diary* was begun as an ordinary travel journal. An initial brief section scarcely differs from his other travel notes. We find the dates of arrivals and departures, and sketchy notes of events, places he visited, and calls he made upon local nobility. The entries appear to have been written down from habit and communicate little of the traveller's or discoverer's joy. But this was not the first time he had travelled through Germany down to Holland; perhaps what he saw offered no new experiences worth noting.

The first stops on the way south were Södertälje and Norrköping. In Linköping he certainly visited his sister and brother-in-law, Anna Swedenborg and Eric Benzelius. The former university librarian had been appointed Bishop of Gothenburg in 1726 and since 1731 had held the same position in Linköping. Leaving his sister and brother-in-law, Swedenborg took the route to Gränna and Jönköping in order to continue to Ystad, which he reached on 27 July. He waited nine days for a favourable wind for further passage, by sea to Stralsund, and then travelled by stagecoach to Hamburg, which he left on 17 August. He crossed the Elbe to Buxtehude in Hanover, at one time Swedish. He noted 'the most charming landscape I have ever seen in Germany; passing through a continuous orchard of apple, pear, plum, walnut, and chestnut trees, and also linden and elms'.[4]

Parenthetically we note that Swedenborg had a great interest in gardens, in horticulture and arboriculture. In the world of his thinking, a well-kept garden is a picture of paradise, resplendent in its colours, fragrant, and divided into sections. He had a weakness for the baroque period's well-trimmed, humanized garden. In an earlier journal, for example, he wrote enthusiastically about the park around Sturehof castle in Eastern Gotland.[5] As we shall see, he himself planned such a landscape in miniature around his newly-purchased house in the Mullvaden block on Södermalm in Stockholm.

Gradually, towards the end of August, he came to Harlingen in Friesland. And here, on the seventh page of the journal, he concludes his travel notes with the words, 'From Harlingen, which is a large town'.[6] The following four pages were torn out.

He travelled further by boat and after a day's journey set foot on land in Amsterdam. At nearby Leiden he could undertake the library research mentioned in his request for leave of absence. He would stay in Holland over the winter and spring, living presumably for the greater part of the time in The Hague. Here he had a longstanding acquaintance, Joakim Fredrik Preis, who had represented Swedish interests in Holland since 1703. When he died in 1759 at the age of ninety, Preis was still in service. In May 1744 Swedenborg left The Hague to live for almost a year in London.

The torn-out pages

Four pages were torn out. If he had continued his travel journal entries in the same brief style he would scarcely have needed the space of all these pages. What had he written?

Perhaps in Amsterdam or The Hague he had had a mind-bending experience of a spiritual or religious nature. Did these pages contain his description of such an event? Why remove them? Much later, in a well-known letter, he would state that his call to a 'sacred office' took place in the year 1743, but in the *Dream Diary* he constantly refers to his vision of Christ in the spring of 1744 as the turning point. [7] And yet another year is mentioned — later on he sometimes gave 1745 as the year when his life's task was determined by a visible divine intervention. There is no clear answer. Perhaps in fact we have two or three events, two or three decisive experiences. In my interpretation, however, I lay emphasis on the great Easter vision in April 1744. Without more detailed information on earlier or later experiences of the same nature, the events documented in the *Dream Diary* stand as the culmination of the great crisis of his life.

Cooled passions?

In the journal we find signs of an early crisis or significant happening during the autumn or winter of 1743. Following the torn-out pages, Swedenborg made an undated, eleven-point summary of important dreams and visions, at the same time as he made notes on changes in his own mental state. We may assume that this summary has regard to what he had just described on the missing pages. The first seven abrupt notes have a special lucid power. Gunnar Ekelöf quoted them in his *Mölna-elegi*; they were 'wreckage on the beaches of sleep, dreams like the ringing of bells from the deep'.[8] Here are the seven lines:

1. In my younger days, and the Gustavian family.
2. In Venice, concerning the beautiful palace.
3. In Sweden, about the white cloud of the sky.
4. In Leipzig, on one lying in boiling water.
5. About one who stumbled with a chain into the depths.
6. Of the king who showed such generosity in a poor farmer's cottage.
7. Of the farmhand who wanted me to depart.[9]

Next on the list come personal observations:

8. On my nightly amusements.
   — wondered at myself that there was nothing left to do for my own glory, which I began to feel very strongly.

—— that I was not inclined towards sexual relations, which I had been all my days.

9. how I have been in wakeful ecstasy almost continuously.[10]

These entries can be assumed to summarize an initial, radical change to the conduct of his life. They correspond to the dated, essential, leading ideas expressed in the journal. We know nothing, however, about their actual form and content.

There are a few more undated notes, and then (after an evident break since the late summer of 1743) on 24-25 March 1744 Swedenborg resumes the dated entries. What follows now is first a day-by-day written account of a religious crisis in process; then, scarcely two weeks later, we read of a decisive, mystical experience: a vision of Christ with an exhortation in obscure words to an unspecified course of action.

Capitulation and crisis

What had happened to the industrious scientist, ceaselessly studying, excerpting, and writing? His plans had become increasingly comprehensive, his ambitions almost without bounds. He had proposed to solve mankind's ancient, central question about God's connection with the individual, the relationship of human reason to the Divine, and the presence of the spiritual in the realm of sensory experience. He wanted to write a religious and philosophical, medical and psychological, encyclopedia. All relevant knowledge would be mobilized in the long series of volumes listed and announced on the first pages of *The Animal Kingdom*. In sum, he would show that faith and knowing were one, that the boundary between them could be crossed. All truth that could be arrived at analytically was integrated in the divine wisdom.

His philosophical and anatomical studies, his reasoning, his somewhat neo-platonic 'doctrines' about the correspondences between what is on earth and what is in heaven, and about the stages of knowledge as steps in 'series and degrees'——all this was to help him and his reader to proceed to insights into a higher sphere of knowing.

The *Dream Diary* is primarily an account of a crisis, but at the same time we can follow how his spiritual experiences were continually connected with his ongoing work on *The Animal Kingdom*. Heavenly inspiration and empirical knowledge went together, and would form a new knowing. Here his extensive physiological and medical learning would be important. The interplay between the brain and the lungs gives us a picture of the circumstances and significance of the divine inflow. The study of the function of the kidneys throws light on the importance of purification for body and soul. He analyses the reason's and the senses' mode of acquiring knowledge. Facts gathered in this process are arranged and explained by an inflow from the Divine, an *influxus*, which makes possible a correct synthesis, where the individual elements are arranged in a higher relationship. A quotation from the journal:

> I saw how everything in an elliptical sphere concentrated itself upward in the highest part, since, in the lowest part, there was something like a tongue from which it spread out. This means, I think, that the innermost was *sanctuarium*, as a center of the globe above, and that such things indicated by the tongue shall be conceived. I believe I am destined to do this, which was inevitably the meaning of the *sanctuarium* I was dealing with and which was, moreover, confirmed by all *objecta scientiarium* represented to me by women, as also that there was a deliberation whether I would be admitted to the society where my father was. [11]

The Animal Kingdom was to be printed in The Hague and London during 1744 to 1745, but only the torso of the planned great encyclopedia came to birth, in three parts published in two volumes, in quarto format.

The crisis which we shall now describe is certainly connected with the intense religious engagement implied in his theory of knowledge about the inflow of the Divine. But equally it was also affected by the magnitude of the task he had taken upon himself, and by his highly accelerated pace of work. Besides, he had come to see that his plans had been conditioned by arrogance, ambition, and self-love. The solution during the period of the *Dream Diary* was an unconditional surrender to the Divine; after this his life and work were to be under divine guidance.

Vision of Christ: 'Well then, do!'

Joy in the midst of the dark night of the senses is 'the soul's happy lot', wrote John of the Cross. This joy reached its high point in a state of nearness or union with God, whose presence became a reality for Swedenborg in The Hague, on 6-7 April 1744, Easter Tuesday. From Good Friday he had been in an elevated state of mind, weeping over his sins and shaken by tremblings, 'inwardly content but outwardly distressed'. He had dreamed of the dissolute King Fredrik's depraved court marshal Erland Broman who had tempted him with his company and appealed to weaknesses in his character. Swedenborg had overcome the enticements and felt himself introduced into heaven as a reward, experiencing 'glory and bliss' that 'no human tongue can utter'. [12]

The notes from Easter Monday and the following night are marked in the margin with three *nota bene*. During the day he had strolled to nearby Delft, and had been in 'the deepest spiritual thoughts, deeper and more beauteous than ever'. [13] In the evening he sat by the fire, watching the flames. He noted their concrete reality; but the outer senses, nevertheless, were deceptive in comparison with God's Word, which was truth itself. He continued:

> I both believed and not believed at the same time. I thought that this is the reason that the angels and God showed themselves to the shepherds and not to philosophers, who let their understanding enter into these matters [. . .] [14]

And here he records his vision of Christ:

> At ten o'clock I went to bed and felt a little better. After half an hour, I heard some din under my head, and then I thought that the tempter left. Immediately a shiver came over me, starting from the head and spreading throughout the body, with some rumbling, coming in waves, and I realized that something holy had befallen me.
>
> Whereupon I went to sleep, and about twelve o'clock, or perhaps it was at one or two in the morning, such a strong shivering seized me, from my head to my feet, as a thunder produced by several clouds colliding, shaking me beyond description and prostrating me. And when I was prostrated in this way, I was clearly awake and saw how I was overthrown.
>
> I wondered what this was supposed to mean, and I spoke as if awake but found that the words were put into my mouth. I said, "Oh, thou almighty Jesus Christ, who of thy great mercy deignest to come to so great a sinner, make me worthy of this grace!" and I clasped my hands and prayed. Then a hand emerged, which pressed my hands firmly.

In a little while, I continued my prayer, saying, "Thou hast promised to receive in grace all sinners; thou canst not otherwise than keep thy words!" In the same moment, I was sitting in his bosom and beheld him face to face, a countenance of a holy mien. All was such that I cannot describe. He was smiling at me, and I was convinced that he looked like this when he was alive. He spoke to me and asked if I have a health certificate; and to this I replied, "Lord, thou knowest better than I." He said, "Well then, do!"—that is, as I inwardly grasped this, "Do love me" or "Do as promised." God give me grace thereto! I found it beyond my powers and woke up, shuddering. [15]

A section of these notes from the *Dream Diary* is reproduced on the following page.

Presence of the Divine

Mystics often describe a sense or feeling of the presence of the Divine. Without attempting to classify different visionary states we can say that the author of the *Dream Diary* was characterized throughout his long life by a striking desire and ability to make his feelings concrete and human. Angels show him truths and regions of heaven. These beings, he wrote in *Conjugial Love*, are 'affections of love in human form. Their ruling affection shines out from their faces, and it is their affection which provides and determines what they wear'. [16] In a corresponding way, self-love's many variants become demons that resemble human beings.

Here the figure of Christ manifested itself as a confirmation and answer to his longing. As Martin Lamm has pointed out, individual elements of this experience would recur several times during the period covered by the *Dream Diary*. The introductory signs would return but Swedenborg had no more clear visions of Christ, and no voices spoke to him. In a note dated 1-2 July he described experiences that began like the occurrences during Easter night; but now without prostration and silently. He saw only a face, 'quite obscurely'—it must have been an angel, he noted. 'This occurred in a vision, when I was neither asleep nor awake'. It was 'the inward human, separated from the outward, who experienced this'. [17]

The divine presence is often marked by experiences of light. As we shall see, these phenomena will come to have another, deeper meaning in Swedenborg's picture of the world. God, Christ was present with every man who opened himself to the being and power of the Divine. 'Behold, I stand at the door and knock!' he read in the third chapter of the Book of Revelation. The one who opens is met by the divine light, we read in his commentary upon the Apocalypse. The divine truth is then engraved on the human heart, and the New Jerusalem is born in the inner man.

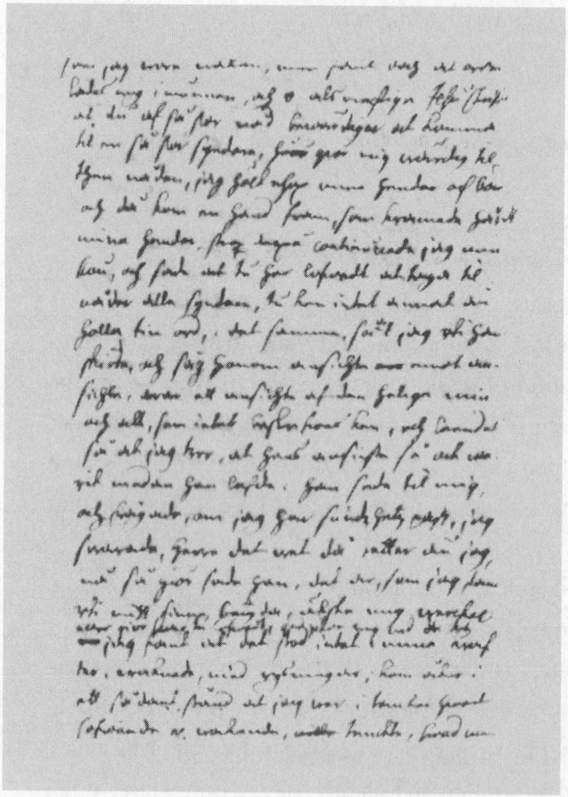

Fig. 19. A page from the *Dream Diary* for 6-7 April 1744: 'I spoke as if awake but found that the words were put into my mouth [...].'

The classical Christian view about the 'inner light' and the ensuing feeling of intense happiness had been brought to the fore in the Swedish revival movement during the early part of the eighteenth century. 'Jesus is coming to his city/This is our inner heart. There he makes our soul rejoice/freed from pain of sin', we read in a well-known pietistic hymn book from 1724, with translations of several songs by Gottfried Arnold and Johann Conrad Dippel.[18] The 'proud and learned' are angered by his presence, the same hymn continues, but the simple, godly Christians perceive the power of God's living word.

The hypnogogic state

It is to be noted that Swedenborg's way of describing and specifying the hour of his night-time experiences seems to indicate that he was in a state between light sleep and wakefulness. This is the hypnogogic state, defined as the half-sleep that occurs before falling asleep or when awakening. Here suggestibility is great: the sleeper 'wakens with a smile on his lips' or in a state of anxiety. Swedenborg, in whose later life sleeping and dreaming were to play a large role, often wrote about this productive intermediate state in the 'spiritual' journal he kept from 1745 to 1765, here called *The Spiritual Diary*.

Visit to London, the Moravians and Count Zinzendorf

Scarcely a month after the Easter vision, in mid-May, Swedenborg left The Hague and moved to London. During the following months the *Dream Diary* records how his relations with the Moravian Brethren developed and intensified. He took lodgings with a well-known member of that congregation, an engraver who lived in Salisbury Court near their chapel in Fetter Lane.[19] He attended their services and seems seriously to have considered joining their church.

The German Count Nikolaus Ludwig von Zinzendorf was the leader of the Moravian Brethren or Congregation of Brothers, also called 'Herrnhuters'. Herrnhut was the name of a village in the count's territory in Saxony, inhabited by Protestants driven out from Bohemia and Moravia.

As mentioned in the chapter on pietism, Zinzendorf called for an intensification, 'subjectivization', and 'spiritualization' of the Christian's personal engagement. A radical rebirth of the whole man was necessary. Like all pietism, the Moravian message built on a two-fold conviction. Man must understand the immense force and capacity of Christ's love, as well as his own personal sinfulness. The whole of Zinzenzdorf's theology builds on the opposition between grace and sin, love and unworthiness. Further, the collective life of the congregation and its organization were important.

It is evident from the *Dream Diary* that the Moravians' tightly knit, sectarian organization was not at all suited to Swedenborg's taste. Later in life he would rather look at the church as a New Jerusalem, given by God, as an open community where regenerated men and women would find rules for their life through divine grace and love.

Swedenborg was drawn to the Moravians' emphasis on a total worship, embracing the whole man without reservation. This was one of the themes he was soon to develop in his book *The Worship and Love of God*. But with the count and his followers this took expression in a strange 'blood mysticism', a mental immersion in Christ's suffering and wounds. This emotionalism must have been foreign to Swedenborg's sober mind and he could never accept Zinzendorf's belief in justification through faith alone.

But in spite of all these reservations he seems to have looked upon his Moravian acquaintances with sympathy. As he would do in his theosophical works, they emphasized a personal relationship with God, regeneration, and the love that a pious man finds in worshipping him. It was these characteristics of pietism that Swedenborg accepted, without regarding himself as a pietist.

Joy and great anguish

After the Easter vision there followed half a year of swings from 'indescribable delight' and inexpressible 'internal joy' to 'anxiety as if one were damned and condemned in hell'. In classical Catholic theology such a drawn-out period, at one and the same time darkness and light, has been called *purgatio* (purification). It can follow upon a few moments of experiencing the presence of the Divine. It is the 'dark night of the soul' that John of the Cross described. After the strong religious experience there usually follows the temptation to be self-satisfied, a feeling of being chosen, the Spanish mystic wrote. A person exaggerates his merits—God shows the way through the darkness and a sense of abandonment, back to the privileged state. It was an asceticism of the understanding, he explained. Reason shall be perfected by faith, a faith which is love, beyond all dogmas and theories. The memory must be emptied, God is loved in the darkness, he wrote.

Swedenborg, whose acquaintance with Catholic mysticism of the 1500s was probably non-existent, is dealing with the same ideas that are timeless, natural, and obvious to all mystics. Our 'will and angry nature' must be forced down by love to God. Self-love, vanity, and sensual enticements must be avoided, and there must be faith without reasoning, he feels. One should trust 'God and Christ and nowise oneself'.[20] But trust does not exclude times of pain, anxiety, doubt; and temptations plague him with 'pain [as when] the root shall be taken out', he writes.

An inexpressible feeling of happiness often runs together with the agony, John emphasized. Swedenborg speaks of an 'interior gladness; but, still, there was a pain in my body for it could not bear the heavenly joy of the soul'.[21]

This inner happiness often seems to have an erotic quality. He is filled with a love 'like that delight a chaste man enjoys when he really is in love and makes love to his spouse. Such an extreme joy was suffused over my whole body, and this for a long while'.[22]

The tension in his soul became too strong. In July 1744 he fell apart. He was quickly looked after and put under the care of a doctor. I have described the course of this sickness in my analysis of the *Dream Diary* and pass by its details here.

Life as sleep

Swedenborg's experiences during the period covered by the *Dream Diary* led him to a new interpretation of the concepts of 'wakefulness' and 'sleep'. To be 'awake' but to give primacy to the experiences of the senses was really, from the Divine's perspective, to be asleep. In Swedenborg's first great commentary on the Pentateuch, he explained his thoughts on the matter:

> It is noteworthy that man places his life in the outer senses and in physical pleasures, yet the life of the outer senses and so the body is only a shadow, and thus is sleep compared with the life of the inner sense, that is, of the natural mind where there are fantasy, imagination, and lusts. Some place their whole life in those, yet it is only sleep in comparison with the life of the more interior faculty, which is properly human. Yet in man this is nothing but sleep compared with his inmost life, which is the life of the soul. And this is nothing but sleep compared with life itself that is of God Messiah, who is Life.[23]

We are awake only when turned to God, and sleep becomes a metaphor for the life dominated by the senses. But man snared in the senses is nevertheless not wholly closed off from the higher and real life. When asleep at night he may, in dreams and visions, meet what is above the senses. 'Only in dreams does Olympus descend to mortals', wrote the Swedish poet Erik Johan Stagnelius at the beginning of the nineteenth century.[24] Swedenborg regarded himself as a dreamer and spirit-seer, called and inspired by God, at home in two worlds. In one of his many anecdotal notes he described how characters in the spirit world wondered about the transitory nature of his presence with them: he would be visible and then would disappear. 'Why?' they asked. Swedenborg answered, 'I am no actor, or Vertumnus, but I am by turns sometimes in light and sometimes in shade to your eyes. So here I am both a stranger and native'.[25]

The question of love

If we consider his journal from the perspective of his later religious writings, a fundamental issue stands out. The journal raises a question about the choice between a life governed by love for oneself or by love to God and the neighbour—not one single choice, but continual choices, decisions that have to be taken throughout life. Man, he wrote much later, becomes stuck in the trap of self-satisfaction, standing still, achieving nothing good.

It was a question of the choice of a path, personal and practical. For Swedenborg, the untiring writer, the problem involved his ongoing, future activity as an author. He thought he had been given an order to stop; but stop for what?

The question returns continually. Glimpses of answers appear, but their wording and clarity are conditioned by the spiritual 'spirals', the circling movements he feels himself experiencing in the constantly on-going battle between body and soul. The flesh rebels, he writes: 'nobody can make himself so free from sin that there is not mixed into every thought much that is unclean or impure'.[26] The question of his future task is put in shade by these analytical swings.

Christ had summoned him to action: 'Well, then do!' What had he meant? In October his state of mind seems to have stabilized and he came closer to an insight into the meaning of the call.

First and foremostly, the scientific work on which he was engaged had its basis in an 'unchaste love'. He ought now to write in another way, he recorded on 6-7 October:

Furthermore something was told about my book. It was said that it would be a *Liber divinus de Dei cultu et amore* [a divine book on the worship and love of God]; I believe there was also something about *spiritibus* [spirits]. I thought I had something on the subject in my work *De Infinito*, but there was no answer as to that. Then I was wrapped up in thought and was informed that *any kind of love* [amor], *no matter for what it may be, as the love for my works on which I am now employed, if I were to love them* [for my own glory] *but not as a medium for the only love which is the love of God and Christ Jesus, this would be a meretricious love.* For the same reason, such love *is always compared to whoredom in the Word of God; such also is the one that I have experienced. But when one has the love of God as the supreme, then one has no other love than that which one finds by devoting all to the service of God.* [27]

The divine book

During the night of 8-9 October Swedenborg felt himself to be in the 'kingdom of innocence'. He went through 'the most beautiful garden that can be imagined' into a long chamber. His continuing words give a picture of his concept of the nature of true literary work. Here, divine inflow is instrumental, and the writer is a vessel for receiving the love and wisdom that colours his text:

> Then I came into a long chamber where beautiful white vessels of milk and bread were, so dainty that something more savory is inconceivable. [28]

A few nights later he had experiences that in spite of earlier warnings encouraged him to continue with *The Animal Kingdom*. A child appears in a dream, to whom Swedenborg said, 'Why do you race about so?' This means, he notes, that he must be calm, and avoid hasty decisions. [29]

The constant friction between body and soul, worldly work and love to God, reappears in the remaining notes of the diary. On 26-7 October, chronologically the last note in the journal, it seems that he is fully clear about the choice that he must make: he will leave what he has in hand and write a new book. Its theme will be the worship and love of God —just the subject he had noted a few weeks prior to this entry:

Afterwards, I was in my chamber with some other acquaintance or relation, and I said that I wished to show him I had better lodgings. I therefore went out with him, first into an adjoining room that extended far, chamber after chamber, but they did not belong to me. Somebody in the bed asked what he wanted; I went out with him, into my parlor. When I opened the door I saw that a whole marketplace was lodged there: right in front of me there was a lot of notions, and beyond it, there appeared the flank of a great palace, but this was taken down. In front and at the sides then appeared plenty of beautiful vessels, porcelain ware it seemed to me, recently put up there; on the side, everything was still being arranged, and then I went into my own little chamber, which was shining too.

This refers to all the work I now enter upon in the name of God, first of all de cultu Dei, *on the side* de amore, *and that I should not draw upon others' notions* [kram also meaning: 'small wares'; 'junk'; 'lumber'; or 'trash'], *but of mine, as it was in the parlor I rented, my chamber, and beside it was the other work, and the rooms at the side did not belong to me.* May God lead me the right way! Christ said that I should not do anything without him.[30]

A few keywords from the October notes recur in this concluding entry: chamber, beautiful vessels, worship, and love. In the dreamer's later developed 'doctrine of correspondences' the house could stand as a symbol of man. The chambers may be a picture of the union of truth and goodness in a proper spiritual state, he wrote in *Arcana Caelestia*, but 'those who possess truths merely in the understanding are not in any chamber of the house, but only in the court'.[31]

The beautiful vessel became a fundamental concept in his theosophy. Man, the vessel, must live in such a way as to receive the Divine that is seeking him.

The words *amor* (love) and *cultus* (worship) appearing in the notes, together with *Deus* (God), formed the main words in the title of the book that he seems to have begun to write immediately after this entry. It was *The Worship and Love of God*, printed in London scarcely half a year after the October dreams.[32]

The inclination to women, true love, and the publication of the *Dream Diary*

The little notebook recording Swedenborg's dreams was published in 1859 through the efforts of the librarian G E Klemming. Ninety-nine copies were printed, with the title *Swedenborgs Drömmar 1744*. 'The small size of the edition', the publisher wrote in a foreword, was due to the 'odd and unusual content, which could easily come into conflict with the law regarding the freedom of the press'. But a year later the book was reprinted, in an edition of a thousand copies.

Klemming was alluding to the strongly sexual character of the entries. Swedenborg noted at the beginning of the journal that he was 'not inclined toward sexual relations, which I had been all my days'.[33] But this statement notwithstanding, in what followed many of the readers found an openness regarding intimate relationships that transgressed all permissible boundaries. Swedenborg was said to be 'sexually obsessed', mentally ill, paranoid. A sixty-year debate followed concerning his state of health, whether he was sane or sick.

The fifty-six year old bachelor was a man of the written word. What was his proper subject? Science and empiricism, or divinely inspired truths? In the dreams these two types of work are now symbolized by women, both enticing him to intercourse. He found that 'all *objecta scientiarum* [were] represented to me by women'.[34] In his dreamed association with these ladies he is certainly 'inclined toward sexual relations':

Throughout the night, something was dictated to me, something holy, which ended with *sacrarium et sanctuarium*. I found myself in bed with one. She said: if you had not said *sanctuarium*, we would do it. I turned away from her; with her hand, she touched me and it got big, bigger than ever. I turned around and applied it; it bent, yet it went in. She said it was long. Meanwhile, I thought that a child must come out of this, and I got off *en merveille* [in a wonderful way].[35]

His interpretation follows:

This signifies the utmost love of the Holy One, for all love originates from that source, constituting a series, in the body manifest in its seminal projection; and when the ejaculation is there and is pure, it answers to the love of wisdom [...][36]

But silence is necessary about these relationships, he noted at the same time: for 'according to worldly reason, it is considered impure, although in reality it is pure'.

The uproar over these learned descriptions of love was increased by the dreamer's way of describing the soul's highest, divine happiness as comparable to sexual orgasm.

Much later in Swedenborg's writings we meet the thought of 'proper' physical love as given by God. In one of his last books, *Conjugial Love*, sexual intercourse between man and woman becomes analogous to the union of wisdom and love, in which wisdom stands for the masculine, love for the feminine. Thus Swedenborg's meetings with different women during the period of his dreams is from this perspective a matter of a search for true love.

The pious aspect of his sexual dreams does not exclude a more worldly side. London of the 1740s offered severe temptations for single men. On several occasions we read of *rebellio carnis*, the rebellion of the flesh. Together with a good friend, Niklas Oelreich, he seems to have made a visit to a brothel, 'although I did not have any intention to proceed into effect', whatever this means.[37] Whatever the circumstances were, we can presume that Swedenborg was no more 'obsessed with sex' than most normal men.

The conclusion of the *Dream Diary*: 'love of the high, maybe'

Thus the *Dream Diary* concludes with a literary *volte-face*. He was ordered to work on a new kind of book, written *ex auditis et visis*, from what he had heard and seen—with divine permission.

The diary ends with several undated notes. The last of them is symbolic:

I thought that a firework burst above me, shedding a shower of sparks of beautiful fire: love of the high, maybe.[38]

Once again: Swedenborg was certainly a believing Christian all his days, from cradle to grave. The warmth and intensity of his faith was growing during the 1730s and 1740s to become the determining factor in his life. He quoted Hugo Grotius approvingly: 'Only the *willing* mind truly worships'.[39]

Swedenborg had no inclination for systematic questioning or for critical analysis. He lived in the century of reason and like so many others sought for explanations of the apparently inexplicable. Synthesis was his domain. Leaving the *Dream Diary* we shall find how he consistently constructs his equations, in which the earthly and the supernatural stand on each side of the equals mark. The sign of equality may be seen as Swedenborg's God.

| *The Worship and Love of God* |

Chapter Fifteen

Seek no more for the source, since you are in its very innermost! [...] Fill your understanding with all that is good from this gushing spring!

Swedenborg: The Worship and Love of God §55

A falling palace

During the night between 26 and 27 October 1744, in a dream or vision, Swedenborg saw a marketplace with all kinds of junk for sale. On one side of the market, a palace was seen, but this stately house was taken down. Its place was filled, instead, with 'plenty of beautiful vessels, porcelain ware it seemed to me, recently put up there; on the side, everything was still being arranged'.[1] The meaning was clear. The goods at this Vanity Fair were his old learning. This knowledge would disappear, the palace of self-conceit would fall.

As we have already seen, the notes continue with a vision of what would come to take the place of the old—a *liber divinus*, a divine book. It would treat of the worship and love of God. The content would be his own, he noted.[2] Nothing of others' notions would be taken. What was his 'own' would come to him as the contents of many 'beautiful vessels' of porcelain. He is given a confirming order: 'Christ said that I should not do anything without him'.[3]

He had at last found his way and understood the meaning of Christ's charge to him on Easter night. As a sign of confirmation from above, he reports that he fainted, that he felt himself near death and saw a divine light. He had been thrown on his face. These strange

179

phenomena reminded him of his experiences in Amsterdam in 1739, he wrote, when he was about to begin his book on *The Economy of the Animal Kingdom*. He continues:

> *This means that my head is thoroughly cleaned and rinsed from all that might obstruct these thoughts, as happened last time, when it gave me the power of penetration, especially with the pen*, which this time too was represented to me insofar as I seem to be writing with a fine hand.[4]

Right worship, true love

The book was thus to treat of the right approach to the Divine. With Swedenborg's background it was natural to think of his own time as worldly and spiritually impoverished. In earlier times mankind had possessed a knowledge of the Divine, now lost. The thought of such impoverishment of knowledge and religion is, of course, a recurring idea. It exists in Plato and Ovid and is found above all in the Bible. In the radical pietism contemporary with Swedenborg, the thought of a successive degeneration became, as we shall soon see, a key for interpreting the Old Testament. In 1734 Swedenborg had already touched on the thought of mankind's great loss. According to his *Principia,* men had lived, before the Fall, in a world of perfect knowledge:

> No man seems to have been capable of arriving at true philosophy since the time of the first mortals, who are said to have lived in a state of spiritual perfection […] They were formed before sin came into the world. They had been created with all possible art and beauty, and with the connection [with the Divine] that is appropriate to this state. All who are governed by an upright mind and […] are intensely desirous of arriving at the same degree of wisdom, which is now lost, [can meet with some success]. But only the true philosopher can understand to what extent this is possible […] One who desires to gain honour and reputation may believe he has reached the goal […] But it is only an imagined wisdom, an hallucination.[5]

The true philosopher is one who is completely upright and who has fully understood how God is to be worshipped, he continued. This applies to the Divine, being the cause of, and present in, all things. He italicizes a few lines:

For […] worship of the Infinite Being can never be separated from philosophy. He who believes himself to be wise and does not recognize a Divine and Infinite Being […] does not have a grain of wisdom.

Swedenborg's 'divine book' was to give the reader an explanation of the meaning of the state of paradise. This was important not least because a return to the wisdom and peace of Eden was possible. The title of the book, *The Worship and Love of God*, points to this return intimated already in Genesis: the serpent's head should be trampled upon and crushed.[6] And worship, *cultus*, was a life of unselfish and practical love to one's neighbour, and the love of God, *amor Dei*, was openness to God's love and wisdom, ever streaming down upon all people turned to God.

These two concepts, the worship of God and the love of God, comprise in themselves what we could call Swedenborg's newly gained moral consciousness. He had been captivated by the enticements of the world: by what he, with almost the same words as the contemporary Swedish poet Johan Runius, called 'voluptuousness, vanity, riches'. Like many of his acquaintances, he had only played the part of a Christian. His worship was only formal, simply following a pattern in society. The *Dream Diary* illustrates his coming to terms with the nature of this form of worship.

True faith was practical and showed itself in good works and in love to our fellow man. This love was a natural consequence of love to God. When we let ourselves be led by a wrong love in our worship, we are to be swallowed by the earth. This is the message we meet constantly in the great journal written from 1745 to 1765, and in most of the works Swedenborg published after his crisis. Those who had been worshippers, but led by a wrong love, often seemed unconscious of the danger of this inconsistency. After death, their spirits continued to mislead the living by the subtle influence of their example and practice.

A few nights before his great call, Swedenborg wrote about the two priests, Korah and Dathan, in the sixteenth chapter of the Book of Numbers.[7] In the desert they had rebelled against Moses. Lighting their censers after this defiance, they were swallowed up by the earth. In their worship they had been led by self-love rather than by love to God:

A number of times I have noticed that there are spirits of various kinds. The spirit of Christ is the only one that carries all beatitude with it. The other spirits entice us in a thousand ways to follow them, but unhappy is the one who does. Once or twice, Korah and Dathan came before me and brought strange fire to the altar but were not able to offer it. Thus it is when another fire is brought in than the one that comes from Christ. I also saw something like a fire that came to me. It is therefore necessary to distinguish between the spirits, which is a thing that cannot be done except through Christ himself and his spirit. [8]

'Man comes closer to God through worship in the same degree that he is joined with him in love', Swedenborg wrote in a fragmentary third part of *The Worship and Love of God*.[9] Such an agreement between worship and love had characterized the state of mankind before the Fall. We should all strive towards that consistency. This message was never fully developed in this little book from 1745, but it became the primary thought in all the works that would follow.

The divine manna of knowledge

The *Dream Diary* crisis came to be centred on a problem of love. What love is required for a 'certificate of health'? The answer was that the driving, transporting feeling must have a divine object. The world and its attractions must fade away, to be replaced by worship that consists of a life of love to the neighbour inspired by God.

It is to be noted that Swedenborg, like so many other mystics and visionaries, always emphasizes that union with or proximity to the Divine is a question of *reception*. God's love descends upon mankind, is present in man. It is a matter of being open, not letting oneself be distracted by false signals from earthly reasoning. Christ's question to Swedenborg on Easter night 1744 regarded his spiritual state. In his dreams he had wanted to become as a child, to live in the kingdom 'where all is innocence'. In such a state of mind he would be 'nurtured into knowledge, as is now, I think, happening to me'.[10]

True knowledge is *influxus*: 'the manna that comes from heaven'.[11]

Contents of the book: the *Dream Diary* as a pattern

The book on *The Worship and Love of God* never became more than a fragment and he abandoned the project after four months' work. Nevertheless he had the first two parts of the manuscript printed. This was done in London in the first half of 1745.

This little book has been thoroughly analysed by Martin Lamm and above all by Inge Jonsson, who has emphasized its place in the intellectual milieu of that day. At the same time, both have brought out its intellectual connection with the *Principia* and *The Infinite,* published in 1734, as well as with the psychology that Swedenborg developed in *The Economy of the Animal Kingdom* in 1740-1. There is also an affinity to *The Soul,* posthumously published under the title *Rational Psychology.*

The Worship and Love of God was intended as a description, at one and the same time poetical and factual, of the first two chapters of Genesis, the story of Creation and the account of Adam and Eve's first days. It is written in a flowing Latin style coloured by Ovid. As in the *Principia*, Swedenborg assiduously uses events and figures from classical mythology in his presentation. The fables are a form of artistic rendering that builds upon correspondences—precisely the congruence that Swedenborg would later make one of the pillars in his theory of knowledge.

Thus the work would be a summary of the knowledge of natural philosophy he had gathered during the fifty-six years of his life, set in a divine perspective. The Swedish literary historian, poet, and admirer of Swedenborg, P D A Atterbom, writing at the beginning of the 1800s, emphasized the unity in Swedenborg's life work, a thought which is developed by most of his students, not least by Martin Lamm. Swedenborg himself also spoke, as has been said, about his own sequential line of development. Most thoughts in the later period exist as intimations or as clearly expressed statements in the earlier works. I shall return to this question later.

The book is divided theatrically into parts, 'acts' and scenes. Its first describes the creation of the universe from the great 'world egg'. The thought goes back to the *Principia*'s theory of the formation of the solar system through explosions in the nebula of the sun. We find similar points in his earlier works when, using mythical allusions, he describes the successive coming into being of the mineral, vegetable, and animal kingdoms. He imagines the earth as the primeval paradise, provided with flowers and animals, but without human beings. And finally, in the fourth scene, man is born as a microcosm and image of the world soul. Adam steps forward to be taught by angelic beings about the order and laws of God's creation.

But the book was primarily intended to give a picture of Swedenborg's own religious insights, such as they appear after the crisis. The drama describes a pendulum movement between the 'wondering joy of natural knowledge and faith's trustful experience of the whole', writes Inge Jonsson.[12] As regards the experiences of faith, the notes in the *Dream Diary*, both chaotic and logical, serve as a suggestive model. On the other hand later, in the theosophical writings, we meet many scenes and thoughts from the poetic paraphrase of the Creation story.

Innocence and knowledge

As Martin Lamm and Inge Jonsson have pointed out, the Adam whose growing up is described in the uncompleted work is just like the perceptive and innocent child that the author of the *Dream Diary* said he himself wished to be.[13] With this first man there was the absolute trust and love that at one time characterized life in the Garden of Eden. For Swedenborg, everyone who turns to God in this way, whether child or adult, becomes 'heavenly', he wrote later. 'The celestial man has the Lord and therefore His kingdom and eternal life as his ends in view'.[14]

In time, according to his repeated statements, Swedenborg himself often attained that spiritual state and the heavenly wisdom that was then imparted to him. This state was of determinative significance to his life and mission:

> I said that [. . .] a person begins to become wise who knows little, virtually nothing from himself as the source. This is the same as to say that he who is nothing is something [. . .] It is then that the Lord is with him for the first time [. . .] his wisdom is then not his own.[15]

Reading advice to a friend, and the divine inflow

The first part of the book was published in January or February 1745, and Swedenborg sent a copy to his friend in The Hague, the envoy Joakim Fredrik Preis. The accompanying letter is dated 11 March, and contains a recommendation. The book was the 'first part of a little piece *The Worship and Love of God*, on which I beg the Herr Envoy kindly to cast his eye, especially at the end, which treats of the first-born's love [*de Amore Primogeniti*]'.[16] Here we meet thoughts and ideas from his earlier period of natural philosophy and from the *Dream Diary*, now clarified in literary form. Preis did not know that this very section could serve as a key to much of what later would become the spirit-seer's theosophy.

We follow Swedenborg's recommendation to the envoy and linger on this part of the text. First we find the already-mentioned emphasis on the divine inflow into the spiritually-prepared man. Adam's heavenly teachers tell him that he must understand the secret of true insight: 'Nothing flows out from you, but all things stream forth from the highest and his love in their order and unity [. . .] nothing is yours [. . .] We, your teachers, are messengers through whom the last stage of outflow passes and returns again to the first, and the first to the last'.[17] In the *Dream Diary* this had implied a total capitulation: 'it is best to surrender unconditionally; and [. . .] be entirely passive'.[18]

Now Adam is instructed by feminine figures embodying wisdom. Everything he sees is a reflection of the love going out from the Divine. Everything in nature is connected to the Divine:

> [. . .] nothing of that which you regard as your own is yours. We [feminine figures of wisdom] are life's forces, or organs and instruments, and thus messengers through which the last goes and returns again to the first, and the first to the last. Therefore everything created flows through you into him, and thus everything created exists to eternity, for subsistence is an eternal existence, and to be preserved is eternally being created [. . .][19]

The idea that all is bent toward its beginning, and the wish to consider man from this perspective, is recurrent in the world of Swedenborg's thought. Death is the beginning of a new life in which the life first lived on earth is incorporated in a supernatural form of love.

Good and evil loves, good and evil spirits

Adam learns that there are good and evil loves, and that they appear as spiritual forces and influences. They support man in his thoughts and intentions: good as well as evil. Here is another of Swedenborg's great subjects, returning in work after work. Love governs our understanding; 'man's life *is* love', he wrote later in his book *De Divino Amore et de Divina Sapienta* (*Divine Love and Wisdom*).[20] And the recurring decisions we must make in our lives about which love will govern us are influenced by the spiritual powers that are always present around us——both angels and demons. Swedenborg always had a strong tendency to express the abstract in concrete, personified terms.

Both good and evil loves are in themselves natural, says the highest wisdom, Adam's female teacher. God had wanted life in its fullness to come to creation's benefit, from heaven as well as from earth. The good was led by God's only-begotten Son, the evil by an autocratic prince of the world with countless servants. In the spirit of the Book of Revelation, Adam now learns that the prince of the world, who was present at creation, was soon seized with arrogant pride, rebelling against the advocates of the good. But apostasy was of no help to him, he would always be obliged to obey every divine command. Nevertheless, he constituted a perpetual threat to heavenly love.

Later Swedenborg would abandon the thought of a 'prince of the world' as the embodied leader of evil. However here, in *The Worship and Love of God*, his figure does appear: subdued, chained, biding his time. He sent his servants from below, through unguarded openings, to gain supremacy gradually by releasing bodily desires, self-love, and love for the world. 'The charioteer of this world controls and guides human reason with his reins'.[21]

The teacher of wisdom emphasized the great importance of learning to know the real nature of our loves. The evil spirits imitated the good. They appeared in disguise, surrounded themselves with servants who praised their doings and defended them. They behaved cunningly, finding ways to impress the innocent. They 'lay out traps and hunting nets [...] place their snares in the shadow of our intellect'.

The author spoke from his own experience. The *Dream Diary* is full of delusive, false loves. Demons tempted him, unsettled his mind, prompted him to speak against his better judgement. On some occasions he had written about what seems to be the dragon in the Book of Revelation:

[I dreamed] that I saw one beast after another, which spread out their wings; they were dragons. I flew above them, yet I ran into one of them. *Such dragons signify amores spurios* [spurious loves]*, which show themselves as if they were not dragons, until their wings are seen* [...][22]

Man, he also wrote, is seduced by evil spirits:

From this and the foregoing, it is found how soon and how easily man is seduced by other spirits, which are represented according to the love of each, since loves are represented by spirits, furthermore, in fact, by women appearing as women in dra— [23]

Adam's guide in the garden tells of circumstances that must have been as strange to the first-born as they were actual and real for Emanuel Swedenborg. The governor of earthly and evil love tempts the weakest souls to his side:

[He entices them] with his tricks [. . .] by displaying the sceptres and purple robes of his power [. . .] To imitate heavenly rule completely he procures for himself servants appearing as intelligence and wisdom, giving them an image of himself [. . .] taking apart and compounding the ideas themselves into forms that please him [. . .] [24]

Adam learns that the consequences are total ignorance, the flight of all truths, and a 'darkness filled with horror'.

In *The Spiritual Diary*, Swedenborg reports on the false angels who wormed their way into heaven to harass him under a false flag. They were often his own deceased acquaintances. During their lifetime they had displayed themselves as pious human beings performing services that were useful to society, but in fact they had been governed by duplicity, greed, and self-love. After death they enticed him to take the wrong path, and tempted him with projects that outwardly could seem to be good, but on closer consideration showed themselves as harmful and evil. These evil spirits were especially active in their attempts to seduce him during the years 1747 and 1748, he wrote. They could fill him with a bad and carnal sense of delight, leading his thoughts astray, enticing him to yield to temptations of all kinds.

Apocalyptic battles

Adam learned that the apostasy of the prince of the world led to yet greater triumphs for the evil. However, the Highest finally lost patience. He decided to bring down the tyrant. In the midst of the thunderous war, a miracle took place. 'Our Love, his first-born, cast himself down among the evil spirits, protecting them from the threatening destruction.'

—

When the Father asked him to move away, the Son, 'from his burning love', refused.[25] Moved by this magnanimity the Highest promised to have compassion on the evil world, 'until it had run the course of its ages, fulfilled itself, and plunged into its winter and night'.

At the same time he gave 'power to our Love to cast the tyrant [...] into chains and to set him free at his own discretion'.

Certainly we are hearing an echo from Swedenborg's studies of the Apocalypse. The battle between good and evil passes through its different phases. During the penultimate combat an angel came down from heaven, with the key to the abyss and a great chain in hand:

> He laid hold of the dragon, that serpent of old, who is the Devil and Satan [...] and he cast him into the bottomless pit, and shut him up, and set a seal on him, so that he should deceive the nations no more till the thousand years were finished. But after these things he must be released for a little while.[26]

Christ and the victory over evil

In veiled words Adam is instructed about Christ's coming. The enemy is bridled when love, which is Christ, 'casts himself into his life'. The Evil, who has made his appearance in heavenly clothing, is forced back to his proper residence, but the prince of the earth is not totally crushed. He and his servants are also part of life. When Christ's love now streams into man unhindered, the enemy is transformed to a 'path or footstool' between heaven and earth. Trusting Providence we can tread upon him without danger, says the angelic wisdom to the first-born.

Like John, the author of the Book of Revelation, Swedenborg sees the course of events from an overall, general perspective. Christ's suffering, death, and resurrection——that 'takes away the sin of the world'——stand in the background. The serpent in the Garden of Eden could not be finally crushed before Jesus came into the world.

Adam was terrified by these battles and the great danger that evil constituted. But in the presence of Wisdom's words about the Son's 'fire of love', he felt a great joy in the innermost of his being, as had the author himself during the crisis he had just gone through. If he kept himself on the right path, the 'internal joy was so strongly awakened [...] that it may be compared to a heavenly joy here on the earth'.[27]

Also in this respect, Adam and Swedenborg had the same existential knowledge:

> [. . .] after he had experienced, with tears of joy, the tender affection that streamed forth from love, he leaned towards his Wisdom, earnestly asking how he could receive the possibility of rejoicing in this love fully. [28]

The answer was not unexpected. It is a matter of continually turning oneself to the highest love, towards the heavenly life. Adam is divided into a higher and lower or inner and outer self. Some things are commanded by heaven, but nature works against them. Thus: 'each and every one carries this enemy with himself, wherever he goes, even if his life is quite irreproachable'.

We shall learn later of how Wisdom brought to Adam and Swedenborg the awareness that earthly life is a long, drawn-out battle against ever-arising temptations. Conversion and rebirth, according to many of the pietists of that day, was an unforgettable, definitive one-time event. Swedenborg understood differently. The battle against evil lasted throughout life, conversion was an on-going process; but in the midst of these attacks, a reborn man could feel secure. The temptations were never greater than could be overcome.

Wisdom's promise

Did Joakim Fredrik Preis read the recommended section to its end? In the last, eighty-sixth paragraph there is a promise to Adam, torn between good and evil. It can be read as a general promise, of interest not only to the first man. The angelic figures of Wisdom now say goodbye to Adam, parting with the message that they are closely tied to him and always nearby:

> We perfect your mind. Therefore, through us you are [God's] image. We behold your love with our eyes, and through us you also may also see him [. . .] Lest we should ever be without him, he has given command to his wisdoms and intelligences, whose soul he is, never to depart from us. Thus by their good offices we [as messengers] enjoy his perpetual presence and life. Let us therefore all be joined together by an eternal bond [. . .] We pledge ourselves to you [. . .]. [29]

Adam's intelligences, already embodied here, would soon change name. They became Swedenborg's angels, always present with men, along with evil's demons.

'Eat not so much!'

The Worship and Love of God thus became only a fragment that concluded as abruptly as did the *Dream Diary*. Perhaps this sudden end is explained by a vision in a London inn in April 1745.

Long afterwards the seer, now an old man, gave an account of what happened to Carl Robsahm, a cashier in the Swedish Central Bank, to whose personal recollections of the ageing Swedenborg I shall return later on. Robsahm's record reads:

> I was in London where I had a private dinner rather late in a restaurant [...] I was hungry and ate with a good appetite. Towards the end of the meal I noticed a kind of blurring in my vision, it grew dark and I saw the floor covered with the nastiest crawling animals, like snakes, frogs, and creatures of that kind. I was amazed, because I was fully conscious and thinking clearly. After a while the prevailing darkness was quickly dispelled, and I saw a man sitting in a corner of the room. Since I was alone, I was quite frightened when he spoke and said, 'Don't eat so much'. Again it grew dark before my eyes, but just as quickly then became clear. And I found myself alone in the room. [30]

Frightened, he hurried home, but he said nothing to his landlord about what had happened. He carefully thought over the event. What he experienced could not been have been a chance occurrence, and it had no physical cause.

Swedenborg continued, according to Robsahm's notes:

> [...] during the night the same man revealed himself to me, and I was not frightened then. He said that he was the *Lord God*, the creator and redeemer of the world, and that he had chosen me to explain the spiritual content of the Scriptures for mankind, and that he himself would explain to me what I should write on this subject. That same night the spiritual world of heaven and hell was opened to me, where I recognized many acquaintances of all estates.

___

Thus he was to lay open the inmost, spiritual meaning of the Bible; this was his life's mission.

'Do not eat so much!' the man at the restaurant had said to him. Perhaps by this Swedenborg had understood that his planning a book on *The Worship and Love of God* was inappropriate, that its form and organization were unsuitable for the task he had now received.

The interruption in his work was presumably also associated with an insight regarding a new problem, one that scarcely belonged in the book on *cultus* and *amor*. Another theme was to have a central place in his thinking during the coming twenty-eight years: the account of man's salvation. Man and woman had been expelled from paradise, gradually sinking into an existence ever more turned from God. Through Christ a possibility for return had been given; the gates to the Garden of Eden were no longer closed, but were now open to reunion with the Divine, to a new blessedness.

But this account of man's salvation required a larger, wider perspective than his book in fable-form provided. The history of humanity's redemption was anchored in the Sacred Scripture, and must be elucidated in a form that would provide a demonstration of the interplay between the Old and New Testaments.

Bible studies

The first two parts of the unfinished manuscript of *The Worship and Love of God* were printed; only a portion of the third part is preserved. Swedenborg now began his life-long studies of the Bible. He prepared a great index of the contents of its books, and of the 'correspondences' he found in the text. About the same time, he studied Hebrew, here probably being able to build on what he had learned at Uppsala roughly forty years earlier. Still in London, he made a compilation of the Bible's prophecies regarding the coming of the Messiah, trying to analyse the characteristics of the coming kingdom of God.[31]

Several smaller manuscripts that witness to his incredible diligence have been published posthumously. He first wrote a short commentary on the Genesis account of creation, verse by verse. Here he made a comparison between the biblical account and the first part of *The Worship and Love of God*. To his amazement, he found that they agreed with each other.[32]

Back at the Board of Mines

Swedenborg left London in July 1745, arriving in Stockholm in August in order to resume service at the Board of Mines. On 17 November he began his first great and systematic bible commentary, published posthumously in English in 1928-48, in nine volumes, as *The Word Explained*. When he commenced this work he wrote this prayer: 'Lord Jesus Christ, lead me to and on the way that you want me to walk'.[33]

Pietism: the old man and the new

Chapter Sixteen

Pietism and enlightenment

Perhaps almost every Christian researcher and philosopher during the age of Enlightenment rejected dogma as the foundation for religious insight. Rather, we must find the truth in accord with our own experience, confident that all empirical knowledge down to the least detail would form a comprehensible whole. Thus, d'Alembert wrote in his foreword to his *Encyclopédie*, there should be no *esprit de système* (mind set), but instead an *esprit systématique* (systematic mind). Consequently, personal experience, instead of fidelity to an official doctrine, stood at the centre of religious experience. The personal religion of the individual became decisive in the movement in the Protestant world usually called 'pietism'. The word comes from the Latin *pietas*, piety.

Christianity, as a whole, had become rigid, 'objectified'. Instead of the evangelists' gospel of love, purity of doctrine was preached as the way to salvation from ever deserved, divine punishment. Luther had constantly spoken of man's burden of sin. Not even the most diligent Christian could effect his salvation through a good life and good works. In works, it was said, there is always a concern for self that God sees through—even if it is nothing other than the egotistical desire to earn divine grace. Man had to trust in God's grace; there alone was forgiveness.

Seen from the pietistic perspective, this easily led to a rigid and paralysed Christianity. In contrast, Pietism taught that Christianity must be both inwardly and practically oriented. Man must be reformed, 'born anew'. The words of the Gospel of John about the new man were a starting point. He who was not born anew could not see the kingdom of God.

The fathers of pietism

The call for inner Christianity and a human union with God found literary expression early in the German priest Johann Arndt's famous *Fyra Böcker om een sann Christendom* (*On the True Christianity*), a book first printed in Sweden in 1647. It was translated into most of the European languages and read in both the Protestant and Catholic world. Here we meet a Christianity where much of the German mysticism of the Middle Ages shines through: above all, Meister Eckhart and Johann Tauler. Almost equally important and widespread was Christian Scriver's devotional manual *Treasure for the Soul*, published 1675-92, translated into Swedish in the 1720s. Here, too, we find a Christian faith of inwardness and personal experience of God.

Philipp Jacob Spener is usually named as the father of organized pietism. He was a priest in Frankfurt am Main in the 1670s. Spener's pietism, urging a renewal of Christian life within the framework of the church, represented an older, conservative, form of the movement. Here the 'general priesthood' would be realized; everyone should know the Bible and live according to its commandments, with private meetings, conventicles, for mutual edification. Theological studies should include the literature of the mystics: Thomas à Kempis, Johann Tauler, and the famous *Theologia Germanica*.

After Spener another priest, August Francke, became the leader of the older German pietistic movement. Francke had gone through a crisis, a penitential struggle and conversion. For him the call to a Christian way of life in its true meaning led to extensive charitable works. He was a pastor in Halle where he established a number of well-known foundations for poor children, and schools of different kinds.

Jesper Swedberg and the older pietism

In Sweden this mild form of pietism, faithful to the church, was accepted by many priests, among them Jesper Swedberg. His high regard for Arndt's and Scriver's works are not the least testimony to this. Pietism's call for practical Christianity was wholly accepted by the bishop. Throughout his life, Swedberg thundered against what he called 'solafideism', the belief that faith was enough to save man from damnation. A Christian's life must stand in accordance with his faith. Swedberg looked upon himself as a pietist, although only in the meaning of the apostle Paul:

> But I defend this: would to God we were all true pietists, such as Paul describes, saying the saving grace of God is revealed to all men. And he teaches us that we should forsake all ungodly and worldly lusts: and live in a chaste, righteous, and godly fashion in this world. And look for the blessed hope and await the glorious appearing of the great God and our Saviour Jesus Christ [...] [1]

Bishop Swedberg, nonetheless, never professed himself to be a 'pietist' in the meaning of the word at that day, asserting that he never read any books with pietistic content; but this latter statement should be taken with a grain of salt, as in his books he often refers to Spener, as well as to Gottfried Arnold.

In the matter of pietism, a bishop in Sweden at that day had to be careful. Many priests in leading positions saw the individualism in pietism as a threat to their own positions of power and thereby also to order in the land. Charles XII was of the same mind; from his camp in Volhynia he had issued a decree against pietism and the dangerous private Christianity. It was 'a strong injunction, and read from all pulpits', wrote the bishop in his memoir.[2] The result was that everyone who sought to live a pious and righteous life risked being accused of being a pietist. Many years later, in 1726, the Estate of the priests in Parliament succeeded in pushing through a strict prohibition against private, domestic religious meetings. It was the so-called 'conventicle bill', repealed only in 1858.

Swedenborg's religious system reflects the thought of restoration that often recurs in pietistic contexts. Here, God had created man in his own image, and the first people lived in community with God; they saw the Divine in all things, without questioning its order. Through sin, the gates of paradise were closed, but God had mercifully decided that man should again be united to Him. God would become man; by this means, God and the Son of Man would again give 'grace and ability, so that man could be united with God, and God be united with him again [...] and impart his holiness and righteousness to mankind'. Bishop Swedberg quotes the words of Genesis about Eve and the serpent: 'The woman's seed shall trample the head of the serpent'. This happened through Christ's life and death. 'And such a union with God and the elect takes place at last in heaven', he writes, citing the Book of Revelation:

Of this John writes, 'and I saw a new heaven and a new earth. For the first heaven and the first earth were passed away. And I John saw the holy city, new Jerusalem, coming down out of heaven from God, prepared as a bride adorned for her husband. And I heard a great voice out of heaven saying, Behold, the tabernacle of God is with men, and he will dwell with them. And they shall be his people, and God himself shall be with them, and be their God'.[3]

Arndt and the bishop's faith

The question about the conditions for divine atonement is naturally a fundamental problem for Christianity. Orthodoxy made a distinction between justification and sanctification, that is, a righteous life through divine grace. In contrast Arndt called for a complete turnabout, a spiritual rebirth, by which man receives power to follow in Christ's path. With Christ's help, man could find the right way and battle against evil's temptations. The Saviour's own life was just such a progressive, ongoing purification:

For this reason Christ had to become man and be conceived of the Holy Spirit [...] yes, for this the Lord's spirit must rest upon him, the spirit of wisdom and understanding, the spirit of knowledge and the fear of the Lord, so that human nature would be renewed in him and by him, and we in him [...] be born anew and become new creatures; so that in place of our foolish spirit we might inherit from him the spirit of wisdom and understanding, in place of our inborn blindness the spirit of knowledge, in place of the spirit of our godlessness the spirit of the fear of the Lord. This is the fruit of the new life and the fruit of the new birth in us [...][4]

In our regeneration, Christ becomes man's model. It is now a matter of gradually, daily improving, and of the old man dying:

[...] as [...] a new man shall daily come forth, so there is no better procedure to find for this than what our Lord Jesus Christ has shown us with his example. Thus it follows further, how Christ's life should be what we reflect and are judged by, and we begin modestly with his poverty, ignominy, contempt, despair, cross, which in Christ's holy life show how our flesh must be crucified, to which equally belong prayer, love, and humility [...] For we must begin with Christ's humanity and in this way ascend to his divinity. Then we see in Christ our dear heavenly Father's heart, and we rest in his love [...] [5]

The bishop voices this thought, chapter after chapter. Arndt summarizes: 'the whole of Christianity consists in the renewal of God's likeness in man and in the uprooting of Satan's likeness'. We find the same line of thought in Scriver.

According to Arndt, this renewal is described already in the Creation story. Each of the six days was related not only to the literal creation but also to man's gradual insights regarding the presence of the Divine in himself.

Radical pietism: Arnold and the Berleburg Bible

Spener had wanted to effect an awakening within the church itself. Thus for him it was never a question of separatism, but of reforms: in general, this was the case with the older, conservative, pietism. But the advocates of the movement's radical wing wanted to go to the root of the evil of the time. The individual's personal relationship with God was emphasised. The significance of the church and its articles of faith was depreciated; the Bible was the only acceptable source. Some of them followed Paul's view that the law is written in all human hearts. For that, not even the Scriptures were needed.

An especially interesting figure within this stream of thought is the Saxon professor and prelate Gottfried Arnold, who died in 1714. From his perspective the history of Christianity was an account of a continuous decline from the time of the first man's ejection from paradise. The Fall had been slowed for a short time by the Lutheran reformation; but churches concerned about the position and power of priests were soon formed. The old faith lived on —not as a church, but with independent individuals, and especially with those who like Arnold and his friends sought the way back to the true and original relationship with God. True Christianity had suffered its first great defeat at the church council in Nicea in 325 AD. Here was the root of the false and dangerous view of God's Trinity as three 'persons', and of faith's anchorage in rigid dogmas.

Jesper Swedberg was well acquainted with Arnold. Among his books the bishop referred primarily to two works, the well-known *Unpartheyische Kirchen- und Ketzerhistorie vom Anfang,* etc (*Objective History of the Church and Heresy*) and *Wahre Abbildung der Ersten Christen im Glauben und Lebe* (*A Picture of the First Christians*). In his *Description of My Life*, Swedberg recommended especially the first of these. 'Here we find much that we are looking for and do not find in other [works].'[6]

In essential aspects, Arnold's interpretation of the Bible is remarkably like Swedenborg's. All things in the text of the Bible are prototypical models, and their historical, rhapsodic character is of secondary importance.[7] Words, concepts, contexts are changed to symbols and correspondences. The history of Israel treats of the human soul and its errors and searching. The flight over the Red Sea, the wandering in the wilderness, and the crossing of the Jordan are a description of the paths of the soul's purification. Israel's obedience and disobedience is the soul's obedience and disobedience. Israel's enemies symbolize the soul's enemies along the way that hinder its reception of the divine love. The individual persons, towns, and places are symbols of good and evil states of the soul, hope and despair, doubt, pure or impure love.

We find this interpretation in Arnold's *Objective History of the Church and Heresy*, from 1699-1700. We meet it also in other texts, above all in the so-called Berleburg Bible published from 1726-42, a new translation with commentaries, produced in Berleburg in North Germany. There, until 1806, the Sayn-Wittgenstein princes ruled over a miniature principality that became a place of refuge for the sectarians persecuted during the 1700s. In this edition of the Bible there is a preface to Genesis that gives a picture of how the Old Testament texts were considered in these pietistic circles:

The first book of Moses [Genesis] deals with the greatest secrets, apostasy as well as salvation [...] Especially in this book man is brought into a theatre, where at the same time he is created by God beautiful and glorious, but due to his own fault becomes miserable and wretched [...] At the same time, God's goodness manifests itself [...] It shows itself especially in his assumption of the human form, and [...] in the word about redemption, a new birth, a second Adam, a holy seed that shall destroy the devil's work in man. This book of Moses is consequently richer in pictures of Jesus Christ and his kingdom than any other book. Words as well as examples show Christ, and speak only of him. Yes, he is the true Noah who comforts the believers in their efforts [...] and who saves his family in God's flood of anger. He is the true Melchizedek, his people's true king of peace and high priest. He is of the [...] seed that comes from Abraham, Isaac, and Jacob. Yes, he himself is Isaac, the only-born and beloved son whom the Father will offer for our sake. Jacob has really seen him and wrestled with him, as God and man [...] [8]

But it was not only Arnold's view of the Trinity and 'theology of the Fall' that drew attention to his religious profile. [9] In German orthodox and political quarters he was accused of holding obscure theories like those propagated by the seventeenth century German mystic Jacob Boehme, and worse: of putting Protestants and Catholics on the same footing, of emphasizing regeneration, and of advancing neo-Platonic emanation theories.

Dippel and faith without theology

Arnold was Johann Conrad Dippel's teacher. Dippel, who died in 1734, was active as a physician, alchemist, and theologian. Due to his constant criticism of the official German Lutheran church and to his polemical disposition, he was compelled to flee from one small German state to another; he published a long series of tracts, most of them objectionable both to a clergy intent on preserving society and to ruling princes. He resided in Stockholm from 1726 to 1728, but was forced to leave Sweden because of his dangerously misleading, subversive ideas. Like Arnold, Dippel helps us to understand Swedenborg's religious contribution and its context.

Dippel's and the radical pietists' primary accusation against the ruling Lutheran hierarchy had regard to the priests' way of conducting their offices. Living Christianity had disappeared from the pulpit. The Christian doctrine was presented as an 'insurance policy against temporal and eternal punishment, and against the wrath of God', wrote Wilhelm Bender in his biography of the reformer. [10]

Thus Dippel preached a non-dogmatic religion, scarcely in need of any outer form of community. Every attempt to organize and dogmatically codify a sect or church immediately led to a boundary-setting divorce from those believing in another way. For those seriously involved in a relationship with the Divine, the church should exist only 'in the spirit'. And for such people no dogmatic articles of faith were needed, and no temple or sacrament. The church in its usual meaning could be justified only as a preparation to the general priesthood of all. Its mission, therefore, should be to abolish itself.

The genuine message of true religion must be concentrated into a few words. We should see beyond the historic content of the Gospels to find the essential, the words about love to God and the neighbour. It was so simple and comprehensible to all that neither learning nor priests were needed.

Dippel and his followers stand close to the idea of the rationalism of the 1700s about moral and religious truths being self-evident to all. This 'de-mythologizing' view of divine revelation makes the Bible a devotional manual based on a few simple truths. Its text was not divinely inspired. It could be an aid to personal regeneration, but only if the reader sees the words as messages of love to God and love to the neighbour. But strictly speaking the Bible was not absolutely necessary. We carry its message within us.

Dippel on regeneration and death

Thus it is in man's serious search for a better life, in his new birth, that Christ comes to meet men. Christ, the Divine in human form, is the life-giving example. Regeneration is made easier and is supported by Christ's example. One must draw forth the living Christ from the Gospels, Dippel proclaimed. He must be born in man, and man shall live in a mystical fellowship with him. This applies to his whole person; suffering and miracles are not the essentials: it has to do with something higher. Those who truly believe know that their salvation can never be based on anything visible or physical. The true religion that bears moral fruit arises when the 'inner Christ' is born and rules in man. Christ shows the way in the long process of dying as to the world and living in God.

We should note that for Dippel regeneration is not something that happens once and for all, but is a process that goes on throughout life. Divine truths are being revealed continually. The thesis of an ongoing, constantly changing, and increasing clarity throws light on Dippel's oft-repeated call that preachers and theologians themselves be reborn.

'The servants of the new covenant are only those who are holy, anointed, and made competent for their office by Christ's spirit.'

Dippel's teaching about the life after death, like so much else in his thinking, stands close to the message that Swedenborg would develop much later. There are no definite 'consequences' levied by God, neither rewards nor punishments. Those who have approached perfection during this life have already received eternal life, Dippel wrote in his *Der von den Nebeln des Reichs der Verwirrung gesäuberte helle Glantz des Evangeli Jesu Christi* (*Outline of the Plan for Blessedness*):

> Did the Saviour himself mean anything else when he says, He who believes in me or gives himself entirely to me shall not be judged, already having eternal life? Would not this one immediately, according to his individual measure, come into the community of the supreme good and eternal joy? And the one who does not believe? Is he perhaps not judged, already carrying his hell and his condemnation within himself? In such a state, is he not hardened in his perverted desires that are imprisoned in the earthly? Is not eternal ruin the natural and necessary consequence of his temporal death?[11]

The falsifier banished

The Swedish clergy naturally looked on Dippel's activity and teaching as a threat against the existing order. He had followers in the highest circles of society, in particular within the nobility, and was known not only as a preacher but also as an alchemist and physician. The king himself is said to have called him to Stockholm to treat his ailments.

But his good connections did not protect him from the hatred of the Swedish clergy. After having been declared *persona non grata* in 1728 he was forced to leave the country and the spreading of his books was prohibited. In spite of the ban, 'Dippelianism' gained new adherents.

Swedenborg and Dippel

Emanuel Swedenborg was well-informed about Dippel and his teachings. The German reformer and his personality are discussed in detail in *The Spiritual Diary*. Swedenborg is highly critical. At the same time he confirms the well-known, convincing impression that the German reformer made on the world around him. Here is a note, presumably from 1748:

I had been with [belonged to?] his followers and I had heard different things that came from his writings. But I could not retain a single one of his statements in my memory and [therefore] could not tell what I thought about what he had written, or what I thought was unreasonable. He behaved in this way towards his followers. He deprived them of an understanding of what is good and true, putting them in a kind of delirium. They understood nothing, but became his followers [...] [12]

Dippel's teaching about God's 'inner word', audible to everyone independently of their religious affiliation, was all too vague for Swedenborg, well-versed in the Bible and scientifically trained. Dippel's thoughts could perhaps contain a certain truth; but when they were presented as being based simply on 'absorption in Jesus', without the necessary anchoring in the Bible, they were transformed into evasive statements, hard to remember and understand. One became inebriated by his message, but the intoxication passed quickly. After Dippel's death Swedenborg met his spirit in the other world:

He came closer, at first black in the face. When the distance became yet shorter, he drew out a greyish, clay flask and offered me a drink. At the same time he intimated that it contained an exceptional wine. I was about to accept, for I did not know who he was. But then I was told that it was Dippel, and that he had come with this flask of wine because he had once used the same trick when he got angry with someone who spoke against him. He had wanted to give this person wine containing something poisonous that damaged his thinking and affected him so that he did not know what he [Dippel] said [...] Besides, he was of such a nature that when he deceived someone it was as if he had taken all understanding about truth and goodness from him [...] [13]

Zinzendorf and Moravian pietism

Dippel's name and teaching thus became topical due to his visit to Sweden at the end of the 1720s, when his writings were propagated and debated. Dippel never surrounded

Fig. 20. The alchemical process, a
metaphor for man's regeneration
(Andreas Libavius: *Alchymia*,
Frankfurt 1606).

The man who strives after
purification and freedom from sin
can be put into a state of union with
the Divine. According to Dippel the
same relationship should apply in
the mineral kingdom. Properly
purified metals could become a
tincture with the power to change
iron into gold. The thought of an
agreement between nature and
spirit, the making of gold and the
ennoblement of the spirit, is
presumably as old as alchemy.
Dippel associated himself with a
tradition. Even if he never
succeeded in his attempts he held
fast to the principle. He also worked
as a physician, asserting that all
sickness was inmostly spiritual. The
cure consisted of spiritual and
physical purification.

Polhem scornfully rejected
Dippel's ideas of making gold and
wrote a verse about his 'ridiculous
philosophy':

Gold made in a chemical way,
never enough will really weigh.
For cooked together in a pot,
it goes on high in smoke and soot
and leaves a learned idiot,
who writes down then a book of rot
that other fools will dearly try
when he himself has gone to die.

Christopher Polhems Efterlämnade Skrifter IV, p 237

himself with organized groups; that aspect seems to have interested him just as little as
dogmatic problems. The restless Dippel, always on the move, contrasts with Count Nikolaus
Ludwig von Zinzendorf, leader of the Moravians, a branch of the pietistic tree known in
Swedenborg's time. It was a well-organized movement. During the 1730s and 1740s the

Moravian Brethren's emotional preaching had made its mark both in Stockholm and in other areas in Sweden. Swedenborg was certainly aware of the main lines of their message, all the more so since Moravians had won several followers in his own Board of Mines.

Their ideas were simple. Religion was piety of the heart. No penance was required: 'Come as you are!' The man who had seen his own imperfection could turn to Christ and take advantage of the grace he communicated. Grace came to its actual expression in Christ's suffering on the cross for mankind's sake, and an empathetic feeling of this suffering was the key to peace for the soul and blessedness. It was a matter of coming to a total and passionate concentration, where Christ would appear before the inner vision of the grace-seeking individual. All the senses must be mobilized, the whole body must participate. At the height of empathy a special, personalized sign might appear—an indication of God's love and presence.

'The theology of suffering and blood is my domain', the count proclaimed.[14]

Since this special form of conversion was a fact, it was important to retain the feeling of blessedness and salvation by Christ's suffering. This took place through a bizarre mysticism in which the Moravians figuratively tried to enter into the wounds of the crucified Saviour. Life was polarized between good and evil, blessedness and rejection. The Congregation of Brethren—yet another name for Zinzendorf's followers—became known for their hymns, written with the purpose of stimulating the members to rapture over the Divine suffering for mankind's sake. All Christians were born from the body of Christ and the blessed moment when the soldier's spear opened his side. This idea took strange expressions in the Moravian hymns:

A little maggot,
In love with my four dear nails,
A heavenly bird of the Cross
Sick from love's agony
For My chest and treasure box.
[…]
Dear little hole in the side,
I will hide myself in you.

For us, the Cross's small friends,

The treasure chest is gladly the same

As the whole lamb. [15]

Swedenborg and the Moravians in London: Zinzendorf and Dippel

It was first in London during the crisis, of spring and summer of 1744, that Zinzendorf's emotionally loaded doctrine became topical for Swedenborg. As we have already seen, he seems to have been captivated by the intensity of the Moravian Christianity. From notes in his *Dream Diary* we read that he visited the Brethren's chapel in Fetter Lane, perhaps considering membership. [16] He boarded with a Moravian and seems to have studied Moravian literature: but the movement's emotionally-charged religiosity, lacking a consistent intellectual basis — like Dippel's preaching — proved unacceptable to the reserved and scientifically trained Assessor. The Moravians were 'enthusiasts': the word comes from Greek and means 'inspired by God', but for Swedenborg this inspiration was only a delirium if the faculty of reason was taken out of play. In *The Spiritual Diary* he describes the Moravians' confusion:

> Their hope follows from their conviction that they are more living than others [...] When they say they are more living than others, and they are asked about what their truth is in outline and how what is good is evident from their life, [they answer,] 'In faith.' [...] All that they call truths are falsities [...] [17]

In a longer note, presumably from the beginning of the 1760s, Swedenborg thought he met Zinzendorf and Dippel together. Dippel was like a wild stag, but bound. The count released his restraints and let the stag (Dippel) loose on the dreamer, who nevertheless escaped. The stag was tied again. It was God's will, noted Swedenborg: because of Dippel's persuasive power he was too dangerous and was not allowed to run free:

> Zinzendorf said that he loved Dippel. But he observed that Dippel [...] was such that he would tear up and devour everything, which he in fact did, in hate-filled tracts. Such was his attitude. I said that his style was as it were full of knowledge and intelligence. But when he revealed his

own feelings he seemed almost insane [...] Zinzendorf's followers say the same of themselves as the Lord said [...] that they are the children of God, that they are adopted, and that they are without sin, that they are truth and life, that God is in them as he was in the Lord [...] [18]

Swedenborg refrains from polemics, presumably with the feeling that the absurdities of these men and their followers were so obvious that polemics were unnecessary.

Swedenborg: a pietist?

If we could ask Swedenborg in his heaven whether when on earth he reckoned himself a pietist, he would probably answer in the negative. He had been called by the Lord and given a mission decisive for mankind. The rider on the white horse in the Book of Revelation bore the name, The Word of God: King of Kings, Lord of Lords. Swedenborg's instruction was, he felt, to explain the Word. He had been forbidden to read theological tracts, he stated on several occasions. The Bible was sufficient.

But the mission had as a tool a man tied to his times. He could only work with the concepts and models of thought of his day. These were found in Arndt, Scriver, Spener, Arnold, Dippel——in the whole stream of thought directed towards personal piety that ran concurrently with the century's faith in human reason and its demand for empirical knowledge and clear thinking.

Chapter Seventeen

Private accounting

Perseverance is one of the seven cardinal virtues. It calls for being faithful to one's intentions, holding fast in faith and vision. Swedenborg filled these requirements to a high degree.

From 1745 to 1765 he kept a journal, in Latin, of his 'spiritual experiences'. He recorded dreams, visions, and ideas—altogether, more than 6,500 notes. They are now published in five volumes as *The Spiritual Diary*.

His notes, short and long, together with the *Dream Diary*, are the most personal Swedenborg ever wrote. We gain a unique picture of his inner life, of temptations and epiphanies, and we also find the repetition of certain key ideas. For instance, he develops his doctrine of correspondences—between the spiritual and the physical—as well as ideas about the spiritual world as the body of Christ, or the grand man, *Maximus Homo*. He describes, in prosaic detail, how new worlds open to his inner vision, sketching maps of heaven, hell, and the transit areas for spirits, as well as countries and towns seen from a supernatural perspective.

And at the same time his journal gives a remarkable description of figures in Swedish political life who had recently died. We see how Swedenborg's personal experiences with corruption, the lust for power, and the desire for revenge among his acquaintances coloured his thinking.

Levels of initiation

The insights that Swedenborg received through divine provision came gradually. Already around the year 1740 he had had experiences of light and visions of a supernatural nature. Part of the Easter vision in 1744 was a feeling that he had been 'inaugurated in a wonderful way'. But as we have seen, it was much later that this 'inauguration' took clear form. In his book *De Coelo et ejus Mirabilibus, et de Inferno* (*On Heaven and its Wonders, and on Hell*), here referred to as *Heaven and Hell*, he wrote about his development as follows:

> I have frequently been permitted both to perceive and to see that there is a true light that enlightens the mind, and it is quite unlike the light called natural illumination. I have been gradually raised into that light; and as I have been raised my understanding has been enlightened until I could perceive what I had not perceived before, and at length such things as could never be grasped by thought from natural illumination.[1]

The first notes: entering the spiritual world

The introductory notes in *The Spiritual Diary* have been recovered from *The Word Explained*, Swedenborg's first great exegesis of the Bible, which he began in November 1745. When writing the notes he realized that they did not belong in his explanation of the Bible, as they referred to his own spiritual experiences. He marked their special character by using wider margins.

These early notes are not without importance for understanding Swedenborg's theosophy. The person Emanuel Swedenborg is usually hidden behind the massive amount of text he produced; but here, in the first notes, he comes into view. He is attacked by spirits and often does not know whether they are good or evil. He writes about the importance of straightforwardness and purity in human character, reacting to the Swedish political world of whose leading circles he was a part. A moral re-armament was required, where man learned how to distinguish clearly between good and evil. In his theosophical and biblical universe a human rebirth, a spiritual revival, became a central factor, brought about through Christ's new coming to earth——not in the form of a new physical presence and activity, but through a proper and true understanding of the meaning of his Word.

Another theme is his amazement and joy over what he feels is a newly acquired ability: he, like no one else, can be together with angels and spirits. He asserts with 'holy earnestness' that he has now been prepared to enter into the higher world:

[. . .] that I have been brought into that kingdom by the Messiah Himself, the Saviour of the world, Jesus the Nazarene. And there I have spoken with heavenly beings, with spirits, and with the dead who have risen, even with those who said they were Abraham, Isaac, Jacob, Esau, Rebecca, Moses, Aaron, and the Apostles, especially with Paul and James. This has now gone on for eight months almost continuously, apart from during my journey from London to Sweden; and then continuously while I wrote these things that are now to be published. [2]

We read in one of the first notes that he writes at the dictation of angel-like children who guide his hand and pen. He is absolutely certain of his unique position in relationship to the Divine. The way in which he feels he is writing stands as a guarantee for the truth, he says somewhat later:

In fact, I have also written whole pages, and the spirits themselves were not dictating the words, but were totally guiding my hand, and so it was they who were writing. And for the sake of experience [they also wrote words] that I myself had not thought, but only the sense of them [. . .] [3]

Later, in 1748, he summed up what he had noted during the three years in which he had kept his journal. Everything was divinely inspired:

[. . .] everything I have written in this book has been solely from living experience, from conversation with spirits and angels, from thought communicated [to me] as if by silent speech, also when I was writing from what was imparted to me by those who were then [with me] while I experienced these things [. . .] Everything written in these three books and elsewhere [. . .] is still from my experience [. . .] from spirits or angels [. . .] [4]

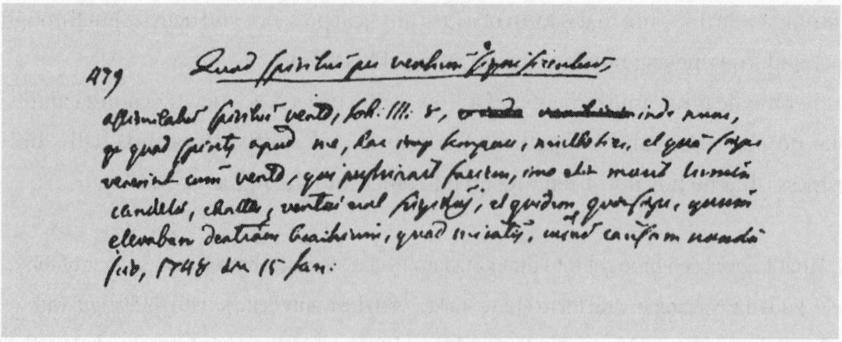
479 Quod spiritus per ventum repraesentantur

assimilatur spiritus vento, Joh: III: 8, ~~...~~ inde nunc, quod spiritus apud me, hac die longaeva, multoties, et quam saepe venerint cum vento, qui perflaverit faciem, imo etiam movit lumen candelae, chartas, ventus erat frigidus, et quidem quam saepe, quum elevabam dextram brachium, quod miratus, nondum causam nosco sum, 1748 den 15 Jan:

Figs. 21, 22. For the graphologically interested we can mention Signe Toksvig's thoughts on Swedenborg's style of handwriting on different occasions. In her biography of Swedenborg she expressed the opinion that his handwriting often took on a special character when he regarded himself to be writing at the dictation of spirits. 'His script is in an angular, slashing, obscure style.' [5] As an example she took his notes from 15 January 1748, n 479 in *The Spiritual Diary*, (see above) where Swedenborg refers to the Gospel of John 3:8: 'the wind blows where it wishes, and you hear the sound of it, but cannot tell where it comes from and where it goes. So is everyone who is born of the spirit'.

Swedenborg's comments in English translation: 'Spirit is likened to wind in John 3:8, and consequently, the spirits present with me at this day, many and most of the times have come with a wind, which stroked my face, indeed even moved the flame of the candle, papers, (the wind was cold,) and this very often when I was raising my right arm. This surprised me, and I do not yet know the reason for it. 1748, the 15th day of January'. The above sample may be compared to the excerpt from the *Dream Diary* on page 168 (Fig. 19). Swedenborg's handwriting when indexing *Heaven and Hell*, below, is contrastingly clear.

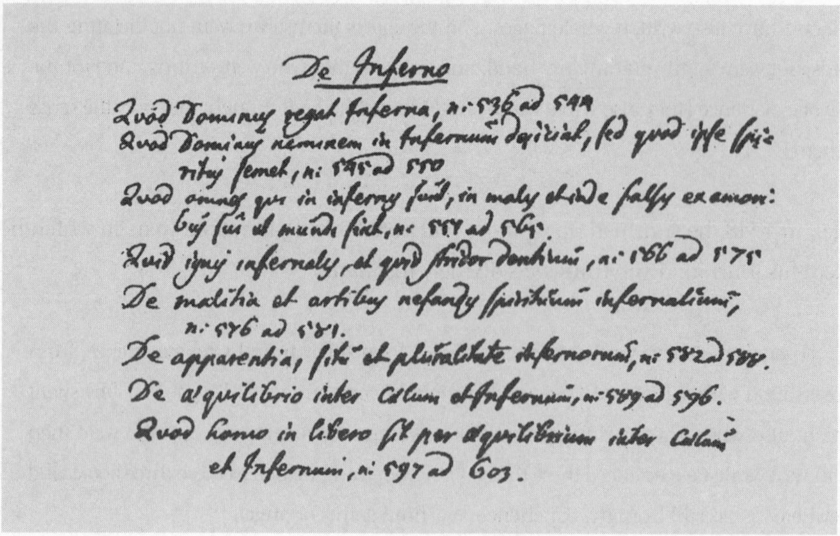
De Inferno

Quod Dominus regat Inferna, n: 536 ad 544

Quod Dominus neminem in Infernum dejiciat, sed quod ipse spiritus semet, n: 545 ad 550

Quod omnes qui in infernis sunt, in malis et inde falsis ex amoribus sui et mundi sint, n: 551 ad 565.

Quod ignis infernalis, et quid stridor dentium, n: 566 ad 575

De malitia et artibus nefandis spirituum infernalium, n: 576 ad 581.

De apparentia, situ et pluralitate infernorum, n: 582 ad 588.

De aequilibrio inter Caelum et Infernum, n: 589 ad 596.

Quod homo in libero sit per aequilibrium inter Caelum et Infernum, n: 597 ad 603.

The journal's psychology

These notes give, above all, a picture of the writer's on-going attempt to find the forces that govern a person's thinking and acting.

It begins with morality. How does a good action look, and what characterizes an evil one? 'Why are the good dumb and the clever evil?' one of Swedenborg's readers, C J L Almqvist, asked much later.

The problem for Swedenborg seems to have a background in his experiences in his nation's political life. As a member of the House of Nobles of the Diet, he had become closely acquainted with leading politicians, men who had high ambitions in Swedish politics and economics. With time he had realized that, for many, personal greed, ambition, and desire for power had been the inner driving force. He may have accepted the divorce between the inner, selfish motives and the publicly professed ambitions as long as the actions of those involved were also of benefit to the country, not simply to themselves.

But his personal experience told him that everyone who attached himself to these figures with divided motives easily became drawn into their hidden calculations, becoming subordinate characters in a theatre piece of state secrets, foreign subsidies, and corruption. Even actors with originally unselfish motives became infected.

During his religious crisis in 1744 Swedenborg had sought to identify the good and evil forces that seemed to be fighting for his inner self. To the assessor, a diligent reader of the Bible, it implied 'testing the spirits' — the expression comes from John's First Letter: 'Every spirit that confesses that Jesus Christ has come in the flesh is of God'. [6]

For Swedenborg the opening of heaven became synonymous with his experience of angels and good spirits. In their spiritual spheres those who were good and those who were evil mixed together with each other, but the wickedness of the evil was more evident in these realms than in the Stockholm of the 1700s. And this was in spite of the fact that the evil (who, like the good, were spirits of those who had at one time lived in the world) attempted to maintain an appearance of pure intentions. He recognised his deceased acquaintances; behind their smiling and genial masks he glimpsed their true faces, twisted by hate, avarice, lust for power, lechery.

The essential constituents in Swedenborg's psychology were a 'mission in life', 'memories', 'forces of good and evil' in the form of spirits, the 'need for purification' and 'unambiguous

Figs. 23, 24. In his dreams or visions Swedenborg believed he saw heavenly landscapes and cities. Once, when witnessing supernatural battles between good and evil spirits, he placed them in a particular city. Upon awaking, he drew its outline in his journal.

motives'. Man is a field of battle, receptive to good and evil. Disunity and mixed motives were always repugnant to Swedenborg. In *Sapientia Angelica de Divina Providentia (Angelic Wisdom concerning the Divine Providence)*, usually referred to as *The Divine Providence*, he condemns the thought of 'two souls in one and the same breast':

> Those who are in evil and at the same time in truths may be compared to eagles. Flying high, they plummet down when they lose their wings. After death [. . .] those who have understood, spoken about, and taught truths, and yet have had no regard for God in their life, fall in the same way. Using their own intellect they raise themselves to the heights, and sometimes enter heaven, lying and saying they are angels of light. But when [unmasked and] deprived of their truths [. . .] they fall down to hell.[7]

Freedom consisted in one's ability to refrain from evil and to let oneself be governed by good spirits. Power from the unseen beings streamed into the visionary, as into every man and woman; their type and strength dependent upon the individual:

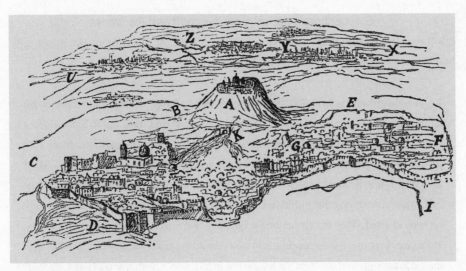

Later editions of *The Spiritual Diary* have attempted to clarify the picture, as may be seen above. (*The Spiritual Diary* n 1857)

[…] spirits streamed into my mind […] In the same way they also streamed into my will and into my very actions. I was led wherever they pleased—through roads and streets, to an inn, and all around—to the point that I was just like a mere passive instrument […] This happened in the same way as when one is driven along by a plainly felt power. Through these experiences, by the divine grace of the Messiah, I have learned most clearly that all human thought, will, and action is guided by the Messiah alone, according to his will. Thus some of his servants, from pure mercy and grace, he leads by means of his heavenly spirits. And some he leads by permission, through other spirits who are not heavenly, all depending on each person's way of living.[8]

Insofar as evil on earth increased, evil spirits were able to diminish the influence of the divine goodness. Evil could appear in disguise and with time it became more and more difficult to 'test the spirits'.

Swedenborg's apocalypse: the chaff and the wheat

But the coexistence of good and evil would soon end. At the close of December 1747 Swedenborg witnessed a revolution in the spiritual world:

> In an uninterrupted spiritual vision, I experienced, and was also now and then taught aloud, that heaven is purged [...] of those who sneak in and dress up, so to speak, in a wedding garment, pretending to be angels. Thus they display themselves as angels, but inwardly they are wolves who are continually leading faithful believers astray. Their trespassing [into heaven] has the following explanation. Such spirits are admitted by the faithful because among the multitude being freed from the pit there are many who have not yet been vastated. They wander among good spirits and angels, sneaking in under angelic guise; and then, using their cunning and their remaining guile, they entice the innocent to their side through intrigues that are second nature to them. The majority of them are those who are steeped in self-love and in various worldly loves. They indeed have stored within themselves [the knowledge] that there is a heavenly marriage—the wedding feast to which the whole world is invited—into which they sneak and afterwards wish to destroy so that they may obtain supreme power and then, from hatred, work against everyone in heaven. How these matters stand, and how [these spirits] were exposed, and how they were cast down from that heaven in groups would take too long to tell. However, they who have been cast down [...] are thrown into a swamp. When they may be delivered from there again, no one can say, for the term of imprisonment in the swamp, and one's depth in it, differ according to each one's wickedness [...] [9]

And here begins a radical cleaning and purification in the spiritual realm, described in detail in *The Spiritual Diary*. The evil are exposed and large numbers of them are cast into the depths and hell, and the good remain in heaven. The criteria were the heavenly disclosure of the inmost love that dominated the spirits during their earthly existence, and a review of the life they had conducted on earth. Ostensible motives were examined and set against hidden purposes. Behind piety a lust for power could show itself; instead of human kindness the driving force might have been a desire for fame. The masks fell away: behind the amiable faces appeared features twisted by hate or perverted lusts.

In the later notes we find detailed accounts of the sifting of the chaff from the wheat. Like Joseph Hall in his treatise *Another World and yet the Same*, published in 1643, Swedenborg draws literal maps of the tracts of evil and foolishness. The Jesuits and the greater part of the Catholic priesthood, on account of self-love and lust for power, are placed in a special subterranean society, 'Babylon'.

According to Swedenborg the majority of the Lutheran priesthood thought that faith alone—not works—was sufficient for salvation. Under the protection of this false concept many had lived their life in sin. Now, after death, they were banished to special quarters in the underworld. Politicians and financiers whose actual driving force had been greed met the same fate.

Beginning of the Last Judgement

A radical upheaval: through their presence in the land of good souls the evil had weakened the influence of the good, thus confusing people on earth. Finally cleansed, a 'new heaven' would take form. It is in fact Swedenborg's own paraphrase of the revelation to John. In the Apocalypse a detailed description is given of how celestial armies, by victories over the powers of darkness, create the conditions needed for a 'new world'. The twenty-two chapters of John's Revelation would be Swedenborg's basic text, subject to comments and inter-pretation in a series of volumes.

The separation of the evil from the good in the spiritual world witnessed by Swedenborg was in actual fact just the beginning of the Last Judgement. It became a long drawn-out process, he later wrote, not concluded until 1757. The judgement had taken place in the spiritual regions, and in Swedenborg's own conscience. He had finally learned to 'distinguish the spirits', and recognise those from his own time. His new insight must have a universal meaning. The Last Judgement was not the end of the world, but the beginning of a new era, the time of the coming of the New Church.

And Christ's promised, new coming to earth? Already in the first notes we find Swedenborg's interpretation of the announcement in the Gospel of Matthew and the Apocalypse concerning the 'coming of the Son of Man'. It is in no way an advent in flesh and blood. It is instead a matter of a new presence, conditioned by man's correct under-standing of the biblical message, and his following it in daily life. As we shall see, due to his insight and interpretation of the Bible, Emanuel Swedenborg regarded himself as called to play a decisive role in this special form of divine advent.

Temptation and freedom

Man is usually led by the desires of his senses. Ever since the Fall we have lived a 'natural life, focused on earthly satisfaction'. But this is the wrong kind of life:

> There can be only one love, and thus only one life. This comes from the Messiah alone. Since the Fall the life that appears in human minds is a nature-based life. It is like the life of the evil genii who were let into heaven in order to sustain and arouse life in those human minds in accord with each man's state of life. These spirits or genii, regarded in themselves, are natural, inwardly being angels of shade, but outwardly like angels of light. Thus they lead an entirely upside down life. [10]

When man gives in to something lower in his thinking, something 'natural', the field is immediately open to evil spirits. But the Messiah saves him from being completely eaten up by evil. In his notes from 1745 to 1746 Swedenborg often speaks about his infestations. During long periods, weeks, months, he says he has been tormented by evil spirits. Jacob's wrestling with the angel in Genesis becomes his own struggle.

Already in the *Dream Diary* Swedenborg defined evil as egotism, self-love. In its essence it is a turning away from the divine influence. It is not man who seeks God, it is God who seeks man—but man will not have him.

The journal is written in a personal form. It is an 'I' who recounts strange experiences, conscious that an outsider must consider them wild fantasies. Thus his freedom, and that of all others, consisted of the ability to withstand evil. And why not give in to it? The writer is immediately clear about the answer. The temptation was in actual fact an attack on his own innermost being, on man's special call. It was a matter of its being blocked, 'numbed'.

There was no in-between, no shortcut. There was only one love, one life. Every compromise was dangerous.

The 'natural' man

But of course it is not only the author, Swedenborg, who falls into darkness by his compromises. It applies to all. The will is free. We know what we will to know, we can see what we will to see. Jacob's wrestling with the angel became, in Swedenborg's interpretation, a picture of his own and humanity's struggle with temptation. We must persevere: victory is certain for the one who does not give up, as is the feeling of divine security given to him who is victorious.

But everyone who gives in, accommodating himself to what is merely natural, sees nothing, understands nothing. Life is captivity or freedom: 'In the world there are only captivity, slavery, and liberation from them'. [11]

Use and purpose

Swedenborg's thinking was always practical. 'Use' and 'purpose' were key words in his century; whole libraries could be filled with volumes focused on the use of economics, physics, philosophy, and theology. Everything or as much as possible should have a tangible anchoring in man's world and be related to concrete human situations. Man was created in the image of God, and all his activities had for Swedenborg a divine aspect, related to the supreme purpose of Creation.

But we are usually unable to distinguish what is in our own highest, best interest, and the useful part we are destined to carry out in our life. The picture of captivity returns:

A state of bondage is seeing and knowing the best [highest] end, yet not being influenced by it, having neither the desire nor the capacity to be moved by it. I found myself in this state of bondage when these things were being written. Still, right now, I could not be freed from spirits who wanted to force me to write these words. When therefore I desired that the love for the end might be aroused, that is, the love of serving the public and promoting uses, [the spirits] brought obscurity upon me. This state came on me gradually, when I could write nothing clearly, other than some things that were dictated to me silently. And yet I did not know whether [what was dictated] was true and good or not true and good. Neither my conviction nor, even less, my affection taught me anything about this. I was taught that truths are mixed with lies [. . .] [12]

Fig. 25. Portrait of Christopher Polhem, who died on 31 August 1751, 89 years old. While the interment was in process Swedenborg saw Polhem's spirit, who asked why people were burying him, in spite of the fact that he was alive. 'He also asked why the priest said that he would arise at the last judgement when in fact he had already been resurrected [. . .] He [. . .] was [already] in his body'. *The Spiritual Diary* n 4773a. An etching based on an oil painting, in the Royal Academy of Sciences, Stockholm.

The thought that all things had a purpose and use was already at hand in *The Economy of the Animal Kingdom* and *The Animal Kingdom*. In Swedenborg's theosophical writings the concept of usefulness as the task and purpose of all living things is a central theme. 'Use' becomes part of man's governing love and, properly understood, a part of his identity.

Portrait from another world

Emanuel Swedenborg was not a closeted scholar whose life was paper and ink. He was a member of the Diet and, if marginally, a politician with sympathies for the Hat Party. In addition, he was one of the leading Swedish experts on mining science. Above all he had powerful relatives within the clergy. Evidently he could socialize with almost everyone, having a pleasant and agreeable manner.

The journal of his spiritual experiences treats of a process through which order was restored to the situation in the spiritual realm, where the evil were separated from the good. As we have seen, this concerned his own large circle of deceased acquaintances. Swedenborg was fifty-seven years old when he began his notes and seventy-seven when he finished the diary. By the end, almost all of his older acquaintances had left this world.

And he seems to have met most of these figures in the spiritual world. He observes them, sometimes speaks with them, noting his impressions, unemotionally, factually. From this perspective the journal of his spiritual experiences becomes a critical examination of many of the best-known figures in Sweden's 'Period of Freedom'. Few of the time's major figures stand up under scrutiny; ambition and greed had been their primary motives in life, though they appeared and acted like true patriots.

Charles XII——whom Swedenborg had dutifully made the object of a poem of praise in 1714——comes off poorly. Swedenborg makes several notes on the absolute monarch. The king's boundless lust for rule seems as great as the strength of his will. He was stubborn to his dying moment and he perverted truth and justice. After death his diabolical nature came into the open:

> [...] he sought for the hell that would obey him, and also searched in heaven for things that could advance his endeavour to subjugate all and to make himself the highest god. [13]

But the king failed after death as he had in life. He then attempted to make himself the highest in hell and from this position enter into negotiations with heaven. This didn't work: he had to content himself with becoming the worst devil of all and he was punished by being taken into a filthy hell, full of pigs. Sometimes the divine love from heaven reached him. He perceived it as a ghastly plague, as if he were being burned by fire.

Eric Benzelius for decades stood very close to Swedenborg. In the preface to *The Infinite,* in 1734, Swedenborg had praised his brother-in-law as an example and teacher, the man who at an early stage had helped the young Swedenborg to choose the right course. Benzelius had died in 1743 as Archbishop of Sweden; it went badly for him in death's kingdom, in Swedenborg's understanding. Here his true nature was revealed. He was a man totally focused on the material and tangible world:

> In the life of the body, he cared nothing at all for the Word, and very little for the doctrine of the Church, but only for worldly things, languages, and questions relating to his country. He had the Word, but it served him only for preaching and not in the least for life and doctrine. He even despised it, and believed nothing, as stated by another in whom he confided

that this was so. He believed a thing to be so, whether or not it was for or against the doctrine of the Church. He loved himself above all things, and esteemed justice and equity as nothing except so far as it might serve for reputation [...] Seen in the light of heaven, he had a horrible form, no longer human. [14]

Other members of the family pass in review. Behind several of the sketchy and often negative portraits there seem to be old disputes about questions of inheritance. Colleagues at the Board of Mines are also described, usually critically, and politicians are also discussed. The two brothers Carl and Fredrik Gyllenborg can be taken as examples. Both were leading members of the Hat Party. Carl was Prime Minister from 1739 to 1746 and was held responsible for the fiasco of the war with Russia in 1741-3, and Fredrik functioned as the powerful whip of the Hat Party and for a series of years as manager of the French subsidies. His posthumous reputation, according to an official investigation into his bankrupt estate, was as follows: religious with pietistic sympathies, winning, charming, but notoriously crooked.

As a member of the Diet and close to the Hat Party, Swedenborg had contacts with the two brothers. Carl died in 1746 and Fredrik in 1759. Did Swedenborg ever analyse the brothers' attitudes and morals during their lifetime? They had both worked for the alliance with France and, like himself, were warmly attached to the Swedish political system.

Had these, and perhaps other good sides, blinded him to Carl's inadequacies from the viewpoint of eternity? In *The Spiritual Diary* all moral compromises are condemned. Carl's spirit ends up in a region occupied by those who deny God, and Fredrik is cast down into his own hell of excrement, which he is never allowed to leave on account of his danger to others.

The former Prime Minister is described as a magician with a beaming face. Armed with the Psalter, a pen knife, and a snuffbox, he let himself be governed by instinct, not from reason. [15] The portrait of his brother is more detailed: 'He was such that he could hold back my thought and divert the heavenly inflow in such a high degree that I could not write what I should'. [16] Swedenborg's key words for Fredrik Gyllenborg are egotism, cunning, and love of intrigue. He belonged to a group of spirits who had their eyes on everything, governed everywhere, rewarded those who obeyed them, and punished those who would not follow. He had been seized with a gradually increasing hatred for Swedenborg: 'He would rather die than desist from murdering me'. According to a later note, the former Hat politician ended up 'almost half-dead' in a cave with a warning sign describing his character.

Memory and reminder

From several viewpoints the journal is one of the most interesting works in Swedenborg's great literary output. Here, together with other notes of a similar nature in the *Dream Diary* and the essay *De Scriptura Sacra seu Verbo Domini* (*The Sacred Scripture or the Word of the Lord, from Experience*), written around 1762, we are given a picture of his spiritual development. And with this we also gain important factors revealing his way of thinking, which otherwise can be difficult to understand.

Swedenborg himself appears to have used his notes as supports and preliminary sketches for his many works. The great diary's descriptions of the Last Judgement return, slightly modulated, in his volumes on the Book of Revelation. The anecdotal 'memorable experiences', inserted in some of his theological works, often go back to his meetings with great spirits from all ages, but edited and streamlined in comparison with the journal.

We also come upon notes, as stated earlier, that seem to apply mostly to his own state of mind and conduct in life. In spite of temptations and attacks from evil spirits, the pages of his journal usually breathe a calm commitment, perhaps synonymous with what one usually means by 'happiness'. He wrote about this condition in October 1748:

Some think that believers should distance themselves from all the delights of life and pleasures of the body. But I can assert that such delights have never been denied me. On the contrary, I have been granted not only to enjoy such pleasures of the body and the senses as are given to others who live, but have also been granted and given joys and happinesses of life that, as I believe, have been enjoyed by no other in the whole world— ones that are greater and more exquisite than any mortal could imagine or even believe. [17]

The Book of Revelation and the keys to heaven

Chapter Eighteen

Here come hard guests, a dangerous cavalry
On horses red, black, and pale, now all these three.
War, hunger, the plague shall so kill all the land,
That for its sins ruined and wasted shall stand.
When Zion shall be built, then shall all cedars fall,
The proud shall be deposed — come, Lord, I call.
Stones and chalk will be the messengers of peace.
Establish soon Your glory as You best know and care.

Ewangeliske Läro-och Bönepsalmer, pp. 150-1

Scenes in the Apocalypse

The Book of Revelation has twenty-two chapters. We find a crowd of figures dramatically presented, and scenes full of colour. The actors are always in motion: arriving or fleeing in battles, sailing across the skies of heaven, punishing or rewarding. At the centre stands a catastrophe, an unheard-of revolution. The universe shakes in convulsions. That cosmic upheaval is followed by silence. A third of mankind perishes. Babylon has fallen.

The scene of its collapse is set against a picture of a quiet river whose banks are edged by budding trees. Behind the devastation stands the Lamb, the sovereign of the world whose wrath has no limit. The Lamb has seven eyes and seven horns. It sends out its angels in mighty battles, to punish, destroy, and purify.

The Lamb's adversary is evil itself: it has mobilized its armies and weapons of destruction, but its defeat is inescapable. Sin's perverted rulers are cast into a bottomless pit. A gate over the opening is closed for all time. The Lamb appears, undeterred by the battles that have been fought. It takes a scroll containing a divine decree and opens it. The Lamb rules to eternity.

The Lamb is quiet and silent, but the hostile monster is as raucous as it is ignorant. It spews a flood of water to engulf the woman clothed with the sun. Around the roaring animal, its hypnotized followers gather to worship it. Its mighty dragon-tail sweeps over the universe, and the stars fall, to move as satellites in the orbit of the beast. They are the fallen angels whose leader is the corrupted morning star.

The Lamb is like the quiet sun, eternally melting the seals of the cosmic secrets. Before the final victory, in musical repetitions, the seven bowls of wrath have been poured out

Fig. 26. The Apocalypse describes the accomplishment of the Last Judgement in the spiritual world. The 'dragon' that persecutes the woman clothed with the sun, in chapter 12, portrays the evil that haunts the heavenly queen. The dragon is conquered and the way is opened for the New Jerusalem to descend. Here is Dürer's famous etching of the scene, from *The Revelation of St John*, 1498.

over depraved mankind, seven thunders have shaken the ground, and seven trumpets have resounded. The stars have fallen, the mountains are set on fire, the wells are poisoned. Evil has been conquered, but returns; yet what is good remains forever, as witnesses or lamenting reminders. The Lamb itself seems to stand outside the course of events. No one knows if it listens to the sad cries or to the songs of praise its worshippers sing before the throne.

Towards the end, the wedding of the Lamb is announced, the blessed are invited, and a rider on a white horse appears. From the rider's mouth comes a sword which is the Word of God and its doctrine. The Word is the most forceful of all weapons. The rider's name is Truth and with his sword he can destroy Gog and Magog, the powers of evil, whose cohorts fall beneath it. All things are made new. A new, holy Jerusalem is formed in heaven and brought down to earth.

The obscure text

The Book of Revelation takes its name from its original Greek title *Apocalypsis* meaning an 'unveiling'. With its obscurity, its play of colours, and its thematic repetitions it became of great significance to Swedenborg's world of thought.

According to the first chapter it was written by John when he was on the Isle of Patmos in the Aegean Sea, 'for the word of God, and for the testimony of Jesus Christ'. He was 'in the spirit', and wrote at the dictation of a 'great voice, as of a trumpet'. The question of whether the writer was also the author of the fourth Gospel, 'the disciple whom Jesus loved', has been discussed for hundreds of years. Whatever the case may be, it can be stated that there are important similarities of thought between the Gospel and the Apocalypse.

The Book of Revelation comes last in the Bible, after the Gospels, Acts, and Letters. This position seems to give John a primary biblical task. Perhaps his short, divinely inspired text should be read as a summary of the content of the two testaments?

Martin Luther found the book difficult to understand. The publishers of the first Swedish translation of the New Testament in 1526 were of the same opinion. According to the preface, the Book of Revelation could have been left out, since no one was in a position to understand what it actually contained. Nevertheless it was included in the New Testament, mostly because many passages used in the Swedish liturgy were quotations from the Johannine prophecies.

Complaints about the cryptic book have been heard from readers and commentators through the centuries. Jesper Swedberg testified to his difficulties regarding its right meaning:

And we may well call John's Revelation a sealed book. It contains many deep secrets and prophecies [. . .] so that many do not understand what is written there, which I myself sometimes also willingly confess, who have little understanding of this very book. For me it is like a closed book, sealed with seven seals.[1]

In the 1703 Swedish translation of the Bible, the Book of Revelation was provided with an introductory explanation. The text was dark, and on that account could lead the reader astray. Therefore it was best to provide an understandable interpretation, insofar as this could be done. Thus John's visions and prophecies treated of the dangers that had faced Christians ever since the beginning: false teachers of the church like Arius and Origen, founders of religions like Mohammed, and above all the popes and their church. The conflicts between good and evil described in the book had to do with the battle between true Christian faith grounded in the Scriptures and false interpretations of different kinds. The conclusion:

> Our sanctity is in heaven, where Christ is, and is not for eyes here in the world, like trash in the marketplace. Therefore, let anger, sectarianism, heresy, and mistaken views do what they may. When only the words of the gospel become pure with us, and we observe and love them, we shall have no doubt that Christ is indeed with and among us, even if conditions turn to the worst. As we see in this book, in the midst of all plagues, wild animals, and evil angels, Christ is nevertheless among us and with his saints, and in time achieves victory.

The Apocalypse's milestones

The determinative events in London in April 1745 have already been described. The essential element in Swedenborg's experiences was the epiphany and the divine command recorded in the notes from October 1744 in the *Dream Diary*. God had appointed him to explain the spiritual content of the Scriptures for mankind. He would also be given instructions about what he should write on this subject.

He was 57 years old. The explanations of the Bible that he was now to begin would keep him occupied for the greater part of the remaining twenty-seven years of his life. The starting point for this enormous work of interpretation was his reading of John's Revelation. Here his task was explained, its meaning, and the consequences for how his authorship would be carried on. And inversely, this divine mission to which he was appointed would give the final explanation of John's prophecies. Swedenborg confirmed his dependence on the Book of Revelation in his last, summarizing work, *Vera Christiana Religio* (*The True Christian Religion*), published in 1771. On the title page we read that the truth of the message in Swedenborg's great book was 'foretold in Daniel 7:13, 14 and in the Book of Revelation 21:1, 2'.

The verses referred to in the prophecy of Daniel describe a vision in which he saw 'one like a son of man', someone who would 'come in the clouds of heaven': 'to him was given dominion and glory and a kingdom, that all people, nations, and languages should serve Him; His dominion is an everlasting dominion which shall not pass away, and His kingdom the one which shall not be destroyed'. Swedenborg read this prophetic passage as a fundamental, divinely inspired statement about Christ's omnipotence and coming. The verses in the Book of Revelation treat of the descent of the New Jerusalem to earth:

> And I saw a new heaven and a new earth, for the first heaven and the first earth had passed away. Also there was no more sea. Then I, John, saw the holy city, New Jerusalem, coming down from God out of heaven, prepared as a bride adorned for her husband.

For Swedenborg these lines would always, from 1744-5 to his death, stand out as if written in fire. Their meaning was that Christ's coming created a new heaven, and that the Christian teaching, rightly understood and applied, would in its turn create a new earth, and this earth would stand in direct communication with the new heavenly, spiritual reality: a new spiritual Jerusalem. For Swedenborg it was a new Christian community, built on the right understanding of the spiritual meaning of the Word. In the form of love, this new church and city would descend to earth to meet properly enlightened human beings. It was the divine marriage between love and wisdom.

Reflections and prophecies

The Apocalypse is a gold mine for those who are interested in 'typology'. Presumably one of the book's original main purposes was to convince the readers, and especially sceptical Jews, that Jesus truly was the Messiah foretold by the prophets. Therefore the frequent citations of, borrowings from, and allusions to the Old Testament, echo unnoticed by the majority of present-day readers. These references are above all to Genesis and Exodus, the Psalms, Proverbs, Isaiah, Jeremiah, Joel, and Zechariah. An analysis of the Apocalypse has shown that in its 404 verses there are 518 quotations from and allusions to the Old Testament. [2]

To Jews versed in the Old Testament and to early Christians these references were more evident than to us. John wanted to fuse the whole Bible together, the Old and the New Testaments. The one could not be understood without the other: the Old Testament witnessed to the New, the New explained the Old. It is the original, primitive Christian conception that was in the highest degree alive also during the first centuries after the Reformation.

Fig. 27. An angel showed John the New Jerusalem:
'And he carried me away in the Spirit to a great and high mountain, and showed me the great city, the holy Jerusalem, descending out of heaven from God, having the glory of God. And her light was like a most precious stone, like a jasper stone, clear as crystal'. Revelation. 21:10, 11. *Biblia Germanica*, 15th century.

Bishop Swedberg's sermons are characterized by this duality, the anchoring of the new covenant in the old, a relation that has explicit, biblical support. The twenty-fourth chapter of Luke's Gospel speaks of Christ's conversation with two disciples on the road to Emmaus: 'And beginning at Moses and all the Prophets, He expounded to them in all the Scriptures the things concerning Himself'.

It was this manner of reading, particularly in relation to the Book of Revelation, that Swedenborg made his own. In the year 1745 he began his first broadly planned interpretation of the Bible, posthumously published under the title *The Word Explained.* Here he analysed his method:

> The ultimate end of creation is the kingdom of God, which is to be established by the Messiah in the heavens and at the same time on earth. From this it follows that there was not one thing that functioned as an intermediate end or means which did not represent that ultimate end in itself, as in a type or effigy. This is true therefore not only of creation and of what was produced on each of its days, but also especially of paradise, Adam, and the state of his integrity and marriage, etc. Wherefore in these, first of all, as in representative mirrors, we may contemplate the state of the future kingdom of God. For individual representations are mirrors of universals [...] since universals are born and exist from their individual elements.[3]

The Apocalypse, therefore, should be understood, according to Swedenborg, as an attempt to show how, since the beginning of creation, God has successively prepared heaven and earth for Christ's coming. Israel had actively participated in this plan of salvation, but rejected the Messiah when in fact he came. The prophetic books speak of Creation, the Garden of Eden, the Fall, the Wandering in the Wilderness, but at the same time also of the coming of the Messiah as foretold by the prophets. All things in these ancient Scriptures were symbols or signs, standing in a special relationship to Christ's life, message, and death. John's purpose, seen from this perspective, was not to foretell the course of development until the end of time. Instead it was a matter of describing, through a series of parallels, the period that began with creation and came to its end and completion with Easter, the resurrection, and the disciples' accounts of the life and teachings of Christ.[4]

Consequently, this spiritual interpretation of the Book of Revelation departs radically from the usual reading. The interpreters often surmised that the text related to earthly caesars, prominent religious figures and their efforts, the Catholic church and its role during different periods of time, etc. Not least, there was speculation about the words concerning the Last Judgement and Christ's returning to earth. With the help of mystical numbers that occur in the text there were attempts to calculate the exact timetable for Christ's coming to earth, and the Last Judgement that was then going to take place. The

German theologian Johan Albrecht Bengel, a contemporary of Swedenborg, was a master of this kind of interpretation. Christ would return to earth in the year 1836, he wrote.

Correspondences

In Swedenborg's last two great works before his crisis, the 'doctrine of correspondence' comes to the fore. Moving by analogy from one concept to another, man could rise step by step to a higher knowing, inaccessible through observations by the senses. Allegories or parables often appear in the Sacred Scriptures. Correspondences can also be expressed 'typologically', he had noted in a posthumously published little work from around 1741, *Clavis Hieroglyphica* (*The Hieroglyphic Key*):

> [It] is done through metaphorical language, in which Christ and the Christian church are pictured in the Jewish church, as also the Kingdom of God and the community of heaven in the Christian church [...] We can be certain in the belief that the whole world is filled with types, but we know only very few of them. For the present time always contains the future, and between [separate] occurrences there is a connection and chain, which is explained by the divine providence's unchanging course and influence.[5]

As a rule we may interpret the Bible in this way, he summarized: 'for the spirit speaks naturally as well as spiritually'.

Swedenborg's close reading of the Book of Revelation seems to have begun in the early 1740s. Already in his notes in the *Dream Diary* we meet the woman and the dragon spoken of in the Apocalypse, as well as accounts of dreams about processions of horses of different colours and other visions, which seem to derive from the Johannine text. He desires to be the man who kills the evil dragon; but he added cautiously that this depended upon what God wanted of him.

The Easter vision reminds us of a scene in the seventh chapter of the Apocalypse: the structure, the questions, and the answers in the *Dream Diary* come very close to the words of John. Here we find the famous passage with the 'great multitude' of those who are saved standing before the throne of God 'clothed with [...] white robes'. 'Who are these people who have been saved from destruction?' a heavenly figure asks. Here follow the words of John:

Then one of the elders answered, saying to me, "Who are these arrayed in white robes, and where did they come from?" And I said to him, "Sir, you know." So he said to me, "These are the ones who came out of the great tribulation, and washed their robes and made them white in the blood of the Lamb. Therefore they are before the throne of God, and serve Him day and night in His temple [. . .] ".

And Swedenborg's note in his *Dream Diary*:

[He] spoke to me and asked if I have a health certificate; and to this I replied, "Lord, thou knowest better than I". He said, "Well then, do!"——that is, as I inwardly grasped this, "Do love me" or "Do as promised".[6]

Thus in these two visions it is a question of a 'certificate of health', spiritual health, and the coming out of 'great tribulation'. Saved? Healthy? In both cases the one spoken to leaves the answer to the questioner: 'Lord, you know'. The conclusion is the same in both texts. In John it was a call to become part of the great multitude in white garments, 'to stand before the throne of God, and serve Him day and night'. In Swedenborg's version, the statement 'Well then, do!' was a matter of 'truly loving', of fulfilling a promise given.

The Book of Revelation became a decisive element in the programme of Swedenborg's life, and he interpreted it in a series of books. The largest work, written from 1757 to 1759, *Apocalypsis Explicata* (*The Apocalypse Explained*), was first published after his death, filling six volumes in a subsequent English edition. He proceeded slowly, with many side excursions. Two of his shorter commentaries, *De Ultimo Judicio* (*The Last Judgment*) and *De Equo Albo* (*The White Horse*), were printed separately in 1758. A summary of his reading of the Book of Revelation was published in 1766 in Amsterdam, entitled *Apocalypsis Revelata* (*The Apocalypse Revealed*).

The Word, Swedenborg's mission, and the actuality of the Last Judgement

Christ was the Word become flesh according to the introduction to the Gospel of John. Swedenborg encountered the same thought in the nineteenth chapter of the Apocalypse:

Then I saw heaven opened, and behold, a white horse. And He who sat on him was called
Faithful and True, and in righteousness He judges and makes war. His eyes were like a
flame of fire, and on His head were many crowns. He had a name written that no one knew
except Himself. He was clothed with a robe dipped in blood, and His name is called The
Word of God. And the armies in heaven, clothed in fine linen, white and clean, followed
Him on white horses [...] And He has on His robe and on His thigh a name written: KING OF
KINGS AND LORD OF LORDS.

For Swedenborg, the first part of the Book of Revelation describes the state of Christianity
as it was in his own time, *in the very moment in time when the Last Judgement takes
place*. He felt that he was a witness to the heavenly scene. He did not see himself as a
prophet: his time was the present and the past. Through his insight into the celestial
sphere, given by a higher power, he understood that the judgement took place in the
spiritual world——*not* on earth. Indeed he could state the time when this occurred: the
year 1757.

What had been previously misunderstood could now be seen correctly. In the preface
to *The Apocalypse Revealed*, he writes:

Everyone can see that the Apocalypse cannot possibly be explained except by the Lord alone.
For each word in the book contains arcana, that could never be known without a particular
enlightenment and thus a revelation. It has therefore pleased the Lord to open the sight of
my spirit, and to teach me. Do not believe, therefore, that I have taken anything there from
myself, or from any angel, but from the Lord alone.

Why this heavenly judgement? During the seventeen centuries since the crucifixion, the
heart of the Christian message had been lost. People no longer knew what was right and
wrong. The Catholic church, with its elevation of the figure of the pope to be Christ's
vicar on earth, was a betrayal of Christian thought. Christian motives had been conflated
with striving after power, worldly and spiritual. And in the Lutheran church hypocrisy
had spread with the doctrine of justification by faith and Christ's vicarious atonement.
This earthly drama had its correspondence in the spiritual world. Now, on the celestial

scene, the chaff was separated from the wheat. The seventh seal was opened, the seven angels each in turn blew their trumpets, and the state of mind of each and all in the world of spirits was examined. The seventh angel gave the signal for the end of the violent trial:

> Then the seventh angel sounded: And there were loud voices in heaven, saying, "The kingdoms of this world have become *the kingdoms* of our Lord and of His Christ, and He shall reign for ever and ever!"[7]

God's heavenly and earthly city: the Second Coming

The long section on the celestial judgement is followed by a concluding part that treats of the heavenly Jerusalem, which descends from heaven to earth. This occurrence was the great and decisive event for Swedenborg and, he was convinced, for all mankind. It is in this connection that the words on Christ's imminent coming were to be understood.

According to the traditional interpretation, the Lord would come with his angels in the skies. It was the 'day of wrath', announced by trumpets. All men, alive and dead, were then to be gathered, and the good separated from the evil. The good would be taken up to heaven, the evil cast down to hell. At the same time a new heaven would be created, and a new earth. The new Jerusalem would descend to earth, where all the good would dwell, both the living and the dead since the beginning of time.

These were absurd ideas, in Swedenborg's view. 'Reason has gone into exile.' Ask anyone at all, he wrote in *The True Christian Religion*:

> What happens if you ask a clergyman or a layman whether they believe all these things for sure? For instance, that the people before the flood together with Adam and Eve, and the people after the flood together with Noah and his sons, as well as Abraham, Isaac, and Jacob together with all the prophets and apostles, and likewise all the rest of human souls, are all still stored in the bowels of the earth or flit about in the ether or the air. Ask whether they believe that souls will be clothed again with their own bodies and coalesce with them, despite the fact that their corpses have been eaten by worms, rats or fish [...] when some have been reduced to skeletons burnt clean by the sun or have dissolved into dust. [...] Ask whether

such things are not paradoxes, which reason can explode as it does contradictions. To this some will have no answer to make. Some will say that this is a matter of faith, 'and we keep our understanding subject to faith.' [8]

No, here was a mistake in the interpretation of the words about the Lord's Second Coming. However, through divine revelations Swedenborg himself had received clarity about the fate of the deceased after death. Their souls do not fly around in the air or wait in the centre of the earth.[9] Man's life continues in a 'substantial body'. Those who come to the abode of the blessed find themselves in a more perfect state than before. If they have lived a life turned from God, they continue as they had been.

The Second Coming had also been misunderstood. It took place solely in and through the Word and therefore consisted of a *deepened understanding* of the Christian message. Through this the new Jerusalem would be created, a communion between God and mankind. It was a 'city of God', to use an expression of Augustine. For Swedenborg as well as for the great apostolic father, this 'city' was nothing other than an invisible community with a unifying link——true faith, true love, true insight.

The communication of this insight was Emanuel Swedenborg's teaching mission.

And the judgement? In John's Gospel we read that 'God did not send His Son into the world to condemn the world'. Each and everyone judges himself. Works are decisive, according to the Apocalypse, and the pattern formed by our deeds is written in the Book of Life. Neither punishment nor reward is a consequence, but a state of mind. This is a recurring thought in Swedenborg.

The judgement is man's meeting with truth, and the existential position he or she takes. When the meaning of the Word is once truly understood, and we live in accord with it, then we return to a heavenly state, to the kingdom of God which, according to the Gospel of Luke, is within man.

Swedenborg's mission

Thus Christ's words to Swedenborg on Easter night in 1744 would change his life. If Christ was the incarnation of the Word, and so was present and accessible after his coming, what was then meant by the repeated words in the Apocalypse regarding Jesus's imminent coming? It could scarcely be a question of a new coming in a physical respect. Christ had indeed already come, and his mission on earth was completed. Should the words on his coming be understood as a *post facto* explanation of the meaning of the first and only coming? Was it not for him, Swedenborg, inspired by God, to illuminate the true meaning of the first advent? If so, he had a divine mission for mankind's spiritual welfare.

He took the question very seriously. If from nothing else, this is clear from *De Messia Venturo in Mundum* (*The Messiah about to Come*), a collection of biblical excerpts made in 1745, though first published in our time. The purpose of the work is clear. Swedenborg wanted to analyse all the texts that could cast light on the chief questions in the Book of Revelation. Primarily it concerned all the prophecies about the coming kingdom of God and the advent of the Messiah.

He summarized his studies in a few lines. The kingdom of God would come, where all mortal beings would live in fellowship with the angels. It was the new covenant between heaven and earth. Jesus Christ was the Messiah spoken of by Moses and the prophets. The Messiah comes to enlighten mankind. This will happen with the help of a servant. All this had been foretold by words and signs.

Swedenborg felt that he had been given a role in the divine scene. Perhaps his reading of the forty-first chapter of Isaiah at this time was especially significant. It speaks of a young woman who is to give birth to a son who was the awaited Messiah. When excerpting Isaiah 41:8-22 Swedenborg underlined the following:

But you, Israel, are my servant, Jacob, whom I have chosen, the descendants of Abraham My friend. You whom I have taken from the ends of the earth, and called from its farthest regions, and said to you, 'You are My servant, I have chosen you, and have not cast you away: Fear not, for I am with you […] '. [10]

The child who would be God's servant had, in the prophet's words, the name Emanuel: the name means 'God with us'. Had not he, Emanuel Swedenborg, also received a Divine call?

Digression on a garden

Chapter Nineteen

Botany's day of glory

Swedenborg's epoch was a time of glory for botany. He had grown up in his father's house on the Uppsala square, with the famous Rudbeck family as close neighbours. Scarcely 30 years before his birth, Professor Olof Rudbeck Sr had laid out his famed botanical garden, constructed symmetrically, with right angles and rectangular sections.

Rudbeck had attempted to catalogue, classify, and describe all the known plants in the world, illustrating them in a huge work, entitled *The Elysian Fields*, but most of the printing plates had been destroyed in the great fire of Uppsala in 1702. Only the first volumes containing some two hundred engravings had been printed before the catastrophe.

Everywhere in Europe we mark the same interest in flora. In Sweden Carl Linnaeus became one of the best-known names in European botany of that day. He was married to Sara Moraea, daughter of the physician Johan Moraeus, Swedenborg's maternal cousin and his tutor in childhood.

Swedenborg's house in Stockholm

In 1743, the year in which the peace with Russia was established in Åbo/Turku,

Swedenborg purchased a small estate in the southern part of Stockholm. It is not known if he moved in after his return to Sweden in 1745-6, or at the beginning of the 1750s. The property was situated on the south side of Hornsgatan, to the west of the sluice between the Baltic Sea and Lake Mälaren. Today the site is occupied by an apartment building numbered 41-45. Several well-known families lived in the neighbourhood: Christopher Polhem, members of the Gyllenborg family, and the bank commissioner Christer Robsahm, whose son Carl would later write his well-known *Anteckningar om Swedenborg* (*Notes on Swedenborg*).

Fig. 28. Vignette on page 1 of *Arcana Caelestia* volume 1. The Royal Swedish Academy of Sciences, constituted in 1739, had chosen the digging man as a symbol for its *Transactions*. In *Arcana Caelestia* the garden stands as a symbol for paradise, and its planting as a picture of the understanding. (Cf. Tore Frängsmyr *Gubben som Gräver*, pp. 8 et seq)

The property comprised slightly more than an acre. Swedenborg's heirs made the following description after his death:

This estate, together with the dwellings and sheds, is protected by a well-made wooden fence with beautiful gates. The gardens (located in the west) are divided into two sections, each covering one-third of the total area [...] The eastern section takes the remaining third. Here the mews are located, as well as a spacious yard. To the south of the yard is Swedenborg's house [...] with a delightful garden with flowers and boxwood figures.[1]

Arcana Caelestia and the planning of the garden

In September 1749 the first volume of *Arcana Caelestia* was published in London by the printer John Lewis. Swedenborg presumably left London in May of the same year, travelling via Amsterdam to Aachen/Aix-la-Chapelle where he passed the winter. He returned to Stockholm in the spring of 1750.

During his stay in Holland he planned his garden. He asked his representative in Amsterdam, the merchant Joachim Wretman, to buy seeds and bulbs for transport to Stockholm. Wretman carried out his assignment and sent instructions for the planting of hyacinths and tulip bulbs; the bulbs must be put into the ground in the autumn, before the frost comes. [2]

For most of the 1750s Swedenborg appears to have stayed in Sweden. During the greater part of this time he continued his work *Arcana Caelestia*, sending the manuscripts in instalments to John Lewis in London. The last, eighth volume was printed in 1756. It was also during these years that the garden was planned and at least partly realized, at the same time as the house was reconstructed. He had a gardener, living in a small house on the north side of the property.

The garden was made up of four sections, grouped around an avenue of lime trees. He probably had flowers and bushes in the south-eastern quarter and kitchen vegetables in the south-western part. On the northern side alongside Hornsgatan, it is presumed that fruit trees dominated. An authority on Stockholm in the eighteenth century, Henrik Alm, drew a map of the garden, placing cold frames and bushes in the north-western quarter.

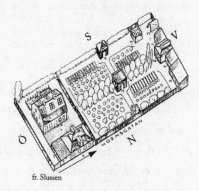

Fig. 29. Swedenborg's house and garden on Hornsgatan according to Henrik Alm's reconstruction. No completely reliable plan exists, of either the house or the garden.

There is an almanac preserved from 1752 in which Swedenborg made notes about his flower beds and garden lawns, interspersed between his comments on the manuscripts he was sending to London for printing.[3]

In front of his house, on the south side, Swedenborg had a small terrace in which he planted boxwood bushes clipped into animal and other figures, like so much else purchased through Wretman in Amsterdam.

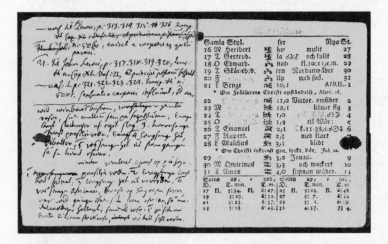

Fig. 30. In his almanac for 1752 Swedenborg recorded his successive mailings to John Lewis. At the same time he made notes about seeds and plantings in his garden. In February he began his notes for the 'large square above on the left side: 1. rose-bed to the bird cage, three kinds of bell roses to the small tree, then cat-mint, Sweet William, liknis [rock lichen?], chalcedonica, at the end spergel [asparagus]. 2. rose-bed'. His notes continue, as may be seen above, on a page inserted in the March calendar: 'at the currant bush, old roses, then mallium as on the bird cage, further on, hollyhocks of some kind. 3. parsley at the top of the transverse bed [...] 4. red beets in the long bed in this direction. 5. rose bed on this side of the stone path and across it. Smaller quarter above to the right. 1. transverse bed, parsley. 2. furthest long row, spinach. 3. long bed of carrots. 4. African rose bed, at the far end, large African, also velvet roses. 5. at the sides white lilium, hollyhocks, at the tree, sunflowers'.

He also planted lemon seeds, artichokes, mulberries, 'peas from America, American corn, and American melon seeds', planes and beeches, as well as a great variety of flowers.

For Swedenborg, trees and flowers all had a useful place in creation; with their aroma and beauty, flowers give happiness to human life, directing man's thoughts to what is good and true. Furthermore, medicinal herbs can heal many sicknesses or be of practical use in other ways. Vegetables and fruits may be served as food. Presumably he wanted to have all categories represented in his garden.

In 1752 he carried out an extensive building project. His garden needed a greenhouse; he solved the problem by converting the second storey of his dwelling to a small conservatory. The floor was covered with tiles, and large studio windows were opened in the roof. In the centre of the garden a pavilion was erected, a copy of a building he had seen in England. According to his heirs' description, the walls were of wood 'in trellis-work, with a flat roof, forming a beautiful, railed terrace, with a round seat in each corner'.

The happiness of heaven — a garden in spirals?

Swedenborg's enthusiasm for gardening was not simply a result of a general interest in flowers. A well-kept, flowering garden was an earthly picture of paradise.[4] The regenerated 'heavenly man' was similar to such a garden, uniting love and wisdom. Regeneration could be described in botanical terms. Man, born anew, begins like a tree from a seed, a picture of truth. The tree grows in stages forming leaves and branches, symbols of the growing human reason. The flowers represented wisdom and the fruit offered a picture of love brought forth into practice. In *Arcana Caelestia* we find a series of pictures of delightful gardens and the world of gardening, always with positive connotations, and contrasted with wild nature, a primitive state, still distant from the caring hands of wisdom and love.

The gardener's work, the turn of the spade in the earth, harmonized with his interpretation of the Bible. The delight of the earthly garden became a picture of heavenly happiness.

In Swedenborg's *Conjugial Love,* published in 1768, he gives an eloquent description of horticulture in paradise. Some spirits are led by an angel to a princely garden:

[…] at the entrance he said: 'This is a magnificent garden, even compared with those in this heavenly community of ours.'

'What do you mean?' they answered. 'There is no garden here. We can see only one tree, with what looks like golden fruits on its branches and its top, and what looks … look like leaves of silver, their edges decorated with emeralds; and under the tree there are children with their nurses'.

To this the angel replied with deep feeling in his voice: 'This tree is in the middle of the garden, and we call it the tree of our heaven; some call it the tree of life. But go on closer and

Fig. 31. The summer house, now in the Skansen Museum Park in Stockholm, is the only building preserved from Swedenborg's estate. In a small wing connected to this pavilion Swedenborg kept his books.

your eyes will be opened and you will see the garden'. They did so, and their eyes were opened, and they saw trees laden with tasty fruits [...]

These trees were planted in an unbroken row, extending outward and running in constant circles or rings, like a never-ending spiral. It was a perfect spiral of trees, in which one species followed another arranged in order of the nobility of their fruits. There was a considerable gap between the beginning of the spiral and the tree in the middle, and this gap sparkled with gleams of light [...] The first trees were the most outstanding of all, luxuriant [...] These were followed by trees that yield oil, and these by trees that yield wine. After this came trees with a fragrant scent, and finally trees with wood useful for making things. Here and there in the spiral or ring of trees were seats shaped out of tree-shoots, brought and woven together from behind [...] There were gates in this unbroken circle of trees, leading to flower gardens, and these leading to lawns, divided into plots and beds. When the angel's companions saw these they cried: 'Here is heaven made visible!'[5]

Does Swedenborg's description of this garden in heaven perhaps better illustrate the plan of his own garden in Stockholm than the sketch made by Henrik Alm? In that case the central pavilion, with its wide outlook, may have been conceived as equivalent to the 'point' that Swedenborg, in his *Principia,* defined as the origin of the universe. From this point, divine power and motion had gone out, always in the most perfect of forms, the spiral.

The heavenly spiral was endless. The blessed in paradise could discern neither its limits nor its end. On the northern side of Swedenborg's garden there was a building with a false door that gave visitors great delight, wrote Carl Robsahm:

> [. . .] when this was opened, another one appeared with a window in it; and as both these doors were directly opposite a green hedge where a beautiful bird cage was placed, and as the window in the inner door was made of a mirror, the effect was most charming and surprising [. . .].[6]

Behind the door there was yet another garden, Swedenborg explained to his visitors. It was the most beautiful of all.

Carl Robsahm was a neighbour of Swedenborg. His *Anteckningar om Swedenborg (Notes on Swedenborg)* are based on recollections of visits to him during the 1760s. His account was dated 29 March 1782.

Departure and the Great Work

Chapter Twenty

> For Mercy, Pity, Peace, and Love
> Is God, our Father dear,
> And Mercy, Pity Peace, and Love
> Is Man, his child and care.
> For Mercy has a human heart,
> Pity a human face,
> And Love, the human form divine,
> And Peace, the human dress.

> William Blake: 'The Divine Image' in *Songs of Innocence*

Resignation from the Board of Mines

Swedenborg resumed his work at the Board of Mines on 19 August 1745. He had made a note about his new, double role already in his *Dream Diary*. No one noticed anything: outwardly he was the same civil servant as before; no one could realize that inwardly he stood at the threshold of a new, radically different task. According to a note made at the time, he could sometimes be in conversation with acquaintances in Stockholm and with angels in heaven simultaneously:

> While I spoke with spirits I was together with friends and others in my own land [. . .] I associated with others as before, and no one noticed that I was also communicating with this heavenly group [. . .] They could not believe other than that I was sunk in my own thoughts.[1]

This state lasted from the middle of April 1745 to January-February 1746, although during the journey home from London he had no heavenly visits, according to a note in *The Word Explained*.[2]

During the spring of 1747 a vacancy for a councillor had arisen on the Board of Mines.

The mining councillors were a rank above the assessors, the position that Swedenborg had held since his appointment in 1716. In a letter to the government the Board proposed that he should now be appointed to the vacant position.[3] If the matter were handled as intended, he would thus, after thirty-one years of service, have been promoted.

But Swedenborg demurred, declining the promotion. In a letter to the king he declared that he was obliged to conclude a work already begun. He therefore asked to be allowed to retire from his post as assessor, requesting that he be given a pension equivalent to half of his salary, 1,800 dalers a year. In the same letter he also applied for permission to leave

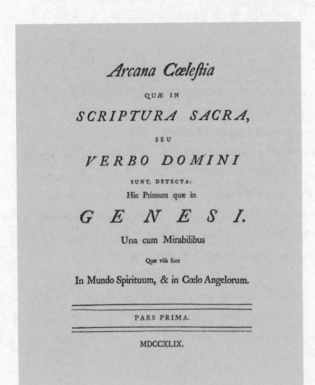

Fig. 32. The title page of *Arcana Coelestia*, published in London in 1749 by the printer John Lewis. The eight volumes, which appeared from 1749 to 1756, were printed without giving the author's name. Swedenborg maintained his anonymity until 1768 when he published *Conjugial Love*. There he presented himself as the author: 'Emanuel Swedenborg, a Swede.'

the country in order to complete the aforementioned work.[4] On 15 June he informed his colleagues that his resignation had been approved and that he had been granted the pension he had requested. The Board in plenary session took note of his retirement, expressing their 'regret at losing such a worthy colleague'.[5] On 17 July 1747, Swedenborg paid a parting visit to his old office on Mynttorget, and a week later he left Stockholm for Holland.

Arcana Caelestia

For nine years, from 1746-57, Swedenborg was absorbed in what he considered as his life's fundamental work, *Arcana Caelestia* (sometimes translated 'Heavenly Secrets'). The full title listed in the first volume gives an indication of its content:

> Arcana Caelestia that have been disclosed in the Sacred Scripture or the Word of the Lord, here first those in Genesis. Together with the marvels that have been seen in the world of spirits and in the heaven of angels.

The eight volumes of *Arcana Caelestia* contain the central ideas in Swedenborg's theosophy; most of his later books are reflections of this work. His name is not given on the title page, as can be seen opposite.

The first Latin edition of *Arcana Caelestia*, filling eight volumes in large octavo format, was printed in London in small quantities from 1749 to 1756. The subject was the inner meaning of Genesis and Exodus, a secret that according to the author had been hidden until this time. The man who rightly understands these two books of the Bible, the Gospels, and the Book of Revelation is, in Swedenborg's view, not simply well-versed in the Bible; such a reader might also have been changed and elevated above the perspective of his earthly existence.

The content of Swedenborg's message, expressed in straightforward but long Latin sentences, was probably not easy to grasp in the author's lifetime. For the reader today the difficulty has increased. The biblical texts and references are not known to the same extent as 250 years ago. In Swedenborg's day everybody was baptized and raised in the Christian faith and, in Sweden, required by law to go to church on Sunday. All citizens knew the chief thoughts of Christian faith; men and women were versed in the Bible, and the words and events of both Testaments were present in daily life. In the Sunday services the sermons, with explanations of the content of the true faith, were a dominant element;

and the truth of Protestant doctrine was, in Sweden, often placed against its opposite, the alleged falsity of the Church of Rome.

Fig. 33. Primarily Swedenborg used two editions of the Latin Bible translation made by Sebastian Schmidius: the version published in 1696 in Strasbourg, and another with the Hebrew text and the Latin translation in parallel columns, published in 1740 in Leipzig. The first page of Genesis in the former version, with Swedenborg's annotations, is reproduced here.

The names and stories of the biblical world were thus constantly present, as on the wall paintings in 'Sveden', the parental home of Jesper Swedberg in Dalecarlia. Large murals in the banquet room depicted King David's adultery with Bathsheba, and his sending of her husband Uriah to die in war. The viewer needed no explanations. Now, for most people, the paintings are unintelligible. We do not know the text that lies behind them.

Creation as regeneration

The creation narrative was a recurring subject of discussion in Swedenborg's time. How could a modern, Christian man, constantly faced with new astronomical, physical, and geological facts, believe that the earth was created in six days? Newton and many others made attempts to unite faith and knowledge. Swedenborg cut the Gordian knot with the same axe-blow used by pietistic authors of his time: the narrative of creation did not treat of the forming of the earth, but of man's regeneration.

The six days corresponded to the same number of spiritual states on the way to life with God which results from receptivity to the divine love. In Lutheran theology this spiritual progress was spoken of as the 'order of grace'; in Catholic quarters the stages were described in terms of 'stations' or 'rooms'. Here, in *Arcana Caelestia*, as in all of Swedenborg's theological texts, the Latin term *status spiritualis* (spiritual state) is an essential concept in regard to human qualities and insight. Our experiences, feelings, and actions are affected by our spiritual state of mind.

For Swedenborg the introductory words about God's creation of heaven and earth became a description of man's initial condition. He was created as a vessel for heavenly and earthly influences. In the biblical text God's spirit hovered over the waters, just as the spirit hovers over man from the moment of his birth. 'The earth was without form and void; and darkness was on the face of the deep': according to Swedenborg these words do not describe an historical event, but the void, the darkness of the state of earthly life, before the new birth. But the divine mercy is always present.

Swedenborg liked to think in terms of sharply marked opposites. The void and darkness were an image of man, irrational and ignorant, directed by his earthly desires and his immersion in their pleasures. But above him God's spirit hovered, a picture of the divine mercy, animating vague notions of difference between good and evil that slumbered on the surface of the waters. When an awareness of these opposites is awakened, a conflict between the evil and good in man begins. If the good is to come forth, its opposition must be cleared away in a process called *vastatio* (laying waste). The old man must die and make place for the new.

This is what is meant by the initial stage of creation, where the battle between good and evil begins. On the *first* day God brought light to the world, and light was separated from darkness. In the process of man's spiritual creation this means a new insight; the good now appears as something higher; and the loves that have dominated him up to this point are to be rejected completely. He understands that the true light is to be found in God. This is the prerequisite for the long process in which he now finds himself involved.

The first day is concluded with the words about evening and morning, recurring through the week of creation: 'and the evening and the morning were the first day'. Swedenborg consistently gives these periods of the day a particular meaning; the dusk of evening is the obscure state that prevails before light, whereas the morning always stands for freshness and clarity, the state when vivifying faith is alive.

The *second* day was characterized by the creation of the firmament. This indicated that man's realization of the difference between good and evil had become definite. He has reached an understanding of his dual nature: he consists of an outer man——the earth——where knowledge comes by way of his earthly senses; and at the same time he has an inner self——the firmament——with an awareness of and insight into the existence of divine good and truth. The waters under the firmament are the knowledge belonging to the old, outer man, while the waters above this canopy are the inner concepts of the new man, now being born.

'And God called the firmament heaven.' Seeking knowledge and comprehension throughout his life, Swedenborg sees the creation of the firmament as a divine act that both separates and unites. Earthly knowledge is bent to heavenly wisdom; man often believes that this knowing comes as a result of his own efforts; but it is through heavenly leading that his efforts for clarity progress from the darkness of evening to the morning light.

During the *third* day of the process an important change occurs on the way towards the repose given on the seventh day. On God's command the waters under heaven will now be gathered to one place 'so that the dry land may appear'. The seeker understands that the higher, God-given knowledge about truth and good reaches him from the inner man. There is now a readiness to receive higher insights that root themselves in man and then grow. It is this increasing knowledge that is described by the coming into being of the vegetable kingdom: 'the earth brought forth grass, the herb that yields seed [. . .], and the tree that yields fruit, whose seed is in itself'.

But a man who is in process of being born anew believes that the seed and growth arise from himself: consequently his life is dominated by the outer side. However, there is now a receptivity to the state in which life and faith are made one.

During the *fourth* day two great lights were brought into the heavens, one for day and one for night: the sun and the moon, and also the stars. For Swedenborg the celestial bodies represent love and faith; love is a sun that enlightens the moon and the stars of knowledge. Love and life, faith and works, can never be separated from each other as they are two sides of the same thing. This is one of Swedenborg's most central thoughts. In *Arcana Caelestia* the concept is given a magisterial formulation:

[…] those who have love have faith as well, and so heavenly life, whereas those who claim to have faith and yet have none of the life inherent in love do not. The life of faith devoid of love is like sunlight devoid of warmth, as is the case in wintertime when nothing grows and every single thing is inactive and dies off. But faith deriving from love is like the sunlight in springtime when everything grows and blossoms, for it is the warmth of the sun that brings it out.[6]

The *fourth* day represents a state where truth, together with loving action, leads to a continually new and increased understanding. We meet this paired relationship in almost every area that Swedenborg touches during his long life; it shows itself as passive and active forces in his theory of the creation of the universe. Wisdom and love flow through the world as cosmic powers, manifesting themselves most clearly in the love of a man and a woman in true marriage. He had written about this happy union before, in the *Dream Diary*:

There was a woman who had a very beautiful estate in which we walked about and whom I was going to marry. Was *pietas*, and moreover, I believe, *sapientia* [wisdom] which owned these possessions. And I was also with her, and loved her in the usual manner, which seemed to stand for the marriage proper.[7]

For Swedenborg, at this early stage, wisdom and love were already the fundamental elements in his view of faith and its subsequent psychology. Wisdom is seen, in the realm of knowledge, as understanding; and love, as will, carries it into practice. He explains this thought in sections 35 and 36 of *Arcana Caelestia*:

Man has two inherent powers, will and understanding. When the understanding is governed by the will they then constitute one mind and so one life; for what a person in that case wills and does he also thinks and intends. But when the understanding is at variance with the will, as it is with people who claim to have faith and yet live otherwise, then a mind previously one is split in two. One half seeks to transport itself into heaven, while the other inclines towards hell. And because the will is what accomplishes everything, the whole man would rush straight into hell unless the Lord took pity on him. People who have separated faith from love do not even know what faith is […] But faith involves not only knowledge of all the things that the doctrine of faith embraces and the acknowledgment of them; it is first and foremost obedience to everything that doctrine teaches. The primary point that it teaches for men's obedience is love of the Lord and love of the neighbour.

During the *fifth* day everything is seen in the new light that is now present in the inner man. Earlier he had attributed all goodness and truth to himself. Now, when the great lights have been lit, his real life begins. The inner man dominates the outer; he no longer has himself as the centre, being in the state where everything is directed to divine purposes. The biblical text speaks of the creation of fish and birds, commanded to be fruitful and multiply. God-given knowledge is endless; one thing known leads to another by inner, hidden connections.

We come to the *sixth* day. Here, according to the Bible, man is created in the image of God. In the ongoing, continuous transformation of the 'old man', the sixth state involves a 'connection with the world of spirits, and through angels with heaven'. The influences of evil, for Swedenborg 'demons' or 'evil spirits', no longer hinder man from placing himself under the leadership of the angels. He can never become a part of the Divine; but on the level of human existence, he is now in harmony with God; he is a 'spiritual' human being. In the outer, he sees the inner. It is precisely this earthly-based aspect of this connection that results in the fact that in the state of the *sixth* day, according to Swedenborg's exposition, man has not yet attained the highest, heavenly level.

'Male and female he created them.' They were blessed by God with the command to be fruitful and fill the earth. As we have already seen, man and woman represent understanding and will, wisdom and love. A third interpretation of the same duality is truth and good. For the spiritual man the union of these two powers is a 'marriage' in which new insights are constantly born. Swedenborg illustrates this thought with the parable of the mustard seed in the Gospel of Matthew. From every one of its seeds a tree grows, larger than all herbs, 'so that the birds of the air come and nest in its branches'.

When the darkness at the start of the *sixth* day is dispersed and morning breaks in, love to God is the dominating force in man. The regenerated spiritual man steps forth; faith has been united with love. 'Then God saw everything that he had made, and indeed, it was very good.'

The interpretation of the Creation narrative is thus far from the literal meaning of the words. Swedenborg had rendered the inner meaning as 'the angels perceive the Word'.[8]

Rest in God

On the *seventh* day God completed his work. The last stage and state is the vision of rest in God. It is a calm that now, in the second chapter of Genesis, is described by 'rain' or 'mist', where the outer man is refreshed by the inner. The conflict is over. The quiet and tranquil repose is like the peace of the Sabbath:

> None but the person who is acquainted with the state of peace is capable of knowing about the serenity of the peace of the external man, which ensues when conflict, the unrest caused by evil desires and by falsities, comes to an end. That state is so joyful that it transcends every idea of joy. It is not just an end of conflict; it is also life coming from an inward peace, influencing the external man in a way that defies description.[9]

This account evidently reflects Swedenborg's own experiences of passing through different, successive states. He often emphasized that in no way was his schema meant as a report of a path leading to a definitive peace and happiness. Regeneration is a continuous process: 'a person's regeneration has a beginning but never ceases; he is continually being made more perfect not only while he lives in the world but also in the next life for evermore'.[10]

Arcana Caelestia and the new man

'Being born again' was, according to the third chapter of the Gospel of John, a condition for man's seeing the kingdom of God. During the 1600s and 1700s this requirement for a new birth was often invoked by believers who were reacting against a petrified Christianity and the tendency to identify the Church with the society and the state; I refer to pietists of various kinds, Methodists, Moravians, English 'Antinomians', and many others.

The concept of this renewal runs like a golden thread through all eight volumes of *Arcana Caelestia*. At one level of Swedenborg's reading of Genesis, Adam and Eve became representatives of a lost civilization. There, man was characterized by a life totally turned to God and by a constant connection with his Creator, but he had instead turned himself towards the earthly world; this is the meaning of the Fall. Yet, as known, the Fall was not conclusive; the head of the serpent would one day be crushed by Adam and Eve's descendant.

The purified and renewed man would thus be able to regain the lost innocence and knowledge of a life led in the presence of God. For Swedenborg this purification from sin came to be the heart of the Gospels' accounts of the life of Christ. The three years covered by the testimony of the four evangelists treated of his victories in earthly temptations. His death on the cross was the final triumph, and his immediate apotheosis and resurrection its natural consequence. Swedenborg's *Arcana Caelestia* consists of a reading of the Bible through which this victorious strife runs as the inner thought, underlying the outer course of events.

For Swedenborg, in the final analysis, the knowledge of divine, higher things was inexpressible: language was inadequate. The only way to attain such insights was through analogies which, by divine grace, the reverent reader of the Bible could perceive. Christ's life was a paradigm for the gradual renewal of man, striving towards God. The Bible's theme is creation, the coming into being of the new man. The word *genesis* means precisely 'birth', 'coming into being'. As a regenerating being, man is on the way back to the original, paradisal state with its life totally turned to God. Every man and woman who in love and action turn themselves to the Divine will find God as in an interior mirror, in themselves. For Swedenborg, God is with each and every human being, but our grasping of his presence and its implications depends on our will.

The Divine Human

An ordinary person, an intensively believing Christian, a prophet, or a mystic can gain the conviction that he has understood God's purpose for our existence. Then everything changes; the language of religion receives a new meaning, the statements of faith a new content. The text receives overtones, echoes, that can be heard only by the divinely initiated and privileged. He becomes one of an endless line of poets and mystics whose experiences and visions are coloured by their longing. They find what they seek——in a flower and in the sun, wrote the Swedish poet Erik Johan Stagnelius, 'in the breath of the roses, in the breeze of the spring'.

In German circles of radical pietism the words of Genesis about man as 'the image of God' had been applied to Christ, who was seen as a second, spiritual Adam.[11] They were following Paul's line of thought in the First Letter to the Corinthians: 'The first man Adam became a living being. The last Adam became a life-giving spirit'.[12] For Jacob Boehme and Gottfried Arnold and his friends, the figure of Christ stood forth as at the same time divine and human, wrestling against the human element in his own nature, to be finally victorious and glorified. This German interpretation is mentioned as a reminder that Swedenborg's vision of Christ had a correspondence on the European continent.

For Swedenborg, Jesus's life in the mirror of the Gospels took the form of a divine lesson. Every detail in the biblical descriptions had to do first and foremost with Christ's own liberation from captivity in a materialistically dominated existence. This is the pattern that Swedenborg found in the biblical text, governing his interpretation. 'Secrets of heaven' were disclosed through this magnifying glass, and the correspondences between innumerable statements and events in the Old and New Testaments appeared. The biblical words became a string of pearls of *dicta probantia* (scripture confirmations) or affirmations of what, by divine grace, he already felt he knew.

Man in the mirror of the Word

The purpose of Swedenborg's detailed commentary on Genesis and Exodus was thus to show how the gradual development of the Divine in Jesus, the human being from Nazareth, is foreseen and elucidated in the Old Testament. However, the text was also applicable to the ordinary human being: Christ showed the way. The books' accounts, from Abraham onwards, were in themselves historically true, but essentially these and the earlier sections were descriptive models. The story of Cain and Abel treats of man's heavenly love; Cain represents rational but dead faith, Abel the love that gives birth to good works. When formalistic faith dominates, genuine love dies. The Flood and Noah's rescue was in actual fact a legend about how proper love and doctrine carry man through the midst of a flood of evil. And the chapter on the tower of Babel treated of misled people who wanted to build their life solely on the basis of their own rationality, a temptation that Swedenborg, like all other human beings, had to overcome.

The Book of Exodus describes the meaning of the new birth. The story of Moses in the bulrushes was an introductory summary of this interpretation. Man, open to the Divine, may have been sunk in spiritual darkness in the same way that the future prophet, as a child, was hidden in a basket of reeds, made watertight with tar. When the Lord approaches, everybody may, like Moses, be saved for a great future.

The flight from Egypt was a story of the soul's departure from sin and breaking free from captivity in barren rationality and blind trust in empirical knowledge. The goal was the land of Canaan, the promised kingdom of love. God intervenes through Moses, punishing, rewarding, explaining, always in accord with the individual's state of mind.

The Children of Israel's way is the path of all mankind. As in Bunyan's *The Pilgrim's Progress* man is constantly facing choices, always meeting temptations, and threatened by imprisonment in false ideas. Every event and stage corresponds to a state of the soul that is characterized by our relationship to God; it is a continuous process of purification and moving towards regeneration.

In the same way the accounts in the Gospels have a dual meaning. They treat of Christ's glorification: how the Divine within him is victorious over his human characteristics. The places and regions which Jesus visited were symbols of different states of spiritual development, Bethlehem, Nazareth, Jordan, the wilderness, Galilee, Judea, the Mount of Olives, Jerusalem. Man's changes of state are also described in Christ's sermons, miracles, and crucifixion; the figures in the Bible are pictures of the readers themselves. We, the reader, are the Scribes and Pharisees, doubting Thomas, Peter who denied, Judas who betrayed. The life of Christ is repeated: the man on the path to regeneration is himself the blind who regained his vision, the lame who could walk, the dead who arose. The water that was changed to wine at the wedding in Cana is a symbol of the Christian's knowledge of truth that is transformed into spiritual wisdom, and so of the total change of life experienced by the man who tries to follow Christ.

'The whole of nature is a theatre representing the Lord's kingdom; and the Lord's kingdom, heaven and the church, is a theatre representing the Lord Himself', Swedenborg wrote in the 1760s in the posthumously-published study, *The Word of the Lord from Experience*.[13]

The one God

God was the source of all truth. How should man, using his reason, comprehend this divinity? Swedenborg, like all other Swedes, was acquainted with the short summary in the Apostles' Creed:

> I believe in God, the Father almighty, creator of heaven and earth.
>
> I believe in Jesus Christ, his only Son, our Lord. He was conceived by the power of the Holy Spirit and born of the virgin, Mary. He suffered under Pontius Pilate, was crucified, died, and was buried. He descended to the dead. On the third day he rose again. He ascended into heaven, and is seated at the right hand of the Father. He will come again to judge the living and the dead.
>
> I believe in the Holy Spirit, the holy catholic Church, the communion of saints, the forgiveness of sins, the resurrection of the body, and the life everlasting.

There was another confession of faith, the Nicene Creed, from the year 325. Here the Son is described in a somewhat different way:

> We believe in one Lord, Jesus Christ, the only Son of God, eternally begotten of the Father, God from God, Light from Light, true God from true God, begotten, not made, of one Being with the Father. Through him all things were made. For us men and for our salvation he came down from heaven; by the power of the Holy Spirit he became incarnate of the Virgin Mary, and was made man.[14]

In *Arcana Caelestia* Swedenborg earnestly warns against a faith in God that sees the

Trinity as *three separate persons*. This was the great danger in the officially-approved confessions of faith: the Christian could scarcely avoid imagining the Trinity as other than three gods. From this follows the doctrine of atonement, where the wrath of the Father is appeased by Christ on the cross, taking on himself the punishment for mankind's trespasses. Swedenborg's polemic against this view of the Trinity would be repeated in all the works he would publish later. The three-headed God was rationally absurd; God was *Dominus*, the Lord. He was the Creator, unknowable because above all human thought, the Preserver of all things. To be seen and understood by man he took on human form in Christ. The Holy Spirit was his power, love, truth, ever present in creation and in the Word, the presence that Swedenborg calls *influx*, inflow.

The concept of God in human form and Swedenborg's emphasis on our ability to live in 'imitation of Christ' led to the purpose of Christ's appearing on earth, a subject that we often meet in his writings, both before and after the 1744-5 crisis. Humankind once lived in paradise, in the presence of God. But experience of the material world's allurements led to sin and the Fall. By God's coming into the world in Christ the way was again opened to paradise.

The Trinity was given a special significance by Swedenborg in *Arcana Caelestia*. God is one, but in this unity a hidden meaning could be distinguished. Firstly there was a purpose or goal, secondly a formative cause, and thirdly an effect. In other words, God was the creator, Christ the materialized Word, and the Holy Spirit the love referred to by Swedenborg as the inflowing Divine.

The divine plan

For years Emanuel Swedenborg had worked with the question of the origin of the universe and the Creator's connection with what he had created. From the moment of the crisis, however, he changed his subject. His question no longer was one of *origin*, but what we today would call the *programme*. God had a plan for his creation. It involved the realization of God's kingdom, on earth and in heaven, a goal that could be achieved by every man. He often quotes the famous proclamation from the Gospel of Luke:

Now when He was asked by the Pharisees when the kingdom of God would come, He answered

——

them and said, "The kingdom of God does not come with observation; nor will they say, 'See here!' or 'See there!' For indeed, the kingdom of God is within you." [15]

The heavenly man could come into being, live, and be active already during earthly life. After death he remained what he had been. God's plan was for all good-willed people to be gathered into a supernatural unity whose magnitude and force would gradually become irresistible, and through its influence would transform the earth and restore the lost paradise. Thus the purpose of creation was a heaven from the human race, but this divine work was far from being finished.

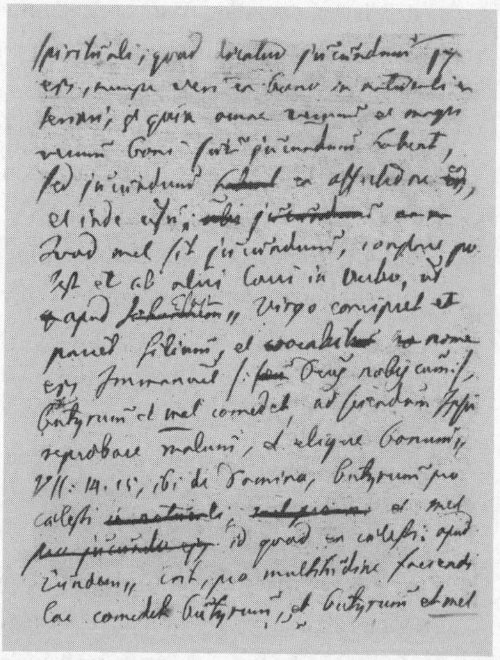

Fig. 34. Detail of *Arcana Caelestia* manuscript.

The Grand Man and anamorphosis

The Pauline concept of 'the body of Christ' often recurs in *Arcana Caelestia*. In this body, according to the apostle, we are all members, each and every one according to his ability: we have the possibility of ascending into this heavenly figure, to our own joy and God's pleasure. For Swedenborg, every man who had tried to follow Christ during his life became, after death, a part of the celestial human structure, not in God, but seen by him. The blessed souls took their abode in *Maximus Homo*, the Greatest or Grand Man. And this heavenly man is heaven itself, the paradise.

To explain the relationship between the parts and the whole Swedenborg referred, several times, to an optical term, *anamorphosis*. The word means 'changed shape'. Anamorphosis was a part of the teaching about perspective and came to be used both as a model for thought and as a method in art. The philosopher Christian Wolff, who often appears in Swedenborg's earlier writings, explains the concept in a book that Swedenborg owned.[16] It was a question of an 'optical miracle'. Disparate fragments spread around a cylindrical or pyramid-shaped mirror and reflected into it formed, when seen from a given point, an integrated picture, in which each separate element took its proper place. The unrecognizable entities seem to fly up to the blank mirror surface, finding their right context. The great French prelate Jacques Bénigne Bossuet used the image in the mirror as a warning to those who denied God. 'Stop, unfortunate soul! If you only find the point from which you should direct your glance, all irregularities will be set right, and you will find wisdom where you had only seen confusion and disorder.'[17]

Around the mirror Swedenborg thought he saw the souls of mankind, each in the form of the love that was dominant during its earthly life. If this love was of a divine character, all the spiritual figures together formed a distinguishable structure in the cylindrical mirror. A large human form stood out. Swedenborg describes the way things are in *Arcana Caelestia*:

The appearance that the Word of the Lord takes on as it is seen by the angels defies description; yet some idea of it may be had by those who have seen in places where curiosities are housed those optical cylinders in which beautiful images are produced from projected components that seemingly lie around without order. But although these components which lie around one another appear to have no form, sequence, or order, and appear to be wholly shapeless projections, yet when they are all directed towards the cylinder they produce a lovely image there. So it is with the Word of the Lord, especially in the prophetical part of the Old Testament.

[...It] is presented before the Lord as the image of a human being in which and by means of which heaven is represented in its entirety, not as it is in fact but as the Lord would like it to be, that is, a likeness of Himself.[18]

In *Arcana Caelestia* as well as in his subsequent works Swedenborg often speaks of the 'Grand Man', a concept which should be understood in the same way as the figure in the mirror. It is scarcely a question of a concrete, giant human figure, but that of an abstract or universal man or maiden: the figure of Christ, or perhaps the Virgin of Wisdom, Sophia. With the expression 'Grand Man' he attempts to communicate a concept of mankind's tasks, its collective possibilities. No human being is quite like another; with the right love, everybody can, in his particular manner, contribute to the perfect divine order.

In the same way, he sees the countless expressions of evil collected into a gigantic monster. This too is a didactic picture: an attempt to reproduce the totality of evil.

Heavenly anatomy

Swedenborg had devoted himself to anatomical studies in Holland, France, and Italy. When he now wanted to give expression to the Divine Human's infinitely numerous facets, it was natural for him to attempt to summarize its characteristics in terms of human anatomy. His point of departure was an analysis of the human body from the sole of the foot to the hair of the head to find every part's function in the whole, or, to employ Swedenborg's language, its use.

Like many others in his century, the anatomically skilled theosopher had an inclination to classify and label whatever he experienced. The souls were angelic figures, populating the Grand Man, and hierarchically ordered into three groups: *heavenly*, *spiritual*, and *natural*. Here too the spiritual state is the criterion. The heavenly individuals have let their earthly life be governed by love for God's goodness, the spiritual by their love of wisdom, and the natural by their faithfulness to the literal meaning of the Word. According to the nature of their love, the heavenly and spiritual angels found their way to different regions in the heart and lungs, the heart being the centre of love, and the lungs the domain of wisdom. Other blessed souls found the function where they fitted in best.

It would take too long to give a detailed account of Swedenborg's concept of the anatomy of heaven. Its interest for us lies not so much in the many parallels between things of the body and those of the spirit, but in his desire to assert the significance of the 'Divine Human' in all contexts. He opposed all forms of absolute idealism; God could never be reduced to an idea, to a concept. He can only be conceived of as a spiritual figure, a 'being'. We can never know him, but he has unveiled himself in the Word, becoming flesh through Jesus Christ. Through life and death Christ revealed himself as both man and God; and in such a way man is able to discover him in himself.

According to Swedenborg's logic, evil and good are always a matter of either/or. In his earthly existence man may be attracted to both evil and good, but the mixture is dangerous: the tearing apart leads to disintegration and the destruction of the image of God in man. But there is always one dominating love in our life, even if we are not aware of it. After death, when we have left our earthly body, that love appears clearly, giving form to our soul. In heaven or its opposite there is no place for split personalities. On this point Swedenborg is emphatic: 'I know with certainty that this is the case'.

Heaven and hell

It *was* possible for man to be free of the burden that had weighed since the Fall. With time, through a new birth, he could *become himself*. He could open closed locks, pass through closed portals, visit new regions never seen on earth. In eternally sunlit landscapes he could find the dwellings of the blessed, living in palaces which were symbols of their wisdom, and wisdom itself was an invitation to go further towards new and higher insights. Their houses lay like clusters of sparkling stars, diamonds, and emeralds, in what seemed like endless, shimmering configurations.

But man could also opt for the promise of happiness held out by his materiality, though it would always be mixed with despair. Here the satisfying of the cravings of the senses was in the centre. In the beginning the joy felt in this gratification was experienced as something ineffable, dizzyingly intense; but it was always followed by an anxiety that was proportionate to the jubilant experience, an anguish that with time passed into agony, and these pains drew man into new pleasures. Gradually he became conscious of his captivity. The violence of the conflict between short-lived satisfaction and new allurements led to a total yielding to blind forces. Life became a self-chosen suffering.

Divine joy

How is God experienced? As light and joy, Swedenborg had written in the *Dream Diary*: a 'heavenly joy here on the earth'. In May 1744 he wrote:

> Yet the internal joy was so strongly awakened, particularly when I was alone, without company, in mornings, evenings, days, that it may be compared to a heavenly joy here on the earth. This I hope to retain as long as, by the grace of our Lord alone, I walk in the pure path and have the right intention; for, if I turn aside to seek my pleasure in worldly things, it vanishes. God knows best whether the internal principle, which is the influx of God's spirit, is there [. . .] I thought that, since I have this heavenly joy, why should I seek for worldly pleasure, which by comparison is nothing, is inconstant, hurtful, opposing, and destructive to the former.[19]

Later Swedenborg would be more precise. God is the source of the collective body of knowledge that the Word communicates to the believing person. The truths of faith could be seen as the face of God in a mirror.[20]

In *Arcana Caelestia* we read of the divine peace and joy that man, resting in God, may enjoy. Swedenborg also often mentions an intense divine light, being at the same time good and truth, or love and wisdom. But perhaps the joy, often described, is the essential characteristic: a happiness steadily and gradually increasing—the closer to the Divine, the greater it becomes. It is our 'affections' that carry this happiness, he notes: a joy so great that some fall into unconsciousness.[21]

One of the most penetrating readers of Swedenborg, the Swedish poet and essayist Vilhelm Ekelund, wrote about the development of Swedenborg's character and the nature of his 'need for happiness'. From his childhood into his old age he saw himself as 'gripped in the drama of the struggle against selfishness and its blinkers', continuing this strife to his last day:

> The uniquely personal nature and tone of Swedenborg's impartiality and magnanimity may appear enigmatic. But as regards his happiness, I experience something extraordinary. A mysteriously powerful sunny warmth is ever the deepest characteristic of the works of truly

great men, a radiation of power from their inner happiness; anyone who has had inner experiences cannot mistake this element in Swedenborg. [22]

Alchemy in the Board of Mines

Swedenborg analysed the meaning of the first two books of the Bible, Genesis and Exodus, sentence by sentence, word by word, wanting to explain how man belonged to God, to demonstrate his proper conduct and correct state of mind. The 'proof' of the truth of his exegesis is that it has been revealed through inner vision and audition, beyond the deceptive sphere of the senses, in the state of mind when man is himself transported to the state of his own inner experience.

Fig. 35. William Blake's picture of the sun, the cocoon, and the butterfly is taken from *For the Sexes: The Gates of Paradise.*
'What is man! / The Sun's Light when he unfolds it / Depends on the Organ that beholds it.
The Pierpont Morgan Library, New York.
PML 63936.

It has sometimes been said that Swedenborg's doctrine is a kind of spiritual alchemy, where the divine fire in the body's decrepit shell corresponds to the burning oven of the gold-maker. As an expert in mining science Swedenborg was a strong opponent of the old legendary art of alchemy, still attempted in the eighteenth century. Metals could be purified, but their essence could never be changed, he wrote. The same thing applied to man, as we have seen.

In his youth the question of the purification and making of gold had been discussed in his own Board, where the President of the Board, Count Gustav Bonde, was an eager alchemist who saw his own body as the true oven, in which the stomach was the appropriate receptacle. After much purification and with the proper golden food, man should literally be able to make gold in himself, Bonde believed.

The clairvoyant Assessor

Chapter Twenty-One

Thoughts and tremulations

According to Christopher Polhem, human thought consists of 'tremulations'. In 1717 Swedenborg published an article in *Daedalus Hyperboreus*, in which he developed his master's idea. Thought was made up of wave motions, a kind of radiation. The theory of tremulation seemed to explain telepathic phenomena, he noted:

> It often happens that one person comes to think about another, and that he then knows what the other is doing and thinking. This [involves the fact that] his membranes are vibrating from the motions in membranes in the other person's brain, in the same way that one string [on a musical instrument] affects another when they are both tuned to the same note. [1]

In a letter to Eric Benzelius dated 3 November 1719 he explained that he had prepared an expanded version of the article, and that his thesis was based on thorough studies of anatomical works. [2] Two days before, he had delivered the new version to the Royal Board of Medicine for their consideration. It was entitled *Anatomi af wår Aldrafinaste Natur, wisande att wårt rörande och lefwande wäsende består af Contremiscentier (Proof that our innermost being consists for the most part of small vibrations, that is, of tremulations*), and in chapter one we read the following:

> Life consists of motion, rest has no part in life [. . .] Vibration is the finest form of movement in nature [. . . it] runs through the membranes and nerves with the speed of lightning. In so doing it produces waves from one end to the other. In a single moment the vibration affects the whole region involved, as for example the vibrations in water or in the atmosphere.

Later, in different contexts, he developed the theme.[3]

Swedenborg's concept of the 'materiality' of thought became one of the starting points for modern parapsychology. According to the Swedish historian of religion Efraim Briem, it could explain telepathy and clairvoyance, as well as otherwise incomprehensible auditory experiences.[4] Present-day parapsychologists have applied the tremulation theory to Swedenborg's own experiences from the spiritual world. When he reported on the ability of the highest angels to communicate without words, was this not a telepathy that took place through vibrations?

During his theosophical period Swedenborg avoided all physical explanations of his spiritual experiences. For him the angels were embodied loves to which his own love carried him. It was a meeting of two spiritual states.

Occult capacity?

It was inevitable that a man like Swedenborg gradually obtained a reputation for possessing occult power. Many were also of the opinion that he was able to discern events occurring hundreds of miles away. He recorded conversations with the spirits of the dead: could he not then convey greetings and ask for information on secrets that the dead had taken with them to the grave? Rumours of his gifts spread across Europe, notwithstanding his clear desire to maintain his anonymity. This alleged ability stirred the interest of Immanuel Kant. The Enlightenment's conviction of the power of human reason in no way excluded a warm interest in what we often call superstition. And after Swedenborg's death the interest in premonitions, signs, predictions, and mysterious interventions, and secret, supernatural knowledge, flowered, not least in his own homeland.

Swedenborg himself was ambivalent regarding supernatural miracles, saying that when we read about them in the Bible we should see them as images of higher truths. 'Miracles do not occur in our days', he wrote to the German priest and theosopher Friedrich Christoph Oetinger. Man's will is free. Miracles would 'be outwardly compelling, without convincing the inner man'. There may possibly be 'signs', he continued. 'These will then serve to illustrate [...] that the truths of the New Church have been accepted.'[5] The fact that he himself had been given the ability to associate with angels, spirits, and demons was quite another matter. This was a natural phenomenon. Everyone who turned to God with the same intensity and love should be able to have the same gift, if God approved.

His own accounts of 'what he had heard and seen' in the invisible world were thus not miracles, 'only' testimonies regarding his conversations with angels and spirits. But he strongly emphasized that the insights he received regarding the innermost meaning of the biblical texts never came from spirits and angels. He was not a medium who was informed through deceased men and women regarding otherwise hidden matters. The source of the knowledge that he enjoyed was the Lord, and no one else. The supernatural souls were simply lines of communication.

In the vast literature on Swedenborg one might speak of three 'extraordinary occurrences' of an asserted occult nature. The first had to do with his vision in 1759 in Gothenburg of a fire on Södermalm in the south of Stockholm. The second concerned the disclosure of the content of a secret letter from Prince August Wilhelm of Prussia to his sister, the Swedish Queen Louisa Ulrika. This episode too can presumably be dated to the year 1759. The assistance that Swedenborg gave to the widow of the Dutch ambassador in finding a lost receipt is the often-described third occurrence.

The fire in Stockholm

Accounts of these three instances exist in several different versions. Regarding the first, the fire in Stockholm, the testimonies are almost identical. Even the critical physician Emil Kleen seems to have accepted the story, suggesting that it could 'possibly be something other than a myth'.[6]

The philosopher Immanuel Kant described what had happened in a letter to a Fräulein Charlotte von Knoblock. The letter is no longer extant but is thought to have been written in 1763.[7] Kant stated that he had gained his information from an English friend whom he had encouraged to visit Stockholm for the purpose of discovering what actually lay behind the 'extraordinary occurrences'. Swedenborg's 'vision' occurred on 19 July 1759. I here reproduce Kant's description of what happened:

> In the year 1759, towards the end of September [sic], on a Saturday, at four o'clock p.m., Swedenborg arrived at Gothenburg from England. Mr William Castel invited him to his house, together with a party of fifteen persons. About six o'clock, Swedenborg left the room, returning to the company quite pale and alarmed. He said that a dangerous fire had just broken out in Stockholm, at Södermalm [. . .] The fire was spreading very fast, he said. He was restless, and went out often. He said that the house of one of his friends was already in ashes, and that his own was in danger. At eight o'clock, after he had been out again, he joyfully exclaimed, 'Thank God! The fire is extinguished, three doors from my house'.[8]

Swedenborg's vision soon became known in the city, located about 250 miles from Stockholm. Next morning Swedenborg was summoned to the governor and questioned about the disaster. He described the fire precisely, how it had begun and ended, and how long it had lasted. Many were troubled on account of their friends and property. The letter continues:

> On Tuesday morning a royal courier arrived at the governor's, with the sad news of the fire, of the loss which it had occasioned, and of the houses it had damaged and ruined. These accounts did not differ in the least from what Swedenborg had communicated [. . .] the fire was extinguished at eight o'clock.

The different versions of the incident, as recorded by R L Tafel, agree in their main points with Kant's account. Afterwards Swedenborg himself confirmed his vision to his friend Christopher Springer, living in London. Another Swede in London, Erik Bergström, also heard Swedenborg affirming the course of events.

It should be noted that Swedenborg's account of the Stockholm fire is of an order different from his recorded connections with the world of spirits. It seems to be a typical 'telepathic' phenomenon. The precise details that Swedenborg gave and his credibility testify to the truth of the account. In connection with this, Kleen recounts a similar vision in his own family. Is it a question of some kind of radiation? he wonders. Kleen doesn't know what to believe.[9]

And what shall we say, eighty years after Kleen? We see the angels and the demons we want to see, and Swedenborg's will was very strong, throughout his life. But could he follow the course of a fire from a distance of 250 miles?

The Queen's secret

The second incident regards a conversation with a deceased spirit about a certain question discussed in a letter during his lifetime.[10] Here we find ourselves in the company of the Swedish monarchy, the most closely involved being Queen Louisa Ulrika and her brother Prince August Wilhelm of Prussia who had died in 1758. There are a number of varying testimonies as to what actually happened. Swedenborg himself was reticent on the matter. In a conversation with Erik Bergström in London he stated that much of what had been reported was true, and much not so. 'The whole thing was perhaps best known in Berlin', he said.

Swedenborg's young friend Carl Robsahm takes up what happened in his *Notes on Swedenborg*.[11] His report contains the main constituents. When at the court Swedenborg was asked by Louisa Ulrika if he would contact her deceased brother in the spiritual world. Swedenborg was to ask him about the content of a letter between the siblings on a particular occasion. A few days later he visited the queen again, reporting what she had wanted to know. The queen was perturbed; no one could have had any knowledge about this except the two who were involved. It should be noted that the queen's contacts with her brother were made at a time when Sweden was at war with Prussia. Presumably the contents of the letter were of a delicate nature.

The account has been changed and provided with extra details by other contemporaries. In one version it did not involve an exchange of letters between the siblings. In another, Swedenborg appears as a henchman of the leading Hats. Two of the prominent members of that party had read the prince's letter containing his pessimistic reflections on the unsuccessful Swedish coup in 1756. They had therefore visited Swedenborg at night, asking him to reveal the prince's views on this to the queen in his forthcoming conversation with her. She was seen as the one who lay behind the unsuccessful revolt, and she might take such a message from Swedenborg as a warning from heaven against engineering a new coup. His strong sympathies for the constitution of 1720 were known to all.

The many pieces of differing information make it impossible to know with any certainty what actually happened. The queen herself was fully convinced of Swedenborg's ability to make contact with those who had died. 'Je ne suis pas facilement dupe', she stressed in this regard: 'I am not easily fooled'.

The lost receipt

The episode of the lost receipt was as well-known as Swedenborg's telepathic awareness of the fire in Stockholm.[12] The Dutch ambassador in Stockholm, de Marteville, died in 1760. After his death his widow was required to pay a large amount of money for a silver service that had been delivered to her late husband by a Swedish goldsmith. The deceased had always been meticulous in money matters. Madame de Marteville was consequently convinced that payment had been made, but she could not find the receipt. According to one version, she had heard about Swedenborg's ability to talk with the deceased and therefore requested him to ask her departed husband where he had put it. Swedenborg answered that he would return to her on the matter. Some time later he told the widow that the receipt was to be found in a secret compartment in a chest of drawers; he had learned this from the deceased ambassador. Madame de Marteville took note of the information about the receipt and found it.

This is the version afterwards given by de Marteville's secretary, and also confirmed by one of Swedenborg's acquaintances. According to other reports——there are ten of them ——Swedenborg's involvement lay entirely on the spiritual plane. He had met the deceased ambassador's spirit and told him his widow's troubles. The diplomat was then reported to have said that he intended to tell her where the receipt was hidden. According to Robsahm, Swedenborg expressly explained that Madame de Marteville herself had found the document without having spoken to him.

Madame de Marteville later married a Danish general. Fifteen years after her first husband's death she was asked in a letter what had actually happened. Since she was indisposed at the moment the general answered in her place, saying that several days after her husband's death Madame de Marteville and some other women visited Swedenborg in his home on Hornsgatan. Their purpose was simply to meet a well-known and remarkable man. They had been received in the second storey of the house in a beautiful room with a large window in the roof. The story about the lost receipt had not been touched upon during the visit. Eight days later the ambassador appeared to his widow in a dream. He pointed out an English writing box where she would find the missing document, as well as a lost piece of jewellery.

This happened at two in the morning, the general wrote. The widow had then risen and found what she was looking for. About eleven the following morning Swedenborg came to her house and asked to be received. Before having heard about the widow's dream and what she had found, he reported that during the night he had met different spirits, among them de Marteville. Swedenborg had wanted to talk with him, but was refused because he needed to visit his wife: he had something important to communicate to her.

Hidden miracles

The accounts of these three incidents could be supplemented with a series of anecdotes and recollections in which Swedenborg describes his meetings and conversations with the spirits of deceased and well-known people.

It is naturally no coincidence that so few 'supernatural' events appear in Swedenborg's biography. When we read the many and varying accounts of the episodes now described, we notice a certain reservation on the part of the spirit-seer himself, as if these occurrences were irrelevant from his perspective. Swedenborg's God did not interfere directly in earthly affairs: everything depended on man himself and on his openness to the inflow of heavenly love.

As we have already seen, no new miracles are done:

The reason why obvious divine miracles do not now take place has been revealed to me. It is because the inward things of faith, which we receive from the Lord, cannot be sown or implanted under compulsion, but only in freedom, thus not amid the anguish and amazement induced by miracles. The things that inflow under compulsion, as when man is influenced by miracles, are of such a nature that they affect a man's interiors and persuade him. But this does not happen in the proper sequence in time or in a proper order [...] [13]

And man's angels, spirits, and demons act only on the internal plane, as reinforcements to his own will and thought.

Mind-reading

Can all the accounts of Swedenborg's 'supernatural' power or knowledge be dismissed? His friend Christopher Springer would have criticised such categorical rejections. Springer lived in London as an expatriate. He had been politically active in Stockholm in his time, with ties to the Cap Party. Towards the end of the 1740s he had been indicted and sentenced to life imprisonment by a special commission of the Diet. The crime was his connections with the Russian ambassador in Stockholm. Using Russian money he had arranged for subsidies to members of the Diet who sympathized with the Caps and wanted to work for good relations with Russia. Besides, he stood as the leading spokesman for an idea with which most of the members of the Diet were uncomfortable: on important questions they should consult with those who had appointed them.

However, Springer succeeded in escaping from prison. He went to Russia and in time settled in London, where in the 1760s he functioned as an intermediary between the Caps and the English government. Here, to his amazement, he was embraced by Swedenborg's good will. He reported on the old man's remarkable characteristics:

All that he told me about my deceased friends and enemies and about the secrets I've had with them was almost unbelievable. He also reported to me the way in which peace was concluded between Sweden and the King of Prussia, and praised my conduct in this matter. He named the high-placed people upon whose services I had relied, despite the fact that this was a deep secret. When I asked him how he had obtained this information, he answered me with a question: 'Who has told me about your dealings with Count Ekeblad? You cannot deny that what I have told you is the truth'. [14]

Claes Ekeblad belonged to the Hats and was Prime Minister from 1761 to 1765. Ekeblad had attempted in vain to bribe Springer in an urgent matter. During a conversation with Springer, Swedenborg had not only stated the nature of the affair but also the exact amount that the Count had promised, 10,000 riksdalers. Swedenborg had heard this in 1771 from the then deceased Ekeblad himself. His revelation made a deep impression on Springer, who after Swedenborg's death often used to tell his friends the story of what happened.

As mentioned, Swedenborg can be regarded as having had sympathies for the policies of the Hats: he had very good friends in that party. Had he heard about the matter and much later remembered its details? Were the discussions with the immaterial figures in the world of the spirits projections of these memories? That Swedenborg would have consciously attempted to dupe Springer or the many others whom he told about his supernatural contacts is, in my opinion, scarcely conceivable.

Kant and Swedenborg

The reports that Kant received about Swedenborg's occult power prompted him to place an expensive order——seven pounds sterling——in London for the eight volumes of *Arcana Caelestia*. In 1766 he published a widely-known book about Swedenborg's *magnum opus*, which he entitled *Träume eines Geistersehrs* (*Dreams of a Spirit-Seer*). The whole work, Kant wrote, was a gigantic mental delusion. As such it was remarkable:

> For a coherent hallucination is a much more remarkable phenomenon than an illusion of the reason, the causes of which are well enough known. This kind of illusion can be prevented by an effort to guide the faculties of the mind. The former on the other hand, concerns the deepest foundation of all judgements, against which the rules of logic have little power [...] [15]

According to the Swedish historian of philosophy Rolf Ejvegård it was not the philosopher David Hume who awakened Kant from his familiar 'dogmatic slumber', but Emanuel Swedenborg. [16] Swedenborg's statements were inaccessible to scientific method, as with all statements regarding the 'thing in itself'. Reason and faith are two different things. Later in life, Swedenborg's inner world——by virtue of its 'ethical character' and logical consistency——would stand for Kant as an unprovable but consistent way of describing the indescribable.

Arcana Caelestia, the Fall and the Ages of Man

Chapter Twenty-Two

Biblical history: an account of man's decline

The leading representatives of the contemporary pietistic movement interpreted the events described in the Old Testament from the perspective of the Fall. Ever since Adam and Eve, man had successively distanced himself from God. He had been driven from paradise and punished with the Fall on account of his godless way of living. In spite of the promise to Abraham, 'the father of the faith', the faith of Israel had declined to a matter of form. Christ had come to earth in order to show, through his message and his example, the way back to man's original relationship with God; but his message was soon forgotten. Like Israel, the church of Rome laid an increasing emphasis on outer forms, while the importance of the intimate relationship with the Creator was neglected. The church became an instrument for the popes' lust for power. Luther and Calvin had wanted to re-establish the genuine faith, the faith that is close to God; but even the Protestant churches became stuck in dogma, outer forms, and desire for power. The Reformation had gone astray, wrote Gottfried Arnold. Before Luther and Calvin there had been *one* sect bringing destruction to faith; as a result of the Reformation there were now *three*.

Churches and spiritual states

Swedenborg's *Arcana Caelestia* can be read as an account of the unceasing changes of state which characterize the human mind. Like the radical pietists, he saw these changes as a progressive decline. Human beings could be grouped according to their spiritual states. He called these groupings 'churches'. The changes of spiritual conditions and their consequences became the history of the churches.

The description of this development appeared as the inner and heavenly text lying within the words of the Scriptures, but not in the Bible as a whole: in the Old Testament the inspired works included the Pentateuch, the Former and Latter Prophets, Psalms, Daniel, and Lamentations; in the New Testament the Gospels and the Book of Revelation. According to Swedenborg these were inspired by God, and thus holy. He did not regard the Letters by Paul as belonging to this group, although in his later years he often referred to them.

Adam and the seventh day

The second chapter of Genesis treats of the seventh day. The Garden of Eden and the creation of woman refer, according to Swedenborg, to the 'inner' story about the birth of the *spiritual man*. The words about God's rest on the seventh day refer to the Creator, but also to the first human beings, represented by Adam. Adam had been created in the image of God. He was a 'heavenly man', as close to the Divine as a human being could come. His love for God was absolute. His inner man, enlightened by the Lord, governed the outer, utterly and completely. His existence had become 'a life *above* the life of questions', to quote the Swedish writer C J L Almqvist in his *Törnrosens Bok* (*Book of the Briar Rose*).

As we have seen, the new birth was fundamental in pietistic preaching, in which Adam was the prototype of man born anew. Here we enter the realm of classic mysticism. The self, the earthly affections and distinctive features of personality, must be eradicated in order for man to be able to enter into *union* with God. Man feels himself transformed. Here are a few lines from the medieval *Theologia Germanica*:

> Every man inwardly enlightened in this way would be able to say, 'I wish I were united with the eternal good as the hand is a part of the body'.

The first, most ancient church

Adam was a biblical symbol for a group of human beings long since disappeared, says *Arcana Caelestia*. Swedenborg called them the *Most Ancient Church*. God had blown the breath of life into Adam's nostrils. The breathing of the first man was such that he and his descendants could have a feeling of the state of love and faith. But nothing could yet be said about this breathing, 'since it is completely hidden from men at the present time'.[1]

We recognize Swedenborg's interest in the technique of breathing: he had learned already as a child to hold his breath to a minimum as a help to concentration during his daily prayers. Now, working on *Arcana Caelestia*, this reduced breathing became instrumental for his communication with the spiritual world. He later considered himself able to bring his breathing into a rhythm corresponding to the general respiration of the heavens.[2]

The garden of Eden and all its trees and plants were for Swedenborg a mirror of man's heavenly state. All things were projections of Adam's divine happiness. He, like all in his faith and state, *was* the garden. In the midst of paradise stood the Tree of Life: a symbol of the happy security of life in this state. Man's inner nature colours his seeing; the character of a good man is reflected in his countenance, and the same applies to the evil person. Here Swedenborg continues on a line as old as mankind. The artist and visionary William Blake described the matter in this way:

> But to the Eyes of the Man of Imagination, Nature is Imagination itself. As a man is, So he Sees. As the Eye is formed, such are its Powers. You certainly Mistake, when you say that the Visions of Fancy are not to be found in This World. To Me This World is all One continued Vision of Fancy or Imagination, & I feel Flatter'd when I am told so.[3]

The birth of Eve

God created man in his own image, Swedenborg read in the first chapter of Genesis, verse 27. Further, 'male and female He created them'. His voluminous manuscripts from the 1740s attest to Swedenborg's continued thoughts regarding the meaning of these words.

In his first great commentary on the Pentateuch, *The Word Explained*, he worked with two Latin translations of the Bible, praised by the Protestants. One was from the

1500s, made for instructional purposes by the Frenchman Sébastien Châteillon, latinized as Castellio. The other was by Sebastian Schmidius, a professor in Strasbourg. His translation belongs to the close of the 1600s; it is a word-for-word rendering, less readable than Castellio's.[4]

Castellio interpreted the Hebrew text of the twenty-seventh verse as if God had created man bisexual, man and woman at the same time: 'In this way God created man like himself, in the image of God, thus as man and woman'. In Schmidius the translation is closer to the original text and to what is internationally common today, as in the New King James Version. Here there is no hermaphroditic implication.

Swedenborg placed the two interpretations side by side. Castellio's suggestion that Adam's original character was bisexual had been repeated by Gottfried Arnold. In *Arcana Caelestia* Swedenborg followed Schmidius's understanding of the text; but the unity and wholeness of personality was, in his theosophical writings, always due to the union of the masculine and the feminine. The woman's creation from the man's rib thus became something more than what the literal meaning indicates.

The account of Eve's coming into existence stood out for Swedenborg as being as radical as the slash of the sword in Plato's *Symposium* which divided the herma-phroditic human being in two: man and woman. Before Adam's deep sleep, man had been a happy combination of wisdom and love, truth and goodness: a union of insight and will forming the axis of power of the human psyche. Now, through Eve's birth, this physical unity was lost. But their first time together, before the appearance of the serpent, did not change the relationship that had prevailed when Adam was still alone. Wisdom and love were clearly divided in the first human couple: but they would always long to be united.

The Tree of Knowledge

In the garden of Eden was the Tree of Life, whose fruits were goodness and truth. But there was also the Tree of the Knowledge of Good and Evil; to taste its fruit was punishable by death: 'in the day that you eat of it you shall surely die'.

And then the serpent entered, tempting man with the promise of knowledge:

You will not surely die. For God knows that in the day you eat of it your eyes will be opened, and you will be like God, knowing good and evil.

The heavenly man had a divine frame of reference. All his thoughts, words, and works were referred to the Lord of creation. But the third chapter of Genesis marks the first radical change in the drama which, according to Swedenborg, is ever ongoing. A new kind of man appeared when Adam and Eve, as representatives of mankind, allowed themselves to be led astray by the serpent's promise of knowledge that would be as great as God's own. The doubting man, the sceptic, was born. From the moment of biting into the apple of knowledge, man made himself the starting point and measure of his knowing; all his impressions, opinions, and ideas now arose from himself. Unity with God was lost.

With Eve's birth the will had left insight's bodily home. The will, love, was thus in Swedenborg's psychology the same as 'man's life'. The will determines the content of knowing. The woman, incarnating love, now saw the knowledge embodied in Adam as her domain. The self, selfishness, took the upper hand. Everything should be ascertained by the standards of the outer man. The inner man's faculty for knowing was left aside; the 'inward' was absorbed in the 'outward'.

The state of the celestial man is such that the internal man is quite distinct from the external, so distinct that he perceives what belongs to the internal man and what to the external man, and how the external man is governed by the Lord through the internal. But because his descendants desired the proprium (that which is one's own), which belongs to the external man, their state became so altered that they no longer perceived any distinction between the internal man and the external. Instead they perceived the internal man as being one with the external, for this is what perception comes to be when man desires the proprium. [5]

Swedenborg's description of this divorce should in no way be read as a drama of the victory of the flesh over the spirit. No, the chief question is man's consciousness and knowledge. 'A life above the life of questions' becomes increasingly difficult; instead of contemplating divine verities, the human *cogito* appears, the thinking self whose thoughts are determined by human will:

Men's desire to probe into mysteries of faith by means of sensory evidence and factual knowledge was not only the cause of the downfall of the Most Ancient Church, that is to say, of its descendants [. . .] it is also the cause of the downfall of every Church. For that desire leads not only to falsities but also to evils of life.[6]

Faith's mystery: man's reason

For Swedenborg this false way of thinking is due to an incorrect starting point. Like so many others throughout the ages he speaks of a reality outside or above the realm of discursive reason, a reality which man is able to experience subjectively under the condition given in his interpretation of the first chapter of Genesis: when man is on the path of being born anew. Here, in this blessed dimension, there are for each and all significant answers to the questions of meaning and purpose.

The great mistake, the catastrophic error of the first men and all their descendants, lies in the way in which this subjective reality has been approached. Scientific experiments and proof can do nothing to establish its actual existence. It is not quantifiable. In the view of the author of *Arcana Caelestia*, it can only be approached if we accept our existence as an *image*. Life is a representation; man inquiring after truth finds himself on a stairway of correspondences whose end is never reached. Allegory is laid upon allegory in a vertical structure where successively we seem to approach the world of wisdom and love.

In the midst of the garden stood the Tree of Life. In the course of events men changed, and consequently also their environment; the Tree of Life was moved to the periphery to be replaced by the Tree of Knowledge. Swedenborg worked in the century of the Enlightenment and factual knowledge. He himself had sought for a universal language of symbols and formulas explaining all the facts of nature, of heaven and earth.

But now he had changed his view in an essential respect. One of the most important differences between the *Principia* and *Arcana Caelestia* regards his view of the potential of human reason. There is a scientific truth, and a spiritual one. We can never, he states in *Arcana Caelestia*, enter into the mysteries of faith solely through the agency of experience and knowledge gathered by the outer senses:

The worldly and bodily-minded man says at heart, Unless I am taught about faith and about things that belong to faith by means of sensory evidence so that I see for myself, that is, by facts so that I understand for myself, I am not going to believe. And he confirms himself in this attitude from the consideration that natural phenomena cannot be at variance with spiritual. Consequently it is from sensory evidence that he wishes to learn about heavenly and Divine matters. But this is no more possible than for a camel to pass through the eye of a needle. The more he wants by this method to become wise, the more he blinds himself, until in the end he believes nothing [. . .] But the person who wishes to be made wise not from the world but from the Lord says at heart that he must believe the Lord, that is, those things the Lord has spoken in the Word, because they are truths. [7]

Nunc licet intrare: Now it is permitted to enter

By the end of his life Swedenborg had published an account of a vision of a church with an inscription over the door: *Nunc licet*. [8] This meant, stated Swedenborg, 'Now it is permitted to enter with the understanding into the mysteries of faith': a motto that can be seen today in many Swedenborgian churches.

Rational human knowledge naturally never lost its significance for Emanuel Swedenborg the theosopher; he valued it even more highly. But divine wisdom and divine love must be understood totally apart from the doctrines being proclaimed by the Christian churches in his time. Their dogmas were incomprehensible, and therefore the old words declaring that reason must be kept in obedience to faith constantly echoed from the church leaders. But true faith *is* rational and easy to understand if the old doctrinal nonsense is cleared away. It is possible to enter with reason into all its secrets. It forms a logical structure, and, note well, one that is consistent and never in conflict with the knowledge that man has gained from experience. It is another matter that its principles cannot be proven and explained in the same way as physical phenomena.

The second, Noachian church

Thus the Fall marks a new era. For Swedenborg and the representatives of radical pietism, consequently, it was not simply a question about the sin of the first human couple. Adam and Eve were symbols of all mankind, fallen away from unconditional faith, that had been replaced by an attitude where man was demanding proof and absolute understanding as a condition of religious conviction. During man's long spiritual history the epochs, the 'churches', have been marked by catastrophes that all arise from man's increasing and at last totally dominating materialism. In Swedenborg's terminology the 'inner man' withered. The fundamental values that belong to faith in God were shared by an ever-diminishing part of humanity.

At last the balance between good and evil was tilted. Swedenborg's God takes action. A new community, a new situation, emerges. But it should be emphasized yet again that Swedenborg's concept of a church in no way means a 'church' in the form of a con-gregation organized in a particular way. It is a question of God's union with the chosen, with those who have chosen to be born anew.

In this way, according to Swedenborg's reading of history, the *first*, *Most Ancient church* was succeeded by *a second*, *Noachian church*. The Flood was a picture of the washing away of the Most Ancient Church, in which man switched his allegiance from the true and good. 'Every intent of the thoughts of his heart was only evil continually', says the sixth chapter of Genesis. Noah symbolizes man after the flood. Because of his righteousness Noah found grace in the eyes of the Lord and was commanded to build a mighty ship, an ark, for himself and his family and for pairs of every animal on the earth. As the flood of sin covers the earth, everything, except those in the ark, is drowned in the massive waters. After forty days of rain and one hundred and fifty days of immersion, the waters flow away, and the ark is stranded on Mount Ararat. God establishes a covenant with Noah: man shall live. The rainbow is set in the sky as a confirmatory sign.

In Swedenborg's reading of the flood, the story of Noah and the ark in its inner meaning is an account of the most ancient, corrupted man's destruction and of the birth of the good man. Noah goes through temptations and difficulties, the symbols of which are Noah and his ark being lifted and falling with the waters, slowly drifting, floating away with hatch closed. The process is set in relief with exact statements of time. It is, as Henry Corbin points out, a description of an initiation process like the accounts we meet in the old alchemical manuscripts.[9]

The flood of sin drowned almost all. In the mass of waters they could no longer inhale what is good: spiritual truth. The fallen people of the Most Ancient Church acted against their better knowledge and by this means profaned the holy. The process of spiritual purification involved a process similar to refinement in Swedenborg's science of mining, a separation of all the dead slag from the glowing mass, the slag being the hardened remains of what at one time had been living faith. Here is the key to the Swedenborgian concept of vastation. [10] The unholy that has been commingled with the holy must be burned away, the profanation cured. Swedenborg regards this as a painful, often long drawn-out process, going on in earthly life as well as after death.

The ark was man, everything alive on board—man, animals, plants—were the good and true things that continued to live with Noah. The majority had forgotten what they had once known, says *Arcana Caelestia*'s interpretation of the sixth chapter of Genesis. But with Noah and those like him there were 'remnants' of what is true and good:

All understanding of truth and will for good perished during the last days of the Church before the Flood [. . .] The people before the Flood were so steeped in dreadful persuasions and filthy desires that not one trace of those goods and truths could be seen. But with those called Noah remnants were left, which however were unable to produce anything belonging to the understanding or the will, only rational truth and natural good. For a person's character determines what it is that remnants can effect. By means of remnants those people were capable of being regenerated. There were no persuasions to thwart or swallow up the Lord's activity by way of remnants. [11]

Using these remnants of knowledge enclosed and preserved in the ark that was his own self, Noah battled against the suffocating flood of sin. When the water receded and the long voyage was over, he was commanded to leave the ark, taking with him every-thing that was alive. God blessed Noah, and entered into a new covenant with him and his descendants.

And by this the *second church* became a fact. In the *first church* man had a direct, wordless connection with the Creator. It was a state of total communion. In this second church the living consciousness of God soon disappeared. The fear of God was roused by the voice of conscience, by ideas that lived on from an older time, legends, traditions, customs. Man could only be instructed by an 'outer way'. Swedenborg continues:

Through the Providence of the Lord, doctrinal matters concerning faith, together with some of the revelations made to the Most Ancient Church, were preserved for the use of these descendants [...] that is to say, [his descendant] was one on whom it was possible to confer charity through cognitions of faith, so that he could act from charity, and from the good which stems from charity recognize what truth is. [12]

Heavenly vision was thus replaced by *conscientia* (conscience). Man had the ability to live in a spiritual state of mind, but not in a heavenly relationship with God. Reason, logical argument, became the decisive factor. At the same time one could make use of the old doctrine of symbols and correspondences that was, we read, the 'knowledge above all knowledges'. [13] But compared to Adam and his like, man's insight in this state was always limited.

From Noah and his descendants the teachings of the *second church* spread over Syria, Egypt, and Babylon, later reaching Greece and Rome. But the spiritual state degenerated, Swedenborg writes. Worldliness and selfishness took the upper hand, religious conscience lost its spiritual content. Worship changed from inner reverence to outer forms.

These changes of man's relationship to the Divine constitute the inner meaning of the first eleven chapters of Genesis. Until Abraham's physical entrance on the scene, everything in this part of the Old Testament should be read as pictures and symbols of inner events. They are important for Swedenborg foremostly because in his interpretation they describe archetypal spiritual relationships. In *Arcana Caelestia* these human states and attributes were linked to the meaning of the Gospels. The states of mind that marked the first churches were the same as characterized the angels. The *first church* were the heavenly angels, who through their love stood in an unbroken, direct contact with the highest love and wisdom. In the *second church* men could be in harmony with those whom Swedenborg terms spiritual angels: blessed on the basis of their love for the neighbour, not directly through an unconditional love for God.

Once again we are reminded of the significance of the Old Testament for Swedenborg. It is the base and explaining complement to the Gospels. In Swedenborg's interpretation the divinely inspired texts are describing and elucidating one and the same thing. How could it be any other way? Christians were not interested in the Old Testament, Swedenborg writes. This was due to the fact that they had not understood the inner meaning behind the literal message. But if we accept the thought that the biblical Word is divine, the conclusion follows that the content must have regard to 'heaven, the church, or faith':

> For where does its life originate except in those things which belong to life, that is, in having every single detail go back to the Lord, who is life itself? Therefore anything that does not interiorly focus on Him has no life; indeed any expression in the Word that fails to embody Him within itself, or does not in its own way go back to Him, is not Divine.[14]

The third, Judaic church

With the *third church* Swedenborg has in view a Jewish form of faith where the most holy is hidden and protected in the *sacrarium* (the blessed shrine). Thus mankind's inmost wisdom is hidden. The third church is 'a representative of a church', distant from the old spirituality: a ritualistic worship of God where form is the very essence.[15] Here we find a formal, customary faith in dogmas and liturgy, and ignorance of their actual content.

During the Middle Ages the eagle was thought to be able to look into the sun, possessing knowledge of the heavenly life. Dante, in the twentieth song of Paradise, listened to the eagle's account of what he had seen, similar to Swedenborg's description of the *third* church. Here man respected the old legends and forms, without understanding them:

> I see thou dost believe, because I say,
> That these things are; the *How* escapes thy sight;
> So, though believed, they're hid, and thou dost stay
>
> Like one who knows a thing by name aright,
> Yet of its quiddity makes no pretence
> To knowledge, till some other give him light.
>
> Predestination! what far depths conceal
> From feeble sight, unable to detect
> The First Cause whole, thy root of woe and weal![16]

Here, as always, Swedenborg saw himself describing timeless occurrences. He depicts the state of obscurity with reference to the Children of Israel's wandering through the wilderness, with the tables of the law in the temple-tent of the Tabernacle. The account of the forty years in the wilderness as such is uninteresting. It acquires a meaning only as a description of captivity and liberation, doubt and faith, despair and joy. From a higher perspective the past and the future are always present. Swedenborg's time is the present.

On the nature of sin and the Messiah's coming

According to Swedenborg's view of history, materialism increased continually within the Jewish church. At the end, the Lord seemed forgotten. Then, when the outer man virtually dominated the inner totally, the Judaic church came to ruin. Its fate was sealed with the coming of the Messiah-Christ.

Thus sin is essentially a turning from God and a trust in one's own earth-bound understanding. The element of sin takes the upper hand, and man loses his ability to see the divine purpose in creation, becoming insensitive to heaven's influence.

A stagnation prevails in which man's life and world risk decaying into a mire. Man's spiritual catastrophes find corresponding expression in recurring calamities, which in their innermost meaning are judgements on a foolish mankind. Christ's coming, life, and death were the judgement on the Judaic church filled with empty forms. In his own life he showed the divine element inherent in every man, thus revealing the constricted or forgotten, spiritual dimension. His life and death became the last judgement upon the *third church*.

But in Swedenborg's view the spiritual wandering in the wilderness continued. The simple meaning of Christ's message was hidden in the Christian churches' false doctrines, and the central experience of God became petrified in empty forms. Now, after one thousand and seven hundred years, the equilibrium must be restored, and false ideas laid bare. A new judgement was at hand. For Swedenborg this was the meaning of the prophecy in the Gospel of Matthew about the coming of the Son of Man in the clouds of heaven with power and glory. And above all he saw in this coming the meaning of the Book of Revelation's announcement of a new heaven and a new earth after the old world's spiritual destruction. A new church, a new state of the human mind, and a new relationship with the Divine was on the way to being established. It was the New Jerusalem, that would come down from God out of heaven, 'prepared as a bride for her husband'.

Here was Swedenborg's great epiphany, his great and life-changing personal revelation. With this New Jerusalem a kingdom of happiness, at the same time heavenly and earthly, would be established. John, the author of the Book of Revelation, seemed to be speaking directly to him:

And I heard a loud voice from heaven saying, "Behold, the tabernacle of God is with men, and He will dwell with them, and they shall be His people, and God Himself will be with them and be their God. And God will wipe away every tear from their eyes; there shall be no more death, nor sorrow, nor crying; and there shall be no more pain, for the former things have passed away". Then He who sat on the throne said, "Behold, I make all things new". And He said to me, "Write, for these words are true and faithful".[17]

These words held a special interest for Emanuel Swedenborg. Schmidius's translation of the Bible was his primary Latin text. Here the verse reads: *Ipse vero erit cum illis, Deus illorum*: 'He himself will be with them, their God'.

Swedenborg's first name, Emanuel, means as said earlier 'God with us'. With God's help he had been called to put all things right again. Through his writings he would explain the meaning of Christ himself. Like Noah he saw himself as an instrument for the divine plan.

Breathing, concentration, and vision

Chapter Twenty-Three

Perfect breathing is utterly and completely obedient to rules of measure, of mental equilibrium [. . .] The most beautiful need is the need to breathe properly. And it is an inestimable treasure, that every moment in its essence is a reminder of this need. From proper breathing goes the path to a continuous, even use of reason. Thereby man possesses the most precious thing in life that can be acquired.

Vilhelm Ekelund: *Ars Magna*, pp. 30-31

The inner meaning of the Word

'Heaven was opened' to Swedenborg in April 1745; the epiphany at the London inn has already been reported. In the divine light he found the interpretation of the text of the Bible that would be his message to humanity. Through God's grace he found himself able to associate with angels and spirits. His last twenty-seven years were filled with visions and communications from the other side. He visited heaven and hell, speaking with spirits of the deceased about life after death in encounters during both day and night.

The Swedenborgian 'doctrine' in its essence is his interpretation of the 'inner meaning' of the text of the Bible due to divine revelations, not primarily his communication with spirits from heaven and hell. God himself was now unveiling concealed connections and hidden contents. Swedenborg 'was enlightened'. Everyone who read the Pentateuch, the histories, the books of the prophets, and the Psalms in the Old Testament, and the Gospels and the Apocalypse, could enter into these secrets. But this entrance was conditional; the understanding of the reader would always depend upon his love for the truth and upon the conduct of his life. In addition, the right insight required hard work:

The internal sense is not only the sense that lies concealed within the external sense [...] but it is also the sense which emerges from a large number of places in the literal sense when they are correctly compared with one another. And it is the sense discerned by those in whom the understanding part of their mind has been enlightened by the Lord. For when enlightened the understanding distinguishes apparent truths from real truths, and in particular falsities from truths, though it does not form any judgements with respect to real truths in themselves. But the understanding cannot be enlightened unless a person believes that love to the Lord and charity towards the neighbour are the chief and essential qualities of the Church. And provided that he is governed by these once he has recognized them he can go on to see countless truths; indeed he can see very many hidden things that have been disclosed to him.[1]

I repeat that Swedenborg's divine mission was precisely to bring this hidden meaning to light; his other spiritual experiences were true and important, but yet of secondary significance in relation to this vocation. These spiritual experiences meant that heaven 'was opened' for him. He met and spoke with angels, with spirits and demons, travelled in paradise and in hell, but this ability was of no direct significance to his interpretation of the Bible. Here he regarded himself as led by God's light. When interpreting the Bible nobody could rely on experiences from the spiritual world. Angels and spirits often wanted to dictate their individual explanations. There were occasions when he did write what they desired, but after doing so he had sometimes been obliged to cross out their words.[2]

Thus he clearly distinguished between the two sources of the contents of his works: the divine love and wisdom and the spiritual world. The title of *Arcana Caelestia* is illustrative: '*Arcana Caelestia* that have been disclosed in the Sacred Scripture or the Word of the Lord [...] Together with the marvels that have been seen in the world of spirits and in the heaven of angels'. The truths of the Word, thus, are 'disclosed'. The marvels in the world of the spirits, on the other hand, have been 'seen'. We find the same emphasis on revelation as the source of a deeper understanding of the biblical Word in other titles of his theosophical works.

Spiritual encounters, spiritual states

Through visions and voices Swedenborg received instruction concerning life in the spiritual realm. He learned about life in heaven and hell and the topography of the spiritual world; he met and talked with deceased figures in heavenly or hellish states. Swedenborg's *memorabilia*, his many notes of an anecdotal nature, refer to this category of experiences.

They were connected with special spiritual states. He was interested in their forms and described them on several occasions. In *The Spiritual Diary* he reviewed four types of visions:

> The first is a sight of sleep, just as real as daytime sight; so I said while actually asleep that if this was sleep, then wakefulness must also be sleep. The second kind is vision with the eyes closed, which is just as real as with the eyes opened, and by which similar objects are presented to view, even more beautiful and pleasant. The same kind can exist with the eyes open, and has occurred two or three times. The third kind is in a state with the eyes open, when those things are portrayed which are in heaven, both spirits and other things. This kind causes symbolic vision, which has become very familiar to me; but it is rather obscure, differing entirely from the commonplace human imagination. The fourth kind occurs when a person is separated from the body, and in the spirit, and then one cannot tell in the least but that one is in a waking state and is then in possession of all one's senses, such as touch, hearing, and sight [...] It is more than the sight of a waking state, because it is an exquisite one, nor does one perceive that state as any different from wakefulness—unless one lapses into a waking state of the body [...] This has been granted me four or five times.[3]

The third stage was the most common. Here he felt that he had been carried into a heavenly or hellish theatre; he observed and discussed, going from one scene to another.

The visions were to become Swedenborg's characteristic mark as a writer and theosopher. He filled book after book with their contents. They could be true or false, depending on whether they were inspired by good or by evil spirits. He emphasized that they were often especially clear just before going to sleep, or in the morning just before he awoke: what today are called hypnogogic, sleep-like states. Sometimes the visions of spirits he had experienced in dreams or in other states of mind were without significance—they were physiologically conditioned or connected with inessential questions, he wrote.[4] Thus by observing himself Swedenborg attained a conscious and well-differentiated understanding of his own experiences and their varying value.

Respiration, thinking, and visions

Swedenborg often declared that his spiritual state depended on his will. He also maintained that concentration and the ability to think presume the regulation of breathing. He had learned to control the motion of his lungs while a child, he reported in *The Spiritual Diary*. During morning and evening prayers in his parental home he had learned to limit his breathing so as to make it almost unnoticeable. The implication: in this way he could hold his thoughts fixed on what was essential, namely God. Much later he elaborated the matter in a letter to Gabriel Anders Beyer in Gothenburg:

> From my 4th to my 10th year, I was constantly in thought about God, salvation, and man's spiritual suffering. Several times I disclosed things that amazed my father and mother, who thought that angels must be speaking through me. [5]

Restrained breathing later, during his scientific period, became a prerequisite for concentration on the problem he had in hand. In the work he began in Amsterdam in 1737, *The Economy of the Animal Kingdom*, he discussed the question of breathing and concentration from an anatomical and physiological perspective. His studies of the human body had shown how the lungs have an effect on the brain and on the fluid from the brain that by way of membranes gives life to the body:

> This general and life-giving relationship is best reflected in the [. . .] breathing of the lungs. For as soon as the brain is active, and thinking deeply, or is occupied with important concerns, the lungs draw their breath tacitly and slowly. The breast either rises to a fixed level, fearing to disturb the quiet of the brain by any deep breath, or else compresses itself, and admits only a small amount of air. When the brain is exhilarated and joyous, the lungs expand and unfold. When its activity is withheld with fear, the lungs are passive. When the brain is disturbed by anger, the lungs are disturbed in the same way. [6]

Concentration presumes control of breathing. All who think intensively are conscious of this. Breathing through the nose can convey odours: therefore, we breathe through the mouth in moments of concentration.

In the last work of scientific character, *The Animal Kingdom* written from 1744 to 1745, we again meet the question of concentration. In this context Swedenborg emphasizes the 'extinguishing of the impure fires of the body and our own delusive lights' as a prerequisite for our understanding of higher truths. We must let ourselves be enlightened entirely by the 'rays of spiritual power'. Then for the first time truths, emanating from that power, flow in, and at length we can 'comprehend by faith those profound miracles that cannot be comprehended by the intellect: and from all these things, in the deep hush of awe and amazement, venerate and adore the omnipotence and providence of the Supreme Creator'.[7]

About correct breathing

Swedenborg's communication with higher worlds was thus not limited to dreams while he slept. Signs and inspiration 'from above' seem to have been a part of his everyday life for a long time. Photisms, experiences of light, he interpreted as confirmations that he was on the right path in his work. Other kinds of signs appeared when he was pondering a problem or embarking upon a new task.

As we have seen, Swedenborg's chief epistemological question as early as the 1730s concerned the connection between empirically proven knowledge and intuitive insight. Already at that time he gave the problem a biblical anchoring. Swedenborg found the answer to his question in the account of the Fall. In paradise man had had an immediate knowledge of the Divine. The question was about how Adam's children, shut out from the garden of Eden and by this also from higher knowledge, could regain their lost privilege.

When Swedenborg pondered this and similar questions he was, according to his own report, in the habit of regulating his breathing. In the *Dream Diary* we have an account that seems to relate his breathing technique to his decisive experience at Easter in April 1744:

I noticed it to be a fact [. . .] that the will has the greatest influence on the understanding. When we inhale, the thoughts fly into the body, and when we exhale, the thoughts are in a peculiar way expelled and rectified; so the very thoughts possess their alternations of activity like the respiration of the lungs. For the inspiration belongs to the will and the expiration to nature, so that the thoughts have their alternations in every turn of respiration because, when wicked thoughts entered, I only had to draw the breath, whereupon they ceased.

Hence, from this may also be seen the reason that, when in deep thought, the lungs are kept in a state of equilibrium and at rest, more according to nature, and that the inhalations are then faster than the expirations, when at other times the reverse is the case; and, furthermore, that a person in ecstasy holds the breath, the thoughts then being as it were absent. Likewise in sleep, when both the inhalation and the expiration are governed by nature, when that is represented which inflows from above. The same may also be deduced from the brain, that by the inhalation all the internal organs together with the brain itself are expanded, and that the thoughts thence have their origin and flux.[8]

Here we find an important personal and concrete confirmation of a theory that he had already formulated. Breath control and the conscious exclusion of sensory input helped him attain the 'transcendental feeling' of coming nearer to the Divine: Adam's privileged state. By being screened off from sensation in this way, new awarenesses come to the surface, perceptions that would otherwise be unknown.

Spirits and 'being in the spirit'

The restrained movement of the lungs became for Swedenborg the practical prerequisite for his frequent contacts with the spirit world: both the light atmosphere of heaven and the gasping vapours of hell. Visually, entrance to the celestial world was marked by an experience of strong light. The light was the wisdom of love, whose brilliance surpassed all worldly luminosity.[9]

In line with Swedenborg's emphasis on correspondences, respiration was as important for angels and spirits as for earthly man. For him the paradise of heaven, as we have seen, took the form of the body of Christ, the 'Grand Man'. It was formed of the blessed souls of the dead. In this supernatural structure there pulsed a heavenly respiration:

There is also a collective breathing, about which I was able to observe [...] that I was then somehow taking part in a collective breathing that was easy and spontaneous; and indeed, that the collective breathing of heaven related to my own breathing as three to one, as did my heartbeat also.[10]

All man's affections are connected with changes of his state of mind, he wrote in *The Divine Providence*. They manifest themselves in the body as organic changes, and are of the same nature as the rhythmic expansions and contractions of the heart and blood vessels that are termed systole and diastole. In the lungs these correspond to the motions of breathing where they are connected with the expansions and contractions of the small lobes.[11] States of mind are in actuality movements in the mind. They consist of the same whirling, spiralling, circular progressions that at one time gave rise to the universe. In Swedenborg's explanation of these respiratory motions we hear an echo of the fundamental thought that he had first developed in his *Principia*, taken up again in *The Divine Love and Wisdom*:

> The state of the natural mind before reformation can be compared to a spiral twisting or bending itself downwards. But after reformation it can be compared to a spiral twisting or bending itself upwards. Wherefore before reformation a man looks downwards towards hell, but after reformation he looks upwards towards heaven.[12]

Every single angel was able to breathe in this way; but they could also choose their own breathing rhythm, he notes in *The Spiritual Diary*:

> I was shown the manner of their breathing, and was instructed that the breathing of their lungs was changed in time, according to the state of their faith, which was before unknown to me, but I can still understand and believe it. For my breathing was developed by the Lord in such a way that I was able to breathe inwardly for a quite a long time without the help of outside air [...] I was also instructed that the breathing is thus directed without my knowledge, so that I may be with spirits, and speak with them.[13]

He classified his observations, as was his custom. Highest in the hierarchy were the angels who stood closest to God; their breathing was minimal, hardly noticeable. Then the breathing grew stronger as the distance from God increased.

Breathing became one of Swedenborg's great themes. Mankind breathed, as did the whole of heaven. The respiration of angels and spirits was conditioned by the state of their love and faith.[14] Here was the reason why evil people after death could not live in the company of the good, he writes in *Arcana Caelestia*:

> When [the evil] come near the good it seems to them as though they are unable to breathe and are so to speak being suffocated. As a consequence they sink down like somebody half-dead, and so like stones, into hell where they regain their ability to breathe along with those who are already in that place. [15]

And conversely, the influence of evil spirits on the good has an equally suffocating effect.

Vision in the spirit

Breathing control, we read, was known to the ancients. Adam, Eve, and their descendants were able to hold open the connection with their Creator precisely through their light breathing, in spite of sin's entrance into the world. The 'inner man' was not yet put in the shade by the outer. The same held true for the prophets of the Old Testament, in Swedenborg's view. They were 'in the spirit', we read in *The True Christian Religion*, the summary of his doctrine written in the last years of his life:

> Since a person's spirit means his mind, 'being in the spirit', a phrase which occurs a number of times in the Word, means the state in which the mind is separated from the body. That was the state the Prophets were in when they saw the kind of things which happen in the spiritual world, so it is called 'the vision of God'. They were then in the same state as that of the spirits and angels of that world. In that state a person's spirit, as the visual capacity of his mind, can be transported from place to place while his body remains in one place. This is the state in which I have been for the last twenty-six years, with the difference that I have been simultaneously in the spirit and in the body, and only at times outside the body. Ezekiel, Zechariah, Daniel, and John the writer of Revelation were in this state [...] [16]

Thought, focused on one single point, helped him to see and understand. The same applied to the angels:

> They see Divine and heavenly things in every single object, and wonderful things in a series

of many objects [...] Thus they see innumerable things at the same time in their order and connection, and this so fills their minds with delight that they seem to be carried away from themselves. [17]

Method or result?

When we examine the spiritual states in which the visionary, the mystic Swedenborg dwelt, we always find a greater or lesser limitation of respiration. Is it then a question of lower or higher degrees of concentration? Or should we consider these states as physical results of holding the breath?

In his biography of Swedenborg, Martin Lamm has a tendency to explain the seer's experiences in the spirit world as having been produced by a lack of oxygen. Ernst Arbman, the Swedish expert on religious psychology, reacted to Lamm's thought with indignation. Breathing was significant to Swedenborg's supernatural experiences, but only as one factor among many that are more important.

Presumably both these points of view are too narrow. Concentration and restricted breathing were two sides of the same thing. Breathing has an effect on sensory consciousness, and sight, hearing, and the sense of touch affect breathing. Swedenborg took up the problem from his own perspective. 'The tool always thinks that it is itself the power', he wrote in *The Spiritual Diary*; but this is a delusion. [18] Man in his quest for knowledge is only an instrument. In actuality all philosophical knowing comes from the Lord. There are two powers behind an acquired insight—one Divine and one human.

Breathing and hesychasm

Swedenborg's interest in breathing techniques and concentration was far from unique. The importance of concentration as necessary for approaching the Divine has always been emphasized by Christian mystics, particularly by those belonging to the Catholic Carmelite order. For the Spanish mystic of the 1500s, Teresa of Avila, it was a matter of an inner journey from room to room in a 'heavenly castle'. The innermost chamber was the bridal room of 'the marriage of the soul' with God.

Among Catholic mystics breathing is seldom seen as a means to approaching the Divine. In the 'mystical theology' that has played a great role in Catholic thinking, this physiological factor of breathing and its restriction is often seen as both a means for concentration and an effect of a state of mind. In a letter to her confessor Teresa of Avila mentioned her states of ecstasy: when they reached their highest degree, her ability to breathe diminished and she lost her power of speech.[19]

In Orthodoxy the control of respiration is of great importance; the term for it, 'hesychasm', comes from the Greek *hesychos* (still, calm). The monks on Mount Athos are said to have used this already in the 1200s. Breathing is restricted to enable the meditating person to obtain tranquillity, in the form of 'quietude in the heart'. The monk wanted to gather and purify his will, thought, and feelings, and to concentrate body and soul on the unity of God. Such meditative prayer brought him near to or into union with the Divine. In a fragment from the Middle Ages the pious soul is given this technical counsel:

> Sit down [...] close the door and raise your mind above what is superficial and incidental [...] and direct your eyes and your mind towards [...] the navel, reduce your breathing through the nose so that you breathe less than normally. Examine the thoughts in your inner parts in search of your heart and the point where all the powers of the soul gather. At the beginning you will find darkness and a stubborn impenetrability; but if you persist, if you practise this day and night, you will——O wonder of all wonders!——find an unlimited happiness.[20]

Through these breathing exercises a way would be prepared for an 'inner prayer'. In *Tales of a Russian Pilgrim* an anonymous monk describes the classical formula for his prayer.[21] As he inhaled he prayed the first words, saying, 'Lord Jesus Christ'. At the same time he attempted to picture the contents of these words. Then he exhaled, concluding the prayer with the words, 'Have mercy upon me'. After many years' practice the praying became continuous: 'My heart dissolved in an unceasing blessedness', he wrote.

But hesychasm's passive and joyous ascent into the Divine is one thing, Swedenborg's concentration another——more directed to knowledge and heavenly insight.

Yoga and Zen

Swedenborg's experiences are to a certain degree the same as those we meet in the techniques of yoga and Zen meditation. The idea behind Indian yoga, as is known, is to free man from material bonds, and in this way to come into contact with a spiritual reality. Here we also find a relation between restricted breathing and experiences of an otherwise inaccessible, higher sphere. After concentration and regulated breathing exercises the yogi sees an 'inner light', equivalent to a state of mind. He has crossed a threshold: gone from 'being' to 'knowing'; he is transformed to that on which he is meditating. He sees everything in its context, from beginning to end, according to the classical handbook *Yoga-Sutra*. He has gone into this higher state with a certain concept in his thoughts. Now he controls the idea or the object from within:

> As on a screen the yogi perceives all the conscious states that the concept can awaken in other human beings. He sees an infinite number of situations that may follow from the same concept. For he is not only united with that notion, but has also entered into its inner dynamics, making its human purposes his own […] [22]

The distracting noise and gaudiness of the sensory world are dampened with the proper breathing technique. The Zen master sits in the lotus position, becoming one with his breathing and the world. His perspective is widened. The crown, trunk, branches, leaves, and roots of existence show themselves in an interplay of surface and depth.[23] The master finds his relationship to existence, and life envelops him.

Swedenborg's task

Comparisons of Swedenborg's experiences with breathing techniques in the West and Orient show similarities regarding the path to concentration. It is a matter of attaining experiences of unity, transcendence; but Swedenborg's ambitious goal and subject give him a particular, individual profile. He saw himself as a chosen instrument with the task of explaining, with divine aid, the inner meaning of the biblical Word. His mission was nothing less than mankind's salvation, not to be swept away or absorbed by a feeling of unity with God and the universe.

The hermeneutic circle

Chapter Twenty-Four

The Word of the Old Testament contains heavenly arcana, with every single detail focusing on the Lord, His heaven, the Church, faith, and what belongs to faith; but no human being grasps this from the letter.

Arcana Caelestia §1

Origen and the spiritual content of the Bible

For Emanuel Swedenborg, all truth is in the Sacred Scripture, his interpretation of the Word *is* his theology and theosophy. The interpretation that we meet in *Arcana Caelestia* is that the Word was directly inspired by God. It is not simply a matter of reading in the right way. The interpreter must also find the 'inner', hidden meaning within the biblical words and accounts; in this, Swedenborg associated himself with a long Christian tradition.

The thought was present already with Paul. In his letters we meet his notion of a 'secret, hidden wisdom of God'. It is not given to everyone but was accessible to the apostle and his friends:

But God has revealed them to us through His Spirit. For the Spirit searches all things, yes, the deep things of God. [1]

To understand the significance of the covenant with God, the literal sense is never adequate, Paul explained to the Corinthians: 'The letter kills, but the Spirit gives life'. [2] The idea of a hidden signification within the literal meaning was systematized in the

---

200s by Origen. A man inspired by Christ, he wrote, can be led by his grace to an understanding of the hidden content of the text. If the veil over the text were to be lifted, constant prayer was required. It was a matter of a divine gift:

> If God did not open our eyes, how would we be able to see these great mysteries that are pictured in the patriarchs and symbolized, at one time by wells, at another by weddings, and at still another [. . .] by unfruitfulness.[3]

Fig. 36. A picture of the three biblical languages: Hebrew, Greek, and Latin —all of equal value. The etching is taken from Sebastian Schmidius's translation of the Bible, *Biblia Sacra sive Testamentum Vetus et Novum ex linguis originalibus in linguam latinam translatum*, 1708.

Every word, every sentence has its hidden signification. The key to Origen's interpretation was Christocentric. Everything in Genesis treats of Christ: Christ is the beginning of all things and the source of all renewal. It is only through allegory that we understand the inner meaning of the Bible. 'To restrict oneself to the letter is to be content with the weak light of prophecy, while Christ's sun casts its light over all things.' Thus it is only through Christ that the whole logical argument of the Scriptures becomes clear. With him the two Testaments stand together as a unity.

From the perspective of the reader, the text of the Old Testament is not to be regarded as providing prophecies of the future. In Origen's *now,* the future is present. In his interpretation, the starting point is the actual coming of the Messiah. Step by step he works through the books of the Old Testament, finding allusions and references to what has already happened, Christ's life and death.

The letter, Augustine, and the hidden wisdom

For Augustine, who lived approximately 200 years after Origen, God's love and man's salvation through the church were the markers that should guide the understanding of biblical texts. But he realized that for the purpose of interpretation 'love' or 'church' were all too wide as rules to give a structure to readings of accounts that were often dark or distant from the gentle Christian message. Consequently he wrote a more detailed statement of the ideas that should lead our seeking for the hidden meaning within the literal text. Some of Augustine's guidelines could just as well have been written by a pietistic interpreter during the first half of the 1700s, or by Emanuel Swedenborg.

First, the reader must always hold in mind the unity between Christ and the church. What applies to Christ also applies to the church, and vice versa. Secondly, the individual elements must be seen in the context of, as a part of, the whole. The Bible treats of God's love. The historical accounts of the Old Testament must be related to Christ. When we read about King Solomon, the wise monarch must be related to Christ's message and today's church. The same relationship holds true overall in the prophetic texts. Thirdly, all references to time have a deeper meaning. As with Origen, prophecies about the future have application to the reader's present.

Spiritual companions

Knowing and understanding stood in direct relation to man's spiritual state of mind, which in its turn is determined by his nearness to God, a principle that presumably has held true in every age. It was present already with Plato, in his words about 'like seeks like'. We meet it not least in the realm of classical Catholic thought, long after Augustine. Faith is formed by love, and love's intensity elevates the soul towards God, to higher and individually-suited levels of knowledge. Action and being go together was one of Thomas Aquinas's most famous sayings, 'The higher on the stairway to God, the clearer the insight'. With Swedenborg, as we have seen, this relative nature of understanding is a continually returning principle.

When Swedenborg was 'in the spirit', he felt that he saw the divine truth enclosed in the Word. It could never be communicated to man directly by God. All our spiritual companions, good and evil, were related as to their character and quality to man's spiritual state:

> [...] it is the Lord Himself who teaches each person by means of the Word. How much he is taught depends upon how far he receives in his will good from the Lord, and he receives the more, the more he shuns evils as sins. Also each person is in the company of spirits as regards his affections and the thoughts they inspire [...] If spirits speak to us, therefore, they do so on the basis of our affections and in accordance with them.[4]

If man changes his will and love, then the spirits and angels who are with him also are changed:

> [...] Since a person is in the company of spirits who share his religion, the spirits who speak with him confirm all the religious principles he has adopted.[5]

'What I have heard and seen'

Some of Swedenborg's best-known works, such as *Heaven and Hell*, announce on the title page that they are accounts of personal experiences, 'what I have heard and seen'. The angels he met were divinely inspired, yet at least in a certain degree still influenced by their own religious conceptions. Consequently, Swedenborg's impressions from the heavenly regions must be coloured by the subjective explanations of the heavenly messengers. Or were these experiences directly communicated to the pious scribe by divine grace?[6] If he relied on spiritual messengers, his accounts could always be contested.

Here is one of the questions that have been discussed by his readers from the time of William Blake to our own days.

In this discussion Swedenborg would certainly have maintained that he wrote as God commanded, and that his words were the divine truth. Of this he was absolutely convinced. This was his continual assurance, the last time given on his death bed.

Will and faith formed a connected whole, this was indeed one of his basic principles. Man's understanding depended on his changing spiritual state and receptivity. Once again: how did this principle agree with Swedenborg's own insight?

The hermeneutic circle

When we approach a text with a preconceived idea of its meaning, we easily find words and sentences proving this opinion. We then go round in what is commonly called a hermeneutic circle.

What did Swedenborg see in his spiritual states? As we have observed, he considered the Gospels to be the keys to understanding the Old Testament, and the Book of Revelation gave a clarifying and eschatological dimension to the whole Bible. Consequently, he came to place the same magnifying glass over most of the biblical texts. Seen through this glass, everything was marked and grouped around the coming of Christ, the life of the regenerating man, and his blessedness in the Garden of Eden before the Fall. The Bible treated of the Fall of man and his restoration by the coming of Christ. The whole must be understood from the particular, and the particular from the whole.

At the same time, as suggested in the chapter dealing with *Arcana Caelestia* and the successive churches, there was another key to his interpretation. The Old Testament was an account of man's gradually increasing distance from God. With this reading, the advent of the Messiah, foretold by the prophets, became all the more urgent since with time mankind had lost the connection with the divine wisdom and love.

In this way, through an existential reading, everything that was incomprehensible or contradictory was moved up to a higher level, where everything appeared comprehensible. The heroes of the Old Testament, with their victories and defeats, became symbols for events and circumstances beyond the quantitative and measurable world; they occurred in another, qualitative reality. The Gospels were interpreted in the same way. Everything is seen from a perspective where human proximity to and distance from the Divine became the criterion. Miracles and obscure passages were consistently placed in categories of divine presence or absence. The miracle of the five loaves of bread and the two fishes referred to spiritual feeding, where bread is love and fishes are truth, against which is set the disciples' little faith and inertia of understanding.

Swedenborg's interpretation of Israel's flight from Egypt

Swedenborg's own hermeneutics followed, generally speaking, the lines that Origen and Augustine had formulated. An example: the flight of the Israelites from captivity in Egypt across the Red Sea. The water opened for the fleeing Israelites, and fell back upon and drowned the pursuing Egyptians. Here is the biblical text from the fourteenth chapter of Exodus:

> Then Moses stretched out his hand over the sea; and the Lord caused the sea to go back by a strong east wind all that night, and made the sea into dry land, and the waters were divided. So the children of Israel went into the midst of the sea on the dry ground, and the waters were a wall to them on their right hand and on their left. And the Egyptians pursued and went after them into the midst of the sea, all Pharaoh's horses, his chariots, and his horsemen. Now it came to pass, in the morning watch, that the Lord looked down upon the army of the Egyptians through the pillar of fire and cloud, and He troubled the army of the Egyptians. And He took off their chariot wheels, so that they drove them with difficulty [. . .] And Moses stretched out his hand over the sea; and when the morning appeared, the sea returned to its full depth, while the Egyptians were fleeing into it. So the Lord overthrew the Egyptians in the midst of the sea [. . .] Not so much as one of them remained. [7]

While 'in the spirit' Swedenborg read in this passage an account of the victory of truth over falsity. When Moses stretched his hand over the sea, this should be read as the dominion of the divine truth over hell. The strong east wind was the means of dispelling falsity. The 'whole night' characterizes the state of temptation endured by those represented by the Israelites. And what happened when the 'waters were divided'? This was the truth that was divided from lies. When the fleeing Israelites marched across the dried-up Red

Sea, they represented those who, led by God, pass through hell uninjured, unharmed by the influence of evil. The Egyptians' pursuit represented the continuing attempt of the evil to reach out and draw the good into its power.

Word for word, line for line, Swedenborg transfers the dramatic flight and fate of the pursuers to the conflict between the two principal forces combatting in moral life. It was the battle that Christ would fight, forever showing the way to victory for goodness and to man's return to the relationship with God that once existed in paradise. The Egyptians' horses, chariots, and riders became, in his reading, symbols of the perverted understanding, false teachings, and resulting arguments of those who are governed by faith separated from charity——the great sin that returns in all of Swedenborg's writings. Seemingly far from the account of the death in the waves suffered by the Egyptian riders, he takes the occasion to describe the further fate of the deceased whom they represent. After death, their false faith appears in all its ugliness. What little these 'Egyptians' may have had soon disappears in the shadows of false belief:

> [...] the hells with which they have been in contact through the evils ruling their life are opened. From there all the evils which they have made their own rapidly converge on them, and the falsities which well out of the evils constitute then the sphere surrounding them [...] Once all this has taken place they are in hell, for they have been shut off from all contact with heaven.[8]

Christianity humanized

Why this kind of interpretation? Symbolic reading was an old tradition, alive also in Swedenborg's own home. It was practised particularly among the radical pietists, by Gottfried Arnold and in the so-called Berleburg Bible, which was influenced by him. This edition of the Bible, in eight folio volumes, printed 1726-42 in the little principality governed by the pietistic princely family of Sayn-Wittgenstein, is a now seldom mentioned monument of radical pietism's view of the Bible. Here we meet not only Arnold, but also echoes of the French 'quietist' Mme Guyon's emphasis on man's inner life and the soul's reception of the divine inflow.

Swedenborg's mission was to provide mankind with a humanized Christianity, freed of all dogmas. Man, liberated through a correct understanding of the Scriptures, would build an earthly New Jerusalem, linked to the congregation of the saints on the other side of the gates of death. This faith in the potential of the individual can be compared with the conviction regarding man's 'absolute capability' that Karl Barth saw as a chief characteristic of the Enlightenment and pietism.[9] The prerequisite for the realization of this 'new' Christianity was its agreement with reason. What was difficult and inaccessible in the biblical texts could be explained simply as the conflict between good and evil. In the New Testament, this combat was concentrated in the figure of Christ himself. He was at one and the same time divine and human, and his life became a battle against man's earthly temptations. In the Gospel of John, we read about the wedding in Cana and the water that was changed into wine. According to Swedenborg the story should be understood as a picture of the glorification of Christ and the regeneration of the divine man.[10] We should all be born anew through successful strife in temptation. In this process, we may see the divine wisdom and the protecting hand of Providence.

Three levels of meaning, three states of mind

Swedenborg's spiritual world was divided into three levels. There was a highest 'heavenly' sphere, a middle 'spiritual', and a lower 'natural' level. These layers could be conceived of spatially, but also as lying on a single plane. There the heavenly formed the innermost, surrounded by the spiritual and outermostly by the natural. The determining criterion was proximity to the Divine, and the degrees of proximity were actually a question of spiritual states. This applied to the mode of life of the individual on earth as well as to his form after death, as an angel or demon.

The Scriptures are God's preaching through the 'mouth of the holy prophets' and his Word made flesh in Christ. The nearer we come to God 'in the spirit', the more we understand. The natural man could never rise above the literal meaning, while the spiritual man saw the inner meaning; and the reader who succeeded in freeing himself from the 'fires of the body' could approach the innermost core of the Word, where we can grasp fragments of God's pure love and wisdom.

This is a leading thought in Swedenborg's hermeneutics. Man in his earthly and after-earthly form *is* his will and understanding. Time and space, the boundary between life and death, disappear. In the highest moments, in instants of clear vision, man is transported to what he perceives as timeless happiness and light, usually hidden (unattainably) to human beings. The circle of interpretation becomes a spiral around a text whose meaning shifts and deepens to eternity.

Moreover, this applies also to the angels. They have all been given their place in the three-level hierarchy, corresponding to their state of love. As interpreters and messengers, they reflect, as said, their own understanding of the Divine, and their movements from place to place are in essence modifications of their spiritual state. As it is with man, so it is with the angels. The highest, most sublime insight can therefore be communicated only through the highest messengers who stand closest to God. Their language is like music, without words. They *are* their truth. When approaching this we can understand their verity.

Once again, the divine message, the divine truth, corresponds to man's spiritual state. For the receiver, past and present are an eternal *now*. In this state words like 'harvest', 'wedding', 'feast', 'bread', 'wine' mean achievement, completion——the decisive event. In the words of Luke, this is the 'great supper' to which all are invited. It is only the 'unrepentant' who send word saying they are prevented from coming. Although invited, they excused themselves: 'I have bought a piece of ground […] I have bought five yoke of oxen […] I have married a wife […] '. [11]

Augustine and the doctrine of states

Beneath Swedenborg's doctrine of states glimmer Augustinian lines of thought. We find the same fundamental ideas in the church father's *Confessions*, from which Swedenborg drew excerpts as he did from many others of his books. The thirteenth chapter of the *Confessions* is an analysis of 'Creation's spiritual value', a subject that must have been of great interest for him. Here we find the essence of Swedenborg's teaching of the relation between understanding and love. Augustine sets man's fall into sin against the words of the coming of light in the biblical account of creation. Light comes in the process of conversion, which has a personal, human correspondence to creation, but not an act of creation in the sense of something definitive and conclusive: creation-conversion must be continually repeated.[12] In connection with the fifth chapter of the Letter to the Romans on the love that is poured into the hearts of all by the Holy Spirit,[13] Augustine describes the transformation of the spiritually-burning man and his understanding of spiritual realities:

> In our heart we reach new heights
> and we sing the hymn of degrees.

Love forms and constitutes man's being, his state. His understanding changes him. Augustine spoke of an 'intelligence of faith'. But the truths of faith should not be seen simply as statements; they were powers that changed human intelligence and the whole man. His proper spiritual attitude is described in the story of the Garden of Eden and the first human beings. Now the tension between the old life and the new appears in and through Christ's life and death. The famous Catholic exegete Henri de Lubac may be quoted in this context:

> All of revelation is organized around a concrete centre, visible in time and space through Jesus Christ's crucifixion and death. This interpretation contains within itself a dogmatic and realized spiritual attitude. The old Christian exegesis constitutes in itself an important aspect of ancient Christian thought.[14]

Inspired books

Swedenborg found the inner meaning only in the 'books of the Word': the parts of the Bible that he regarded as being 'inspired'.[15] Paul's letters, according to Swedenborg, did not belong to this category. In his *The Spiritual Diary*, Swedenborg made long notes about his meetings with the 'apostle to the gentiles'. It was evident that Paul had no mind for the inner meaning of the Word. He never spoke about what Christ had taught and never dealt with his parables. He did not know what heaven was. Paul was full of his own importance, according to Swedenborg. Perhaps Swedenborg reacted against Paul's rhetoric? Swedenborg's simple, easily understood, logically-phrased message is far from the style of the more sophisticated Paul. Swedenborg's originally negative attitude to Paul changed with the years.

In a letter to the German priest Friedrich Christoph Oetinger in 1766 Swedenborg communicated that he had spoken with Paul for a whole year.[16] Perhaps they gradually understood that they had much in common? In his last monumental work, *The True Christian Religion*, he often referred to the apostle, without polemics.

Swedenborg in daily life: portrait with a double-exposure

Chapter Twenty-Five

> Those who have something significant to teach are essentially only those who understand the supreme art of opening oneself without reserve to the divine: the sun-drenched, the superior. Here creed is a matter of no importance, here Swedenborg and Goethe meet each other [...] Goethe says that the happiest man is one who is in the position to build a bridge between his maturity and his childhood. Perhaps we find such a return in Swedenborg's works [...]
>
> Vilhelm Ekelund: *På Hafsstranden* (*On the Seashore*) p. 8.

Small needs, great industry

For our notion of Emanuel Swedenborg's personality we have two kinds of source. First we have written observations made by his contemporaries. Second, there is the picture hidden in his works. We begin with notes from his own time, all relating to the period after 1745.

As to his appearance, his contemporary, Carl Gustaf Tessin, a Hat politician and once Prime Minister, noted that Swedenborg was an image of his father, but not as tall. He had 'feeble eyes, a large mouth, and a pale complexion'; he was 'friendly, agreeable, cheerful, and talkative'.[1] According to the German-Dutch businessman John Christian Cuno, he looked, even as an old man, like the portrait in the engraving published in *Principia* (Fig. 12) in 1734, when he was in his mid-forties. 'The eyes have retained their beauty', he wrote.[2] Yet the lines around the mouth must have changed as he lost his teeth when getting older.

He dressed in the fashion that was in style in his youth: a jacket buttoned up to the neck, breeches, shoes with buckles. He wore a wig of the kind often used by men of the upper class of his time.

His house has been described by Carl Robsahm, whose account, dated 1782, describes the property as it was in the 1760s. The unique nature of his sketch may excuse the length of this quotation:

Swedenborg's property was about a stone's throw in length and in breadth. The rooms of his dwelling-house were rather small and plain, but comfortable for him, though scarcely for anyone else. Although he was a learned man, no books were ever seen in his room, except his Hebrew and Greek Bible, and his manuscript indexes to his own works, by which, in making quotations, he was saved the trouble of examining all that he had previously written or printed [...] For the sake of the public that came to see the old gentleman, generally from curiosity, he had a pretty summer house built in his garden in 1767; to one side of this house was his handsome library, and in the wing that stretched out on the other side were garden-tools. He had also another summer house put up in the middle of his garden, according to the plan of one he had seen in England on a gentleman's estate; and still another, which was square, with four doors, which could be changed into an octagon by opening the doors across the corners of the room. In one corner of his garden he had constructed a maze of boards, entirely for the amusement of the good people that would come and visit him in his garden, and especially for their children; and there he would receive them with a cheerful countenance, and enjoy their delight at his contrivances.

Among these things I must also mention a false door which he had made; and when this was opened, another one appeared with a window in it; and as both these doors were directly opposite a green hedge where a beautiful bird cage was placed, and as the window in the inner door was made of a mirror, the effect was most charming and surprising to those who opened it with the intention of entering Swedenborg's 'other garden', which, as he used to say, was much more beautiful than his first one. Swedenborg gained much pleasure from this arrangement, especially when inquisitive and curious young ladies came into his garden.

In front of his house there was an ornamental flower bed on which he spent considerable sums of money. Here he had some of those singular Dutch figures of animals, and other objects shaped out of box-trees; but he did not keep up this bed in his later years. The cultivation of the garden and its produce he left to the gardener.

The fire in the stove of his small study was never allowed to go out, from autumn, throughout the whole winter, until spring; for as he always needed coffee, and as he made it himself, without milk or cream, and as he never had any definite time for sleeping, he always required a fire.

His bedroom was always without fire; and when he went to bed, he covered himself with either three or four woollen blankets depending on the severity of the winter; but I remember one winter so cold that he was obliged to move his bed into his study.

As soon as he awoke, he went into his study, where he always found glowing embers, put wood on the burning coals, and a few pieces of birch-bark, which for convenience he used to purchase in bundles, so as to be able to make a fire speedily; and then he sat down to write.

In his drawing-room was the marble table which he afterwards presented to the Royal Board of Mines; this room was neat and genteel, but plain.[3]

To the picture of the drawing room we can add a few details as noted by Jonas Odhner, later vicar of Lyrestad and progenitor of the many followers of Swedenborg with the same name who still live in the USA. As a young man he visited Swedenborg in 1769, then eighty-one years old, and noted that in the room there was a painting of Charles XII in a battle scene, the framed patent of nobility of his family, and a few pieces of Louis XV style furniture. In the bedroom hung a newly painted portrait of himself.[4]

His lifestyle was always strikingly simple, at home and abroad. During his long stays in foreign countries he lodged with craftsmen, where travel cost him no more than if he had lived at home, wrote Anders Johan von Höpken.[5] The one luxury he seemed to allow himself was snuff: its dust may still be found in his manuscripts. Before his call he often bought books, without being a book collector. Instead of keeping originals he often copied extended excerpts into manuscript notebooks.

His customs at meals, in any case later in life, were very frugal. His midday meal consisted of a bread roll, soaked in warm milk. He did not eat in the evening when at home, Robsahm declares. His consumption of coffee has already been mentioned. When invited out he drank wine, but very moderately.[6]

Into his old age he moved quickly and lightly. His hygiene was certainly that of the 1700s, far from our concept of what is proper. When he lay dying in London in 1772 he was often visited by the Swedish priest Arvid Ferelius, who stated that one of Swedenborg's peculiarities was that he never washed his face and hands, nor did he brush his clothes.

It was unnecessary, he explained; dust and dirt did not stick to him. This statement must rest on a misunderstanding, wrote R L Tafel in his edition of *Documents concerning Swedenborg*.[7] Robsahm has emphasized the contrary: Swedenborg always insisted that there be a 'big bucket of water' in his room.[8]

He clearly had an economical disposition. We quote Robsahm once again:

> Swedenborg did not appear to give alms to beggars, and he was asked why. He said: 'Most of the poor are either lazy or vicious; further, handouts are often harmful to those that receive them. Nevertheless, there is nothing wrong if anyone from plain goodness of heart takes pity on the indigent.' He did not lend money; for, said he, this is the quickest way to lose it. He added that he needed all his money for his travels, and for the printing of his works.[9]

It should be noted that according to unconfirmed reports, Swedenborg made an annual donation to the poor in his congregation.[10]

His health was unusually strong. We know of only two periods of long sickness: in Paris in 1713, and his collapse in London in the summer of 1744. Robsahm reports that he suffered from gallstones in his old age.[11]

Good health was a prerequisite for the long journeys. He always travelled in an 'open, iron carriage, without a servant', wrote Robsahm.[12] It must have been very uncomfortable; flexible wagon springs had not yet appeared in his time.

Pleasant, learned, and odd

Swedenborg made a pleasant impression: thin and lean, talkative and smiling, wrote the librarian Carl Christopher Gjörwell, who visited him in his garden in 1764. He was working then with his flowers.[13]

Anders Johan von Höpken had known him for forty-two years, and 'visited him almost daily' during his last years. In a letter to the Danish Commissioner General Christian Tuxen, dated 11 May 1772, thus some months after Swedenborg's death, von Höpken gave the following description of the personality of the deceased:

> I have lived long in the world, moving in broad social circles and having enjoyed numerous

opportunities of knowing men as to their virtues or vices, their weakness or strength; and as a result of this, I do not recollect having known any man of more uniformly virtuous character than Swedenborg: always contented, never fretful or morose, although throughout his life his mind was occupied with sublime thoughts and speculations. He was a true philosopher, and lived like one; he laboured diligently, and lived frugally without being extreme; he was constantly travelling, and his travels cost him no more than if he had lived at home. He was gifted with a most happy genius, and a fitness for every field of knowledge, which made him shine in all those which he embraced. He was, without contradiction, the most learned man in my country [...] [14]

Such words of praise are blended with criticism and wonder regarding Swedenborg's accounts of his experiences in the spirit world. When Carl Gustaf Tessin visited him in Stockholm in the summer of 1760 Swedenborg told him and his friends about his contacts with the recently deceased Countess Sack. Tessin made the following note quoted already: 'I do not know if I should call a weak-minded man happy or unhappy, a man who finds delight in what he imagines'. [15]

Cuno took the same position. Here is his experience in Amsterdam in 1769:

It soon become known in town that I associated with this remarkable man; and everybody troubled me to give them an opportunity of making his acquaintance. I advised the people to do as I had done, and to call upon him, because he willingly conversed with every honest man. Mr Swedenborg moves in the world with great tact, and knows how to address the high as well as the low. I should have liked very much to introduce him into our club, because he told me that he was fond, occasionally, of playing a game of l'hombre; but as I knew that he did not stop anywhere after seven, and as no High German and only very little French is spoken in our circle, I had to give up [...] Once, however, at the urgent request of the wife of my friend Mr Nicolaus Konauw, I agreed to bring him to dinner. The old gentleman consented and was prepared at once to go. Mr Konauw sent his carriage for us. On presenting ourselves [...] we found among other guests the two Misses Hoog, who had been highly educated [...] in the higher, especially the philosophical, sciences. Mr Swedenborg's deportment was exquisitely refined and gallant. When dinner was announced, I offered my hand to the hostess, and quickly our young man of eighty-one years had put on his gloves and, with an uncommonly charming gesture, presented his hand to Miss Hoog. Whenever he was invited out, he dressed properly and becomingly in black velvet; but usually he wore a brown coat and black trousers. [16]

On this occasion he ate unusually much, to Cuno's surprise. However, 'they could not prevail on him to take more than three glasses of wine, which were half filled with sugar'. The conversation turned upon a certain distinguished personage in The Hague, a former ambassador, who had died some time ago:

'I know him!' Swedenborg exclaimed, 'although I never saw him in his lifetime [...] he was a widower. But he has already married again in the spiritual world, and he now has a wife for all eternity, who is more perfectly in harmony with his disposition than the one with whom he lived in this world.' This remarkable story naturally gave rise to many questions; all of which he answered. The ladies also were so well-bred and discreet as to content themselves with the answers he gave them.

Self-portrait from youth and the great crisis

Thus friends and acquaintances saw the older Swedenborg as a highly educated man with great ambitions, constantly at work, pleasant, economically independent. He was deeply religious, and very particular. To penetrate these outer characteristics we go to his letters and writings.

In early letters and books, as we have seen, we meet a young man of very strong ambitions. His vitality, his energy, and his desire to make a name for himself seem boundless. He would like most of all to produce something 'new', a *novitas*, every day, he writes to Benzelius in January 1718. He also wanted to exchange his place in the Board of Mines for something better suited to his talents in mathematics or in chemistry. Whatever position he gains, no one is going to regard him as unworthy of it, he wrote. His practically minded brother-in-law seems to have warned him that his self-reliance and dynamic intellect could raise bad feelings and envy among powerful people, but Swedenborg did not intend to listen to this advice. On the contrary, he had 'always striven after becoming an object of envy, and as time passed he would probably be even more envied'.

Such a self-image could not be maintained in the long run; scarcely ten years later he had come to other thoughts. In actuality the desire for fame and self-love blocked man's faculty of understanding, we read in the introduction to *The Economy of the Animal Kingdom*. Here he formulated what can be seen as a point of departure for the way of life he would try to lead during his theosophical period. The highest form of knowing descended from the highest source, received in the brain as intuition, inborn with artists.[17] But this faculty of reception can also exist with others, and be successively trained through habit and conscious exercise until finally it is always at hand. Those who have had experiences of such higher knowing recognize it immediately by a multitude of signs:

> When, after a long course of reasoning, they make a discovery of the truth, straightway there is a certain cheering light, and joyful confirmatory brightness, that plays around the sphere of their mind; and a kind of mysterious radiation—I know not whence it proceeds— that darts through some sacred temple of the brain. [18]

A double-exposed picture: Swedenborg and Vilhelm Ekelund

The great crisis in 1744 concerned the dichotomy between egotism and love of God. This contrast also becomes a chief theme in many of Swedenborg's theosophical works. Through his analysis of this tension and its implications his books constitute a full-length self-portrait, unique of its kind in Swedish literature.

The Swedish reader who has best drawn the main lines of this portrait into words is the poet and writer of the early 1900s, Vilhelm Ekelund. On the basis of Swedenborg's works, his individual experiences, and his way of writing, Ekelund emphasized characteristics regarding Swedenborg's view of the conditions and possibilities of creativity. The articulation of these distinctive traits captures much of the essential in Swedenborg's own psychology. Ekelund's aphoristically formed analyses produce a double-exposed picture in which we perceive both him and his subject.

Ekelund underlines the significance of childhood impressions for the adult theosopher: 'His regeneration must have had a long and deep history. He sees himself involved in such a drama'.[19] Swedenborg often speaks of the importance of early experiences of what is good and true. He called them *reliqui* (remnants), impressions that remain, stored up in man, to appear later as an alternative to worldly ways.

Swedenborg emphasizes this starting point as early as the eighth paragraph of *Arcana Caelestia*. In what we can read as a description of his own life crisis he writes that the circumstances under which a choice is made are often associated with 'temptation, misfortune, and sorrow'. His own temptations and setbacks often regarded, as we have seen, the goals he had set up and the possibility of reaching them through science. During his crisis he came to understand that his inmost motivations were his own self-love and ambition, 'the devastating effect of selfishness on the life of truth', in Ekelund's words.

In his dreams Swedenborg heard his father's exhortations to a Christian life and a close and ardent relationship with God: the 'mystical' union. His own crisis led to a rebirth, a 'regeneration', radically changing him inwardly, and sometimes also outwardly, into a new man. It was, in Ekelund's words, 'the conclusive establishment of the character'. In Catholic and pietistic quarters this is the stage of purification; Ekelund spoke of an 'enlargement of the personality'. Man born anew looks on his earlier life as filled with ambition and greed.

Swedenborg's crisis led to what Ekelund calls 'the opening of the inner elements of man'. He realized that 'selfishness is [...] for him completely identical with ignorance'. Ekelund:

> Note how Swedenborg at the beginning of his enlightenment clings to the memory of the state of blessedness experienced in vision, and how he attempts to call it back [...] Preserving and nursing such a desire would be the real formative process [...]

Swedenborg saw his own crisis as a paradigm for the regeneration that every man ought to go through. His description of the successive creation of man in the first chapter of *Arcana Caelestia* may thus be seen as an account of his own.

Ekelund, Swedenborg, and temptations

Robsahm repeats the servants' story of Swedenborg's recurring groaning and battling against temptations during the night, torments which the master explained as coming from evil spirits. Sometimes he could be lying in bed for several days in such anguish, according to Robsahm:

> When such a time was past and his household folk asked him about the cause of his misery, he said, 'Praise God! It's all over now. You should not be concerned about me. For everything that happens to me occurs with the Lord's permission, and he does not let it go on longer than he sees that I can bear it.

Temptations were regarded by Swedenborg as elements in the continual, lifelong strife that was regeneration. They neither could nor should be avoided. Christ's life and suffering on the cross had been just such a victory over enticements to evil. Man should follow his example.

Ekelund often returns to Swedenborg's attitude towards allurements that should be rejected. As always, he applies Swedenborg's words about the conditions of man's relationship to God on an intellectual and artistic level. Yielding to temptations becomes equivalent to capitulating and standing still, to spiritual drought:

> For Swedenborg temptation refers to attacks on the innermost in man's love in life and spirit, the barring of Divine influence, the paralysis of the power of faith. It regards the power of spiritual renewal, productivity in its deepest and most comprehensive sense. [20]

For Ekelund such yielding leads to what in the Middle Ages was called *acedia*: to distraction, resignation, distress, thus the same tribulations as those that Swedenborg was facing:

> It may be interesting to remember how the great characters in classical antiquity comported themselves in such situations. For no one should make us imagine that we here are facing something particular for Christians or a pathology related to Christian faith; it is rather a trait, characteristic for mankind.

Spirits and angels

For Ekelund, the avid seeker and reader, Swedenborg's teaching about angels is an account of the 'houses of the soul' visited by the spirit-seer. He quotes a sentence from *Arcana Caelestia*: 'For when spirits come to a person they enter into possession of his entire memory and call forth from it the things suited to them'.[21] Angels, for Swedenborg, arouse the remnants of happiness from the depths of man's past.[22] In human cultural traditions we always find a relationship to the Divine for the man or woman who is truly willing to be its disciple.

On the opposite side, Swedenborg speaks of hidden places where secrets from the past are stored away. Evil spirits discover them at once. Ekelund has the same experience: 'Is there anything shameful that passed under their nose that they did not know how to ferret out and drag into the open and hold up for your view and enjoyment!'[23]

Rules of life

In the essay on Publius Syrus Mimus that concluded the young Emanuel Swedenborg's years of study at Uppsala, he had rephrased and commented on statements by this Stoic teacher of ancient wisdom. Towards the end of the 1730s Swedenborg's interest in the conduct of life and self-control became noticeable. During the crisis of 1744 the question of 'victory over one's self', also a theme of Publius Syrus Mimus, took a central place. Concentration on a new task seemed to presuppose discipline and total involvement, a careful life: 'Tomorrow is yesterday's disciple', Publius Syrus Mimus had written.

An aid to such an inner composure and 'spiritual thoughts' was the control of breathing, upon which we have already touched. Ekelund returns often to this question, and seems himself to have regarded the 'breathless' instant as the special moment of insight. 'The lesson to be learned about Swedenborg's way of breathing is perhaps more adventurous than all his visions of spirits', he wrote. It involves a 'measured engagement' or pursuit, an emphasis on a strictly regulated manner of living. Through this discipline Swedenborg's life and personality form a link in a long chain of human tradition:

Perfect breathing is wholly measured concentration [...] The most beautiful need is the need to breathe properly. And it is a priceless treasure, that every moment in its essence is a reminder of this need [...][24]

Heavenly clarity, self-love's darkness

Swedenborg's conduct of life was now dictated by insight into what Ekelund called 'the devastating effect of selfishness on the life of truth'. It was a matter of guarding and maintaining a state of mind. Swedenborg saw himself and every human being as a 'receiving vessel' for good or evil. Being receptive to what is good required a strictly controlled conduct of life, what Swedenborg called *cultus*, usually translated as 'worship'. But the concept needs to be clarified; according to Ekelund it concerns 'rituals, adoration, carefulness, and prudence of an unusual nature'.

Swedenborg's way of living had probably always been spartan. After his crisis the regularity in his life seems to have been almost total, in spite of his long journeys. In his role as a member of the Diet he appeared publicly with political and economic contributions; but when fulfilling his divine mission through his writings, he did not wish to have his name mentioned. This anonymity was, in Ekelund's view, not simply maintained for reasons of caution and concern for his safety in Sweden at that day, where it was a crime to spread 'misleading religious doctrines'. Swedenborg was primarily anxious to avoid polemics and being disturbed in what he regarded as his God-given, receptive state. The first human beings, before the Fall, had lived in a constant relationship with the Divine, he wrote in *Arcana Caelestia*. It was this spiritual condition that he sought and often felt himself to have attained. Swedenborg's description of this ideal state presumably corresponded to Ekelund's own experiences, in which the question of how to maintain a spiritual state of openness and receptivity stands in the centre. We quote Swedenborg regarding the ideal state of mankind before the Fall:

> In each object [. . .] they used to perceive something Divine and heavenly. For example, when they saw any high mountain they did not perceive the idea of a mountain but that of height, and from height they perceived heaven and the Lord. That is how it came about that the Lord was said to 'live in the highest' [. . .] The same applies to all other objects [. . .] When they perceived the morning they did not perceive morning time itself [. . .] but that which is heavenly and is a likeness of the morning and of the dawn in people's minds. [25]

Here we find Swedenborg's correspondences as spontaneous inspirations. The doctrine of correspondence is indeed part of man's nature, wrote Ekelund:

> To be sufficiently filled with [unselfish] love was always the goal striven after by all sages. But they always came to the same result as Dostoevsky: life in and for itself always appeared to them as something insufficient. Man cannot love something sufficiently in any other way than as a sign, as a representative [of something higher], be it the sun or a flower or a human being [...]

Swedenborg's teaching about the importance of the state of mind for human insight was in complete agreement with Ekelund's own thinking. Writing about this relationship, he paints simultaneously a picture of his model and of himself:

> [...] however much we may seek to elevate ourselves intellectually and morally, we always fall back to the level of our love: this is the glorious and merciless truth that Swedenborg constantly teaches [...] It is a matter of *being* [...] From love follows order in the understanding [...] hate conveys disorder [...] [26]

Many observers give reports of Swedenborg's calm, harmonious state of mind. When we stand before the works of Swedenborg and other great men, we feel, in Ekelund's words, a 'powerful radiation of their inner happiness'. The visionary, as we have seen, often mentioned his *jucunditas* (joy and felicity):

> God Messiah is everywhere [...] This presence, by the divine mercy [...] of God Messiah, it has been allowed me to experience; as was the case in London, in the street and at home, and in the church in Stockholm. Hence the presence can be deduced, and so can be described. It is an inmost affection, which can never be described; and even if it were described in many words, yet the subject would never be exhausted. Moreover, there are other presences which manifest themselves by peace, felicity, and a more interior sense, which I have frequently experienced during two years. These presences also cannot be described, for there is a manifest sense of felicity [...] [27]

Knowledge and felicity

A typical characteristic of the former scientist was his delight in knowledge that seemed to reveal itself to him when he was 'in the spirit'. Ekelund emphasizes that the 'opening of his inner sight' always seemed to convey a knowledge, an insight, which is independent of dogmatic systems.

All deeper understanding was for Ekelund always filled with delight: 'Knowledge of the highest joy and the way to attain it is the most important and precious'. The acquired insight is never isolated, but leads on to new discoveries. In what could be a paraphrase of a passage in *Arcana Caelestia*, Ekelund writes about these 'chains of truth':

> For the truths that have been assimilated lead [. . .] into wide fields, since every truth has infinite extension, and is connected with manifold others. [28]

These internal connections between truths became a recurring thought with Ekelund. Swedenborg was convinced that the intensity of the experience of truth could be especially great in genuine marriage love. Ekelund reminds us of the title of the book, *De Amore Conjugiali,* usually translated *Conjugial Love*. The full title reads *The delights of wisdom concerning marriage love, after which follow the pleasures of insanity concerning licentious love*. In the relationship between a couple who allow their love to be in harmony with love to God, there comes a sense of understanding and wisdom filled with endless pleasure.

For Swedenborg and Ekelund will and love were two sides of the same thing. Both before and after his crisis Swedenborg seems to have been a man possessed of unusual perseverance, a 'yearning for felicity' in Ekelund's terminology. After his crisis in 1744 Swedenborg seems as if carried on a wave, urging him to communicate the divine message; everything else in his life was of secondary importance.

Insanity too has its pleasure, a sensual delight, but it is unappealing to everyone who has experienced the higher satisfaction. Ekelund dwells often on the visionary's descriptions of the contrast between the highest happiness and spiritual darkness: 'Swedenborg is right: one's own self is hell, that is to say, evil'. For Swedenborg spiritual darkness was connected with his having given in to the self-love that always exists in man. This is valid for all, Swedenborg wrote: even the angels had such experiences of falling from a higher state to a lower one. His many descriptions of the miserable existence of the damned came, according to *Heaven and Hell*, from what he had heard and seen. In Ekelund's opinion these accounts were also a matter of Swedenborg's own observations about the ravages of selfishness in himself. Darkness is punishment; the great crisis in Swedenborg's life concerned just such a 'flight from the self'.

Portrait and self-portrait

Vilhelm Ekelund's psychological analysis of Swedenborg can thus be seen as a self-portrait. For Ekelund, however, the similarity was never simply a question of a relation between a particular reader and a chosen author. The descriptions of spiritual conditions and relationships that he found in Swedenborg were universal. They applied to everybody who with 'higher purposes' was seeking after 'objectivity' in the sense of knowledge vouchsafed to men and women who at least temporarily succeed in freeing themselves from egotism:

> The sacrifice of personality, that played such an important role in the inner life of well-known characters of different creeds, is an ideal to which even worldly education must return. Harmony and the cultivation of truth are empty words without such a renunciation. How do I unite nature and grace? was the constant problem for the religious person. How do I unite nature and art, the naïve brutality of the personal, the egotism, and the ambition with a pure life of truth? How do I free myself from the tyranny of vulgar instincts and give my heart the power and purity without which all culture is hypocrisy and miserable chattering?[29]

For Ekelund the intensely religious and the artistically creative man wrestles with the same problem: 'the innermost need, the motive, and the pain have the same essence'. Ekelund's world of thought illuminates Swedenborg's great panorama, just as Swedenborg's work contributes to the explanation of Ekelund himself.

Emanuel Swedenborg (1688-1772).
Painting by Per Krafft d.ä. (Grh 1040). PHOTO: The National Museum of Fine Arts, Stockholm.

Emanuel Swedenborg.
Painting by Carl Friedrich Brander. Nordiska museet, Stockholm.

Jesper Swedberg (1653-1735).
Painting by Okänd konstnär (Grh 1008). PHOTO: The National Museum of Fine Arts, Stockholm.

Sara Behm (1666-96).
Painting by Okänd konstnär. Nordiska museet, Stockholm.

Charles XII (1682-1718).
Painting by David von Krafft (Drh 376). PHOTO: The National Museum of Fine Arts, Stockholm.

Christopher Polhem (1661-1751).
Painting by David von Krafft (Grh 1015). PHOTO: The National Museum of Fine Arts, Stockholm.

Louisa Ulrika (1720-82).
Painting by Alexander Roslin (Drh 35).
PHOTO: The National Museum of Fine
Arts, Stockholm.

Anders Johan von Höpken
(1712-89).
Painting by K F Brander (Grh 1517).
PHOTO: The National Museum of Fine Arts,
Stockholm.

Fredrik I (1676-1751).
Painting by Martin van Meytens d.y. (Drh 1355). PHOTO: The National Museum of Fine Arts, Stockholm.

Ulrika Eleonora (1688-1741).
Painting by Martin van Meytens d.y. (Drh 401). PHOTO: The National Museum of Fine Arts, Stockholm.

Chapter Twenty-Six

But the living all mistakenly
stress what separates.
Angels often do not know if they move among
the living or the dead. The eternal flood, deafening,
drags all the ages through both realms.

R M Rilke: Duino Elegies, First Elegy

Vanity fair and the Last Judgement

In the year 1756 France, Russia, Austria, and the German-Roman Empire declared war against Frederick the Great's Prussia and Hanoverian England. A year later Sweden joined the nations battling against Frederick, though he was the brother of the Swedish queen. With good fortune in war and French money there was a possibility of winning back some of the Pomeranian territory that had been lost at the Peace of Nystad in 1721. Swedenborg's friend and a member of the Hat party, Anders Johan von Höpken, was Prime Minister and as such the highest official in the government responsible for initiating hostilities. The Parliament was not consulted.

Sweden's financial position had become increasingly weak during the 1750s. The economy worsened as a result of the costs of war, in no way covered by the promised French subsidies. Paper money was printed without funds to cover its value, and abroad the Swedish currency fell quickly. For Swedenborg this meant an increase in the cost of printing, unless when abroad he had direct access to foreign currency.

During these years Swedenborg observed an increasing moral decay. The poet Gustaf Fredrik Gyllenborg, whose uncle was the notoriously corrupt Fredrik Gyllenborg, described the situation in his poem 'Contempt for the World':

I'm now racking my brain, new riddles to answer:

Rich and mighty you'll be? Take money and squander,

One builds great castles, and owns not a stone,

One strives for honour, and pretends to be democratic.

One has his own wife for his friend's jollity,

One joins in a pair, from each other to flee.

One speaks of all, while knowing nothing,

One lies to friends while socializing,

One says black is white, and makes it believable [...] [1]

It was now, in 1757, that according to Swedenborg's testimony the Last Judgement took place in the spiritual world that he felt himself able to visit. He then saw clearly what he had perhaps sensed and suspected earlier. From the celestial realms deceased persons known to the visionary were cast down into appropriate hells. The hypocrites and liars were unmasked, and people who had presented themselves as exemplary figures had their inner nature laid bare.

In 1758 Swedenborg was seventy years old. During the spring or summer he travelled to London. This was a year of culmination in his authorship. At Lewis's he published his now best-known work, *Heaven and Hell*. As a subtitle the anonymous author added 'According to what I have heard and seen'. Besides this he published four smaller works: *De Telluribus in Mundo Nostri Solari* (*Worlds in Space*); *The Last Judgment*; *De Nova Hierosolyma et ejus Doctrina Coelesti* (*The New Jerusalem and its Heavenly Doctrine*); and *The White Horse*. He also worked on his first great commentary on the Revelation of John. This was first printed after his death, in 1785, under the title *Apocalypsis Explicata*. It filled four volumes in Latin.

Angels, the Bible, and Luther

Heaven and Hell treats of the life after this one, and of angels and demons. Swedenborg's intensive involvement with the world of angels is incomprehensible without a look backwards.

Angels are often mentioned in the Scriptures, mostly in the Old Testament. During the long wandering in the wilderness the children of Israel are led by an angel. In the Book of Psalms we read about the angels guarding the pious in all their ways: 'They shall bear you up in their hands, Lest you dash your foot against a stone. You shall tread upon the lion and the cobra, The young lion and the serpent you shall trample under foot'. [2]

We meet angels also in the New Testament, above all at the annunciation to Mary and at Christ's empty grave. Jesus himself speaks of angels, but without mentioning their life and tasks. In the first chapter of the Gospel of John they appear in a prophecy: 'you shall see heaven open, and the angels of God ascending and descending upon the Son of Man'. [3] And from this viewpoint the apocryphal Book of Tobit is significant: here the hero is led by the archangel Raphael.

Thus the angels are 'intermediate beings' standing near to God. Luther did not deny their significance. The feast of the angels, Michaelmas, is still celebrated in most Lutheran churches, but the reformer warned against superstition. Angels were not needed after Christ's birth because there was the divine Word in the gospels, and God's face was to be seen there. Generally speaking, according to Luther, man should not rely on private revelations: doing so involved a contempt for God and his means of grace. We should never turn to angels for information on spiritual questions:

> If God wants to speak to me in a dream or in my sleep and give me signs and warnings about temporal things, as he did to the Wise Men when they wanted to return to Herod, I am content with that. For the eternal life, however, I need no new revelation. And [...] if such should reach me, I would be suspicious [...] on account of the Satan's roguish deceitfulness [...] For God reveals himself completely and richly enough in baptism and in the priestly office. [4]

Death as the gateway to life

Who were the angels? What happens after death? Do the decomposing parts of the body remain in the graves from death until the trumpets of the Last Judgement announce that the day of wrath has come? Or is death the passage to a new life? Christ's words to the thief on the cross are sometimes cited as an argument for an immediate transition from one existence to another: 'today you will be with Me in Paradise'. [5]

According to Catholic faith an intermediate period follows after death when souls are purified from earthly sin. Protestants rejected the thought of such a purgatory. Some were of the opinion that the soul slumbered in its grave, in an unconscious state. Calvin thought that the soul rested, but was conscious of standing before God's face.

The Swedish church manual did not hesitate. Man had come from earth, and to earth he would return; then, 'Jesus Christ, your Saviour, will awaken you on the last day'. It was the day of judgement, when the sheep would be separated from the goats. In Bishop Swedberg's hymn book he inserted a song by the Swedish poet Lasse Lucidor, describing what awaited the evil man:

O body and limb: Shake and tremble, shiver and shudder.
My hair, stand on end. My thought descends
to the depths of the abyss and sees
the anguish gnawing all, but not devouring. [6]

As we have seen, the bishop himself had a somewhat different conception of the matter. We must distinguish between body and soul. The body becomes earth, 'but the spirit, which does not pass away or rot like the body, comes without any detour or delay directly to God'. And in the presence of God the soul will give an account of its life. Each and everyone comes to eternal happiness or to an equally eternal suffering.

As regards the fate of the spirit after death, Emanuel Swedenborg had essentially the same conception as his father. The difference was that with the son it was not at all a question of faith but a matter of certainty, based on actual experience. From April 1745 and throughout his life Swedenborg had by divine grace, according to his own often repeated assertions, received a special ability to cross the boundary between life and death. In conversations with angels, spirits, and demons he had been able to form an exact understanding of this passage. Moreover, he had been given the opportunity to travel in regions of heaven and hell. He also had information on the fates that befell those who had not qualified for heaven during life on earth. From *Arcana Caelestia* to *The True Christian Religion* his books are full of accounts of what he has 'heard and seen' in these realms, inaccessible to others. It is primarily these accounts that created Swedenborg's reputation. The doctrine itself—which for Swedenborg naturally was the most important —was regarded as secondary.

The passage and the inner memory

Usually the deceased does not immediately understand that he has left the earthly life, wrote Swedenborg. The soul instantly enters a special spirit world, neither heaven nor hell. It functions as a kind of supernatural transit area.

Here his life seems to be the same as he had led before death. In the beginning we look the same, and behave in our usual way. But with death the mask that life has laid over man's face soon falls away. Swedenborg cites the Gospel of Luke:

Whatever you have spoken in the dark will be heard in the light, and what you have spoken in the ear in inner rooms will be proclaimed on the housetops. [7]

We then acquire our right and final form: the essential form and posture we ourselves have given our life on earth. We take up this life in our spiritual body.

This body is structured by what Swedenborg calls the inner memory. There everything we have longed for and have been doing during life is registered. But in his earthly existence man knows nothing about this inner faculty. Here we use our outer memory. In comparison with the inner memory it is incomplete and weak, with large gaps:

People who are governed by false persuasion and evil desire imbibe and retain all things that suit them, for these things enter into them like water into a sponge [...] But those who believe in truth and have an affection for good retain all things that are true and good, and are consequently being perfected all the time [... through] instruction. [8]

It is this spiritual bodily form that lives on to the fullness of time. The body and the soul lie like a fallen tree: it is too late for change. [9] We see what we want to see, we understand what we want to understand.

At this stage, before a person's nature is unquestionably revealed, a clarification of the spiritual profile of the deceased may be necessary. With or without angelic help the spirit then undergoes a *vastatio* (purification), or a *devastatio* (devastation). [10] Swedenborg distinguishes the outer and the inner aspects of man in the same way that he distinguishes between the outer and the inner memory. We may outwardly appear to be good but in our innermost be evil. In a similar way the inwardly good person may be burdened with outer, loosely attached evils. The good man is purified from his evil, and the evil one from his overlay of good. In each case his true self comes forth.

Swedenborg frequently describes his visits in these middle states. Some spirits may wait a long time for their final destination to become clear. There may be good qualities in the inner memory that conflict with bad ones in the outer memory. Both Luther and Melanchthon were such cases: they waited more than two hundred years.[11] Swedenborg had long conversations with Luther in particular. He attempted to convince the reformer about his faulty doctrine of justification and the absurdity of his refusal to believe in free-will. Gradually Luther let himself be convinced. Swedenborg had then been visiting him daily. Luther had adopted these mistaken beliefs in his zeal to battle Catholicism. When he finally came to clarity he smiled at his own stupidities, the visiting Swede noted. Melanchthon also came to better thoughts after conversations with Swedenborg. The good that was in their inner memory had at long last taken control over the outer, and heaven was opened for the two men.

Angelic states of mind

That God would punish man was an irrational thought in Swedenborg's view. If we are to use the word 'punishment' at all, it is man who punishes himself. Nor can there be any purging fire that burns away the sins of the deceased. Sin originates in a perverse love. If we have no genuinely good love during earthly life, there is nothing that can be done about it. Once again, as the tree falls, so it lies. [12]

Heaven is not a limited space but an ever-expanding gathering of souls whose states of mind develop forever. Here dwell the angels, the blessed, who during their lives have chosen to be governed by love to God and their fellow man. Those with similar angelic loves gather to each other in communities. The angels are images of the Lord, but they are not divine. They have never lost their *proprium* (the sense of being independent beings with good and bad characteristics). The angels' state of mind inspires them to see well planned, handsome cities, beautiful palaces, parks and gardens. When their *proprium* dominates, their spiritual state is changed, and with it also their environment. The exterior 'noble castles, sky-high towers, and cathedral arches' are as in Shakespeare's

The Tempest only projections of the thoughts and feelings of the blessed. But still tangible: the supernatural figures find pleasure in their gardens, in nature, and in the beautiful halls of heavenly palaces.

Here there is neither time nor space. The subjective nature of the exterior explains the changing sceneries and the rapid movements of the blessed. August Strindberg was an attentive reader of Swedenborg and described the world of dreams in a way that immediately takes one's thoughts to the spiritual journeys described in Swedenborg's works:

> Men and women are split, doubled [...] evaporate, are condensed, flow out, gather. But the dreamer's consciousness stands over the changing scenery; for there are no secrets here, nothing inconsequential, no scruples, no law. He does not judge, he does not approve, he is only relating [...] [13]

The angels' life and service

The meaning of blessedness and the life of the angels have been discussed in all ages. What are the angels doing? Do they gather in praise around the Lord of the universe, simply enjoying eternal and blessed rest? As we have seen, motion, activity, growth were fundamental factors in Swedenborg's view of life. To stand still was unproductive and perhaps equivalent to spiritual death. Consequently the angels were always at work: each and every one found the task that best suited his or her love. Those seeking knowledge could be assured that they would always, to all eternity, penetrate further and higher into divine wisdom. Activity in heaven was necessary, Swedenborg wrote in a well-known 'memorable relation', that begins his book *Conjugial Love*. [14]

In Swedenborg's presence an angel trumpeted and called together brilliant minds from the whole Christian world to tell what they thought about heavenly joy and blessedness. One group expressed the thought that being happy in heaven was simply a matter of being admitted there, another that blessedness was conversation with angels. A third group thought that heavenly joy was the continual pleasure of delicious dinners with Abraham and his descendants. Others supposed that it was dwelling in the Garden of Paradise; still others thought that felicity was in heavenly power, splendour, and riches. A sixth group saw heavenly happiness as consisting in continually praising the Lord.

Fig. 37.   The river is flowing so beautifully
            Rosalduna is sailing, forward, mild, beautiful,
            The river flows slowly to secret, pious regions,
            The sailing there is beautiful
            At Rosalduna's sides stand a boy, a girl,
            Wondering, they look forward to the sky.

The Swedish poet C J L Almqvist, deeply influenced by Swedenborg's theosophy, described the angels' upbringing of children after their death: 'One song described Rosalduna's sailing trip […] It is a scene from that world of life, called the world of spirits. Infants, boys, and girls who had died on earth are brought to the company of angels; and one of the higher women spirits, Rosalduna, is the teacher for some of them. When the instruction has come to an end, she embarks upon a ship, sailing away to their eternal home'. *Book of the Briar Rose*, Stockholm 1833.

They were all mistaken. Each and all were given the opportunity to try out their ideas, but after a short time all of them were bored.

At the end comes the moral. The angel with the trumpet declared:

You can now see that the joys of heaven and everlasting happiness are not places, but are the conditions of a person's life [. . .] it is service which holds together love and wisdom [. . .] Everyone who becomes an angel carries within himself his own heaven. For man is by creation a small-scale effigy, image and model of the great heaven. The human form is nothing else. Therefore each person comes into the community in heaven of which he is formed as a particular effigy. [15]

Thus blessedness consists in activity that is of use to the whole. Its form and expression is always related to the angel's character. Some are teachers for adults or small children. Others are priests and preachers. As mentioned, angels may become increasingly wise, to their own delight.

Angels have important tasks on earth; in this earthly life we all have two angels beside us, suitable to our spiritual state. The word 'angel' comes from the Greek and means 'messenger'. The angels receive divine instructions, and communicate them to men.

The experiences and facts in the angels' outer memory have slipped out of mind. Angels therefore have no past. What they know is in their activity, Swedenborg writes. Those who come into their presence understand their language. The closer to God they are, the quieter they become; then they communicate through their inner strength without words.

If earth is a nursery for heaven, heaven is in its turn a path towards greater perfection. No one can become perfect: that would involve an impossibility, a standing still. But the life of the angels is never led in the same direction unceasingly, forward and upward. Sometimes their love cools and with it also their wisdom. Light and warmth are then changed to twilight and a feeling of uneasiness. So must it be, Swedenborg reports. Even in heaven variation is necessary.

Most things in Swedenborg's view of creation are divided into three levels. We find a threefold division in heaven: there are heavenly, spiritual, and natural angels. They dwell in corresponding heavens: the heavenly, spiritual, and natural. The highest of all states is the third and inmost. Here the angel is so near to the divine truths that he identifies himself with them. The wisdom of these angels is like an 'amazingly beautiful palace'.[16] The angels of the second degree, the spiritual, see the inner meaning in all things, but without the clarity that characterizes those in the innermost heaven. In the first and outermost heaven are the natural angels, with lower and natural insights.

Who were Swedenborg's angels?

Good men and women become angels after death. Could man become an angel already in this life? No, we must first pass through the gates of death. But good people here on earth could become like angels. In a dream or vision Swedenborg had been informed that the people who were nearest to God lived in Africa. There they thought in an 'inner way', living in communities governed by laws of mutual love. On one occasion he sketched a map of the African continent showing where these people would be found. His opinion of the characteristics and life of the black peoples would, as we shall see, leave its tracks in history.

Swedenborg's way of thinking was always concrete: he avoided abstractions as much as possible. Thus for him the angels were embodiments of love and wisdom, incarnated states of mind. [17]

His meetings with the angels were always meetings between states, his own and the angels'. His communication with their feelings or loves was like meetings with faces. No face was like another, as no spiritual states could ever be identical. The angels nearest God radiated light and life, he wrote, so intensively and varyingly that no painter could ever portray them.

Thus travels in the spirit world were the same as spiritual changes of state: 'In this way I have been transported by the Lord to the heavens [...] by my spirit being transported, while my body remained behind in its place'.[18] This thought is often repeated in Swedenborg's writings. After his call in 1744-5, the whole of his spiritual energy seems to have been concentrated on his divine mission. While writing *The Word Explained* he sought intensively for guidance. In December 1745, eight months after the definitive and final call, he noted the following regarding his God-given instruction: 'As for me, there has not been the least moment of thought, affection, persuasion that came [from myself]'.

[This] is a fact which, for the space of eight months, has been so sensible to me that there was not even the least thing which did not flow in from without [...] The reason why angels flow in is because of their activity [...] they are active forces. Such also will men become after death [...] [19]

The angels' faces and bodily forms lose their resemblance to those they had on earth. Swedenborg could nevertheless recognize them again, providing he had known something about their life on earth. He himself had had a loving relationship with his mother Sara Behm and his stepmother Sara Bergia, who died in 1696 and 1720 respectively. In his *The Spiritual Diary* these two women, 'my mothers', appear on just one occasion:

Spirits known to me told me that my mothers said they had tidy homes where they lived, but which could not be shown to me. Other spirits might then get an idea of them. They said that houses were given to them, and that they were changed [from time to time]. They always had some task to do [...] and were happy [...] [20]

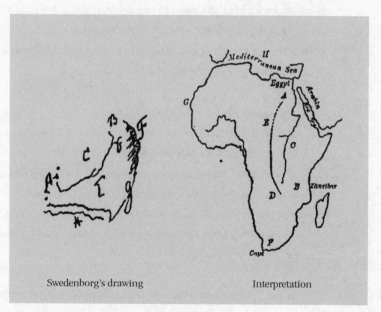

Fig, 38. Swedenborg met wise Africans in the spirit world: 'they had the truths of the church within themselves.' He sketched a map of the continent in his journal. Its first English publishers clarified the map (*The Spirtual Diary* n 5946). The most pious Africans were believed to dwell east of Sierra Leone. The Swedish alchemist August Nordenskjöld sought for them, with catastrophic results.

Swedenborg's drawing

Interpretation

'Abraham does not know us'

Abraham in his heaven did not recognize his descendants: 'Abraham did not know us.' In *The Word Explained* Swedenborg several times cites the 63rd chapter of Isaiah, showing the great distance between the man who has been raised to God and earthly human beings:

> The angels do not know us. For a long time I believed that the innermost ... angels knew what I was doing and thinking [...] But they knew nothing [...] So it is God the Messiah alone, who acts through his angels [...] This is what is meant by the words, 'Abraham does not know us.' Today by means of a certain abstract thought, something ascended [from me] to the angels. They were moved by this, speaking to me through the spirit. Nor do the angels want to know what happens on earth, because they are aware that everything here is perverted and destroyed [...] [21]

In spite of this estrangement, man has been given the ability to be together with them, Swedenborg emphasized in *Arcana Caelestia*; but usually we could not know who an angel had been during his earthly life. A year before his death Swedenborg wrote to a German prince who had asked to be informed about several deceased friends. He told the prince that the angels have forgotten their earthly names, and had been given new ones corresponding to their states. If he were to meet them in the spiritual world, he needed to know something about them. The letter continues:

> For this reason when I wish to speak to anyone, I must think of and put forth some idea of his character, and then, if he is not altogether too distant from me, he either becomes present, or I speak with him from afar, yet never by merely naming the person. Pardon me therefore, most noble Duke, for being unable to satisfy your command and desires with regard to the four persons, as I would do most willingly if it had been possible. I speak daily with a great many persons, also with such as held positions of great dignity, without my knowing who they were or what kind of persons they had been in the world. Possibly some one of the four mentioned by you was among them [...] [22]

If the prince had read Swedenborg's *Heaven and Hell*, he could have known more from the author's accounts of his meetings with angels. Sometimes he felt that an angel was an acquaintance from childhood, while others were totally unknown. Those who appeared as childhood friends were such as were in a state similar to Swedenborg's own. Those who were unfamiliar to him had another frame of mind.

The darkness of the evil

Angels are with man, fostering his good will; but in doing so they are never alone. Also at our side are evil spirits, demons. These too have at one time been living men and women. After death their true character showed itself: their dominant love had been evil. In the same way as the angels form a heaven, all those who have chosen states of evil arrange themselves in a contrasting dark shadow-shape of the home of goodness, consisting of innumerable hells.

The dead, good and evil, are in our midst:

Man is totally unaware of the fact that the Lord is governing him by means of angels and spirits, and that at least two spirits and two angels are present with everyone [...] As long as [a person] is unregenerate, evil spirits reside with him, who have such dominion over him that angels, though present, can accomplish little more than simply distract him from plunging into utter evil and so divert him towards something good [...] When however he is regenerate it is the angels who then have dominion, and they breathe into him every kind of good and truth, as well as a horror and dread of evils and falsities. Angels do indeed lead, yet they are but servants, for it is the Lord alone who, by means of angels and spirits, governs a person. Now because this is done through the ministry of angels, it is said here [Genesis 1: 26] in the plural, 'Let Us make man in Our image'. [23]

In the region between heaven and hell all the outer characteristics thus disappear, and our inner, hidden features are revealed. Those who are oriented toward material things, more or less evil, come to rest in the place or that corresponds to the state of their love. Gluttons continue to gorge themselves, wiping the sweat from their forehead in the same way as during earthly life, complaining of their colic. The intriguers in Swedish political life continue fabricating their schemes to all eternity. Swedenborg describes hells, where the inhabitants live in the same godless state as during life on earth: the inferno of the deceivers; the quarters of the unjust; biased judges; the hellish sewers of the murderers. They have all chosen their fates during life on earth and by this also after death. Hell's inhabitants accept their surroundings and are scarcely conscious of their situation:

> I have heard that the infernal spirits neither see nor feel these things [...] partly because they are as in their own atmosphere, and thus in the delight of their life, partly because their situation corresponds to the evils and falsities in which they are. For fire corresponds to hatred and revenge, smoke and soot to the false ideas arising from these [...] [24]

Their desperate situation is only revealed for a few moments when a visitor from the heavenly realms passes by: as did Swedenborg for the purposes of study, with angels as guides. Then the devils can suddenly be struck by a horrible suspicion that there is, perhaps, another and better life.

The topography of hell is described by the visiting Swede. Key words in his tours of the underworld stage are 'caves' and 'caverns', 'holes', 'animal dens', 'ruins of burnt-down houses and cities', 'bordellos full of rubbish and excrement'. But the demons are in a relatively balanced equilibrium; they are in the evil that filled their heart during their earthly life.

The attack of the demons: man's temptations

In the world as seen by Swedenborg, evil spirits are the inevitable companions of every human being. They reveal their presence through temptations, enticements to deviations from the narrow way. Between the powers of good and evil there is a continual conflict, with man as the arena. When choosing good, he is encouraged by angels, in the opposite case by demons:

> Spirits from hell are constantly on the attack, and angels provide protection [...] The angels [...] also dispel any strange and new influences which can produce evil effects. In particular the angels call forth the forms of good and truth residing with a person and set them opposite the evils and falsities activated by the evil spirits. As a result the person is

in the middle and is not conscious of the evil or of the good; and being in the middle he is in freedom to turn towards one or towards the other. [25]

Unlike the angels, the evil spirits were often recognizable. During his journeys in the lower world Swedenborg often met infernal beings from his own circle of acquaintances. As we have seen in the chapter describing his journal from 1745-65, he records how malicious relatives and well-known, now deceased politicians plague him with toothaches or itching, or disturb his peace of mind in other ways.

He saw the angels in connection with his Bible studies, and in dreams and visions. The demons seemed to turn up most frequently in dreams. When he awoke he sometimes made sketches of the landscapes of hell, or illustrations of the revolutions in heaven recorded in the Book of Revelation.

Are punishments eternal? Can man be persuaded to give up the state that he finds most delightful? Within the 'New Church' this problem has been discussed through the centuries: there is a whole body of literature on the question. The tree lies as it fell, Swedenborg wrote. What did he mean?

Politics: the art of the possible

Chapter Twenty-Seven

The Holy Scripture pictures the whole world as a kingdom ruled by God alone, and to whose peoples he gives their masters, good and evil, to be the instruments of his mercy or justice. These masters, who are those who hold the highest powers, one must love and respect, and obey their instructions [. . .] And consequently there is a complete agreement between the light of the Holy Scripture and our conception of politics.

François Fénelon [1]

The Pomeranian war

Heaven and Hell and *The White Horse* were published in London in 1758. Five years would pass before Swedenborg left another manuscript at the printers in Amsterdam or London. In the interval he drafted his long exposition of the Apocalypse, and works on heavenly wisdom and providence that would be published in 1763 and 1764. At the same time, during the beginning of the 1760s, he was active in Swedish politics.

Many years prior to this Sweden had come to enter the so-called 'French system'. France, together with Poland, Sweden, and Turkey, was to attempt to hold back the Russian efforts at expansion in Europe. Now France had entered instead into a treaty with Russia. Frederick the Great of Prussia saw himself in the process of being surrounded by hostile powers, and in 1756 he attacked neighbouring Saxony. England and Hanover under King George II were his allies. The French ambassador in Stockholm promised the Swedish Hat-party government under Anders Johan von Höpken great advantages, money and regained territory, in return for Swedish involvement in the war. Through the peace treaty in Stockholm in 1720 King Frederick's father, Frederick William I, had won southern Pomerania and Stettin from Sweden. Here, now, it was suggested, was a possibility for revenge.

In 1757 Sweden's government joined the warring entente without the Diet's approval, promising 20,000 men to Swedish Pomerania for attacks on Prussian territory. Sweden had thus manoeuvred herself into a strange diplomatic constellation by virtue of the fact that her queen, Louisa Ulrika, was the Prussian king's sister.

The Swedish army was poorly equipped. Von Höpken and his government realized that the promised French subsidies would in no way cover the costs, but too late. Money must be found, in spite of the fact that decisions regarding taxation or loans required the agreement of the Diet. The government solved the problem by ordering the Central Bank to print more money.

The Diet in Stockholm

The Diet met in Stockholm in October 1760. The political climate was the worst imaginable for von Höpken and his government. According to Carl Gustaf Tessin, the nation faced an 'unexpected war, exorbitant inflation, an unbearable foreign exchange rate, a shameless luxuriance, a devastating cost of living'.[2]

The war and its costs, the financial policy, the well-placed politicians' way of enriching themselves using their position: all this created a situation where even the Hat Party members criticized the government. Some kind of accountability for the government's misuse of power was required. The attacks concentrated on von Höpken and two other members of the government. In February 1761, von Höpken submitted his resignation.

Swedenborg's appeal

Here Emanuel Swedenborg enters the scene. In the days following von Höpken's resignation, Swedenborg formulated a memorandum to the four Estates. Von Höpken was a man of honour, he wrote. The Diet should continue to give him the trust he deserved, for he had always been inspired by an honest and patriotic will. 'I am well acquainted', Swedenborg wrote, 'with his good intentions'. As regards the war, von Höpken had recommended that only 6,000 men be sent to Pomerania. If the proposal of the prime minister had gone through, the French subsidies would have been sufficient with no loan needed for armaments and maintenance.[3]

Thus Swedenborg vouched for von Höpken's good intentions. A half-year later the four

Estates declared that all three of the accused enjoyed their full confidence. Von Höpken would afterwards re-enter the government, although only for a short time. Behind the speedy counter-action lay many votes: Swedenborg's significance in this undertaking was presumably peripheral. His contribution is of interest mainly on the personal plane.

Absolute monarchy and Catholicism

Swedenborg also wrote another, longer *Humble Memorandum* to the Estates, presented to the Diet in July 1761.[4] Its background was firstly the war and the government's responsibility. Secondly, we find references to King Adolf Fredrik and Queen Louisa Ulrika's unsuccessful coup in 1756. The royal couple and their followers had wanted to put an end to the prevailing parliamentary system and give the king real power. Those responsible had been executed. The royalty had been humbled; if the king were to continue with attempts to undermine the constitution, he risked his throne.

In connection with these events, Swedenborg expresses his strong faith in Sweden's constitution. Thus his document begins with a defence of von Höpken and the other criticized members of the government.

In the first place, they had always stood up for Sweden's excellent constitution, in every way opposing all attempts directed towards the restoration of absolute monarchy. In connection with praising the merits of the three statesmen, he described the dangers of royal political sovereignty, of the perils of which he had personal experience. However, his reasoning also gives expression to his own religious standpoint and his abhorrence of papal power. Absolute monarchy could easily give in to Catholic enticements. The church of the pope, the great whore of the Book of Revelation, had lured to itself not only Swedish monarchs like King Sigismund and Queen Christina, but absolute monarchs in Germany had also succumbed to the Vatican's temptations. In the constitution established in 1720 there were built-in guarantees against such catastrophes.

His second line of argument is one of principles of foreign policy. In entering the war on the continent, von Höpken and his colleagues had only acted in accordance with the existing Swedish-French alliance. The Diet, the Secret Committee, and the government had respected this treaty and found it in agreement with the kingdom's interests ever since the acceptance of the new constitution. He continues:

The principal reason for this is that France is far from Sweden. Our geographical positions necessarily preclude the recurrence of any difficulties between us respecting the partition of lands and provinces. France can look upon the increasing wealth, industry, and prosperity of Sweden without jealousy. This cannot be expected from England; for since that country and Hanover have been united under one sovereign, and since as Elector of Hanover he has come into the possession of lands which formerly belonged to Sweden, his interests are turned against us, and ours against him. This situation cannot be overlooked or forgotten by either party. Until this problem has lost its actuality, our respective interests must remain irreconcilable.[5]

Anders Nordencrantz and the excellent constitution

A French observer must have found a curious contradiction between Swedenborg's praise of the French alliance and his support of Sweden's constitution. From the French perspective the Swedish internal political situation was comparable to the notorious disorder in Poland. The king was practically powerless. The government's position and authority was influenced by the political winds in the Diet, and the changes of those winds depended on the bribes that foreign powers would present. Consequently, seen from the French perspective, the only way of getting order and consistency in Swedish politics was to bring about a radical change in the Swedish political system. Above all, it was necessary to give essential influence to the king.

Later, when the Cap Party had regained power, disposed toward friendly relations with Russia, Paris would explain that its patience was at an end. Subsidies of all French money would be withheld until there was a change in the ruinous constitution.

In Swedenborg's view, the Swedish constitution was among the best in the world.[6] He had on many earlier occasions touched on the 1720 constitution and its implementation, but only superficially. During the Diet of 1760-2, in several addresses and memoranda he reviewed and explained his position regarding the Swedish form of government where he himself functioned as a member of the Diet. In this way he was replying to the criticism that had begun to be heard from different quarters in the country.

The immediate cause of Swedenborg's argument was a 690-page document written by the economist and Cap Party politician Anders Nordencrantz. The book was a strongly critical attack on current policy in the economical and political spheres: a system of warring cliques, anarchy, corruption, and economic chaos. Besides, there was a dangerous integration of the legislative and the judicial powers: the Diet's deputations functioned in reality, according to Nordencrantz, as courts. The government, considering the book as dangerous, ordered that it should be available to the public only after approval by the Estates.

Swedenborg's contribution rests on a comparison between absolute rule and popular rule.[7] A democratic system always involves risks and drawbacks, but the dangers are much greater by far with an absolute ruler. It was easy to enumerate Swedish shortcomings and improper actions. The same applied to Holland and England, which together with Sweden had the best forms of government in the world. But men are not perfect, and there will always be misconduct; no perfect system of rules will ever exist.

Continuing his detailed analysis Swedenborg argued that Nordencrantz never took up the positive sides of the present system, only the negative; but when we concentrate exclusively on injustices and faults, being blind to positive elements, we are treading a dangerous path. Criticism becomes amplified and even balanced citizens can feel tempted to change and ruin the social calm and order.

Our system of government has a particular advantage, Swedenborg writes in his memorandum, because everything is arranged in chain-like systems, with higher and lower levels of authority. We see the Swedenborgian concept of series and degrees, now transferred to the political sphere. Above all the citizens stands the king, who was to live according to the law of the land, providing a supreme example to all. Below him stands the judiciary, from the Supreme Court (over which the king presides) to the Court of Appeal to the District Courts. The same principle holds in matters of civil law. At the head stands the king with the national government, below whom are the provincial governors and the sheriffs and local officials.

The laws, made by the representatives of the people in the Diet, should regulate all activity. 'Law is justice, and all justice worth the name is Divine', he had written in a little book, entitled *The New Jerusalem and its Heavenly Doctrine*, published in 1758.[8]

Swedenborg was a fervent supporter of a parliamentary system controlling practically all political power. The ultimate authority should proceed from the Diet, notably the legal system. A separation of powers of the type proposed by the famous French philosopher Montesquieu was foreign to him.

Justice is a scale with two pans, he explains at the end of his *Humble Memorandum*. Completely opposed to the thought of separating the legislative from the judicial powers Swedenborg refers to a special, extraordinary committee set up by the four Estates to investigate the unsatisfactory conditions to which Nordencrantz had called attention. Here the mistakes should be corrected and those having acted with evil intention would be punished. But when mistakes have been made as a result of human weakness, they should be excused. However the committee must be cautious:

> [...] above all I hope care will be taken lest by an enumeration of too many short-comings it creates among the people themselves, and among the now assembled Estates, discontent with the excellent government established among us. For in that case, in accordance with the old proverb, it might be that in avoiding Charybdis one falls into Scylla, and that from the egg which is supposed to contain a bird of paradise there is hatched a basilisk.[9]

Politics and the divine order

Swedenborg paints a picture of a political utopia, far from the polemics and intrigues at the Diet which met in 1760. His political thoughts reflect his religious convictions. In all matters there is a divine order from which comes all wisdom and truth. Love to God and the neighbour, practically applied, is man's task and vocation.

The body of society is like that of the heavenly 'Grand Man'. On a celestial plane, all the parts of the body work together for the common good. Every part of the body has its tasks, and all are under the loving and wise leading of the head.

Swedenborg saw the nation and its mode of government in a similar way. Man, as a citizen, is a member in a body. The royal Majesty himself, the head, had been given strongly limited powers in the forms of government established in the 1720s. The king guaranteed law and order. He could be likened to the 'king that the children of Israel set up over themselves', Eric Benzelius had explained in a sermon at the conclusion of the 1723 session of the Diet. The king's power thus proceeded from the people. As with King David, his highest and sacred duty was to hold unswervingly to the ten divine commandments.

In accord with the same view, the leaders of the Diet were an embodiment of the nation, the people themselves. In this political body unity and order were not merely practical, necessary terms: concord was God's purpose. In contrast, absolute monarchy, where a single individual sees himself as the man who carries out what is really the community's task, actually involves a denial of the higher purposes of social life.

Those reading Swedenborg's contributions to the meeting of the Diet in 1760 presumably found Nordencrantz's concrete critique more urgent than the assessor's pious hopes, warnings, and concerns for the constitution. The abuse had gone too far, quite apart from the war and the costs of war. Von Höpken himself joined in the criticism, denouncing 'the boundless, indecent plundering of public resources'.[10]

The Diet was dissolved in 1763. At the turn of the year 1761-2 the two combatants, Swedenborg and Nordencrantz, had perhaps become reconciled in spite of their conflicting differences. Swedenborg's old friend Niklas von Oelreich, known from the *Dream Diary* and the escapades in London in 1744, belonged to the Caps and was an associate of Nordencrantz. On New Year's Eve 1761 he wrote the following message to Swedenborg:

> Herr Nordencrantz, Councillor of the Board of Commerce, invites the Assessor and me to come to church tomorrow morning at ten, and to have dinner with him afterwards. He will send his carriage, and at the aforementioned time I will call for the Assessor with the carriage. I am very anxious that you two will become good friends.[11]

Nordencrantz continued his battle against rule by the Estates and against the Hats' misuse of power as long as he lived. Neither did Swedenborg change his opinions. Both died in 1772. The same year the new king, Gustaf III, with French economic encouragement, put an end to the 'Period of Freedom's' supposed anarchy through a quiet revolution, without bloodshed.

Money from Paris and 'a good king'?

Chapter Twenty-Eight

Swedenborg's money

Arcana Caelestia was printed in London, 1749-56, in eight volumes in quarto format. The publisher was John Lewis at 1 Paternoster Row, near Saint Paul's Cathedral. The edition was small, about 500 copies, and the cost of printing was paid by Swedenborg himself. With the help of notes preserved in Swedenborg's manuscript, we can reckon that the total cost of the project, for all eight volumes, was £1,600 pounds.[1] From 1758 to 1771 he would publish six more large volumes and a long series of smaller writings. An approximate calculation of his total printing costs from 1745 to his death in 1772, including *Arcana Caelestia*, indicates a sum of £3,200 pounds. The value of the Swedish riksdaler in relation to the English pound and the Dutch florin sank greatly during the period.

In the 1910s and 1920s Frans G Lindh, a well-known Swedish New Church man, examined documents archived in Sweden containing information on Swedenborg's income and expenses. The results of his efforts were printed in the Swedish *Nya Kyrkan Tidning* (*Journal of the New Church*), published in 1927-30.[2] He estimated that Swedenborg's purchase of pounds (or, when the printing was done in Holland, of florins) cost him altogether a little more than 198,000 riksdalers. Lindh had then taken into consideration the riksdaler's fluctuating value at the time of each printing. According to Lindh Swedenborg's income from pension and interest during the same period amounted to 5,000 riksdalers per year, totalling about 125,000 to the day of his death.

In connection with the war with Russia in 1741-3, a declaration of personal income was set up as the basis for the armament tax. Swedenborg declared his interest income for the year 1742 as 3,000 riksdalers. Calculated at 5 per cent, the amount of his income-producing capital would then have been approximately 55,000 riksdalers. In addition to this there was his salary from the Board of Mines, 3,600 riksdalers. His total annual income was thus 6,600 riksdalers. In 1747 Swedenborg resigned from his service on the Board. He received an annual pension of 1,800 riksdalers, half of his salary. When the interest income that he reported in 1742 is included, his annual income then became 4,800 riksdalers.

More than 20 years later, in 1765, Swedenborg tabulated his assets. He then seems to have possessed about 60,000 riksdalers in capital. At his death in 1772 the total value of his estate was approximately 55,000 riksdalers.

Again: his known income amounted to no more than, at the highest, 5,000 riksdalers per year, approximately 130,000 during the whole period. His assets remained the same through the years. Lindh's conclusion is that Swedenborg had a patron or benefactor who paid for the publication of his writings. This unknown guardian patron was, according to Lindh, none other than the King of France, Louis XV, who allotted the Swedish theosopher an annual pension of 5,000 riksdalers, corresponding to 2,500 French livres.

To clarify Swedenborg's scarcely transparent financial situation we shall first consider his inheritance and the economic situation in Sweden, then the question of his possible financial assets abroad originating from Sweden, and finally the question of support from France.

Inheritance and iron-works income

His father was, as we have seen, the son of a well-to-do mine-owner; and his mother, Sara Behm, was very wealthy. From 1718 to 1735, Swedenborg inherited parts of the estates of his mother, stepmother, maternal uncle, and father. We gain a notion of his assets in 1729 when he sold to Fredrik Gyllenborg his portion in a mining property that he had inherited from Sara Behm. The purchase price was 45,000 riksdalers.

During 1728, he sold the estate that he had inherited from his maternal uncle Albrecht de Behm. How much he received from the sale is unknown. It should, by Lindh's estimate, have amounted to at least 30,000 riksdalers. In 1734 the printing costs of the three, richly illustrated folio volumes on subjects of natural philosophy——*Principia* and the subsequent works regarding iron and copper——were approximately the same as he had gained from the large sale of property in 1729, that is, around 45,000 riksdalers.

Swedenborg also sold the property that he had inherited from his stepmother Sara Bergia to Fredrik Gyllenborg, but not until 1742. He then received 36,000 riksdalers of which however only 6,000 was in cash. He later succeeded in obtaining a further 10,000 riksdalers of the outstanding sum, but the remaining 20,000 seems to have been lost in the Gyllenborg bankruptcy.

The inheritance from his father was relatively small, estimated at ca. 5,000 riksdalers. Thus his total inheritance, converted to cash, in the end brought him between 100,000 and 125,000 riksdalers.

During the 1720s and 1730s Swedenborg was a mine-owner, receiving an income from the export of iron ore. We know from a preserved letter, written in 1722, that he had money on deposit in the Balguerie Bank in Amsterdam, presumably his shares of the payments coming in from the sale of the ore. By that time he had plans to publish works outside Sweden. It would have been in his interest to reserve capital abroad that would be secure from possible swings in the value of the Swedish riksdaler.

'So that no one may know how much I am worth'
In the beginning of 1748 he sent a letter from Amsterdam to an accountant at the Bank of Sweden in Stockholm. The rough draft of the message reads as follows:

> At the time of my departure my account was not reviewed, and although I did not issue any payment order, to keep things right I should like to issue such an order. When you have finished, would you, Sir, please [. . .] put it in a [plain] envelope and seal it, and give it to [my] business agent Petter Hultman, who will forward it to me. Seal the envelope well, so that no one may see my account [. . .] [3]

Petter Hultman was Swedenborg's trusted business confidant. Lindh emphasizes Swedenborg's intriguing instruction that the letter be carefully sealed so 'no one may see my account'. Just this sentence is repeated, deleted, and underlined several times in the draft. Originally Swedenborg had written, 'so that no one may know my currency'. Above the words 'no one' we read the abbreviation 'Hultm'. Thus not even Hultman, who was thoroughly acquainted with Swedenborg's business activities and assets, was to know in what currency the deposit had been made into his account in the Bank of Sweden.

It was a respectable amount that was on deposit in Swedenborg's account, which was opened in October 1746, when a little more than 5,000 riksdalers was deposited under the heading 'Diverse'. The following year the account was credited with an additional 3,000 riksdalers under the same heading. Later, on 4 June 1747, the sum of 10,240 riksdalers was deposited by 'Gother' and on the 27th of the same month 11,800 by 'Jennings'. In July there followed a deposit by 'Gyllenborg' of 1,800 riksdalers. At the time of the letter to the accountant at the Bank of Sweden there were thus nearly 32,000 riksdalers in the account.[4]

Who were the depositors? Engelbert Gother was a well-known Stockholm citizen and one of the leading members of the Hat Party. Frans Jennings was a naturalized Swede of British origin who had been ennobled in 1742. He was a manufacturer and exporter, married to the daughter of the wholesaler Jean Bedoire, who presumably functioned as one of the financial middlemen for French subsidies to Swedish Hat politicians.

And 'Gyllenborg'? Supposedly it was Fredrik, the distributor of the French money mentioned in the previous chapter. French subsidies were for many years given to the Hat party, termed 'the Patriots' by the French Embassy in Stockholm when reporting to Louis XV in Versailles.

Why did Gother, Jennings, and Gyllenborg pay these large amounts into Swedenborg's account? Why should the matter be kept secret? Who lay behind the deposits totalling 8,000 riksdalers, covered under the word 'Diverse'? Lindh starts from the assumption that the depositors wanted to hide something. It must, however, be pointed out that as regards Gother and Gyllenborg this could be a matter of quite normal transactions. Gother had assumed a debt obligation of 10,000 riksdalers from Peter Schönström, son of Jesper Swedberg's brother who when ennobled had taken the name 'Schönström'.[5] Was this perhaps simply a repayment? And Gyllenborg had a debt of 30,000 riksdalers to

Swedenborg from the sale of property; it might have been a matter of a normal payment of interest.

Lindh, however, takes for granted that it was a matter of French money. Here is his argument. The first entry under 'Diverse' was for exactly 5,049 riksdalers. 'If Petter Hultman had seen the information hidden in the blue envelope', Lindh wrote, 'his trained business-eye would at once have recognized that the 5,049 riksdalers corresponded to 2,500 French livres converted at the current rate'. And perhaps he also would have understood that the combined total of deposits, 30,139 riksdalers, was the equivalent of 15,000 livres.

Did Swedenborg have an annual French 'pension' of 2,500 livres during this period? Lindh wonders. Were the six deposits a prepayment for six years?

The sum of a little more than 30,000 riksdalers corresponds approximately to the cost of printing the first two volumes of *Arcana Caelestia*, together with expenses for translating and printing the second volume in English. According to Lindh's calculations these expenses did amount to about 25,000 riksdalers. Lindh reproduces the records preserved at the Bank of Sweden. According to these Swedenborg withdrew 18,000 riksdalers in both 1749 and 1750, a total of 36,000 riksdalers.

Lindh's studies of preserved notes and his estimation of Swedenborg's printing costs leads him to presume that from 1746-71, a period of 25 years, Swedenborg received an annual pension of 2,500 French livres, equivalent to 5,000 riksdalers, from an unknown source. Is this plausible? We have already seen that earlier he had an account with Balguerie in Amsterdam. Could not the money have come entirely or partially from there? And who can say with certainty that the capitalized interest income corresponds to his wealth? He could naturally have lent money without interest, or with a clause about the interest being due on the date of the loan's maturity.

Thus about 200,000 riksdalers is 'missing', according to Lindh. This was a large amount, corresponding to 56 times Swedenborg's annual salary before pension, the value of almost thirty-five residential estates of the kind he bought in 1743. If Swedenborg had been the owner of such a large amount of capital in the 1740s would not such a possession have become known in Sweden, where very little could be hidden within the narrow leading circles? There were speculations about his financial situation, Robsahm reported:

Many in his lifetime wondered about where Swedenborg gained enough money to be able to make such trips and pay for such expenses, but when one took into consideration his frugal lifestyle and the small expenditures on his travels, only a moderate amount of capital was needed.[6]

Robsahm also believed that the industrious author's many books did not end up 'lying in the bookshops, but always gave him resources'. But what we know about the small editions and modest sales scarcely supports this supposition. Furthermore the publisher John Lewis stated that Swedenborg directed that the entire proceeds from the sale of *Arcana Caelestia* were to be given to the Society for the Propagation of the Gospel in Foreign Parts, a British organization formed in 1701.

Money in new ways: Rudenskjöld's question

In the beginning of the 1750s Swedenborg appears to have closed his account at the Bank of Sweden. Why? Perhaps he thought that larger deposits would follow, and in such case the money ought to come to him in a more comfortable and discreet way, directly by way of the large European trading houses, Lindh supposes. Payments could then be made to him in those cities, Amsterdam and London, where he printed his books, and Hultman's role could be reduced to management of Swedenborg's household and Swedish business affairs.

At the Royal Library in Stockholm, in the so-called Engeström Collection, there is a document that seems to speak for Lindh's thought.[7] It is a signed, undated answer by Swedenborg to a question that was put to him by Count Carl Rudenskjöld, a member of the government. At the top of the folio-size paper stands Swedenborg's name as a heading, in Engeström's handwriting. This is followed by an empty space where we can clearly see that a piece of paper, once pasted there, has been taken away. Beneath the now disappeared small document Engeström made this note:

The above question has been written by Count Rudenskjöld at the request of a foreign minister. Assessor Emanuel Swedenborg has written this quite remarkable answer with his own hand.

After this Swedenborg's message is pasted in:

These 14,300 riksdalers in copper coin are paid through a bill; I received them in Amsterdam, besides this [they still] owe me 30,000 riksdalers.　　　　　　—Emanuel Swedenborg

The communication is undated. Who was the 'foreign minister'? Why did Engeström think that Swedenborg's answer was so remarkable? Who ripped Rudenskjöld's question out of the manuscript, and why? Rudenskjöld was a known Hat, from 1747 to 1765 the Secretary of State in the foreign ministry.[8] According to the well-known expert on Swedish political life in the 1700s Carl Gustaf Malmström, Rudenskjöld received an annual pension from France amounting to more than 15,000 livres, following the Hats' fall from power in 1765. Was it possibly a French diplomat who had asked him to check whether Swedenborg had received his pension?

The Hats and the Caps in foreign policy

'French money'? The assumption cannot be rejected as totally incredible. The question must be seen in its historical context. The Swedish constitution of 1720 gave in practice the political power to the four Estates. After the retirement of the Prime Minister Arvid Horn in 1738, foreign subsidies became an increasingly important factor in the play of Swedish politics. Through secret financial support, France, Russia, England, and Denmark sought to secure a Swedish foreign policy that corresponded to their interests. The chief question concerned the Swedish position towards the arch enemy Russia. The Nordic War of 1700-18 had ended with a devastating defeat; Sweden had lost the Baltic provinces to Russia. After the peace treaty the bitter feelings slowly settled, but in the 1730s a younger generation of politicians successfully launched the idea of a war of revenge.

This question about a new war became an issue that divided political life. Most of the Hats in the Diet supported the thought of militant action against Russia, whereas their opponents, the Caps, were against any form of armed action: on the contrary, Swedish foreign policy should strive to establish trusting relations with St Petersburg.

Sweden and the 'French system'

The so-called French system was personally directed by Louis XV. Good relations and alliances with Prussia, Poland, Turkey, Denmark, and Sweden would create a French-led counterweight to Russia and England. The return of the Baltic provinces to Sweden would diminish the Russian dominance around the Baltic Sea and in Europe in general. From this perspective a Swedish war of revenge was of interest; therefore the French endeavoured to win, through the use of promises and money, the Swedish Diet's sympathies for an anti-Russian policy. On the other side the Caps were encouraged by Russia and, occasionally, English money.

It is significant that this form of continental foreign policy, perfected during the 1700s, was usually led by a small, closed group. It was often carried out through bypassing the normal, established political channels, including the embassies. Thus a diplomacy arose in which silence and secrecy were both the means and the goal. France's Louis XV was the master of these contacts and negotiations, *Le Secret du Roi*.[9]

France's foreign policy interest in Sweden explains the flood of money that washed over the Swedish political scene from the end of the 1730s to Gustaf III's constitutional reform in 1772. During the Hats' long period in power, from 1738 to 1765, the French-Swedish relations and the French influence in Stockholm became so dominant that the Court of St James found it meaningless to maintain an English representative in the Swedish capital.

The provision and final use of the subventions are difficult to analyse in detail, since the individuals involved usually erased the traces of the foreign liberality. This applies to the great Hat leaders like Fredrik Gyllenborg, Anders Johan von Höpken, and Carl Fredrik Pechlin, as well as to many other less significant beneficiaries. The foremost sources of information are the French diplomatic reports from Stockholm. In the correspondence of the French envoys from the 1740s to the 1760s in the Quai d'Orsay's archive there is scarcely a report that did not take up some aspect of the distribution of the financial support to the party's issuing agents, or sometimes to the direct receiver. The account statement is usually paired with supplications for still larger sums, and optimistic promises of coming successes for the French cause.

Subsidies, how much and to whom?

Thus it was a matter of large sums. At the Diet of 1746-7 the French ambassador had spent something over a million riksdalers, of which the portion for the House of Nobles was distributed by Fredrik Gyllenborg.[10] The sums distributed at the time when *Arcana Caelestia* was published cannot be determined.

Receipts from the end of the 1760s are preserved in the archives of the French Foreign Ministry.[11] As an example it can be mentioned that in December 1768 and the whole of 1769, according to receipts, the Hats' treasurer and subsidy distributor Fredrik Ulrik von Rosen received 6,884,846 riksdalers from Paris. This colossal sum was intended to cover the purchase of powers of attorney to assure the 'correct' voting at the Diet beginning in the town of Norrköping in the spring of 1769, as well as payments for travel to and from the city, clothes for three hundred nobles, food and lodging for six hundred men, etc. Seen from Paris's perspective, the Diet was important. The Caps had been in power since 1765, and it was now a matter of securing victory for the Hats.

How did those receiving these French subsidies look on the matter? Perhaps as help for a good cause, as support that for natural reasons, and also out of respect for their donor and the international situation, must be kept secret? Or as a necessary evil? Count Carl Gustaf Tessin, during his career as member of the government, ambassador, tutor to Crown Prince Gustaf, and Prime Minister, was known for his catastrophic private economy, often being on the brink of ruin.[12] But in spite of proposals from the French side, he refused to accept what others requested, the French foreign minister reported. Later, we read, Tessin changed his mind.

Those who distributed the subsidies were naturally exposed to great temptations. In political circles in Stockholm and at the French Embassy, it was well-known that Gyllenborg and his successor, Pechlin, had not always used the French money in the proper way, but to promote their own financial interests.[13]

With the approval of the French king and sometimes his foreign minister, support was given to individual Swedes. In the lists established by the French ministers in Stockholm giving names and amounts we never find Swedenborg's name; but these lists give no definite answers, as they also include gratuities to unnamed figures, designated simply by the letter 'A', Anonymous.

Further, the distributor of subsidies to the Hats had not necessarily any knowledge of money that came *directly* from Louis XV. Not even the heads of the French embassies were always informed about such transactions.

Why Swedenborg?

As a member of the House of Nobles, head of his family, and a man with close contacts with leading Hat politicians, Swedenborg was a politically interesting figure. He was not a party follower, neither a faithful Hat nor a Cap. In domestic politics he was a warm supporter of the prevailing political system and the dominant position of the Estates. As an expert in mining, he agreed with the Hats' trade and commerce policies. His memorandum from 1734 can probably be considered as the model he held for Swedish foreign policy throughout his life. In principle he took a negative position to a war of revenge against Russia. It was, he felt, a matter of keeping his country outside all international conflicts, and instead building Sweden into something like a great economic power, but he always strongly emphasized the importance of close and friendly relations with France, and for the French officials in Stockholm he was an 'ami' and 'patriote'.

Swedenborg's group of acquaintances belonged to the circle of the Hats. His famous brother-in-law, Bishop Eric Benzelius, was a powerful Hat till his death in 1743. As we have seen, Swedenborg had close connections with the powerful Gyllenborg family, and from the 1730s with Anders Johan von Höpken, a Hat and head of the government from 1752-61. Von Höpken was usually in good favour in Paris. He obviously regarded the subsidies from Paris as something quite natural, requesting and receiving French money for himself, according to the French Stockholm reports. Through von Höpken, Swedenborg had a channel to the Hat leadership and the highest political power in the country even after Fredrik Gyllenborg's death in 1759.

His esteem for von Höpken was not only politically motivated, but probably also connected with his appreciation of Swedenborg's religious message. Von Höpken is known to have advocated that Swedenborg's doctrine should be propagated in the non-European colonies that Sweden might eventually acquire, though in Swedenborg's homeland such a reform would be impossible, according to the old statesman.

If Swedenborg received money from the Swedish Hats or from Versailles, he certainly regarded such support as the finger of God. It would have been taken as help from above, a grace from the same source as the message he was commissioned to present to humanity.

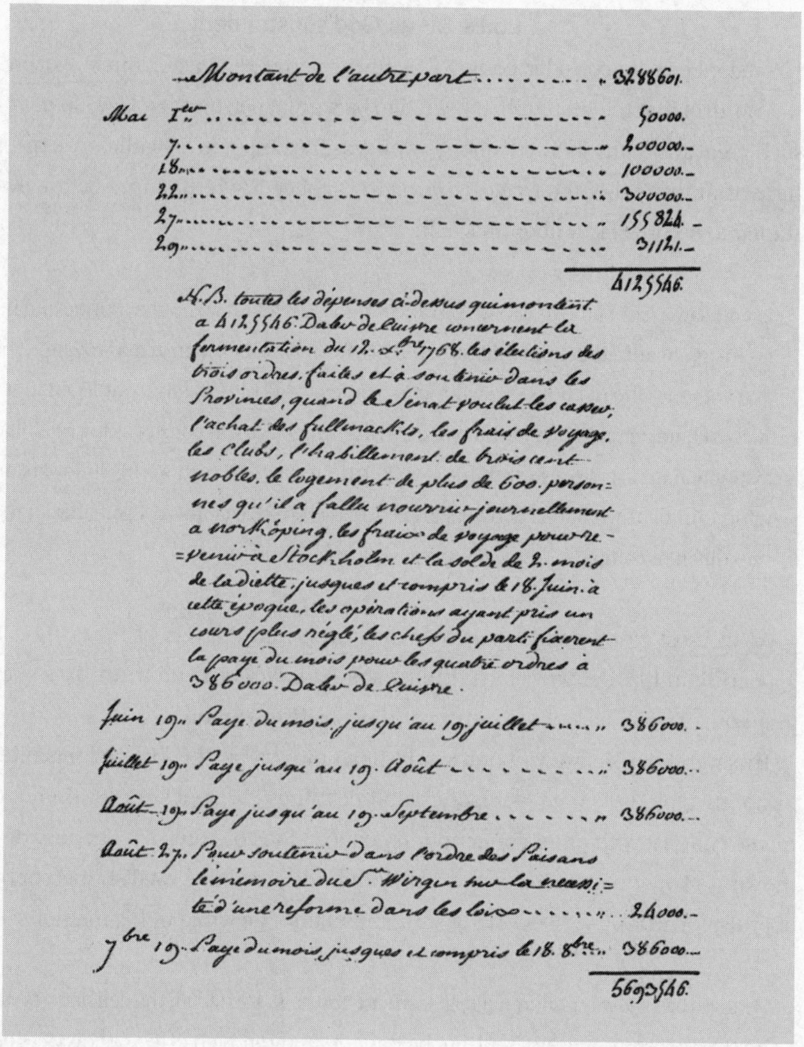

Montant de l'autre part .... 3288601.

Mai	1er	50000.
	7	200000.
	18	100000.
	22	300000.
	27	155824.
	29	31121.
		4125546.

N.B. toutes les dépenses ci-dessus qui montent a 4125546. Daler de Cuivre concernent la fermentation du 19. Xbre 1768. les élections des trois ordres. faites et à soutenir dans les Provinces, quand le Senat voulut les casser, l'achat des fullmackts, les frais de voyage, les Clubs, l'habillement de trois cent nobles. le logement de plus de 600. personnes qu'il a fallu nourrir journellement a Norrköping. les frais de voyage pour revenir à Stockholm et la solde de 2. mois de la diette, jusques et compris le 18. Juin. à cette époque. les opérations ayant pris un cours plus réglé, les chefs du parti fixerent la paye du mois pour les quatre ordres à 386000. Daler de Cuivre.

Juin 19.	Paye du mois, jusqu'au 19. juillet	386000.
Juillet 19.	Paye jusqu'au 19. Août	386000.
Août 19.	Paye jusqu'au 19. Septembre	386000.
Août 27.	Pour soutenir dans l'ordre des Paisans le mémoire du Sr. Wirgin sur la necessité d'une reforme dans les loix	24000.
7bre 19.	Paye du mois, jusques et compris le 18. 8bre	386000.
		5693546.

Fig. 39. From the French Embassy's account of expenses for the Diet in Norrköping in 1769 and its continuation in Stockholm. The amounts accounted for in May have been used to 'purchase letters of attorney, travel costs for Diet members, Hat clubs, clothes for three hundred noblemen, lodging for more than six hundred, for whom we have also paid daily for their meals in Norrköping, travels to Stockholm [in connection with the change of location of the Diet], and payment to the Diet for two months [. . .] ' Until 7 October 1769 expenses for the Diet amounted to 5,603,946 riksdalers. (*Mémoires et Documents*, *Suède*, vol. 32, folio 193, verso, from the Archives des Affaires Etrangères, in Paris.)

Louis XV as God's instrument

If Swedenborg did consider Louis XV as his personal benefactor, directly or indirectly, it was natural that the monarch appeared to be a great personality. Few are portrayed with such great sympathy in Swedenborg's works as the despot in Versailles. We meet the king himself at the end of the *Dream Diary* in October 1744, the night before Swedenborg started to become clear about his call:

> Later I saw a great king, the king of France, who went about without a retinue and had such an insignificant household that he could not from this be recognized as royalty. There was one with me who did not seem willing to acknowledge him as king, but I said that he is of such a character as to care nothing about such things. He was courteous towards all without distinction and spoke also with me. As he left, he was still without his followers and took upon himself the burdens of others and carried them like clothes. Thereafter, came into a very different company, where there was much more splendor. [14]

As in most cases, Swedenborg's dreams have many layers of meanings. The kings appearing in his nightly visions usually stand for wisdom and truth. It is worth noting that Louis XV was part of the same world of positive symbols.

In several works Swedenborg would heap praises on the king in Versailles. He was 'innocent', 'pious', 'polite', 'proposed sublime things', 'a great king'. Swedenborg's judgements contrast with other contemporary conceptions of Louis XV. The Duc de Choiseul, the king's Foreign Minister, would not have understood the Swedish theosopher's words of praise. The king was 'devoid of soul and talent', he wrote in his memoirs:

> He loved evil the way children like to torment animals. He had all the deficiencies we find in an utterly corrupt and dark soul, but he was not strong enough to live out his vices openly as often as would have been natural to him [...] He would, for example, following Nero's model, have gladly seen Paris burn from his vantage point in Bellevue [...] [15]

Swedenborg regarded the French queen, Maria Leszczyńska, with the same goodwill. She was the daughter of Charles XII's protégé Stanislaw Leszczyński, for a short period

King of Poland. In connection with her father's flight from his native land after the collapse of the Swedish armies, she came and stayed for three years in the peaceful town of Christianstad in the southern part of Sweden.

A detail: when Countess Ulla Tessin and her husband were presented at Versailles the queen greeted her in Swedish, 'Good morning, dear hearts!'

Did she perhaps greet Swedenborg in the same way? Whatever, he also dreamt of her as a sympathetic figure:

> Then I saw the queen; and when a chamberlain came and bowed before her, she made just as deep a reverence, and there was nothing of pride in her. *This means that in Christ there is no pride at all* […] *The queen, who is* sapientia [*wisdom*], *is of the same nature; she has no love of self* […] [16]

Louis XV and the Jansenists

But there was also another reason for Swedenborg's praise for France's ruler, probably more important than financial generosity. Louis XV appeared to Swedenborg as a leader of the battle conducted on Catholic ground against the pope and Rome.

Here French *Jansenism* comes into the picture. This was the movement that took its name from the theologian and bishop from the Netherlands, Cornelius Jansen, who died in 1638. It spread in France, with the convent of Port Royal outside Versailles as the centre. Just as the later Protestant pietists did, the Jansenists called for a personal conversion and regeneration and a life in accordance with the Ten Commandments: man had to choose between God and the world. The Jansenists repudiated the pope's claim to stand as the representative of Christ on earth. They were also known for their accusations against the Jesuits, regarding them as the papal power's chief tool, all too ready to overlook evils and willing to compromise to achieve higher goals.

In Rome this individualistically coloured but nevertheless Catholic and severe Christianity appeared as a threat to the unity of the church. Later, in 1713, Pope Clement XI issued a Bull against the Jansenists, the so-called *Unigenitus*, (God's only-begotten son).

Louis XIV and his great-grandson Louis XV came to be regarded as favourably inclined towards this movement. France, more than other Catholic states, had long emphasized its independence of the papal power. It took expression in the so-called Gallicanism, negative towards all 'ultramontane' striving, the claim of power not only over the church-state of Rome, but also over the lands *ultra montes*, on the other side of the Alps. From Swedenborg's perspective this negative attitude towards Rome was in every way praise-worthy: condemnation of the religious and secular pretensions of the pontiff runs like a scarlet thread through his works. In the seventeenth chapter of the Book of Revelation the 'great whore' sitting on the scarlet beast was for Swedenborg and a great number of Protestants a symbol of the Word of God profaned by the papal church.

Thus for the Swedish theosopher, Louis XV became a leader in the battle against Rome. The king's exemplary posture is mirrored in Swedenborg's dreams. He records a conversation with the deceased Louis XIV, who in the spiritual world had 'a position of high dignity'. Louis XIV had counselled Louis XV to reject the papal bull against the Jansenists:

> King Louis XIV, who had been king of France a long time ago, suddenly went under me, and descended by means of ladders to a place below me, a little towards the front [...] he told me that he had spoken to the now reigning king of France, and that he had exhorted him, in various ways, to desist from the Bull Unigenitus, which he had laid before the Parliament. He told me some things which he had said to him, amongst others that he must entirely abandon it, and that unless he did so misfortune would befall him [...] This happened on 13 December 1759, near about the eighth hour.[17]

A few years later the Jesuit Order was forbidden by Parliament to work in France, and the prohibition was confirmed in 1764 by Louis XV. It was good news for Swedenborg; for him the Jesuits were poisonous serpents.[18] The action was understood as a blow against the papacy, so much the more as the Order came to be proscribed in other countries also. In the end, in 1773, the pope himself found it advisable to go with the flow of the times, and the Society of Jesus ceased to exist, and was not re-established until 1814.

There could be a break between the papal church and France, Swedenborg wrote in *The Apocalypse Revealed*, published in 1766.[19] The Jansenists had already provided a good example.

Piety, Wisdom, and Providence

Chapter Twenty-Nine

He knew that Glory and Hell too
Are in your soul, with all their myths;
He knew, like the Greek, that the days
Of time are Eternity's mirrors.

Jorge Luis Borges, 'Emanuel Swedenborg'[1]

Crisis in Sweden, Swedenborg in Stockholm

The great 'Seven Years War' began in 1756. On one side was the alliance of Prussia and Great Britain; on the other was the coalition of France, Austria, Russia, and Saxony, joined by Sweden in 1757. The Swedish contributions were practically without military significance, but with the help of Queen Louisa Ulrika a separate peace agreement was struck with her brother, the Prussian king. It was signed in Hamburg in 1762 without territorial secessions.

The Hat government manoeuvred in a deepening economic crisis, with a steadily decreasing value of the currency to the detriment of both wage earners and owners of capital. The situation worsened when an international trade crisis became apparent in 1763, resulting in the bankruptcy of several Swedish enterprises. The lame efforts in the continental war, the irrational Swedish constitution, and the nation's economic impotence led to the recall of the French ambassador and the termination of the subsidies from the legation in Stockholm.

In the spring of 1763 Swedenborg was in the Swedish capital. In spite of the fact that his writings were published anonymously, rumours were now spreading of his claimed divine calling. In a theological bibliography published in 1763 he was named as the author of *Arcana Caelestia*, as well as of later theosophical works. He had now become known as a mystic, spirit-seer, and prophet.

That summer, a well-known magazine, *Den Svenska Merkurius* (*The Swedish Mercury*), contained a notice of his impending departure from the country:

> Herr Assessor Swedenborg, known for his learned work and remarkable ideas, in spite of his mature age left Stockholm in June on the ocean voyage that would take him to Holland. There he is going to publish several works of a doctrinal nature.[2]

Literary situation

The 75-year-old man now had *Arcana Caelestia* and *Heaven and Hell* behind him. A fundamental idea in *Arcana Caelestia* was the process of rebirth he had described as the spiritual content of the creation story. He had presented a comprehensive synthesis embracing the whole Bible. Man's destiny and purpose was to return to a paradisal state. The necessity of this return had been emphasized in the Gospel of John: only the regenerated man could see the kingdom of heaven. Further, in *Heaven and Hell* he had described the states that awaited man after death.

In the same year that *Heaven and Hell* was printed, 1758, he had also published a summarizing 'catechism', *The New Jerusalem and its Heavenly Doctrine*. His next task was to describe, in detail, the faith that was at once the means and the goal for the regenerated man. Now, in Amsterdam in 1763, he published four small works, often called 'the four doctrines', in which he clarified his message. The subjects are first and foremost his view of Christ as God, and Christ's mission on earth: *Doctrina Novae Hierosolymae de Domino* (*The New Jerusalem's Doctrine of the Lord*). In a second book he develops his concept of the biblical Word and the relation of its literal sense to its spiritual meaning: *Doctrina Novae Hierosolymae de Scriptura Sacra* (*The New Jerusalem's Doctrine of the Sacred Scripture*). In a third, *Doctrina Vitae pro Nova Hierosolyma ex Praeceptis Decalogi* (*The Doctrine of Life for the New Jerusalem*), he gives a practical description of Christian life in accordance with the Ten Commandments; and in the fourth, *Doctrina Novae Hierosolymae de Fide* (*The New Jerusalem's Doctrine of Faith*), he presents faith as the regenerated man's reception of love and wisdom.

These four books are essentially systematic restatements of teachings published in his earlier works. In the same year that he published 'the four doctrines' he sent yet another book to the printer which he entitled *Angelic Wisdom concerning the Divine Love and Wisdom*. The book is an attempt to give a theoretical 'explanation' of his concept of God and of man's situation in relation to him.

Swedenborg's God and the connection between God and man

For Leibniz and Wolff God was the perfect intelligence, the infinite rationality, from which creation came forth as the best of all possible worlds. Leibniz and his disciples envisaged God as an all-embracing being, and from this vague concept they drew sweeping conclusions concerning the supreme ruler's characteristics and will. God was an independent, self-sufficient being, by definition absent from man, who could never experience his presence. On the other hand, we could study his wisdom in all the details of creation, and human reason, human logic, was the same as God's thinking.

For Swedenborg such objectification was absurd. The Divine could never be understood using human ideas and supposedly logical conclusions drawn from abstract concepts.[3] Inevitably, earth-bound limitations always crept into such scholastic thinking, leading man astray. Nothing more than omnipotence and the will to create could, using logic, be attributed to God.

Knowledge of God, his essence and nature can, according to Swedenborg, be given to man only through a personal, *existential* experience, in love to God and in a life of love to the neighbour. At certain moments everybody could feel the presence of the Divine; if this feeling made a sufficiently deep impression, it could lead to a radical change of the human being, a new birth.

The nature of love

God *is* love. Through creation God had wanted to make his will manifest: creation must be seen as an act of love. God had made man in his image, and for Swedenborg love is the life of man.

He does not attempt to give a rationally satisfying, systematic, and logical explanation of the concept of God; instead he invites his readers to become engaged in the main thoughts of his teaching. Man's will is free: if he allows himself to be convinced of true teaching about God, the Bible, faith, and the right way to live, his view of life and his relationship to the surrounding world will be changed. Truth is existentially experienced, giving birth to a new man with new perspectives.

'Man knows that there is such a thing as love, but he does not know what love is': this is the first sentence of *The Divine Love and Wisdom*. Swedenborg continues:

> He is completely unaware that love is his very life, not only the general life of his whole body, and of all his thoughts [...] A wise man can perceive this when it is asked, 'If you remove the affection which is of love, can you think or do anything? Do not thought, speech, and action grow cold to the extent that the affection which is of love grows cold? And do they not grow warm to the extent that this affection grows warm?' A wise man perceives this simply from experience that it is so, and not from any knowledge that love is the life of man [...] If we think of the sun's heat in the world, we can have some idea of love as being the life of man. We know that heat is a kind of life that is common to all forms of vegetation [...] But when heat recedes in the time of autumn and winter, the plants are stripped of these signs of their life, and they wither. It is the same with love in man, for heat and love correspond to each other. Therefore love also is warm.

To the natural sun there corresponded a 'spiritual sun', the divine love. Man's relationship to this source, distant or close, was a question of degrees, a concept that Swedenborg always had in mind. Just as the determination of longitude was decisive for the commander wanting to determine his position at sea, the spiritual degrees of height measured the distance from God. The latitude alone could never give information about a position, whether at sea or in the spiritual domain.

Degrees of love, degrees of wisdom

Swedenborg had already in *The Economy of the Animal Kingdom* and *Arcana Caelestia* transferred his system of degrees from the physical into the spiritual realm. In *The Divine Love and Wisdom* he now uses this concept as an element in his theosophy; without an understanding of the significance of these degrees profound insight was excluded.

There were two kinds of degrees, he taught. First, a chain of 'degrees of height', clearly distinguished from each other, which linked God with creation. Seen from the source itself, these degrees diminished in love and intensity down towards the zero point. From the perspective of the seeking, god-fearing individual, they were steps from coldness up towards ever-greater warmth, of increasing proximity to the Divine. These degrees must be clearly distinct and separate from each other: continuous grades would have implied that creation was a part of the Divine, but man could as little become one with God as nature could.

Every degree was three-fold. Just as God had a purpose in his creation, everything must be considered as an element in a long series of purposes, one within every degree. Each purpose was realized with the help of what philosophers somewhat confusingly call a *cause*. By this is meant the structure that makes the purpose possible, just as the clock's purpose is to measure time and the cause is the clockwork itself. The *effect*, the result or 'use', is the concrete consequence of the realization of the purpose by means of the cause.

Thus, by means of a series of degrees what is of God descends into creation. The purpose is consequently the highest element in each degree. Each degree of height is different, yet always an outflow from God. The highest is therefore always to some extent present on every step of the ladder.

Each degree of height, each 'longitude', forms the starting point for a degree of breadth, a 'latitude'. These parallels indicate various degrees of clarity, light and darkness, or intensity. The horizontal plane is always related to the vertical. To illustrate his thinking, Swedenborg takes a cone as his example. The cone, divided into three sections (a higher, a middle, and a lower) is a picture of the divine inflow. When the cone is compressed like a closed telescope, the highest becomes the innermost section, followed by the middle and the outer, in concentric circles. Swedenborg often returns to this system of defining spiritual positions:

> Without a knowledge of these degrees nothing can be known either of how the three heavens are distinct from each other or of how the love and wisdom of the angels there are distinct from each other. Nor without a knowledge of these degrees can anything be known of the distinction between the interior faculties of human minds, thus nothing of their state in

regard to reformation and regeneration, nor of the distinction between the exterior faculties of the bodies of both angels and men; and nothing whatever can be known of the distinction between spiritual and natural, thus nothing about correspondence [...] Those who have no knowledge of these degrees can never discern causes with any power of judgement. They discern only effects, and for the most part they judge causes from these, by induction on the same continuous level of effects; yet causes produce effects not by continuous degrees but by discrete degrees. [4]

Standing before the effects in the world of the senses, we must always look for their purpose. And this purpose is always something useful, beneficial to the whole, an outflow of the reason, truth, and utility in the divine love. When we clearly distinguish the purpose we can gradually see a new cause and a new effect grow forth on a higher plane on the ladder of degrees, and here we discern a new divine thought. Thus man in the process of regeneration ascends towards greater clarity and insight in progressive stages.

It is to be noted that the degrees of knowledge are also states of mind: degrees of happiness and feelings of peace, resulting from a temporary absence of tension between questions and answers. These experiences and feelings have always been described by mystics throughout time as 'inexpressible' and 'boundless'.

But the system of degrees is also applicable in down-to-earth, practical contexts. In every phenomenon the scientist must look for its purpose; and this purpose is its *use*. In several of his writings Swedenborg argues against the ideas of his distant relative Carl Linnaeus, although without ever mentioning his name. [5] The 'King of Flowers' had in his 'sexual system' classified flowers using stamens and pistils, male and female, basing it on the structures of the plants, but he should instead have analysed their purposes in creation, the use each flower performed.

Wisdom the garment of love

Love's outer form is wisdom, Jacob Boehme had written in his book *Beschreibung der drei Principien Göttlichen Wesens* (*The Three Principles of the Divine Being*). Gottfried Arnold, inspired by Boehme, wrote a book about the divine *Sophia*, the Greek word for 'wisdom'. Wisdom and love were dependent on man's nearness to God. Sagacity's form and content were the right understanding of God's Word. Wisdom did not consist in special notions or ideas, wrote J C Dippel, but lived 'in the new [regenerated] being and its perfection'.[6]

As with Arnold and Dippel, the divine wisdom became a fundamental concept for Swedenborg. Boehme and Arnold conceived of wisdom as a feminine, active power, but for Swedenborg it was masculine, and passive; the active love, giving power to wisdom, was feminine. The regenerated man found himself, as we have seen, in a divine light, in the divine wisdom and love. This was the state of truth. Wisdom was in the Word that became flesh, and therefore in Christ's preaching. The wisdom of the Son of Man was dictated by love, bringing man back to the original innocence and simplicity of creation, to the tree of life in paradise.

Swedenborg's teaching about love and wisdom, as we have seen, can be related to events in his own inner life. In parallel with the Last Judgement that he had witnessed, he had experienced such a judgement in his own spiritual space so that he could distinguish the evil from the good. In the same inner space love and wisdom meet in a marriage, giving birth to new truth, new insight.

Perhaps Swedenborg's 'inner space' and his way of describing its spiritual components can be classed among the more remarkable elements in Swedish literature, and in the literature of the world in general. Czeslaw Milosz has himself thought about this. With a reference to Osip Mandelstam's essay on Dante, he asks the question whether the Swedenborgian *doctrine* is not secondary to this inner theatre, and its psychological space. Everyone who approaches the Word properly in thought and action will come close to the divine humanity, drawing near to the Divine through his state of mind. Swedenborg's theosophy is a teaching about man's seeking and finding in *his own self* something of the love and wisdom of God as a hidden treasure.

The Divine Providence

Thus God had created the universe with his wisdom. Swedenborg's next work, printed in 1764, was entitled *Angelic Wisdom concerning the Divine Providence*, here shortened to *The Divine Providence*. Its main theme is God's preservation of his creation and his leading of man.

The problem of the divine providence was eagerly discussed during the period of the Enlightenment. God must be rational; therefore his creation must be purposeful, characterized by wisdom. The meaningless destruction of the city of Lisbon in an earthquake in 1755 is frequently referred to as a catastrophe for this optimistic faith in providence. Voltaire's *Candide*, written in that year, was conceived as a satire on the thought of God's omniscience, wisdom, and loving care.

For Swedenborg providence took the form of a divine project, an overall plan. God's purpose was to create a heaven from the human race, and the constant goal was therefore mankind's ever-closer conjunction with the Divine. When Swedenborg describes the ways of providence it is done from the point of view of the regenerated man, thus from the same perspective as in the book on love and wisdom.

Each man had a destiny provided by God. If he chose to turn to God and to live a life of love to the neighbour, he was acting in harmony with this plan. God's way of influencing him was imperceptible:

> If man were to notice that he was always being led away from what delights him intrinsically, he would become enraged [. . .] To avoid this the Lord's care is invisible [. . .] He leads man by his providence imperceptibly as a ship is carried by a favourable current [. . .] Therefore man always feels that he is independent [. . .] [7]

We should emphasize immediately that, in Swedenborg's view, providence applied solely to man's spiritual state. God did not intervene in earthly events: prevention or alleviation of catastrophes, injustices, cruelties were not a priority in his sphere of action. His concern was man's eternal life: on earth, man must bear his cross.

This thought leads on to the principle that no one can be influenced through miracles to choose the path of regeneration: this would be the same as an outer coercion. God never intervenes forcefully, according to Swedenborg, through outer means such as miracles, visions, misfortunes, and the like. Choice must be made freely:

> If man were to perceive and feel the operation of divine providence, he would not act from freedom in accordance with reason, nor would anything seem to him to be his own.

It would be the same if he had foreknowledge of events. In such cases he would have nothing for which he was personally responsible, and the question of whether he did evil or good would lose its meaning.[8]

If we truly want to perceive the divine order and find our place in a higher context we must make a basic decision to follow God's purposes. No one can serve two masters; no one can enter into God's love and wisdom without a strong will to remain there to the end of life.

'The Secret of Swedenborg'

God neither recompenses nor punishes. God is never angry. Man had made the great mistake of projecting his own weakness and his own feelings onto his image of God. We have not been willing to accept the implications of the nature of the Son of Man, simultaneously divine and human. The American author Henry James Sr published a book in 1869 with almost the same title as this biography—*The Secret of Swedenborg*. The secret was the Swedish theosopher's synthesis of providence and Christ, God and man.

Through his life and death on earth Christ had shown the Divine that exists within every human being, as a potential. Man was not only *created*, but also *creating*, James emphasized. His duty was to contribute, according to his qualifications and conditions, to the welfare of society through active love towards the neighbour. He must thus attempt to suppress his own egotism. God-Christ was present in man, and it is our duty to make him visible by following his example. This requires a surrender. The good shepherd gave his life for the sheep, and in a similar way we must try to live our life for others. Once again: God *is, exists* for man only as an existential experience. It is first in this dimension, James writes, that we experience what is divine and meaningful in our lives. Here is the essence of the secret:

Spiritual Christianity means the complete secularization of the divine name, or its identification henceforth only with man's common or natural want, that want in which all men are absolutely one [. . .] and its consequent utter estrangement from the sphere of his private or personal fulness, in which every man is consciously divided from his neighbour: so that I may never aspire to the divine favour, and scarcely to the divine tolerance, save in my social or redeemed natural aspect; i.e. as I stand morally identified with the vast community of men of whatever race or religion, cultivating no consciousness of antagonist interests to any other man, but on the contrary frankly disowning every personal hope towards God which does not flow exclusively from his redemption of human nature, or is not based purely and simply upon his indiscriminate love to the race.[9]

The regenerated man allows the Divine to live in the depth of himself. In *The Divine Providence*, as in so many other works, Swedenborg emphasizes the totality of man's engagement. 'The Lord acts from man's inmosts and at the same time in his outmosts.'[10] The whole personality must be engaged, thought alone is not enough.

God seen from behind

The words 'sorrow', 'pain', 'doubt', 'compassion' are seldom seen in Swedenborg's vocabulary. When they do occur, it is usually in connection with temptation or attacks by evil spirits who arouse the person's own evils and falsities. Swedenborg's outward life was apparently happy, without devastating catastrophes. After 1745 he was borne along by what he conceived of as his call, a wave that washed away all usual earthly cares.

The regenerated man sees providence not 'face to face', but from the back. People totally concentrated on nature do not believe at all in a divine care for the human race. The world seems all too evil:

What is divine providence when the wicked are advanced to honours and acquire wealth more than the good [...]? Those who do not believe in God [...] can inflict injuries, loss, misfortunes, and sometimes death on the believing and god-fearing, and harm them with cunning and malice. Therefore they think, 'Do I not see [...] as in clear daylight that treachery and evil prevail over fidelity and justice if a person by trickery only can make them appear to be trustworthy and fair? [...] Nothing of the divine providence appears to be present [...]'[11]

Against this usual view of things Swedenborg brings in another perspective. The believing observer realizes that the divine providence can never be seen in its wholeness. Faith is a trust, a confidence that everything happens for the best in a perspective which includes an acceptance of the life after death. All is present in the divine plan for the increasingly close conjunction of the human race with divine truth and goodness, thus with a heaven in constant development.

The regenerated man understands that an insight into the ways of providence is impossible. If there were to be such knowledge, man would lose faith in his own abilities and free will. He would try to interfere with what was already determined, as if he were God's equal.

Love and will

The divine invitation to a doubting, hesitating man involves, according to Swedenborg, the call for a clear, distinct decision. We must choose: good and evil can never be woven together. He quotes the 16th chapter of the Gospel of Luke:

> No servant can serve two masters; for either he will hate the one and love the other, or else he will be loyal to the one and despise the other. You cannot serve God and mammon. [12]

This theme often appears in Swedenborg's writings, most clearly in *The Divine Providence*. The call for moral purification had been given concrete expression in *The Spiritual Diary*. Among contemporary politicians and officials he had met different kinds of hypocrisy, corruption, and openly-professed Christianity which cloaked criminality. In *The Divine Providence* we find long accounts of different kinds of this duplicity.

Behind the words we glimpse the dilemma of Emanuel Swedenborg, member of the Diet. How should we consider the spiritually-dead politician who did what was useful, in spite of selfish and low motives? Can a man who has regard only for his own advantage see that God exists? he asks, rhetorically: 'A smoke like that of a house on fire surrounds him, a cloud through which no spiritual truth in its own light can pass. I have seen that smoke around the hells where such people dwell'. [13]

The theme of man's double nature is closely connected with the notion of justification through faith *and* works. The thought of 'faith alone' as Swedenborg found it in official Lutheran documents of confession was a fatal misunderstanding. In *The Divine Providence* he adduces his father's polemic against the supposedly 'great faith' of Lutheranism and quotes a famous essay, written by his father, entitled *Reflections on the Excuses of the Unrepentant*:

In Sweden the religion of faith alone is accepted, but at the same time it is plainly taught that there is no faith that is separate from charity or without good works. This is placed in all Psalm books as a kind of appendix, called 'The Excuses of the Unrepentant'. Here we read the following: 'Those who are rich in good works show by this that their faith is rich, since when faith is saving it operates through love. Yes, justifying faith is never solitary or separate from good works, since there is no good tree without fruit, sun without light [...]'[14]

It is a question of being sincere, of moral integrity. Swedenborg directs his attack against priests who do not live as they teach, against politicians who turn a blind eye to the justice they say they are advancing, against married men who profess concern for marriage while considering their spouses as sexual objects, against unfair judges. Once again we may quote Bishop Swedberg's discourse:

Always remember that Christ, who is a Saviour, did not drive Moses, the accuser of sin, out of his church. For Christ had not come to set aside the law and the prophets [...] but to fulfil. For we Christians must not trust in the Gospel in such a way that we completely forsake the Law; we must rather work in fear and trembling that we may be saved. We must lead our life as if we were still under the severe reign of Moses, but in the firm trust that we are saved and blessed through Jesus Christ alone.[15]

All are invited to the heavenly marriage described in the Gospel of Matthew. The bishop and his son both point to the famous parable: those who have not prepared themselves for the celebration are turned away. This thought was necessary for Swedenborg's explanation of the world. God had created man in his image, and given him a nature that was like his own. The Fall was simply a consequence of man's distancing himself from this likeness. The drama continues as promise and fulfilment, new falls and new sequels, leading and enlightening.

'Tyger! Tyger! burning bright'

Swedenborg states his thinking in terms of contrasts. Wisdom is set against darkness and confusion, providence's general goodness against individual evil. We are presented everywhere with clear opposites, he later wrote in *Conjugial Love*:

> There is nothing in the universe that does not have its opposite. Opposites are not relative, but absolute [...] light is contrary to darkness, heat is opposite to cold [...] day to night, summer to winter [...] [16]

From Swedenborg's perspective the negative had a value only as something hostile, the conquest of which contributed to the victor's spiritual growth.

William Blake was at times a dedicated reader of the Swedish visionary's writings. Swedenborg emphasized the significance of what is good but, according to Blake, was blind to the legitimate place of the evil in our life. Our earthly days were an eternal battle between the good and the bad forces. The dragons must be defeated, but they could never be rooted out. In chains, they were present in the moment of the victor's triumph. They *must* be present there, as a threat and reminder. Life for Blake was a 'marriage between heaven and hell'. This is the idea behind his famous poem on the tiger's evil and beauty:

> Tyger! Tyger! burning bright
> In the forests of the night,
> What immortal hand or eye
> Could frame thy fearful symmetry?
>
> In what distant deeps or skies
> Burnt the fire of thine eyes?
> On what wings dare he aspire?
> What the hand dare seize the fire?
>
> What the hammer? what the chain?
> In what furnace was thy brain?
> What the anvil? what dread grasp
> Dare its deadly terrors clasp?

When the stars threw down their spears,

And water'd heaven with their tears,

Did he smile his work to see?

Did he who made the Lamb make thee?[17]

The tiger's burning eyes and deadly claws were comparatively uninteresting to Emanuel Swedenborg. He saw himself as the interpreter of a heavenly message about love and wisdom; and here life's shadows fall into the background. In his youth he had very much wanted to make a new discovery every day, to be envied by all. Now, instead, the daily victory over the incessantly appearing self-love stood in the centre, over what Swedenborg in his *Dream Diary* called 'that dreadful apple [...] the root of Adam and original sin'.[18] The author of the diary had found his way out of the dark forest: 'since I have this heavenly joy, why should I seek for worldly pleasure, which by comparison is nothing, is inconstant, hurtful, opposing, and destructive to the former'.[19] The Creator and the lamb are contrasted with the tiger, burning in the forests of the night, which with God's help it was always possible to overcome.

Marriage on earth, marriage in heaven

Chapter Thirty

I enter now in marriage true,

with my best friend on earth

and as Christ's face presents itself in him

so let me at this blessed change

remember both when with you I'll be united;

in marriage here on earth […]

'Wedding song' at the marriage of the pietist priest Erik Tolstadius to Margareta Ariosa,

Stockholm 1724[1]

Oetinger's question

In the years 1763 and 1764 Swedenborg had no less than seven works printed in Amsterdam concluding with *The Divine Providence*. In August 1764 he returned to Stockholm. When he made a new trip to Amsterdam in July 1765, he stayed for a few days in Gothenburg while waiting for a sailing ship. Here he met Doctor Gabriel Beyer, master in classical languages of the college in that city, a meeting with significant consequences.

Swedenborg's torrential flood of publications could scarcely go unnoticed in the Europe of that day. All his theosophical works had been printed anonymously but it gradually became known that the Swedish philosopher and mining scientist was the author. One reader, who later became well-known, was a priest in Württemberg, Friedrich Christian Oetinger. After having thoroughly studied *Principia* and the first two volumes of *Arcana Caelestia*, he published, in 1765, a treatise in two parts called *Swedenborgs und Anderer irdische und himmlische Philosophie* (*Swedenborg's and Others' Earthly and Heavenly Philosophy*). Here we read a German translation of the descriptions of the world of spirits, heaven, and hell that had been inserted between the opening chapters of *Arcana Caelestia*. Oetinger wrote to Swedenborg asking for information concerning questions raised by many readers.[2]

Oetinger had found the descriptions of the spiritual world enriching, but when it came to Swedenborg's interpretation of the Bible he was critical. He asked two questions: first, did Swedenborg consider himself as having sole rights to the definitive key to the interpretation of the biblical texts? Must not each reader find his way to *his* own truth, all the more so since only a few could have access to his writings? Secondly, why could he not provide a sign from above convincing those who were doubtful about his doctrine? Swedenborg claimed, after all, to have communication with the spiritual world.

Oetinger was anxious to have clarifying answers, not least because his book had been much discussed, and quickly confiscated. The excerpts from *Arcana Caelestia* that he had reproduced were considered unsuitable by the authorities, and he had been exhorted to answer a long series of questions on his intentions with the book and its actual content.

Swedenborg responded that the time of miracles was past; besides, such wonders had never helped anyone to true faith.[3] Think of the Children of Israel and God's miracles in Egypt, or of the scant effect that the descent of Jehovah on Mount Sinai had upon the Israelites! As to the question about his exclusive privilege as revelator, Swedenborg called attention to the rationality of his doctrine. What was rational was also true. Why had he alone been chosen by God? This resulted from the fact that through the Lord's providence he had first been initiated into the sciences. His knowledge of nature had been a prerequisite for insights into spiritual things; between natural and spiritual things there are always correspondences. To this divinely-provided preparatory period was added the fact that he had always loved truths 'in a spiritual way', not for the sake of honour or gain. There was only one way to open the church, which for a long time had been ensnared by false teachings. This opening was now possible by a correct understanding, inspired by the Lord.

The marriage of wisdom and love

Swedenborg was a bachelor throughout his life. The picture of monogamous, spiritual, and physical marital-love became a concrete picture of the inexpressible happiness of the union of truth with goodness, of the embrace of wisdom and love. It was not only a tangible picture but also for Swedenborg the best way to explain a tenet in his own message: wisdom and love as the two divine forces that form existence. All can participate in mankind's never-ending celebration of the union of the good and the true. There, the categories of time and space disappear: all things are in the process of being consummated.

Beyer, Swedenborg's first disciple, asked in a letter in February 1767 about an essay that Swedenborg had promised on this subject. Swedenborg answered that he had already touched upon these questions in four books which he listed. He continued:

[...] and there will be still more concerning them in the ARCANA OF ANGELIC WISDOM CONCERNING CONJUGIAL LOVE; for to write separately concerning the Divine attributes would be to raise the thoughts too high without the assistance of anything to support them. For this reason the subjects have been dealt with in series together with other things that fall within the understanding.[4]

The principle of duality

The marriage union was an expression of the duality that Swedenborg found as a principle throughout creation. It was for him simultaneously a physical and a metaphysical axiom. We have already met this notion in his *Principia*, where the active elements are uniting with the passive in the earliest stages of creation, bringing matter and the universe into being.

In Swedenborg's *The Spiritual Diary*, we follow his thinking on marriage and love from 1745 to 1765. In *Arcana Caelestia* he develops his characteristic 'metaphysics of love' for the first time. The starting point here is, as it so often is in his theosophical works, the biblical account of creation.

The inner meaning of the first chapters of Genesis here unfolded did not apply to the creation of the world: it was a description of the spiritual stages of regeneration. The seventh day symbolically pictured man's ultimate endeavour to be formed into an image of God. This, when it happens, occurs through a faith involving *reason* and *will*. In the Swedenborgian world these concepts stand for *masculine* and *feminine*:

Male and female He created them. What 'male and female' mean in the internal sense was very well known in the Most Ancient Church [...] But [...] among later generations [...] this arcanum was lost. Marriages gave them their highest forms of happiness and delight [...]

They were internal men [...] external things, they did no more with than take them in with their eyes, but their thoughts involved what those things represented [...] in their form reflecting celestial things, and in so doing mirroring the Lord, who was everything to them. Consequently they reflected the heavenly marriage [...] which [...] was the source of the happiness in their marriages. For this reason they called the understanding in the spiritual man Male and the will Female, and when the two acted as one, they called it Marriage.[5]

Swedenborg's divine mission was precisely to remind his readers of this venerable, general, and universally applicable thought of a covenant, demonstrating its reality in a time of secularized enlightenment. From this angle of approach, his essential subject became the problem of reunification, the obliteration of earthly tension in a higher world.

Within the relationship of a man and woman, not only in marriage but in all earthly contexts, Swedenborg perceived an attraction between love and wisdom, between the true and the good, will and understanding. The man was rationality that longs for love, woman was love seeking rationality.[6] On all levels there was a tense relationship that was first eased when the union was complete. Everything is striving for this synthesis of understanding and will. The one cannot be thought of apart from the other. What is love without rationality? It is irrationality, since the understanding teaches what and how something should be done. On the other hand rationality without love produces nothing more than calculated self-interest. Love and rationality live in marriage, always acting in unison. Good and truth are united: 'Such a marriage exists in all things created by the Lord in the universe'.[7]

Thus we come to his conclusion: God himself is love and wisdom in union.[8] On the human plane we meet these two components in the spiritual relationship between husband and wife, and in their bodily conjunction. God's plan was that everything should be united anew in obedience and love to the Creator. This presumed man's sanctification, the opening of the mind to the inflow of the divine love and wisdom. Such a reception was a step towards the realization of the heavenly formative work, the *civitas Dei*, which Swedenborg, in following John, refers to as the New Jerusalem. Something resembling human marriage is present everywhere, he wrote in *Arcana Caelestia*. We meet it as a conjunction between good and truth, or oppositely as the union between evil and falsity.

'Indeed everything contains a marriage or coupling together of its own on which its very continuance depends.'[9]

Unity

The relation between understanding and love, man and woman, is for Swedenborg never a relationship in which one is subordinate to the other. The one complements the other, each is a different side of one and the same thing. With man wisdom matches his love, and love matches his wisdom. In this thinking we glimpse the Platonic tale mentioned earlier about man once having been bi-sexual, hermaphroditic. When this wholeness was cleft in two by the gods, man and woman arose as independent beings, always longing to be reunited:

> That's how, long ago, the innate desire of human beings for each other started. It draws the
> two halves of our original nature back together and tries to make one out of two and to heal
> the wound in human nature.[10]

On the earthly human level, this amalgamation is a prerequisite for the continuation of mankind. In the Swedenborgian world of correspondences we find the same complementary relationship on a higher level. Man's worship through right living is met by God's love. To God's wisdom there answered the love professed in his church: the church was 'the bride of Christ'.

It is thus to be underlined that in Swedenborg's thought true marriage, the true amalgamation, is always a reflection of God's union with mankind. Here is the fundamental, dominating analogy between what is earthly and what is heavenly. Such marriages were scarce, in the 1700s, but before the Fall, when the heavenly element in the earthly was evident to all, every marital union reached this perfection.

Marriage and virtue

The doctrine of the unity of apparent opposites is most clearly expressed in Swedenborg's book on marriage, published in 1768 with his name on the title page.[11] The long Latin title in English translation reads *The Delights of Wisdom relating to Conjugial Love followed by the Pleasures of Insanity relating to Licentious Love*, usually referred to as *Conjugial Love*.

According to contemporary descriptions of customs, in middle-class and higher circles, faithfulness in marriage was a virtue from which dispensation was generously granted. Before the erotically inexhaustible Fredrik I had gone to his Hessian forefathers, his own royal example was known to all. In the same year that *Conjugial Love* was published, Louis XV entered into his long and public relationship with Mme du Barry; her predecessor Mme de Pompadour had died in 1764.

The book was Swedenborg's last great creative work, comparable in weight and originality with *Arcana Caelestia* and *The Apocalypse Revealed*. His next and final great work, *The True Christian Religion*, published in 1771, is of another nature: as we shall see, essentially a summary of his theosophy, and a defence against the accusations of heresy that Swedish prelates were then directing at him.

Life is a nursery for heaven, Swedenborg wrote in his conclusion to *The Economy of the Animal Kingdom*. In *Conjugial Love*, this often recurring thought is further developed but from a new perspective. Human beings mature naturally in marriage: in the best case, living together led to a gradual ennoblement of both husband and wife. This sanctity of marriage was in the interest of society, and above all a true love and marriage was pleasing to God. The love in marriage continued after death and contributed to strengthening and enriching the paradise that awaits in heaven.

Swedenborg's view of marriage and of men and women's complementary nature was different from what we meet in the Swedish church handbook, issued in 1693. Here the man was presented as having been created to rule over the woman, and woman's duty was to be subservient to him. Swedenborg must have heard the introductory words of the wedding ceremony many times:

You must carefully remember that God himself has [. . .] placed the man as the woman's head, that he shall be her superior, govern her in the fear of God for what is best, thereto love her, as Christ loved the congregation [. . .] And as the man is gifted with greater intelligence and a stronger nature than woman, he should also use such gifts of God to aid and not to oppress her [. . .] Likewise, the woman shall be obedient to the man, love him, regard him as her head and superior, keeping in mind that she has been created to be a help for the man [...] For the woman has been created for the sake of the man, and not the man for the sake of the woman [...] [12]

The priest would remind the bridal couple that in their life together they should have 'God in mind'. The man's and the woman's sensuality was natural, but was never to take the upper hand. When the ceremony was reaching its conclusion, the priest would again emphasize the importance of purity in their married life together:

And give your blessing to them and preserve them, O Merciful Father, from the devil's incitements [...] so that they be not deceived by impure lusts and unchastity, but may in genuine faith and harmonious love live together to a ripe old age [...]

The married state

Swedenborg's view of marriage gives no place to the harsh, male-dominated view in the official church handbook. In the romantic currents of the 1800s it stood out as an example of the right relationship between men and women, on earth and in heaven. In Swedish literature we discern this in several works, particularly in the prose and poetry of C J L Almqvist.

Sweden's legal code of 1734 begins with a section on marriage. [13] The text of the law seems to confirm the view of the relationship between man and woman that we met in the church handbook. It presents a clearly practical view of marriage. Marriage was the basis for society's existence, the framework of all social order, the prerequisite for the agrarian economy and the birth and raising of children.

Marriage in Catholic societies had the character of a sacrament, and therefore was indissoluble. In Lutheran Sweden marital union was no longer definitive, although divorce was possible only on the basis of certain carefully listed grounds: in the first place, sexual unfaithfulness. The lifelong character of the relationship, and the roles and responsibilities of the man and the woman, were emphasized very strongly in the texts prescribed for the obligatory ceremonies.

As a scientist, philosopher, and theosopher, the Assessor in the Royal Board of Mines was, like the taxonomist Linnaeus, a constantly analysing, classifying, labelling, and arranging observer. God's own order was reflected in the proper use of reason. We can never have a clear understanding of any phenomenon without reference to a general source and universal principles. Classification implies setting clearly defined elements in their places: everything of a 'mixed', blurred nature disappears.

As we have seen, Swedenborg's psychology was dialectic. We meet the same perspective when it comes to judging the character of a marriage. Either we open ourselves to the divine love, or we do not. If man receives the divine *influxus* the marital love becomes pure, anchored in the divine purpose. Man and woman then replenish the earth for the

Fig. 40. Who has understood what is involved in the heavenly marriage? This was a prize question in one of Swedenborg's 'memorable experiences'. The competition took place in heaven. The Africans won and were rewarded with a diamond-studded head-piece. The picture is taken from *The New Jerusalem Magazine* for 1790, the first of a long series of British Swedenborgian magazines to be published.

use of mankind. Or, in the other case, when turning away from divine influence, marriage becomes superficial, far from the innermost, divine purpose.

But, as is usually the case for Swedenborg, psychological and moral uniformity is seen as an ideal, difficult or almost impossible to attain during earthly life. His account of the many forms of sexuality indicates that he had a very clear understanding of the shifts and duplicity in human emotional life. As regards both marriage and man's individual character, the dominant moral quality may be hidden during life. But after death our true and unequivocal self appears.[14]

A catalogue of adulteries

To put the concepts in order, Swedenborg makes a schema of the character of adultery and its varying degrees of gravity.[15] The starting point is a melancholy analysis of the fragility of earthly marriages. Their defectiveness is often connected with the fact that the marital union has been based on wrong premises: the families had wanted to secure wealth and position, or the bride and bridegroom themselves had striven to consolidate security and power. As a result sexual love decreases gradually, and man and woman become indifferent to each other. Swedenborg makes a map or catalogue of the unhappy marriages he has met, and the causes of their failures. Strife about power and money, dissimulation, lies, new public or secret sexual relationships are described by Swedenborg in a way that for him is unusually down to the earth. He himself was unmarried; his descriptions of conventional marriages and the glowing, hidden hatred between husband and wife thus go back to what he has heard and seen in real life. We meet echoes of his analyses in the works of August Strindberg, a fervent reader of Emanuel Swedenborg.

Swedenborg's analysis and classification partially follows the Swedish law on marriage from 1734, where the union's holiness and central significance are emphasized by the care and severity with which adultery is treated.

But with Swedenborg the different deviations from true marriage as established by God are not judged from the point of view of civil law. Instead, the criterion is the degree to which adulteries have harmed true marital love. The offence is serious in the degree to which it brings about such destruction, in the last resort a consequence of the sinners' turning themselves away from the divine influence.

His views and groupings of the different offences are well analysed by the Finnish expert on Swedenborg, Sverker Sieversen.[16] When it comes to sexual activity between the unmarried, of urgent interest to Swedenborg himself in his younger days, he develops the topic at some length, discussing the case of those who 'for various reasons cannot yet enter into marriage, and due to lust cannot govern their desires'. Apparently referring only to men, Swedenborg finds that such individuals may enter into a stable relationship with a mistress, with the understanding that she is unmarried and not a virgin. In this way disorderly relationships can be avoided, lust can be moderated, health-destroying debaucheries lose their attractiveness, and infectious diseases as well as adultery may be avoided.[17]

As is evident it is a highly male oriented viewpoint. It conflicts with the law of 1734 where copulation between two unmarried individuals was punishable.[18] Swedenborg's conception of a bachelor's possibility of regulating his sexual life would later be much discussed: the Swedenborgian position was attacked as encouraging immorality.

Politics and concubines

Swedenborg's religiously-based marriage ethic was an ideal, reality was another matter. He lived in the century of 'gallantry'. Erotic allusions were the spice of conversation in the higher levels of society. Men and women openly discussed things that always happened, but usually quietly. In Sweden King Fredrik officially took a 'concubine' at the side of Queen Ulrika Eleonora, the sister of Charles XII. Her name was Hedvig Taube, sixteen years old, though the king was fifty-four. Her father, an admiral, was rewarded by being given a count's coronet, and the girl was made a princess of the Holy Roman Empire with the name Hessenstein. They had several children. Leading figures within the Hat Party looked with understanding on the king and his mistress, not least Fredrik Gyllenborg, well-known by Swedenborg.

At Versailles Louis XV's publicly-known concubines became figureheads of the royal despotism. Mme de Pompadour and her successor Mme du Barry became *de facto* what in France were called 'wives at the left'. The queen, Maria Leszczyñska, seven years older than the king, seems to have looked on her husband's side-connections with equanimity.

Swedenborg, who dedicated his great work on copper in 1734 to King Fredrik 'with admiration and respect', appears to have accepted his concubinage with Hedvig Taube. The same applies also to the French monarch's amorous life. In *Conjugial Love* we also find exceptions to the requirement for faithfulness in marriage that seem to have been formulated with regard to the marriages of convenience that were then the rule within royal and socially highstanding families. A married man could under certain circumstances enter into a relationship with another woman. Such was the case when the wife's advanced age led to infertility and a distaste for the physical intimacies of marriage, but the husband's desire was unchanged.[19] In good legal style there is also a general clause: there could be other, similar causes justifying an extra-marital relationship.

Heavenly marriage, the delights of the angels

Swedenborg had a pessimistic view of the marriages in his day. Men and women no longer realized that the earthly dwelling place of the Divine is in a marriage where there is faith in God and mutual love, where feminine will and love is met by masculine knowledge and wisdom. Nor did people want to understand that it was a matter of classic roles, strictly monogamous, where the sexual element is present, but in an ennobled form. The union, at the same time both physical and spiritual, produces those very delights of wisdom that are mentioned in his great marriage book's long title: *The Delights of Wisdom concerning Conjugial Love.*

'Delight' that is at the same time happiness and enjoyment takes the form of an ennobled intercourse in the spirit of chastity and shared love for marriage and for God. If this chaste union is rare among human beings living on earth it is, according to Swedenborg, characteristic of the togetherness of male and female angels. The angels in the highest heaven are examples of this degree of intercourse, whose intensity is in proportion to the tender heat of their love. Their capacity and inclination for this kind of love seems endless: he met angels telling him of their willingness and readiness for intercourse, lasting thousands of years. Their married intercourse continues during sleep, all through the night, we read. 'They say they cannot live any other way, since marriage love is just such an intimate union.'[20] At home they are always naked, he notes, but outside the home they are dressed in loin-cloths.

And their pleasures, it appears from another report, surpass those of all other loves. But at the present day, true marital love is so seldom seen on earth that its happiness can only be described by referring to the angels' own accounts:

> Angels have said that its inmost delights, those of the soul, the first point reached by the conjugial influence of love and wisdom, or good and truth, coming from the Lord, are imperceptible and therefore inexpressible, being at once feelings of peace and innocence. But as they come down they become more and more easily perceived, in the upper levels of the mind as blessedness, in the lower levels as bliss, in the chest as the pleasant sensations these give, and spreading out from the chest into every part of the body, and finally uniting at the lowest level to produce the greatest of delights [...] [21]

In the heavenly marriage, happiness is complete. In one of the 'memorable experiences' where Swedenborg recounts his visions of this felicity, he reports that the angels learned of his interest in marriages after death. The heavens were opened to him:

> One morning I looked up into heaven and [...] there was to be seen a chariot coming down from the highest or third heaven, containing what seemed to be one angel. But as it approached, it seemed to have two angels in it. The chariot seen from afar sparkled like a diamond, and had harnessed to it foals as white as snow. The travellers [...] called out to me, 'You would like us to come closer, but be careful then that the fiery radiance, which is from the heaven we come down from, does not strike too deep [...]' 'I will be careful,' I replied, 'come closer.' They did so, and turned out to be a husband and wife. 'We are a married couple,' they said. 'We have lived a blessed life in heaven from the earliest time, which you call the Golden Age. We have been perpetually in the bloom of life, in which you see us today.' [22]

It was a picture of marriage love. Swedenborg reports that the man looked to be between adolescence and adulthood with eyes shining with the light of wisdom: a sparkling light that illuminated the interior of his face. His wife was both visible and invisible, like her indescribable beauty. In her countenance there was a glow as from a flaming light, blinding him:

she spoke to me. 'What can you see?' she asked. 'I can see nothing but conjugial love and the form it takes,' I answered. 'But I both see and don't see.' At this she turned sideways on to her husband, and then I could gaze at her more fixedly. Her eyes flashed with the light of her heaven, a fiery light [. . .] which derives from the love of wisdom [. . .] I was surprised to see that the colours changed as she turned towards or away from her husband [. . .]

As the fruits of their life together, the united pair receives a spiritual offspring: new truths, new kinds of usefulness.

Immorality in hell

The question of man's moral state and the love that governed him in life is given a definite answer after death, when we are stripped of our physical nature, and our character stands visible in its nakedness. As a contrast to the description of angelic marriages Swedenborg also reports on infernal sexuality. We read about different kinds of adultery, the lust of defloration, the longing for sexual variety, the urge to rape, the wish to destroy innocence. Just as Linnaeus had studied the relation between stamens and pistils in flowers, during his long life the methodical Assessor made his own observations of the different forms of human lust.

Those who had let themselves be led in their marriage by other motives than creation's fundamental purpose of union between love and wisdom found themselves opposing goodness in the sphere most suitable to them. This applied not least to the promiscuous, who on account of their sensuality tend to distance themselves from the true, marital, and monogamous form of life. In the infernal life, heaven's blessedness is changed into the 'pleasures of insanity'.[23] As usual in the Swedenborgian doctrine of the life after death, it is not a question of punishment, but a matter of a personally chosen state of mind, whose misery is seldom or never evident to those who become accustomed to these perverted pleasures during their life on earth. But a vague idea of higher and purer spheres may give them a momentary glimpse of their real situation:

Those who in the natural world have been confirmed adulterers, on perceiving the sphere of conjugial love coming down from heaven, immediately either run away and hide in caverns or […] become furiously angry and rage like furies […] I could hazard the opinion that, if you asserted that everything has its opposite, and that therefore conjugial love must have its opposite, adulterers would reply that there is no opposite to this love […] No one knows good from a consideration of evil, but evil from a consideration of good. For evil is in thick darkness, but good in light. [24]

Swedenborg's descriptions of hell are soberly objective; only occasionally is he, like Dante, gripped with sympathy for the sinners and their lot. One of these distant, unemotional reports regards the everyday life of those men who during their earthly existence had been aroused to conquer women by force. It is their lot to deal with sly prostitutes who pretend to lead a pure and chaste life:

[…] when the rapist approaches and touches them, they […] take refuge, as if terrified, in a room where there is a couch or bed, lightly barring the door behind them while they lie down. From that position they use their skill to excite the rapist to an overbearing passion to break down the door, rush in and assault them. When this happens, the whore sits up and begins to fight the rapist punching and scratching, scoring his face and tearing his clothes, and shouting out in a frenzied voice to her fellow whores, as if calling on her servants for help, 'Thief, robber, murderer!' While the rapist is achieving his purpose she weeps and wails; and then after the rape she throws herself on the floor wailing and crying 'Horrors!' Then in a serious voice she threatens the rapist that unless he pays a heavy fine for his rape, she will encompass his ruin […] they look at a distance like cats […] After a number of such bawdy contests they are taken out and transferred to a cavern […] But because of their foul smell […] they are banished to the borders of the western region. There seen at distance they look emaciated, as if made of bones covered only with skin, and from far off like panthers. [25]

The theosopher's heavenly bride

Swedenborg's insights into the problems that can arise in marital life have been interpreted as indicating that he is describing his own experiences from long periods of living together with a woman. We know of his interest in women, and his strong sexual inclination, displayed in the *Dream Diary*. Regarding more lasting relationships with women we have only scant information given by Carl Robsahm, according to whom Swedenborg as a young man had a 'mistress', whom however he gave up when she showed herself unfaithful. Nobody in Swedenborg's wide circle of acquaintances ever mentioned such a relationship: is it possible that Robsahm, in fact, is referring to Swedenborg's one-time planned betrothal to Emerentia Polhem?

Given the importance he attached to the heavenly marriage it would appear to be quite natural for him to speculate about who would be his companion in the future life, all the more so since he saw himself as having access to special information from that realm. According to one of Swedenborg's early English biographers, J J Garth Wilkinson, Swedenborg had pointed out Countess Elisabeth Stierncrona Gyllenborg as his heavenly wife-to-be: the information is said to go back to a communication from the English Member of Parliament Charles Augustus Tulk. [26]

Since 1759 Elizabeth Stierncrona had been the widow of the bankrupt and loose-living Fredrik Gyllenborg. She went to the spiritual world in 1769, three years before Swedenborg. She was very pious, and is described as a singularly good-hearted woman. She wrote and published a devotional book in two volumes: *Marie Bästa Del* (*Mary's Better Part*). In the preface to the book she made a glowing declaration of love for the departed swindler who had been her husband. She was an 'inconsolable widow', we read. Would she forget her loving affection when she met Emanuel Swedenborg in a better world?

Chapter Thirty-One

Christt: the natural point

Swedenborg had presented his model for the origin of the universe in his *Principia*. The book was printed in 1734, when he was 46 years old. The Swedenborgian cosmogony proceeded from what he called the 'natural point'. This was an entity assumed by reason, literally a starting point. It was a mathematical or, rather, geometrical point. Swedenborg's great German teacher Christian Wolff had described it in his book on geometry, also translated into Swedish. It was inaccessible, incomprehensible to reason and to our scientific instruments:

> The geometricians have had sufficient reason to regard a point as indivisible, although the imagination can just as little form one as can our hands using drafting tools; namely, so that it is not part of a line, which must be carefully avoided when doing geometry. [1]

The point became the bridge between the infinite and the finite. It had arisen through whirling movements in the infinite. And through these movements centripetal and centrifugal movements arose in the finite.

In the same year Swedenborg also published a small book, entitled *The Infinite and*

Final Cause of Creation. Here he made a dizzying parallel. In his cosmogony the point corresponded, on the spiritual level, to God's coming into the world, his incarnation as Christ. In Swedenborg's conception of the universe, Jesus's life and preaching was the *Divine Human*. Christ was the spiritual bridge between the finite and the infinite. Christ had always been present in the prophecies of the Old Testament; now he came forward into open view in the 'new covenant'.

Physics and mystic

In the colossal literature on Swedenborg there is a tendency to regard his life's work, science, philosophy, and theosophy as an unbroken whole. From the viewpoint of the Swedenborgian New Church there is a tendency to see a clear line running through all he wrote. 'It is the besetting sin of Swedenborg researchers', writes Inge Jonsson, 'to interpret earlier stages in the light of later developments and to presume logical connection and consequence where the sources reveal rather a joy in hypothesizing and a rich phantasy'.[2]

The warning is well-founded. Swedenborg himself took up the question in his *Dream Diary* and in *The Spiritual Diary*.[3] From science and philosophy no one could draw conclusions regarding divine truths. These must come forth from the power of the spirit; 'the verities are not my own', he wrote in the *Dream Diary*. It was another thing to discern later a rational agreement between the two spheres.

The Interaction of the Soul and the Body

The problem is discussed in *De Commercio Animae et Corporis* (*The Interaction of the Soul and the Body*), printed in London in 1769. Someone had asked him why from being a philosopher he had become a theologian. Swedenborg answered that he had always been a 'spiritual fisherman'. Asked to explain what he meant he gave an answer typical for himself and his time:

A fisherman, in the Word, in its spiritual sense, signifies a man who investigates and teaches natural truths, and afterwards spiritual truths, in a rational manner.[4]

The notion of Christ as the connection between the infinite and the finite, God and man, is the main thought in this book. The divine love and goodness were streaming into man's soul as a constantly shining spiritual sun. However, by this alone no relationship was established. Conjunction with God was dependent on man himself. Everything depended on his will to receive the 'love that courses through the world', to use the words of the Swedish poet and historian Erik Gustaf Geijer.

For Swedenborg this was simultaneously a contribution to a current philosophical debate and to a thought fundamental to his whole doctrine. Through this divine inflow a man receives wisdom, he writes in his book on the soul-body interaction. He is filled with love to God and the neighbour, and his reason is enlightened. It is his soul that receives the divine inflow, which then via his reason streams into his body's senses, speech, and movements. The spiritual becomes human and is adapted to the level and state of the receiver. He summarizes:

> The understanding in a man can be raised into the light, that is, into the wisdom in which
> are the angels of heaven, according to the cultivation of his reason; and his will can be
> raised in like manner into the heat of heaven, that is, into love, according to the deeds of his
> life; but the love of the will is not raised, except so far as the man wills and does those things
> which the wisdom of the understanding teaches.[5]

To illustrate his line of thought Swedenborg records a 'memorable experience' where actual philosophers of his day appear and hold a discussion on a heavenly stage.[6] Swedenborg had asked God that he might be allowed to converse with disciples of Aristotle, Descartes, and Leibniz, and this was granted. The philosophers themselves appeared, laurelled, and surrounded by their disciples. Behind Leibniz stood a person well-known to the spirit-seer: it was Wolff, 'holding the skirt of his garment'. A spirit entered, torch in hand. He shook his light before the philosophers' faces, with the result that they were taken by a desire to argue and discuss:

> Then the Aristotelians, who were also Schoolmen, began to speak, saying, 'Who does not see
> that objects flow through the senses into the soul, as man enters through the doors into a
> chamber, and that the soul thinks according to such influx? When a lover sees [...] his

bride, does not his eye sparkle, and transmit the love of her into the soul? When a miser sees bags of money, does he not burn towards them with every sense, and then cause this ardour to enter the soul, and excite the desire of possessing them? [...] Are not the senses of the body like outer courts, through which alone entrance is obtained to the soul? From these considerations and innumerable others of similar nature, who can conclude otherwise than that influx proceeds from nature, or is physical?'

After this Aristotelian thinking, tied to human conceptions, Descartes' supporters take up the issue. No name is mentioned, but we sense the French priest Malebranche in the Cartesian group. Now the celebrated concept of 'occasionalism' is presented: there is no direct influence between soul and body. But God always has 'occasion' to establish a spiritual connection and by this means an influence.

The Cartesians put their fingers to their foreheads as an indication of deep thought:

Ah, you speak from appearances. Do you not know that the eye does not love a virgin or a bride from itself, but from the soul; and likewise that the senses of the body do not covet the bags of money from themselves, but from the soul; and also that the ears do not devour the praises of flatterers in any other manner? Is it not perception that causes sensation? And perception is of the soul, and not of the bodily organ. Say, if you can, what causes the tongue and lips to speak, but the thought; and what causes the hands to work, but the will? And thought and will are of the soul, and not of the body. Thus, what causes the eye to see, and the ears to hear, and the other organs to feel, but the soul? From these considerations, and innumerable others of a similar kind, everyone, whose wisdom rises above the things of the bodily senses, concludes that there is no influx of the body into the soul, but of the soul into the body.

Now it was the turn of Leibniz's followers, particularly Christian Wolff, the one who was clutching his master's robe. Both the Aristotelian and the Cartesian arguments are partially correct, but we will solve the controversy, says their spokesman:

There is not any influx of the soul into the body, nor of the body into the soul; but there is a

———

unanimous and instantaneous operation of both together, to which a celebrated author has assigned an elegant name, by calling it Pre-established Harmony.

So, three different opinions. Now the spirit shook his torch behind the combatants' heads, and they became confused, knowing neither what was right nor what was wrong. To determine the truth they requested that lots be drawn, which was granted. Each philosopher took a sheet of paper and wrote down his opinion, and put his lot in the hat. On one paper could be read 'physical influence', on another 'spiritual influence', and on a third 'pre-established harmony'. Then one of the participants drew a paper out of the hat, and read 'spiritual influence'. All agreed that this must be accepted to be the truth.

The account concludes with an angel explaining that the result of the lot-drawing was divinely ordained, and that the words 'spiritual influence' contained more truth than the participants understood. The angel does not develop his thinking, but for the reader of Swedenborg's writings it is immediately clear. Spiritual influence is permanent, always present, but whether man will receive it depends on him.

Swedenborg the mystic

The author of the book on the connection between soul and body looked on himself as a specially privileged person, a *mystikós*, as the word reads in Greek. In his books, letters, and conversations he averred that he had a call, that he was chosen by God, and that his mission was to explain the meaning of the Christian message. It was God himself who through a flood of light and truth had given him the ability to understand the Word. He was not a prophet, as he explained on several occasions, he did not foresee the future. His time was the present, and his mission was a matter of enlightening readers in his own and coming times. The past was of interest only as a matter of clarification, of explanation. Søren Kierkegaard formulated the same thought about a hundred years later:

The past is not reality, for me; only what is present is reality for me. What you are living in at the moment is reality: for you. And thus every person can be contemporary only with the time in which he is living, and also with one more, with Christ's life on earth, because Christ's earthly life, the holy history, stands alone for me, outside history [...][7]

They who have received the gift of living in the divine wisdom and love lead their lives outside of time, Swedenborg reported. In the spiritual world there is no time, only a succession of changing states.

Attack and self-defence

Chapter Thirty-Two

The Gothenburg circle and the question of orthodoxy

During the 1760s Swedenborg had acquired followers in Gothenburg. It was a little group, consisting for the most part of teachers, priests, and public officials, among whom the lecturers Gabriel Beyer and Johan Rosén were the most active. Another early follower, the businessman Sven Wenngren, reported later on their meeting in Gothenburg. Swedenborg was en route to England and was waiting for his ship to leave the port:

During his stay [. . .] Dr Beyer accidentally met him socially and, according to what I have heard, was then entertaining the same opinion about him as did many other learned men in the country, namely, that he was insane. Thus Beyer was surprised when he observed that Swedenborg spoke very sensibly, not showing any signs of that infirmity of which he was suspected; he invited Swedenborg to dine with him the day following, in company with Dr Rosén. After dinner, Dr Beyer expressed a desire, in the presence of Dr Rosén, to hear from him a full account of his doctrines, upon which Swedenborg, animated by the request [. . .], spoke so clearly and in so wonderful a manner on the subject that the Doctor and his friend were quite astonished. They did not interrupt him; but when the discourse was ended, Dr

Beyer requested Swedenborg to meet him the next day at Mr Wenngren's, and to bring with him a paper containing the substance of his discourse so that he might consider it more attentively. Swedenborg came the following day, as he had promised, and, taking the paper out of his pocket, in the presence of the other two gentlemen, he trembled and appeared much affected, the tears flowing down his cheeks. Presenting the paper to Dr Beyer, he then said, 'Sir, from this day the Lord has introduced you into the society of angels, and you are now surrounded by them'. They were all greatly affected. He then took his leave, and the next day embarked for England.[1]

The meeting with Beyer would lead to Swedenborg's abandoning his role as a visionary who was relatively unknown and difficult to understand: a role that he had filled for two decades. Now he became the best-known and most disputed Swedish religious figure in the latter part of the 1700s. Beyer, convinced of the truth of his teaching, devoted the rest of his life to Swedenborg's doctrine, writing a dictionary of biblical 'correspondences' as explained in the master's writings. In 1767-8 he also published a collection of sermons in which the Gospels were explained in accordance with Swedenborg's doctrine, without however mentioning his name.

The collection of sermons had been properly approved by the ecclesiastical authorities. But the following year Peter Aurelius, a priest in the diocese, wrote a critical review of the book, alleging that it contained doctrinal mistakes inspired by Swedenborg. The reviewer and the Bishop of Gothenburg, Erik Lamberg, have gone down into posterity as the local leaders of the judicial and administrative undertaking that was now to begin, not aiming directly at Swedenborg himself, but at Beyer and his friend Rosén. They were both members of the Cathedral Chapter and were requested to give an account of their position regarding Swedenborg's teaching: it contained dangerous departures from the fundamental principles of ecclesiastical orthodoxy, particularly his rejection of the orthodox conception of the Trinity and his criticism of the accepted doctrine regarding the Christian's justification by faith.

A protracted case

A long, drawn out, investigation began.[2] The government and the authorities in Stockholm were clearly troubled by the disturbance that the orthodox priests in Gothenburg had stirred. Swedenborg was a well-known man, with good connections in the highest places. Besides, he was eighty-one years old and could be expected to leave this world soon.

Swedenborg felt compelled to defend himself, causing him to define his position in regard to the current ecclesiastical opinions and political realities differently from his earlier method. Above all, he wanted to show the agreement between his own comprehensible and rational doctrine and the biblical texts. But it was not only these elements in his theology that took expression in his letters and writings during these years; at the same time the disquieting and supernatural aspects became evident. According to rumours some members of the clerical Estate set his mental health in question: his reports of meetings with the spirits of the deceased and of his travels in heaven and hell could indicate mental disturbances.

The question of his health during these years was often discussed. Shortly after Swedenborg's death Anders Johan von Höpken wrote a letter to a friend of the deceased, Commissioner General Christian Tuxen, admitting his own indetermination regarding Swedenborg's personality: 'In spite of his genius [...] there is [nevertheless] something unusual, extravagant, that could resemble a disturbed brain'.[3]

The matter was taken up at a meeting of priests in the diocese of Gothenburg, as well as in the Swedish government, at Uppsala University, and before the appropriate Court of Appeal. From 1768 onwards Swedenborg gave up his earlier anonymity entirely.

At approximately the same time as the Diet opened in Norrköping in 1769, he travelled to Amsterdam, to write and publish an apology, entitled *Summaria Expositio Doctrinae Novae Ecclesiae* (*A Brief Exposition of the Doctrine of the New Church*). The little book was presented as an outline of a larger work that would be completed in the coming years. It consists, essentially, of a review in twenty-five articles of the Catholic and Protestant views on the question of the atonement, being the foundation of the new church that he regarded himself as called to herald. In the last article he made a most offensive statement: Catholics could enter the New Church more easily than Protestants.

When he finished his book, he received a sign from above that what he had written had gained heaven's approval:

When the *Brief Exposition* was published the angelic heaven, from east to west and from south to north, appeared purple-coloured with the loveliest flowers; this happened before my very eyes and before those of the kings of Denmark and others; on another occasion it appeared as if it were beautifully aflame.[4]

Swedenborg was well aware that the contents of the book could be dangerous for him; it involved a turning point in Christian theology. It would be best if the book remained unknown in Sweden, he wrote to Beyer and von Höpken, who each received a copy. In a letter to Beyer, dated in April 1769, he declared that nobody in Gothenburg, except the receiver, could understand it. Swedenborg had, however, sent it to 'all the professors and priests in Holland and [...] to the principal universities in Germany'.[5] He had published it in Latin, but intended to have it printed in French and English also.

Departure for Paris and a 'secret purpose'

While the documents in the case against Beyer and Rosén continued to meander between different departments in the Swedish administration, Swedenborg left Amsterdam for Paris. In several letters to Beyer he had spoken of his approaching departure: he emphasized that the journey 'was undertaken for a purpose that must remain a secret'.[6] The Swedish Diet had assembled in Norrköping that spring and the Hats were preparing to recapture power from the Caps who had ruled since the previous Diet in 1765-6. Was the task a political mission for the Hats?

This was probably not the case, but rather a question of a French translation and printing of the *Brief Exposition*, although no version in French appeared during his lifetime. From later French information it appears that the French censor had given him permission to publish the book on condition that London or Amsterdam was given as the place of publication, a condition which Swedenborg refused.[7]

The Interaction of the Soul and the Body: answer to criticism in Amsterdam

In July he had travelled further to London. Here an English edition of the *Brief Exposition* was soon ready for distribution to local bishops and to others who ought to read the work. In London he also had printed the pamphlet, *The Interaction of the Soul and the Body*.

This little book should be regarded as a part of his defence against the attacks on his writings. As we have seen, Swedenborg had an admiring and intelligent friend, John Christian Cuno, active in Amsterdam. In a long letter to the eighty-one year old author, dated 8 March 1769, Cuno had made a balanced assessment of his reading of all the works of a theosophical nature that Swedenborg had published, with the exception of *Arcana Caelestia*. Cuno was full of admiration for great parts of the content, but there was a fundamental fault: a very important question was never answered, neither in his *Brief Exposition* nor in his previous works. 'Royal ambassadors have credentials without which they are neither accepted nor listened to. You present yourself before the world without credentials as an ambassador from heaven', Cuno wrote, with this blunt advice:

'I implore you! Why do you not convince the incredulous world of this your legitimate mission? It is your duty to set forth your mission publicly, which is such as has never been entrusted to any man since the time of the first human being. You must demonstrate it, with all the attendant circumstances which you can truthfully adduce, and totally remove from the minds of your readers all doubts. If you refuse to do so, you must not take it amiss, if in the whole world you do not find a single reader willing to believe you.

It is stated that you verbally reported from the spiritual world a conversation which the Queen of Sweden once had in the natural world with her brothers, the King and the Prince of Prussia, at Charlottenburg, close to Berlin; and that the Queen, who knew that no one was secretly present who could have related the least word of it, was compelled to acknowledge that you reported this conversation in its least details [...] You yourself have told me that this occurrence has actually taken place. Tell it then to the unbelieving world. You owe this to the cause of truth. You have at least a Queen and a great King for your witnesses. Perhaps they will suffice [...][8]

In paragraph after paragraph Cuno hammers home the point that the burden of proof rests on the author, claiming that he has been inspired from heaven:

No one, I think, will deny that in the biblical literal sense there is a spiritual sense. I willingly admit that you are most versed in that spiritual sense; nay, I acknowledge it with admiration.

Your little treatise *The White Horse* would please me above your other works, if towards the close you did not rashly deny that the apostolic epistles of Paul, Peter, John, James, and Jude were divinely inspired, because, in your opinion, they have no internal sense. You were the only one who could see the inner meaning, and so there was no inner meaning in their letters.[9]

Cuno's respectful but very critical letter contained the same thought advanced at approximately the same time by von Höpken, and probably by many others. Swedenborg answered in writing, providing information that as to its thoughts and words is almost the same as we find in the twentieth paragraph of *The Interaction of the Soul and the Body*. The proof that Cuno desired was stated in the lines already quoted in part in our previous chapter:

I was once asked how, from a philosopher, I became a theologian; and I answered, "In the same manner that fishermen were made disciples and apostles by the Lord: and that I also had from early youth been a spiritual fisherman." On this, my questioner asked, "What is a spiritual fisherman?" I replied, "A fisherman, in the Word, in its spiritual sense, signifies a man who investigates and teaches natural truths, and afterwards spiritual truths, in a rational manner."[10]

Cuno could then read that Swedenborg's questioner found himself convinced by this argument. He was an intelligent man, the author of the letter and the book stressed. Strengthened by the conversation, his partner in the dialogue had added that 'the Lord alone knows who is the proper person to apprehend and teach those things which belong to His New Church'.

Swedenborg's answer to Cuno and other doubting readers was thus that his scientific and philosophical theses agreed with the thoughts he had advanced after being called to proclaim Christianity's true message.

The open letter

On his return to Stockholm Swedenborg soon became aware that what originally had been a case against the two lecturers in Gothenburg was now directed against him and his works. He arranged to have a large number of copies of the work on *Conjugial Love* sent from Amsterdam to the Diet in session at Norrköping in 1769. His intention was to distribute it widely: to the royal couple, the Council of the Realm, the bishops, and other noteworthy Swedes. At the instigation of the Bishop of Linköping Petrus Filenius, the books were impounded. Filenius, who was married to the daughter of Eric Benzelius and Anna Swedenborg, functioned as the Diet's spokesman for the priesthood. The book, according to Filenius, could not be brought into the country until its agreement with the true evangelical doctrine had been proven. Swedenborg was informed further that a special commission would investigate all his theosophical works with the same purpose.

At approximately the same time he received information that according to rumours reported in a Gothenburg newspaper he would be forced to leave the country due to a French deportation application. [11] He had come into print with new revelations from the world of spirits, but could the French people really assess the light in his message? asked the anonymous correspondent, who was very probably referring to the work about the doctrine of the new church recently published in Amsterdam.

In this situation it was time to put up a defence. The caution he had shown when presenting his *Brief Exposition* had to be given up. On 30 October he wrote a letter to Beyer on the questions that now demanded clear answers. The letter could 'be copied and printed', he suggested. [12]

He argues passionately first against Filenius and Swedish theologians in general. The confiscation of *Conjugial Love* was illegal, so much the more so since the book did not have a theological character but dealt mostly with moral problems; the Swedish theologians refused to use their understanding in questions of faith, and therefore came to wrong conclusions. In the letter he also summarized the arguments that in his view showed that his doctrine was in agreement with the Lutheran confessions of faith and that orthodox Swedish theologians had misunderstood the texts.

A short time before the letter was written, Beyer's wife had died in childbirth. On her deathbed she had been visited by the Dean of the cathedral and another priest. [13] Both had adjured her to disavow her belief in the Swedenborgian doctrine. Beyer had informed Swedenborg about this and Swedenborg's long answer concluded with a word of consolation. He had met Beyer's wife in the spiritual world. The two priests, visiting the dying woman, had seduced her faith and led her thoughts in the path of the dragon spoken of in the Book of Revelation. The dragon and his company had been cast down from heaven and were full of hate for everything that had to do with the New Church. Swedenborg continued:

> Your late wife was with me yesterday, and she related much of what she had thought, and what she had spoken of with you [...] and [...] with her seducers. Were I present with you, I would be able to tell you much about these things, but it is not permitted to write it. [14]

Beyer understood the permission given to print the letter as a recommendation, and hurried to do it. The document intensified debate about Swedenborg himself and the conflict over his doctrines. Bishop Lamberg wrote to the Cathedral Chapter in Gothenburg that the letter had 'caused him and all who read it the greatest dismay'. The priesthood now had a new inducement to work with real seriousness on the Swedenborg question.

'Apostasy from the pure evangelical doctrine?'

The excitement over the question of Swedenborg's doctrinal purity naturally strikes us as remarkable from the perspective of our time. According to the Swedish Criminal Code of 1734, 'apostasy from the pure evangelical doctrine' was in no way risk-free:

> If anyone departs from the true evangelical doctrine and adopts one that is heretical, and does not permit himself to be corrected, then he shall be banished from the kingdom, and enjoy neither the rights of inheritance nor civil rights within the kingdom of Sweden [...] Anyone who disseminates heretical doctrines either at home or abroad, and does not desist after being warned, shall also be expelled from the kingdom [...]

The prescriptions of the law seem to have been put into effect by a Royal Resolution dated 26 April 1770. [15] In the case against Beyer and Rosén 'Swedenborg's errors are obvious': Bishop Lamberg was to inform the two men of this opinion. He was also to communicate to them that the fact that Swedenborg's ideas had not actually been refuted was due to obvious reasons: 'It merely shows that no one who has read these writings has found it necessary to refute irrational matters, which fall to the ground by themselves, but which through a public review could become generally known'.[16] The two lecturers were to be informed that the government would give them time for consideration and that they must be seriously urged to desist from their mistaken thinking in the future. Till further notice they were to be suspended from teaching theology.

Swedenborg felt that he had been confidentially assured by highly-placed persons that nothing would happen to him. Feeling threatened and insulted he wrote to King Adolf Fredrik, requesting his protection. He repeated what he had communicated to the royal family: the Saviour had revealed himself to him, commanding him to write what he had written. By divine grace he had received the ability to be in the company of and converse with the angels and spirits. Beyer and Rosén, he said, had been innocent victims of cruel persecution. The priestly witch-hunt had also involved his own books, with false accusations:

> If now the rumor which is spread abroad is true, that such are the contents of the letter that was sent from the office of the Chancellor of Justice to the Consistory in Gothenburg, it follows therefrom that my books are characterized as heretical [...] with myself unheard. This is the reason [...] why I fly to your Royal Majesty for protection; for that has befallen me which has never yet befallen any one in the Kingdom of Sweden since the introduction of Christianity [...][17]

He had not been privy to the letters, accusations, or minutes of the proceedings that pertained to his case. He asked that he might have access to all of the transactions. The matter was important, and he must be given the right to defend himself: 'This concerns not only my own writings but also [...] myself personally and my good name and reputation'.

The investigation dragged on, presumably in accord with the desire of the king and the government. Gradually things quietened down, and the whole matter was closed in 1778, six years after Swedenborg's death.

Return to Amsterdam: beginning of the great defence

But for the main protagonist, the conflict was not finished at all. In July 1770 Swedenborg left Stockholm for Amsterdam in order to compose a great summarizing account of his theosophy, at the same time both a clarification and a defence. His *Brief Exposition* and his little volume on *The Interaction of the Soul and the Body* had been preparations for what was now to follow. Cuno, both admiring and sceptical, described his impressions of the eighty-three year old Swedish seer in a letter written in January 1771:

> You ask me what this old man is now doing? I will tell you. He eats and drinks very moderately, but sleeps pretty long, and thirteen hours are not too much for him. When I informed him that his work *The Earths in the Universe* had appeared in a [German] translation, his eyes, always smiling, became twice as bright. He is now indefatigably at work; yea, I must say that he labours in a most astonishing and superhuman manner at his new work. Sixteen sheets, in type twice as small as those used in his former works, are already printed. Only think! for every printed sheet he has to fill four sheets in manuscript. He now has two sheets [16 pages] printed every week [...] His work is to consist, as he says himself, of eighty printed sheets [640 pages]; he has thus already calculated that it cannot be finished before Michaelmas [in September]. [18]

Swedenborg has a title for his new book, Cuno continues. It will be called *The True Christian Religion, containing the whole theology for the New Church, predicted by the Lord in Daniel 7: 13, 14, and in the Apocalypse 21: 1, 2, by Emanuel Swedenborg, servant of the Lord Jesus Christ*. Cuno could not conceal his astonishment that on the title page Swedenborg should declare himself to be the servant of the Lord Jesus Christ, but he was told that the declaration was written by express command. Cuno continues:

> You can scarcely believe with what confidence the old gentleman speaks of his spiritual world, his angels, and of God Himself. If I were to give you only a summary of our last conversation, it should fill many pages [...] In it things were said that made my ears ring, but which I pass over, in order not to be too precipitous in my judgment. I am quite willing to confess that I do not know what to make of him.

Swedenborg appears to have finished the manuscript in the summer of 1770. The printing in Amsterdam was completed in June 1771. The book is in octavo format and with its index comprises 541 pages. [19]

The true Christian religion: defence and summary

Chapter Thirty-Three

In Great Eternity, every particular Form gives forth or Emanates

Its own peculiar Light, & the Form is the Divine Vision

And the Light is his Garment. This is Jerusalem in every Man [...]

Blake: 'Jerusalem' [1]

True Christianity

In the book of Daniel and in the Apocalypse Swedenborg had read about the coming of a new heaven and new earth. What was coming was a new message of Christ, rightly interpreted and at last presented as the true Christian religion. This interpretation was his call and mission as 'servant of the Lord Jesus Christ'. Swedenborg had exposed himself to attack; according to the Swedish Chancellor of Justice, his religious thinking was heresy. Defence was urgent, he was well aware of his age and time was short.

The True Christian Religion, printed in Amsterdam in 1771, became a comprehensive work, with fourteen massive chapters. Swedenborg here followed the arrangement usually used by Lutheran theologians in their *Loci*: collections of passages from the Bible to prove and illustrate the Christian faith. More than he had ever done earlier, he presented his message so that it could be accepted by orthodox Lutheran critics. It was not simply a matter of terms, but also of biblical quotations. As George F Dole has pointed out, he is working with a broader biblical base than hitherto.[2] He now refers often to the epistles in the New Testament, something relatively unusual in Swedenborg's earlier works. Paul's writings, he had said, were not divinely inspired: consequently they had no inner, spiritual meaning.[3] But in *The True Christian Religion* he often quotes them: Swedenborg presumably wanted to show the compatibility of his thoughts with the Lutheran tradition.

To illustrate his theological presentation, Swedenborg inserts a great number of 'memorable experiences' which were records of his visionary experiences in the spiritual world. They constitute, he seems to say, the supernatural evidence of his doctrine: in heaven the arguments of those who stand in doubt and opposition are overthrown. Swedenborg, who on earth stuttered and was usually disinclined to discussion, takes the lead in these heavenly debates. His opponents accept his arguments, or disappear to regions where their misconceptions are accepted.

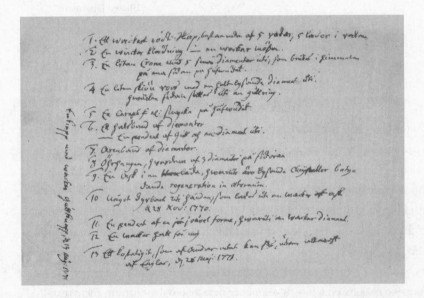

Fig. 41. The power of Swedenborg's dreamed or visionary experiences is illustrated by a list of gifts he had received in the spiritual world. The list was written on the inside of the cover of his own copy of *The True Christian Religion*. The Stockholm librarian G E Klemming, who sold the book to the American New Church priest W H Benade, made this tracing of the list of spiritual valuables. The list was included as an appendix in the 1859 edition of the *Dream Diary*:
  1. A beautiful red chest, consisting of 5 compartments, 5 drawers in each compartment.
  2. A beautiful shirt — a beautiful cap.
  3. A small crown set with 5 diamonds, which is worn in heaven on the side of the head.
  4. A small beautiful rose set with a gleaming diamond, which is then set on a gold ring.
The thirteen items on the list conclude with a practical present, received on 13 August 1771: A cane with a beautiful golden head.[4]

Cuno was amazed at the pace at which the old man worked. This speed may be partly explained by the fact the book is essentially a marshalling of pre-formulated thoughts. According to John Faulkner Potts's *Swedenborg Concordance*, no work of Swedenborg's contains so much reworked material as *The True Christian Religion*. Such borrowing from earlier works is natural; the book is a summary of twenty-five years of teachings.

The book begins with his understanding of God as the Creator, the Son of Man, and the Holy Spirit, and continues with the subjects of the atonement and the significance of works, free will, regeneration, baptism, and the Holy Supper. All this leads up to his final topic: the Lord's coming through the Word and the resulting new heaven and new church. The fourteen chapters can be summarized in four main points: the concept of the unity of God, clarity in the question of good and evil, the doctrine of the new man, and the preparation for a new spiritual church, the 'New Jerusalem'. Most of this has been touched on in the previous chapters. Here I limit myself to Swedenborg's own conclusions.

The Apocalypse and Swedenborg's mission

The Book of Revelation and the Gospel of Matthew had spoken of Christ's second coming to earth. As Swedenborg understood these books, it was never a question of the Saviour's physical return. The new coming would be in and through the Word. The Christians of his day had held to the literal meaning of the Bible and the official formularies of faith. It was Christianity in name only: its innermost meaning remained hidden. Such Christians had not turned to the Saviour himself and worshipped him as mankind's only God. Christ had been conceived of as a mediating being, below and outside the Great Divinity.

'Behold, I make all things new!' declares the Book of Revelation. This renewal was effected through Emanuel Swedenborg, who upon divine command explained the holy biblical texts in *The True Christian Religion* and all the works he had published since his call. Thus Swedenborg emerged as 'servant of the Lord Jesus Christ'. Here is his explanation of his divine mission, certainly difficult for Bishop Lamberg and his fellow priest the cathedral Dean to accept:

Since the Lord cannot show Himself in person [in the clouds of heaven . . .] and yet He predicted that He would come and found a new church, which is the New Jerusalem, it follows that He will do this by means of a man, who can not only receive intellectually the doctrines of this church, but also publish them in print. I bear true witness that the Lord has shown Himself in the presence of me, His servant, and sent me to perform this function. After this He opened the sight of my spirit, thus admitting me to the spiritual world, and allowing me to see the heavens and the hells, and also to talk with angels and spirits; and this I have now been doing for many years without a break. Equally I assert that from the first day of my calling I have not received any instruction concerning the doctrines of that church from any angel, but only from the Lord, while I was reading the Word.[5]

Before the reader had come this far, he had learned that Christianity 'is now for the first time arising [...] God the Father, the Son and the Holy Spirit are acknowledged as one [...] in one person'.[6]

The law in our hearts and ecumenical thoughts

The dogmatic position of the Swedish priesthood regarding the 'true evangelical doctrine' contrasted with the ecumenical streams that were flowing powerfully on the continent from philosophers and radical pietists. Samuel von Pufendorf, Hugo Grotius, the great Leibniz, and many others worked for Christian unity. Gottfried Arnold and his disciple Johan Conrad Dippel went further than the philosophers. They saw no need, generally speaking, for official confessions of faith. Man had the Word of God within himself, Dippel wrote. He could support his view with Paul's statement that even 'the pagans have the law in their hearts'.

In a concluding chapter on the 'end of the age', Swedenborg argued passionately against the claim of all churches and sects to represent the one, definitive truth, maintaining that all others were in darkness. His position had appeared already in earlier writings, but never so clearly as here. Man can always find arguments for false thoughts and doctrine: we 'resemble owls which can see light in the shades of night, and in the daytime find the sun and its rays thick darkness'.[7] What fool 'does not believe his folly is wisdom, and wisdom folly?'

Natural light by itself will not allow it to be recognized that a church has reached its end, that is to say, has nothing but false doctrines, at least until truth sheds its light from heaven [...] Everyone is so made that he can see and grasp truth on hearing it. But if he has convinced himself of false doctrines, he cannot bring truth into his understanding so as to lodge there, since it finds no room; and if by chance it does get in, the crowd of falsities gathered together there throws it out as not belonging.[8]

He did not consider his own writings, his own interpretation of the Bible, as a *doctrine*, using the term with the meaning of official statements like the Augsburg Confession. The true Christian religion in its absolute simplicity was natural and incontestable.

Swedenborg's secret: eternity is now

Swedenborg perceived a new community, a new Jerusalem, to be built in heaven and on earth. The tie binding it together is the unity given to its members by God through the inflow of his spirit. This is the real understanding, the real content, of the Christian message. Everything is the work of the Spirit, foretold by the prophets and hidden in the words of the Gospels and the Apocalypse.

The new, heavenly Jerusalem would descend from heaven to earth. The 'city of God' was a utopia that would be realized only slowly and gradually. But *the individual man and woman* could already live in this community now on the personal plane. Like the angels, everybody ought to become a 'heaven in miniature'.[9]

The thought of the presence of eternity here and now is expressed clearly in the Gospels and by Paul. It had also been the heart of what Bishop Swedberg called the 'mystical union'. In his *Description of My Life* he had reminded his children about a sermon that he had preached in 1714 at a meeting of priests in his diocese. There he reminded the assembled clergy of Paul's Letter to the Colossians:

This mystery is made known to me by revelation [...] It is given to me to preach the riches of the mystery which has been hidden from the beginning of the world and time eternal, which is Christ in you: whom we preach [...] that we may present every man [as] perfected in Christ Jesus.[10]

'Everything with Christ! Die with Christ, be buried with Christ, be resurrected with Christ, and be made living with Christ', the bishop preached. Emanuel Swedenborg would have been able to take the words as a summary of his own message.

What would Jesper Swedberg have thought of Emanuel's conception of his high calling? There are a few lines in the *Dream Diary* where at an early stage, 1744, the bishop appears in a dream to urge his son to go forward with care:

> It seemed as if I were racing down a stairway. I touched each step only a little and came safely down all the way without danger. There came a voice from my dear father, 'You are making such an alarm, Emanuel!' He was said to be angry but would calm down. This means that I made use of the cross too boldly yesterday, but, by the grace of God, I passed through this out of danger. [11]

The voice of the fatherly scolding echoes down through the centuries. The word 'alarm' means 'frighten', we read in Jesper Swedberg's *Schibboleth. Swenska språkets rycht och richtoghet* (*Shibboleth. The Proper Use of the Swedish Language*). [12]

Above all the bishop would probably have been negative towards Emanuel's lack of interest in the new church's order and organization. For Jesper Swedberg the church was in no way merely the 'congregation of the saints', it was also a state within a state, a political entity having a strong worldly involvement in the four-Estate Diet. About this, Swedenborg is quiet. Just as with Arnold and Dippel, for him the heavenly city on earth occasionally becomes visible through the witness given by the lives of its members: they are good trees, 'known by their fruits'. The new Jerusalem, the true church, does not form a sect. When Swedenborg's mission was accomplished, the question of the exact time for the coming of the Heavenly City becomes meaningless. It is here already, as long as one single person understands his message and lives according to it.

The disciples' commission

Swedenborg finished *The True Christian Religion* on the nineteenth of June 1770. The occasion was observed in heaven, he wrote. There the Lord called together his twelve disciples. They had followed Christ on earth, and now he sent them out through the whole spiritual world, where they were to preach the gospel that the Lord God Jesus Christ reigns.[13] In accord with the Book of Daniel and the Apocalypse, they were also to preach that his kingdom would be forever and ever. This was the meaning of the words in the Gospel of Matthew regarding the angels being sent forth: 'And He will send His angels with a great sound of a trumpet, and they will gather together His elect from the four winds, from one end of heaven to the other'.[14]

Death is my reward

Chapter Thirty-Four

Faithful God, in this need
Let me not be abandoned;
Come to my aid
Be my support
That my anxiety be driven away;
I am of your body beauteous
A lovely limb and sapling green;
In peace let me leave this world.

Jesper Swedberg's hymn book [1]

Sickness and death

On 29 March 1772, Emanuel Swedenborg died in London. He was then eighty-four years old. Since the summer of 1771 he had rented rooms with the wig-maker and barber Richard Shearsmith and his wife. They were simple pious people, living in Clerkenwell, at 26 Great Bath Street, north of the Thames. It was the second time he had taken lodgings there. Shearsmith appreciated his good fortune; when Swedenborg was his tenant everything went well for him.

Some years later two British followers of the Swedenborgian teaching asked the Shearsmiths to make a legally-attested statement of what they knew about Swedenborg's last days. [2] The couple reported that just before Christmas 1771 he had suffered a stroke. He lost the ability to speak and was in a lethargic state for several weeks. He ate nothing, taking only tea and water, sometimes a few teaspoons of red currant jelly. About three weeks after the stroke he regained his ability to speak. His health improved to some degree. As usual he now ate toast and drank tea and coffee. A few friends visited him sporadically; seemingly, he did not want to receive strangers. Approximately a month before he died, he told Elizabeth Reynolds, then a servant of the Shearsmiths, that he was going to die on a certain day. As far as she could remember he expired on just the day he had foretold.

421

His memory and understanding functioned normally. At about five in the morning on Sunday the twenty-ninth of March he asked Elizabeth Reynolds and Mrs Shearsmith, who perhaps were both sitting by his bed, what the time of day was. After they answered that it was about five o'clock, he said, "Dat be good, me tank you, God bless you", or something like that. And ten minutes later he sighed gently and gave up the spirit in great stillness.

Pastor Ferelius and Swedenborg

During Swedenborg's sickness Arvid Ferelius, pastor of the Swedish London congregation, paid several visits to his lodgings. He had worked in the city since 1761 and had often met the famous Assessor.

Ferelius was often requested to give an account of what he knew about Swedenborg's last days. According to the preserved notes, the pastor once visited the sick man for the purpose of giving him the Lord's Supper. When entering Shearsmith's house he heard a noise from the room where Swedenborg was lying. The woman who attended the sick man reported that this sound had gone on during the last few days. From within the sick room Swedenborg, happy and delighted, greeted him. "Welcome, good gentleman! God has now freed me from the evil spirits that have been attacking me during these last days. Now good spirits have returned." Ferelius replied, "Herr Assessor, I have heard that you were ill, and as pastor of the Swedish church I have regarded it my duty to visit you". Whenever the priest visited, he asked Swedenborg if he thought he was now going to die. This time, Swedenborg answered affirmatively.[3]

On an earlier occasion the priest took up the question of his writings and their value:

Many people think that the only purpose behind your new theological system has been to make a name for yourself and become famous. You have achieved this purpose in the highest degree. If this has been the case, it is now your duty to the world to deny what you have written, entirely or partially, especially since this world can give you no further advantage. You shall certainly soon leave it.

At this Swedenborg arose halfway from his bed, and laying his healthy hand on his breast, responded to the exhortation with a 'certain zeal':

As true as you see me before your eyes, so true is everything that I have written; and I could have said more, had it been permitted. When you enter eternity, you will see everything, and then you and I shall have much to talk about.[4]

Ferelius asked him if he was prepared to take the Lord's Supper. Swedenborg answered, "That is a good suggestion, although actually I do not need this sacrament since I am already a member of the higher world. But I will now take communion to show the close association that exists between the invisible church and the visible. Have you read my thoughts on the sacrament of the altar?" Ferelius answered by asking if he confessed that he was a sinner. Swedenborg: "Certainly, as long as I bear this sinful body".

Ferelius continued: 'With much devotion he uncovered his head, folded his hands, and read the confession of sins and received the holy sacrament. Afterwards he presented me with a copy of his large work, the *Arcana Caelestia*, of which only nine copies remained unsold, which were to be sent to Holland'.

In March and April 1772, Ferelius's period of service in London was concluded, and he travelled home to become vicar in Skövde, a town in the Skara diocese. Ferelius's final official duty in London was to conduct Swedenborg's funeral. As thanks he was given Swedenborg's Hebrew Bible, in two quarto volumes, underlined everywhere. According to the priest, that had been Swedenborg's only reading matter during his last stay in London.

Ferelius's thoughts about Swedenborg

Ferelius, in contrast to his successor in the Swedish church in London, Aaron Mathesius, was friendly towards Swedenborg and had a certain familiarity with his writings. Swedenborg had sometimes attended the morning service in the Swedish church, and afterwards usually dined with the pastor or some other Swede. He had told one of his countrymen that spirits disturbed him during these services, protesting against the priest, especially when he spoke of the Trinity as three separate gods.

Did the pastor believe the assurance Swedenborg gave him before the Lord's Supper? The dying man had sworn that everything he had written was true. He had explained the true meaning of the Bible and opened the way for the coming of the New Jerusalem, and through this for a communion between believers on earth and the celestial congregation of the saints. For years he had spoken daily with spirits, demons, and angels.

What would one believe of a man who, when the pastor called, said that he had been visited, well before being taken ill, by the apostle Peter: who sat (Ferelius was told) right in front of Swedenborg at his desk.[5] The pastor was also assured by Christopher Springer that his friend Swedenborg had reported an other-world conversation with the chamberlain Ulrik Fredrik von Höpken, touching upon the political views held by Springer and von Höpken during their years together in Uppsala.

The many questions about Swedenborg's spiritual health and good faith could seem contradictory, not least because the old man throughout his life had been politically active in the House of Nobles, writing numerous memoranda on topics concerning the economy and constitutional law, generally regarded as sensible and important. He had been an excellent mining engineer, one of the best in the land, and besides this during the 1730s a noted Christian philosopher. And obviously he was also most capable regarding his private economy; otherwise he could scarcely have financed the large publication of books during the past two decades.

Perhaps the pastor felt approximately the same as Swedenborg's highly placed friend Anders Johan von Höpken. According to him everything in Swedenborg's works was sensible and clear, with one exception: von Höpken could never accept his *memorabilia*, his 'memorable experiences', his accounts of meetings and discussions in the spirit world, his conversations with Luther and Calvin, Leibniz and Wolff, Descartes and Newton. The Prime Minister had told him that these heavenly debates should be omitted from his books. But Swedenborg insisted that they were important, being exact accounts of his experiences.

And what should one think of the extraordinary tales of his occult powers? Ferelius was certainly acquainted with the story of Mme de Marteville's lost receipt, Swedenborg's awareness in Gothenburg of the fire in Stockholm, and other accounts of a similar nature.

Swedenborg's lifestyle, his meagre diet, his unusual concentration on what he believed to be his divine task, gave him a unique position. He was a very likeable person, in the pastor's estimation. In a letter in 1780 Ferelius gave a picture of Swedenborg as he saw him in London during his last ten years:

Someone might think that Assessor Swedenborg was eccentric and whimsical; but the very reverse was the case. He was very easy and pleasant in company, talked on every subject that came up, accommodating himself to the ideas of the company; and he never spoke on his own views, unless he was asked about them. But if he noticed that anyone asked him impertinent questions, intended to make sport of him, he immediately gave such an answer that the questioner was obliged to keep silence [...][6]

The pastor must have been struck by the fact that the sick man seemed to meet death without any anxiety whatsoever. Everyone who has a relationship with the Lord during his earthly life has a foretaste of the eternal life, Swedenborg said in 1769 to his friend Cuno, then he does not attach so much importance to this quickly disappearing worldly existence. Cuno noted that Swedenborg once had said that he would invite musicians if the Lord told him that he was about to die the following day. Then for one last time in this world, he would feel truly happy.[7]

The day of death foreseen

Did Swedenborg foresee the day of his death? The matter has been discussed back and forth. Besides the statement by the servant girl Elizabeth Reynolds, Samuel Smith touched on the question in reference to an exchange of letters, no longer extant, between Swedenborg and the Methodist leader John Wesley.[8] In February 1772 Swedenborg was said to have written a note to Wesley proposing a meeting, as in the spiritual world he had learned that Wesley wanted to speak with him. Wesley answered that he had in truth hoped for a meeting with Swedenborg, but that he was just about to make a long trip far from London. Could they meet later?

It would not be possible, Swedenborg is said to have answered: he would be leaving this earth on 29 March.

Whether or not the date is correct is of no particular significance. Swedenborg, eighty-four years old and half-paralysed, must have realized that his life was moving quickly towards its close. For him this was no great catastrophe, but just the opposite: death was for him a reward, a continued life in the body of Christ.

The burial was arranged by the Swedish businessman Carl Lindgren. A bill of currency exchange for £400 was found in Swedenborg's wallet. Ferelius officiated at the funeral, which took place on 5 April. Swedenborg was buried in a vault in the Swedish chapel in Prince's Square, the body having been placed in a sealed lead coffin.

Ferelius returned to Sweden and Skövde. He was regarded as influenced by Swedenborg's teaching. His three daughters married men who are known to have been active members of the New Church. Ferelius was not the only follower of Swedenborg's teachings in this part of Sweden. The Skara diocese was to become, together with Stockholm, the most receptive to the New Church's message in Swedenborg's native country.

Chapter Thirty-Five

Swedenborg in Sweden: the first hundred years after his death

Swedenborg's contributions to science and natural philosophy soon became obscured by his theosophy. His Christian message was not formally prohibited, neither in Scandinavia nor on the Continent and in Great Britain, although in Sweden his teaching was looked upon as suspect in official quarters. Dr Gabriel Beyer, a high school lecturer, had been forbidden to give instruction in Christianity, but was never brought to a secular court; nevertheless the local ecclesiastical authorities considered him 'heretical'. No freedom of the press existed for publications of a religious character; it was introduced only in 1809 and 1812. Consequently when Beyer was to print his dictionary of the 'correspondences' that Swedenborg had used in his interpretation of the Bible, this had to be done in Amsterdam.

In spite of official opposition to Swedenborg's doctrines by the Swedish church, the so-called 'Swedenborgianism' spread quickly.[1] Anders Johan von Höpken, the former Prime Minister, observed that an increasing number of laymen and priests were influenced by the teachings about the New Church.

Swedenborg's influence was particularly strong in the diocese of Skara, where the well-known Dean of the Cathedral, Anders Olofsson Knös, while not openly taking a position in favour of Swedenborg's teachings, became the first and most important spokesman for the spirit of the New Church.

Knös and his successors laid emphasis on man's regeneration and his duty and ability to shape his life with Christ as the perfect example. Following Swedenborg's teaching, but usually without mentioning his name, a simple and rational, evangelical Christianity was emphasized: a spiritual and Swedenborgian renewal within the framework of the official Swedish Church. It was only much later, in 1866, that an independent Swedish Swedenborgian congregation was founded, having its own priests from 1874.

Before then, fourteen years after his death, the first Swedish association of laymen dedicated to Emanuel Swedenborg was formed with the brothers August and Carl Fredrik Nordenskjöld as the main promoters. It was called the *Exegetiska och Philantropisken sällskapet* (*Exegetic and Philanthropic Society*), under the presidency of Governor Sven Liljenkrantz; and Anders Johan von Höpken, who however never attended the meetings, was its most prominent member. The purpose was to discuss, spread, and translate Swedenborg's works. Printing could be done only in excerpts, as articles, which were then published in the Society's magazine, *Samlingar för Philantroper* (*Transactions for Philanthropists*).

Already, in the early stages, a particular aspect of Swedenborg's message came into the foreground. In his accounts of what he had 'heard and seen', he had described his crossings

Fig. 42. The first theological work of Swedenborg that was published in Sweden was his 'catechism', *The New Jerusalem and its Heavenly Doctrine*. It was issued in 1787 in *Transactions for Philanthropists*. The book is said to have escaped censure thanks to the influence of Prince Charles, the king's brother, who was interested in Swedenborg. The title page was illustrated by Johan Fredrik Martin. The picture represents the judgement on the old church and the birth of the new through a heavenly revelation.

of the boundary between the natural and the supernatural worlds. The significance of the world of spirits and angels was now, after his death, brought to the fore, often overshadowing the core of his teaching: his reading of the Bible and the message of the coming New Jerusalem. Swedenborg's doctrine was taken as a foundation for fanciful occultism and utopianism. In the first hundred years after his death, his world populated by good and evil spirits, the notion of correspondences between higher and lower things, and the significance he gave to man's dreams came to be interpreted in ways that would not have pleased their originator. Towards the end of the 1700s Swedenborg's doctrines were often taken as justification for spiritism, 'animal magnetism', exorcism, and esoteric secretiveness.

In Sweden, this occurred partially within the framework of the system of secret societies favoured by King Gustaf III and his brother Charles. It was these quaint, fantastic movements that the Swedish poet Johan Henrik Kellgren gathered together into a bundle of one and the same folly: 'gold-makers, Swedenborgians, mesmerisers, somnambulists, mediums, treasure-seekers, numerologists, makers of mystical panaceas'. Kellgren's connection of Swedenborg with his occult-minded admirers was certainly understandable; but in relation to Swedenborg's writings these obscure off-shoots represented a corruption.

Early Swedish Swedenborgianism would also take on a social and utopian aspect. The adventurous August Nordenskjöld allied himself with another well-known New Church figure, Carl Bernhard Wadström. In 1789 Nordenskjöld published, in London, a *Plan for a free society on the coast of Africa*, that was conceived of as an earthly materialization of the New Jerusalem described in the Book of Revelation as explained by Swedenborg. It was to lie on the west coast of that continent. As we have seen Swedenborg once had a vision, telling him that the people closest to the angels were the black Africans living in the interior of that region.[2]

British efforts to abolish the slave trade in 1787 led to the foundation of Freetown in the present-day Sierra Leone. Freed slaves would be sent there, an idea probably inspired by Wadström. August Nordenskjöld travelled to this part of Africa, making, in 1792, a journey into the interior. But instead of angels he found aggressive blacks, perhaps mistakenly taking him for a slave trader. Mistreated, he succeeded in returning down towards the coast, but died on his raft upon his arrival.

Fig. 43. Carl Bernhard Wadström reading
Swedenborg's *The Divine Providence* with his ward
Peter Panah. Painting by C F von Breda, London,
1792, in the Nordic Museum, Stockholm

The visionary, imaginary, and utopian line taken by Swedenborg's followers could also lead to concrete social results. The thought of a just society, characterized by Swedenborg's doctrine of man's obligation to love his neighbour, presumably lay behind Wadström's well-known fight against slavery. His battle is regarded as having contributed to the British decision in 1807 to put an end to slavery in the British Empire.

The rational Englishmen

Sweden was a sinful and unrighteous land, Swedenborg wrote in *The Spiritual Diary*: as a nation, after Italy and Russia, Sweden and the Swedes were the worst in Europe.[3] But he had high regard for England and its inhabitants; we read that Englishmen when hearing truths have the capacity of seeing them before their eyes, and adapt their behaviour accordingly.[4]

Swedenborg's teachings found their most active and influential adherents in England. During Swedenborg's last years of life there were a few people in London who regarded his writings as the basis for a complete renewal of religion. After 1772 the Anglican priest

Thomas Hartley together with Swedenborg's physician, Husband Messiter, formed a core from which an organized New Church would develop.

In 1773 a young Manchester priest, John Clowes, happened to read *The True Christian Religion*, which affected his view of life. He soon became the main translator of Swedenborg's works into English.

Robert Hindmarsh, who became a well-known printer, began to study Swedenborg's works in 1783. During the 1780s and 1790s a great number of Swedenborg's writings in English and Latin were to be published in his print shop in London. Hindmarsh formed a study group in 1783 that in the following year developed into a 'Theosophical Society' for the furtherance of Swedenborg's teachings, as well as for the spread of his writings. The Society brought together a group of priests, officials, physicians, artists (among them the later well-known sculptor and artist John Flaxman), musicians, and lawyers.

More directly than in Sweden, the early receivers of Swedenborg's teachings in England were attracted to the renewal of Christian doctrine that his works implied. Followers drawn from both the Church of England and other Christian bodies found that his exposition of the nature of the Trinity, man's regeneration, and justification was in harmony with their understanding of the Bible. His communication with the spiritual world does not seem to have been emphasized in England to the same degree as it was in so many quarters in Sweden.

At the same time as a number of people attracted to the new teachings hoped and worked for the renewal of the existing bodies of the Christian Church, the first independent Swedenborgian Church was founded in London in 1787. This took place in spite of John Clowes's strong protests and assertions that in time the Church of England would become favourably disposed towards the influences of Swedenborg's doctrines, and that sooner or later the Anglican bishops would themselves revise their liturgical forms and doctrinal articles accordingly.

The new chapel lay off Great Eastcheap, between the Tower of London and St Paul's Cathedral. Above the entrance stood the inscription that later would be found in a number of the Swedenborgian churches around the world: 'Now it is permitted'—words which Swedenborg had seen over the door of a temple in heaven.[5] In the year 1789 the first 'General Conference of the Church of the New Jerusalem' was held; in the list of participants we find the water-colourist, engraver, and poet William Blake, and his wife Catherine. Blake's works would be characterized by Swedenborgian thought, sometimes accepting, sometimes rejecting them.

From England the Swedenborgian doctrines came to the USA. Compared with Europe there was little attachment to tradition here, and no suspicious state church. Boston and above all Philadelphia became centres of the New Church. In 1817 the first 'General Convention of the New Church' was held, a meeting of the New Church Christians in the country. Swedenborg's followers would gradually branch and split due to differing interpretations of doctrinal matters. A common characteristic of the American churches has been emphasis on instruction in schools, where the children would be given religious knowledge at an early stage, becoming formative for their adult life. In the USA the New Church never became a mass movement any more than in Sweden and England. Although schools, academies, and large libraries were erected with the help of believing businessmen, the number of church members has always been relatively few, and membership has often continued from generation to generation.

There is not room here for a description of this reception of Swedenborg's message during the 1800s. The always small numbers of followers may perhaps be explained partially by the radical requirement of a new birth and new life that are fundamental in Swedenborg's message. Perhaps the usual institutionalized forms of Christianity have been seen as less demanding, for both priests and congregations?

When will the New Jerusalem come?

'I am often asked about the New Church and when it will come', Swedenborg wrote to Gabriel Beyer three years before his death, stating that he usually replied that the New Church would become a reality gradually, as the doctrine of justification by faith and Christ's vicarious suffering was rooted out of the minds of those on earth.[6] The *Brief Exposition* would certainly be significant in this context, the author believed. Beyer should keep in mind that the Christian church was not established immediately after Christ's resurrection, it grew step by step. The same would be the case with the New Church. He should also remember the twelfth chapter of the Book of Revelation and the episode of the woman who gave birth to a son. She was clothed with the sun, the moon was under

Fig. 44. 'In the end the heavenly Jerusalem shall descend to earth.' From Albrecht Dürer's *The Revelation of St John*, 1498

her feet, on her head was a crown of twelve stars, and she was persecuted by the seven-headed red dragon. In the fourteenth verse Beyer found an answer to his question:

> The woman was given two wings of a great eagle, that she might fly into the wilderness to her place, where she is nourished for a time and times and half a time, from the presence of the serpent.

For Swedenborg the woman represented the whole company of those who form the New Church, and her son was the true doctrine. The woman/assembly was given the ability to withstand the attacks of the dragon; though small, it would increase in significance and strength, and would finally appear in purity and power.

According to Swedenborg, John describes the constant, implacable attacks of the Protestants and Catholics against the true doctrine, and the New Church's increasing strength through continual repulses of these confrontations. In the fourteenth chapter Christ manifests Himself:

> And I looked, and behold, a white cloud, and on the cloud sat One like the Son of Man, having on His head a golden crown, and in His hand a sharp sickle.

The sickle goes through the old church, corrupted by false doctrines, and at last the heavenly Jerusalem shall descend to earth; but an exact answer to the question of the time of its coming can never be given. In heaven, time and space are appearances that portray the angels' states of mind. The angelic host grows in number and power, in pace with the state of progress on earth. And the *status mundi*, the condition of the world, is slowly improving: for a time and times and half a time.

Endnotes / Chronology

Swedenborg's Library

Bibliography / Index

Endnotes

Texts referenced in the notes have been given short titles. Full titles and details of publication are given in the bibliography.

Many quotations within the text have been modified by the translator for the sake of greater consistency of style. The notes below refer to their published source.

Introduction
1 ELLIOTT, J, (ed.), *Small Theological Works and Letters*, p. 247.
2 For further details about Swedenborg's breakdown, see BERGQUIST, *Swedenborg's Dream Diary*, pp. 52-9, 251-3.
3 PROUST, *In Search of Lost Time*, vol. I, *Swann's Way*, p. 52.
4 SWEDENBORG, *The True Christian Religion*, §508.
5 SANDSTRÖM, *En ny Kristen Kyrka*, p. 20.
6 LAMM, *Swedenborg* (Stockholm, 1915).
7 *Tessin och Tessiniana*, pp. 357, 368.
8 KLEEN, *Swedenborg*, pt 1, p. xiii.
9 SCRIVER, *Siäle-Skatt*, vol. I, p. 125.
10 LAMM, *Swedenborg* (Paris, 1936), p. xxii.

Chapter 1
1 SWEDBERG, J, *Lefwernes Beskrifning*, §51.
2 ibid., §109.
3 SWEDBERG, J, *Gudelige Döds Tankar*, in the dedication to Charles XII, §19.

4   WAHLSTRÖM, B, *Studier över Tillkomsten av 1695 års Psalmbok*, p. 226; and WAHLSTRÖM, B, 'Herde och Hosbonde', in *Karolinska Förbundets Årsbok*, p. 38 ff.
5   RHYZELIUS, 'Biskop A. O. Rhyzeli Antenckningar om sitt Lefverne', p. 81.
6   cf. SWEDENBORG, *A Brief Exposition of the Doctrine of the New Church*, §§13-15.
7   SWEDBERG, J, *Ungdoms Regel och Ålderdoms Spegel*, p. 523.
8   See Bibliography, section C: *Jesperi Swedbergii, Doct. et Episcopi Scarensis, parentis optimi, canticum svecicum...*
9   Ecclesiastes 12:1,6.
10 SWEDBERG, J, *Lefwernes Beskrifning*, §101 ff., 180, 362-3.
11 ibid., §398.
12 SWEDBERG, J, *Festum Magnum*, §§86, 91.
13 SCRIVER, *Siäle-Skatt*, vol. I, p. 112; WAHLSTRÖM, B, 'Karl XII:s Änglar', in *Karolinska Förbundets Årsbok*, p. 105 ff.
14 SWEDBERG, J, *Lefwernes Beskrifning*, §§783-800.
15 SWEDBERG, J, *Ungdoms Regel och Ålderdoms Spegel*, p. 318.
16 SWEDBERG, J, *Lefwernes Beskrifning*, §362.
17 ibid., §362.
18 ibid., §§594, 596.
19 ibid., §607.
20 ibid., §§257-8.
21 ibid., §§72-3.
22 SWEDBERG, J, *Sanctificatio Sabbati*, p. 494 ff.
23 HELANDER, J, *Haquin Spegel, hans Lif och Gärning intill år 1693*, p. 181.
24 SWEDENBORG, *The Spiritual Diary*, §2821; cf. SWEDENBORG, *Arcana Caelestia*, §647.

Chapter 2

1   The Gregorian system was introduced into Britain in 1752.
2   LINDH, 'The Entry of Swedenborg's Birth', in *New Church Life*, 1915, pp. 70-2.
3   SWEDBERG, J, *Lefwernes Beskrifning*, §375.
4   ibid., §377.
5   ELLIOTT, J, (ed.), *Small Theological Works and Letters*, p. 241.
6   SWEDENBORG, *The Spiritual Diary*, §3464.
7   SWEDENBORG, *Arcana Caelestia*, §5135.
8   SWEDBERG, J, *Lefwernes Beskrifning*, §255.
9   ibid., §365.
10 SWEDBERG, J, *Ungdoms Regel och Ålderdoms Spegel*, p. 429 ff.
11 BRECKLING, *Then sidste basun öfwer Tyskland til at upwieckia werlden ifrå syndennes sömn*, translated from German into Swedish by Jesper Swedenborg, with an autobiographical preface by the translator.
12 LINDROTH, *Uppsala Universitet 1477-1977*, p. 69.
13 SWEDBERG, J, *Dextra sors docensi et dicendi seu Ludus Literarius*, §5.
14 SWEDBERG, J, *Ungdoms Regel och Ålderdoms Spegel*, pp. 441-2.
15 PRICE, 'The Curricula in Swedenborg's Student Years, 1700-1708', in *The New Philosophy* (1932-5).

16 FRÄNGSMYR, *Wolffianismens Genombrott i Uppsala*, pp. 46-7.

17 ERIKSON, A, (ed.), *Letters to Erik Benzelius the Younger from Learned Foreigners*, vols. I-II; and ERIKSON, A, and NYLANDER, E N, (eds.), *Letters from Erik Benzelius to his Learned Friends*.

18 SWEDBERG, J, *Dextra sors docensi et dicendi seu Ludus Literarius*, §8.

19 SWEDENBORG, *Selected Sentences*, in *The New Philosophy* (Jan-Mar 1967), p. 332.

20 STROH, A H, (ed.), *Opera Quaedam*, vol. I, p. 201-2.

21 ibid., p. 203-4.

Chapter 3

1   TAFEL, R L, (tr., ed. and comp.), *Documents concerning the Life and Character of Emanuel Swedenborg*, vol. II:1, pp. 3-4.

2   ACTON, (tr. and ed.), *The Letters and Memorials of Emanuel Swedenborg*, vol. II, pp. 768-70.

3   STROH, A H, (ed.), *Opera Quaedam*, vol. I, p. 207.

4   Castellio [1515-1563] was a Frenchman, with the French name Sébastien Châteillon.

5   cf. SWEDENBORG, *Arcana Caelestia*, §§1799, 1834.

6   STROH, A H, (ed.), *Opera Quaedam*, vol. I, p. 210.

7   ibid., p. 207.

8   ibid., p. 210.

9   ibid., p. 219.

10 ibid., p. 207.

11 ibid., p. 214; and ACTON, (tr. and ed.), *Letters and Memorials*, vol. I, p. 30.

12 LINDROTH, *Kungl. Svenska Vetenskapsakademiens Historia 1739-1818*, pp. 444-5; and NORDENMARK, *Swedenborg som Astronom*, p. 243 ff.

13 SWEDBERG, J, *Lefwernes Beskrifning*, §884 ff.

14 ibid., §593.

15 HELANDER, H, (tr. and ed.) *Emanuel Swedenborg, Ludus Heliconius and other Latin Poems*, p. 192 ff.

16 ibid., p. 193.

17 SWEDENBORG, *Arcana Caelestia*, §9140.

18 BENZ, *Emanuel Swedenborg: Visionary Savant in the Age of Reason*, p. 31 ff.

19 cf. ACTON, (tr. and ed.), *Letters and Memorials*, vol. I, p. 40.

20 cf. ibid., p. 51.

21 SWEDBERG, J, *Lefwernes Beskrifning*, §134.

22 HELANDER, H, (tr. and ed.), *Emanuel Swedenborg, Camena Borea*.

Chapter 4

1   RUNIUS, J, 'Tilflycht i Nöden,...'

2   Minutes of the Secret Committee, no. 36; GRAUERS, 'Några Bidrag till Oppositionens Historia under Karl XII', in *Karolinska Förbundets Årsbok*, pp. 196-230.

3   STROH, A H, (ed.), *Opera Quaedam*, vol. I, p. 227.

4   HELANDER, H, (tr. and ed.), *Emanuel Swedenborg, Camena Borea*.

5   cf. ibid., p. 10.

6   cf. Chapter 27 herein: 'Politics: the art of the possible'.

7   HELANDER, H, (tr. and ed.) *Emanuel Swedenborg, Festivus Applausus in Caroli XII in Pomeraniam suam adventum*.

8   ACTON, (tr. and ed.), *Letters and Memorials*, vol. I, p. 64.

9   SWEDBERG, J, *Lefwernes Beskrifning*, §620.

10 Isaiah 58:12.

Chapter 5

1   STROH, A H, (ed.), *Opera Quaedam*, vol. I, p. 252.

2   ibid., p 230-1; and ACTON, (tr. and ed.), *Letters and Memorials*, vol. I, p. 65.

3   STROH, A H, (ed.), *Opera Quaedam*, vol. I, p. 233-5.

4   ibid., p. 235.

5   SWEDENBORG, *The Spiritual Diary*, §§4691, 4693.

6   ERIXON, S, *Sveden*, p. 58.

7   SWEDENBORG, *The Spiritual Diary* §§4835, 5133.

8   ACTON, (tr. and ed.), *Letters and Memorials*, vol. I, p. 122.

9   cf. ibid., vol. I, pp. 125-6.

10 ibid., vol. I, pp. 127-8, 135.

11 STROH, A H, (ed.), *Opera Quaedam*, vol. I, p. 329; cf. ACTON, (tr. and ed.), *Letters and Memorials*, vol. I, p. 459.

12 STROH, A H, (ed.), *Opera Quaedam*, vol. I, p. 286.

13 ibid., vol. I, p. 279; cf. ACTON, (tr. and ed.), *Letters and Memorials*, vol. I, pp. 174-5.

14 BERGGRÉN, P G, 'Karl XII's Galärtransport från Strömstad till Idefjorden och striderna därstädes år 1718', in *Karolinska Förbundets Årsbok*, p. 169.

15 STROH, A H, (ed.), *Opera Quaedam*, vol. I, p. 288.

16 SWEDENBORG, *The Spiritual Diary*, §4704.

Chapter 6

1   POLHEM, C, *Christopher Polhems Brev*, p. 163.

2   POLHEM, C, *Christopher Polhems Efterlämnade Skrifter*, pt III, p. 65.

3   ibid., pt III, p. 3.

4   ibid., pt III, p. 312.

5   POLHEM, C, *Christopher Polhems Brev*, p. 95.

6   DESCARTES, *Discourse on Method*, Discourse 5, p. 72.

7   POLHEM, C, *Christopher Polhems Efterlämnade Skrifter*, pt III, p. 314.

8   POLHEM, C, *Christopher Polhems Brev*, p. 164.

9   SWEDENBORG, 'Bewis at wårt lefwande wesende består merendels i små darringar thet är tremulationer', in *Daedalus Hyperboreus*, no. 6, pp. 13-14; cf. *On Tremulation*, tr. C T Odhner, p. 6.

Chapter 7

1   STROH, A H, (ed.), *Opera Quaedam*, vol. I, p. 289.

2   TAFEL, R L, (tr., ed. and comp.), *Documents...*, vol. II:1, p. 437.

3   POLHEM, C, *Christopher Polhems Brev*, p. 130.

4 ACTON, (tr. and ed.), *Letters and Memorials*, vol. I, p. 193.

5 SWEDBERG, J, *Lefwernes Beskrifning*, §948 ff.

6 The Diet was composed of the four 'Estates' or Houses of Nobles, Clergy, Burghers, and Peasants. The constitution adopted in 1719 provided that while the Diet was not sitting the king should rule jointly with a council which had been elected by the Diet.

    Elections to the Diet were held each third year. The House of Clergy was composed of the archbishop and the bishops, with vicars and assistant vicars in each diocese electing their representatives. The burghers in each town elected their representatives to the House of Burghers, the size of each town governing the number elected. In each parish the property-owners elected one of their number to sit in the House of Peasants.

    When the Diet was in session it elected a 'Secret Committee', consisting of 50 noblemen, 25 clergy, and 25 burghers. This committee controlled finances, legislation, and foreign policy, although the House of Peasants had to be consulted on matters of taxation. In 1742 the House of Peasants won a place on the Committee. To have legal power any measure had to pass three of the four Estates while the Diet was in session. The Secret Committee was abolished in 1772.

7 ACTON, (tr. and ed.), *Letters and Memorials*, vol. I, p. 237.

8 ibid., vol. I, p. 215.

9 ibid., vol. I, p. 224.

10 ibid., vol. I, pp. 333-4.

11 SWEDENBORG, *The Spiritual Diary*, §4722.

12 ibid., §6049.

Chapter 8

1 STROH, A H, (ed.), *Opera Quaedam*, vol. I, p. 292; cf. ACTON, (tr. and ed.), *Letters and Memorials*, vol. I, p. 215.

2 ACTON, (tr. and ed.), *Letters and Memorials*, vol. I, p. 255.

3 SWEDENBORG, *Some Specimens of a Work on the Principles of Chemistry, with other treatises*, pp. 1-2.

4 ACTON, (tr. and ed.), *Letters and Memorials*, vol. I, p. 260.

5 TAFEL, R L, (tr., ed. and comp.), *Documents...*, vol. II:1, p. 5.

6 STROH, A H, (ed.), *Opera Quaedam*, vol. I, p. 226.

7 LINDQVIST, S, *Technology on Trial*, p. 159 ff.

8 LINDERHOLM, *Sven Rosén och hans Insats i Frihetstidens Radikala Pietism*. Concerning the students Leopold and Stendahl, see ODENVIK, N, *Leopold och Stendahl*.

9 LINDH, 'Swedenborgs Ekonomi', in *Nya Kyrkans Tidning*. No modern valuation of the riksdaler can be calculated in view of the fluctuating state of the Swedish economy in Swedenborg's time.

Chapter 9

1 *Receuil des Instructions données aux Ambassadeurs de France, Suède*, p. 407.

2 PERRAULT, *Le Secret du Roi*, vol. I, p. 82 ff.

3 See note 6 to Chapter 7.

4 SWEDENBORG, *Projekt* (Codex 56, Royal Academy of Sciences); English tr. in, ACTON, (tr. and ed.), *Letters and Memorials*, vol. I, pp. 468-75.

5 ibid., p. 469.
6 ibid., pp. 469-70.
7 ibid., p. 470.
8 ibid., p. 472.

Chapter 10

1 SWEDENBORG, *The Principia*, vol. I, p. 53.
2 SWEDENBORG, *Swedenborg's Treatise on Copper*, vol. I, Preface, p. ix.
3 SWEDENBORG, *The Principia*, vol. II, p. 243.
4 ibid., vol. I, p. 50.
5 ibid., vol. I, p. 35.
6 *The Emerald Table* is traditionally ascribed to Hermes Trismegistos.
7 GYLLENSTEN, *Palatset i Parken*, p. 131.
8 SWEDENBORG, *The Infinite and Final Cause of Creation*, p. 230.

Chapter 11

1 All information concerning Bishop Swedberg's last moments, his death, and the funeral are taken from BENZELIUS, J, *Christelig Lik-predikan öfwer Doctor Jesper Swedberg*, and the adjoined account of his life, read at the funeral.
2 ACTON, (tr. and ed.), *Letters and Memorials*, vol. I, p. 476; ACTON, *The Green Books*, February 1736.
3 SWEDBERG, J, *Lefwernes Beskrifning*, §994 ff.
4 SWEDENBORG, *The Spiritual Diary*, §§6028, 6034, 6044.
5 ibid., §5896.
6 1 Corinthians 13:12.
7 ACTON, *The Green Books*, March 1736.
8 TAFEL, R L, (tr., ed. and comp.), *Documents...*, vol. II:1, p. 76.

Chapter 12

1 ACTON, A, (tr. and ed.), *A Philosopher's Note Book*, p. 164 ff.; cf. JONSSON, I, *Swedenborgs Korrespondenslära*, p. 24.
2 CAMPBELL MOSSNER, *Bishop Butler and the age of reason*, p. 35.
3 Cited in MALMESTRÖM, *Ur Linnés Tankevärld och Religiösa Liv*, pp. 47-8.
4 SWEDENBORG, *The Spiritual Diary*, §§4727, 4744.
5 ibid., §§4727-8.
6 ibid., §4851.
7 KLEEN, *Swedenborg*, pt I, p. 259.
8 NEWTON, *Principia* from French translation, Paris 1756, vol. I, p. 10.
9 SWEDENBORG, *The Principia*, vol. I, p. 32.
10 SWEDENBORG, *The Spiritual Diary*, §767.
11 STROH, A H, (ed.), *Opera Quaedam*, vol. I, p. 338; ACTON, (tr. and ed.), *Letters and Memorials*, vol. II, p. 528.

Chapter 13

1 BERGQUIST, *Swedenborg's Dream Diary*, §282, p. 316.
2 SWEDENBORG, *The Economy of the Animal Kingdom*, vol. I, §41.
3 ibid., vol. I, §270.
4 SWEDENBORG, *Arcana Caelestia*, §1001.3.
5 SWEDENBORG, *The Economy of the Animal Kingdom*, vol. I, §259.
6 SWEDENBORG, *The Cerebrum*, vol. II, facing Ruysch *Epist.*, Tab. VIII, fig. 3.
7 JONSSON, *Swedenborgs Korrespondenslära*.
8 SWEDENBORG, *Arcana Caelestia*, §2991.
9 The French passage reads:
> La Nature est un temple où de vivants piliers
> Laissent parfois sortir de confuses paroles;
> L'homme y passe à travers des forêts de symboles
> Qui l'observent avec des regards familiers.
10 SWEDENBORG, *The Economy of the Animal Kingdom*, vol. II, §363.
11 ibid., §366.
12 BERGQUIST, *Swedenborg's Dream Diary*, §11, p. 88.
13 TAFEL, R L, (tr., ed. and comp.), *Documents...*, vol. II:1, p. 85.

Chapter 14

1 *Constitutiones Nationis Dalekarlo-Vestmannicae...*, p. 14.
2 BERGQUIST, *Swedenborg's Dream Diary*, §67, p. 141.
3 ACTON, (tr. and ed.), *Letters and Memorials*, vol. I, pp. 497-8.
4 BERGQUIST, *Swedenborg's Dream Diary*, §7, p. 85.
5 TAFEL, R L, (tr., ed. and comp.), *Documents...*, vol. II:1, p. 7. The Journal entry was for 15 May 1733.
6 BERGQUIST, *Swedenborg's Dream Diary*, §10, p. 86.
7 cf. ACTON, (tr. and ed.), *Letters and Memorials*, vol. II, pp. 679, 682, where 1743 is given in letters to Thomas Hartley and Dr Messiter, both dated 5 August 1769.
8 EKELÖF, Gunnar, *Poems 1927-1962*, p. 341.
9 BERGQUIST, *Swedenborg's Dream Diary*, §11, p. 88.
10 ibid., §12, p. 89.
11 ibid., §213, pp. 247-8.
12 ibid., §40, p. 119; §44, p. 121.
13 ibid., §50, p. 124.
14 ibid., §49, p. 124.
15 ibid., §§51-4, pp. 125-6.
16 SWEDENBORG, *Conjugial Love*, §42.3. English versions have been variously entitled *Conjugial Love*, *Married Love*, and *Love in Marriage*.
17 BERGQUIST, *Swedenborg's Dream Diary*, §§209-10, p. 244.
18 *Ewangeliske Läro...*, pp. 174-5; cf. LIEDGREN, *Svensk Psalm och Andlig Visa*, p. 362 ff.
19 BERGQUIST, *Swedenborg's Dream Diary*, p. 53.
20 ibid., §254, p. 293.
21 ibid., §79, p. 148.

22 ibid., §88, p. 155.

23 SWEDENBORG, *The Word Explained*, §5150.

24 See STAGNELIUS, *Collected Writings*, p. 227.

25 SWEDENBORG, *The True Christian Religion*, §280.

26 BERGQUIST, *Swedenborg's Dream Diary*, §109, p. 172.

27 ibid., §250, p. 290.

28 ibid., §257, p. 295.

29 ibid., §263, p. 298.

30 ibid., §§277-8, pp. 313-14.

31 SWEDENBORG, *Arcana Caelestia*, §10110.

32 Swedenborg presented a copy of Part I of the book to the Royal Society, London, on 28 February 1745; Part II was published in mid 1745.

33 BERGQUIST, *Swedenborg's Dream Diary*, §12, p. 89.

34 ibid., §213, p. 248.

35 ibid., §171, p. 211.

36 ibid., §172, p. 212.

37 ibid., §200, p. 231.

38 ibid., §285, p. 319.

39 SWEDENBORG, *The Economy of the Animal Kingdom*, vol. II, §331.

Chapter 15

1   BERGQUIST, *Swedenborg's Dream Diary*, §277, p. 313.

2   ibid., §250, p. 290.

3   ibid., §278, p. 314.

4   ibid., §282, p. 316.

5   SWEDENBORG, *Principia*, vol. I, §4, pp. 34-5.

6   Genesis 3:15.

7   BERGQUIST, *Swedenborg's Dream Diary*, §247, p. 287.

8   ibid.

9   SWEDENBORG, *The Worship and Love of God*, §122, p. 267n.

10 BERGQUIST, *Swedenborg's Dream Diary*, §259, p. 296; §267, p. 304.

11 ibid., §199, p. 231.

12 JONSSON, *Swedenborgs Skapelsedrama 'De Cultu et Amore Dei'*, p. 122.

13 BERGQUIST, *Swedenborg's Dream Diary*, §259, p. 296.

14 SWEDENBORG, *Arcana Caelestia*, §81.

15 SWEDENBORG, *The Spiritual Diary*, §2060.

16 ACTON, (tr. and ed.), *Letters and Memorials*, vol. I, p. 500.

17 SWEDENBORG, *The Worship and Love of God*, §57.

18 BERGQUIST, *Swedenborg's Dream Diary*, §266, p. 303.

19 SWEDENBORG, *The Worship and Love of God*, §57.

20 SWEDENBORG, *Divine Love and Wisdom*, §1.

21 SWEDENBORG, *The Worship and Love of God*, §§72, 75.

22 BERGQUIST, *Swedenborg's Dream Diary*, §271, p. 308.

23 ibid., §252, p. 292; the paragraph ends abruptly.

24 SWEDENBORG, *The Worship and Love of God*, §§72, 75.

25 ibid., §78.

26 Revelation 20:2-3.

27 BERGQUIST, *Swedenborg's Dream Diary*, §201, p. 233.

28 SWEDENBORG, *The Worship and Love of God*, §79.

29 ibid., §86.

30 ROBSAHM, *Anteckningar om Swedenborg*, §15; cf. TAFEL, R L, (tr., ed. and comp.), *Documents...*, vol. I, pp. 35-6. Robsahm's description is partly equivalent to notes in two of Swedenborg's works, posthumously published: *The Word Explained* §3557, and *The Spiritual Diary* §397; but this similarity does not prove that it concerns his first divine calling-vision. Furthermore we cannot exclude that the dates given refer to the date of writing the note, but not to the day of the experience itself. Robsahm does not mention the year of the experience; but according to Swedenborg's words in his *Responsum* from 1769 it was in the year 1743 that the Lord appeared to him, calling him to his holy task. The experience recorded in connection with the meal was probably not later than his call. As to the year 1743, it may be a misprint for 1745, even if we take into account that Swedenborg's 'life crisis' in 1743-4 also involved spiritual experiences and revelations, as we see in his *Dream Diary*. During the spring and summer of 1745 Swedenborg was in London. It would thus be correct to set 1745 as the year of departure for the 'later' Swedenborg, the theosopher and exegete. For further discussion of Robsahm's recollection cf. REGAMEY, A G, 'The Vision in the Inn', in *The New-Church Magazine*, 1966, pp. 36-9.

31 *The Messiah about to Come*.

32 SWEDENBORG, *The History of Creation*, §§9-10.

33 On p. 127 of the manuscript of Codex 38, *The Messiah about to Come*; see ACTON, *An Introduction to The Word Explained*, p. 122.

Chapter 16

1   SWEDBERG, J, *Lefwernes Beskrifning*, §176.

2   ibid., §§174-5.

3   ibid., §799; Revelation 21:1-2.

4   ARNDT, *Fyra Böcker om een sann Christendom/genom Johan Arndts*, book I, ch.3, §6 ff.

5   ibid., book II, foreword.

6   SWEDBERG, J, *Lefwernes Beskrifning*, §§867-8.

7   HOFMANN, *Theologie und Exegese der Berleburger Bibel (1726-1742)*, p. 189.

8   *Berleberg Bibel*, vol. I.

9   SCHRADER, 'Pietistisches Publizieren unter Heterodoxieverdacht. Der Zensurfall "Berleburger Bibel" ', pp. 79-80.

10 BENDER, *Der Freigeist aus dem Pietismus*, p. 166 ff.

11 CHRISTIANUS DEMOCRITUS, *Der von den Nebeln des Reichs der Verwirrung...von Christiano Democrito*, questions 54-6.

12 SWEDENBORG, *The Spiritual Diary*, §3486.

13 ibid.

14 In *The Spiritual Diary* §4749m, Swedenborg comments that the Moravians 'so frequently

mention the blood of the Lord'.

15 Reference in RADLER, *Kristendomens Idéhistoria från Medeltiden till vår Tid*, p. 250.

16 BERGQUIST, *Swedenborg's Dream Diary*, pp. 29-38.

17 SWEDENBORG, *The Spiritual Diary*, §6043.

18 ibid., §5995.

Chapter 17

1 SWEDENBORG, *Heaven and Hell*, §130.

2 SWEDENBORG, *The Word Explained*, §475.

3 ibid., §1150.

4 SWEDENBORG, *The Spiritual Diary*, §2894; cf. ibid., §1647.

5 TOKSVIG, *Emanuel Swedenborg. Scientist and Mystic*, pp. 211-16; the quotation is from p. 212.

6 1 John 4:2.

7 SWEDENBORG, *Divine Providence*, §20.

8 SWEDENBORG, *The Word Explained*, §943.

9 SWEDENBORG, *The Spiritual Diary*, §409.

10 SWEDENBORG, *The Word Explained*, §986.

11 ibid., §3119.

12 ibid., §4477.

13 SWEDENBORG, *The Spiritual Diary*, §4748.

14 ibid., §5722.

15 ibid., §5008.

16 ibid., §5161; see also ibid., §§5983-4.

17 ibid., §3623.

Chapter 18

1 SWEDBERG, J, *Guds Barnas Heliga Sabbats Ro*, Sermon no. 3, for Michaelmas Day.

2 *New Catholic Encyclopedia*, 1976, article 'Apocalypse'.

3 SWEDENBORG, *The Word Explained*, §5.

4 cf. CORSINI, *Apocalisse prima e dopo*; ULFGARD, *Feast and Future*, p. 16 ff.

5 SWEDENBORG, *Hieroglyphic Key*, Example XXI, Rules 2-4, pp. 33-4.

6 BERGQUIST, *Swedenborg's Dream Diary*, §54, p. 126.

7 Revelation 11:15.

8 SWEDENBORG, *The True Christian Religion*, §770.

9 ibid., §771.

10 SWEDENBORG, *The Messiah about to Come*, ch. vi, §13, p. 18.

Chapter 19

1 ALM, 'Emanuel Swedenborgs Hus och Trädgård', in *Samfundet S:t Eriks Årsbok 1938*, p. 151 ff.

2 TAFEL, R L, (tr., ed. and comp.), *Documents...*, vol. II:1, p. 234.

3 The notes, difficult to read, have been analysed by A H STROH, in *Anteckningar i Swedenborgs Almanacka för år 1752, förvarad å Kungl. Biblioteket i Stockholm*; here Stroh's interpretation of the text is used.

4   cf. SWEDENBORG, *Arcana Caelestia*, §§79, 225.

5   SWEDENBORG, *Conjugial Love*, §13. The Swedish specialist in Swedenborg and the history of science, David Dunér, has indicated this paragraph and its significance to me.

6   TAFEL, R L, (tr., ed. and comp.), *Documents. . .*, vol. I, pp. 32-3; cf. ROBSAHM, *Anteckningar om Swedenborg*, pp. 53-4.

Chapter 20

1   SWEDENBORG, *The Word Explained*, §943, see also §§1003, 3347.

2   ibid., §1003.

3   ACTON, *The Green Books*, vol. II, 2 June 1747, p. 732.

4   ibid., vol. II, 2 June 1747, p. 732.

5   ibid., vol. II, 15 June 1747, p. 75.

6   SWEDENBORG, *Arcana Caelestia*, §34.2.

7   BERGQUIST, *Swedenborg's Dream Diary*, §179, p. 216.

8   SWEDENBORG, *Arcana Caelestia*, §64.

9   ibid., §92.

10 ibid., §8326.

11 cf. BOEHME, and the works of ARNOLD, F, mentioned in the bibliography. The theme is treated in BENZ, *Adam. Der Mythus vom Urmenschen*. For the contemporary discussion and the attitude of German priests, see SCHRADER, 'Pietistisches Publizieren unter Heterodoxieverdacht. Der Zensurfall "Berleburger Bibel" '.

12 1 Corinthians 15:45.

13 SWEDENBORG, *On the Sacred Scripture or the Word of the Lord from Experience*, §34.

14 The Apostles' Creed and the Nicene Creed are quoted from *The Alternative Service Book of the Church of England*, 1980.

15 Luke 17:20-21.

16 BALTRUSAITIS, *Anamorphoses ou thaumaturgus opticus*, pp. 115-16. The work of Wolff here referred to is *Elementa Matheseos Universae*, vol. II, ch. 5, pp. 113-15; cf. TALBOT, 'Swedenborg and the holographic paradigm', in *Emanuel Swedenborg. A Continuing Vision*, p. 443.

17 BALTRUSAITIS, *Anamorphoses ou thaumaturgus opticus*, p. 221.

18 SWEDENBORG, *Arcana Caelestia*, §1871; cf. SWEDENBORG, *The Spiritual Diary*, §2164.

19 BERGQUIST, *Swedenborg's Dream Diary*, §201, p. 233.

20 SWEDENBORG, *Arcana Caelestia*, §1871.

21 ibid., §4529.

22 EKELUND, *På Hafsstranden*, p. 199.

Chapter 21

1   SWEDENBORG, 'Bewis at wårt lefwande wesende består merendels i små darringar thet är tremulationer', in *Daedalus Hyperboreus*, no. 6, pp. 13-14; cf. *On Tremulation*, tr. C T Odhner, p. 6.

2   STROH, A H, (ed.), *Opera Quaedam*, vol. I, p. 292.

3   SWEDENBORG, *Notes and observations on C Wolff's 'Empirica'*, in *Psychologica*, §§15-20.

4   BRIEM, 'Swedenborg och den moderna Parapsykologien', in *Från Skilda tider*, p. 75.

5   ACTON, (tr. and ed.), *Letters and Memorials*, vol. II, p. 626, in a letter to F C Oetinger of 11

November, 1766. The quoted phrase 'Miracles do not occur in our days' is from a later letter to Pastor Venator of 13 July, 1771, in ibid., p. 750.

6   KLEEN, *Swedenborg*, pt II, p. 472.

7   For a background to and reproduction of Kant's letter, see TAFEL, R L, (tr., ed. and comp.), *Documents...*, vol. II:1, pp. 620-30, 635-6, 653-4; for further analysis of Kant's views on Swedenborg, and the dating of Kant's letter, see BENZ, 'Spiritual Vision and Revelation', in *The New Philosophy*, Jan-Jun 2001, ch. VI, pp. 7-52.

8   cf. TAFEL, R L, (tr., ed. and comp.), *Documents...*, vol. II:1, p. 629.

9   KLEEN, *Swedenborg*, pt II, p. 475.

10 TAFEL, R L, (tr., ed. and comp.), *Documents...*, vol. II:1, pp. 647-66.

11 ROBSAHM, *Anteckningar om Swedenborg*, p. 61.

12 TAFEL, R L, (tr., ed. and comp.), *Documents...*, vol. II:1, pp. 633-46.

13 SWEDENBORG, *Miracles*, §4, pp. 7-9.

14 TAFEL, R L, (tr., ed. and comp.), *Documents...*, vol. II:1, p. 533.

15 KANT, *Träume eines Geistersehrs*; cf. *Dreams of a Spirit-Seer*, p. 50.

16 EJVEGÅRD, 'Kant om Swedenborg', in *Värld och Vetande*, p. 56 ff.

Chapter 22

1   SWEDENBORG, *Arcana Caelestia*, §97.

2   ibid., §3884.

3   BLAKE, Letter to Dr John Trusler (1735-1820), 23 August 1799, in *Complete Writings*, p. 793.

4   *Biblia Sacra ex Sebastiani Castellionis interpretatione*, vol. I, Leipzig 1726, was in Swedenborg's library.

5   SWEDENBORG, *Arcana Caelestia*, §159.

6   ibid., §127.

7   ibid., §128.

8   SWEDENBORG, *Vera Christiana Religio*, §508.

9   CORBIN, *Face de Dieu, Face de l'Homme*, pp. 41-162.

10 SWEDENBORG, *Arcana Caelestia*, §§19, 410, 1106.

11 ibid., §635.

12 ibid., §§609, 615.

13 ibid., §§3021, 4280.

14 ibid., §2.

15 ibid., §4288.2.

16 DANTE, *Paradise*, vol. III of *The Divine Comedy*, Canto 20, ll. 88-93, 130-132.

17 Revelation 21:1-5.

Chapter 23

1   SWEDENBORG, *Arcana Caelestia*, §7233, for further explanation of the internal sense, see also §§334-46.

2   cf. SWEDENBORG, *The Word Explained*, §1892.

3   SWEDENBORG, *The Spiritual Diary*, §§651, 653.

4   SWEDENBORG, *The Word Explained*, §1892.

5   ACTON, (tr. and ed.), *Letters and Memorials*, vol. II , p. 696.

6   SWEDENBORG, *The Economy of the Animal Kingdom*, pt 2 (in vol. II), §10.

7   SWEDENBORG, *The Animal Kingdom*, §464.

8   BERGQUIST, *Swedenborg's Dream Diary*, §§111-12, pp. 174-5.

9   cf. SWEDENBORG, *The Interaction of the Soul and the Body*, §6.

10   SWEDENBORG, *The Spiritual Diary*, §605.

11   SWEDENBORG, *The Divine Providence*, §319.

12   SWEDENBORG, *The Divine Love and Wisdom*, §263.

13   SWEDENBORG, *The Spiritual Diary*, §3317.

14   cf. SWEDENBORG, *Arcana Caelestia*, §9281.

15   ibid., §3894.

16   SWEDENBORG, *The True Christian Religion*, §157.

17   SWEDENBORG, *Heaven and Hell*, §270.

18   SWEDENBORG, *The Spiritual Diary*, §649.

19   ARBMAN, *Ecstacy or Religious Trance*, vol. I, p. 272 ff.

20   ELIADE, *Le Yoga. Immortalité et Liberté*, pp. 74-5.

21   *Récits d'un Pèlerin Russe*, p. 46 ff.

22   ELIADE, *Le Yoga. Immortalité et Liberté*, p. 96.

23   HOF, *Bli mer Människa*, p. 212.

Chapter 24

1   1 Corinthians 2:10.

2   2 Corinthians 3:6.

3   ORIGEN, *Omelie sulla Genesi*, p. 17.

4   SWEDENBORG, *On the Sacred Scripture or the Word of the Lord from Experience*, §29.2.

5   ibid.

6   cf. SWEDENBORG, *The Divine Providence*, §135; and SWEDENBORG, *The True Christian Religion*, §779.

7   Exodus 14:21-5, 27-8.

8   SWEDENBORG, *Arcana Caelestia*, §8210.2.

9   BARTH, *Die protestantische Theologie im 19. Jahrhundert*, p. 18 ff.

10   SWEDENBORG, *Arcana Caelestia*, §2649.

11   cf. MILOSZ, *La Terre d'Ulro*, p. 206; Luke 14:16-24.

12   Swedenborg wrote repeatedly that remaining in existence is perpetual creation; cf. *The True Christian Religion*, §§35, 46, 224.

13   Romans 5:5.

14   LUBAC, *Exégèse Médiévale. Les Quatre Sens de l'Écriture*, vol. I, pp. 16-17.

15   SWEDENBORG, *The White Horse*, §16.

16   TAFEL, R L, (tr., ed. and comp.), *Documents. . .*, vol. II:1, p. 256.

Chapter 25

1   *Tessin och Tessiniana*, p. 356-7.

2   TAFEL, R L, (tr., ed. and comp.), *Documents. . .*, vol. II:1, pp. 450, 453.

3   ROBSAHM, *Anteckningar om Swedenborg*, p. 30 ff.; cf. TAFEL, R L, (tr., ed. and comp.), *Documents...*, vol. I, pp. 31-3.

4   *Nya Kyrkans Tidning*, no. 9, 1923. According to the editor of the magazine, Odhner's report contains some details which seem to be taken from other texts regarding Swedenborg's dwelling.

5   TAFEL, R L, (tr., ed. and comp.), *Documents...*, vol. II:1, p. 407.

6   ROBSAHM, *Anteckningar om Swedenborg*, p. 31; cf. TAFEL, R L, (tr., ed. and comp.), *Documents...*, vol. I, p. 32.

7   TAFEL, R L, (tr., ed. and comp.), *Documents...*, vol. II:1, p. 561.

8   ROBSAHM, *Anteckningar om Swedenborg*, p. 31; cf. TAFEL, R L, (tr., ed. and comp.), *Documents...*, vol. I, p. 32.

9   ROBSAHM, *Anteckningar om Swedenborg*, p. 53; cf. TAFEL, R L, (tr., ed. and comp.), *Documents...*, vol. I, p. 42.

10   *Strödda anteckningar, hörande till Swedenborgs lefverne*, p. 10.

11   ROBSAHM, *Anteckningar om Swedenborg*, p. 38; cf. TAFEL, R L, (tr., ed. and comp.), *Documents...*, vol. I, p. 36.

12   ROBSAHM, *Anteckningar om Swedenborg*, p. 49; cf. TAFEL, R L, (tr., ed. and comp.), *Documents...*, vol. I, p. 41.

13   GJÖRWELL, *Anmärckningar i Swenska Historien,* vol. I, p. 220 ff.

14   HÖPKEN, A J von, 'Avskrifter av v Höpkens brev', MS in Royal Library, Stockholm, Ep Sign 14; cf. TAFEL, R L, (tr., ed. and comp.), *Documents...*, vol. II:1, p. 407.

15   *Tessin och Tessiniana*, p. 368; cf. TAFEL, R L, (tr., ed. and comp.), *Documents...*, vol. II:1, p. 401.

16   TAFEL, R L, (tr., ed. and comp.), *Documents...*, vol. II:1, pp. 448-50.

17   SWEDENBORG, *The Economy of the Animal Kingdom*, §19.

18   ibid.

19   EKELUND, *På Hafsstranden* [*On the Sea-shore*], p. 194. All quotations from Ekelund are, if no other source is mentioned, taken from this book, pp. 191-220.

20   EKELUND, *Lyra och Hades*, p. 85.

21   SWEDENBORG, *Arcana Caelestia*, §6811.

22   cf. ibid. §§1680.2, 2574.2.

23   EKELUND, *Spår och Tecken*, p. 132.

24   EKELUND, *Ars Magna*, p. 30.

25   SWEDENBORG, *Arcana Caelestia*, §920.1.

26   EKELUND, 'Kunskapslif - Erfarenhet', in *Sak och Sken*, pp. 82-3.

27   SWEDENBORG, *The Word Explained*, §4663.

28   EKELUND, *Lefnadsstämning*, no. 138, p. 86.

39   EKELUND, 'Kunskapslif - Erfarenhet', in *Sak och Sken*, pp. 87-8.

Chapter 26

1   CREUTZ, *Vitterhetsarbeten af Creutz och Gyllenborg*, p. 115.

2   Psalm 91:12, 13.

3   John 1:51.

4   The words about Luther's attitude and the quotation are taken from HARDT, 'Luther och Mystike',

in *Nya Väktaren*, no. 12, pp. 518-19.

5   Luke 23:43.

6   Hymn 479 in the 1694 edition of the hymn book [*Psalm-Boken, Then Svenska*] and 409 in the 1695 edition.

7   Luke 12:3.

8   SWEDENBORG, *Arcana Caelestia*, §2490.

9   Ecclesiastes 11:3.

10 cf. SWEDENBORG, *Heaven and Hell*, §551 ff.

11 SWEDENBORG, *The True Christian Religion*, §§796-9.

12 SWEDENBORG, *Arcana Caelestia*, §4588.

13 STRINDBERG, *Ett Drömspel*, in *Nationalupplagan,* vol. XLVI, p. 7.

14 SWEDENBORG, *Conjugial Love*, §2 ff.

15 ibid., §10.7,8.

16 SWEDENBORG, *Heaven and Hell*, §270.

17 SWEDENBORG, *Arcana Caelestia*, §5133.

18 SWEDENBORG, *Heaven and Hell*, §192.

19 SWEDENBORG, *The Word Explained*, §1147.

20 SWEDENBORG, *The Spiritual Diary*, §4181.

21 ibid., §206.

22 ELLIOTT, J E, (ed.), *Small Theological Works and Letters*, pp. 305, 307.

23 SWEDENBORG, *Arcana Caelestia*, §50.

24 SWEDENBORG, *Heaven and Hell*, §585.

25 SWEDENBORG, *Arcana Caelestia*, §5992.

Chapter 27

1   FÉNELON, F, *Grundläggande til en Beskrifning öfwer Borgerlige Samhälsens...*, pp. 191-2.

2   *Tessin och Tessiniana*, p. 190.

3   TAFEL, R L, (tr., ed. and comp.), *Documents...*, vol. I, p. 537.

4   ibid., vol. I, pp. 511-15.

5   cf. ibid., vol. I, pp. 540-1.

6   ibid., vol. I, p. 513.

7   ibid., vol. I, pp. 511-15.

8   SWEDENBORG, *The New Jerusalem and its Heavenly Doctrine*, §322.

9   TAFEL, R L, (tr., ed. and comp.), *Documents...*, vol. I, pp. 514-15.

10 HÖPKEN, A J von, *Skrifter*, vol. I, p. 124.

11 ACTON, (tr. and ed.), *Letters and Memorials*, vol. II, p. 596.

Chapter 28

1   See HYDE, J, (ed.), *A Bibliography of the Works of Emanuel Swedenborg, original and translated*, nos. 549-64 for details of the manuscripts, and no. 565 for publication details and printing costs.

2   LINDH, 'Swedenborgs Ekonomi', in *Nya Kyrkans Tidning*, May-June 1927 to June 1930.

3   ibid., September-October 1929, p. 85.

4   ibid., pp. 89-90.

5   SWEDENBORG, E, *Skrifter och handlingar rörande Assessor Emanuel Swedenborg*, Royal Library, Stockholm, Sign I, p. 58.

6   ROBSAHM, *Anteckningar om Swedenborg*, pp. 53-4; TAFEL, R L, (tr., ed. and comp.), *Documents...*, vol. I, p. 42.

7   The 'Autografsamlingen', Em. Swedenborg. Lars von Engeström (1751-1826) was a well-known Swedish diplomat and collector of manuscripts and rare books. His collection of manuscripts is now in the Royal Library, Stockholm.

8   In this capacity he was the head of Swedish foreign policy. From 1741 to 1746 he had been Sweden's envoy to Berlin.

9   See STIEGUNG, *Ludvig XV:s Hemliga Diplomati och Sverige 1752-1774*.

10 MALMSTRÖM, *Sveriges Politiska Historia från Konung Karl XII:s Död till Statshvälf-ningen 1772*, vol. III, pp. 420-1.

11 Dépenses de l'Ambassade 1759-1772, Quai d'Orsay, from, *Mémoires et Documents, Suède*.

12 ibid.

13 ibid.

14 BERGQUIST, *Swedenborg's Dream Diary*, §274, p. 310.

15 DE CHOISEUL, E F, *Etienne François de Choiseul, Duc: Mémoires*, p. 192.

16 BERGQUIST, *Swedenborg's Dream Diary*, §275, p. 311.

17 SWEDENBORG, *The Spiritual Diary*, §5980.

18 ibid., §4470.

19 SWEDENBORG, *The Apocalypse Revealed*, §740.

Chapter 29

1   Borges, translated by R Howard and C Rennert, in SWEDENBORG, *The Spiritual Diary* (London, 2002), vol. I, p. xlvi.

2   *Den Svenska Merkurius* [*The Swedish Mercury*], June 1763, p. 462; cf. TAFEL, R L, (tr., ed. and comp.), *Documents...*, vol. II:2, p. 704.

3   SWEDENBORG, *The Divine Love and Wisdom*, §§1-5.

4   ibid., §185.

5   BERGQUIST, 'Linné och Swedenborg: spegelbilder i svenskt 1700-tal', in *Världarnas Möte*, nos. 1-2, p. 1 ff.

6   SEEBERG, *Gottfried Arnold*, p. 558.

7   SWEDENBORG, *The Divine Providence*, §186.

8   ibid., §176.

9   JAMES Sr, H, *The Secret of Swedenborg*, pp. 175-6.

10 SWEDENBORG, *The Divine Providence*, §124.4.

11 ibid., §175.

12 Luke 16:13.

13 SWEDENBORG, *The Divine Providence*, §250.4.

14 ibid., §258.6; SWEDBERG, J, *Betrachtelser om the Obotferdigas Förhinder*, p. 323 ff.

15 ibid.

16 SWEDENBORG, *Conjugial Love*, §425.1.

17 BLAKE, 'The Tyger', from *Songs of Experience*, in *Complete Writings*, p. 214.

18 BERGQUIST, *Swedenborg's Dream Diary*, §75, p. 146.

19 ibid., §201, p. 233.

Chapter 30

1   LIEDGREN, *Svensk Psalm och Andlig Visa: Olaus Petri-föreläsningar i Uppsala*, p. 365.

2   ACTON, (tr. and ed.), *Letters and Memorials*, vol. II, pp. 624-6; Swedenborg's Letter to Beyer, in *Samlingar för Philantroper*, no.1.

3   ACTON, (tr. and ed.), *Letters and Memorials*, vol. II, p. 627 ff.

4   ELLIOTT, J E, (ed.), *Small Theological Works and Letters*, p. 223; *Samlingar för Philantroper*, no. 1.

5   SWEDENBORG, *Arcana Caelestia*, §54.

6   Swedenborg pursued this theme all his life — it appears as early as his short academic thesis in 1709; cf. HALLENGREN, *Framtiden i Äldre Tid*, pp. 54-5.

7   SWEDENBORG, *The Divine Love and Wisdom*, §409.

8   ibid., §§33, 170.

9   SWEDENBORG, *Arcana Caelestia*, §747.

10 PLATO, *The Symposium*, no. 191.

11 SWEDENBORG, *Conjugial Love*, §147; *Doctrine of Life*, §71, in *The Four Doctrines*.

12 cf. HELLSTEN, *Kyrklig och Radikal Äktenskapsuppfattning i Striden Kring C J L Almqvists 'Det Går An'*; see also BERGQUIST, *Biblioteket i Lusthuset. Tio uppsatser om Swedenborg*, p. 100 ff.

13 *Sveriges Rikes Lag. Gillad och Antagen på Riksdagen år 1734* [*The Law of the Kingdom of Sweden, approved by Parliament in 1734*], the section about marriage, chapters 1-17.

14 SWEDENBORG, *Heaven and Hell*, §577.2.

15 SWEDENBORG, *Conjugial Love*, §479.

16 SIEVERSEN, *Sexualitet och Äktenskap i Emanuel Swedenborgs Religionsfilosofi*.

17 SWEDENBORG, *Conjugial Love*, §459.

18 *Sveriges Rikes Lag. Gillad och Antagen på Riksdagen år 1734* [*The Law of the Kingdom of Sweden, approved by Parliament in 1734*], the section about crimes, chapter 53.

19 SWEDENBORG, *Conjugial Love*, §459.

20 SWEDENBORG, *On Marriage*, §66, in ELLIOTT, J E, (ed.), *Small Theological Works and Letters*, p. 129.

21 SWEDENBORG, *Conjugial Love*, §69.

22 ibid., §42.

23 ibid., pt 2 'voluptates insaniae de amore scortatorio' (§423 ff.).

24 ibid., §425.

25 ibid., §512.

26 TAFEL, R L, (tr., ed. and comp.), *Documents. . .*, vol. I, p. 699; WILKINSON, C J, *James John Garth Wilkinson*, p. 234.

Chapter 31

1   WOLFF, C von, *Baron von Wolff's Geometrie i sammandrag*, p. 15.

2   JONSSON, *Swedenborgs Korrespondenslära*, p. 32.

3 BERGQUIST, *Swedenborg's Dream Diary*, §13, p. 90.

4 SWEDENBORG, *The Interaction of the Soul and the Body*, §20.

5 ibid., chapter XII, heading.

6 ibid., §19.

7 KIERKEGAARD, *Indøvelse i Christendom* [Practice in Christianity], from *Søren Kierkegaards Samlede Værker* [The Complete Works of Søren Kierkegaard], vol. XII, p. 84.

Chapter 32

1 HJERN, *Swedenborg och hans Vänner i Göteborg*, p. 11, with reference to an article in *The New Jerusalem Magazine* (1790), pp. 41-2; cf. TAFEL, R L, (tr., ed. and comp.), *Documents...*, vol. II:2, pp. 699-700.

2 KAHL, *Nya Kyrkan och dess Inflytande på Theologiens Studium in Sverige*, no. 1; SUNDELIN, *Swedenborgianismen Historia in Sverige under förra århundradt*, p. 58 ff.; HJERN, *Swedenborg och hans Vänner i Göteborg*.

3 HÖPKEN, A J von, 'Avskrifter av v Höpkens brev', MS in Royal Library, Stockholm, Ep Sign 14.

4 HJERN, *Swedenborg och hans Vänner i Göteborg*, p. 46; SWEDENBORG, *Sketch of an Ecclesiastical History of the New Church*, no. 7.

5 ACTON, (tr. and ed.), *Letters and Memorials*, vol. II, p. 672.

6 ibid., vol. II, p. 660.

7 The information is given in the preface to the first French edition of *The True Christian Religion*, which appeared in Paris in 1802. According to one of the editors Swedenborg had asked the French censor Chevreuil for permission to print *Vera Christiana Religio* in France, but this request probably concerned his *Summaria Expositio*, since Swedenborg's great final work was not yet written when he left Paris in 1769; cf. TAFEL, R L, (tr., ed. and comp.), *Documents...*, vol. II:2, pp. 700-1.

8 cf. ACTON, (tr. and ed.), *Letters and Memorials*, vol. II, pp. 652-3.

9 cf. ibid., vol. II, p. 655.

10 SWEDENBORG, *The Interaction of the Soul and the Body*, §20.

11 ACTON, (tr. and ed.), *Letters and Memorials*, vol. II, p. 690.

12 ibid., vol. II, p. 695; the letter was published in Swedish and translated into English and Latin to be printed in London in 1769.

13 SUNDELIN, *Swedenborgianismen Historia in Sverige under förra århundradt*, p. 74.

14 ELLIOTT, J E, (ed.), *Small Theological Works and Letters*, pp. 237, 239.

15 SUNDELIN, *Swedenborgianismen Historia in Sverige under förra århundradt*, p. 90 ff.

16 See TAFEL, R L, (tr., ed. and comp.), *Documents...*, vol. II:1, p. 367.

17 ACTON, (tr. and ed.), *Letters and Memorials*, vol. II, p. 725.

18 TAFEL, R L, (tr., ed. and comp.), *Documents...*, vol. II:1, pp. 482-3.

19 HYDE, J, (ed.), *A Bibliography of the Works of Emanuel Swedenborg, original and translated*, no. 2725.

Chapter 33

1 BLAKE, 'Jerusalem', ch. 3, plate 54, in *Complete Writings*, p. 684.

2 DOLE, 'A Rationale for Swedenborg's writing sequence 1746-1771', in *Emanuel Swedenborg:*

A Continuing Vision, p. 293 ff.

3 cf. ACTON, (tr. and ed.), *Letters and Memorials*, vol. II, pp. 612-13; SWEDENBORG, *The Spiritual Diary*, §4824.
4 cf. TAFEL, R L, (tr., ed. and comp.), *Documents. . .*, vol. II:2, pp. 747-8.
5 SWEDENBORG, *The True Christian Religion*, §779.
6 ibid., §700.
7 ibid., §759.1.
8 ibid., §759.3.
9 SWEDENBORG, *Heaven and Hell*, §73.
10 I quote here from Swedberg's own version of Colossians 1:26-28 in his *Lefwernes Beskrifning*, §763.
11 BERGQUIST, *Swedenborg's Dream Diary*, §123, p. 183.
12 SWEDBERG, J, *Schibboleth. Swenska språkets rycht och richtoghet*, §249.
13 SWEDENBORG, *The True Christian Religion*, §791.
14 Matthew 24:31.

Chapter 34

1 SWEDBERG, J, *Then Swenska Psalmboken*, Ps. 461, v. 3.
2 TAFEL, R L, (tr., ed. and comp.), *Documents. . .*, vol. II:1, pp. 577-9.
3 ibid., vol. II:1, pp. 556-7.
4 ibid., vol. II:1, pp. 557-8.
5 ibid., vol. II:1, p. 558.
6 ibid., vol. II:1, p. 560.
7 ibid., vol. II:1, p. 454.
8 ibid., vol. II:1, pp. 564-71.

Chapter 35

1 Regarding the development of 'Swedenborgianism' during the first decade and thereafter, refer to JONSSON and HJERN, *Swedenborg. Sökaren i Naturens och Andens Världar. Hans verk och efterföljd*, p. 140 ff., see also the works of Karin Johannisson, Harry Lenhammar, Marguerite Beck Block, and Carl Theophilus Odhner listed in the Bibliography.
2 SWEDENBORG, *The Spiritual Diary*, §§4777, 4783.
3 ibid., §§5037, 5043.
4 ibid., §5629.
5 SWEDENBORG, *The True Christian Religion*, §508.
6 ACTON, (tr. and ed.), *Letters and Memorials*, vol. II, pp. 630, 668.

Chronology

Events related to Swedenborg's life	Publications: titles given in English	Contemporary events
1682		Birth of future Charles XII.
1685		Birth of Bach and Handel.
1687		Newton: *Philosophiae Naturalis Principia Mathematica.*
1688 29 January: birth in Stockholm, son of Jesper Swedberg, regimental chaplain, and Sara Behm.		
1688-9		The 'Glorious Revolution' in Britain.
1689		Queen Christina of Sweden dies in Rome.
1690		Locke: *Essay concerning Human Understanding.*
1691 Jesper Swedberg is pastor in Vingåker.		

1692 Move to Uppsala: Jesper Swedberg appointed professor of theology at the University.		
1696 Death of Emanuel's mother and elder brother; Johan Moraeus is his tutor.		Toland: *Christianity not Mysterious.*
1697 Jesper Swedberg marries Sara Bergia.		Charles XI dies, succeeded by Charles XII; Pierre Bayle: *Dictionnaire Historique et Critique.*
1698 Family moves into house owned by Jesper Swedberg on Stora Torget, Uppsala.		
1699 Emanuel enrols in Uppsala University and Västmanland-Dala students' association.		Arnold: *Unpartreyische Kirchen- und Ketzerhistorie.*
1700		Russia, Saxony, and Denmark attack Sweden: Charles XII lands at Själland and peace is concluded with Denmark; battle at Narva: Russians defeated.
1701-06		Charles XII involved in war in Poland; Act of Settlement in Britain (1701): British monarchs must be Protestants.
1702 Great fire in Uppsala.		Swedish town Nyenskans on Bay of Finland captured by Russians; Czar Peter begins to build St Petersburg west of the Swedish fortress there.
1703 Jesper Swedberg and Sara Bergia move from Uppsala to Brunsbo and the		

Skara diocese; Emanuel lodges in Uppsala with his newly-married brother-in-law Eric Benzelius and Anna Swedberg.		
1704-09 Emanuel continues studies at Uppsala.		
1704		Charles XII deposes August 'the Strong' of Saxony from Polish throne, and with Swedish support chooses Stanislaw Leszcyñska as king of Poland; Newton: *Optics*.
1706		Peace of Altranstadt; August of Saxony abdicates from Polish throne.
1707		Charles XII begins campaign against Russia.
1709 Leaves Uppsala after defending his thesis entitled *Selectae Sententiae*.	*Selected Sentences*.	Swedish defeat at Poltava; Charles XII flees to Turkish territory; Stanislaw deposed by August of Saxony.
1710 First foreign journey: to England, lodges in London.	*Joyful Ovation on the Victory over the Danes*.	Swedish Baltic provinces seized by Russians; Danes conquered at Helsingborg by Swedish army led by Magnus Stenbock; plague in Sweden; foundation of 'Guild of the Curious'; Berkeley: *Treatise concerning Human Knowledge*; Leibniz: *Theodicée*.
1711 In London: studies mathematics, mechanics, astronomy; lives with craftsmen, learning their trades.		Jesper Swedberg: *Godly Thoughts* in which he criticizes the king for his involvement with the Turks and his refusal to return to Sweden; Stanislaw and his court flee to Christianstad where they stay for three years.

1712 Stays in London till turn of 1712-3, then travels to Holland.		Episcopal seat at Brunsbo burns down.
1713 In May leaves Holland and travels to Paris to continue his studies.		Russian offensive, totally occupying Finland in 1713-4; Charles XII imprisoned by Turks in Bender; Swedish government summons the Diet in Stockholm, requesting the king to conclude the war; Jesper Swedberg openly criticizes the king; Peace of Utrecht ends the War of the Spanish Succession.
1714 Leaves France in May or June to return to Sweden via The Hague and Hamburg; stops at Greifswald and Rostock.	*Heliconian Sport.*	Charles XII forbids the Diet to gather, and rides from Turkey to Stralsund and Swedish territory, Finland and the Baltic provinces still in Russian hands; George I of Hanover succeeds to throne of Great Britain.
1715 Stays in Stralsund until April-May.	*The Northern Muse, A Joyful Ovation* printed at Griefswald.	Sweden loses German provinces; Stralsund falls to Prussian troops; Charles XII escapes to Skåne, makes headquarters at Ystad then at Lund; Louis XIV dies and is succeeded by five-year-old Louis XV; Jacobite uprising in Scotland.
1716 Works with Christopher Polhem; December, they visit Charles XII in Lund; appointed Extraordinary Assessor in Board of Mines.	*Daedalus Hyperboreus* (*The Northern Inventor*) first issued with Swedenborg as editor; writes short articles on technical and practical subjects, published posthumously.	Charles XII's first and unsuccessful attack on Norway; death of Leibniz.

1717 Under Polhem's oversight works on locks at Trollhättan for canal between Gothenburg and Stockholm, studies the founding of salt-works and a dry dock at Karlskrona.	*Information about the Tin-ware of Stjernsund, its Use, and the Method of Tinning.*	
1718 Co-operation with Polhem continues; supervises transport of Swedish ships overland to Idefjord.	*Algebra, composed in Ten Books*; *Attempt to find the east and west longitude by means of the moon* reprinted and revised in several later editions.	Charles XII's army invades Norway in autumn; on 30 November the king is shot at Fredrikshald.
1719 All technical operations stopped due to funding shortage; relations with Polhem cease; in May, 147 families of commoners ennobled, including Emanuel and his siblings who assume the name Swedenborg.	*The Motion and Position of the Earth and Planets*; the final issue of *Daedalus Hyperboreus*, containing article *Proof that our Inner-most Being consists [...] of [...] Tremulations*; *On the Height of Water and Strong Tides in the primeval world*; *Proposal for the System of our Coinage and Measurement*; *Description of Docks, Sluices, and Salt-works.*	Ulrika Eleanora queen of Sweden; peace with Hanover; Swedish withdrawal from Bremen and Verden; The Swedish Society of Learning and Literature formed in Uppsala in succession to the Guild of the Curious.
1720 Emanuel's stepmother dies; Jesper Swedberg marries his third wife, Christina Arrhusia; Emanuel participates in the Diet.	*Anatomy of our Finest Nature* presented to the Board of Medicine; *Fall and Rise of Lake Wenner* in *Acta Literaria Sueciae*.	Ulrika Eleanora abdicates and is succeeded by her husband Fredrik I; peace with Prussia and Denmark; Swedish withdrawal from parts of Pomerania; new Constitution with a parliamentary form of government proclaimed by Diet and government.
1721 Second foreign journey, to Hamburg, Amsterdam, Liège, partly to publish theoretical and practical material.	*Some Specimens of a Work on the Principles of Chemistry, with other treatises by Emanuel Swedenborg;*	Peace of Nystad; Sweden loses Ingermanland, Estland, Livland, parts of Karelen, province of Viborg, and Ösel and Dagö to Russia; Fénelon:

	New Observations and Discoveries respecting Iron and Fire.	*Télémaque* (critical of political absolutism) published in Swedish.
1722 In Leipzig at turn of year; returns to Sweden via Hamburg in July.	*Miscellaneous Observations*; *Modest Thoughts on Inflation of Swedish Currency.*	
1723 Participates in Diet; submits several memoranda of importance on promoting export of Swedish iron.	*Memorandum on the balance of Trade*; *Memorandum regarding the Establishment of Iron Works in Sweden.*	
1724 Promoted in Board of Mines as a salaried Assessor.	*Memorandum regarding Production of Iron and Copper.*	Publication of Breckling: *The Last Trumpet over Germany* in Swedish, translated from German by Emanuel's brother Jesper Swedenborg; birth of Immanuel Kant; Bach: *St John Passion.*
1725 Reviews possibilities of using steam engines in Swedish mines; during this and coming years makes extensive travels in mining districts for the Board of Mines.		
1726 Participates in Diet.		Private religious meetings banned; radical pietist J C Dippel enters Sweden; The Berleberg Bible published.
1727 Stays in Sweden until his foreign journey in 1733.		Dippel active in Stockholm and begins his chief work *Demonstration of Evangelical Truth.*
1728		Dippel expelled from Sweden; Leibniz: *Monadology* published posthumously.

1729	Manuscript of *Fundamental Principles of Natural Things based on experiments and geometry.*	Dippel: *Demonstration of Evangelical Truth.*
1730		Episcopal seat at Brunsbo burns down for second time.
1731 Participates in Diet.		Voltaire: *Charles XII*, in which the king is presented as both a classical hero and the cause of Sweden's defeat.
1733 Third foreign journey to Denmark, Germany, and Bohemia, partly for mining research.		
1734 Returns in July; participates in Diet; submits Memorandum to Diet on importance of Swedish policy of peace and desisting from war of revenge against Russia.	*Philosophical and Mineralogical Works I-III: part I, Principles of Natural Things (Principial); part II, On Iron; part III, On Copper; Outlines of a Philosophical Argument on the Infinite; Mechanism of the Interaction between the Soul and the Body;* Outline of a memorandum concerning Swedish military involvement in Poland and war against Russia.	Conflict on the succession to the Polish throne; the Swedish Prime Minister Arvid Horn considers military support for Stanislaw Leszcyñska; Voltaire: *Lettres Philosophiques.*
1735 Jesper Swedberg dies.		New religious regulations directed against pietism; Linnaeus: *Systema Naturae.*
1736 Jesper Swedberg's burial at Varnhem church; fourth foreign journey: leaves Sweden in July; arrives in Paris in September where he stays for one and a half years.		
1737 In Paris, studying anatomy.		

1738 Leaves Paris for Turin and Milan; arrives in Venice in April; continues in August via Florence to Rome.	1738-40, writes three works on the physiology of the brain, posthumously published as *The Cerebrum*.	During the Diet of 1738-9 Arvid Horn, Prime Minister since 1720, resigns; the long period of peace, characterized by a conciliatory policy towards Russia, ends.
1739 Leaves Rome in February; stays at Amsterdam during the summer; the Vatican places *Principia* on the Index.	Begins *The Economy of the Animal Kingdom*.	Hat Party politician Carl Gyllenborg is Prime Minister.
1740 Returns to Stockholm in the autumn; participates in the Diet of 1740-1.	Publishes *The Economy of the Animal Kingdom, part I*.	
1741 Participates in Diet; elected to Royal Academy of Sciences.	*The Economy of the Animal Kingdom, part II; The Soul* published posthumously.	Sweden declares war on Russia.
1742 Participates in Diet.	*A Hieroglyphic Key* published posthumously; works on *The Animal Kingdom*.	Diet in 1741-2; the Swedes capitulate at Helsingfors; Handel: *The Messiah*.
1743 Participates in Diet; leaves Sweden again; in Amsterdam from August; at the turn of the year to The Hague; buys house and garden on Hornsgatan, Stockholm.	Continues *The Animal Kingdom*; begins *Dream Diary:* published post-humously.	Eric Benzelius dies; peace with Russia at Åbo, with small surrender of territory; Adolf Fredrik of Holstein-Gottorp chosen to succeed to Swedish throne.
1744 Religious crisis at The Hague during spring, with a vision of Christ and call, 6-7 April; leaves The Hague and travels to London in May.	*The Animal Kingdom I, II*; concludes *Dream Diary*; *The Senses*: published posthumously;	
1745 April: 'Heaven and hell opened' after a vision; returns to Sweden in August; begins study of Hebrew.	Begins collection of Bible passages *The Messiah about to Come*: published posthumously; *On the Worship and Love of God*; begins a biblical	

	commentary *The Word Explained*: published posthumously; starts journal *The Spiritual Diary* and continues it until 1765.	
1746 Participates in Diet.		Prime Minister Carl Gyllenborg dies; birth of Gustaf Adolf, son of Adolf Fredrik and Lovisa Ulrika.
1747 Participates in Diet; requests retirement from Board of Mines; leaves Sweden for Holland.		C G Tessin, Hat politician, becomes Prime Minister.
1748 Begins *Arcana Coelestia*; travels to London in December.		La Mettrie: *L'Homme Machine*.
1749 Leaves London for Aix-La-Chapelle (Aachen) where he spends the winter.	*Arcana Caelestia* vol 1 published in London.	
1750 Returns to Stockholm via Amsterdam in spring/summer.	*Arcana Caelestia* vol 2; English translation of the volume also published	Bach dies.
1751 Participates in Diet.	*Arcana Caelestia* vol 3.	Polhem dies; Fredrik I dies; Adolf Fredrik becomes king; publication of French *Encyclopédie* begins.
1752 Participates in Diet.	*Arcana Caelestia* vol 4.	A J von Höpken, also a Hat, succeeds C G Tessin as Prime Minister.
1753	*Arcana Caelestia* vols 5, 6.	Gregorian calendar introduced into Sweden: dates move forward 11 days.
1754	*Arcana Caelestia* vol 7.	
1755 Participates in Diet.	*Memorandum on Distribution of Brandy in Sweden*.	Earthquake in Lisbon.

1756	*Arcana Caelestia* vol 8.	King Adolf Fredrik's unsuccessful coup; the 'Seven Years' War' begins.
1757 States that he witnessed the Last Judgement in the spiritual world.	Begins work on *The Apocalypse Explained*.	Sweden declares war against Prussia and joins in Seven Years' War; birth of William Blake.
1758 In London.	*The Worlds in Space; Heaven and Hell; The Last Judgment; On The New Jerusalem and Heaven's Teaching for it; The White Horse.*	
1759 Returns from England during summer; vision of fire in Stockholm.	Stops work on *The Apocalypse Explained*: published posthumously.	Fredrik Gyllenborg dies; Voltaire: *Candide*; Handel dies.
1760 Participates in Diet.	Four memoranda to Diet on economic questions.	Nordencrantz: *Proposal to the Estates of the Diet on the Constitution*.
1761 Participates in Diet; episode of Mme de Marteville and the lost receipt.	Memorandum to Diet: *Modest Thoughts on Upholding and Strengthening Freedom in the Country*, defensive of the Period of Freedom's Constitution against criticism by Nordencrantz; *The Process of Inlaying Marble*; article in *Transactions of the Royal Academy of Sciences*.	Claes Ekeblad becomes Prime Minister.
1762 Participates in Diet, which is now closed.	*On the Word of the Lord, from Experience*: published posthumously.	Sweden's participation in the Seven Years' War ceases; peace in Hamburg.
1763	*The Four Doctrines; Continuation on the Last Judgment; The Divine Love and Wisdom.*	

1764	*Divine Providence.*	
1765 Leaves active session of Diet and travels to Amsterdam to publish *The Apocalypse Revealed*; begins correspondence with F C Oetinger.		Economic crisis in Sweden; Caps take power 1765-6; C G Löwenhielm becomes Prime Minister.
1766 In April travels from Holland to London; on 19 May submits the final version of his proposals for finding the longitude to the Royal Society of Sciences in London; returns to Sweden in September and may have attended closing of the Diet.	*The Apocalypse Revealed*; *A New Method for Determining the Longitude at Sea.*	Kant: *Dreams of a Spirit-Seer, illustrated by the Dreams of Metaphysics.*
1767		G A Beyer publishes anonymously a collection of sermons, strongly influenced by Swedenborg.
1768 Cathedral chapter in Gothenburg decides to present the question of the doctrinal purity of Swedenborg's teachings for consideration by the Estate of priests.	*Conjugial Love.*	
1769 April: departs to Amsterdam and Paris; returns to Gothenburg in September-October; doctrinal purity of his writings reviewed by special commission appointed by the priesthood.	*A Brief Exposition of the Doctrine of the New Church*; *The Interaction of the Soul and the Body*; Swedenborg's letter to Beyer is published.	Diet in Norköping; Hats retake power; for a period the Swedenborg family is represented by Emanuel, son of Jesper.
1770 Royal action against Beyer and Rosén in Gothenburg; Swedenborg's doctrines condemned; he writes to the king requesting protection against unjust		

attacks; leaves Sweden for Amsterdam in July.		
1771 Paralysed by a stroke in London shortly before Christmas.	*The True Christian Religion*; new edition of *Modest Thoughts on the Deflation and Inflation of Swedish Coinage*; writes *Coronis*, published posthumously.	Adolf Fredrik dies during visit of Prince Gustaf to Louis XV in Versailles; radical pietist T Leopold dies in Bohus prison after 43 years of captivity.
1772 29 March: dies in London; on 5 April, Pastor Arvid Ferelius conducts his funeral in Swedish church, Prince's Square.		Gustaf III's revolution and abolition of parliamentary rule; Poland partitioned for the first time.

Contents of Swedenborg's Library

The list is a revised and completed version of the *Förtekning på Afl. Wälborne herr Assessor* Swedenborgs *efterlämnade wackra Boksamling, i åtskilliga Språk och Wetenskaper, som kommer at försäljas på Bok-Auctions-Kammaren i Stockholm d. 28 Nov. 1772* [List of the Deceased Honourable Mr Assessor Swedenborg's Beautiful Book Collection in Various Languages and Disciplines Which are to be Sold at the Book Auction Chamber in Stockholm on 28 Nov. 1772]. The list was printed in Stockholm the same year. From the printed list are included the first part, pages 1-8, and 'Appendix A', to which the catalogue gives the description: 'beautiful and to a great part rare and well conditioned books'. The remaining part of the books in the catalogue probably did not belong to Swedenborg.

The comments following the entries, in square brackets, are explanations, corrections and suggestions for abbreviated or unclear titles in the catalogue. After this are scientific and philosophical works in which the author in question is mentioned by Swedenborg, although these indications are far from complete.

The annotations to the titles listed indicate the following:

A1   the book is listed in Appendix 1 to the Auction Catalogue.
N   a book which once belonged to Swedenborg which does not appear in the Auction Catalogue.
NSL   such a volume is held by the Swedenborg Library, Bryn Athyn, Pa.
RSAS Swedenborg's own copy of one of his works, now held in the Library of the Royal Swedis Academy of Sciences, Stockholm; Codices of his unpublished works are also held in this Library.

The following annotations indicate that the book is cited or its author is referred to in these works by Swedenborg:

CE   *Cerebrum*

AK   *The Animal Kingdom*

MO   *Miscellaneous Observations*

EAK   *Economy of the Animal Kingdom*

PC   *Principles of Chemistry*

PN   *Philosopher's Notebook*

PR   *Principia*

PT   *Psychological Transactions*

SPT   *Scientific and Philosophical Treatises*

ABRAHAMSSON, F, *Swerikes Rijkes Landslag med Drysells Reg*, vols. I-II (Stockholm, 1726), 4to.

Acta Eruditorum Lipsiensiae p. annis 1720-3, vol. II, 4to.

AGRICOLA, G, *De Re Metallica* (Basel, 1657), fo. [cit. Codex 84; PR II, III].

ALBERTUS, M P M, *Porta Lingua Sanctae, h. e. Lexicon Novum Hebraeo-Latino-Biblicum* (Budisse, 1704), 4to.

N   ALIMARI, D, *Longitudinis aut terra aut mari investigandae methodus adjectis insuper demonstrationibus et instrumentorum iconismis* (London, 1715) [cit. 26 June 1716, to E Benzelius].

Anon., *Bedencken von Kunst- u. Natur-Kammern*, fo.

Anon., *Beschreibung von der Ursprung der Natur und Naturlichen Dinge* (Leipz., 1728), 8vo.

Anon., *Beschreib. von Spiritu Vitrioli* (Hamb., 1725), 4to.

Anon., *The Complete Duty of Man* (London, 1763), 8vo [in the catalogue of the Swedenborg Library, Bryn Athyn, 'A Vonn' is given as the author. Richard Allestree, Provost of Eton College, is sometimes mentioned as the author of the book. No edition from 1763 has been found; the year of printing should probably be 1764].

Anon., *De Glandulis* c. fig. defekt, 8vo.

Anon., *Denckwürdigkeiten des Carlsbad* (Eger, 1731), 8vo.

Anon., *Den Höga Wexel-Coursen, med Swaret, den låga Handels-Balancen* (1744), 4to.

Anon., *Entdeckte Grust natürlicher Geheimnisse* (1727), 4to.

Anon., *Erfindung einer Seigerung u. Erzbeizung* (Francf., 1690), 12mo.

Anon., *Histoires Tragiques & Galantes* a. fig., 2 vols. (Paris, 1715), 8vo.

N   Anon., *History of Learning* [cit. SPT].

Anon., *Instrumenta Meteorognusiae inserv* (Wittenberg, 1725), 4to [unidentified].

A1   Anon., *Leben und Thaten Ihr. K Maj.t in Schweden Caroli XI* (Leipz., 1697), NB. det enda man hafwer af denne store Konung [NB. The only work existing concerning this great king]. Geschichte der Könige in Schweden. Ib. 8vo.

A1   Anon. (S F), *Lebens- Beschreibung des Carl XII u. des Czars*, 8 vols. (Nürnb., Francf. u. Leipz., 1703-17), 12mo.

N   Anon., *Letter to Sir Jacob Banck* [cit. 15 November 1712, to E Benzelius].

Anon., *A Manual of Doctrine, or a Second Essay to bring into the form of Question and Answer the Fundamental Doctrines of the ...Brethren* (London, 1742), 12mo.

Anon., *Méthode de resource des problèmes des Mathémat*, vol. II (1708), 4to.

Anon., *Neu verbessert, und vermehrte Denckwürdiges Kayser Carls-Baad* (Eger, 1731).

Anon., *Pforte zu dem Chymischen Kleinod.* (Nürnb., 1728), 12mo [unidentified].

Anon., *Saltz und Berg-Geist* (1717), 4to [unidentified].

A1 Anon., *Thaler-Cabinet; d. i. Historisch. Critische Beschreibung der R Thaler welche heis 2½ Seculum geschlagen* (Königsb. u. Leipz., 1735), 8vo.

A1 Anon., *Tragicum Theatrum Londini. celebrat* (Amst., 1649), rar. 8vo [Description of the events related to the fall and execution of King Charles I in 1649].

Anon., *Unterricht von Gold u. Silber machen* (Stockh., 1726), 8vo [unidentified].

Anon., *Utkast til jemnförelse imellan den Bibliska och Werldsliga Historien* (Stockh., 1760), 8vo [unidentified].

Anon., *Voyage aux Côtes de Guinée & en Amerique c. fig. par Mr. N.* (Amst., 1719), 8vo [unidentified].

A1 ARCKENHOLTZ, J, *Mémoires conc. Christine de Suède*, vol. I (Amsterdam, 1751), c. fig. num. 4to.

N ARISTOPHANES, *Comediae* [cit. PR].

ARISTOTELES, *Thesaurus, Cura Sanflori* (Paris, 1583), 12mo [possibly a later edition of *Aristotelis Stagiritae Thesaurus Commentariolis illustratus. Quatordecim Libris distinctum, auctus et postremo recognitius. In quo universae philosophiae praeceptiones explicantur. Petro Sanfloro Monpeliensi Medico auctore*, Paris, 1576].

N —— *De Secretiore Parte Divinae Sapientiae secundum Aegyptios* [The More Secret Part of Divine Wisdom according to the Egyptians], in *Opera Omnia* (1572) [though now not recognised as a work by Aristotle] [cit. PT].

A1 AUBERY, L, *Mémoires pour servir à l'hist. de Hollande &c. ou les causes des divisions de cette République* (1680), rare, 12mo.

BACCUS, A, *De Thermis* (Patavia, 1711), fo. [Andrea Bacci, *De thermis, lacubus, balneis et fontibus totius orbis*, publ. 1571 in Venice] [cit. PR II, III].

N BACON, F, *De Verulam. Angliae Cancellarii De Augmentis Scientiarum Lib. IX.* (Lugd. Batavorum: officina Adriani Wijngaerden, 1652), 12mo [cit. PR II, III] [On the inside of the cover: 'Emanuel S(wed)berg 170(9)'. In another handwriting: 'affinitis dilectissimus dono, nunc Erici Benzelii'. Diocesan Library, Linköping].

BAIER, J J, *Oryktographia Norica* (Norimb., 1708), a 2 ex., 4to [The title probably means 'The presence of mines in Noricum', a Roman province located between the Donau and the Alps Alperna].

N BAKER, T, *Reflections upon learning* [cit. April 1711 and August 1712, to E Benzelius].

BARCHHUSEN, J C, *Elementae Chemiae, quibus subiuncta et confectura est Lapidis Philosophici imaginibus representata,* c. fig. (Lugduni Batavarum, 1718), 4to [cit. PR II, III]

Barnabae Epistola & Hermae Pastor, Gr. & Lat. (1685), 12mo.

BARON, R, *Metaphysica generalis* (Lugdeb., 1654), 8vo [The history of metaphysics].

BARTHOLIN, T, *Anatomia* (1666), 8vo [cit. CE; EAK II, III; AK II; Codex 74].

BAUSCH, J L, *De Lapide Haematite et Aetite* (Lipsia, 1665), 8vo [cit. PR II, III].

—— *De Coeruleo et Chrysicolla* (Jenae, 1688), 8vo.

BECHER, J J, *Opuscula Chymica* (Norimberg, 1719), 8vo.

—— *Mineralisches ABC* (Nurnb., 1723), 8vo [cit. PR II, III].

—— *Grosse Chymische Concordantz* (Halle, 1726), 4to.

A1 BECHMANN, F, *Theologia Conscientiaria, sive de Casibus Conscientiae adornatus imprimis in gratiam eorum, qui ad Sacrum Ministerium adspirant* (Francf & Lips., 1694), 4to

BECKE, D von der, *Experimenta…circa natural. rer. Principia* (Hamburg, 1674), 8vo.

BEHRENS, G H, *Curioser Hartzwald* (1720), 4to.

BENTZ [?], *Thesaurus Processuum Chemicos* (1715), 4to [cit. PR II].

BERGER, G, *De Thermis Carolinis* (1709), 4to [cit. PR II].

Bergs-Ordningarne, eller Kungl Stadgar, Förordningar, Privilegier och Resol (Stockholm, 1736), 4to.

BERNOULLI, J, *Nouvelle Théorie de la Manoeuvre des Vaisseaux* c. fig. (Basle, 1714), 8vo.

BEVERLAND, A, *De stolatae virginitatis jure* (Lugd., 1680), 8vo [The catalogue gives the title as 'De violatae'; the book is about the legal rules referring to the virginity of brides].

An English Bible (London, 1599), 4to.

Biblia Hebr. cum interpr. Pagnini & Montani (Lips., 1657), fo.

Biblia Hebr. cum N. Testam. Graeco, 8vo [unidentified].

Biblia Hebraica cura M. Christiano Reineccio (Lips., 1739), 4to.

Biblia Sacra ex interpr. Em. Tremellii & Junii, vol. II (Amst., 1632), 12mo.

Biblia Sacra ex recent. Im. Tremellii & Junii (Hanov., 1596), fo.

N *Biblia Sacra, sive Testamentum Vetus et Novum ex linguis originalibus in linguam latinam translatum a Sebastiano Schmidt* (Argentorati, 1696) [With Swedenborg's comments in the margin. The Bible was given by Swedenborg's heirs to the Royal Academy of Sciences in Stockholm. The book, which is in quarto, was partly published photolithographically by R L Tafel, Stockholm, 1872].

Biblia Sacra Vulgatae Editionis (Colon.,1647), 8vo.

Biblia Sacra, Seb. Castellionis, vol. II (Lips., 1738), 4to.

Biblia Sacra ex interpr. Sebast. Castellionis, vol. IV (Lond., 1726), 12mo [After vol. II, two numbered volumes follow in the catalogue, indicated 'Dito Dito'. This evidently refers to other parts of the Castellio Bible].

Novum Testamentum Gr. Lat. cura Leusden (Amst., 1741), 12mo.

Novum Testamentum interprete Castellione (Amst., 1681), 8vo.

Bibliotheca Chemica (Nürnb., 1727), 8vo.

Bibliothèque Raisonnée des Ouvrages des Savans, vols. 27 & 28 (Amst., 1741), 8vo [cit. PN].

BILBERG, J, *Elementa Geometriae* (Stockholm, 1691), 8vo.

BILFINGER, G B, *De Harmonia Animi & Corporis praestabilita* (Francf., 1725), 8vo [cit. PN].

BLANCART, S W, *Neues Licht vor die Apotecker* (Leipzig, 1700), 8vo.

BOERHAAVE, H, *Institut. & Experimenta Chemiae*, vol. II (Paris, 1724), 8vo [cit. PC; PR III].

—— *Aphorismi de cognoscendis & curandis Morbis* (Paris, 1728), 8vo.

—— *Institutiones Medicae* (Paris, 1735), 8vo [cit. CE; AK III].

—— *Aphorismi de cognoscendis & curandis Morbis* (Lugd., 1737), 8vo [cit. PR III; EAK I, II; AK I, II].

The Book of Common Prayer (London, 1711), 12mo.

BORRI, G, *La Chiave del Gabinetto* (Geneva, 1681), 12mo.

BOYLE, R, *Opera Varia* (Genève, 1680), 4to [cit MO].

N BREGMAL, J F, *Hydro-Analyse des Minerales chaudes et froides de la Ville Imperial d'Aix-la-Chapelle* (Liège, 1703) [cit. MO].

N   —— *La Circulation des Eaux, ou l'Hydrographie des Minerales d'Aix et de Spa* (Liège, 1719) [cit. MO].

BROMEL, M von, *Mineralogia et lithographica Svecana* (Stockholm, 1740), 8vo.

BRUCKMANN, F E, *Magnalia Dei in locis subterraneis, oder Unterirdische Schatz-Kammer*, c. fig. (Braunschweig, 1727), fo. [cit. Codex 81; PR III].

BRUCKMANN [?], *Historia Naturalis Lapidis Asbesti* (1727), 4to [cit. PR II].

BRUGENSIS, F L, *Loca insigniora Rom. correctionis in Lat. Bibliis* (1657), fo.

BRUNNICH, M T, *Entomologia, sistens insectorum tabulas systematicas* (Kjöbenh., 1764), 8vo.

BÜNTINGEN [?], *Sylva Subterranea* (Halle, 1693), 12mo.

BURNET, T, *Telluris Theoria Sacra* (Frankf., 1691), 12mo.

BUXTORF, J, *Lexicon Chaldaicum, Talmudicum et Rabbinicum* (Bas., 1639), fo.

CAESIUS, B, *Mineralogia* (Lugd. 1636), fo. [cit. PR III].

CALSATUS, P, *Dissertationes physicae de igne* (Francf., 1688), 4to.

CANEPARIUS, P M, *De atramentis* (Roterd., 1718), 4to [cit. PR II].

N   CARERI, G, *Voyage du Tour du Monde*, tr. from the Italian by L M N (Paris, 1719) [cit. PT].

N   CASSEBOHM, J F, *De Aure Humana* (Halle, 1735) [cit. Codex 58].

A1   CHEMNITZ, B P v., *Belli Sueco-Germanico*, vol. I (Stettin, 1648), fo.

A1   —— *Königlichen Schwedishen in Teutschland gefürten Kriegs Erster Theil* (Stettin, 1648), fo.
       —— *Königlichen Schwedishen in Teutschland gefürten Kriegs Erster Theil* (Stettin, 1653), fo.

CHERUBIN (d'Orleans, Le père), *La Dioptrique Oculaire*, c. tab. (Paris, 1671), fo.

Ciceronis Paradoxa (Paris, 1733), 4to.

Collectanea Chymica Leydensia (1726), 8vo.

Collectanea Chym. Metallurgica curiosa (Lips., 1715), 8vo.

A1   COSTER, J, *Theoriae & Praxis affectum Corporis hum.* (Francf., 1663), 4to.

CREQUINIÈRE, M de la, *Conformité des Coutumes des Indiens au celles des Juifs & des autres peuples*, S. Tit. (Bruxelles, 1704), 12mo.

A1   CURTIUS, Q, *Historia Alexandri M. e. not. Var.*, c. fig. (Lugdeb. B., 1649), 8vo.

DAMPIER, W, *Nouveau Voyage autour du Monde*, vols. I & III (Rouen, 1715), 8vo.

Dictionnaire Français-Alleman (Genève, 1683), 8vo.

Dictionnaire Français & Latin (Lyon, 1725), 8vo.

Dictionarium Lat. Gallicum (Amst., 1732), 8vo.

DIEREVILLE, *Relation du Voyage du Port Royal de l'Academie* (Amsterdam, 1710), 12mo [The Catalogue has: '…du Voyage du Portugall…'].

N   DIODORUS, *Bibliothecae Historicae* (1559) [According to the catalogue of the Swedenborg Library, Bryn Athyn, A Acton noted in their copy as follows: 'E. S. had a copy of this edition bound in parchment. It is now in the library of Director Carl Saluhr, Laxå, Sweden'].

NSL   DRANGEL, E, *Anmärckningar til Swerige Rikes Lag* (Stockholm, 1766).

DUHRE, A G, *Wälmenta tanckar om laboratorio Mathem. Oecon* (Stockholm, 1722), 4to.

DUVERNEY, J G: see MISCHEL.

EHRHART, B, *Dissertatio de Belemnitis Svevicis* (1727), 4to [The title in English is 'Fossils of Cuttlefish in Schwaben'].

Endters Probier-Buch (Francf., 1703), fo.

A1   EUREMONT, St, *Oeuvres mélées de St. E.*, 11 parts in one volume (Paris, 1688), 12mo.

Executions-Werket, Förordn. angående.

FEBURE: see LEFÈVRE.

FLORUS, L A, *Res Romanae c. not. Pontani*, 12mo.

A1   ‒‒ *c. not. J. Graevüe Var.*, cum fig. aen. (Amst., 1680), 8vo.

A1   FONTAINE, J de la, *Fables Choisies*, vols. I & II, av. fig. (La Haye, 1688), 8vo.

FORELIUS, D, *Consultatio de Calendarii correctione* (Holmiae, 1719), 4to.

A1   *Förråd av Handlingar i Nordiska Historien*, all four parts (Stockh., 1753), 4to.

GANS, J L, *Corallorum Historia* (Francf., 1620), 8vo.

GAUTRUCHE, P, *Historia Poetica* (Antw., 1690), 8vo.

GEBER, *Curieuse Vollständige Chymische Schriften* (Frankf., 1710), 8vo.

GEMMA, *Unterricht von Edelgesteinen* (1719), 8vo.

Gesangbuch der Evangel. Brüder-Gemeinen, 2: ter Th., 8vo.

GILBERT, [W], *De Magnete* (Lond., 1600), 4to [Gilbert, William (1544-1603), *Physiologia nova, sive Tractatus de Magnete, Magnetisque Corporibus, et de magno Magnete Tellure*] [cit. Codex 81].

GIRARD [?], *Tables des Sinus tangentes & secantes* (1726), 12mo [unidentified].

GLAUBER, J R, *Furni novi Philosophici* (Amst., 1651), 8vo [cit. PR II].

    ‒‒ *Kern der Glauberischen Schriften* (Leipz., 1715), 4to.

GRADIN, A, *A Short History of the Bohem. Morav. Church* (Lond., 1743), 8vo.

Grammaire Anglaise (Lond., 1741), 8vo.

GREENWOOD, *English Grammar* (Lond., 1737), 12mo.

GREGORY, D, *Elem. Astron. Phys. Geometr.* (Genevae, 1726), 4to [cit. Codex 86; PR].

A1   GROTIUS, H, *Historia Gothorum, Vandalor. & Longobardor* (Amstelod., 1655), 8vo.

    ‒‒ *De Veritate Religionis Christianae* (Amsterd., 1662), 8vo.

GRUNDEL, *Underrätelse om Artilleriet* (1705), 4to.

GULIELMINUS, D, *Excertitatio Physico-Medica de Sanguinis Natura & Constitutione* (Vened., 1701), 8vo.

GUSI, *Zeughaus der Natur*, c. fig. (Francf., 1714), fo.

GUSTAVE ADOLPHE, *Recueil des Sentimens & des Propos de Gustave Adolphe, Roi de Suède* (Stockh., 1769), 12mo.

A1   GYLDENSTOLPE, M, *Descriptio Sueciae* (Aboae, 1650), [Bound together with?] *Rota Fortunae* (Abo, 1647), rare, 8vo.

A1   ‒‒ *Politica ad moderniorum imperii Sueo-Gothici Statum accommodata* (Aboae, 1657), rare, 8vo.

N   HALLEY, E, *General Chart, showing at one view the variation of the compass in all those seas with which the English navigators were acquainted* (1701) [PR I].

N   ‒‒ (ed.), *Miscellanea Curiosa*, in 3 vols. [cit. 15 November 1712, to E Benzelius].

HARTMANN, J, *Tractatus physico-medicus de Opio* (Wittenb., 1635), 8vo [cit. PR III].

HARTSOEKER, N, *Suite des Conjectures Physiques*, c fig. (1712), 4to.

    ‒‒ *Recueil de plusieurs pièces de Physique* (Utr., 1722), 12mo.

N   HAUKSBEE, F, *Physico Mechanical Experiments* (1709) [cit. 15 November 1712, to E Benzelius].

N   ‒‒ *Experimenta Antleae Suae* [cit. 2 May 1722, to E Benzelius].

HAUSENII, *Elem. Matheseos* (1734), 4to [unidentified].

HEDERICUS, B, *Lexicon Manuale Graecum* (Lond., 1739), 4to.

HEISTER, L, *Compend. Anatom.* (Norimb., 1732), 8vo [cit. CE; EAK I, II, III; PT; AK I, II].

HELLOT, J, *Elemens de la Philosophie de l'art du feu* (Paris, 1651), 8vo.

HELLWIG, C von, *Lexicon Medico Chymicum* (1718), 8vo.

HELVETIUS, J F, *Vitulus Aureus, quem mundus adorat, in quo tractatur de rarissimo naturae miraculo transmutandi metalla* (Francf., 1726), 8vo.

N   HELWIG, G A, *Lithographia Angerbergica*, 23 vols. with plates (Königsburg, 1717, 1720) [cit. MO].

HENCKEL, J F, *Flora Saturnizana*, c. fig. (Leipz., 1722), 8vo.

—— *Pyritologia oder Kiess-Historie* (Leipz., 1725), 8vo [cit. PR II, III].

—— *De Argenti cum acido Salis communis combinatione* (Dresd., 1727), 8vo [cit. PR II, III].

HENEL, A J von, *Det 1729 florerande Sverige* (Leipzig, 1730), 4to.

HERBERT, T, *Relation du Voyage de Perse & des Indes Orient* (Paris, 1663), 4to.

HIERNE, U, *Actorum Chymicorum … tentamina* (Holmiae, 1712), 4to [cit. PC; PR II, III].

HOFFMAN, F, *Observat. Physico Chemicae* (Halae, 1722), 4to [cit. PR II (?)].

—— *Opuscula Physico-Medica*, 2 vols. (Ulmae, 1725), 8vo [cit. PR II].

HOFFMAN, J M, *Acta Laboratorii Chemici* (Norimb., 1719), 4to.

HOFSTETERN, *Von Güte des Zinober* (1711), 4to.

HORATIUS, *Opera c. not. Minelli* (Lips., 1721), 12mo.

Justitiae-Werket, 2 del. 2 vols, 4to.

KAPP, J E, *Dissertatio de Xiccone Polentino cancellario* (1733), 4to.

A1   KEDER, N, *De Argento Bunis insignito*, c. fig. cen. (Lips., 1703), 4to.

A1   —— *Bunae in nummis*, c. fig. (Lips., 1704), 4to.

A1   —— *Numi Antiqui Suecani ex Arg. praestantiss*, c. fig. (Lips., 1706), 4to.

A1   —— *Numer. in Hibernia curor. indagatio*, c. fig. cen. (Lips., 1708), 4to.

KELLNER, D, *Berg- und Saltzwercks-Buch*, (Francf., 1702), 8vo [2 copies listed].

—— *Officina Chymico Metallica curiosa* (Nordhausen, 1723), 8vo [cit. Codex 84].

KERTZENMACHER, F, *Alchimia*, c. fig. (1720), 8vo.

KIRCHER, A, *Magnes sive de arte magnetica* (Col. Agr., 1643), 4to.

—— *Magnitrium Naturae Regnum* (Amsterdam, 1667), 12mo.

KIRCHMAIER, G K, *Hoffnung besserer Zeiten durch das Edle Bergwerck* (Wittenb., 1698), 4to.

KÖNIG, E, *Regnum Minerale* (1743), 4to [cit. PR II, III].

KRAUTERMANN, V, *Der ackurate Schneider und Künstliche Probierer* (Francf. u. Leipz., 1717), 8vo.

—— *Regnum Minerale* (Francf., 1726), 8vo.

KUNCKEL von LÖWENSTERN, B J, *Ars Vitriaria* (Francf. u. Leipzig, 1689), 4to [cit. PR II].

—— *Laborat. Chymicum* (Hamb., 1722), 8vo.

KURTZEN, *Untersuchung der Oelberschen gesund-Brunnen* (Hanov., 1728), 8vo [unidentified].

A1   LAMBERTY, De, *Mémoir. pour servir à l'Histoire du XVIII Siècle, cont. les Neg. des Traités &c sur les affaires d'État* (La Haye, 1724-1728), tom. 1, 2, 3, 4, 6, vol. 5, 4to.

LANCISIUS, G M, *De Motu cordis*, c. fig. (Neap., 1738) 4to.

LEEUWENHOEK, A van, *Briefen*, vol. III (Delft, 1696), 4to.

—— *Epistolae Physiologicae* (Delphis, 1719), 4to.

    — *Opera Omnia.* (Lugud. Bat., 1722), 4to [cit. CE (?); Codex 57].

    — *Arcana Naturae detecta*, c. fig. (Lugd. Bat., 1722), 4to.

    — *Continuatio Arcana Naturae* (1722), 4to.

LEFÈVRE, N [in catalogue, FEBURE], *Traité de la Chymie* (Paris, 1669), 12mo [cit. PR II (?)].

LEHMAN, J C, *Bescreib. einiger neu erfundenen Pischwerke* (Leipz., 1716), 4to [cit. PR III].

    — *Von den Blumen-Garten*, vol. II (1718), 4to.

LEIBNIZ, G W, *Tentamina Theodicaeae*, 2 vols. (Francf., 1739), 8vo.

LÉMERY, N, *Cours de Chymie* (Paris, 1683), 8vo.

    — *Neue curieuse chymische Geheimnisse des Antimonii* (Dresden, 1709), 8vo.

    — *Volständiges Materialen Lexicon* (Leipz., 1721), fo.

    — *Cours de Chymie, oder der vollkommene Chymist* (Dresden, 1726), 8vo [cit. PC].

N   LESLIE, *Truth of Christianity* [cit. August 1712, to E Benzelius].

LEUTMANN, J G, *Neue Anmerckungen v. Glass-Sleiffen* (Wit., 1718), 8vo.

    — *Vulcanus famulans, oder Sonderbare Feuer-Nützung*, c. fig. (Wittenberg, 1723), 8vo.

    — *Instrumenta Meteorognusiae inserv* (Wittenb., 1725), 8vo.

A1   LIPSIUS, J, *Epistolae* (Antwerp, 1605), fo.

LOCCENIUS, J, *Hist. rerum Svecicarum* (Upsaliae, 1662), 8vo.

LOESCHER, A G, *Commentatio Physica de Phenomeno septentrionali luminose* (Wittenb., 1728), 8vo.

LÖHNEYSS, G E von, *Gründlicher und ausführlicher Bericht von Bergswercken*, c. tab. (Stockholm u. Hamburg, 1690), fo.

LÖWE, C P, *Speculum religionis Judaicae* (Stockh., 1732), 8vo.

NSL LUND, B, *Excercitium academicum* (Stockholm, 1699).

MALEBRANCHE, N, *De inquirenda veritate* (1689), 4to.

N   MALPIGHI, *De Bombyce*, in *Opera Omnia*, vol. II (Lugdum Batavorum, 1687), fo. [cit. SPT; PT; EAK; AK; Codex 74].

MANGET, J, *Theatrum Anatomicum*, c. tab. Vol. II (Genev., 1717), fo.

MARRIOTTE, E, *Grund-Lehren d. Hydrostatick u. Hydraulik.* (Leipz., 1723), 8vo.

MARTENEZ, M, *Novum Dictionnaire, Gr. Gall. ac Belg.*, 2 Ex. (Amst., 1730), 8vo.

MARTIN, B, *The Elements of all Geometry*, c. fig. (Lond., 1739), 8vo.

N   MASSILIUS, A F, Count, *Danubii Pannonico Mysici*, vol. III (The Hague, 1726), [cit. Codex 88]. *Matrikel öfwer Sw. Riddersk. och Adel.* (Stockh., 1731), 8vo.

MELLE, J à, *De lapidibus figuratis*, c. fig. (Lubec., 1720), 4to [MO, 1847, pp. 149-153; SPT].

MENLÖS, D, *Kort Beskrifn. af d. Hydrostatiska Wågbalken* (Stockholm, 1728), 8vo.

A1   MERCUTIO, S V, *Historia des Tempi Correnti*, Tom. I-II, vol. 3 (Genève, 1646-7), 4to.

A1   MESSENIUS, J, *Tombae Veter., Regnum Reginar. Ducum & Hervum Sueco-Goth* (Holmiae, 1611), 8vo.

A1   — *Sueopenta-protopolis f. de Upsalia, Sigtuna, Scara, Birca & Stockholmia* (Holmiae, 1611), 8vo.

A1   — *Retorsio Imposturar. Petri Parvi Rosefontani contra Suecor. Gothorumque Nationem* (Holmiae, 1612), 8vo.

A1   — *Specula* (Holmiae, 1612), 8vo.

A1   — *Chorographiae Scandinaviae* (1615), 8vo.

A1   — *Chronicon. Episcopor. Sueco-Gothiae & Finlandiae*, vol. 6 (1685), 8vo.

Miscellanea Berolinensia, c. fig., vol. II, 4to.

MISCHEL [?], *Abhandlung vom Gehör* (Berlin, 1732), 8vo [German translation of J G Duverney's *Tr. de l'Orange de l'Ovie*].

A1 MOINE DE L'ESPINE & J LE LONG, *Den Koophandel van Amsterdam* (Amst., 1719), 8vo.

MORGAGNI, J B, *Adversaria Anatom.*, c. fig. (Lugd. Bat., 1723), 4to [cit. CE; EAK I, II; AK I, II].

MOSHEIM, J L von, *Institutiones Historiae ecclesiasticae antiquioris et recentioris* (1764), 4to.

MUSSCHENBROEK, [P van], *Physicae experiment.* (Lugd. Bat., 1729), 2 ex., 4to.

— *Tentamina Exper. Natural.*, c. fig. (Lugdeb., 1731) 4to.

MYLIUS, G F, *Memorabilium Saxoniae Subterraneae* (1720), 4to [Bound with VOLKMAN, H, *Silesia subterranea*].

NEHRMAN EHRENSTRÅLE, D, *Inledning til Then Swenska Jurisprudentiam Civilem* (Lund, 1729), 4to.

NEMEITZ, *Nachrichten von Italien* (Leipz., 1726), 8vo [cit. Codex 88].

NERI, A, *Ars Vitriaria* (Amster. 1686), 12mo [cit. PR II, III].

A1 NESTESURANOV, I [?], *Mémoires du Règne de Pierre le Grand*, vol. III (La Haye, 1726), 8vo.

NEWTON, I, *Philosophiae Naturalis Principia Mathematica* (London, 1687), 4to.

NORDENCRANTZ, A, *Memorial wid Riksdagen* (1760), 4to.

N NORRIS, *Reflections upon the conduct of human life* [cit. April 1711 and August 1712, to E Benzelius].

NUCK, A, *Sialographia & Adenographia*, c. f. 2 vols. (Lugd., 1722), 8vo [Sislographia (?), 'adenographia': 'Description of the lymph': an edition from 1696 is referred to in CE; EAK I, II, III; AK I].

— *Experimenta Chirurgica* (Lugdeb., 1733), 8vo.

N ORSCHALK, A, *Von neuen Zeigerung* (Frankfurt, 1690) [cit. Codex 84].

OVIDIUS, N P, *Metamorphosis Admod. Minelli* (Lips., 1714), 12mo [cit. PR I; PT].

— *Operum Tom. I & Fastorum Libri* (Amst., 1649), 12mo.

PACCHIONUS, A R, *Dissert. Physico Anatomicae* (Roma, 1721), 8vo [cit. CE; EAK I, II].

A1 PATIN, G, *Lettres de Guy Patin* (Paris, 1685), 12mo.

PISO, N W, *De Medicina Brasiliensi def.* (Amsterdam, 1658), fo.

N PLINY, *Naturalis Historia,* lib 2 [cit. PR].

N PLOTINOS, *Opera Philosophica* (Basel, 1580) [This book belonged to Georg Stiernhielm, 'the father of Swedish poetry, who, according to his inscription on the front page, regarded it as his 'animi pabulum diu esuritum'—'a spiritual nourishment for which I have long since been hungering'. On the same page is Swedenborg's autograph, 'Emanuel Swedberg 1705'. The book is now in the Diocesan Library in Linköping, Sweden].

POLENIUS, J, *De Motu Aquae*, c. fig. (Batavii, 1717), 4to.

POLHEM, C [in catalogue PÅLHEIMER], *Daedalus Hyperboraeus* (1716), 8vo.

(*En bunde*) *Predikningar och Disputationer* [A bundle of sermons and dissertations], 4to.

Psalmbok, Sw. [no title], 8vo.

PUTONEUS (pseud. C G Meiningen), *Historische und Physicalische Beschreibung der See-Würmer* (Leipzig, 1733), 8vo.

RÉAUMUR, R A F de, *L'art de convertir le Fer forgé en Acier* (Paris, 1722), 4to.

Recueil des Sentimens & des propos de Gustave Adolphe Roi de Suède: see GUSTAVE ADOLPHE.

REDOLIN [?], *Sehenswürdige Prag* [unidentified].

REEVES, G A, *New History of London* (London, 1764), 8vo.

Register for the year 1759, The Annual (London), 12mo.

RELAND, A, *Palaestina* (Norimb., 1716), 4to.

Relation du Voyage de Perse & des Indes Orientales (1663): see HERBERT, T.

N   REYNEAU, C R, *Usage de l'Analyse ou la Manière de l'appliquer à découvrir les proprietés des Figures de la geometrie Simple et composée, a resoudre les Problemes de ces Sciences et les problemes des Sciences Physico-Mathematiques, en employant le Calcul Ordinaire de l'algebre, le Calcul Differentiel et la Calcul Integral*, vol. II (Paris, 1708), 4to [RSAS; on title page: Emanuel Swedberg, Parisiis 1713. 1 Sep. 15 Libres.].

N   RICCIOLI, G B, *Almagestum novum, astroniam veteram novamque coraplectens* [cit. PR II].

RICHTERN, C F, *Die höchst-nöthige Erkentnis des Menschen* (Leipz., 1729), 8vo [translated by Swedenborg, SPT].

ROBERTSON, W, *Thesaurus Linguae Sanctae* (London, 1680), 4to.

ROGISSARD, *Grammaire* (Hag., 1738), 8vo.

ROHR, J B von, *Physikalische Bibliothek* (Lips., 1724), 8vo.

A1   ROSINI, J, *Romanae Antiquitates c. not. The. Dempsteri &c. cum Corn. Schrevelii*, c. fig. aen. (Lugdeb. Bat., 1663), 4to.

ROSSINI, P, *Il Mercurio erante* (Roma, 1732), 12mo.

RÖSSLER, B, *Speculum Metallurgiae Politissimum* (Dresd., 1700), fo.

A1   ROTHMAN, *Om Skjäl och Orsaker till Swenska Folkets Utflyttning* (Stockh., 1765), 8vo.

N   RUDBECK Sr, O, *Atlantica, sive Manheim, vera Japheti posterum sedes ac patria*, 4 vols. with plates (Uppsala, 1675-6), fo. [cit. MO; SPT].

RÜDIGER, A, *Physica Divina.* (Franc., 1716), 4to.

— see also WOLFF, C von.

RUIPHIUS [?], *Observationes. Anatom. et Chirurg.*: See the following entry.

RUYSCH, F, *Observat. Anatom. et Chirurg.*, c. f. (Amst., 1691), 4to.

A1   SAHLMON, I, *Hollands Stats-och Commercie-Spegel, föreställande, under vissa anmärckningar, de förente Noderländernes republique...*, I-II (Stockh., 1731), 8vo.

SARETS [?], *Concernant les Arts & Métiers* (Paris, 1716), 8vo [unidentified].

SCHELHAMMER, G C, *De Nitro.* (Amsterd., 1709), 8vo.

SCHREIBER, T, *Kurzer historischer Bericht von Aufkunft und Anfang der Braunschweig... Bergwerke* (1678), 4to.

SCHURIG, [M], *Spermatologia* (Francof., 1720), 4to.

— *Chylologia* (Dres., 1725), 4to [cit. CE; AK I, II].

— *Muliebra* (Dres. & Lips., 1729), 2 copies, 4to [cit. Codex 88].

— *Parthenologia* (Dres. & Lips., 1729), 4to.

— *Gynaecologia* (Dres. & Lips., 1730), 4to.

— *Syllepsiologia* (Dres. & Lips., 1731), 2 copies, 4to.

— *Embryologia* (Dres. & Lips., 1732), 2 copies, 4to [cit. Codex 53].

SCHWENKE, T [in the catalogue 'SCHASENCHE'], *Sanguinis Historia* (Hag., 1743), 8vo.

SCHÜTTE, J H, *Oryktographia Jenensis, sive Fossilium & Mineralium in agro brevissima descriptio* (Lipsiae et Susati, 1720), 8vo.

SINCERUM, A, [*Der Wohl-erfarne*] *Saltpetersieder und Feuerwerk* (Francf., 1710), 8vo.

Sivers Evangelische Reden (Norrköpping, 1746), 8vo.

SNELLEN, P, *Dissert. Phys.- Chem. qua Salis communis triumviratus* (Amst., 1714), 8vo.

SOHREN, P, *Musicalischer Vorschmack der jauchzenden Seelen im ewigen Leben. Das ist neu-ausgefärtigtes…Lutheranisches Gesangbuch…neben…einem schönen Gebetbuch* (Hamburg, 1683), 8vo.

N   SOPHOCLES, Σκολια παλαια τον πανυ δοκιμον και τον του Τρικλινιου εις Σοφοκλεους επτα τραγψδιας (Kantabrigia, 1669) [With autograph 'Emanuel Swedberg 1706'; probably a gift to Eric Benzelius in 1709. In the Diocesan Library, Linköping].

A1   SPANHEIM, F, *Le Soldat Suédois, ou Histoire de ce qui est passé en Allemagne depuis l'entrée du Roy de Suède en l'année 1630* vols. I-II (1633), 8vo.

A1   [SPEGEL, H], *Then Swenska Kyrko-Historia* vols. I-II (Linköping, 1707-8) 1. *Som innehåller kopnungars och andra regenters namn* (1708). 2. *Som innehåller biskoparnas namn, lefwenes-och ämbetsförrättningar* (1707), 4to.

N   — *Skrifteliga Bewis hörande til Swenska Kyrko-historieneller Biskops Chrönikan, uthur gambla hand skrefna böcker, och til en stor del af sina originaler sammansköte (af H Spegel) och nu i dagsliuset utgifne (af E Benzelius)*, 2.ne Band (Upsala, 1716), 4to.

STAHL, G E, *Bedancken von der Verbesserung der Metallen* (Nürnb. Altd., 1720), 8vo.

— *V. d. Minerali- u. Metallischen Körper* (Leipz., 1720), 8vo.

— *Anweisung zur Mettallurgie* (Leipz., 1720), 4to.

— *Fundam. Chymiae dogmatica et rationalis* (Norimb., 1723), 4to [cit. PR II].

N   STEPHANUS, H, *Lexicon GraecoLatinum seu, Epitome Thesauri Graecae Linguae* (Ebrodunum), 8vo. [The title page bears these signatures: Jesper Swedberg An. 1674, 5 Aug. Em: Swedberg 14 Sept. Anno 1700. In the Library of The General Conference of the New Church, London].

STIERNMAN, A A, (ed.), *Alla riksdagars och mötens beslut 1521-1731*, vol. I (Stockholm, 1727), 4to.

STOCKIUS, C, *Clavis Linguae Sanctae Veris Testamenti* (Jenae, 1744), 8vo.

STURM, J C, *Colleg. Experimentale* (Norimb., 1701), 4to.

N   SUETONIUS, C T, *Opera* (Trajecti ad Rhenum, 1690) [In the Catalogue of the Swedenborg Library, Bryn Athyn, A Acton wrote: 'E. S. had a copy of this edition. It was stamped in gold letters on the outside of a handsome brown calf binding 'Em. S.', and on the back 'Suetonii tom I, Suetonii Tom II'. E. S.'s copy is in the library of Kammarskrifvaren Albert Hallberg, Gothenborg, who received it from Torsten Rosell of Upsala. This copy has notes in Swedenborg's writing which have been copied in pencil in the present volume (in the Swedenborg Library)'].

N   SWAMMERDAM, J, *Bybel der Natuure* (Leyden, 1737) [cit. Codex 53, 57]. In a letter to State Councillor A J von Höpken dated 10 April 1760, Swedenborg wrote: 'When I had the honor of being with your Excellency, I promised to send you my *Regnum Animale*, but when I looked for it, I found it was gone, and then remembered that it had been given to the Library in Stockholm. Therefore, in order to fulfill my promise, I now send in its place Swammerdam's *Biblia Naturae*. This book will be of no use to me hereafter, for I have turned my thoughts from natural things to spiritual'. [A Acton: Letters and Memorials vol. II, p. 528].

SWEDBERG, J, *America Illuminata*, (Skara, 1732), 4to.

SWEDENBORG, E, *Ludus Heliconius, sive Carmina Miscellanea* [Greifswald, 1714 ?], 2 copies, 4to. [Hyde 38 or 39: the book was reprinted in Skara in 1716].

N — *Underättelse, om thet Förtenta Stiernesunds arbete, thess bruk, och förteckning* (Ups., 1717), 4to [Hyde 104; Swedenborg's own copy, RSAS].

— *Regelkonsten, författad i tijo böcker*, 6 issues (Upsala, 1718), 8vo [Hyde 116].

— *Om Jordenes och Planeternas gång och stånd* (Skara, 1719), 8vo [Hyde 124].

N — *Förslag til wårt Mynts och Måls Indelning* (Stockholm, 1719), 4to [Hyde 138; Swedenborg's own copy, RSAS].

— *Prodromus Principiorum Rerum Naturalium, sive Novorum Tentaminum Chymiam et Physicam Experimentalem geometrice explicandi* (Amst., 1721), 4to [Hyde 157].

— *Miscellanea Observata circa res naturales* (Lips., 1722), 6 copies, 8vo [Hyde 175; Swedenborg's own copy, RSAS].

N — *Prodromus Philosophiae Ratiocinantis de Infinito* (Dresden & Leipzig, 1734), 8vo [Hyde 244; Swedenborg's own copy, RSAS].

N — *Oeconomia Regni Animalis*, vols. I and II (Amsterdam, 1740-1), 4to [Hyde 288, 289; Swedenborg's own copy, RSAS].

— *Opera Mineralia. Regnum Subterraneum Minerale. De Cupro*, vol. III (Dresd. & Lipsia, 1734), fo. [Hyde 230].

N — *Regnum Animale*, vols. I and II (The Hague, 1744), vol. III (London, 1745), 4to [Hyde 437-438; Swedenborg's own copy, RSAS].

N — *De Cultu et Amore Dei*, vols. I and II (London, 1745), 4to [Hyde 458, 459; Swedenborg's own copy, RSAS].

N — *Arcana Coelestia*, vols. I and II (London, 1749-50), 4to [Hyde 565, 571; copies of these volumes annotated by Swedenborg, in the Library of the Swedenborg Foundation, West Chester, Pa].

N — *De Ultimo Judicio, et de Babylonia Destructa* (London, 1758), 4to [Hyde 1166; Swedenborg's own copy, RSAS].

N — *De Nova Hierosolyma et ejus Doctrina Coelesti* (London, 1758), 4to [Hyde 1210; Swedenborg's own copy, RSAS].

N — *De Equo Albo* (London, 1758), 4to [Hyde 1313; Swedenborg's own copy, RSAS].

N — *Apocalypsis Revelata* (Amsterdam, 1766), 4to [Hyde 2195; Swedenborg's own copy, RSAS].

N — *Methodus Nova Inveniendi Longitudines* (Amsterdam, 1766), 4to [Hyde 171; Swedenborg's own copy, RSAS].

N — *De Amore Conjugiali* (Amsterdam, 1768), 4to [Hyde 2400; Swedenborg's own copy, RSAS].

N — *Summaria Expositio Doctrinae Novae Ecclesiae* (Amsterdam, 1769), 4to [Hyde 2475, 2476; Swedenborg's own copies of the first edition and the first English version, RSAS].

N — *De Commercio Animae et Corporis* (London, 1769), 4to [Hyde 2536; Swedenborg's own copy, RSAS].

N — *Responsum ad Epistolam ab Amico ad me scriptam* (London, 1769), 8vo [Hyde 2593, 2598; Swedenborg's own copies of the first edition and the first English version, RSAS].

N — *Vera Christiana Religio* (Amsterdam, 1771), 4to [Hyde 2725; Swedenborg's own copy, RSAS].

Swensk Psalmbok [no title], 8vo.

TARNOVIUS, *Gramat. Hebr. Biblica* (Rost., 1712), 8vo.

———

A1 TESSIN, C G, *Bref till en ung Prins 1751 och til en stadigare Prins 1753 jemte Högbemälte unge Herres Swar.* (Stockh., 1753), Edit. på Regal P. nitide Exempl., 4to.

Teutsch-Lat u. Franskt Dictionarum (Bas., 1683), 8vo.

N THEOPHYLACTOS SIMOCATTA, Θεοφυλακτου απο επαρχον του Σιμοκατου τα Ευρισομενα απαντα (Heidelberg, 1599). *Theophylacti Simocati, expraefecti, Quae reperiri potuerunt omnia. Naturalium quaestionum dissertatio; Historiarum orientalis imperii Mauric., imper. Aug., epitome librorum VIII (ex Photio); De Legationibus exterarum gentium ad Romanos, et Romanorum ad exteras gentes; Epistolae morales, rusticae et amatoriae.* Ex bibliotheca And. Schotti. [With autograph 'Emanuel Swedberg 1704, gåva t Eric Benzelius 1709'. In the Diocesan Library, Linköping].

THUMMIG [THUMIGIUS], L P, *Institut. Philosoph. Wolfianae* (1729), 8vo.

A1 TYPOTIUS, J, *Relatio de Regno Sueciae & Bellis civilibus Sigismundi & Caroli D. & Majorum* (1678), 8vo.

VALENTINUS, M B, *Vollständige Schau-Bühne* (Francf., 1714), fo.

— *Aurifodina Medica*, c. fig. (Giessae & Francof., 1723), fo.

VALLEMONT, L de, *La physique occulte, ou Traité de la Baguette Divinatoire et son utilité pour la découverte des sources d'eau, des miniers, des trésors cachez, des voleurs et des meurtriers fugitifs* (Amsterdam, 1696), 12mo.

VENERONI [catalogue, 'VENEROSI'], *Le maître Italien ou la Grammaire Françoise et Italienne* (Venet., 1735), 12mo.

VERHEYEN, P, *Corporis humani Anatomia*, c. fig. (Napoli, 1734), 2 vols., 4to.

— Supplementum til Dito, 4to.

VIGANI, G F, *Medulla Chemiae* (Lugdeb., 1693), 8vo.

VIRGILIUS, M P, *Opera c. not. Varior,* vol. II (Lugd. B., 1680), 8vo.

VLACQUE, A, *Tabellen der Sinuum Tangentium* (Amst., 1695), 8vo.

VOLKMAN, H, *Silesia subterraneae*, c. fig. (1720). 4to [Bound with MYLIUS, G F, *Memorabilium Saxoniae Subterraneae*].

WAHLBERG, S, *Götha Rikes forne Hofwud-Stad Skara in flore et Cinere* (Stockh., 1729), 8vo

WHEELER, G, *Voyage de Dalmatie, de Grèce & du Levante*, c. fig. (Amst., 1689), 8vo.

WILLIS, T, *Opera Omnia,* c. fig. (Genev. 1676), 4to [cit. Codex 86; CE; PR II; EAK I, II; AK I, II, III].

WINSLOWE, J B, *Exposition Anatomique de la Structure du Corps Humain*, vol. V (Paris, 1732), 8vo [cit. EAK I, II, III; AK I, II].

WOLFF, C von, *Allerhand nützliche Versuche…zu…Erkäntniss der Natur u. Kunst*, vol. 3 (1721), 8vo.

— *Vernünfftige Gedancken von der Absicht der natürlichen Dinge* (Francf. und Leipzig, 1726), 8vo.

— *H Christ. Wolffens Meinung von dem Wesen der Seele. H. Rüdigers Gegenmeinung* (Leipzig, 1727), 8vo.

— *Ontologia* (Francf., 1730), 4to [cit. Codex 37, 88; EAK II].

— *Cosmologia* (Francf. & Lips., 1731), 4to [cit. Codex 37, 88; EAK II; PT].

— *Elem. Matheseos Universae*, vol. II (1733), 4to.

N WOTTON, *Reflections upon the antient and modern learning* [cit. August 1712, to E Benzelius].

ZAHN, J, *Telescopium* (Norimb., 1702), fo.

Remarks

Many authors represented in the library are referred to in Swedenborg's works without naming the titles of their books, for example:

AGRICOLA, G: Codex 81, 82, 83, 85.

ALBINUS, B S: Codex 57.

BOERHAAVE, H: PR II; Codex 57, 65.

BOYLE, R: PR II, III; EAK; AK.

CANEPARIUS, P M: Codex 85.

DESCARTES, R: Codex 86.

ERKER, L: Codex 84.

EUCLID: Codex 36.

GLAUBER, J R: Codex 83; PR II, III.

HENCKEL, J F: Codex 81.

HOFFMAN, J M: Codex 81.

KELLNER: Codex 84.

KEPLER, J: Codex 86.

LANCISIUS, G M: Codex 57, 74.

LEEUWENHOEK, A van: PR II, III; CE; PT; EAK I, II; Codex 53, 57; AK I, II, III.

LEFÈVRE, N: PR II.

LEIBNIZ, G W: Codex 86.

LÉMERY, N: PR II, III; PC.

LÖHNEYSS, G E von: Codex 81.

LÖHREN: Codex 82.

MUSSCHENBROEK, P: Codex 86; PR II, III.

NUCK, A: Codex 57.

POLHEM, C: Codex 86.

RICHTER: Codex 88.

RIDLEY, H: Codex 57, 88.

ROUMETTE: Codex 86.

RÖSSLER, J E: Codex 81, 82, 85.

RUYSCH, F: CE; EAK I, II, III; AK I, II.

SWAMMERDAM, J: PR II, III; EAK II, III; AK I, II, III.

VALENTINUS, M B: Codex 81; PR II.

VIEUSSENS, R de: Codex 57, 65, 88.

VOLKMAN, H: Codex 81.

WILLIS, T: Codex 57, 65.

WINSLOW, J B: Codex 57, 65, 88.

WOLFF, C: see Hyde 225, MS no longer extant.

Bibliography

A   Unpublished material
B   Published works
C   Swedenborg's Writings
D   Collected editions of letters, notes, etc., by or about Swedenborg printed, published, or compiled after his death
E   Volumes of Essays, Handbooks, Concordances, Catalogues

A Unpublished material

ACTON, A, *The Green Books*, vols. I-X. Manuscript in the Library of the Academy of the New Church, Bryn Athyn, USA. From its Foreword: 'The Academy Collection of Swedenborg Documents...is the only fairly complete record of its kind, the result of many years of careful labor...It accounts for every document by or concerning Swedenborg known so far, including those published in Tafel's *Documents Concerning Swedenborg* (London, 1875-1877)'. The majority of the 3,096 documents are reproduced in the languages in which they were written, and also in English translation. The documents are arranged in chronological order. Then a reference is given to the collection where the original document is to be found, stating its date and subject matter. Microfilm copies of *The Green Books* are in the Library of the Swedenborg Society, London, and the Royal Library, Stockholm.

BESKOW, P, 'Om ingen frågar mig, så vet jag vad tiden är...', lecture on 'Berget', in Rättvik on 7 June, 1998.

—— *Bibeln i Kyrkan eller den Hermeneutiska Circkeln*, (MS).

Correspondence politique, *Suède* (1744-72) from the Archives des Affaires Etrangères, in Paris.

HJERN, O, 'Skaraswedenborgianismen', lecture in Skara, October 1998.

HÖPKEN, A J von, 'Avskrifter av v Höpkens brev', MS in Royal Library, Stockholm, Ep Sign 14.

Mémoires et Documents, *Suède* (1744-72) from the Archives des Affaires Etrangères, in Paris.

MONTAN, E W, *Personförteckning öfver Ridderskapets och Adelns riksdagar 1719-1809*, Swedish State Archives, R 6012, 6011.

SWEDENBORG, E, *Skrifter och handlingar rörande Assessor Emanuel Swedenborg*, Royal Library, Stockholm, Sign I, p. 58.

—— *Åtskillige konceptpapper af Emanuel Swedenborg*, Royal Library, Stockholm. Sign. Engeström, C IV 1.14.

—— *Drömmar 1744*, Royal Library, Stockholm, Sign I, p. 57.

——*Almanacksanteckningar af år 1752*, I, p. 56.

—— *Brev från Em. Swedenborg 1769*, Royal Library, Stockholm, (various notes) Sign, Autografsaml.

B Published works

ACKROYD, P, *Blake* (London, 1995).

ACTON, A, *An Introduction to The Word Explained. A Study of the Means by which Swedenborg the Scientist and Philosopher became the Theologian and Revelator* (Bryn Athyn, 1927).

ALLEN, E F, 'Swedenborg's Philosophy as a Whole', in *The New Philosophy* (Bryn Athyn,Jan-March 1984 and issues through to Jan-March 1988).

ALM, H, 'Emanuel Swedenborgs Hus och Trädgård', in *Samfundet S:t Eriks Årsbok 1938* (Stockholm, 1938), p. 151 ff.

ALMQVIST, C J L, *Murnis eller De Dödas Sagor* (Uppsala, 1960).

—— *Törnrosens Bok. Ormus och Ariman* (Stockholm, 1838).

ALMQVIST, D, 'Några Karolinska Kanalprojekt', in *Karolinska Förbundets Årsbok* (Lund, 1935), pp. 112-56.

ALMQVIST, J A, *Bergskollegium och Bergslagsstaterna 1637-1857* (Stockholm, 1909).

ANDRAE, T, *Mystikens Psykologi. Besatthet och Inspiration* (Uppsala, 1926).

ANGELUS SILESIUS (pseud. Johannes Scheffler), *L'Errant Chérubinique*, tr. R Munier (Paris, 1970, 1993).

ANNERSTEDT, C A, *Upsala universitets historia*, vol. II:2 (Uppsala, 1909).

ANTÓN PACHECO, J A, *Symbolica Nomina* (Barcelona, 1988).

—— 'Foreword', in *La Sabiduria de los Angeles* [Sp. tr. of Swedenborg, *Divine Love and Wisdom*] (Madrid, 1988).

—— *Un Libro sobre Swedenborg* (Seville,1991).

—— *Prosa de Cámara. El Fantasma* (Imprenta de la Disputación Provincial, 1993).

—— 'Swedenborg y la Religiosidad Romántica', in *Isidorianum*, no. 4 (Seville, 1993), pp. 99-114.

ARBMAN, E, *Ecstacy or Religious Trance in the experience of the ecstatics and from the psychological point of view,* vol. I (Uppsala, 1963).

ARNDT, J, *Fyra Böcker om een sann Christendom/genom Johan Arndts,... stoore flijt, grundeligen vthur then h schrifft sammansatte; och förswenskade af Stephan L. Murano* (Stockholm, 1647).

—— *Fünff geistreiche Bücher vom wahren Christenthum* (Frankfurt am Mayn & Leipzig, 1678).

—— *Das erste Buch von wahren Christenthum* (Riga, 1679).

ARNOLD, G, *Wahre Abbildung der Ersten Christen im Glauben und Lebe* (Frankfurt am Mayn, 1696).

—— *Unpartheyische Kirchen-und Ketzerhistorie vom Anfang des Neuen Testaments biss auf dass Jahr Christi 1688*, vols. I-IV (Frankfurt am Mayn, 1699-1700).

—— *Gottfried Arnold: in Auswahl* [Selected writings, ed. E Seeberg], from the *Mystiker des Abendlandes* series (Munich, 1934).

ARRHENIUS, S, 'Emanuel Swedenborg as a Cosmologist', in *Opera Quaedam aut inedita aut obsoleta de Rebus Naturalibus*, vol. II (Stockholm, 1908).

ASSUNTO, R, *Infinita Contemplazione: Gusto e Filosofia dell'Europa barocca. Studi e testi destoria e critica dell'arte* (Naples, 1979).

ATTERBOM, P D A, *Svenska Siare och Skalde eller Grunddragen af Svenska Vitterhetens häfder. Samlade skrifter*, vol. I (Örebro, 1862).

AUGUSTINUS, *De Spiritu et Anima,* ed. J-P Migne, vol. XI of *Patrologiae cursus completusomnius SS. Patrum, doctorum scriptorumque ecclesiasticorum sive Lainorum, sive Graecorum, Patrologia Latina* (Paris, 1887).

—— *De Doctrina Christiana,* no. 32 of the series *Corpus christianorum. Series Latina* (Turnhout, 1962).

—— *Les Confessions,* in *Œvres de Saint-Augustin,* Series 2, vols. XIII-XIV, ed. M Skutella, tr. E Tréhorel and G Bouissou (Paris, 1962).

—— *La Genèse au sens littéral en douze livres,* in *Œvres de Saint-Augustin,* Series 7, vols. XLVIII-XLIX, tr. P Agaësse and A Solignac (Paris, 1972).

AUMANN, J, *Spiritual Theology* (London, 1995).

BALTHASAR, H URS von, *Parole et Mystère chez Origène* (Geneva, 1998).

BALTRUSAITIS, J, *Anamorphoses ou thaumaturgus opticus* (Paris, 1984).

BARTH, K, *Die protestantische Theologie im 19. Jahrhundert* (Zurich, 1947).

BAUDELAIRE, C, *Les Fleurs du Mal* (Paris, 1857).

BELFRAGE, E, *1600-talpsalm. Litteraturhistoriska Studier* (Lund, 1968).

BENDER, W, *Der Freigeist aus dem Pietismus. Ein Beitrag zur Entstehungsgeschichte der Aufklärung* (Bonn, 1882).

BENZ, E, *Swedenborg in Deutschland* (Frankfurt am Main, 1947).

—— *Emanuel Swedenborg. Naturforscher und Seher* (Munich, 1948; 2nd edition edited by F Horn, Zurich, 1969); tr. N Goodrick-Clarke as *Emanuel Swedenborg: Visionary Savant in the Age of Reason* (West Chester, 2002).

—— *Adam. Der Mythus vom Urmenschen* (Munich, 1955).

—— *Vision und Offenbarung. Gesammelte Swedenborg-Aufsätze* (Zurich, 1979); tr. A Heron as 'Spiritual Vision and Revelation', in *The New Philosophy* (Bryn Athyn, Jan-June 2000 — Jan-June 2001).

BENZELIUS, E, *Predikan...hållen i Stockholm, vid Riksdagens slut åhr 1723, then 17 October in för Kongl. Maij:t samt Ridderskapet och Adeln* (Uppsala, 1723).

—— 'Democriti Ponenda, eller jakande frågo-satser', in A Rydelius, *Anmerkningar til Christiani Democriti så kallada Demonstratio evangelica,* 2 vols. (Linköping, 1732-6).

—— see also ERIKSON, A.

BENZELIUS, J, *Christelig Lik-predikan öfwer Doctor Jesper Swedberg* (Linköping, 1736).

BERGGRÉN, P G, 'Karl XII's Galärtransport från Strömstad till Idefjorden och striderna därstädes år 1718', in *Karolinska Förbundets Årsbok* (Lund, 1920).

BERGQUIST, L, *Swedenborgs Drömbok. Glädjen och det stora kvalet* (Stockholm, 1988); tr. A Hallengren as *Swedenborg's Dream Diary* (West Chester, 2001).

—— *Biblioteket i Lusthuset. Tio uppsatser om Swedenborg* (Stockholm, 1996).

—— 'Swedenborgs Galenskap', in *Mänskliga Gränsområden. Om extas, psykos och galenskap* (Stockholm, 1996), pp. 127-43.

—— 'Linné och Swedenborg: spegelbilder i svenskt 1700-tal', in *Världarnas Möte,* nos. 1-2 (Stockholm, 1998), pp. 1-22.

Berleburger Bibel, Die, 8 vols. (Berleburg, 1726-42).

BESKOW, B von, *Minne öfver Assessoren i Bergskollegium Emanuel Swedenborg* (Stockholm, 1860).

(BEYER, G A), *Nya försök til Upbygglig Förklaring öfwer Evangeliska sön- och högtidsdags-texterna, i afsigt på en Hand-Postilla* (Gothenburg, 1767).

—— *Index Initialis in Opera Swedenborgii Theologica* (Amsterdam, 1779).

Biblia Sacra ex Sebastiani Castellionis Interpretatione eiusque Postrema Recognitione praecipue in Usum Studiosae Iuventutis Denuo Evulgata (Leipzig, 1750)

Biblia Sacra, sive Testamentum vetus et Novum ex linguis originalibus in linguam Latinam translatam a S. Schmidt, Argentorati MDCXCVI. Ad fidem exemplaris annotationibus E. Swedenborgii manu scriptis locupletati...descriptum...edidit R. L. Tafel (Stockholm, 1872).

Biblia, Thet är All Then Heliga Skrift På Swensko; efter Konung Carl then Tolftes Befalning... (Stockholm, 1703).

Bidrag till Svenska Kyrkans och Riksdagarnas Historia från 1650 till Närvarande Tid (Stockholm, 1835).

BLAKE, W, *Complete Writings*, ed. G Keynes (Oxford, 1972).

BLOCK, M B, *The New Church in the New World: a Study of Swedenborgianism in America* (New York, 1932, 1984).

BOEHME, J, *Om de fyra Lynnena, Gudomlig syn, Om Födelse på nytt, Mysterium pansophicum*, tr. E(rik) H(ermelin) (Stockholm, 1918).

BORGES, J L, *Borges Oral* (Buenos Aires, 1979).

BRATTGÅRD, H, *Bibeln och Människan,* (Lund, 1955).

BRECHT, M, 'Die Berleburger Bibel. Hinweise zu ihrem Verständnis', in *Pietismus und Neuzeit* (Gottingen, 1982), pp. 162-200.

BRECKLING, F, *Then sidste basun öfwer Tyskland til at upwieckia werlden ifrå syndennes sömn*, tr. Jesper Swedenborg (Skara, 1724).

BREDBERG, S, *Resedagbok: Greifswald-Wittenberg-Leiden-London. Västgötamagistern Sven Bredbergs Resedagbok 1708-1710 med inledning utgiven av Henrik Sandblad* (Skara, 1982).

BRIEM, E, 'Swedenborg och den moderna Parapsykologien', in *Från Skilda tider. Studier tillägnade Hjalmar Holmquist* (Stockholm, 1938).

BRING, S E, 'Några bref från Casten Feif till Christopher Polhem', in *Karolinska Förbundets Årsbok* (Lund, 1911).

BROBERG, G, 'Swedenborg och Uppsala', in *Världarnas Möte* (Stockholm, 1960).

BROCK, E J, 'New Church Epistemology', in *The New Philosophy* (Bryn Athyn, Jan-March to Oct-Dec 1984).

BUISSON, F, *Sébastien Castellion. Sa Vie et son Œuvre 1515-1563,* vol. I (Paris, 1892).

BUNYAN, J, *Christens Resa* [Sw. tr. of *Pilgrim's Progress*] (Stockholm, 2nd edition 1866).

CAMPBELL MOSSNER, E, *Bishop Butler and the age of reason* (New York, 1936).

CARLSSON, I, *Parti-partiväsen-partipolitiker, 1731-43* (Stockholm, 1981).

CASSIRER, E, *Die platonische Renaissance in England und die Schule von Cambridge* (Leipzig, 1932).

—— *Die Philosophie der Aufklärung* (Tübingen, 1932).

—— *Descartes: Lehre-Persönlichkeit-Wirkung* (Stockholm, 1939).

CHRISTIANUS DEMOCRITUS (pseud. J C Dippel), *Der von den Nebeln des Reichs der Verwirrung gesäuberte helle Glantz des Evangeli Jesu Christi, oder Schrifft- und Wahrheitsmässiger*

Entwurff der Heilsordnung, in 153 Fragen aus einander gelegt...von Christiano Democrito (Stockholm, 1727).

—— *Vera Demonstratio Evangelica, das ist ein in der Natur und dem Wesen der Sachen selbst so wohl, als in Heiliger Schrifft gegründeter Beweiss der Lehre und des Mittler-Amts Jesu Christ durch Christianum Democritum von Mitternacht mit sich zurück in Teutschland gebracht...oder Communication desjenigen, was in Schweden mit ihm passiret* (Frankfurt & Leipzig, 1729).

Concordia Pia (Norrköping, 1730).

Constitutiones Nationis Dalekarlo-Vestmannicae Upsaliae Die X Maji MDCC. Datae. Jämte några anteckningar om Emanuel Swedenborgs studenttid i Uppsala 1699-1709 (w. foreword by Helge Ruuth, Uppsala, 1910).

CORBIN, H, *Le Paradoxe du Monothéisme* (Paris, 1981).

—— *Face de Dieu, Face de l'Homme* (Paris, 1983).

CORSINI, E, *Apocalisse prima e dopo* (Turin, 1980).

CREUTZ, G P, *Vitterhetsarbeten af Creutz och Gyllenborg* (Stockholm, 1795).

CROUZEL, H, *Origène* (Paris, 1985).

'Curricula in Swedenborg's Student Years. Catalogue of the public lectures of the Upsala professors ...from 1700-1708', tr. E S Price, in *The New Philosophy* (Bryn Athyn, Jan 1932-Jan 1935).

CURTIUS, E R, *Europäische Literatur und lateinisches Mittelalter* (Tübingen, 2nd edition 1993).

DANTE ALIGHIERI, *Paradise*, vol. III of *The Divine Comedy,* tr. D L Sayers and B Reynolds (London, 1962).

DE CHOISEUL, E F, *Etienne François de Choiseul, Duc: Mémoires* (Paris, 1790).

DE GEER, L, *Anders Johan von Höpken: minnesteckning* (Stockholm, 1882).

DEGHAYE, P, *La Sagesse dans l'Œuvre de Jacob Boehme. Cahiers de l'Hermetisme* (Paris, 1983).

—— *La Mystique Protestante.* Oetinger. *Bible de tous les Temps. Le Siècle des Lumières et la Bible* (Paris, 1986).

DELLNER, J, *Den Wolffska Filosofien och Svensk Teologi*, vol. I (Stockholm, 1930).

DESCARTES, R, *Les Traitez de l'Homme et de la Formation du Foetus, et mis au jour depuis sa mort, par Mr Clerselier...* (Amsterdam, 1680).

—— *Discourse on Method,* tr. F E Sutcliffe (London: 1968).

—— *Valda Skrifter,* tr. with intr. by K Marc-Wogau (Lund, 1990).

DIPPEL, J C: see CHRISTIANUS DEMOCRITUS.

DOLE, G F, 'A Rationale for Swedenborg's writing sequence 1746-1771', in *Emanuel Swedenborg: A Continuing Vision* (New York, 1988).

DUCKWORTH, D, *A Branching Tree. A narrative history of The General Conference of the New Church* (London, 1998).

DUNÉR, D, *Om det Oändliga och det Ändliga i Emanuel Swedenborgs 'De Infinito' (1734)*, thesis handed in to Lund University, Philosophy Institute (Lund, 1997).

—— 'Swedenborgs Spiral', in *Lychnos* (Uppsala, 1999).

DUPLEIX, Sc., *Corps de Philosophie contenant la Logique, la Physique, la Metaphysique, et l'Ethique* (Geneva, 1636).

EDEL, L, *Henry James. The Untried Years: 1843-1870* (New York, 1953).

(EHRENHEIM, F W von), *Samlingar i allmän physik, 1:a delen: fragmenter af natur-philosophiens och natur-lärans historia. D:o af meteorologiens*, vol. I (Stockholm, 1822).

EJVEGÅRD, R, 'Kant om Swedenborg', in *Värld och Vetande* [World and Knowledge], nos. 2-3 (Linköping, 1993).

EKELÖF, Greta, and STROH, A H, *Kronologisk Förteckning öfver Emanuel Swedenborgs Skrifter 1700-1772* (Uppsala, 1910).

—— *An Abridged Chronological List of the Works of Emanuel Swedenborg* (Uppsala and Stockholm, 1938).

EKELÖF, Gunnar, *Poems 1927-1962* (Stockholm, 1965).

EKELUND, V, *På Hafsstranden* (Stockholm, 1922).

—— *Sak och Sken* (Stockholm, 1922).

—— *Lefnadsstämning* (Stockholm, 1925).

—— *Lyra och Hades* (Stockholm, 1930).

—— *Spår och Tecken* (Stockholm, 1934).

—— *Ars Magna* (Hälsingborg, 1955).

—— *Hemkomst och Flykt* (Lund, 1972).

EKERWALD, C-G: see Section D.

ELIADE, M, *Le Yoga. Immortalité et Liberté* (Paris, 1983).

EMERSON, R W, *Representative Men* (London, 1899).

ENESTRÖM, G, 'Meddelande om Svedenborgs Matematiska Arbeten', in *Öfversigt af Kongl. Vetenskaps-Akademiens Förhandlingar*, no. 8 (Stockholm, 1889).

—— 'Emanuel Svedenborg Såsom Matematiker', in *Bihang till Kungl. Svenska Vetenskaps-Akademiens Handlingar. Afdelning 1, Mathematik, astronomi, mekanik, fysic, meteorologi och beslagtade amnen*, vol. XV, no. 12 (Stockholm, 1890).

ERIKSON, A, (ed.), *Letters to Erik Benzelius the Younger from Learned Foreigners,* vol. I, 1697-1722, vol. II, 1723-43 (Gothenburg, 1979).

ERIKSON, A, and NYLANDER, E N, (eds.), *Letters from Erik Benzelius to his Learned Friends* (Gothenburg, 1983).

ERIXSON, S, *Sveden. En Bergsmansgård i Stora Kopparbergslagen* (Stockholm, 1934).

Ewangeliske Läro- och Bönepsalmer eller Andelige Sånger öfwer alla sön-, fäst- och helgedags ewangelier (Stockholm, 1724).

FANT, E M: see KNÖS, C J.

FÉNELON, F, *Grundläggande til en Beskrifning öfwer Borgerlige Samhälsens...Nödwändigheter...efter Herr Franciscus de Salignac De la Mothe Fénelons Grundsatser,* tr. from French by E Reuterholm (Norrköping, 1765).

Formula Concordia (Leipzig, 1756).

FORSSELL, H, 'Minne af Erkebiskope Doktor Eric Benzelius den yngre', in *Svenska Akademiens Handlingar* (Stockholm, 1883).

FRÄNGSMYR, T, *Geologi och Skapelsetro. Föreställningar om Jordens Historia från Hiärne till Bergman* (Uppsala, 1969).

—— *Wolffianismens Genombrott i Uppsala. Frihetstida Universitetsfilosofi till 1700-talets mitt* (Uppsala, 1972).

—— *Svärmaren i Vetenskapens Hus. Idéhistoriska essäer* (Stockholm, 1977).

—— *Gubben som Gräver. Människer och Miljöer i Vetenskapens Värld* (Stockholm, 1989).

French Poetry, 1820-1950, tr. W Rees (London, 1990).

FRESE, J, *Andelige och Werldslige Dikter* (Stockholm, 1726).

GJÖRWELL, C C, *Anmärckningar i Swenska Historien,* vol. I (Stockholm, 1786).

GOLDMANN, L, *Racine* (Paris, 1956).

—— *The Philosophy of the Enlightenment. The Christian burgess and the enlightenment* (London, 1973).

GRAUERS, S G, 'Några Bidrag till Oppositionens Historia under Karl XII', in *Karolinska Förbundets Årsbok* (Lund, 1921), pp. 196-220.

GROTIUS, H, *De Veritate Religionis Christianae* (Amsterdam, 1662).

GUSTAFSSON, L, *De Andras Närvaro. Essäer om Konsten som Kunskapskälla* (Stockholm, 1995).

GYLLENBORG, E, *Marie Bästa Del, eller Then ena Nödwändiga; Genom Underwisningar och Påminnelser, Angånde then Christna Trons Lärostycken, och Wåra Åligganden och Skyldigheter,* vols. I-II (Stockholm, 1756-60).

GYLLENBORG, G F, *Mitt Lefverne 1731-1775. Självbiografiska Anteckningar. Med Anmärkningar Utgifna af Gudmund Frunck* (Stockholm, 1885).

—— see also CREUTZ, G P.

GYLLENHAAL, M, *John Flaxman's Illustrations to Emanuel Swedenborg's Arcana Coelestia* (thesis submitted to the Temple University Graduate Board, 1994).

GYLLENSTEN, L, *Lotus i Hades* (Stockholm, 1966).

—— *Diarium Spirituale* (Stockholm, 1968).

—— *Palatset i Parken* (Stockholm, 1970).

HAFENREFFER, M: see SWEDBERG, J (1714).

HALL, J, *Another World and yet the Same. Bishop Joseph Hall's Mundus alter et idem*, tr. and ed. by J M Wands (New Haven, 1981).

HALLENGREN, A, *Framtiden i Äldre Tid* (Gothenburg, 1987).

—— *Universum som Hieroglyfisk Text* (Stockholm, 1989).

—— 'Kristendoms Plotinos', in *Lychnos* (Uppsala, 1991).

—— *Tingens Tydning: Swedenborgstudier* (Stockholm, 1997).

—— *Öarna under Vinden: Färder i Swedenborgvärlden* (Stockholm, 1997).

—— see also ROBSAHM, C.

HAMMARSKÖLD, L, *Historiska Anteckningar Rörande Fortgången och Utvecklingen af det Philosophiska Studium* (Stockholm, 1821).

—— *Grunderna för Skönhetsläran i Tvenne Afhandlingar* (Phosphoros, 1813).

HAMNGREN, H, *Anamorfoser* (Stockholm, 1975).

HARDT, T G A, 'Luther och Mystike', in *Nya Väktaren*, no. 12 (Stockholm, 1991), p. 518 ff.

HELANDER, H, 'Om Swedenborgs Latin', in *Svensk Kyrkohistorisk Årsskrift* (Uppsala, 1989), pp. 57-96.

—— (tr. and ed.) *Emanuel Swedenborg, Camena Borea, edited with introduction, translation, and commentary* (Uppsala, 1988).

—— (tr. and ed.) *Emanuel Swedenborg, Festivus Applausus in Caroli XII in Pomeraniam suam adventum, edited with introduction, translation, and commentary* (Uppsala, 1985).

—— (tr. and ed.) *Emanuel Swedenborg, Ludus Heliconius and other Latin Poems, edited with introduction, translation and commentary* (Uppsala, 1995).

HELANDER, J, *Haquin Spegel, hans Lif och Gärning intill år 1693* (Uppsala, 1899).

HELLMAN, E, *Den Svenska Bibeln Genom Tiderna* (Stockholm, 1968).

HELLSTEN, S, *Kyrklig och Radikal Äktenskapsuppfattning i Striden Kring C J L Almqvists 'Det Går An'* (Uppsala, 1951).

HENNING, K S, *Johan Conrad Dippels Vistelse i Sverige samt Dippelianismen i Stockholm 1727-1741* (Uppsala, 1881).

HERDIN, K W, *Bidrag till Uppsala Stads Byggnadshistoria* (Uppsala, 1932).

(HITCHCOCK, E A), *Emanuel Swedenborg Skildrad Såsom Hermetisk Filosof samt en Kort Jemförelse mellan Swedenborgs och Spinozas Läror. Anteckningar af en Amerikanare,* tr. C Wingstedt (Stockholm, 1862).

HJERN, O, *Swedenborg och hans Vänner i Göteborg* (Stockholm, 1990).
— see also JONSSON, I.
— see also ROBSAHM, C.

HOF, H, *Bli mer Människa* (Simrishamn, 1985).

HOFMANN, M, *Theologie und Exegese der Berleburger Bibel (1726-1742)* (Gütersloh, 1937).

HOLCOMBE, W H, *Tänkespråk om det Nya Lifvet* [Sw. tr. of *Aphorisms of the New Life*] (Stockholm, 1895).

HOLMQUIST, H, *Från Swedenborgs Naturvetenskapliga och Naturfilosofiska Period* (Helsingfors, 1913).

HOLST, W, *Carl Gustaf Tessin under Rese-, Riksdagsmanna-och de Tidigare Beskickningsåren* (Lund, 1931).

HÖPKEN, A J von, *Skrifter*, ed. C Silfverstolpe, vols. I-II (Stockholm, 1890-3).

HORN, F, *Schelling and Swedenborg. Mysticism and German Idealism*, tr. G F Dole (West Chester, 1997).

HULTCRANTZ, J V, *The Mortal Remains of Emanuel Swedenborg* (Uppsala, 1910).

INGEBRAND, S, *Bibeltolkningens Problematik* (Stockholm, 1966).

JAMES Sr, H, *Substance and Shadow* (Boston, 1863).
— *The Secret of Swedenborg. Being an elucidation of his doctrine of the divine human humanity* (Boston, 1869).

JOHANNISON, K, *Magnetisörernas Tid. Den animala magnetismen i Sverige* (Uppsala, 1974).
— *Kroppens Tunna Skal* (Stockholm, 1997).

JONSSON, I, *Swedenborgs Skapelsedrama De Cultu et Amore Dei. En studie av motiv och intellektuel miljö* (Stockholm, 1961).
— 'Köpenhamn-Amsterdam-Paris: Swedenborgs Resa 1736-1738', in *Lychnos* (Uppsala, 1967-8).
— *Swedenborgs Korrespondenslära* (Lund, 1969).
— *Emanuel Swedenborg* (New York, 1971).
— *Visionary Scientist. The Effects of Science and Philosophy on Swedenborg's Cosmology* (West Chester, 1999).
— *Den Sköna Lögnen* (Stockholm, 1986).
— *I Symbolens Hus: Nio kapitel litterär begreppshistoria* (Stockholm, 1983).
— (with HJERN, O) *Swedenborg. Sökaren i Naturens och Andens Världar. Hans verk och efterföljd* (Stockholm, 1976).

JOSEFSON, R, *Andreas Knös Teologiska Åskådning* (Uppsala, 1937).

JUNG, C G, *Psychology and Alchemy,* from *The Collected Works of C G Jung* (London, 1968).

KAHL, A J, *Nya Kyrkan och dess Inflytande på Theologiens Studium in Sverige. Ett bidrag till sednare tidens Swenska Kyrkohistoria,* nos. 1-4 (Lund, 1847-64).

—— *Narratiuncula de Vitis Hominum in Swedenborgii Diario commemoratum*, in J F I Tafel's edition of *Diarium Spirituale*, vol. VII, part III (Tübingen & London, 1853).

KÄLLSTRÖM, A, *Bidrag till den Svenska Pietismens Historia* (Stockholm, 1894).

KANT, I, *Träume eines Geistersehrs* (w. 1766; Leipzig, 1880); tr. E F Goerwitz, ed. F Sewall as *Dreams of a Spirit-Seer* (London, 1900; repr. New York, 1969).

KIERKEGAARD, S, *Indøvelse i Christendom* [Practice in Christianity], from *Søren Kierkegaards Samlede Værker* [The Complete Works of Søren Kierkegaard], vol. XII (Copenhagen, 1929).

KLEEN, E A G, *Swedenborg. En Lefnadsskildring*, parts 1-2 (Stockholm, 1917-20).

KNÖS, A, *Om Naturlig och Uppenbarad Religions principer och samband*, tr. with historical background J Dellner, 2 vols. (Nyköping, 1939-1941).

KNÖS, C J, *Vita Jesperi Swedberg…pars prior…venia ampliss. fac. philos. Upsal. Praeside mag. Erico M Fant…publico examini subjicit Carolus Johannes Knös* (Uppsala, 1787).

KÜTTNER, J, 'V N Tatiscevs Mission i Sverige 1724-1726', in *Lychnos* (Uppsala, 1990), pp. 109-64.

LAGERCRANTZ, O, *Dikten om Livet på den Andra Sidan. En bok om Emanuel Swedenborg* (Stockholm, 1996).

LAMM, M, *Johan Gabriel Oxenstierna. En Gustaviansk Natursvärmares Lif och Dikt* (Stockholm, 1911).

—— *Swedenborg. En studie öfver hans Utveckling till Mystiker och Andeskådare* (Stockholm, 1915); tr. into French by E Söderlindh, with a 'Preface' by P Valéry, as *Swedenborg* (Paris, 1936); tr. into English by T Spiers and A Hallengren, with a 'Preface' by P Valéry, as *Emanuel Swedenborg. The development of his thought* (West Chester, 2000).

—— *Upplysningstidens Romantik*, vols. I-II (Stockholm, 1918-20).

LEIBNIZ, G W von, *Essais de Theodicée sur la Bonté de Dieu, la Liberté de l'Homme et l'Origine du Mal* (Amsterdam, 1720).

—— *Valda Skrifter*, tr. K Marc-Wogau (Stockholm, 1959).

LENHAMMAR, H, *Tolerans och Bekännelsetvång. Studier i den Svenska Swedenborgianismen 1765-1795* (Uppsala, 1966).

LIBAVIUS, A L, *Alchymia* (Frankfurt, 1606).

LIEDGREN, E, *Svensk Psalm och Andlig Visa: Olaus Petri-föreläsningar i Uppsala* (Stockholm, 1926).

—— *Den Svenska Psalmboken* (Stockholm, 1952).

LINDBORG, R, *Descartes i Uppsala. Striderna om 'nya filosofien' 1663-1689* (Uppsala, 1965).

LINDERHOLM, E, *Sven Rosén och hans Insats i Frihetstidens Radikala Pietism* (Uppsala, 1911).

LINDH, F G, 'The Entry of Swedenborg's Birth', in *New Church Life* (Bryn Athyn, 1915), pp. 70-2.

—— 'Swedenborgs Ekonomi', in *Nya Kyrkans Tidning* (Stockholm, 1927-30).

—— *Swedenborgs Adelskap* (Stockholm, 1936).

LINDQVIST, S, *Technology on Trial. The Introduction of Steam Power Technology into Sweden, 1715-1736* (Stockholm, 1984).

LINDROTH, S, *Kungl. Svenska Vetenskapsakademiens Historia 1739-1818*, vol. I (Stockholm, 1967).

—— *Svensk Lärdomshistoria*, vol. II, *Stormaktstiden* (Stockholm, 1975).

—— *Svensk Lärdomshistoria*, vol. III, *Frihetstiden* (Stockholm, 1978).

—— *Uppsala Universitet 1477-1977* (Uppsala, 1976).

LINNÉ, C von, *Skrifter af Carl von Linné*, vols. I-V (Uppsala, 1905-13).

LITZELL, G, *Svedberg och Nohrborg. En homiletisk studie* (Uppsala, 1910).

LOCKE, J, *An Essay concerning Human Understanding* (Cambridge, MA, 1931).

—— *The Reasonableness of Christianity* (Oxford, 1998).

LOVEJOY, A O, *The Great Chain of Being. A study of the history of an idea* (Cambridge, MA, 1942).

LUBAC, H de, *Histoire et Esprit. L'Intelligence de l'Écriture d'après Origène* (Paris, 1950).

—— *Exégèse Médiévale. Les Quatre Sens de l'Écriture,* vols. I-II (Paris, 1959).

MALEBRANCHE, N, *Recherche de la Verité,* vols. I-II (Paris, 1910).

MALMESTRÖM, E, *Carl von Linnés Religiösa Åskådning* (Stockholm, 1926).

—— *Ur Linnés Tankevärld och Religiösa Liv* (Uppsala, 1932).

MALMSTRÖM, C G, *Sveriges Politiska Historia från Konung Karl XII:s Död till Statshvälf-ningen 1772,* vols. I-VI (Stockholm, 2nd edition 1893-1901).

MANDELSTAM, O, *Entretien sur Danta* [French tr. of *Razgovor o Dante*], tr. from Russian by L Martinez (Paris, 1977).

MILOSZ, C, *La Terre d'Ulro* (Paris, 1985).

NATHORST, A G, *Emanuel Swedenborg as a Geologist* (Stockholm, 1908).

New Catholic Encyclopedia article 'Apocalypse' (New York, 1976).

NEWTON, I, *Philosophiae Naturalis Principia Mathematica* (Amsterdam, 1687).

—— *Principes mathématiques de la philosophie naturelle,* tr. la Marquise du Chastellet (Paris, 1756).

NICHOLSON, G, *A Dictionary of Correspondences, Representatives, and Significatives, extracted from the Writings of Emanuel Swedenborg* (1841; repr. New York, 1955).

NORDBERG, J, *Karl XII,* vols. I-II (Stockholm, 1740).

NORDENMARK, N V E, *Swedenborg som Astronom*, in *Arkiv för Matematik, Astronomi och Fysik*, vol. 23 A, no. 13 (Stockholm, 1933).

NORDENSKJÖLD, C F: see *Samlingar för Philantroper.*

NORSTRANDH, O, *Den Äldre Svenska Pietismens Litteratur* (Stockholm, 1951).

NYLANDER, E N: see ERIKSON, A.

ODEBERG, H, *Skriftens Studium. Inspiration och Auktoritet* (Norrköping, 1954).

—— *Kristus och Skriften* (Karlskrona, 1970).

ODELBERG, W, 'Emanuel Swedenborgs Kranium —— förlorat och återbördat. En sällsam Historia', in *Arte et Marte*, Annual no. 37 (Stockholm, 1983), p. 1 ff.

ODENVIK, N, *Eric Tolstadius* (Stockholm, 1942).

—— *Leopold och Stendahl* (Stockholm, 1950).

ODHNER, C T, *Annals of the New Church, with a chronological account of the life of Emanuel Swedenborg,* vol. I, 1688-1850 (Bryn Athyn, 1904, 1932).

ODHNER, J D, 'Translator's Corner', in *The New Philosophy* (Bryn Athyn, Jan-March 1984), p. 263 ff.

OETINGER, F C, *Swedenborgs und Anderer irdische und himmlische Philosophie,* vols. I-II (Frankfurt & Leipzig, 1765).

—— *Die Lehrtafel der Prinzessin Antonia, herausgegeben von R Breymayer und F Häussmann,* vols. I-II (Berlin & New York, 1977).

OLSSON, A, *Den Okända Texten,* (Stockholm: 1987).

ORIGEN, *Omelie sulla Genesi,* tr. M I Danieli (Rome, 1978).

PASCAL, B, *Tankar och Smärre Skrifter,* vols. I-II, tr. R Hejll (Stockholm, 1929).

PATTISON, M, 'Tendencies of Religious Thought in England, 1688-1750', in *Essays and Reviews by eminent English Churchmen* (New York, 1874).

PERRAULT, G, *Le Secret du Roi*, vol. I (Paris, 1992).

—— *L'Ombre de la Bastille* (Paris, 1993).

PLATO, *The Symposium*, tr. C Gill (London, 1999).

PLEIJEL, H, *Der schwedische Pietismus in seinen Beziehungen zu Deutschland* (Lund, 1935).

—— 'Karolinsk Kyrkofromhet, Pietism, och Herrnhutism 1680-1772', in *Svenska Kyrkans Historia*, vol. V (Stockholm, 1935).

PLOTINUS, *Enneads,* tr. A H Armstrong, parts I-VII (Harvard University Press, 1966-88).

POLHEM, C, *Christopher Polhems Brev*, with an introduction and commentary by A Liljencrantz (Uppsala, 1941-6).

—— *Christopher Polhems Efterlämnade Skrifter*, parts I-IV, rev. A Liljencrantz (Uppsala, 1952-3).

POPE, A, *The Works of Alexander Pope,* vol. III. (London, 1797).

PRICE, E S, 'The Curricula in Swedenborg's Student Years, 1700-1708', in *The New Philosophy* (Bryn Athyn, 1932-5).

PROUST, M, *In Search of Lost Time,* vol. I, *Swann's Way,* tr. C K Scott Moncrieff and T Kilmartin, rev. D J Enright (Guernsey, 1996).

Psalmbok, Den Svenska Psalmboken av Konungen Gillad och Stadfäst år (Stockholm, 1937).

Psalm-Boken, Then Svenska (Stockholm, 1694) —— see also SWEDBERG, J.

Psalm-Boken, Then Svenska (Stockholm, 1695) —— see also SWEDBERG, J.

QUENNERSTEDT, A, 'Karl XII i Lund', in *Karolinska Förbundets Årsbok* (Lund, 1912).

RADLER, A, *Kristendomens Idéhistoria från Medeltiden till vår Tid* (Lund, 1988).

RAINE, K, *The Human Face of God. William Blake and the Book of Job* (London, 1982).

RAMSTRÖM, M, *Om Emanuel Swedenborg som Naturforskare och i Synnerhet Hjärnatom* (Uppsala, 1910).

Receuil des Instructions données aux Ambassadeurs de France, Suède (Paris, 1885).

Récits d'un Pèlerin Russe à son Père spirituel, tr. J Gauvin from les Cahiers du Rhône (Paris, 1963).

REGAMEY, A G, 'The Vision in the Inn', in *The New-Church Magazine* (London, 1966).

RHYZELIUS, A O, *The Utwaldas Inskrifning. Ericus Benzelius Begrafwen* (Linköping, 1743).

—— 'Biskop A O. Rhyzeli Antenckningar om sitt Lefverne', in selected edition by J Helander (Uppsala, 1901).

ROBSAHM, C, *Anteckningar om Swedenborg. Med en inlande Självbiografisk text av Emanuel Swedenborg: Svar på Brev från en Vän,* ed. A Hallengren, with a postscript by O Hjern (Stockholm, 1989).

ROSE, J S, 'The Ornaments in Swedenborg's Theological First Editions', in *Covenant,* vol. I, no. 4 (Bryn Athyn, 1998), pp. 293-362.

RUNIUS, J, *Dudaim*, vols. I-II (Stockholm, 1714-15).

—— 'Tilflycht i Nöden, Eller Swea-Rikes ödmiuka Supplique Til Gud Alsmächtig', in *Svenska Författare,* vol. IV.1 (Stockholm, 1950).

RUYSCH, F, *Opera Omnia Anatomico-medico-chirurgica, huc usque edita quorum...cum figuris aeneis,* vols. I-II (Amsterdam, 1738).

RYDBERG, S, *Svenska Studieresor till England under Frihetstiden* (Uppsala, 1951).

RYDELIUS, A, *Anmerkningar til Christiani Democriti så kallada Demonstratio Evangelica,* 2 vols. (Linköping, 1732-6).

—— *Nödiga Förnufts Öfningar* (Linköping, 2nd edition 1737).

RYMAN, B, *Eric Benzelius d y. En Frihetsida Politiker* (Stockholm, 1978).

SAHLBERG, G, *Gustaf Fredrik Gyllenborg: Hans liv och dikting under frihetstiden* (Uppsala, 1943).

Samlingar för Philantroper, ed. C F Nordenskjöld, 4 parts (Stockholm, 1787).

SANDSTRÖM, E, *En ny Kristen Kyrka* (Stockholm, 1948).

SCHLIEPER, H, *Emanuel Swedenborgs System der Naturphilosophie, besonders in seiner Beziehung zu Goethe-Herderschen Anschauungen* (Berlin, 1901).

SCHRADER, H-J, 'Pietistisches Publizieren unter Heterodoxieverdacht. Der Zensurfall "Berleburger Bibel" ', in H G Göpfert & E Weyrauch (eds.): *'Unmoralisch an sich …': Zensur im 18 und 19 Jahrhundert*, vol. XIII of *Wolfenbütteler Schriften zur Geschichte des Buchwesens* (Wiesbaden, 1988), pp. 66-88.

SCRIVER, C, *Siäle-Skatt, in hwilken Uppbyggeligen och Trösteligen handlas om thenmennskliga Siälens höga werdighet, diupa och ömkeliga syndafall, bettring och förnyelse genom Christum. .., vols. I-VI*, tr. A Münchenberg (Stockholm, 1723).

SEEBERG, E, *Gottfried Arnold. Die Wissenschaft und die Mystik seiner Zeit. Studien zur Historiographie und zur Mystik* (Darmstadt, 1964).

—— see also ARNOLD, G.

SEWALL, F, *Swedenborg and Modern Idealism* (London, 1902).

—— *Swedenborg and the Sapientia Angelica* (London, 1910).

SIEVERSEN, S, *Sexualitet och Äktenskap i Emanuel Swedenborgs Religionsfilosofi* (Helsingfors, 1993).

SIGSTEDT, C O, *The Swedenborg Epic. The Life and Works of Emanuel Swedenborg* (New York, 1952; London, 1981).

SJÖDÉN, K-E, 'Swedenborg in France' [Eng. tr. of *Swedenborg en France*], tr. K-E Sjödén, ed. M Y Gladish, in *The New Philosophy* (Bryn Athyn, 1994-7).

SOBEL, D, *Longitude. The true story of a lone genius who solved the greatest scientific problem of his time* (London, 1996).

SOURY, G, *Aperçus de Philosophie Religieuse chez Maxime de Tyr, platonicien éclectique* (Paris, 1942).

STAFFORD, B M, *Body Criticism. Imagining the unseen in Enlightenment art and medicine* (Cambridge, MA, 1991).

STAGNELIUS, E J, *Collected Writings,* vol. III (Stockholm, 1833).

STENSTRÖM, T, *Existentialismen i Sverige. Mottagande och Inflytande 1900-1950* (Stockholm, 1984).

STIEGUNG, H, *Ludvig XV:s Hemliga Diplomati och Sverige 1752-1774* (Lund, 1961).

STRINDBERG, A, *Ett Drömspel*, in *Nationalupplagan,* vol. XLVI (Stockholm, 1988).

—— *Religiös Renässans*, in *Nationalupplagan,* vol. LXVIII (Stockholm, 1988).

Strödda Anteckningar, hörande till Swedenborgs Lefwerne (Karlshamn, 1821).

STROH, A H, *Anteckningar i Swedenborgs Almanacka för år 1752, förvarad å Kungl. Biblioteket i Stockholm* (Stockholm, 1903).

—— *Catalogus Bibliothecae Emanuelis Swedenborgii. Förteckning på afl. Wälborne Herr Assessor Swedenborgs efterlämnade Boksamling… som kommer at försäljas på bokauktionskammaren i Stockholm d 28 Nov. 1772* (Stockholm, photolithographic edition 1907).

—— *Grunddragen af Swedenborgs Lif* (Stockholm, 1908).

—— *Några Vittnesbörd om Vetenskapsmannen Swedenborg samlade af Alfred H Stroh* (Stockholm, 1909).

—— 'Notes on the development and texts of Swedenborg's early philosophy of nature and Principia', in *Opera Quaedam*, vol. III (Stockholm, 1911).

—— 'Swedenborg's Contributions to Psychology', in *Transactions of the International Swedenborg Congress 1910* (London, 1912).

—— 'Swedenborg's early life, scientific works, and philosophy', in *The New-Church Magazine* (London, 1915).

—— see also EKELÖF, Greta.

SUNDELIN, R, *Swedenborgianismen Historia in Sverige under förra århundradt* (Uppsala, 1886).

Svenska Merkurius, Den [*The Swedish Mercury*], June 1763, p. 462.

Svensk Teknikhistoria (Hedemora, 1989).

Sveriges Rikes Lag. Gillad och Antagen på Riksdagen år 1734 (Stockholm, 1780), chapters 1-17, 53.

SWAMMERDAM, J, *Biblia Naturae,* vol. I (Leyden, 1737).

SWEDBERG, J, *Then Swenska Psalmboken, med the stycker som there til höra* (Stockholm, 1694).

—— *Betrachtelser om the Obotferdigas Förhinder*, included in the 1694 *Psalm-Boken* and thereafter in the 1695 *Psalm-Boken*.

—— *Dextra sors docensi et dicendi seu Ludus Literarius* . . .(Skara, 1708).

—— *Ungdoms Regel och Ålderdoms Spegel, af Salomos pred:s XII cap., förestält i en visa med thess förklaring i två predikningar, hållne til afsked i Upsala åhr 1703* (Skara, 1709).

—— *Cathechismi gudeliga öfning. Jemte tröstrikt samtal med en högt bedröfvad siäl, angående svår kenning af ungdoms brist och annor synd* (Skara, 1709).

—— *Herre, ho tror wår predikan? In ett gudeligt bref, tå the fast sorgeliga tidender om the swenskas nederlag i Ukrainien, i augusti månad innewarande åhr i wiszhet förspordes...* (Skara, 1709).

—— *Gudz Barnas Heliga Sabbats Ro uti christeliga predikningar öfver söndagz och högtidzdags evangelierna. Vinterdelen Skara 1710, Våhrdelen* (Skara, 1712).

—— *Gudelige Döds Tankar, them en christen altid, helst i thessa dödeliga krigs-och pestilens tider bör hafwa skrifne och utgifne* (Skara, 1711).

—— *Gudz heliga ödnalag, wid menniskions timeliga och ewiga welferd eller oferd. Wyrdsamliga foresteld, wid prestamötet, uti en Christelig predikan, i Skara domkyrkio, then 17. junii 1712* (Skara, 1713).

—— *En liten bok, innehållande ens Christens tro och lefverne. Utdragen af D. Matthias Hafenrefferi. Här vedertagen skolbok. Och nu ånyo förswenskad* (Skara, 1714).

—— *Schibboleth. Swenska språkets rycht och richtoghet* (Skara, 1716).

—— *Festum Magnum, Stora syndares store högtid...* (Skara, 1724).

—— *America Illuminata. Skrifwen och utgifwen af thess biskop* (Skara, 1732; Stockholm, 1985).

—— *Sanctificatio Sabbati, Sabbatens helgande enfaldeliga foresteld uti högtiders och söndagars epistlars gudeliga betrachtande* (Norrköping, 1734).

—— *Jesper Swedbergs Lefwernes Beskrifning*, pt 1 (Lund, 1941).

SWEDENBORG, J: see BRECKLING, F.

TALBOT, M, 'Swedenborg and the holographic paradigm', in *Emanuel Swedenborg. A Continuing Vision* (New York, 1988).

TEGNÉR, E, *Esaias Tegnérs Brev,* ed. N Palmborg, vol. II (Malmö, 1954).

TERESA OF AVILA, *Den inre Borgen* (Helsingborg, 1974).

Tessin och Tessiniana. Biographie med anekdoter och reflexioner, samlade utur framledne riksrådet, greve C G Tessins egenhändige manuscripter (Stockholm, 1819).

THANNER, L, *Revolutionen i Sverige efter Karl XII:s död. Den inrepolitiska maktkampen under tidigare delen av Ulrika Eleonora d y:s regering* (Uppsala, 1953).

Theologia Germanica. En ädel liten bok. Theologia Germanica i Martin Luthers utgåva; om livet i Gud som det präglar livet i världen, tr. with intrd. B Hoffman (Skellefteå, 1985).

THOMPSON, E P, *Witness against the Beast. William Blake and the Moral Law* (Cambridge, 1993).

THORILD, T, *True Heavenly Religion Restored. Samlade skrifter av Thomas Thorild* (Stockholm, 1934).

TOKSVIG, S, *Emanuel Swedenborg. Scientist and Mystic* (New York, 1983).

TOTTIE, H W, *Jesper Swedbergs Lif och Verksamhet. Förra och senare delen* (Uppsala, 1885-6).

TRULSSON, L, *Ulrik Scheffer som Hattpolitiker. Studier i Hattregimens Politiska och Diplomatiska Historia* (Lund, 1947).

UEBERWEGS, F, *Grundriss der Geschichte der Philosophie der Neuzeit. Dritter Teil: Die Neuzeit bis zum Ende des achtzehnten Jahrhunderts* (Berlin, 1914).

ULFGARD, H, *Feast and Future. Revelation 7:9-17 and the Feast of Tabernacles* (Stockholm, 1989).

VÄRILÄ, A, *The Swedenborgian Background of William James' Philosophy* (Helsinki, 1977).

VOLTAIRE, *Elements de la Philosophie de Newton*, from *Œuvres Completes de Voltaire* [The Complete Works of Voltaire], vol. V (Paris, 1855).

—— *Letters on England*, tr. L Tancock (Harmondsworth, 1980).

VOSS, K-L, *Christianus Democritus. Das Menchenbild bei Johann Conrad Dippel* (Leiden, 1970).

WAHLSTRÖM, B, *Studier över Tillkomsten av 1695 års Psalmbok* (Uppsala, 1951).

—— 'Johan Jacob Leibnitz och Güldene Äpffel in Silbernen Schalen. Ett bidrag till kännedomen om den arndtinfluerade asketiken', in *Svensk Kyrkohistorisk Årsskrift* (Uppsala, 1954), pp. 31-48.

—— 'Herde och Hosbonde. Jesper Swedbergs tillfällighetsdikter till Karl XII', in *Karolinska Förbundets Årsbok* (Stockholm, 1955), pp. 78-88.

—— 'En Politisk Bönepsalm från Brunsbo år 1711', in *Karolinska Förbundets Årsbok* (Stockholm, 1956), pp. 173-86.

—— 'Karl XII:s Änglar', in *Karolinska Förbundets Årsbok* (Stockholm, 1960), pp. 105-18.

WAHLSTRÖM, L, *Revolution och Religion: ur den franska Revolutionens Själsliv* (Stockholm, 1936).

WARNOCK, M, *Existentialism* (Oxford, 1977).

WIJKMARK, H, *Wolffs Filosofi och Svensk Teologi. Strövtåg i 1700-talets disputationslitteratur. Bilaga till Nya Elementarskolans Årsredogörelse* (Stockholm, 1914-15).

WILKINSON, C J, *James John Garth Wilkinson* (London, 1911).

WOLFF, C F von, *Vernünfftige Gedancken von den Absichten der naturlichen Dinge* (Frankfurt & Leipzig, 1726).

—— *Philosophia prima sive Ontologia, methodo scientifica pertractata* (Frankfurt & Leipzig, 1730).

—— *Elementa Matheseos Universae*, vols. I-II (Geneva, new edition 1732).

—— *Philosophia rationalis sive Logica, methodo scientifica pertractata* (Frankfurt & Leipzig, 1732) from *Gesammelte Werke* [Complete Works], ed. J Ecole, Series 2, vol. I (Hildesheim, 1983), pp. 538-1275.

—— *Baron von Wolffs Geometrie i sammandrag*, tr. C Stridsberg (Stockholm, 1793).

WUNDT, M, *Die deutsche Schulphilosophie im Zeitalter der Aufklärung* (Hildesheim, 1964).

ZIMMERMANN, R C, *Das Weltbild des jungen Goethe. Studien zur hermetischen Tradition des deutschen 18 Jahrhunderts*, vol. I (Munich, 1969).

ZINN, E, *Die Theologie des Friedrich Christoph Oetinger* (Gütersloh, 1932).

C Swedenborg's Writings

Titles are listed in their original language, followed by the current English translation (where there is one). Works are listed in chronological order of publication, or composition for those works published posthumously.

Published by Swedenborg

Selectae Sententiae (Uppsala, 1709).
> *Selected Sentences*, tr. A Acton, in *The New Philosophy* (Bryn Athyn, Jan-March 1967), pp. 305-70.

Jesperi Swedbergii, Doct. et Episcopi Scarensis, parentis optimi, canticum svecicum, 'Ungdoms Regel och Ålderdoms Spegel', ex Ecclesiast. c. XII. Latino carmine exhibitum ab Emanuele Swedbergio, filio (Skara, 1709).
> 'The Swedish Poem *Ungdoms Regel och Ålderdoms Spegel* (from Ecclesiastes, ch. 12) by J Swedberg, Doctor of Theology and Bishop of Skara, my dear father, translated into Latin verse by Emanuel Swedberg, his son', in *Ludus Heliconius and other Latin poems*, tr. H Helander (Uppsala, 1995).

Ludus Heliconius (Greifswald, 1714; rev. edn., Skara, 1716).
> *Ludus Heliconius and other Latin poems*, Latin text and English translation by H Helander (Uppsala, 1995).

Festivus Applausus (Greifswald, 1714, 1715).
> *Festivus Applausus*, Latin text and English translation by H Helander (Uppsala, 1985).

Camena Borea (Greifswald, 1715; publ. under name of E.S., a Swede).
> *Camena Borea*, Latin text and English translation by H Helander (Uppsala, 1998).

Daedalus Hyperboreus, Issues 1-6 (1716-1718) of which 1-5 were printed in Uppsala in 1716 (no. 5 issued in 1717), and 6 was printed in Skara in 1718. Emanuel Swedenborg was the editor, major contributor and publisher of this periodical written in Swedish, of which there is currently no complete English translation.

Underrätelse, om thet förtenta Stiernsunds arbete, thess bruk, och förtening [Information about the tin-work of Stiernsund, its use, and tinning] (Stockholm, 1717; publ. anon.).

Regel-Konsten Författad i tijo böcker (Uppsala, 1718).
> *Algebra, composed in Ten Books*, tr. J N Cossham, MS in Swedenborg Society Archives (B/102), n.d.

En ny Räkenkonst, som omwexlas wid 8 i stelle then wahnliga wid thalet 10... (Carlsgraf, 1718).
> *A New System of Reckoning which turns at 8 instead of the usual turning at the number 10...*, tr. A Acton (Philadelphia, 1941).

Eman. Swedbergs...försök att finna östra och westra Lengden igen, igenom månan, som til the lärdas ompröfwande framstelles [Attempt to find the east and west longitude by means of the moon, which is submitted for the reconsideration of the learned] (Uppsala, 1718). Reprint with alterations of the text in *Daedalus Hyperboreus*, issue 4.

Om Jordenes och Planeternas Gång och Stånd (Skara, 1719).
> *The Motion and Position of the Earth and Planets*, tr. L P Ford (London, 1900, 1915).

Om Wattnens Högd, och förra werldens starcka ebb och flod. Bewis utur Swerje framsteld (Uppsala, 1719).
    On the Height of Water and Strong Tides in the primeval world, tr. J E Rosenquist, in *Scientific and Philosophical Treatises* (Bryn Athyn, 1992).

Förslag til Wårt Mynts och Måls Inledning, så at rekningen kan lettas och alt bråk afskaffas [Proposal to divide our money and measures, so that the calculation would be easy and all fractions be abolished] (Stockholm, 1719; publ. anon.).

Underrettelse om docken, slysswercken, och saltwercket [Description of docks, locks, and saltworks], (Stockholm, 1719).

Prodromus Principiorum Rerum Naturalium sive Novorum Tentaminum Chymiam et Physicam (Amsterdam, 1721; publ. anon.).
    Some Specimens of a Work on the Principles of Chemistry, with other treatises by Emanuel Swedenborg, tr. C E Strutt (London, 1847; Bryn Athyn, 1976).

Nova Observata et Inventa Circa Ferrum et Ignum... (Amsterdam, 1721; publ. anon.).
    New Observations and Discoveries respecting Iron and Fire..., tr. C E Strutt, in *Some Specimens of a Work*... (London, 1847).

Methodus Nova Inveniendi Longitudines Locorum Terra Marique ope Lunae (Amsterdam, 1721; publ. anon.). The book also includes the articles *Artificia nova mechanica receptacula navalia et aggeres aquaticos construendi* [*A new mechanical plan of constructing docks and dykes*], *Nova constructio aggeris, sive moliminis aquatici* [*A new construction of a dam or mole*], and *Modus mechanice explorandi virtutes et qualitates diversi generis et constructionis navigiorum* [*A mode of discovering the power of vessels*], which are, as below, translated by C E Strutt, in *Some Specimens of a Work*... (London, 1847).
    A New Method of Finding the Longitude of Places, on Land or at Sea, by Lunar Observations, tr. C E Strutt, in *Some Specimens of a Work*... (London, 1847).

Miscellanea Observata (parts 1-3, Leipzig, 1722; part 4, Hamburg, 1722).
    Miscellaneous Observations, tr. C E Strutt (London, 1847; Bryn Athyn, 1976).

Oförgripelige Tanckar om swenska Myntets Förnedring och Förhögring (Stockholm, 1722; Enlarged edn. Uppsala, 1771).
    Modest Thoughts on Inflation of Swedish Currency, tr. A Acton & B A H Boyeson, rev. & ed. G Dole, in *Studia Swedenborgia*, vol. VI (Jan. 1987).

Emanuelis Swedenborgii Opera Philosophica et Mineralia [Philosophical and Mineralogical Works], 3 vols. (Dresden & Leipzig, 1734):
    Tomus I. *Principia Rerum Naturalium sive Novorum tentaminum phaenomena mundi elementaris philosophice explicandi* (Dresden & Leipzig, 1734). *The Principia; or, The First Principles of Natural Things, being attempts toward a philosophical explanation of the elementary world*, tr. A Clissold, 2 vols. (London, 1846; Bryn Athyn, 1976).
    Tomus II. *Regnum Subterraneum sive Minerale De Ferro* (Dresden & Leipzig, 1734).
    Tomus III. *Regnum Subterraneum sive Minerale De Cupro et Orichalco* (Dresden & Leipzig, 1734). *Swedenborg's Treatise on Copper*, 3 vols., tr. A H Searle (London, 1938).

Prodromus Philosophiae Ratiocinantis de Infinito et Causa Finali Creationis (Dresden & Leipzig, 1734).
    The Infinite and Final Cause of Creation, tr. J J G Willkinson (London, 1847, 1992).

Oeconomia Regni Animalis in transactiones divisa... 2 vols. (Amsterdam & London, 1740-1; publ. anon.).

    The Economy of the Animal Kingdom, tr. A Clissold, 2 vols. (London, 1845-6; Bryn Athyn, 1955).

Regnum Animale, 3 vols. (vols. I-II The Hague, 1744; vol. III London, 1745).

    The Animal Kingdom, tr. J J G Wilkinson, 2 vols. (London, 1843-1844; Bryn Athyn, 1960).

De Cultu et Amore Dei, 2 pts (London, 1745).

    The Worship and Love of God, tr. A H Stroh and F Sewall (Boston, MA, 1914; London and West Chester, 1996).

Arcana Coelestia, 8 vols. (London, 1749-1756; publ. anon.; revised edn. in 12 vols., ed. P H Johnson and others, London, 1949-1973).

    Arcana Caelestia, tr. J E Elliott, 12 vols. (London, 1983-1999).

De Telluribus in Mundo nostro Solari, quae vocantur Planetae (London, 1758; publ. anon.).

    The Worlds in Space, tr. J Chadwick (London, 1997).

De Coelo et ejus Mirabilibus, et de Inferno, ex auditis et visis (London, 1758; publ. anon.).

    Heaven and Hell, tr. J Ager, rev. and ed. D H Harley (London, 1958).

De Ultimo Judicio (London, 1758; publ. anon.).

    The Last Judgment, tr. J Chadwick (London, 1992).

De Nova Hierosolyma et ejus Doctrina Coelesti (London, 1758; publ. anon.).

    On The New Jerusalem and Heaven's Teaching for it, tr. J Chadwick (London, 1990).

De Equo Albo, (London, 1758; publ. anon.).

    The White Horse, tr. B S Willmott (London, 1955).

Doctrina Novae Hierosolymae de Domino; Doctrina Novae Hierosolymae de Scriptura Sacra; Doctrina Vitae pro Nova Hierosolyma ex praeceptis Decalogi; Doctrina Novae Hierosolymae de Fide (Amsterdam, 1763; publ. anon.).

    The Four Doctrines, tr. J F Potts, ed. A S Sechrist (New York, 1984).

Continuatio de Ultimo Judicio (Amsterdam, 1763; publ. anon.).

    Continuation on the Last Judgment, tr. J Chadwick, in *On the Last Judgment and the Destruction of Babylon* (London, 1992).

Sapientia Angelica de Divino Amore et de Divina Sapientia (Amsterdam, 1763).

    Angelic Wisdom concerning the Divine Love and Wisdom, tr. C and D H Harley (London, 1969, 1987).

Sapientia Angelica de Divina Providentia (Amsterdam, 1764; publ. anon.).

    Divine Providence, tr. W C Dick and E J Pulsford (London, 1949).

Apocalypsis Revelata (Amsterdam, 1766; publ. anon.).

    The Apocalypse Revealed, tr. F F Coulson, 2 vols. (London, 1970).

Delitiae Sapientiae de Amore Conjugiali (Amsterdam, 1768).

    Conjugial Love, tr. J Chadwick (London, 1996).

Summaria Expositio Doctrinae Novae Ecclesiae (Amsterdam, 1769).

    A Brief Exposition of the Doctrine of the New Church, tr. R Stanley (London, 1952).

De Commercio Animae et Corporis (London, 1769).

    The Interaction between the Soul and the Body, tr. J Whitehead, in *Miscellaneous Theological Works* (New York, 1913; West Chester, 1996).

Vera Christiana Religio (Amsterdam, 1771).

    The True Christian Religion, tr. J Chadwick, 2 vols. (London, 1988).

Published Posthumously

Anatomi af wår Aldrafinaste Natur, wisande att wårt rörande och lefwande wäsende består af Contremiscentier (first published in *Daedalus Hyperboreus*, issue 6, 1718; This expanded version of the essay, sent to Eric Benzelius, was written in 1719).

On Tremulation, tr. C T Odhner (Boston, MA, 1899).

Sit felix faustumque—Principia Rerum Naturalium ab experimentis et Geometria Sive ex Priori Educta (1720).

The (Minor) Principia or the First Principles of Natural Things deduced from experiments and geometry, tr. I Tansley (London, 1913).

Itinerarium ex annis 1733 et 1734 (w. 1733-4; Tübingen, 1840) and *Mina Resors Beskrifning* [Description of my journeys] (w. c. 1710-39; first publ. in A Kahl's Latin tr. as *Itinerarium*, Sectio Secunda, ed. J F I Tafel, Stuttgart, 1844).

Swedenborg's Journals of Travel, tr. R L Tafel, in *Documents concerning the Life and Character of Emanuel Swedenborg*, vol. II:1 (London, 1877).

Comparatio Ontologiae et Cosmologiae Generalis Dominis Christiani Wolfii cum Principiis *nostris* Rerum Naturalium [A General Comparison between Christian Wolff's Ontologia and Cosmologia and our Principles of Natural Things], MS (1733) printed in *Opera Quaedam*, vol. II, pp. 193-206.

Notae ex Wolfii Psychologica Empirica, MS (1733).

Notes and Observations on C Wolff's Empirica, tr. A Acton, in *Psychologica* (Philadelphia, 1923).

Projekt (1734).

Project on War with Russia, tr. A Acton, in *Letters and Memorials of Emanuel Swedenborg*, vol. I, pp. 468-75.

Transactiones de Cerebro; prima, secunda, et tertia (1738-40).

The Cerebrum, tr. A Acton, 3 vols. (Bryn Athyn, 1976).

Clavis Hieroglyphica (w. 1741-1742?; London, 1784).

A Hieroglyphic Key, tr. J J G Wilkinson (London, 1847).

Ontologia (1742).

Ontology, tr. A Acton (Boston, MA, 1901).

Psychologia Rationalis, eller De Anima (1742).

Rational Psychology, tr. N H Rogers and A Acton (Philadelphia, 1950; rev. Bryn Athyn, 2001).

Swedenborgs Drömmar 1744 jemte andra hans anteckningar, ed. G E Klemming (w. 1744; Stockholm, 1859).

Swedenborg's Dream Diary, ed. L Bergquist, tr. A Hallengren (West Chester, 2001).

De Messia Venturo in Mundum (1745).

Concerning the Messiah about to Come, tr. A Acton (Bryn Athyn, 1949).

Historia Creationis a Mose tradita. Ex Smidio et ex Castellione (1745).

The History of Creation, tr. A Acton in *The Word of the Old Testament Explained*, vol. I (Bryn Athyn, 1928), pp. 3-30.

Experientiae Spirituales, ed. J D Odhner, 6 vols. (w. 1745-65; Bryn Athyn, 1983-97).

The Spiritual Diary, tr. G Bush (vols. I-IV), J H Smithson (vols. I-III), and J F Buss (vols. IV-V), 5 vols. (London, 1883-1902); vol. I also tr. A W Acton (London, 1962); rev. edn. (vol. I, tr. Acton; vols. II-III, tr. Bush & Smithson; vol. IV, tr. Bush & Buss; vol. V, tr. Buss), 5 vols. (London, 2002–).

Explicatio in Verbum Historicum Veteris Testamenti (1746).

The Word of the Old Testament Explained, tr. A Acton, 10 vols. (Bryn Athyn, 1928-51).
De Miraculis (1749?).
    Miracles, Latin/English edition, ed. and tr. P H Johnson (London, 1943; rev. 1947).
Ödmjukt Memorial (1755).
    Memorial on Distillation, tr. A Acton (of an incomplete draft), in *Letters and Memorials*, vol. II (Bryn Athyn, 1955).
Apocalypsis Explicata (w. 1757-9, 4 vols., London 1785-89; revised edition in 6 vols., ed. S H Worcester, New York, 1884-5).
    The Apocalypse Explained, tr. J Whitehead, 6 vols. (rev. ed. New York and West Chester, 1980-95).
De Athanasii Symbolo (1759-60).
    The Athanasian Creed, Latin/English edition, ed. and tr. D H Harley (London, 1954).
Oförgripeliga Tanckar om Rikets Upprätthållande och befästande i sin Freihet: memorial till Riksdagen (1761).
    Inoffensive Thoughts concerning the Upholding and Strengthening of the Kingdom in its Freedom, tr. A Acton, in *Letters and Memorials*, vol. II (Bryn Athyn, 1955).
De Scriptura Sacra seu Verbo Domini, ab experientia (1762).
    On the Sacred Scripture or the Word of the Lord from Experience, tr. J Chadwick (London, 1997).
De Ultimo Judicio (posth.) (1762).
    On the Last Judgment and the Destruction of Babylon, tr. J Chadwick (London, 1992).
De Conjugio (1766).
    On Marriage, tr. J E Elliott, in *Small Theological Works and Letters* (London, 1975).
Historia Ecclesiastica Novae Ecclesiae (1770).
    Sketch of an Ecclesiastical History of the New Church, tr. J Whitehead, in Posthumous Theological Works, vol. I (West Chster, 1991).
Coronis seu Appendix ad Veram Christianam Religionem... (1771).
    The Coronis, tr. J F Buss (London, 1893; rev. edn. London, 1931).

D Collected editions of letters, notes, etc., by or about Swedenborg printed, published, or composed after his death

ACTON, A, (tr. and ed.), *A Philosopher's Note Book: excerpts from philosophical writers and from the Sacred Scriptures on a variety of philosophical subjects together with some reflections, and sundry notes and memoranda by Emanuel Swedenborg* (Philadelphia, 1931).
    —(tr. and ed.), *Psychological Transactions,* (Philadelphia;1955; rebound with editorial additions, 1984).
    — (tr. and ed.), *The Letters and Memorials of Emanuel Swedenborg,* 2 vols. (Bryn Athyn, vol. I 1948, vol. II 1955).
EKERWALD, C-G, (tr.), *Memorabilier: minnesanteckningar från himlar och helveten (hämtade ur* Vera christiana religio*)* [Memoranda from heaven and hell, extracted from *The True Christian Religion*] (Stockholm, 1988).
ELLIOTT, J E, (ed.), *Small Theological Works and Letters* (London, 1975).
FOX, L and ROSE, D L, (eds.), GLADISH, D and ROSE, J, (tr.), *Conversations with Angels. What Swedenborg heard in heaven* (West Chester, 1996).
LE BOYS DES GUAYS, J F E, *Uppenbarelse-boken till dess andeliga mening efter 'Apocalypsis*

Revelata' och 'Apocalypsis Explicata' af Emanuel Swedenborg jemte andeliga meningen af 25 kapitel hos Mattheus, efter 'Arcana Coelestia' af samme författare [Sw. tr. of *L'Apocalypse dans son sens spirituel, d'après* l'Apocalypse révélée *et* l'Apocalypse expliquée *d'Emanuel Swedenborg, suivie du sens spirituel du vingt-quatrième chapitre de Matthieu, d'après des Arcanes célestes du même auteur*], tr. J A Sevén (Christianstad, 1859).

STROH, A H, (ed.), *Scientific and Philosophical Treatises 1716-1740* (Bryn Athyn, 1905-8; 2nd edn. edited and rearranged by W R Woofenden, Bryn Athyn, 1992)

—— (ed.) *Opera Quaedam aut inedita aut obsoleta de Rebus Naturalibus,* 3 vols., published by the Royal Swedish Academy of Sciences (Stockholm, 1907-11).

—— *Resebeskrifningar af Emanuel Swedenborg under åren 1710-1739,* (Uppsala, 1911).

TAFEL, R L, (tr., ed. and comp.), *Documents concerning the Life and Character of Emanuel Swedenborg,* vols I, II:1, II:2 (London, 1875-7).

'Utdrag af några bref från Emanuel Svedenborg til åtskillige des Vänner', in *Samlingar för Philantroper*, 1st issue (Stockholm, 1787).

WHITEHEAD, J, (tr. and ed.), *Miscellaneous Theological Works* (New York, 1988).

—— (tr. and ed.), 'Autobiographical Letters', in *Posthumous Theological Works*, vol. I (West Chester, 1996), pp. 1-5.

E Volumes of Essays, Handbooks, Concordances, Catalogues

BERGMANN, H and ZWINK, E, (comp.), *Emanuel Swedenborg 1688-1772: Naturforscher und Kundiger der Überwelt* (Stuttgart, 1988).

BROCK, E J, and others, (eds.), *Swedenborg and his Influence* (Bryn Athyn, 1988).

HYDE, J, (ed.), *A Bibliography of the Works of Emanuel Swedenborg, original and translated* (London, 1906).

LARSEN, R, and others, (eds.), *Emanuel Swedenborg: A Continuing Vision* (New York, 1988).

POTTS, J F, (comp.), *The Swedenborg Concordance: a complete work of reference to the theological writings of Emanuel Swedenborg*, 6 vols. (London, 1888-1902; 1988-92).

WAINSCOT, A S, (comp.), *Additions to Hyde's Bibliography* (London, 1967).

WOOFENDEN, W R, *Swedenborg Explorer's Guidebook: a Research Manual* (West Chester, 2002).

| Index |

89, 91, 92, 93, 94, 95, 96, 97-100, 125,
132, 145, 158, 160, 192, 203, 204, 220,
245, 246, 264, 265, 320, 354, 387
Boehme, Jacob 199, 255, 372, 373; *The
Three Principles of the Divine Being*
372
Boerhaave, Herman 45
Bohuslän (province) 70
Bollnäs 1
Bonde, Count Gustaf von 96, 265
Borges, Jorge Luis 367 'Emanuel
Swedenborg' 367
Bossuet, Jacques Bénigne 260
Boston, U S A 432
Bothnia, Gulf of 159
Boyle, Robert 87
brain 28, 78, 79, 150, 156, 165, 294, 267,
321, cortex of the brain 123, 152-3;
spirituous fluid 149-50
breathing 17, 279, 291, 294, 295, 296, 298,
299, 300, 324
Breckling, Friedrich 98-9; *The Last Trumpet
over Germany* 98-9
Breda, Carl Friedrik von 430
Bredburg, Sven 34
Bremen 72
Briem, Efraim 268
Brink, Elizabeth 62
British Empire; see England
Broman, Erland 166
Brunsbo 24, 25, 31, 32, 40, 55, 57, 66, 86,
87, 99, 124, 125, 126, 157
Brunswick 95, 114
Buddenbrock, General Henrik Magnus 159
Bullenaesia, Anne Petersdotter 1
Bullenaesius, Petrus 1
Bunyan, John 256; *The Pilgrim's Progress*
256

Cain 256
Calderón de la Barca, Pedro 139
calling, Swedenborg's Divine; mission x,
226, 235, 338, 367, 418
Calvin, John xvii, 277, 332, 424

Cambridge 36
Cambridge Platonists, the 37
Cana, The Wedding at 257, 310
Canaan 10
Caps and Hats (political parties in Sweden)
24, 106, 158, 159, 218, 220, 271, 274,
275, 315, 329, 345, 346, 348, 351, 356,
359, 360, 361, 362, 363, 367, 390, 406
Carelia 72, 93
Carmelite Order 299
Carolinian Era 70
Cartesian 12, 27-8, 31, 78, 400
Casaubon, Isaac 34-5
Cassini, Jacques 44
Casteja, Charles Louis, Count de 105-6
Castel, William 270
Castellio, Sebastian (Sébastien Châteillon)
34, 280
Catholic Church, Roman (Church of
Rome) 194, 232, 248, 277, 300, 322, 331,
334, 347, 365, 366, 387, 405, 434
Catullus, Gaius Valerius 41
Celsius, Nils 88
Charles XI 3, 15, 20, 26, 84
Charles XII 3, 4, 16, 20, 24, 49, 50, 51, 52,
53, 65, 68, 69, 71, 72, 73, 82, 83, 84, 103,
106, 107, 159, 195, 219, 317, 364, 390,
398
Charles, Prince 428-9
Charlottenburg 407
chastity 391
Choiseul, Etienne François de Choiseul, Duc
de 104, 364
Christ, Jesus; see also, Second Coming of
Christ, 9, 10, 11, 85, 122, 123, 139, 157,
163, 164, 166, 167, 168, 170, 171, 172,
173, 179, 182, 188, 191, 192, 195, 196,
199, 200, 201, 203, 204, 209, 215, 254,
258, 262, 277, 288, 296, 301, 304, 305,
310, 311, 312, 323, 331, 368, 373, 378,
385, 397, 398, 399, 401, 413, 415, 417-9,
425, 432, 434
Christianstad 365
Christina, Queen of Sweden 347